MANGA KAMISHIBAI

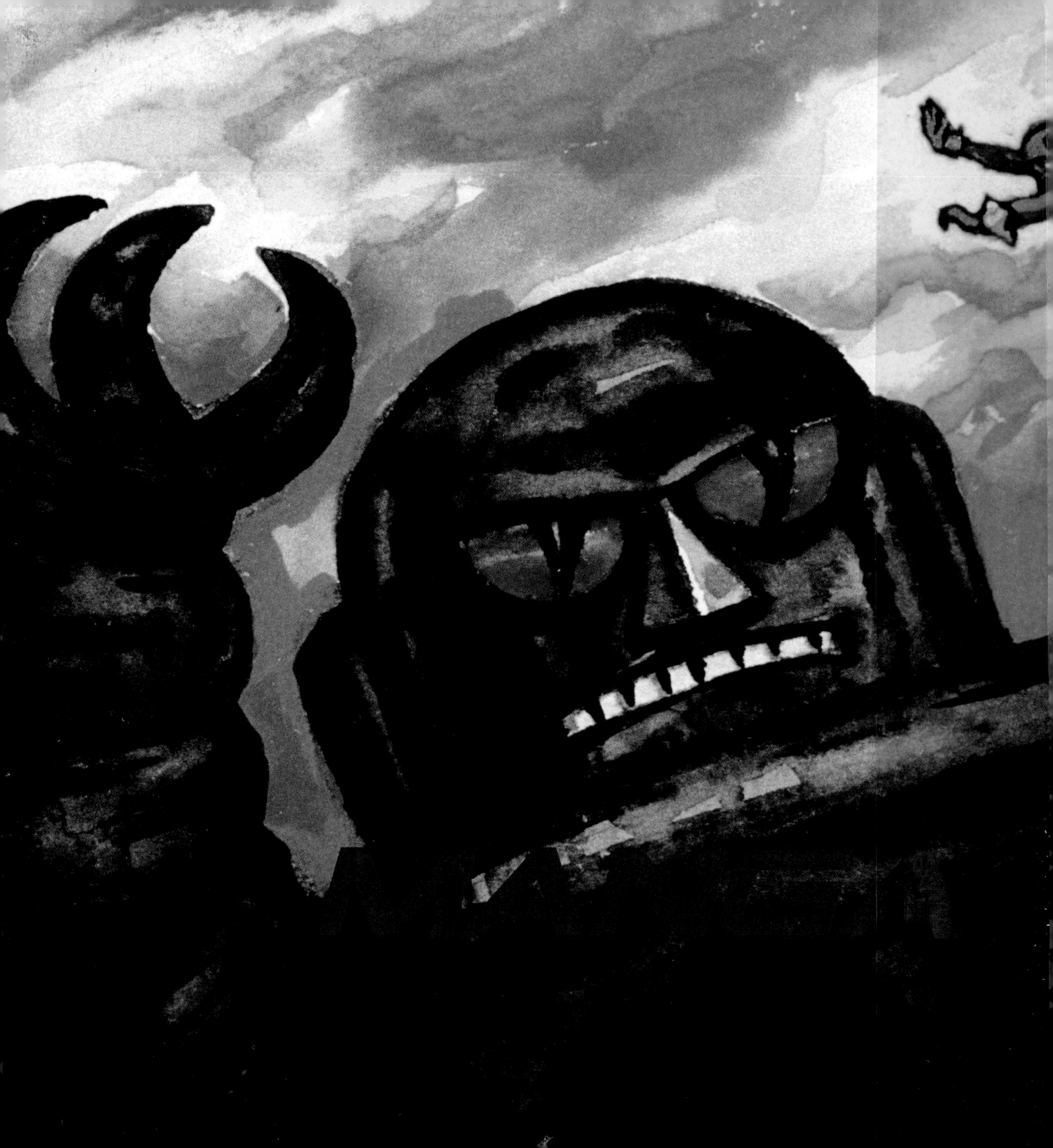

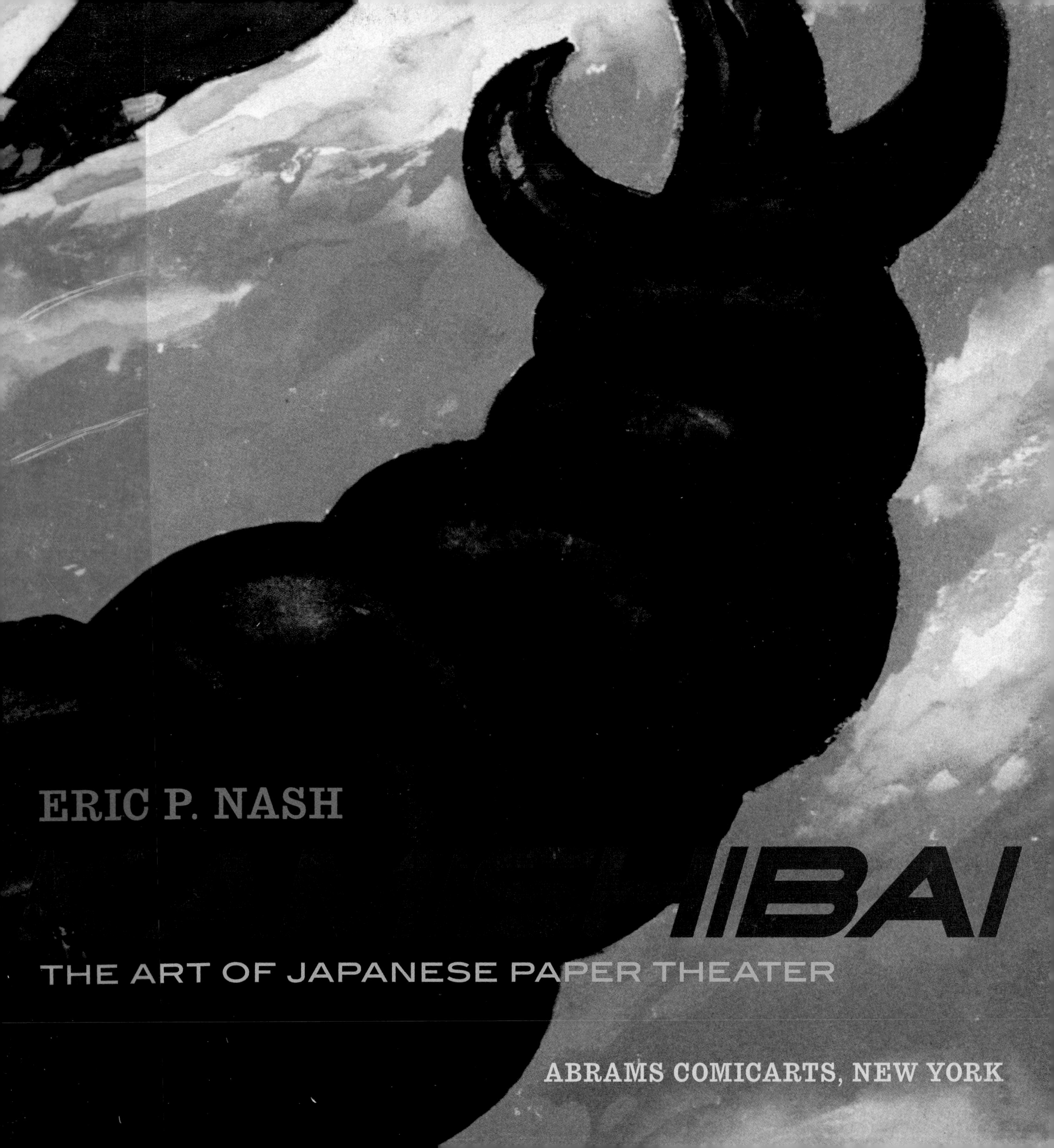

ERIC P. NASH

HIBAI

THE ART OF JAPANESE PAPER THEATER

ABRAMS COMICARTS, NEW YORK

FOR MY MOTHER, SISTER LAURA, AND NEPHEWS THEODORE AND LIONEL.

✦

EDITOR: SOFIA GUTIÉRREZ
PROJECT MANAGER: CHARLES KOCHMAN
DESIGNER: LAURA LINDGREN
PRODUCTION MANAGER: ALISON GERVAIS

LIBRARY OF CONGRESS CATALOGING-IN-PUBLICATION DATA
NASH, ERIC PETER
  MANGA KAMISHIBAI : THE ART OF JAPANESE PAPER THEATER / BY ERIC P. NASH,
VARIOUS ILLUSTRATORS.
    P. CM.
  ISBN 978-0-8109-5303-1
  1. KAMISHIBAI. I. TITLE.
  PN1979.K3N37 2009
  372.66—DC22   200805435

PRINTED AND BOUND IN CHINA
10 9 8 7 6 5 4 3 2 1

ABRAMS COMICARTS BOOKS ARE AVAILABLE AT SPECIAL DISCOUNTS WHEN PURCHASED IN QUANTITY FOR PREMIUMS
AND PROMOTIONS AS WELL AS FUNDRAISING OR EDUCATIONAL USE. SPECIAL EDITIONS CAN ALSO BE CREATED TO
SPECIFICATION. FOR DETAILS, CONTACT SPECIALMARKETS@HNABOOKS.COM OR THE ADDRESS BELOW.

HNA ▮▮▮▮▮
harry n. abrams, inc.
a subsidiary of La Martinière Groupe
115 WEST 18TH STREET
NEW YORK, NY 10011
WWW.HNABOOKS.COM

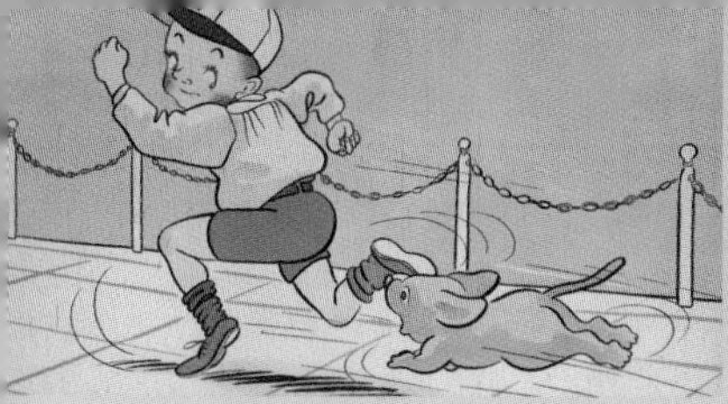
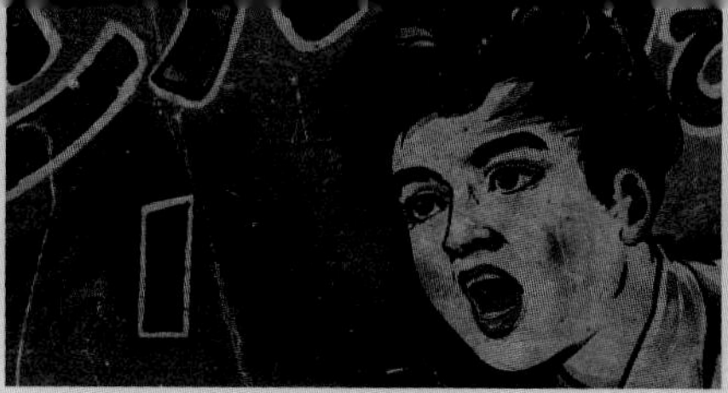
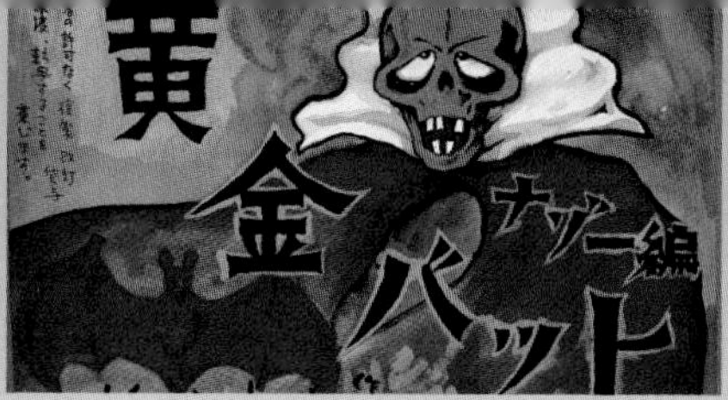
黄金
ナゾー編
バット
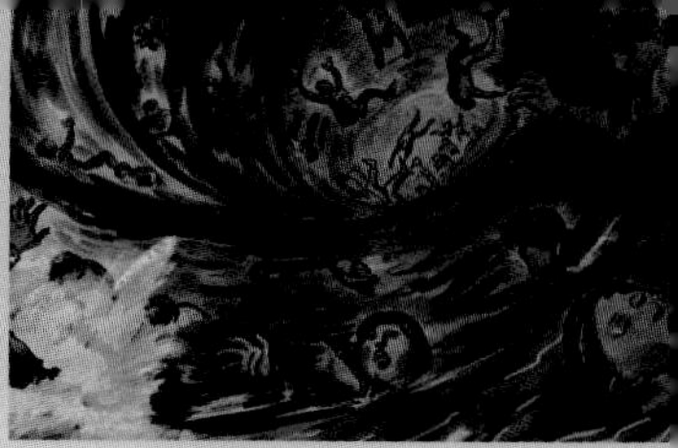

Contents

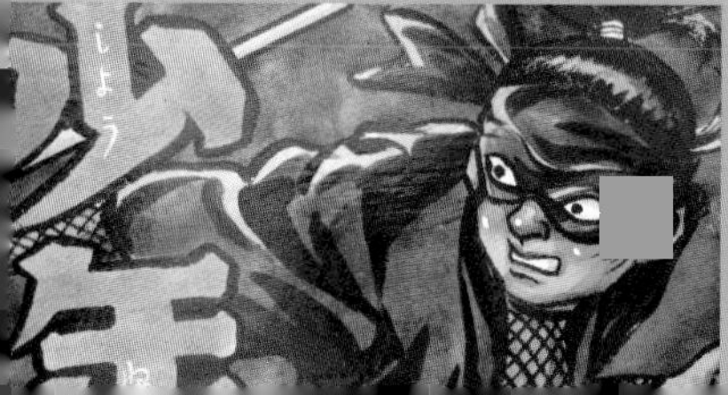
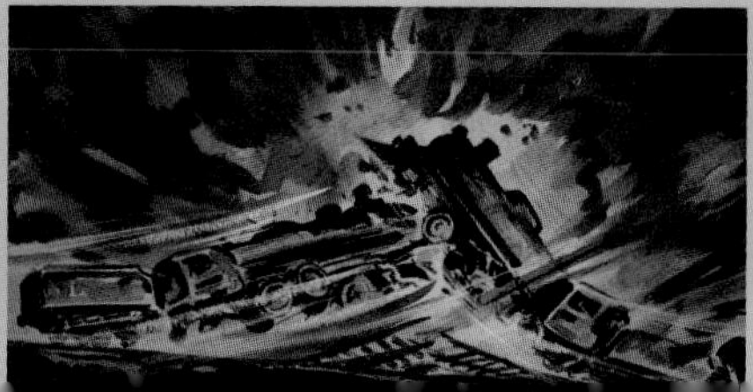
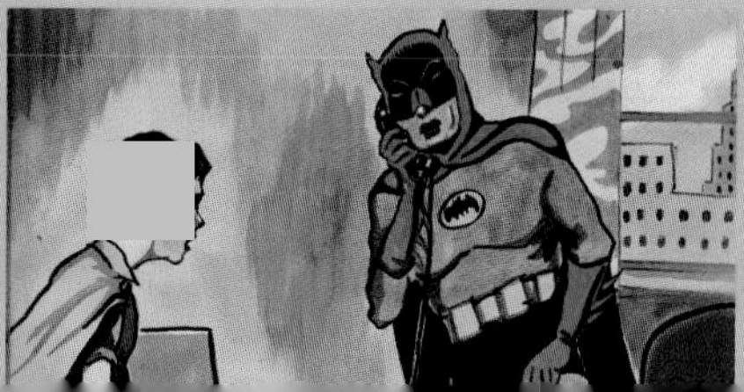
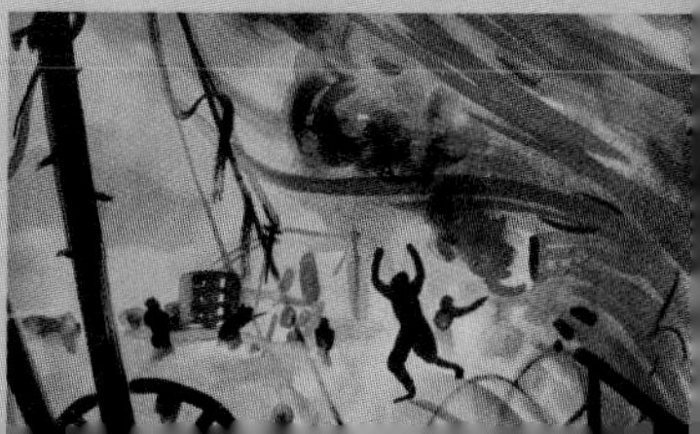

INTRODUCTION BY FREDERIK L. SCHODT

Old memories are washing over me. I'm looking at photographs I took on June 24, 1981, of Masao Morishita, one of the last true *kamishibai* narrators. One shows him standing proudly next to his bicycle, a big wooden box on the back containing the tools of his trade. Others show him selling

candy to eager children in a local park and then narrating *kamishibai* to them. The photos are all black and white, shot with old-fashioned Kodak film, and it reinforces the sense of a different era.

By 1981, *kamishibai* had largely disappeared from the streets of Japan and there wasn't much information available on it, either. I took the photos when doing research for my first book on manga, because I had heard how many manga artists had emerged from the *kamishibai* industry—how *kamishibai* in fact had helped create modern manga. Friends had introduced Morishita-san to me as one of only fifteen *kamishibai* narrators—down from thousands in the immediate postwar period—who still practiced the art the old way, the way it had been before television, manga, and daily animated shows became ubiquitous.

I met Morishita-san in an old, crowded area of Tokyo. Perhaps because *kamishibai* was regarded as a dying, if not dead, art form, I had expected an older, frail-looking person. He was fifty-eight, very short, bald, and toothless, and he reminded me a bit of Yoda in *Star Wars*, but Morishita-san was also lively, grinning, and eager to talk. He wore sandals and nondescript gray clothing, and he looked happier than many people in Japan. He had been doing *kamishibai* performances for over thirty years, and he said his father, then eighty-eight years old, still gave performances in rest homes.

Morishita-san proudly showed me the illustrated storyboards he used. True *kamishibai* street performers, he said, only used hand-painted, original art, and never the mass-produced, printed panels sometimes used by teachers in schools. His were glued on cardboard and lacquered so the rain would not ruin them; on the back they had the basic elements of the illustrated drama outlined in pencil, but like most performers he had all the stories memorized and could easily improvise if necessary.

I walked with him to a nearby park and marveled at his ability to balance such a big box on his bicycle. When fully loaded with panels, a frame to display them, and ingredients for candy in various drawers, it weighed over sixty pounds. Sure enough, when we arrived fifteen to twenty children were already eagerly waiting, money clenched in their hands. Mr. Morishita walked around in a circle, clacking two wooden sticks together to officially announce his presence, and then he began selling candy. The show being free, he made his money from the candy, but this was time-consuming because it was traditional Japanese candy, consisting mainly of colorful gelatinous little blocks and sticky red pastes applied to or sandwiched between crackers, and it had to be assembled. The candy was very inexpensive, and it was clear to me that traditional narrators never got rich. Due to bad weather, most could only work an average of twenty-three days a month.

A gong in the park signaled the start of Morishita-san's *kamishibai* performance. He divided it into three parts—a quiz, where children who answered correctly received candy; a comic tale; and an adventure/horror story. In looking at the photographs, I see that Morishita-san covered many of the same stories showcased in this book, including *Ôgon batto* (Golden Bat). He supplied the voices for dialog, narration, and sound effects, and the children were riveted by his performance.

When it was all over, Morishita-san lamented to me that modern children studied too much and didn't have enough free time. Television had also changed them, he said, for they didn't laugh out loud the way they used to; they also tended to anticipate the endings of the *kamishibai* stories, which made it difficult for him. But they loved the interaction between the narrator and the audience. He said, "*Kamishibai* are a two-way street, as opposed to television, which is a one-way form of communication. Moreover, *kamishibai* are a source of moral teaching . . . television today has no moral emphasis . . . and it is something the children need."

As the years have passed, I have wondered what became of Morishita-san. And I have always been fascinated by *kamishibai*. When I heard that Abrams ComicArts was publishing Eric P. Nash's *Manga Kamishibai* and was asked to write this introduction, I was delighted. Traditional *kamishibai* culture may have been buried by more modern media, but in this beautifully designed, colorful, informative book, it lives on. I am sure that Morishita-san would have been very happy and proud.

FREDERIK L. SCHODT is an author, interpreter, and translator who has written extensively on Japanese culture and Japan-U.S. relations. His latest book is The Astro Boy Essays: Osamu Tezuka, Mighty Atom, and the Manga/Anime Revolution.

GLOSSARY

akabon— "red book"; an early form of manga named for its red covers

anime—Japanese animation

banzai—Salute or cheer meaning "May you live 10,000 years"

bento—wooden lunch box

benshi—live narrators who accompanied silent film

bokken—a wooden sword

bushido—the samurai chivalric code

butai—a miniature stage

chambara—the genre of swordfighting stories, particularly in film

chibi—little, or superdeformed, characters for humorous effect

cosplay—fans dressing in the costume of manga characters

coujinshi—manga produced by amateurs

denki kamishibai—"electric paper theater," i.e., television

emaki—illustrated scrolls

emonogatari—illustrated storybooks

etoki—pictorial storytelling

figyura—figurine

gaito kamishibai—street-corner kamishibai

gekiga—serious or dramatic comics, as opposed to cartoons

genbaku no ko—children of the bomb

gesaku—playful stories

geta—traditional wooden footwear

hentai—sexually perverted subject matter

hibakusha—survivors of the atomic bomb

higa—underground images

hiyogoshi—clapping sticks

jidai geki—period dramas set in feudal Japan

kai—society or association

kamishibai—street theater using painted illustrations

kamishibaiya—a kamishibai performer

kanji—ideograms

Kansai—western Japan

kashihon—a lending-library system for manga

kashimoto—a kamishibai dealer

katana—Japanese sword

kawaii—cute

kendo—the art of fighting with wooden swords

kibyoshi—"yellow-covered book," a predecessor to comic books from Edo-era Japan

kokusaku kamishibai—war propaganda *kamishibai*

kyoiko kamishibai—educational *kamishibai*

kyokan—the group spirit formed by listening to *kamishibai*

maido—French maid outfits

manga—"foolish drawings"; Japanese comics

manga eiga—"moving manga"; early Japanese animation

manga-ka—a manga creator

manji—ancient Buddhist swastika symbol

maru—a crow-quill pen

mukashi mukashi—a long, long time ago

mukokuseki—statelessness

nozoke megane—a 3-D viewing apparatus

oji—uncle

pika-don—the atomic bomb

ronin— "wave men"; masterless samurai cast adrift on the sea of fate

rori-kon—Lolita-style

sanryu—third-rate

SCAP—Supreme Commander, for the Allied Pacific

shakuhachi—a wooden flute

shojo manga—stories for girls

shonen manga—stories for boys

tachie—"stand-up pictures"

taishu engeki—a form of street theater

tanuki—badger spirit

tokko—thought police

ukiyo-e—"pictures from the floating world," prints from Edo-era Japan

utushie—storytelling with slide images

yaoi—a popular genre of homoerotic comics

yamato damashii—the spirit of Japan

waraie—giggle pix

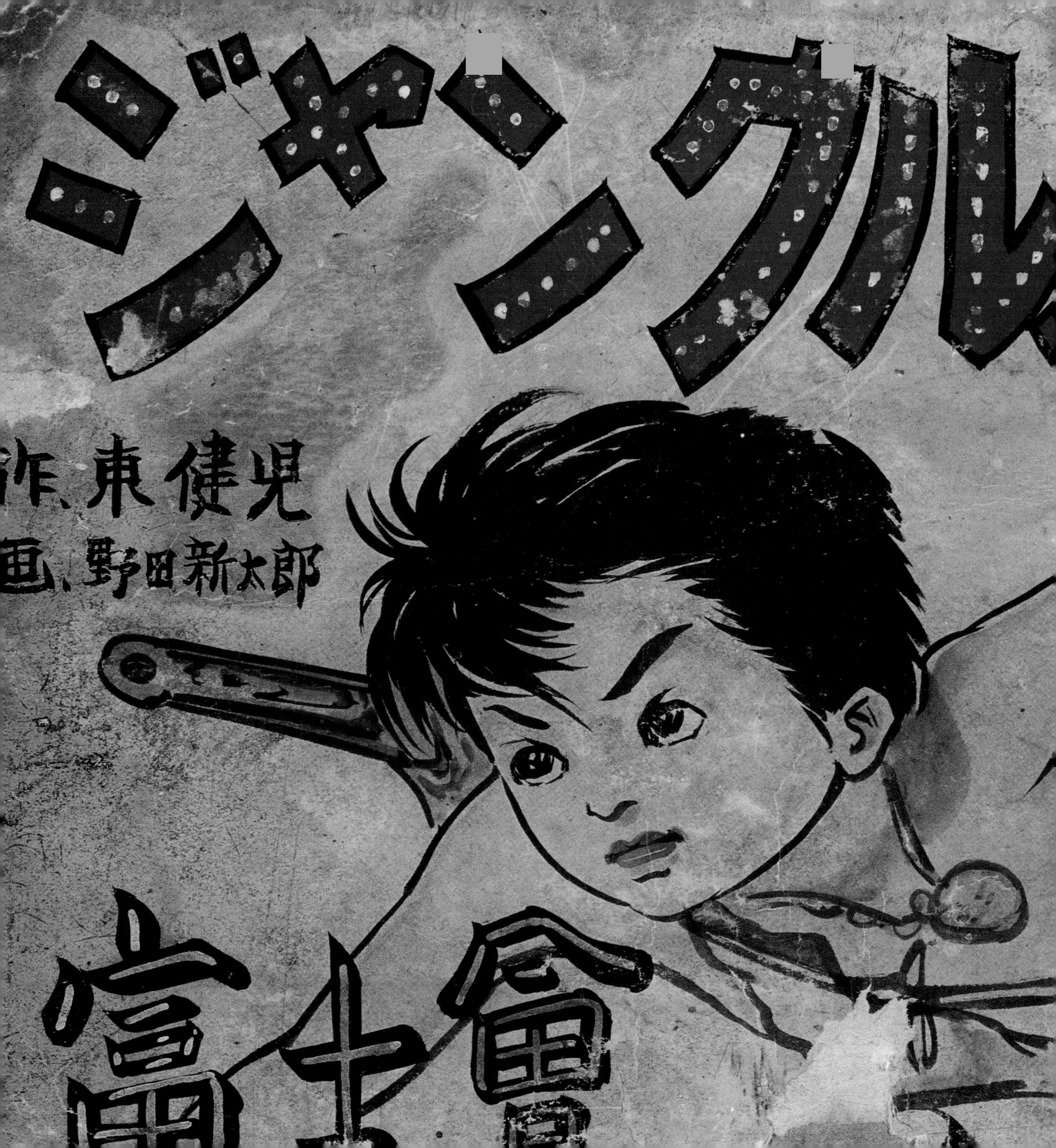
ジャングル
作、東健児
画、野田新太郎

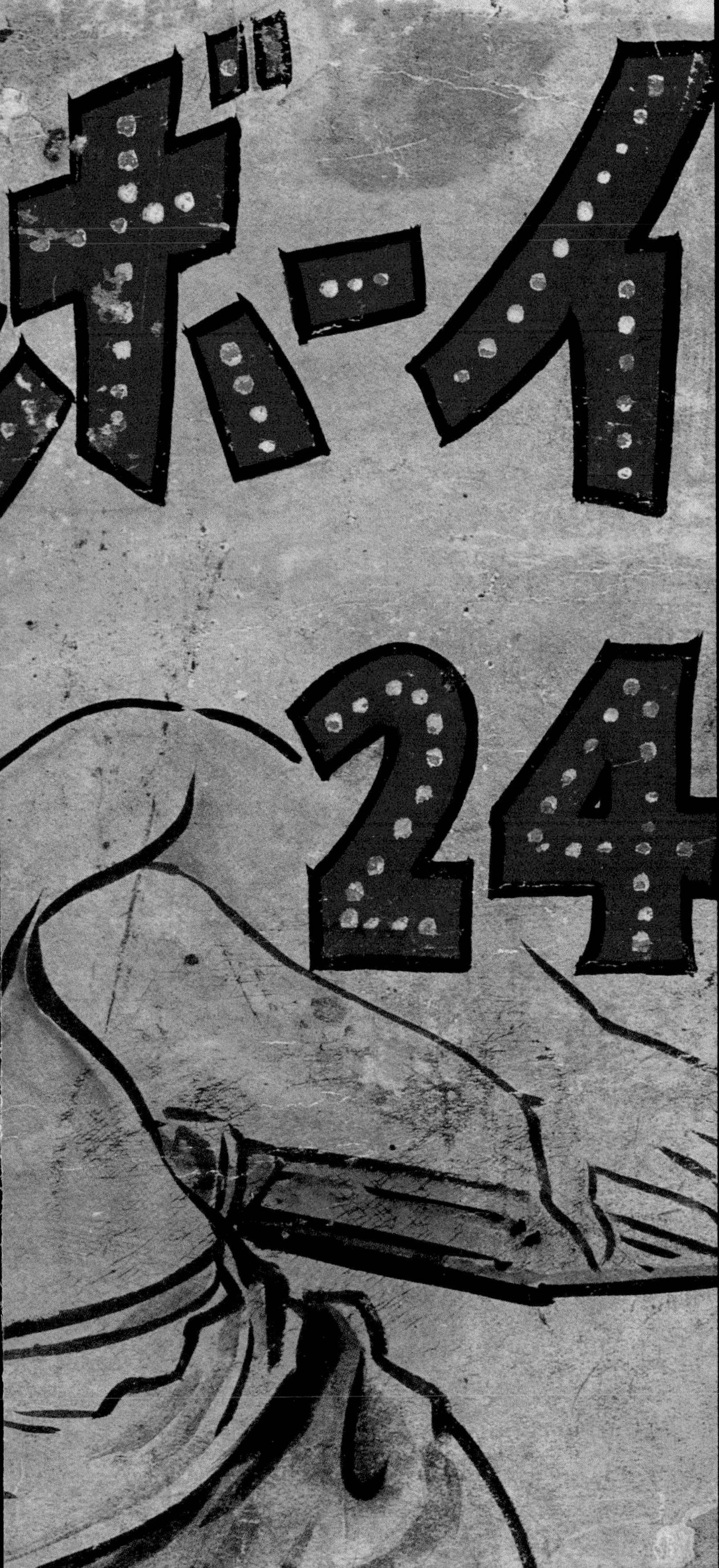
ボーイ
24

RAISING THE CURTAIN

◀ **Jungle Boy**: Rendered in simple outlines and flat poster colors that look remarkably contemporary, Jungle Boy was one of the first popular paper theater characters. Jungle Boy's writer, Kenji Azama, was heavily influenced by Western juvenile authors and characters, including Rudyard Kipling (Mowgli from *The Jungle Book*) and Edgar Rice Burroughs (*Tarzan*).

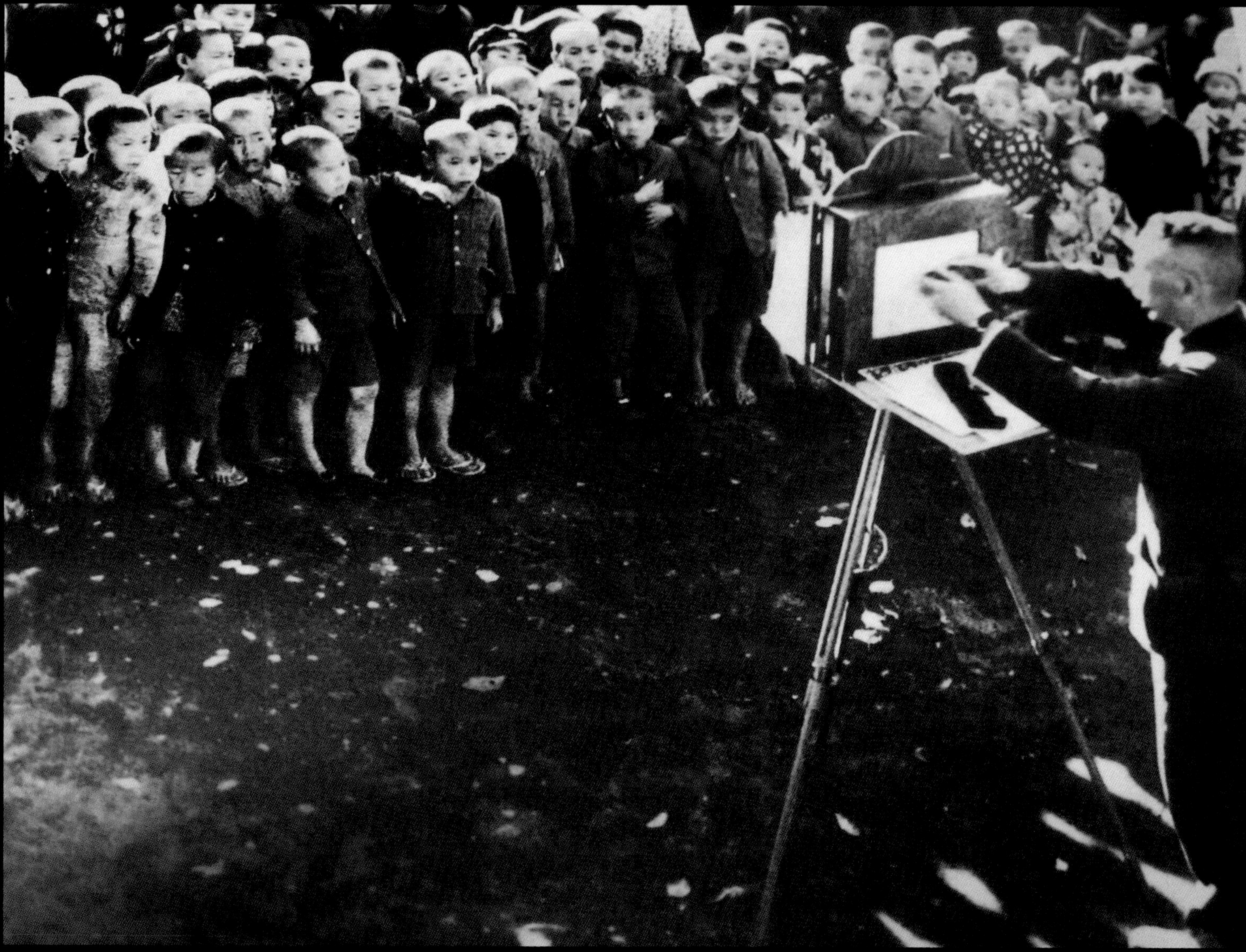

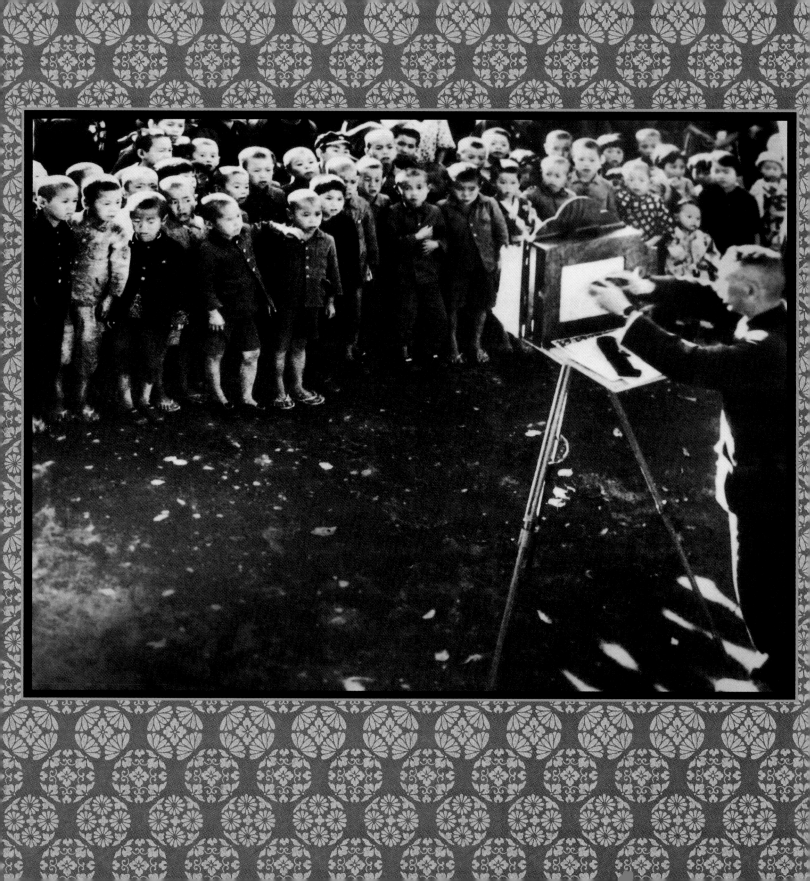

Before manga (Japanese comics) and anime (animation) hit the West with the force of a tsunami, there was an earlier popular art form known as *kamishibai*—paper theater.

Kamishibai were picture stories enacted by itinerant storytellers with illustrated boards set in a Punch and–Judy–like stage. No one knows the exact origins of this type of storytelling: *Kamishibai* appeared "like the wind on a street corner" in the Shitamachi section of Tokyo, Japan, around 1930, one observer noted. At its height in the ruined landscape of post-war Japan, more than 5 million children and adults were entertained by *kamishibai* daily.

If most Japanese pop culture, from videogaming to toy merchandising, is based in manga, manga has its roots in *kamishibai*. Serious manga about adventure, action, and sex (called *gekiga* to distinguish them from funny cartoons), can be traced directly to the *kamishibai* stage.

Street-Corner Theater: *Kamishibai* first appeared in the 1930s, "like the wind on a street corner." A *kamishibaiya*—paper theater storyteller—sets up his miniature *butai* (stage) in a bygone Tokyo of crooked lanes and *geta*-shod urchins. The stage is operated by sliding out successive images painted on heavy poster board. Before World War II, all *kamishibai* were original, hand-painted works of art.

Just as bonsai create a miniature forest, *kamishibai* is a microcosm of twentieth-century Japanese history. *Kamishibai* is not only the story of a lost medium, but a cross-sectional look into the cultural mindset of a people who experienced the worldwide Depression of the 1930s, imperialist expansion in World War II, and crushing defeat and encounter with the West other during American occupation.

***Kamishibai* Woman**: A rare photo of a female *kamishibaiya* from the 1930s. Original works of art were produced by writers and artists belonging to a *kai* (society), and then rented out by dealers (*kashimoto*) for a small fee to storytellers, who eked out marginal profits by selling sweets to children.

Behind the Scenes: A young lad peeks at a *kamishibaiya*'s wares as he tells a samurai story. In the 1950s, nearly 5 million people a day were entertained by *kamishibai* men. Except for a few stars, many of the writers and illustrators have slipped into anonymity.

Typically, the *gaito kamishibaiya* (street-corner *kamishibai* storyteller) would park his balloon-tired black bicycle at a familiar intersection and bang together his *hiyogoshi* (clapping sticks) to announce his presence and drum up anticipation for his picture show. He would unfold a *butai*, a miniature wooden proscenium complete with a satin curtain, to hold the illustrated boards that would slide in. The sharp clack of the *hiyogoshi* was as thrilling as the chimes of an ice cream truck in suburban America. Children gravitated to the storytellers whom they called *ojisan kamishibai* (*Uncle Kamishibai*).

Kamishibai kids crowd around a *butai* in the 1930s. *Kamishibai* dates to a bygone era when children spent languorous afternoons under the spell of *kamishibaiya*, rather than cramming in schools. One *kamishibai* man described the idyll in haiku style: "The ambience of *kamishibai* at fall of evening, fireflies on a darkening street corner."

Kamishibai takes us back to a Tokyo of an earlier time, a city of crooked dirt lanes, tilting two-story structures, and crowds of grimy urchins shod in wooden geta. *Kamishibai* men made an uncertain living by selling sweets as the price of admission to their fantastic little tales. A good *kamishibai* man ran the gamut of voices and facial expressions for his paper plays, from mincing female tones to gruff samurai expostulations.

"You have to create an atmosphere," one veteran *kamishibai* storyteller said. "If I am performing a samurai *kamishibai*, I really have to sound like a samurai."

Kamishibai had its Golden Age, just as American comics did. In 1933, 2,500 kamishibaiya in Tokyo put on their thimble-size theater shows ten times a day for audiences of up to thirty children, reaching a daily total of 1 million kids.

Golden Age *kamishibai* show all the breakneck excitement of American radio and Saturday-afternoon movie serials, with jutjawed heroes, damsels in distress, intercut action, and hairbreadth escapes. There are enough lost Inca gold and heroes wielding bullwhips for an *Indiana Jones* sequel. The repertoire of underground lairs, hooded henchmen, and giant robots is foreign but strangely familiar. *Kamishibai* resembles manga in its dizzying range of genres, including one of the world's first illustrated costumed super heroes, Golden Bat, in 1931, who edged out Lee Falk's Phantom by several years. Traditional folktales like those about Momotaro, the boy who was born from a peach and went on to become a samurai, were played alongside the pulp escapism of Tiger Boy and the courtly Lion Man (who could have walked out of Cocteau's *Beauty and the Beast*).

Kamishibai featured some of the world's first illustrated super heroes with secret identities, like the Prince of Gamma, a boy in a Peter Pan costume with the ability to fly and whose alter ego is a street urchin. The episodic science-fiction serial followed the interstellar adventures of a young alien prince. In one adventure with close parallels to *Twenty Thousand Leagues Under the Sea*, Prince Gamma responds to reports of a giant crablike creature disrupting shipping lanes and drowning passengers. The prince discovers that the sea monster is actually a cleverly disguised submarine, captained by a Nemo-like figure with a strong resemblance to Gumby. Gamma rescues the captive professor, reunites him with his daughter, and flies away before he can be thanked. In another episode he saves the inhabitants of a planet from a veiny, laser-eyed brain creature. A closing shot of the young prince walking into the crepuscular cityscape is as moodily evocative as any final panel of a Steve Ditko *Spider-Man* comic.

Golden Mask: A historical fantasy by way of Hollywood.

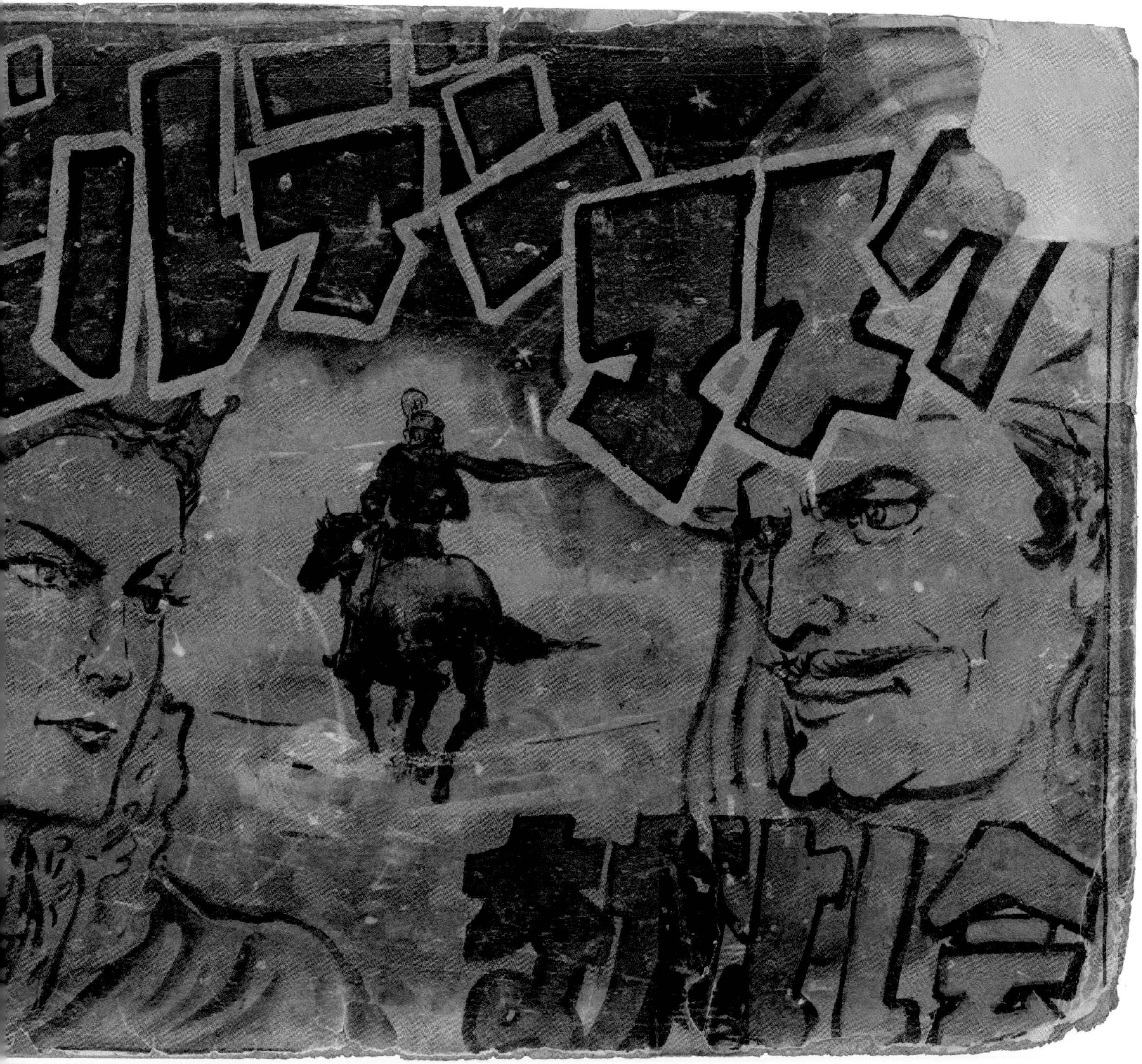

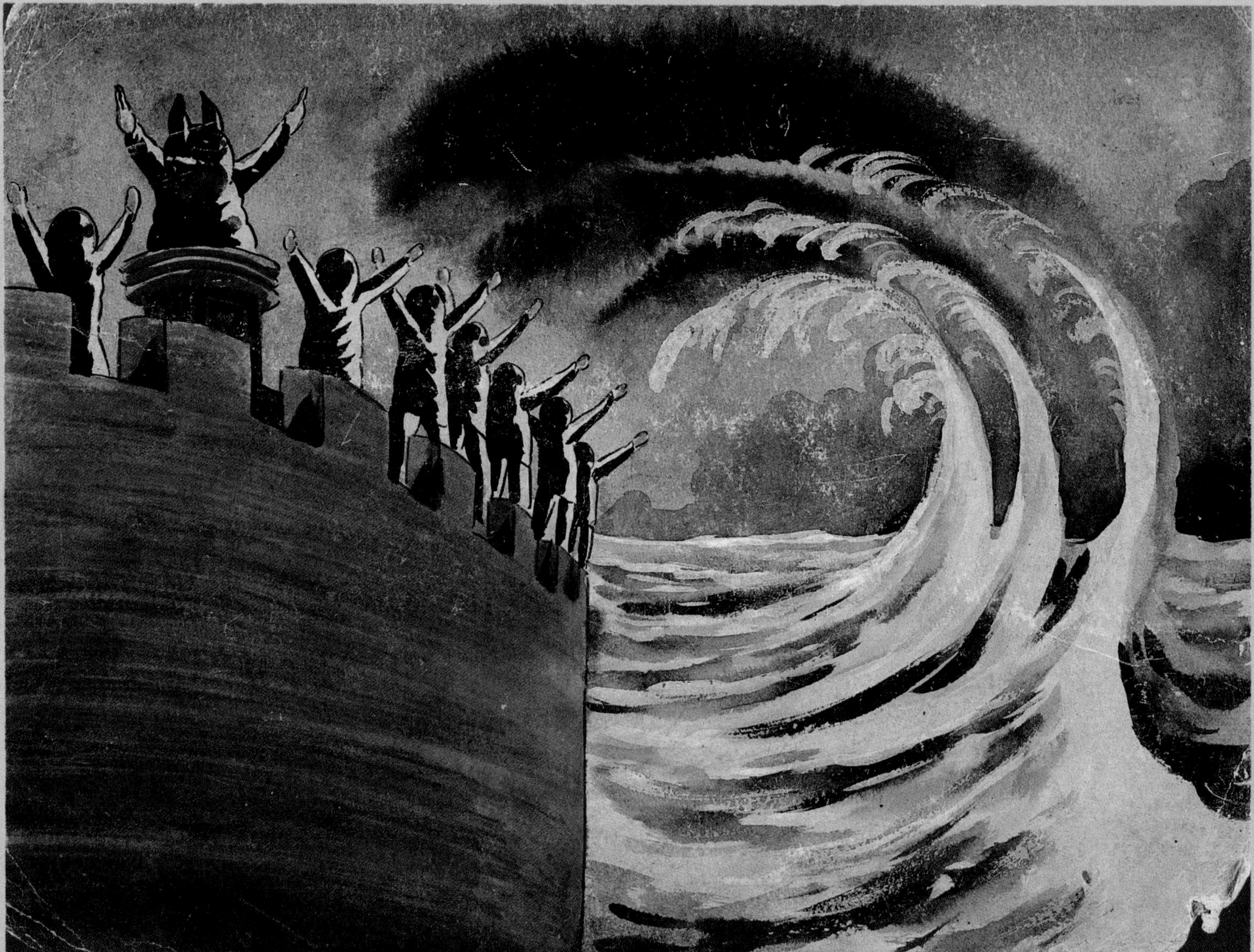

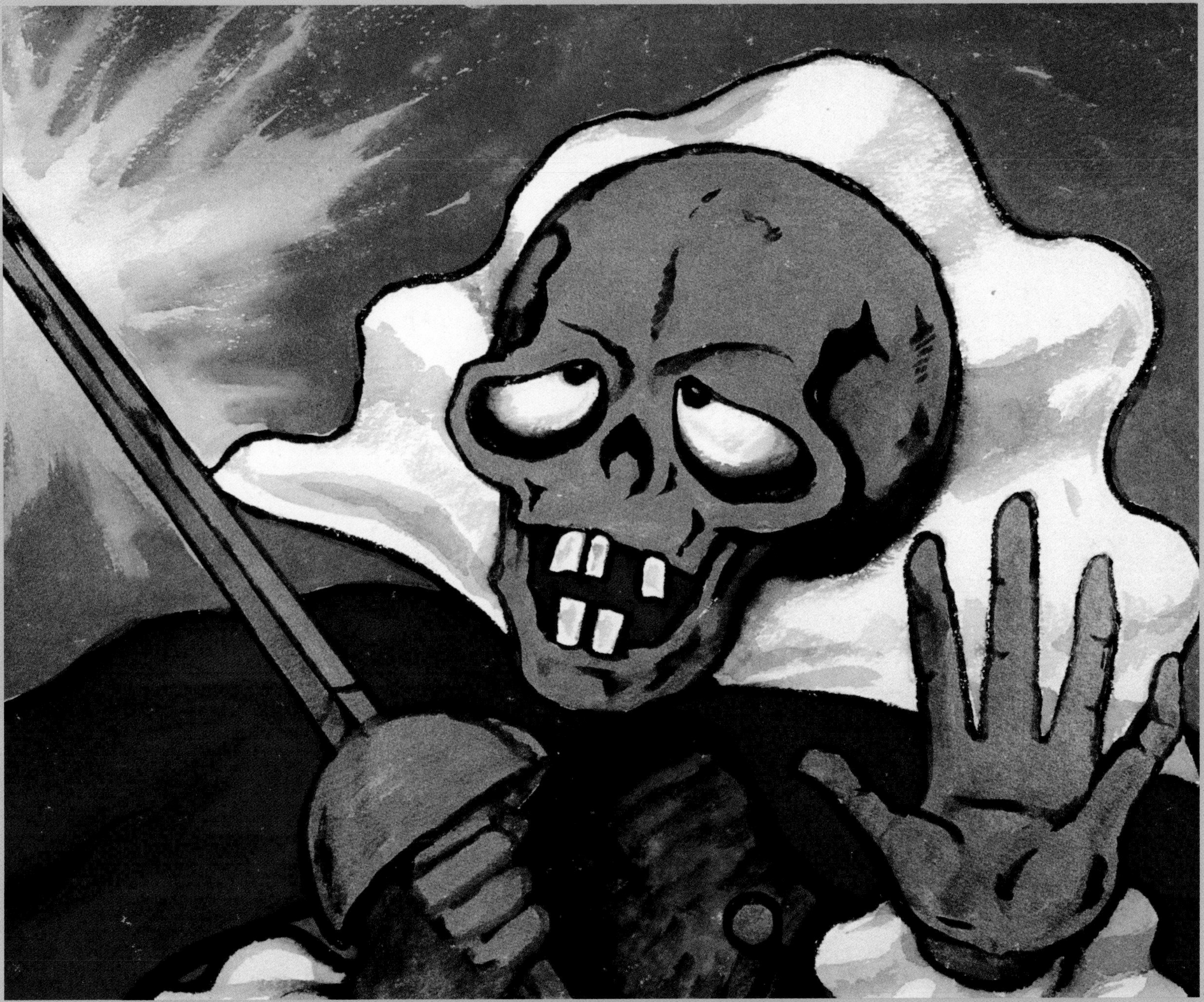

Golden Bat, a supernatural being from Atlantis 10,000 years in the future, who debuted in 1931, is one of the world's first costumed super heroes, predating Lee Falk's the Phantom by five years. Scripted by Ichiro Suzuki and illustrated by Takeo Nagamatsu, the skull-faced, cross-eyed, super hero was the most popular character of *kamishibai*'s Golden Age. The stories about Golden Bat were ahead of their time in featuring space aliens, rocket ships, dinosaurs, and giant robots.

少年

1
女忍者
作画 左久良五郎
三邑会

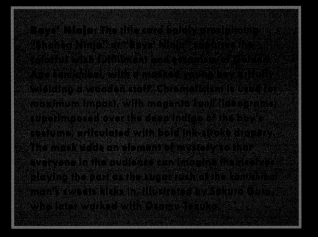

Boys' Ninja: The title card boldly proclaiming "Shonen Ninja" or "Boys' Ninja" captures the colorful wish fulfillment and escapism of Golden Age *kamishibai*, with a masked young boy artfully wielding a wooden staff. Chromaticism is used for maximum impact, with magenta *kanji* (ideograms) superimposed over the deep indigo of the boy's costume, articulated with bold ink-stroke drapery. The mask adds an element of mystery so that everyone in the audience can imagine themselves playing the part as the sugar rush of the *kamishibai* man's sweets kicks in. Illustrated by Sakura Goro, who later worked with Osamu Tezuka.

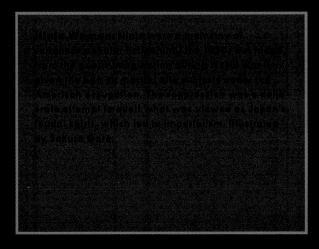

Ninja Woman: Ninja were a mainstay of Japanese popular fiction until the 1930s but faded from the public imagination during World War II, given the ban on martial arts subjects under the American occupation. The suppression was a deliberate attempt to quell what was viewed as Japan's feudal spirit, which led to imperialism. Illustrated by Sakura Goro.

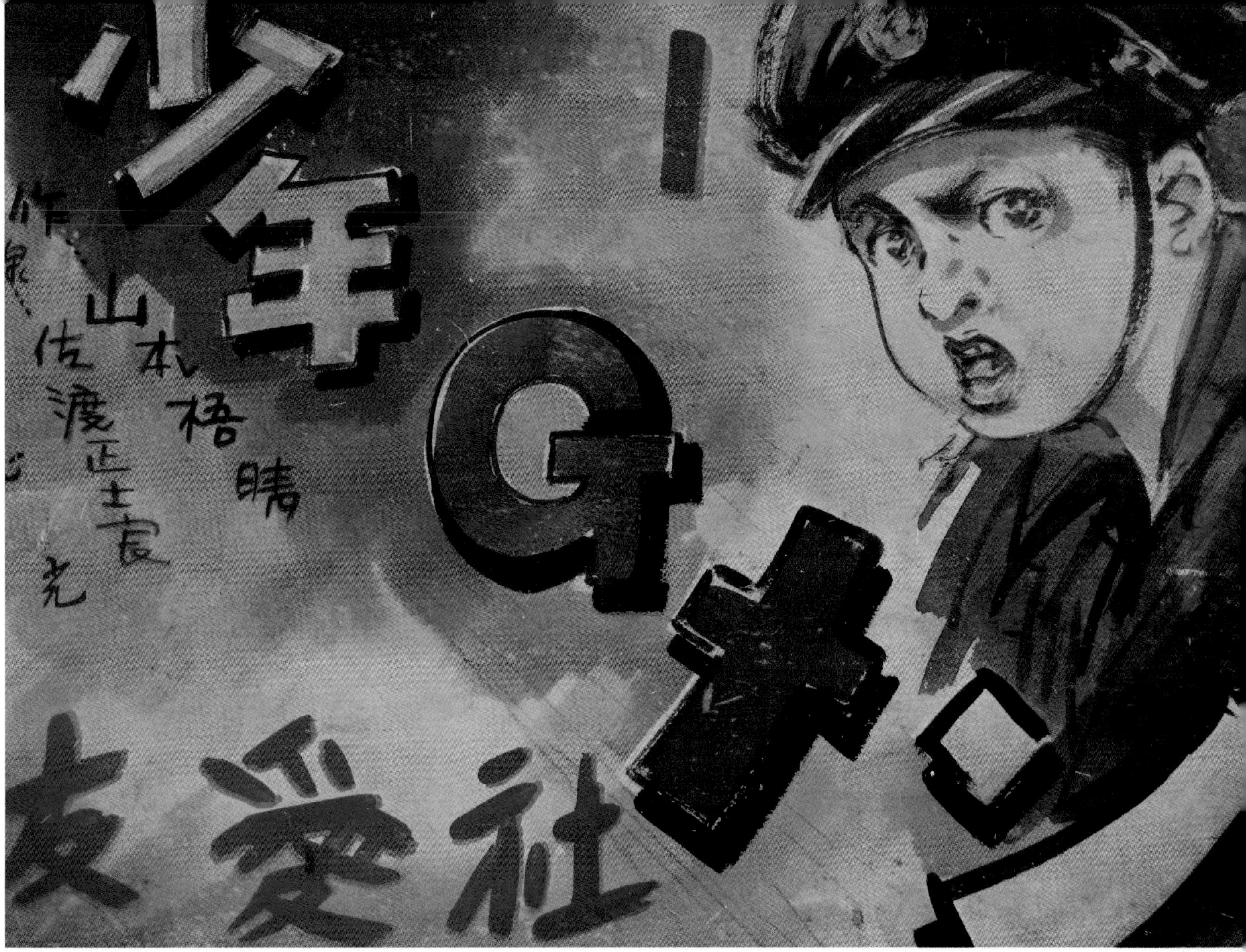
少年G
友愛社

From early on, *kamishibai*, like manga, were divided into *shonen* (boys') and *shojo* (girls') stories. There were enough boys' ninja, girls' ninja, and junior G-men stories for everyone. Costumed adventurers and tales of brave *ronin* battling supernatural forces abound. *Kamishibai* men usually performed a set formula of three tales: a funny story with comic characters, followed by a melodrama for girls, and an adventure or period piece for boys. In one picaresque boys' ninja serial, a young ruffian dares to take on a convoy of black-clad ninja carrying a palanquin.

Shojo kamishibai featured young girls as protagonists, and focused on

Gee, How I'd Like to Be a G-Man: Written by Gosei Yamamoto and illustrated by Seishiro Sawatari, *Boys' G-man* tips its police cap to American movie serials like Universal's *Junior G-men* of 1940. The character's face is unusually modeled with chiaroscuro light and shadow, a development of Renaissance painting as opposed to traditional Japanese art's conveyance of volume through intensity and tonality of line.

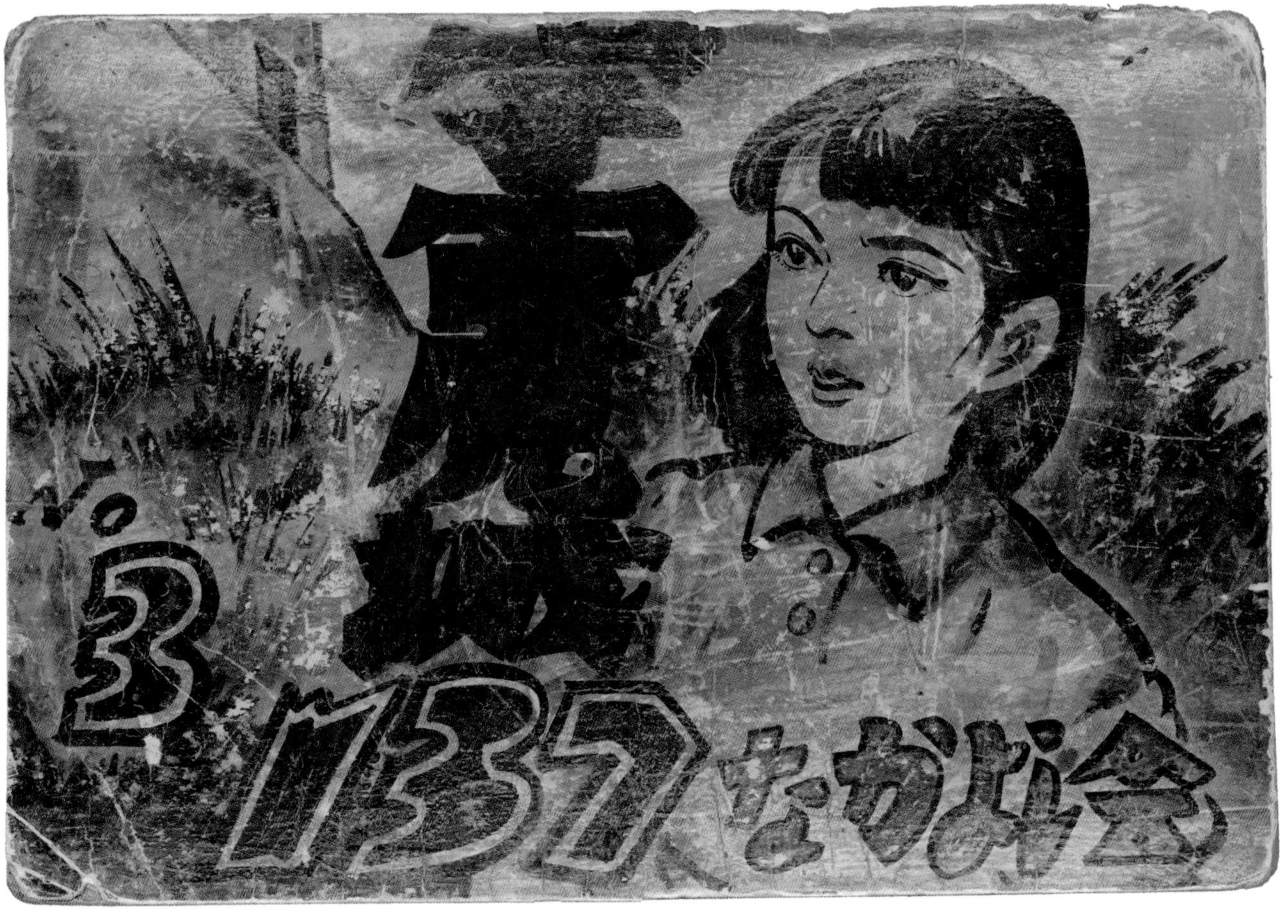
No. 3
137
なかよし会

more down-to-earth scenarios like a girl being teased in class. Sentimental stories often brought adults in the audience to tears. Unscripted except for the order of the pictures, early *kamishibai* were an opportunity for the storyteller to try out new stories and gauge the audience reaction, like a stand-up comedian refining his routine.

A cornerstone of *kamishibai* and a mainstay of today's manga and anime is children in peril, as in *Naruto* and *Full Metal Alchemist*. In *kamishibai*, children are shown solving crimes, shooting guns, piloting boats, and generally outwitting grown-ups. *Kamishibai* creators took inspiration from popular movies and fiction for the juvenile audience: Kipling's Mowgli, Tarzan, Robin Hood, and *The Prince and the Pauper*. Creators also looked to Dickens

Demon Castle of Outer Space: Like movie studios and comic book houses, the *kai* (societies) put their imprint on productions by matching a bullpen of scriptwriters and illustrators.

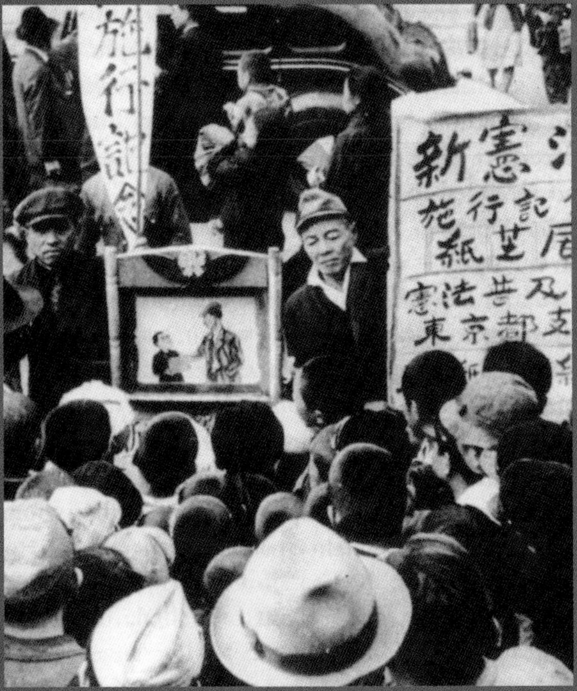
新憲
施行記
紙芝居
憲法普及
東京都支

Farewell to Feudalism: When the American-drafted constitution, with its controversial Article 9 that forbade Japan from ever rearming itself, was unveiled on May 3, 1947, many adults first heard the news announced by *kamishibai* men.

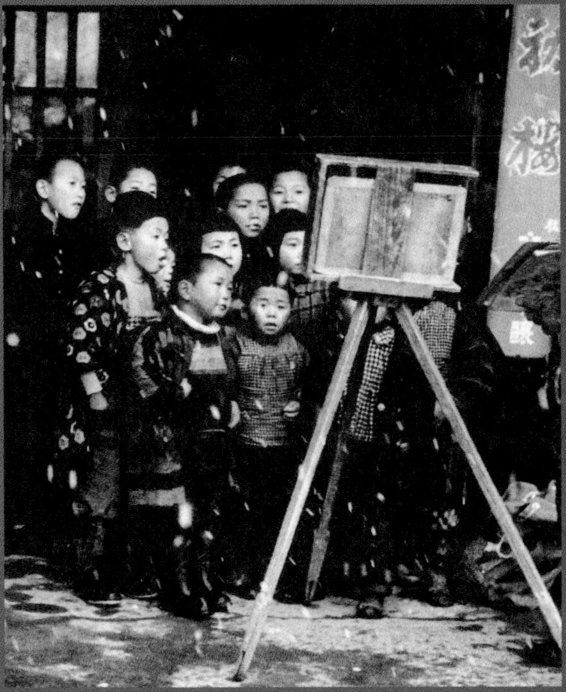

The Storyteller's Art: Children huddle under the shelter of an eave on a snowy Tokyo afternoon, transfixed by a storyteller's magic. *Kamishibaiya* usually divided their performances into three parts: a funny tale featuring comic characters; a *shojo manga* (story for girls, often a domestic drama); and a *shonen manga* (boys' adventure story featuring tales of derring-do), categories that carry over into manga today.

for his ability to construct long story arcs spanning many installments. The rivet-head realism of Jules Verne's nineteenth-century technology influenced the look of many science-fiction *kamishibai* as well as Osamu Tezuka's *Astro Boy* in 1952.

During World War II and the American occupation, *kamishibai* also functioned as a kind of evening news for adults. When the new constitution forbidding warfare was announced on November 3, 1946, many adults heard the news from their local *kamishibai* man.

Like the congressional hearings into American comic books as a corrupter of youth, *kamishibai* was investigated and censored a number of times in its colorful past before it was put to use by the government itself. The medium was considered so powerful that the Tokyo Trials after the war examined *kamishibai*'s role in furthering the Japanese war effort.

Kamishibai's demise neatly overlaps with the end of the occupation in 1952 and the advent of television in Japan in 1953. *Kamishibai* was so engrained in Japanese life that when television was first introduced it was known as *denki kamishibai* (electric paper theater).

Japanese adults can still recall the scent of roasting sweet potatoes and chestnuts emanating from the *kamishibai* man's cart in the dwindling days of autumn as they returned home from school. As the tale reached its climax in the gathering twilight, voice and images formed a bridge between poverty and dreams.

One *kamishibai* man lamented in haiku style the passing of the medium to television: "*The ambience of* kamishibai *at fall of evening, fireflies on a darkening street corner.* A screen can't compare to that."

PRINCE OF GAMMA AND THE SEA MONSTER

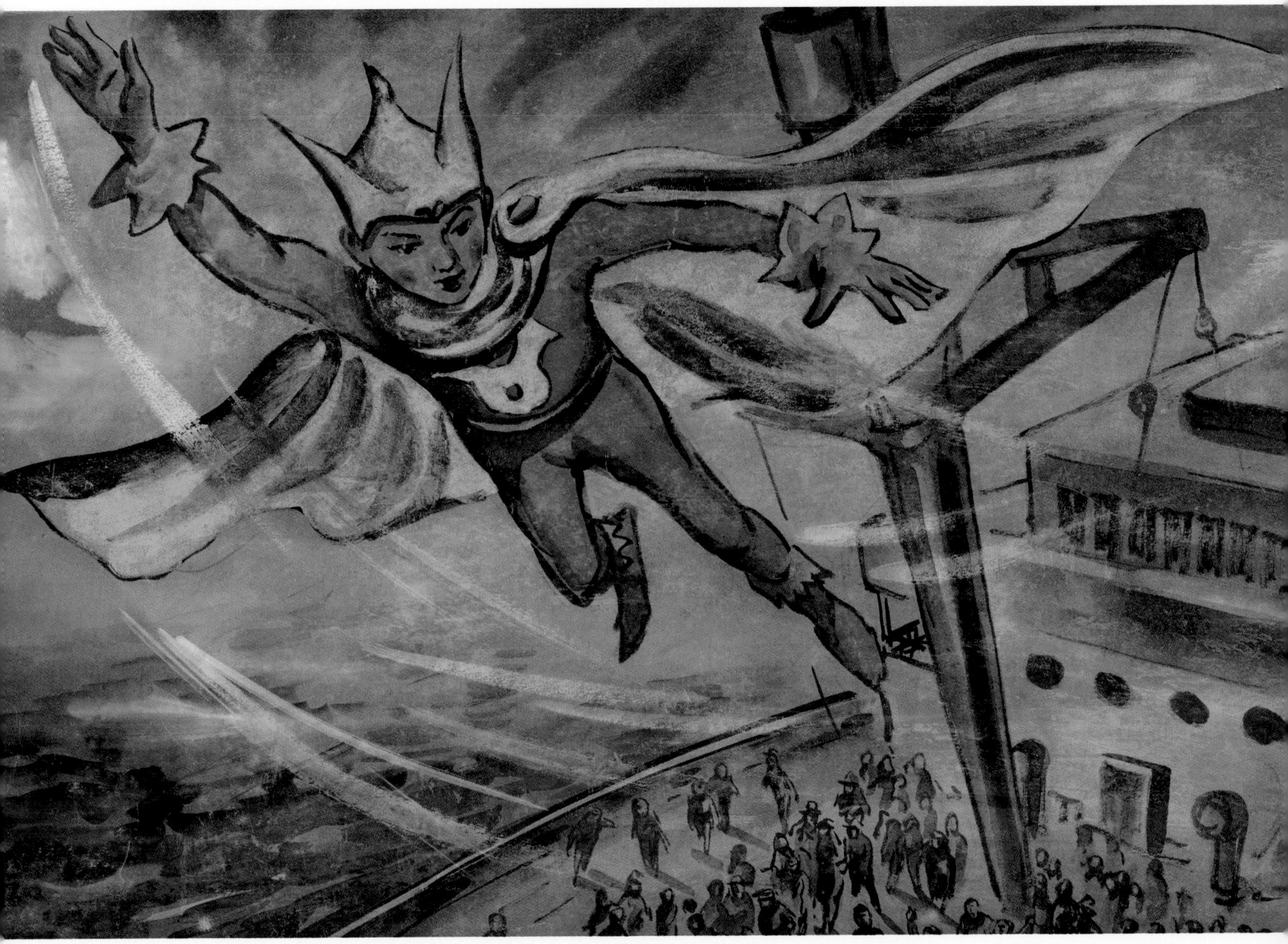

Prince of Gamma, featuring an interstellar hero by way of J. M. Barrie's *Peter Pan*, was from the nuts-and-bolts school of science fiction. In this episode, Prince of Gamma takes on a mad captain of a sea-monster-like submarine, à la Jules Verne.

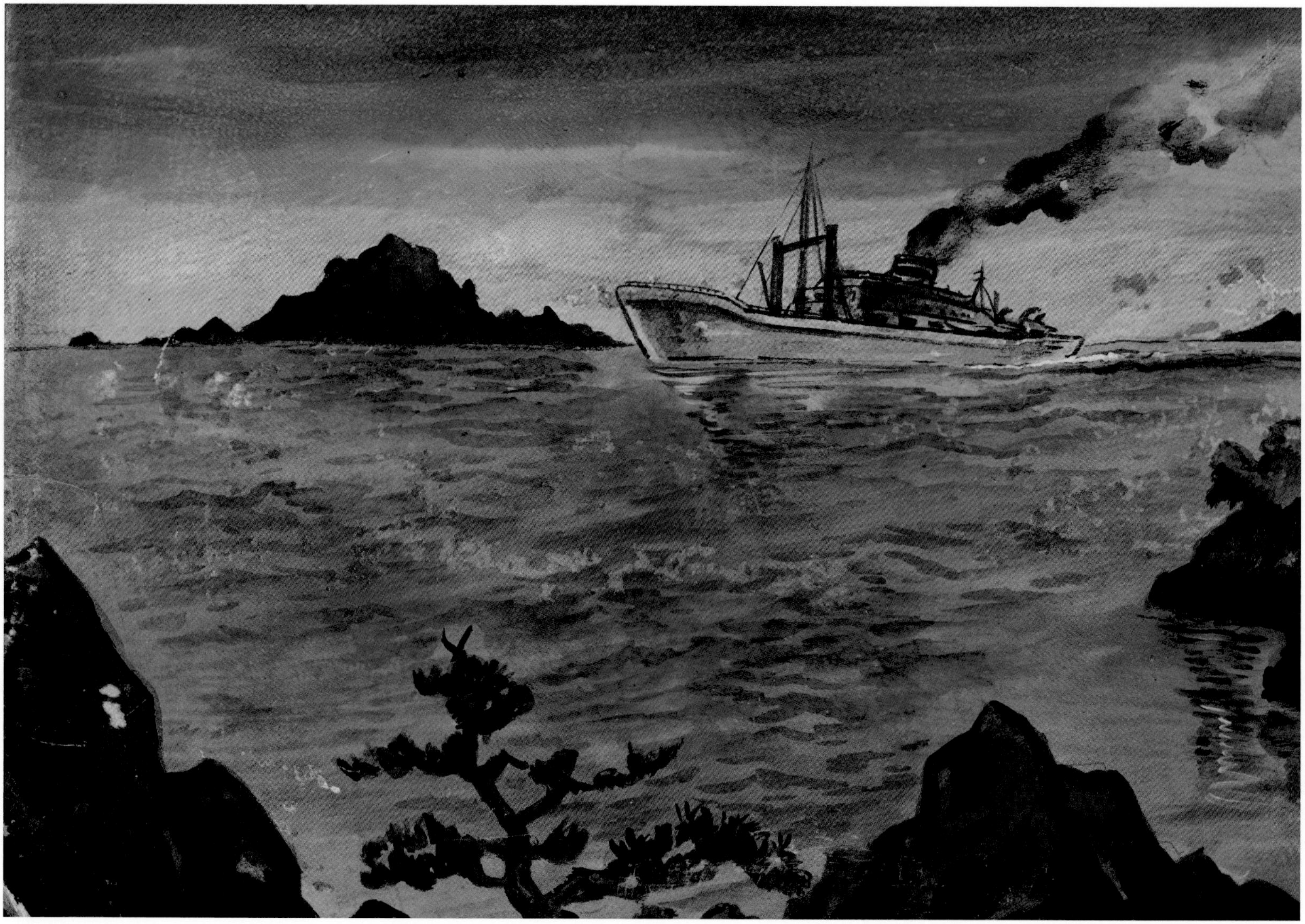

Fantastic Voyage: A steamship traverses a calm sea at sunset in the opening scene of this adventure patterned after Jules Verne's *Twenty Thousand Leagues Under the Sea*.

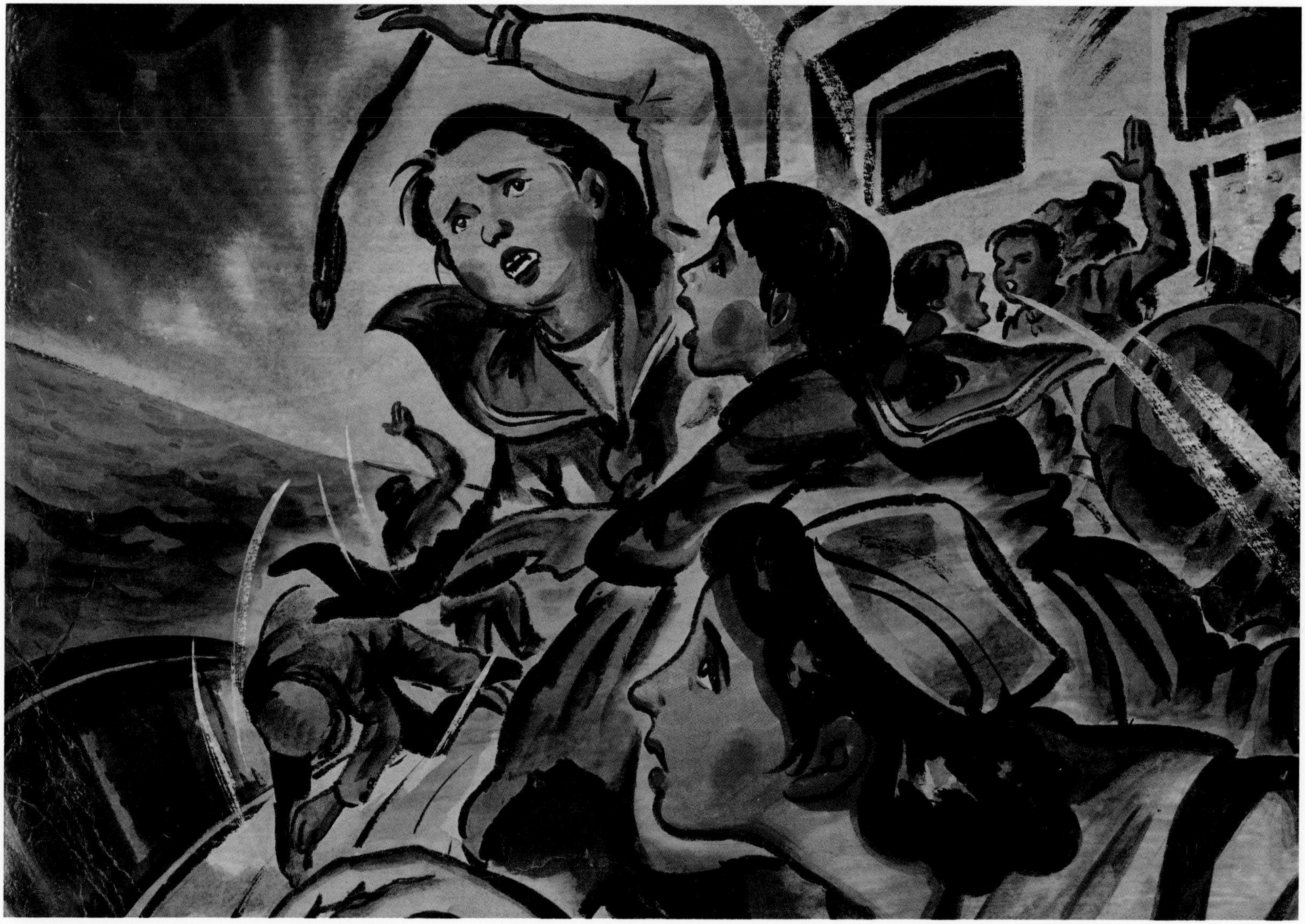

Overboard: The ship rocks violently, with cartoon motion lines rendered in feathered brushstrokes. The *kamishibai* teller would give voice to the screams of the passengers and use special effects like drums and gongs to convey the chaos. The young girls in the center are wearing middy blouses, still worn today by Japanese schoolgirls.

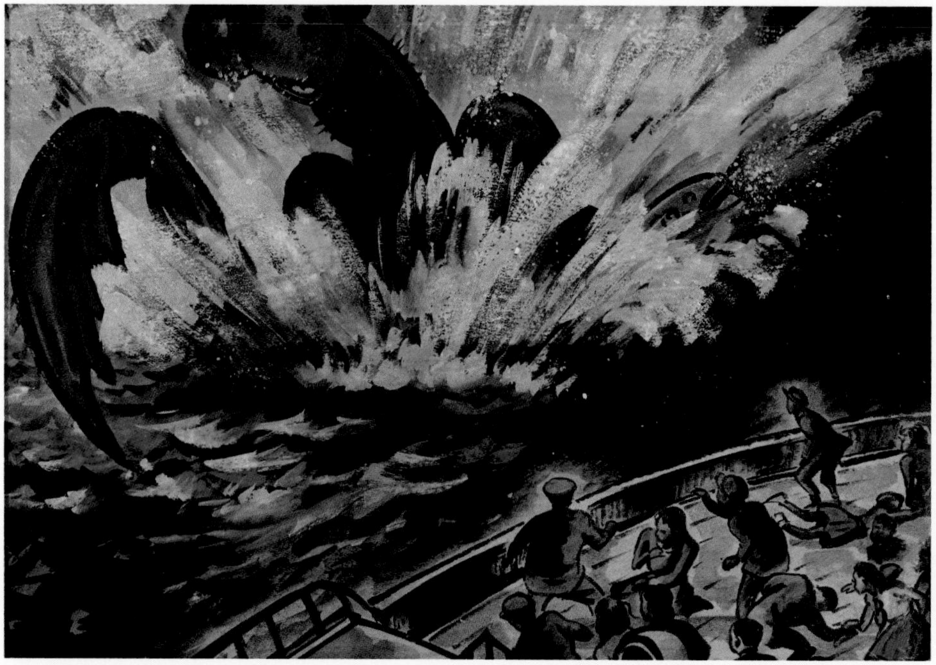

ABOVE King Crab: A crablike sea monster appears off the bow in a colorful spray of water. Some censors claimed that *kamishibai* colors were "too stimulating" to young minds.

RIGHT Splash Page: The bug-eyed monster sinks the steamer with the swipe of a giant claw. *Kamishibai* were drawn with heavy India ink brushstroke outlines and painted in with layers of watercolor and an overlay of tempera paint. A brief summary of the action was written on the reverse side of the panel for the *kamishibaiya* to extemporize upon. Street-corner storytellers were constantly under the scrutiny of police and local authorities to censor their sometimes lurid contents, often on the pretext that the candy sold was unsanitary and that the crowds of children created traffic problems.

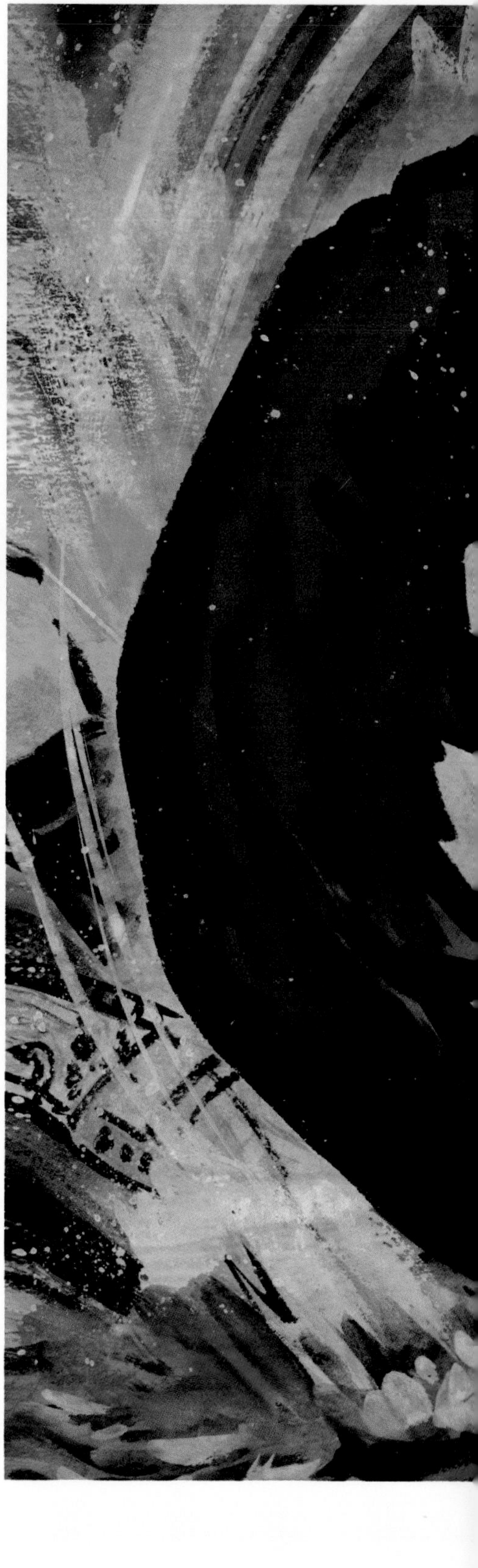

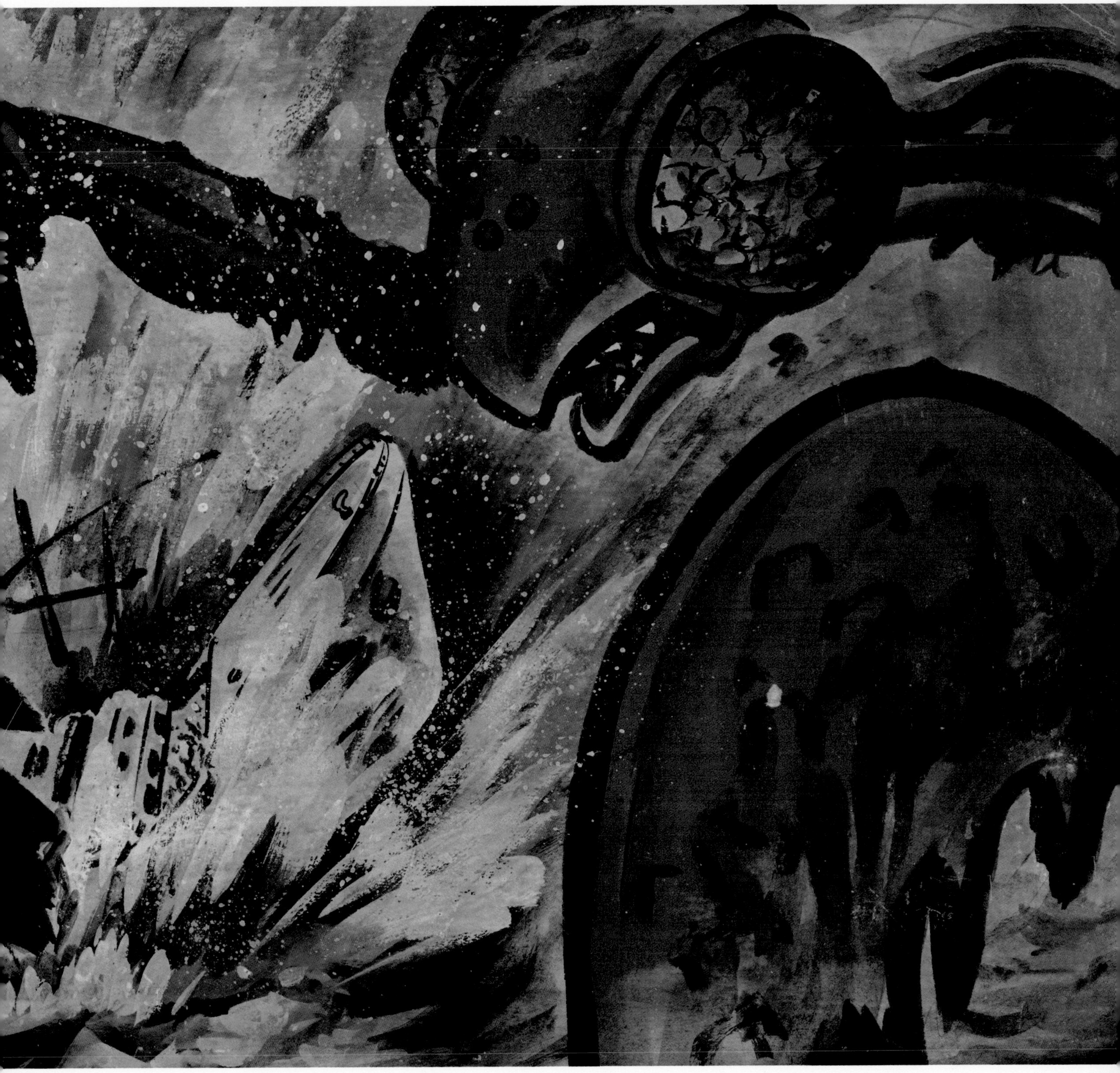

ABOVE Maelstrom: The eye of the *kamishibai* artist is more akin to the deep focus of a movie camera than to the flat perspective of landscape painting. Children would be immediately drawn into this story by images of the drowning girl and boy in the foreground, and by the horrifying downward spiral in which bodies are pitched into the air. A common motif of children in peril follows through from Grimm's fairy tales to Dickens to *kamishibai* to *Harry Potter*, and the latest J-horror flick of demon children.

OPPOSITE, TOP Shipping News: In a pre-TV era, news of the sea monster's attack hits the streets of Tokyo (the newspaper reader oddly resembles R. Crumb in one of his cityscapes). In the 1920s, a new type of newspaper for working-class readers featured, for the first time, comic strips. Later, borders between serialized newspaper novels, *kamishibai*, manga, and film would become quite fluid.

OPPOSITE, BOTTOM Anchorman: A strange being from another planet with powers and abilities far beyond mortal men, Prince of Gamma flew through the air with a cape and had superstrength like a well-known American super hero (i.e., Superman). Here, the Prince smashes a giant anchor against one of the sea monster's "eyes"—a plate-glass portal.

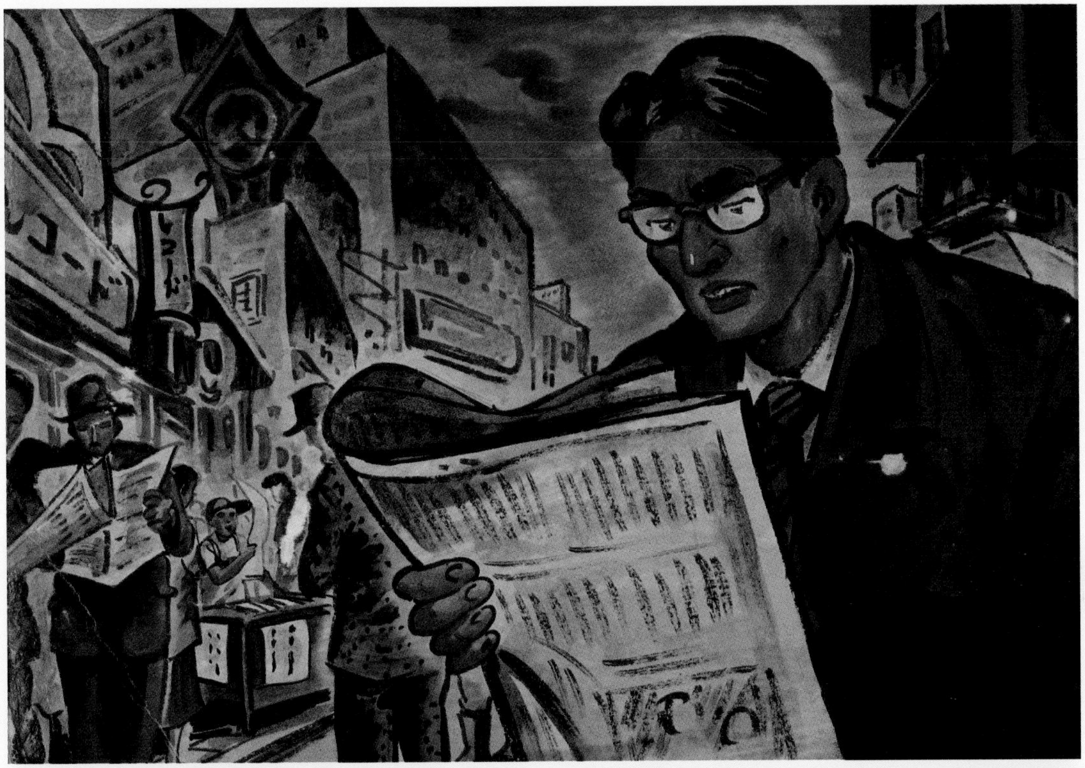
レコード

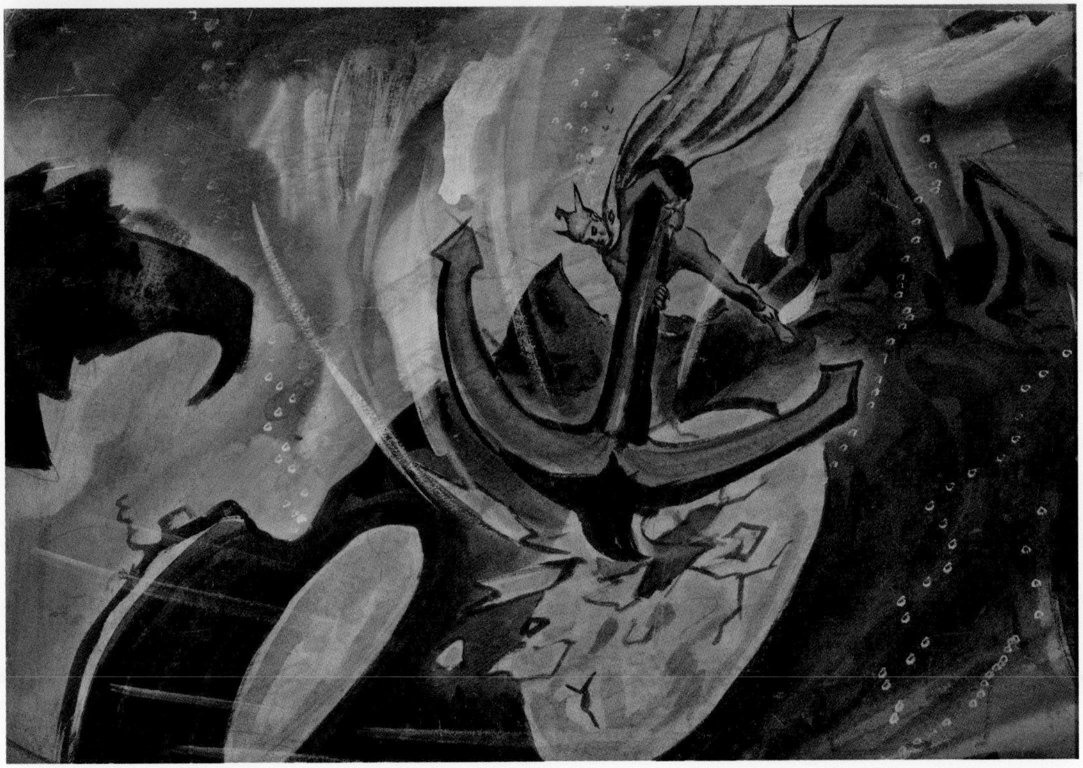

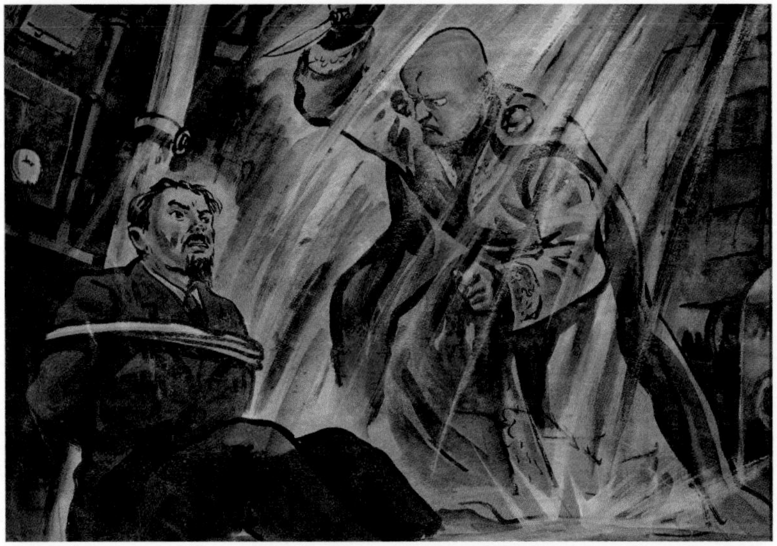

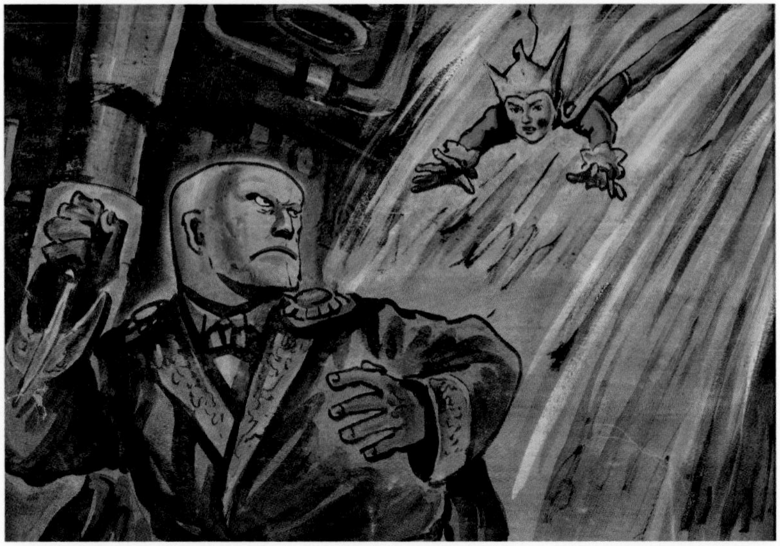

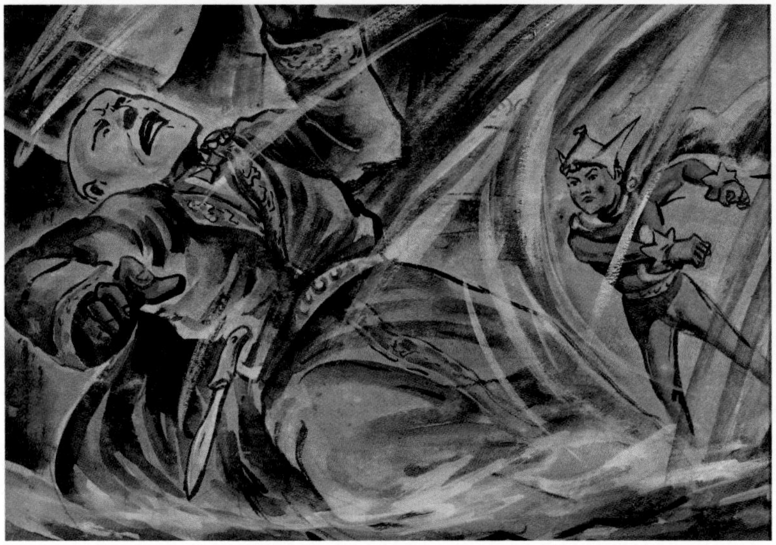

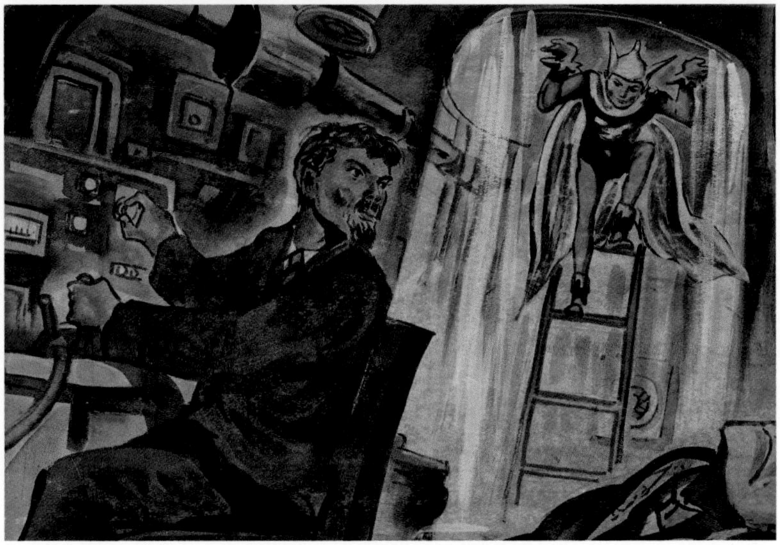

TOP LEFT Storyboards: The evil submarine captain, who looks more like Gumby than Captain Nemo, is about to stab his hostage when water sluices in from above. The characters' poses magnify the menace of the knife and the vulnerability of the brave professor. *Kamishibai* resemble film storyboards in selecting key action sequences.

TOP RIGHT Closely cut action gives an impression of cinematic movement, as the bald-domed bad guy with epaulets and a bow tie turns to see Prince of Gamma descending upon him in a rainbow of color. The panel is framed from a low angle to maximize the action.

BOTTOM LEFT In a flurry of painted motion lines, Prince of Gamma pastes Baldy on the chin with a good old roundhouse right, like in an American action reel, rather than using Japanese martial arts. The *kamishibaiya* would vocalize all three characters in the scene as well as the roar of the water and the sound of the sock on the jaw.

BOTTOM RIGHT The Prince seals the hatch as the professor takes over the controls (which look no more complex than an old Ford V-8). The villain is reduced to a jutting jaw in the lower right-hand corner.

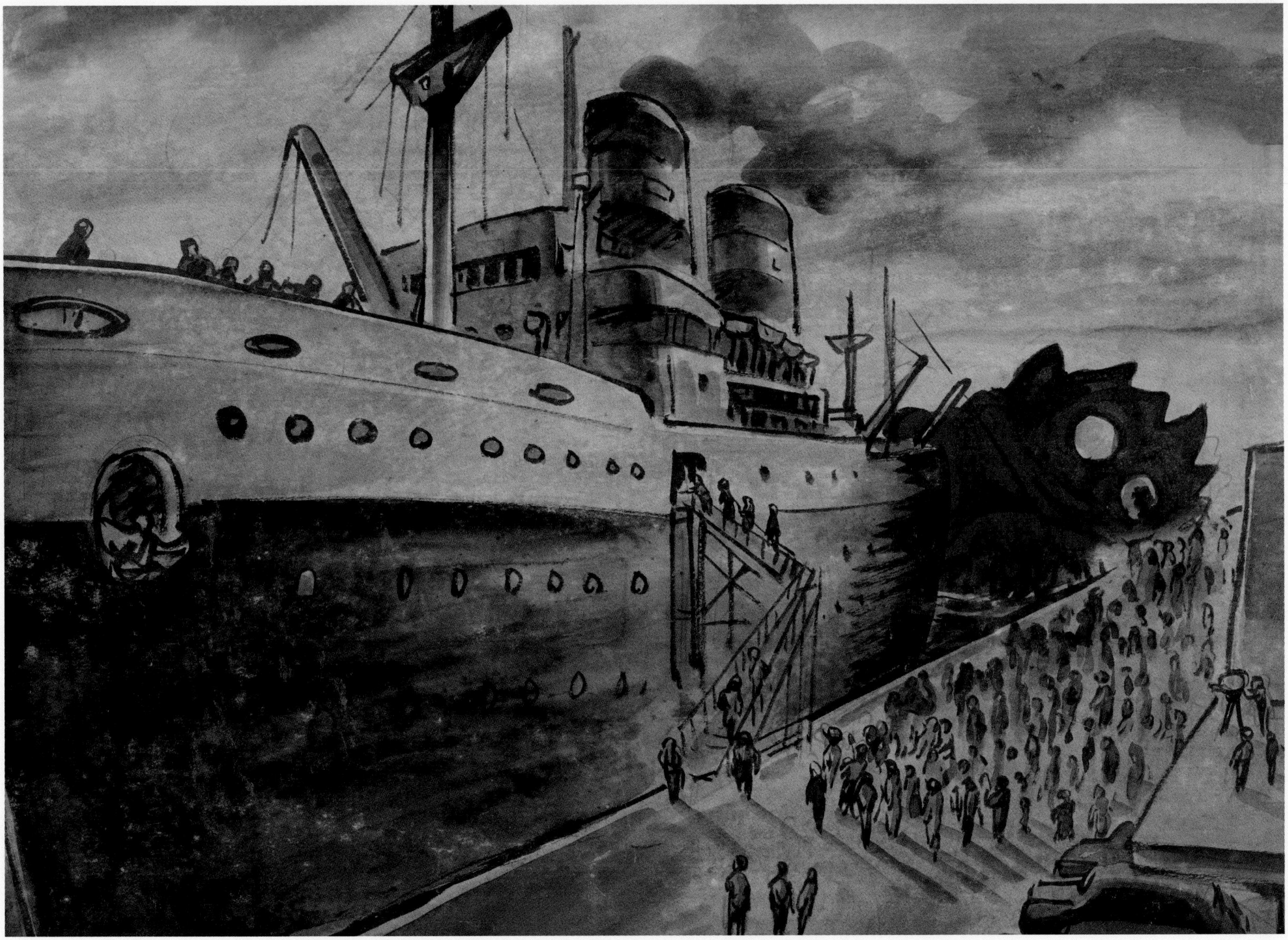

Little Nemo: A steamer hauls to port the shattered hull of the "sea monster," looking like a deflated Macy's balloon, as an eager crowd stands by. The scene is strongly composed with the diagonal of the dock, the towering wall of the steamer's hull, and the once-mighty submarine in the background.

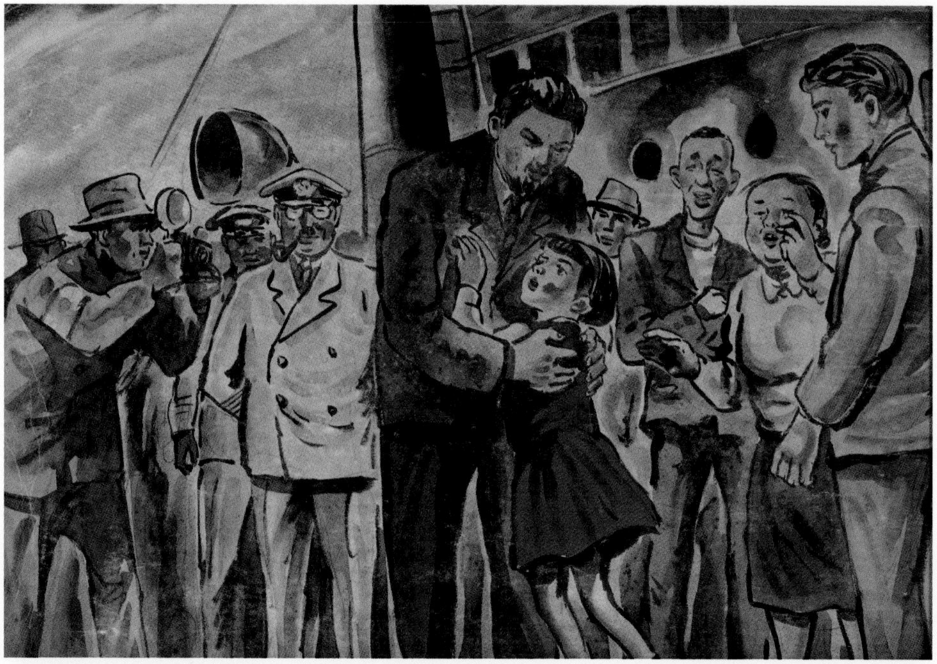

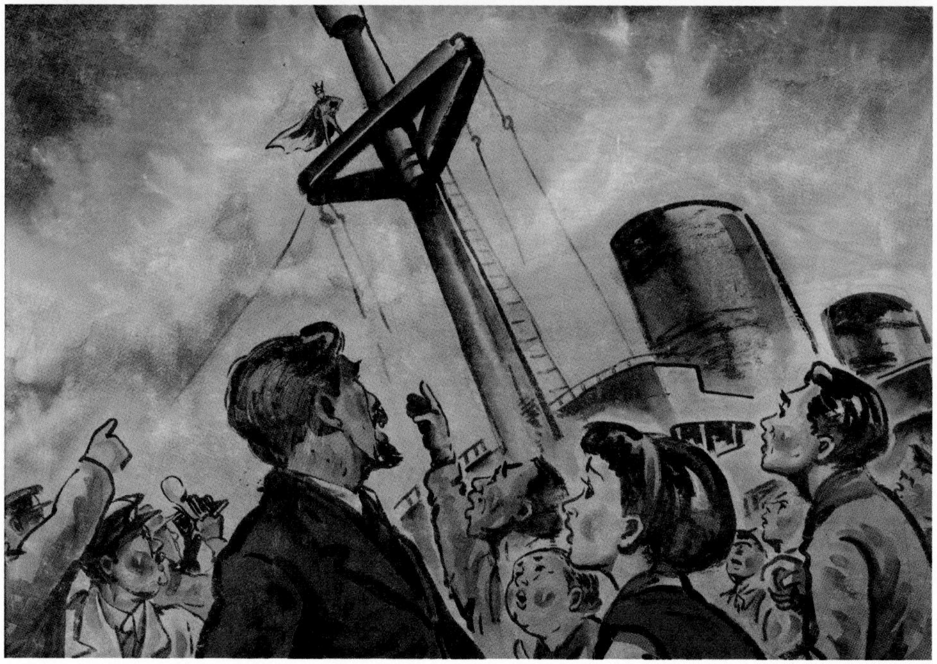

TOP What's Up, Dock?: The professor is reunited with his loving daughter, as a cast of characters looks on approvingly and an old-style news photographer pops a flashbulb.

BOTTOM Master and Commander: Prince of Gamma observes the reunion from atop a mast and flies away before he can be thanked for his heroics.

PRINCE OF GAMMA IN DEMON CASTLE OF OUTER SPACE

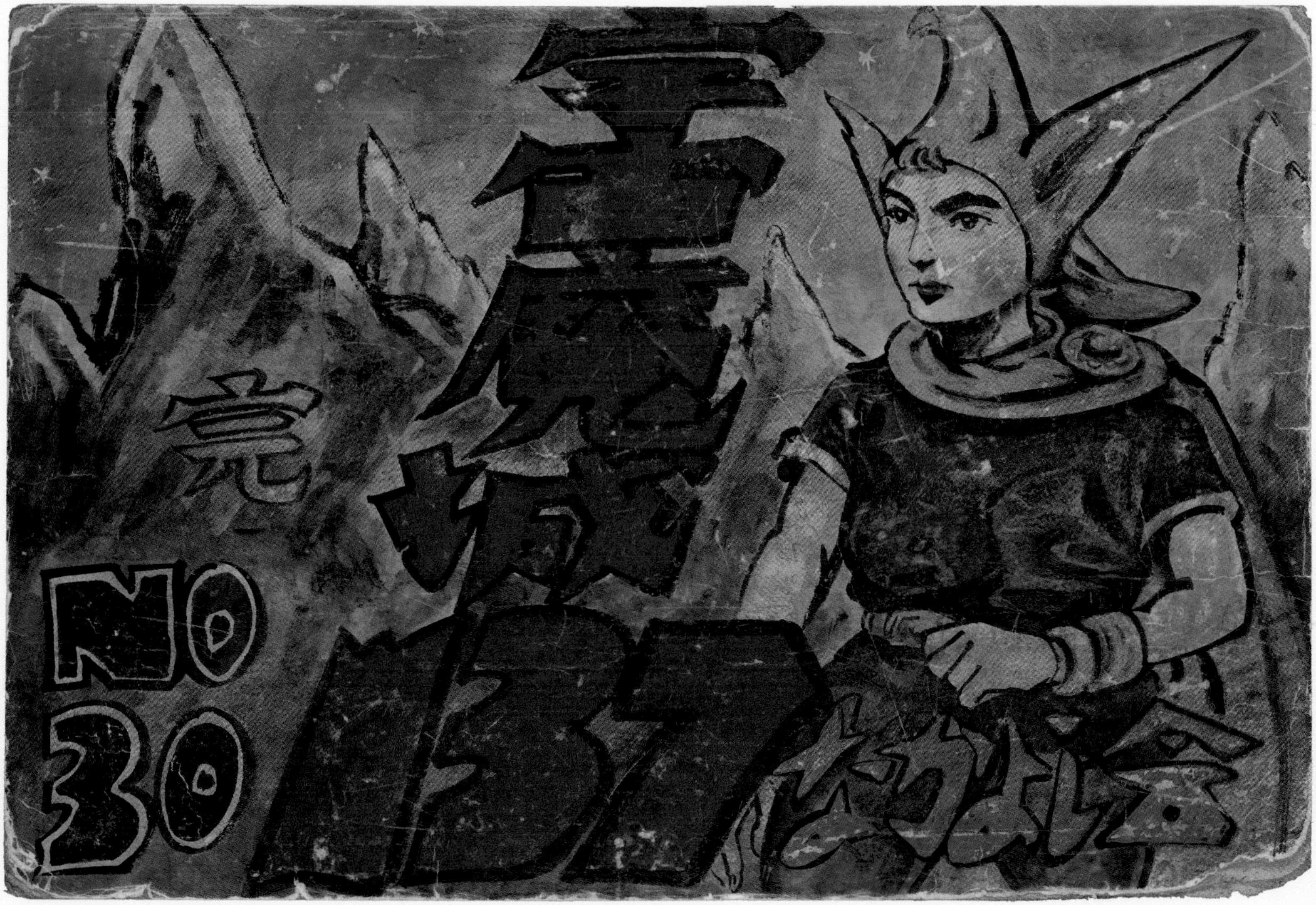
完
NO 30

Star Wars: Prince of Gamma takes on an alien monster in this chapter of *Demon Castle of Outer Space*. In a fascinating bit of transcultural borrowing, the title letters slant away from the viewer as they did in the old *Flash Gordon* serials, a trick picked up by George Lucas for the opening credits of *Star Wars*.

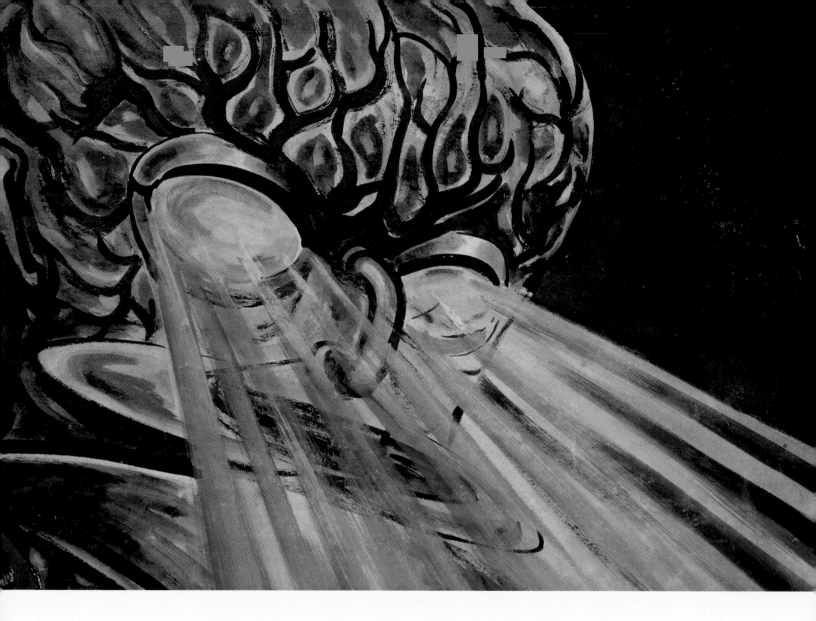

The Eyes Have It: In this spacey *Prince of Gamma* episode, a monster with an exposed cerebrum (not a very intelligent design, if you think about it, because it leaves him extremely vulnerable) resembles the Braniac alien in the classic 1955 cheapie *This Island Earth*. The prismatic colors of the rays shooting from the creature's eyes and his pulsing scarlet veins play up the immediacy of the *kamishibai* experience. A talented *kamishibaiya* would entertain his audience by voicing the monster's otherworldly commands.

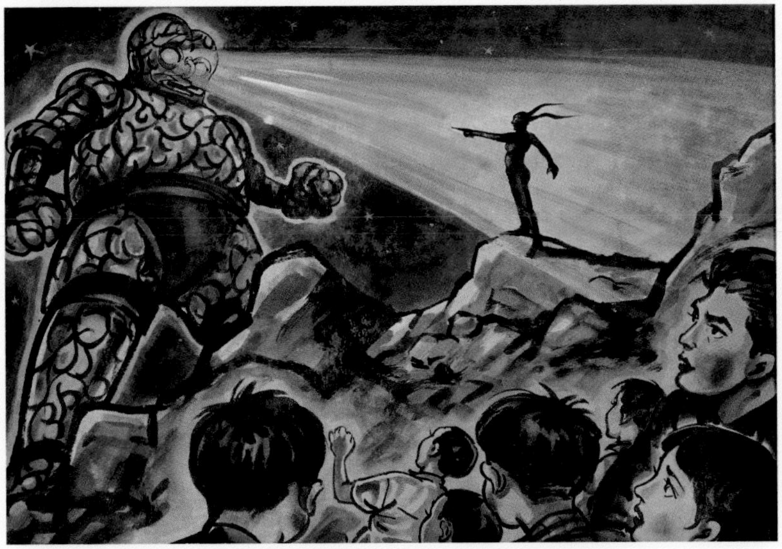

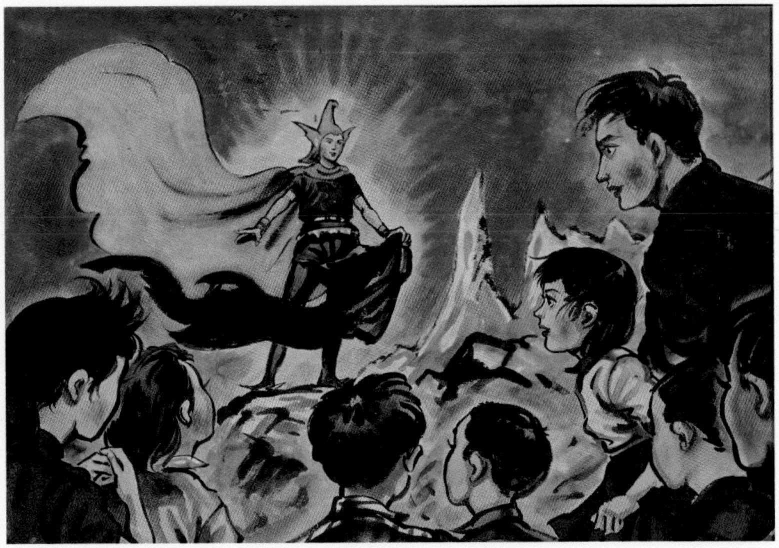

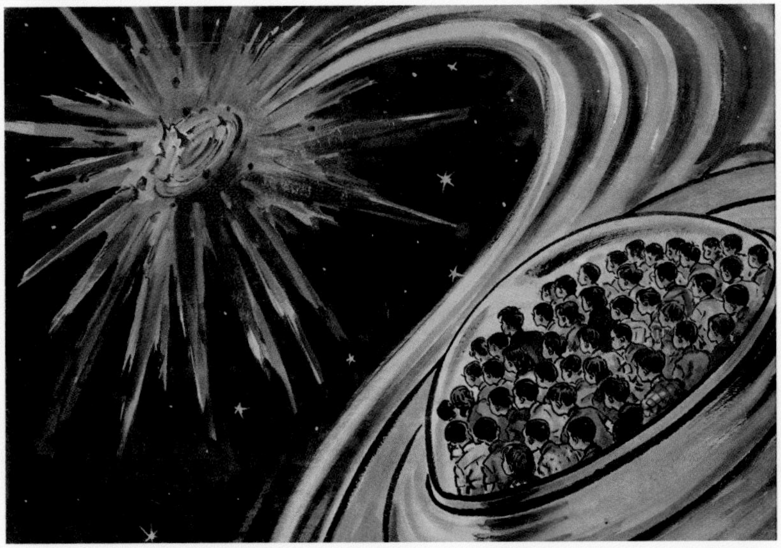

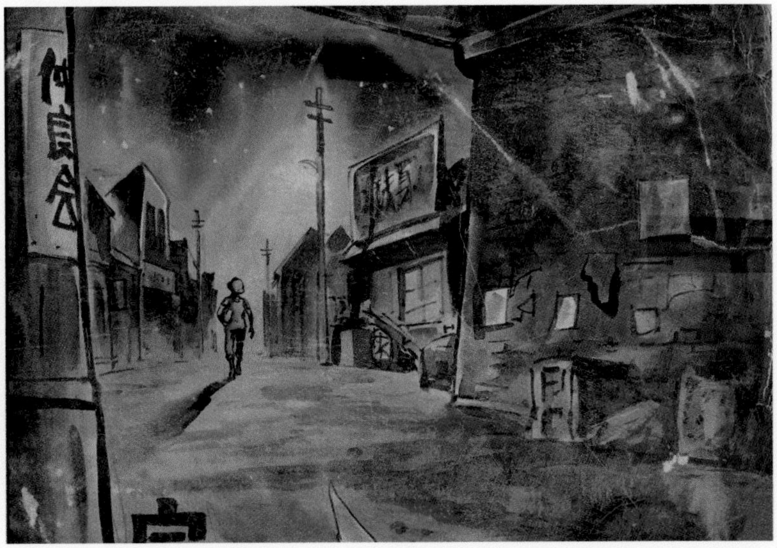

TOP LEFT Gamma Rays: Prince of Gamma defies the giant alien as the shot widens to reveal the captives of the rocky planetoid, who look remarkably like those in the crowd scenes in the previous *Gamma* episode, down to the rendition of the boys' and girls' faces.

BOTTOM LEFT The Floating World: In a sweeping science-fiction image, the Prince transports the populace from the endangered moonscape in a flying saucer. The crowded bubble of people spirals out in a streaming series of brushstrokes from the detonating planetoid.

TOP RIGHT Caped Crusader: The Prince protects the crowd from the alien's rays with his mantle. The inward-facing crowd is a stand-in for the *kamishibai* audience.

BOTTOM RIGHT Secret Identity: Prince of Gamma was one of the first super heroes to have an alter ego as a tatterdemalion street urchin, a dual-identity motif that may have been inspired by another juvenile classic of Western literature, *The Prince and the Pauper*. The dingy Tokyo neighborhood filled with refuse and lean-tos has the wistful crepuscular quality that characterized Steve Ditko's end panels of Spider-Man returning to the contradictions of his quotidian life as the teenage Peter Parker. (The bill posted on the telephone pole in the foreground bears the name of the production company, Good Friends Society.)

METAMORPHOSIS OF THE WHITE FOX SPIRIT

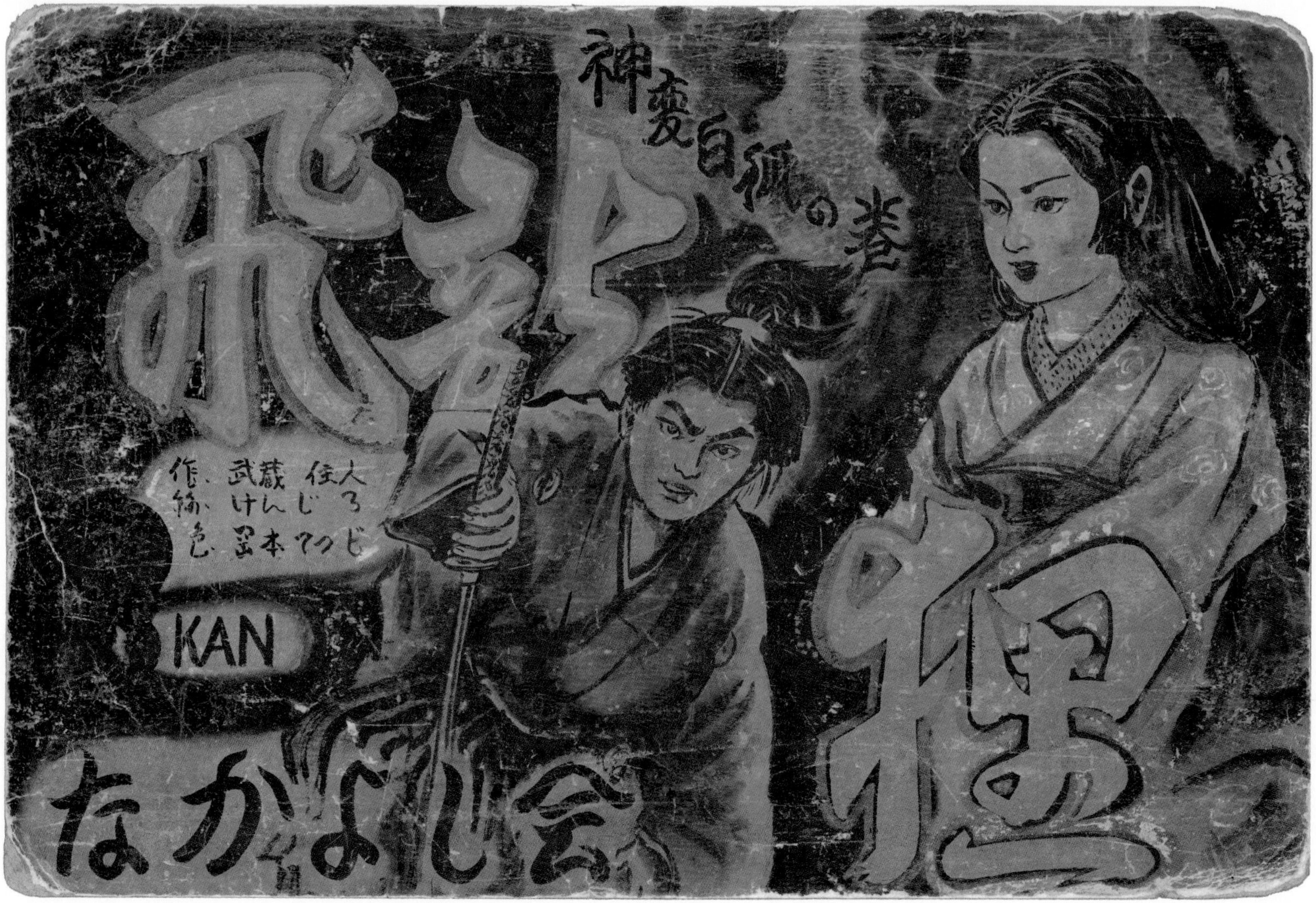
神変白狐の巻
KAN
なかよし会

Flying-Dragon Tanuki: The Japanese fondness for supernatural stories is seen in this episode about friendly flying badgers versus an evil White Fox Woman, entitled *Metamorphosis of the White Fox Spirit.*

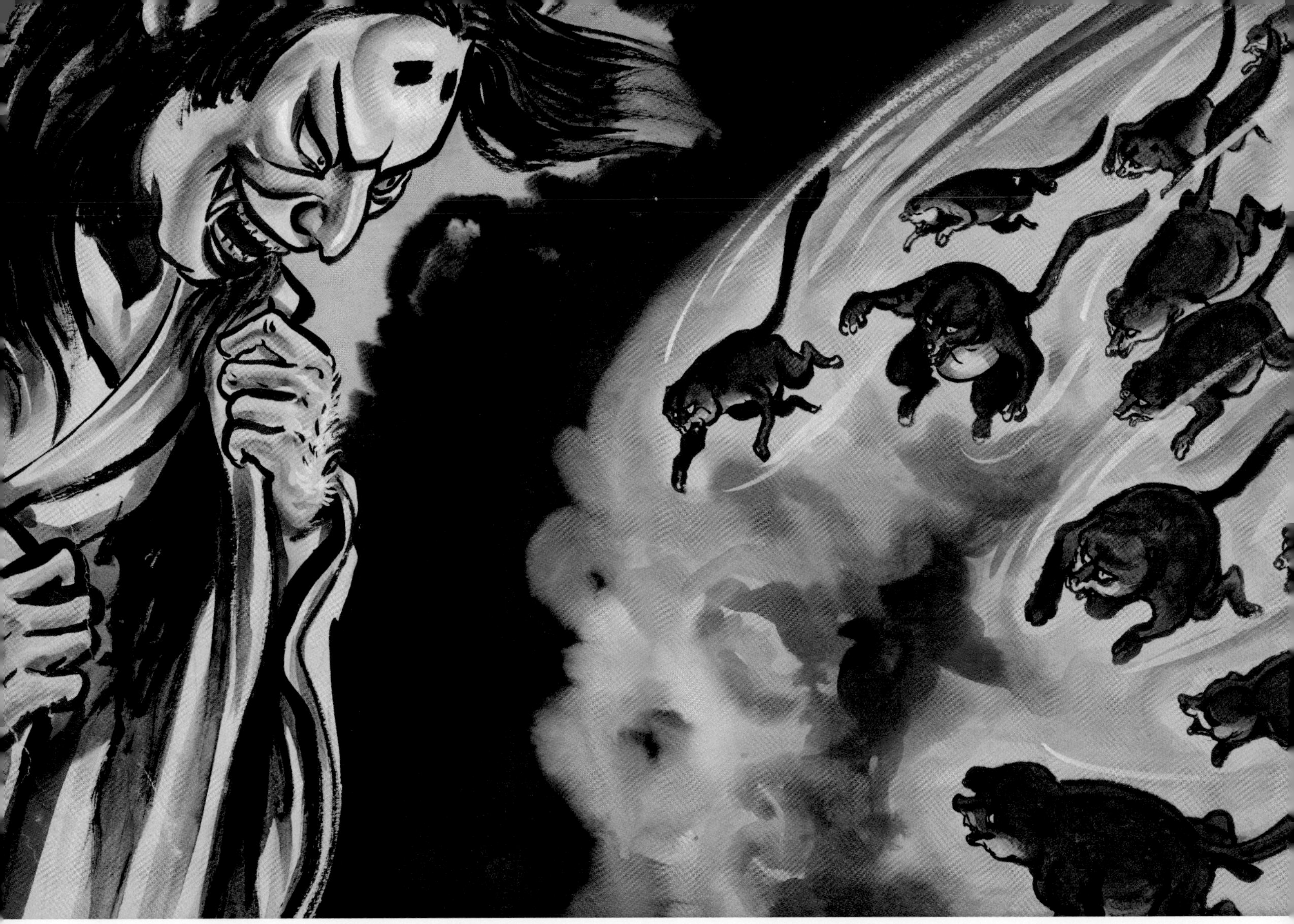

Badgering the Witness: The female White Fox spirit is associated with transformation and black magic in folklore, while the *tanuki* (badger spirit) is a hugely popular trickster figure. Many Japanese restaurants feature a statue of a *tanuki* with gimlet eyes, a fishing pole, a flask of sake, and a straw hat slung around his neck.

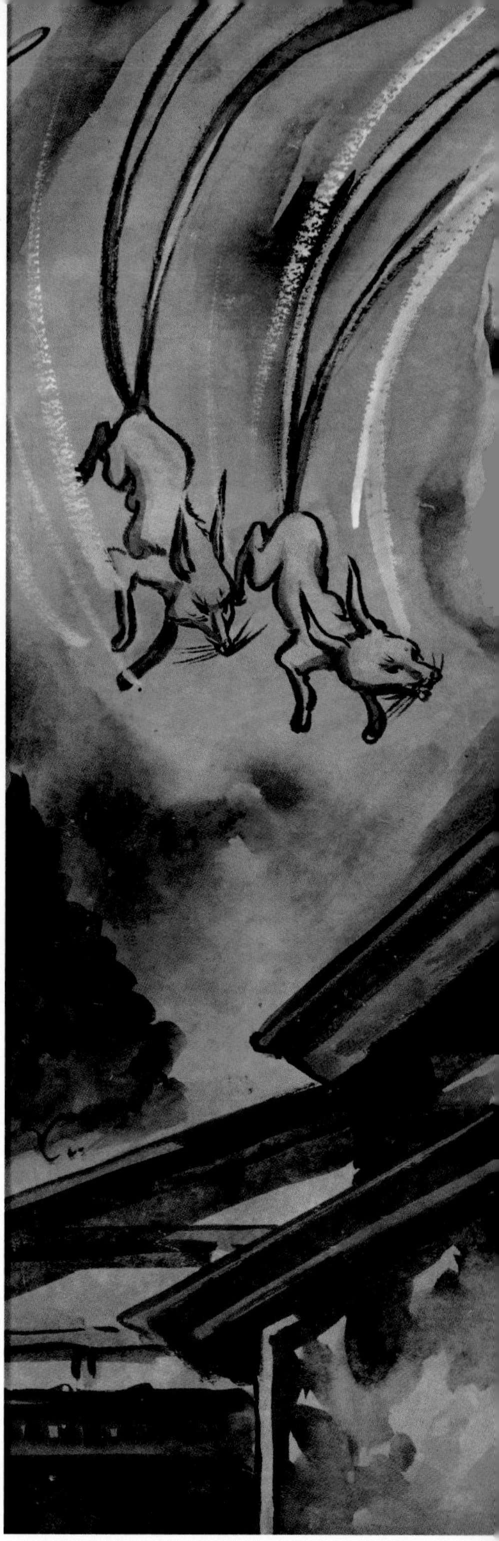

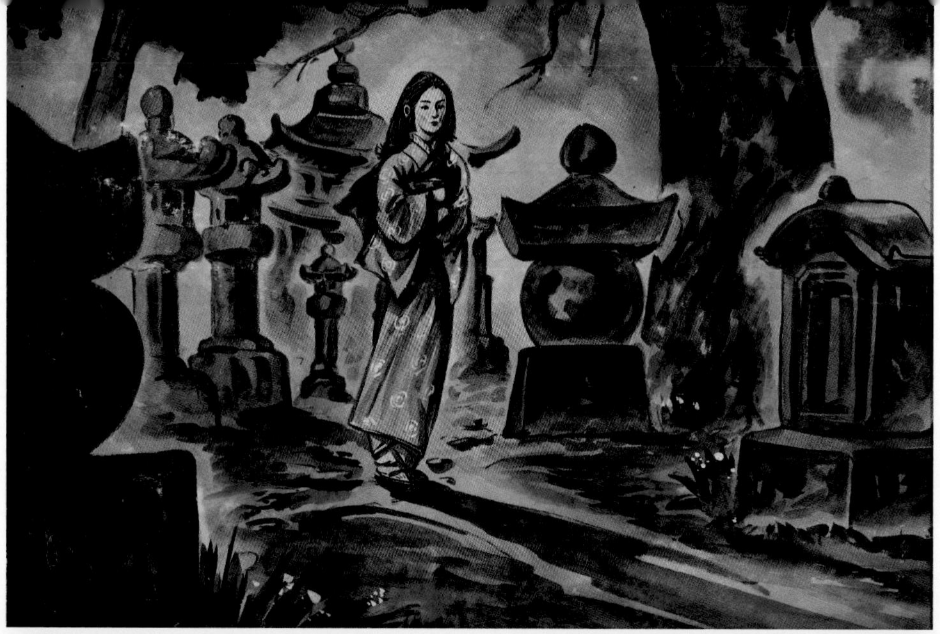

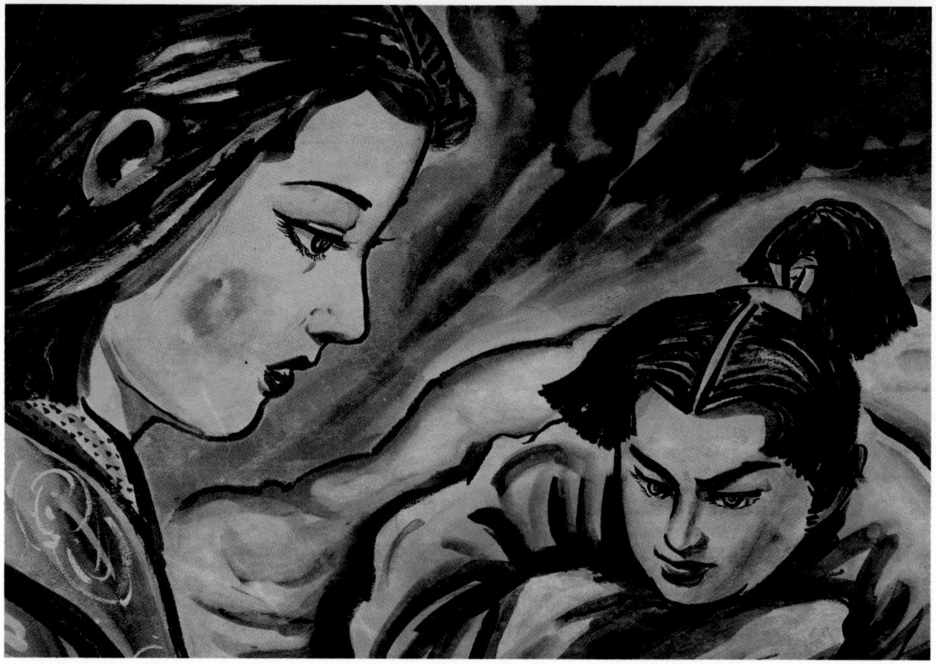

TOP **Grave Mission:** A noblewoman slips silently past ceremonial urns in a moon-shadowed cemetery to seek help from a young samurai against the attack of the White Fox Woman.

BOTTOM **Shelter from the Storm:** The young samurai vows to protect her.

RIGHT **Great Balls of Fire!:** Flying fox spirits with elongated tails rain down fire on the roof of the noblewoman's house. Unlike Japanese painting that counterbalances mass and empty space, this image is composed symmetrically along Western classical lines, with the triangular roof placed centrally between the elongated fox tails and the twin balls of flame.

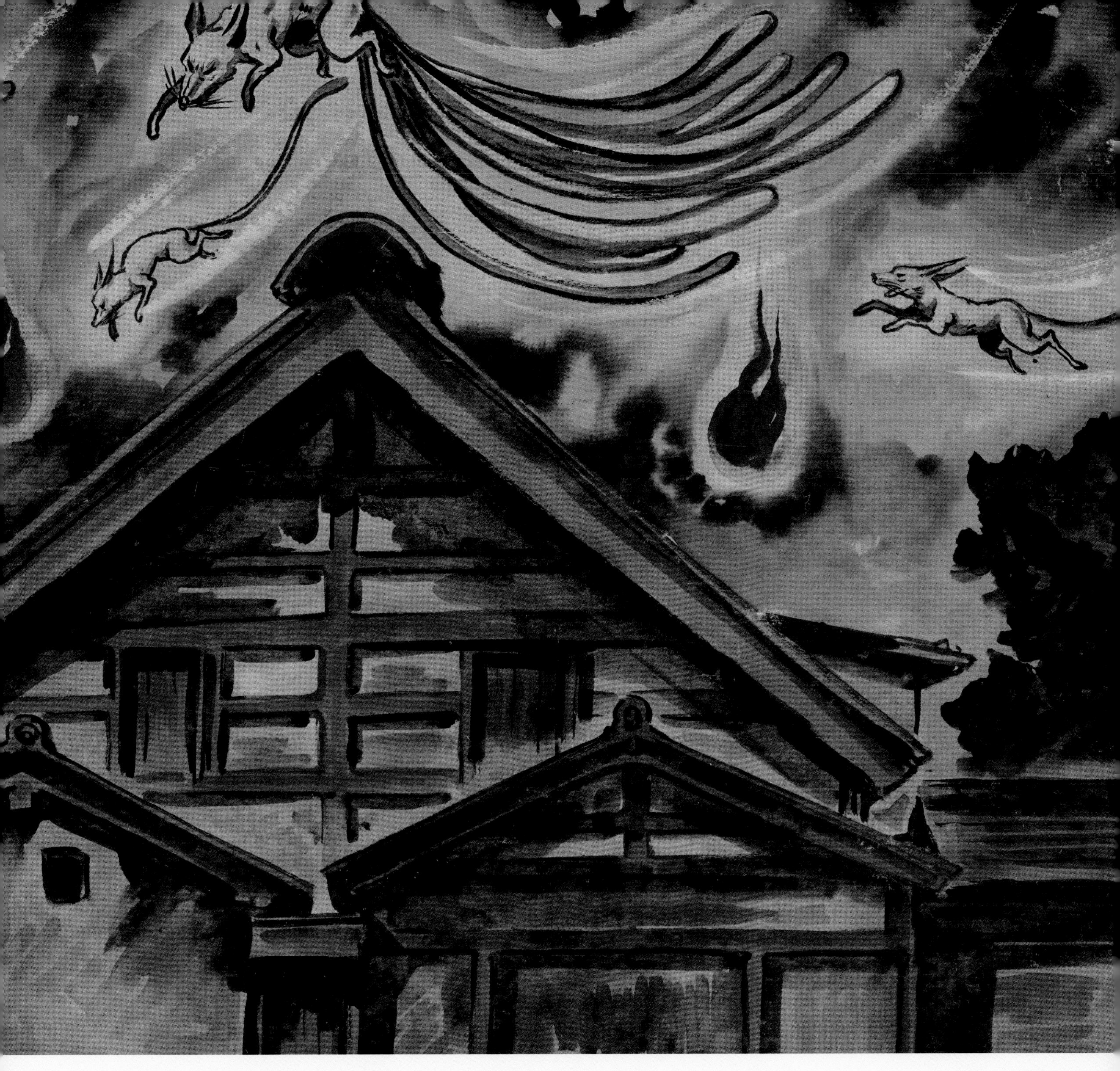

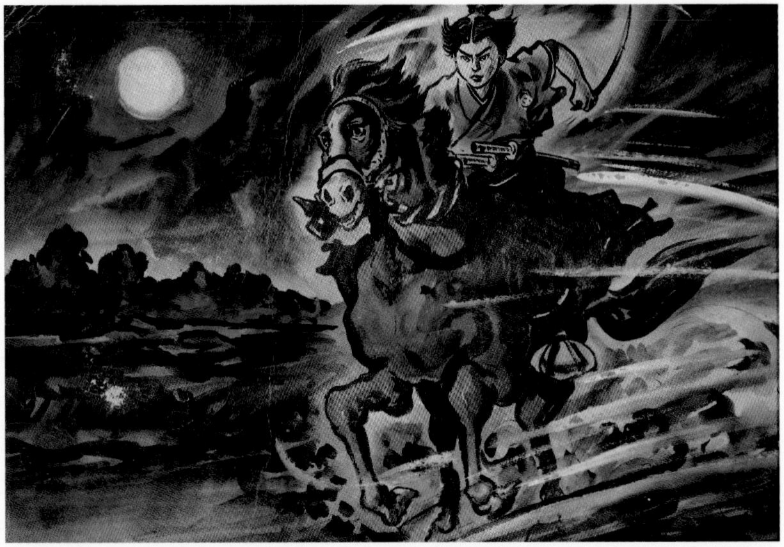

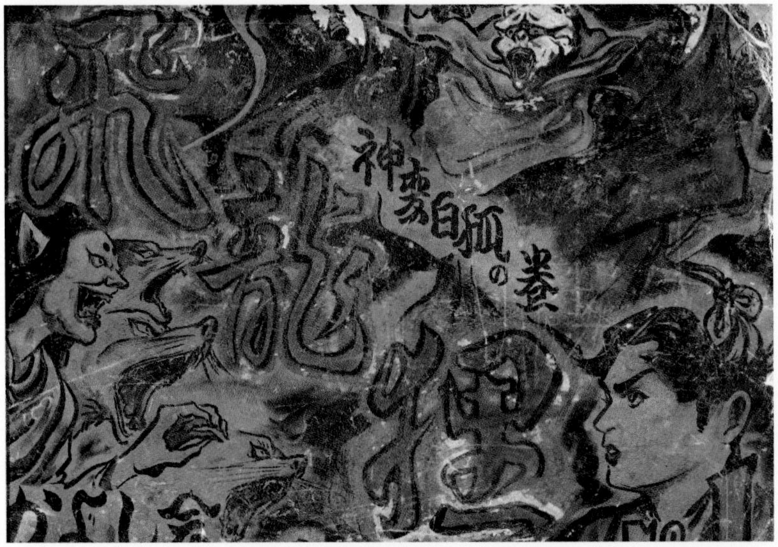

神変白狐の巻

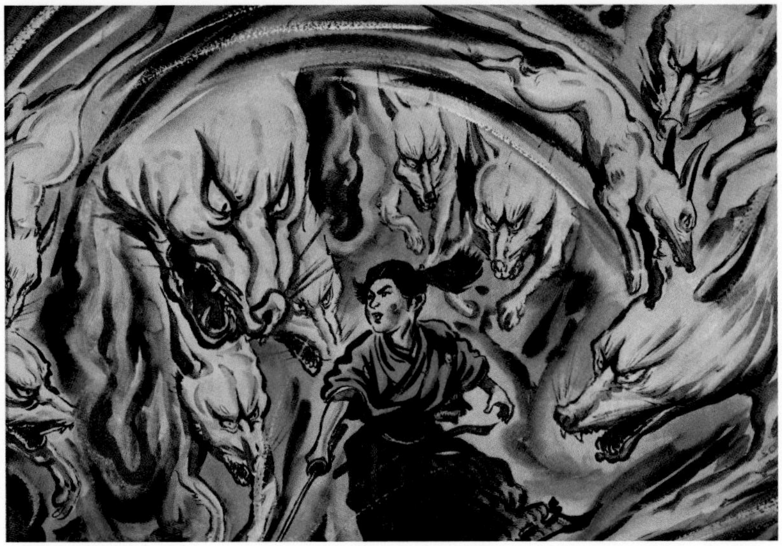

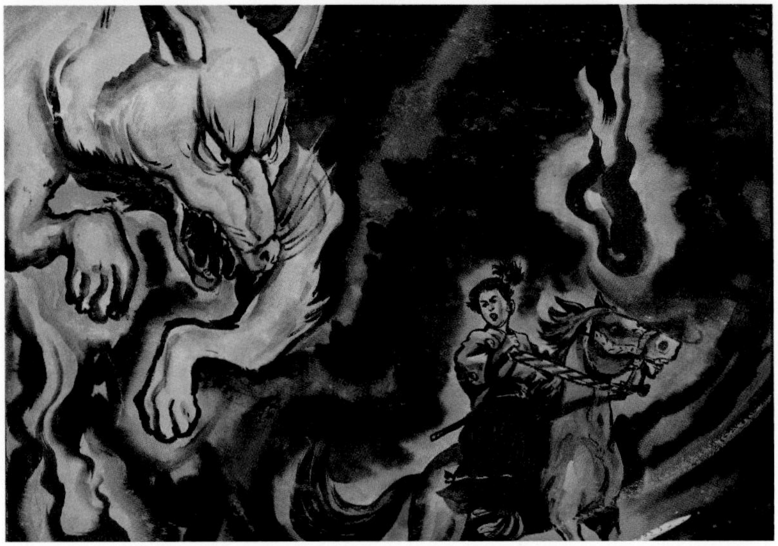

TOP LEFT Foxy Lady: The title card for the first episode of *Flying-Dragon Tanuki* shows the red-robed badger king facing off against the White Fox Woman and a skulk of foxes.

BOTTOM LEFT Firefox: An evil White Fox hurls a fireball across the hero's trail. This paper play is a street-corner version of the ghostly tales in Noh drama.

TOP RIGHT Ghostbuster: The story begins *in medias res* at a heart-thumping pace, as the gallant young samurai gallops under a moonlit sky to the rescue of the noblewoman menaced by the White Fox Woman.

BOTTOM RIGHT Outfoxed: In a vivid image that maximizes the difference in perspective between foreground and background, the boy samurai is attacked by a pack of flying foxes.

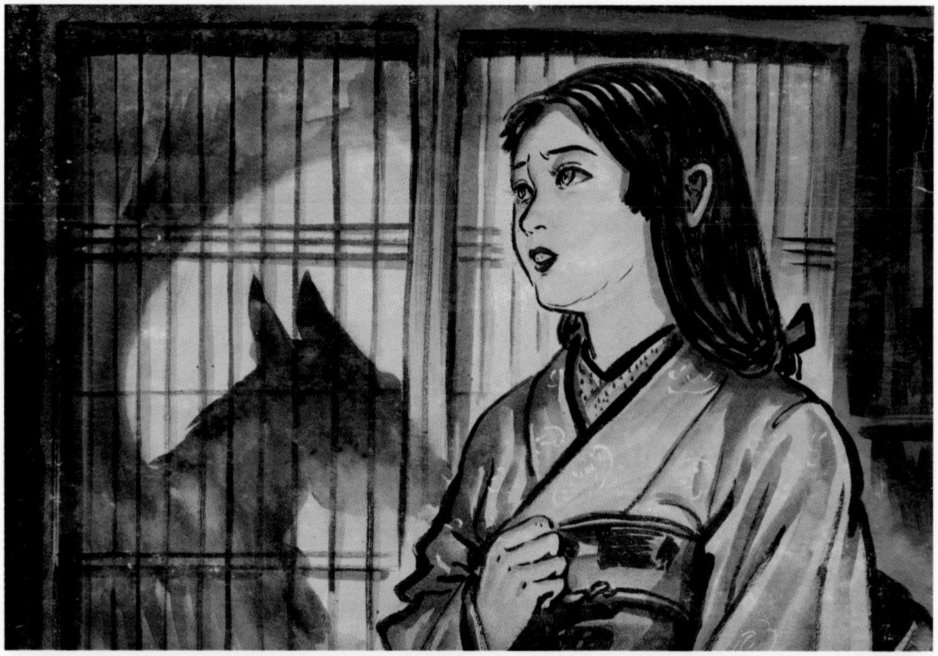

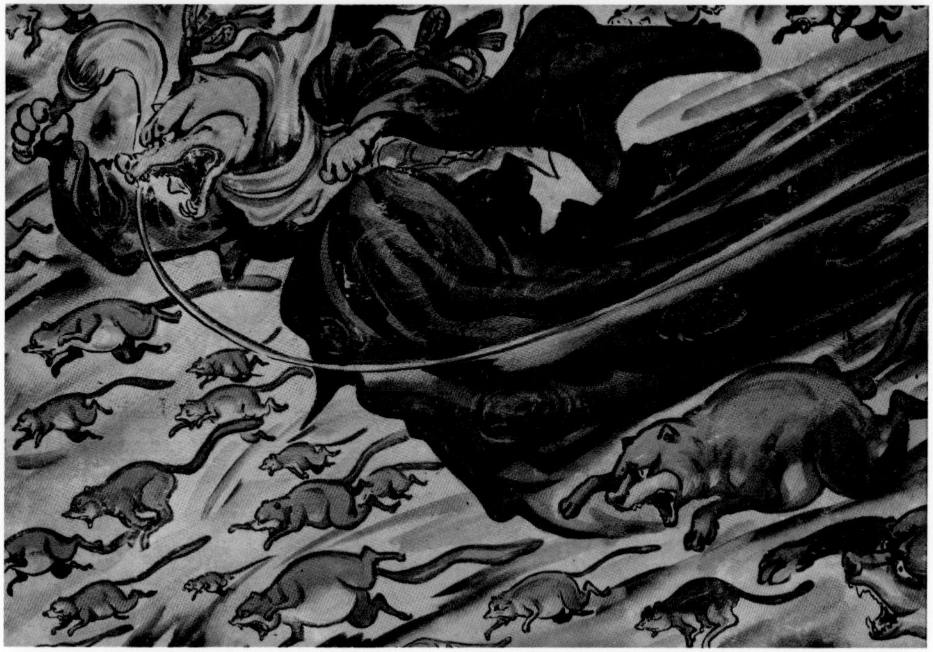

TOP Lady in Waiting: The noblewoman nervously awaits the arrival of her hero as the horse's head appears in silhouette.

BOTTOM Forward, Flying Badgers!: The badger king leads his Flying-Dragon Tanuki into battle against the White Foxes.

NINJA BY NIGHT

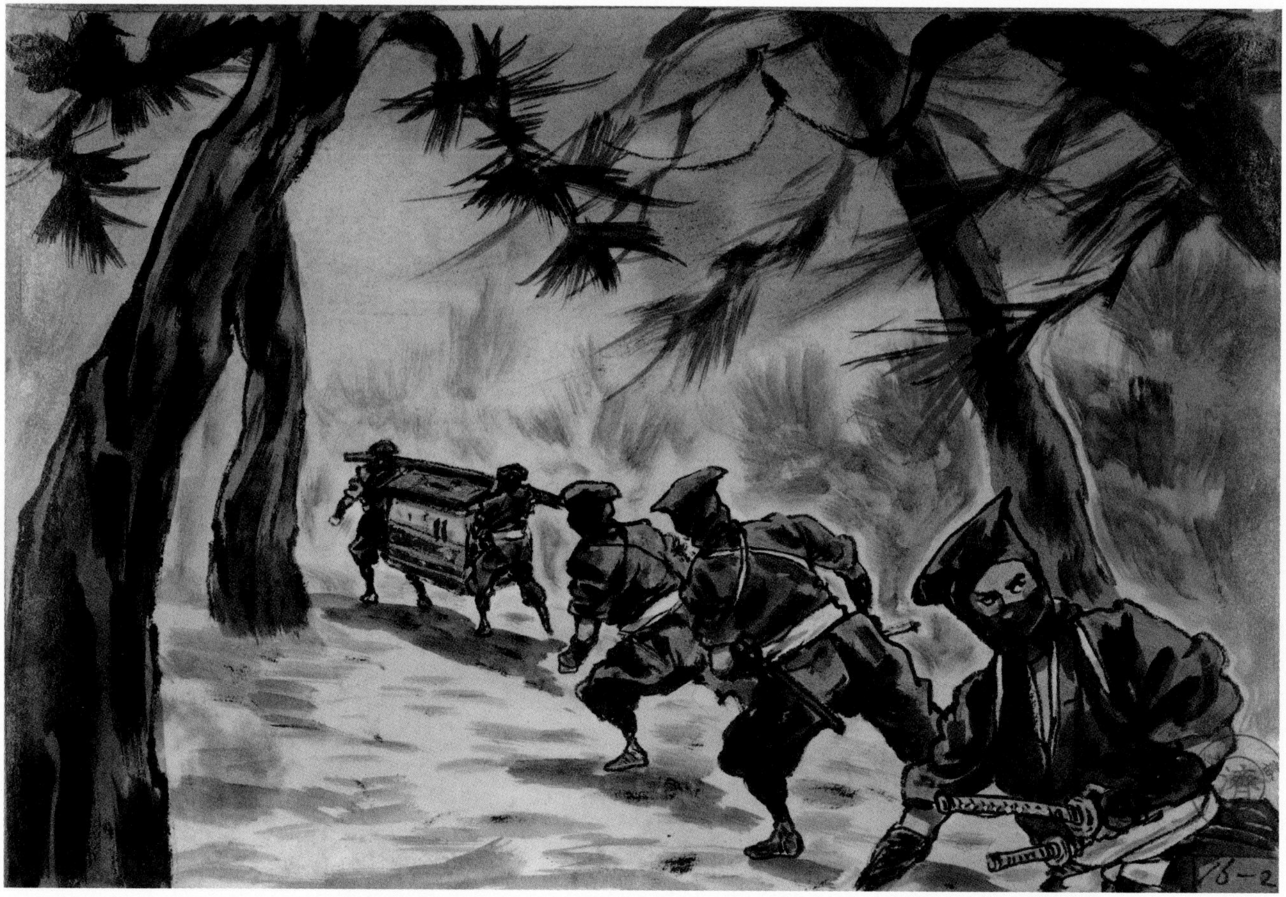

ABOVE Ninja by Night: A *shonen* ninja story opens as hooded spies bear a mysterious noble in a palanquin through a nocturnal forest, rendered in brushy paint strokes. The face looking out of the frame anticipates movement to the next panel. The *kamishibaiya* relates his tale by calling attention to successive elements in the image that contain a built-in narrative drive.

OPPOSITE, TOP *Ronin* Roadblock: The main character makes his debut as a wild-haired young *ronin*, a masterless samurai who dares to interrupt the palanquin's progress. Strong verticals of the trees on the left and the grouped heads of the ninja clan form a frame-within-the-frame often used in Japanese cinema.

OPPOSITE, BOTTOM Lone *Ronin*: Hands on their *katana* hilts, the ninja angrily accost the young interloper. The unarmed boy stands his ground unfazed and tells them they may not pass through his section of the forest. Free spirits who do not play by the rules are a staple of Japanese popular entertainment, from Mushashi to Toshiro Mifune's *Yojimbo* to the films of Beat Takeshi, functioning as a safety valve for a society highly governed by social mores. The price these characters pay, especially onerous in the Japanese mind, is loneliness and isolation, like this wild child of the forest. The characters' self-sufficiency, despite the sense of community that the Japanese value most, makes them an object of fascination.

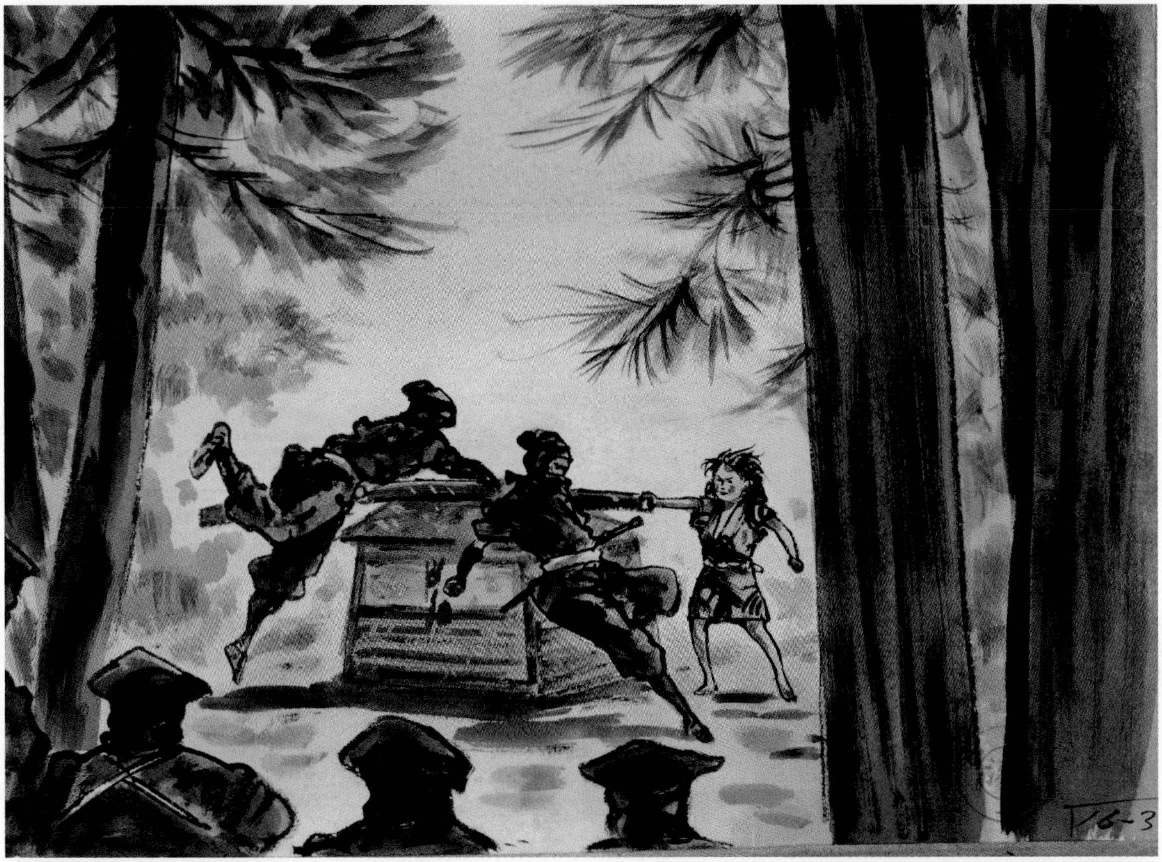
T16-3
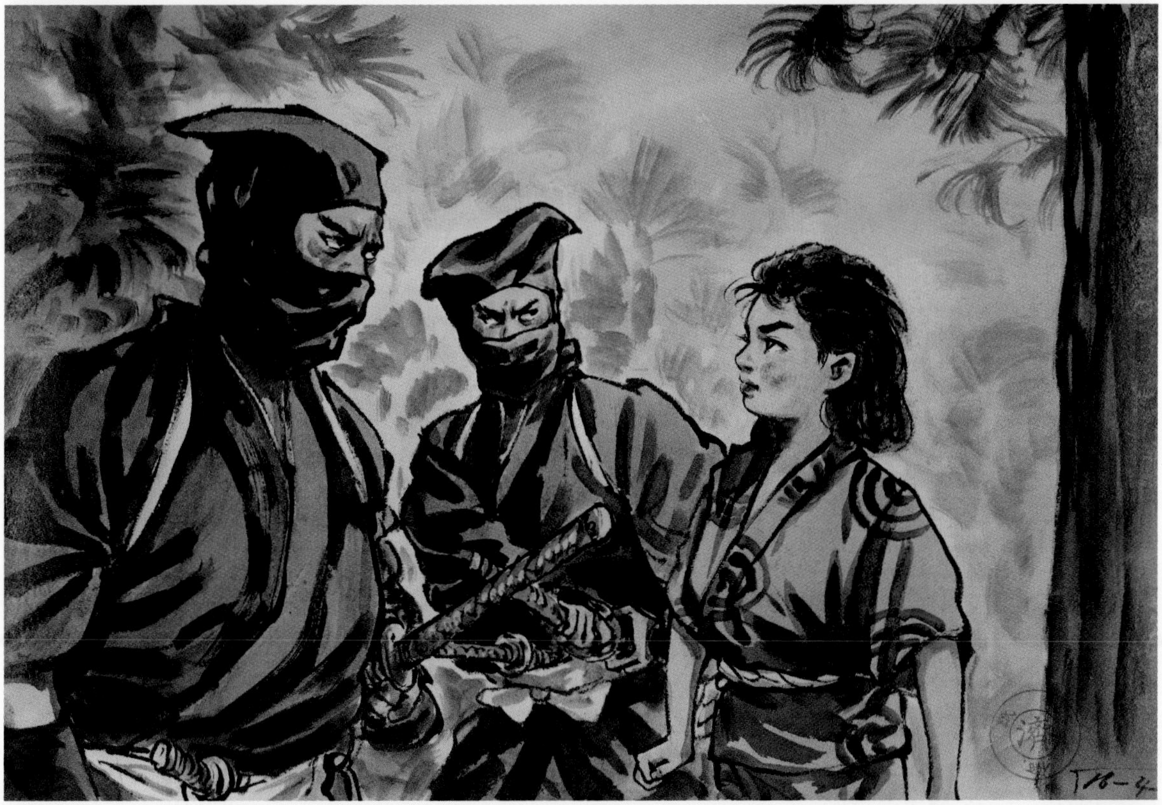
T16-4

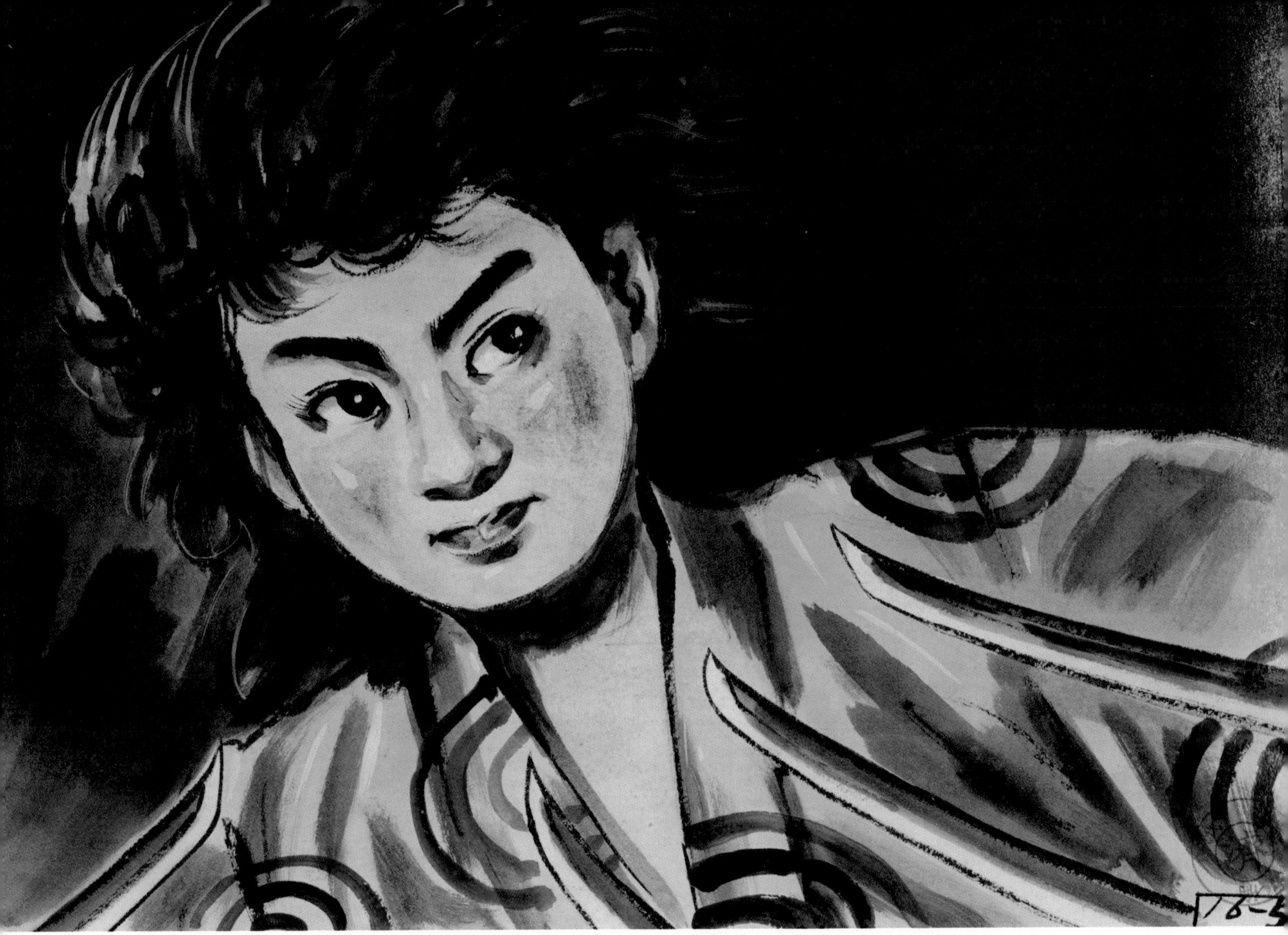

Wild Child: A close-up shows the cinematic moment of truth as the boy stares down his assailants' drawn blades. The close cropping of the frame highlights the vulnerability of his neck to the sword tips, while his tranquil but determined expression speaks of his strength of character in contrast to his unruly mop of hair, which reveals his wild nature. The folk hero Musashi was also frequently pictured as a kind of divinely inspired wild man, as in Takehiko Inoue's manga series *Vagabond*, which has sold more than 22 million copies. There was a storytelling art in the timing of the *kamishibaiya*'s revealing of the next image, sometimes slowly, drawing out the suspense, or rapidly like an old-fashioned screen wipe in film.

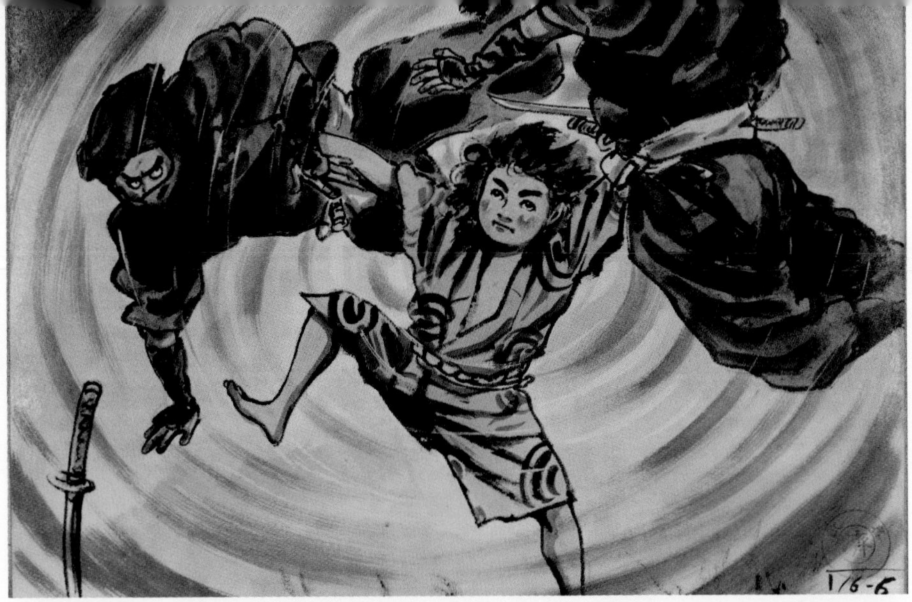

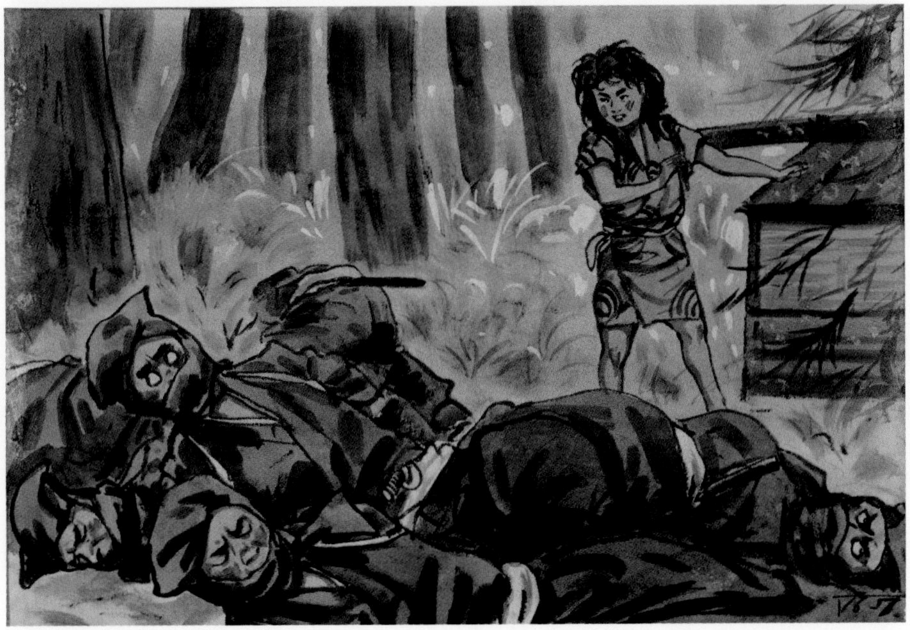

TOP *Ronin, Jr.*: In a pin-wheeling flurry of judo throws, the boy reveals his martial-arts prowess. The composition is top-heavy, emphasizing the ninja's precarious predicament. *Kamishibai* often show children in unchildlike activities—riding, shooting, piloting boats, and generally outwitting adults—like Jimmy Sparks, the boy who controls the stick shift of the original giant robot Gigantor (known as *Tetsujin 28-go* in Japan).

BOTTOM One-Man Band: The band of ninja lie defeated in a trussed clump at the feet of the boy *ronin*, filling a third of the foreground. Each ninja's face is an expression of distress, though only the eyes are visible. The boy points to the palanquin, leading to the next question in the narrative: Who's inside?

ABOVE **Close Encounter:** The palanquin's occupant reveals himself to be a mightily ticked-off samurai bearing short and long swords. The focal point of the composition is the meeting between the samurai's scowling gaze and the boy's mocking expression. The image is framed by an overhanging pine bower rendered in stylized, delicate brush strokes.

RIGHT **To the Point:** The boy dodges the samurai's sword thrust by making a head-high standing leap, a staple in martial arts films all the way up to Quentin Tarantino's *Kill Bill*. Motion lines converge in strokes of green watercolor, drawing the eye to the sword tip and empty space below the boy's bare foot. Like Jack Kirby, Steve Ditko, and Gil Kane in American comics, *kamishibai* artists were adept at capturing the maximum point of impact.

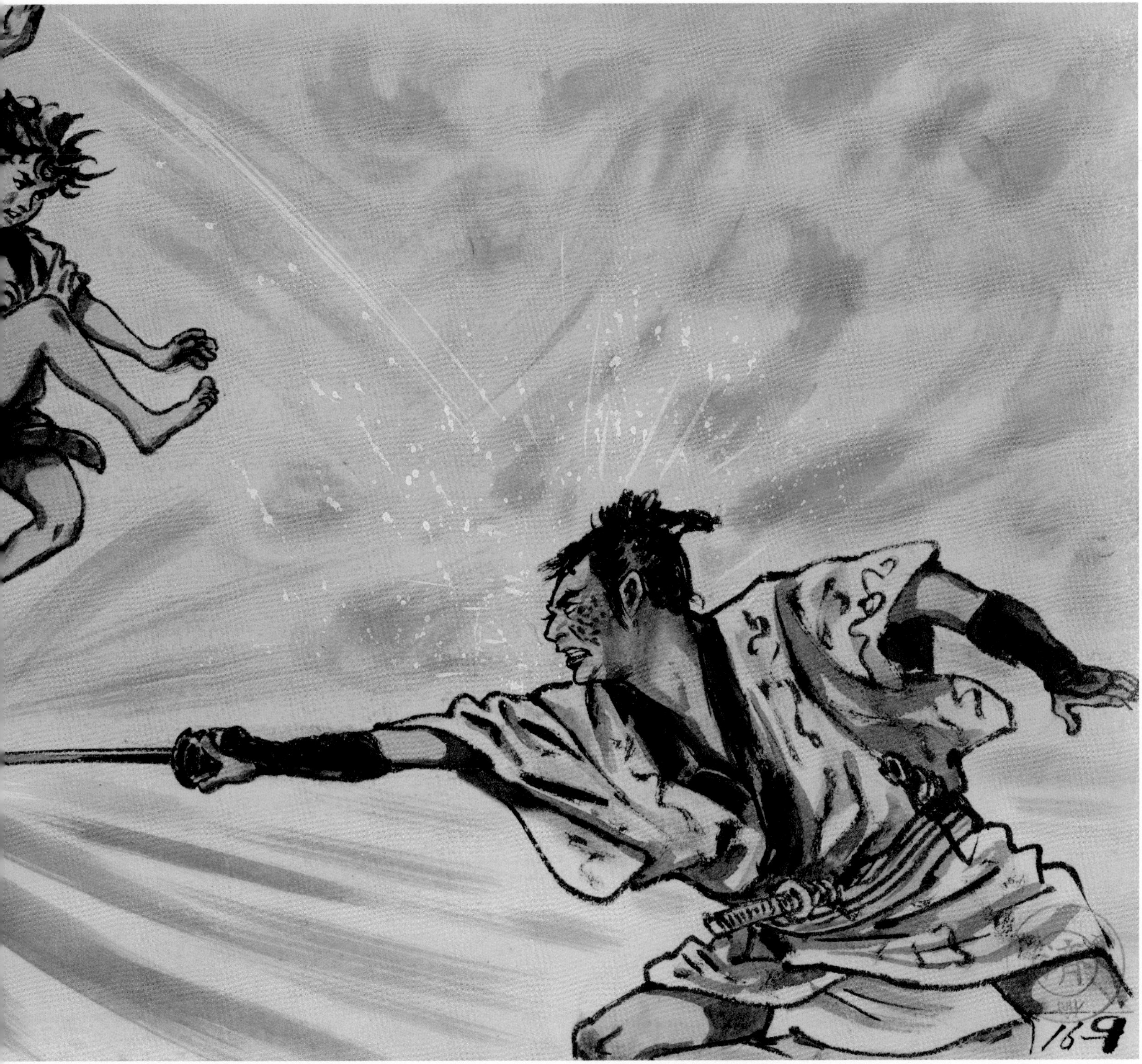
169

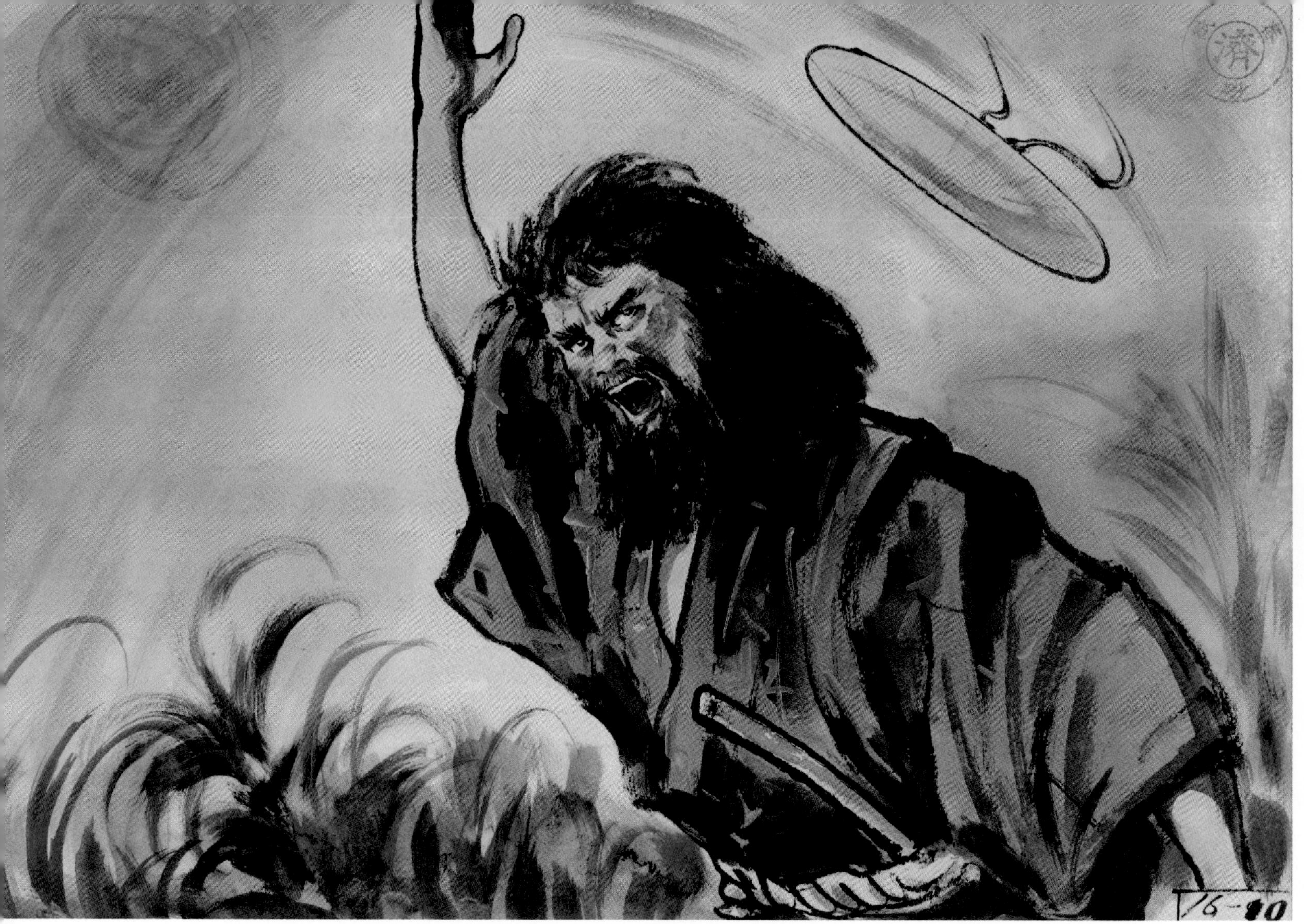

The Last Straw: A ninja disguised as a peasant with a bushy beard tosses his straw hat aside and calls for an attack. He carries a wooden stick rather than a *katana* in his rope *obi* (sash). In feudal Japan, only the samurai warrior caste was allowed to bear swords, leading to the rise of "empty-handed" martial arts like karate and judo for commoners to defend themselves in a bandit-plagued land. Postwar *yakuza* gangster films introduced handguns into the mix, but they look like peashooters compared to the firepower of American action flicks. Using firearms was considered beneath the dignity of the samurai class.

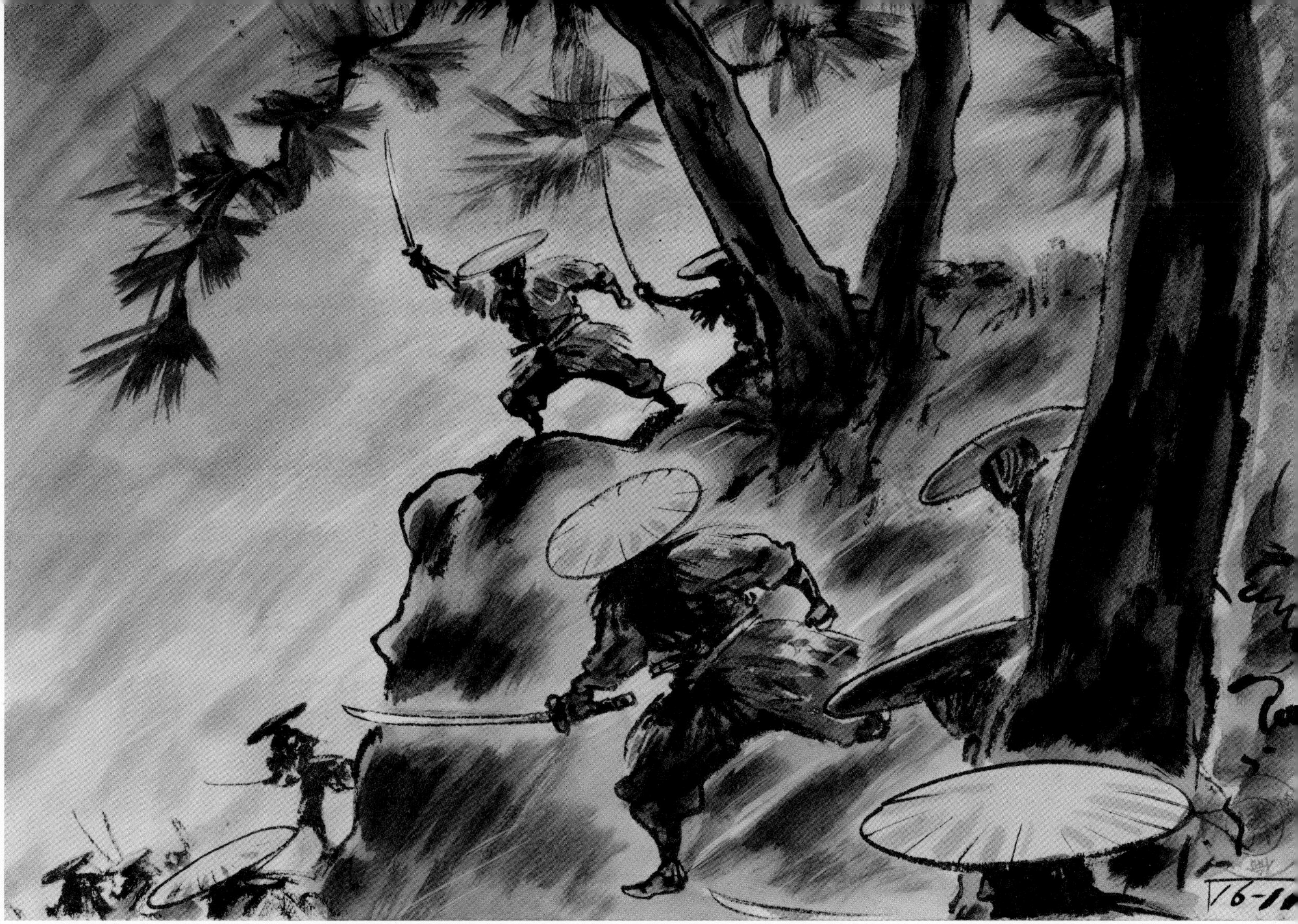

Straw Men: Straw-hatted ninja disguised as peasants descend in a composition that resembles landscape painting, with the mass of rocks asymmetrically balanced against the space of an empty sky. Traditional Japanese ink painting had a set repertoire of brush techniques for depicting trees and rocks—one of the expressive names for rendering rock is "wrinkles on a cow's neck."

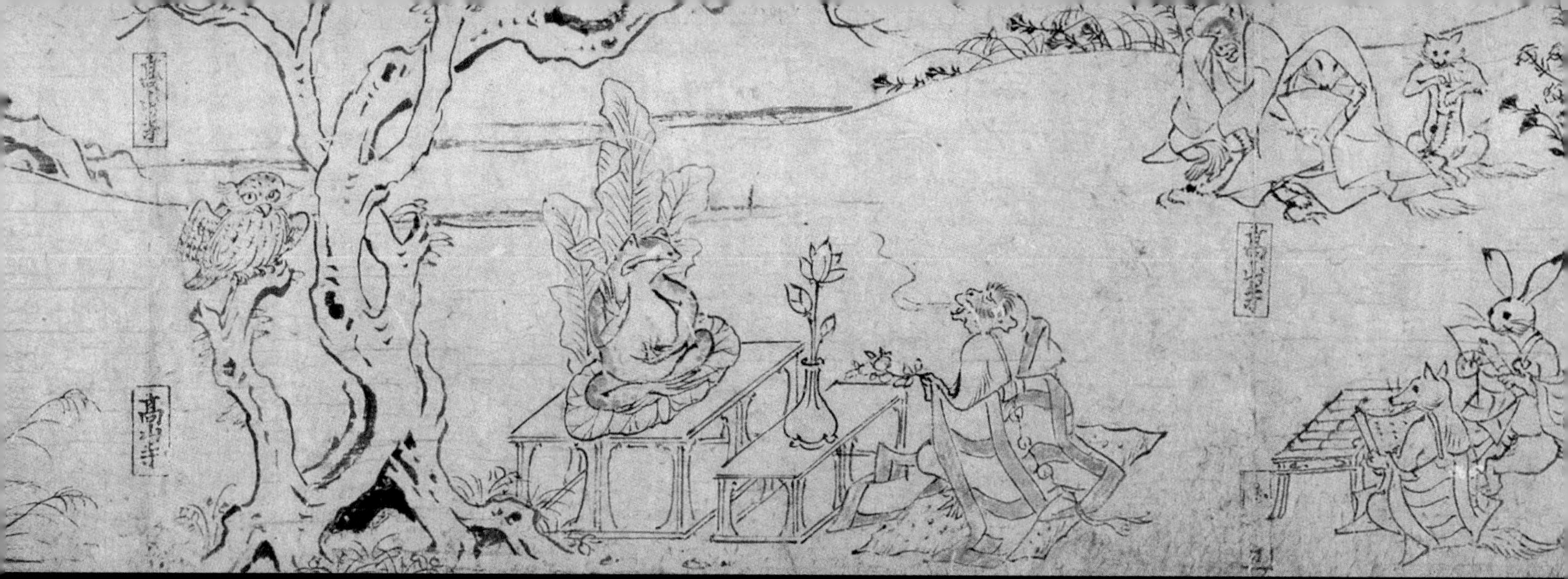
高山寺
高山寺
高山寺

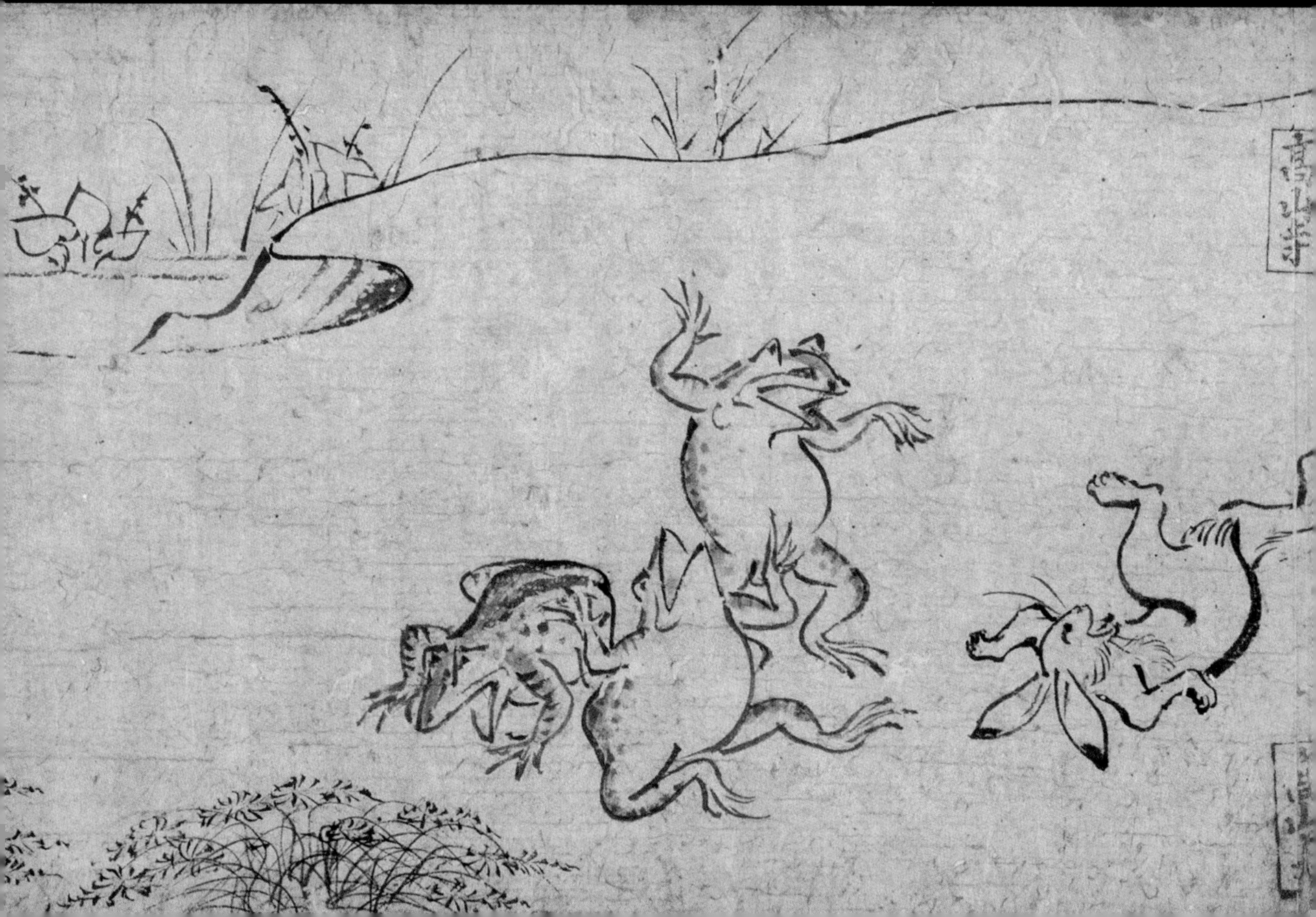
高山寺

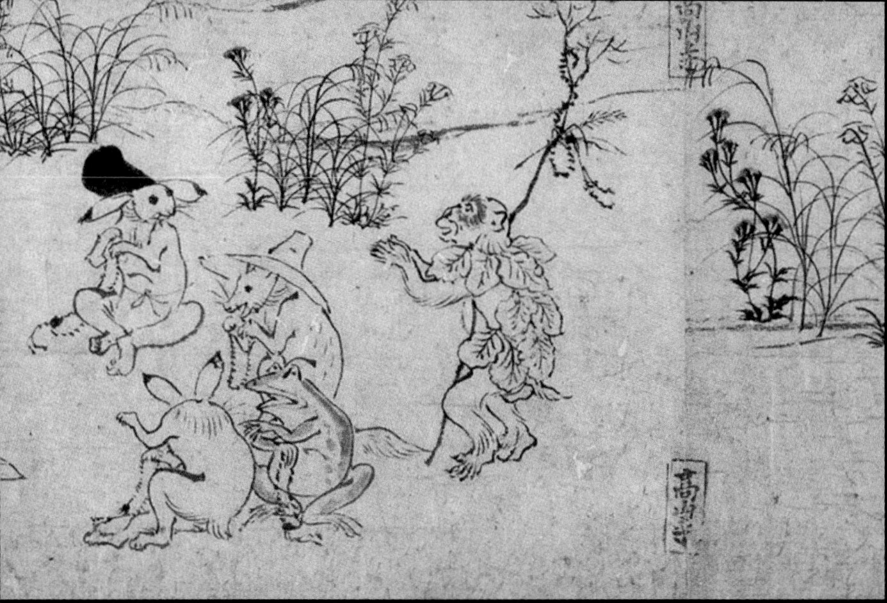

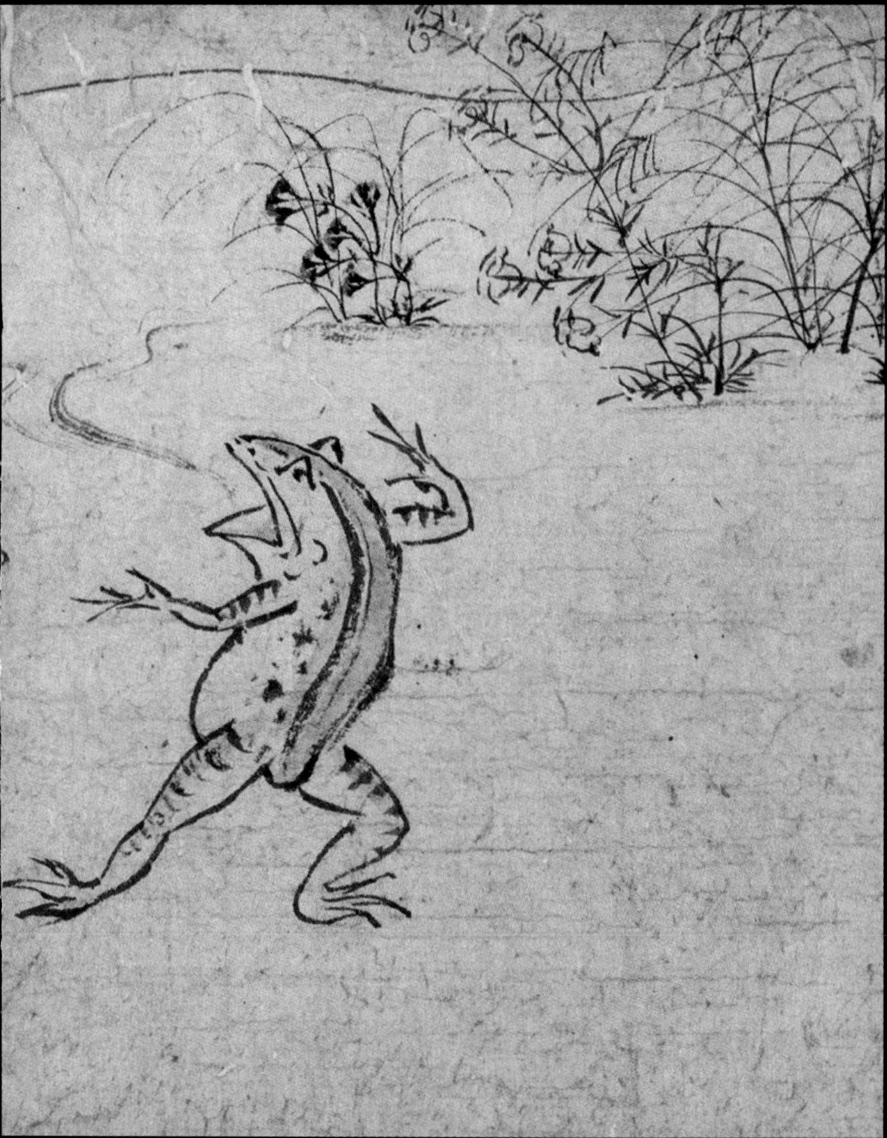

FROLICKING CRITTERS

◀ The roots of manga can be traced back nearly a millennium ago to *emaki*—illustrated scrolls like *Choju giga*, (*Frolicking Critters*), attributed to the painter-priest Toba Sojo (1053–1140) in the twelfth century. With a delightful economy of line in a few exquisitely varying brushstrokes, a gloating bullfrog flips a bunny rabbit in a judo throw while his fellow frogs laugh convulsively. *Emaki* scrolls measured a foot wide and were up to forty feet long. This scroll is unusual among *emaki* in that it contains no text, only animal caricatures that satirized Japanese society. Even the gust of air escaping from the sumo frog's mouth has its counterpart in the mushroom-shaped puffs of air depicting manga characters sighing.

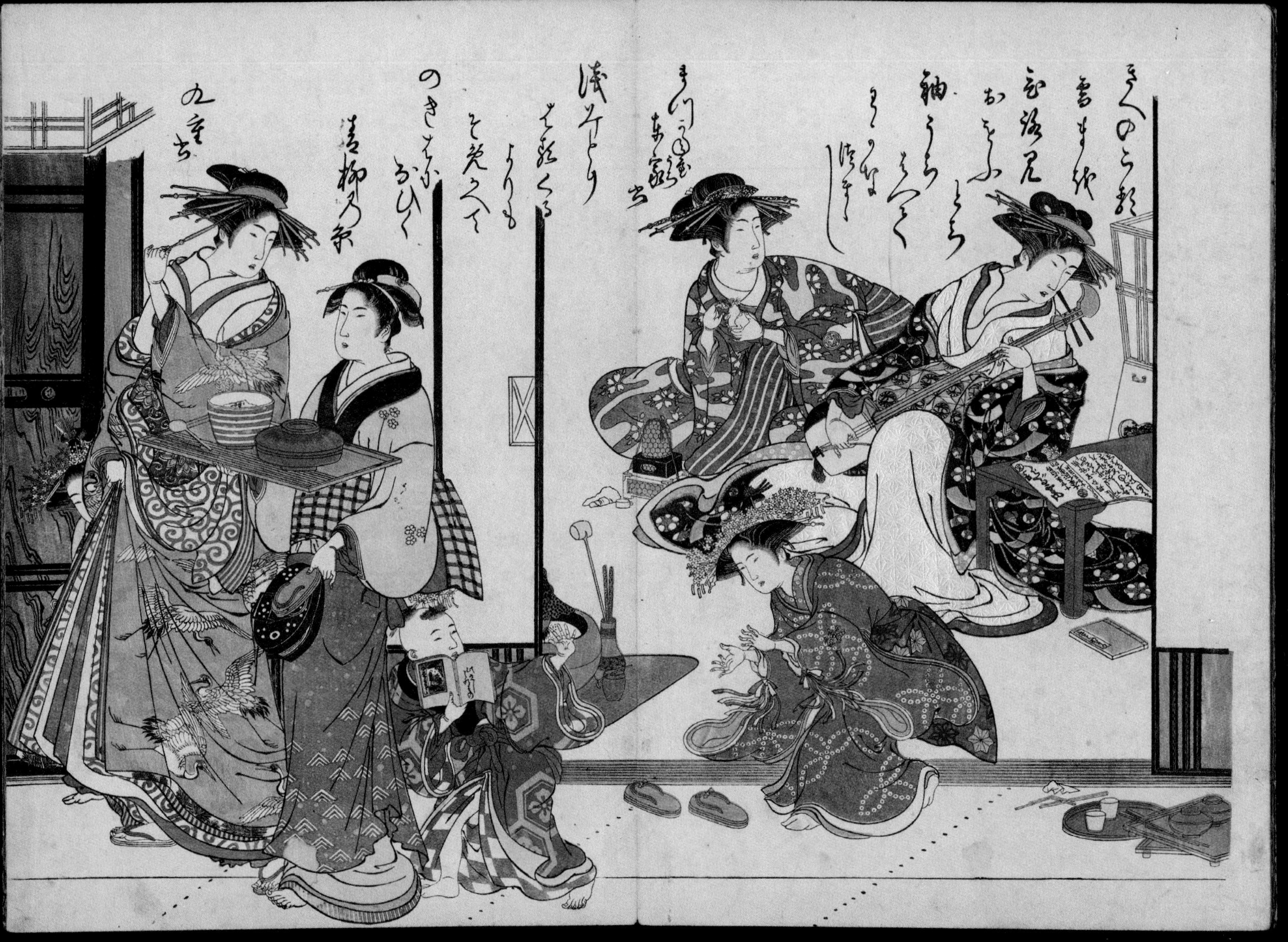

Kamishibai's earliest forerunner is *emaki* (illustrated scrolls) produced by Buddhist monks in the eighth century, hundreds of years before the Bayeux tapestry.

Emaki were used by monks as a pictorial aid in recounting the history of their monasteries—an early example of combining spoken words and pictures to tell a story (the audiovisual filmstrips of their day).

The tradition of *etoki* (pictorial storytelling) has deep roots in Japan, dating back to twelfth century scrolls of **C**hoju **G**iga (or *frolicking critters*) by the abbott **T**oba **S**ojo, with anthropomorphic drawings of a sumo-wrestling frog vanquishing a bunny rabbit while his fellow amphibians laugh their guts out. The scrolls are up to forty feet long and are deemed national treasures. The humorous sketches can be seen as a direct antecedent of the folk figures that populate *kamishibai* and manga today.

During the long period of peace under the Tokugawa Shogunate from 1603 to 1868—known as the Edo period for the new government capital, later renamed Tokyo—the arts, literature and performance flourished, notably *ukiyo-e* (colored prints of "floating world" leisure pursuits including theater, teahouses, and courtesans). The vividly colored woodblock printing process was perfected and mass produced in the mid-1700s.

Comic Book: Japan has one of the oldest traditions of comics in the world. This 1984 woodblock print, charmingly titled *A Pageant of the Latest Beauties, Their Calligraphy Mirrored*, by Edo-era artist Kitao Masanobu, shows a young courtesan in training (third from left) reading a *kibyoshi* (a yellow, soft-covered booklet like a comic that featured images and text). The comic book shown here is thought to be called *Best Man in Japan*. *Kibyoshi* were often satires of social life within the rarefied walls of the floating world, or pleasure quarters of Edo, the old capital of Japan, later named Tokyo.

With a population of more than 1 million people by the late eighteenth century, Edo was not only the largest city in the world, but also the most literate. Edo high society amused itself with another printed art form that closely resembled *kamishibai* and manga known as *kibyoshi* (yellow-covered book). *Kibyoshi* were typically thirty pages of woodblock prints hand-stitched into soft covers, similar to poetry chapbooks. Like *ukiyo-e* prints, *kibyoshi* mainly concerned themselves with the pleasures of the floating world, but they were also used as instruments of political satire. The Edo-era woodblock print **A Pageant of the Latest Beauties, Their Calligraphy Mirrored** from 1784, showing courtesans in the Yoshiwara pleasure district, is thought to be one of the first depictions anywhere of a person reading a comic book.

The word *manga* was coined in 1814 by the master printmaker Katsushika Hokusai (1760–1849), recognized around the world for his **Thirty-six Views of Mount Fuji** including the perhaps single-most-celebrated Japanese image, **The Great Wave Off Kanagawa**. Manga (loosely translated as foolish or irresponsible drawings) is a combination of two *kanji* (ideograms): *man* (meaning rapidly thrown off) and *ga* (for drawing). The sense is that the drawings have a spontaneous, irrepressible nature, drawn in spite of the artist. Hokusai used the word to refer to his quick sketches and caricatures of Japanese village life. Between 1814 and 1834 he produced fifteen volumes of acutely observed yet free and fluid drawings of villagers bathing, eating, and wrestling. His faces have a compressed graphic grotesquerie like Chester Gould's Dick Tracy villains. His sketch of opium smokers with elongated crazy-straw necks is as funny as any underground comix image.

Shadow puppetry and various forms of magic-lantern shows adopted from the West also had their vogues. *Utushie*, in which slide images were projected onto a screen using a kerosene lamp, is considered a forerunner of

Fangirl: Kitagawa Utamaro's portrait of the young geisha Ochie from his series *Edo's Celebrated Beauties* (c. 1792–93) may be the earliest picture anywhere of a teenager reading a comic book (bubblegum, rock and roll, and greasy pompadours didn't follow until after the American occupation). The Edo era even had its own version of underground comix, with a genre of racy pictures, called *higa* (underground images) or *waraie* (giggle pix) like the men's humor digests *Laff* and *Breeze*, with low-down jokes and long-stemmed beauties.

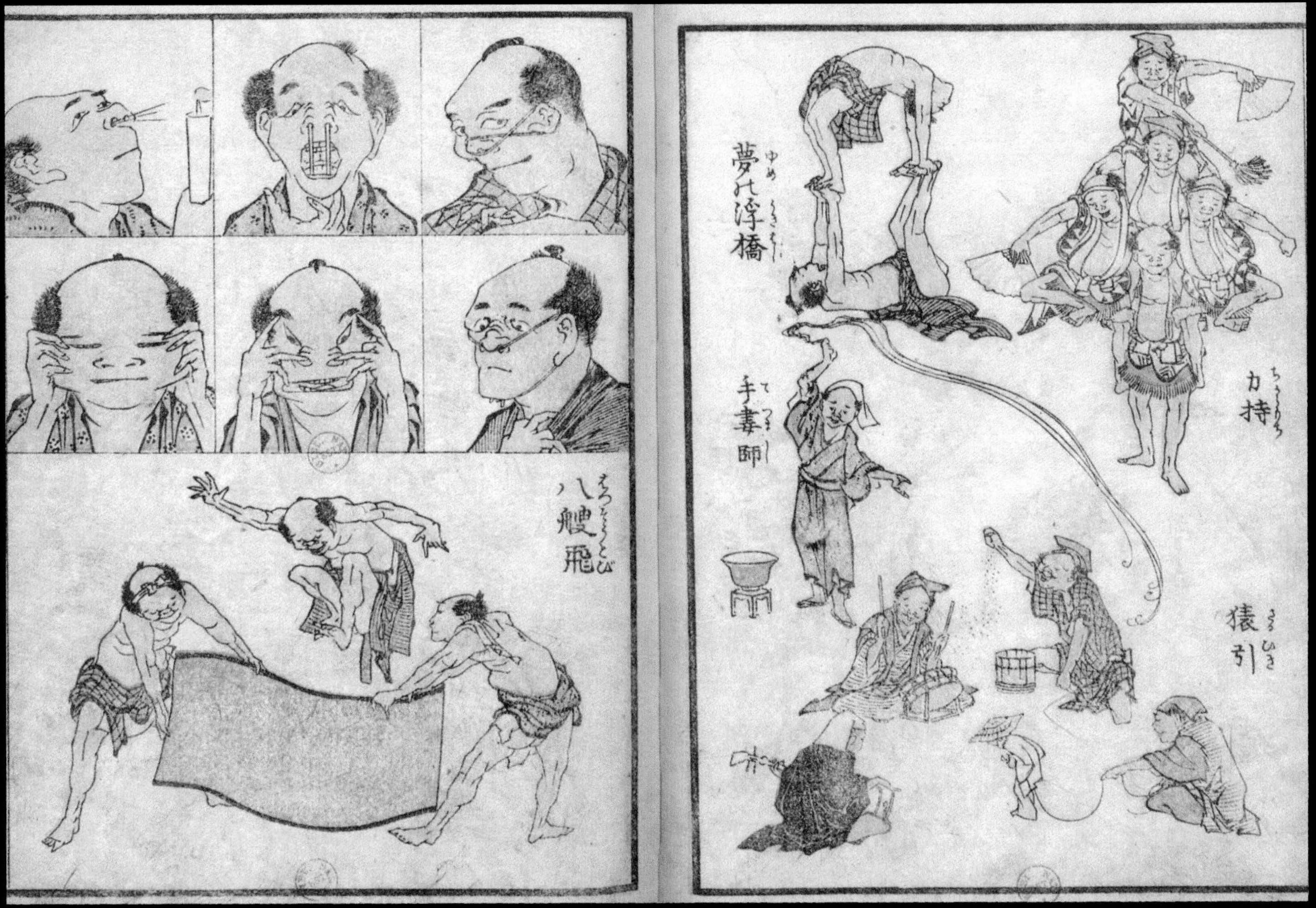

夢の浮橋
力持
手妻師
猿引
八艘飛

[redacted]

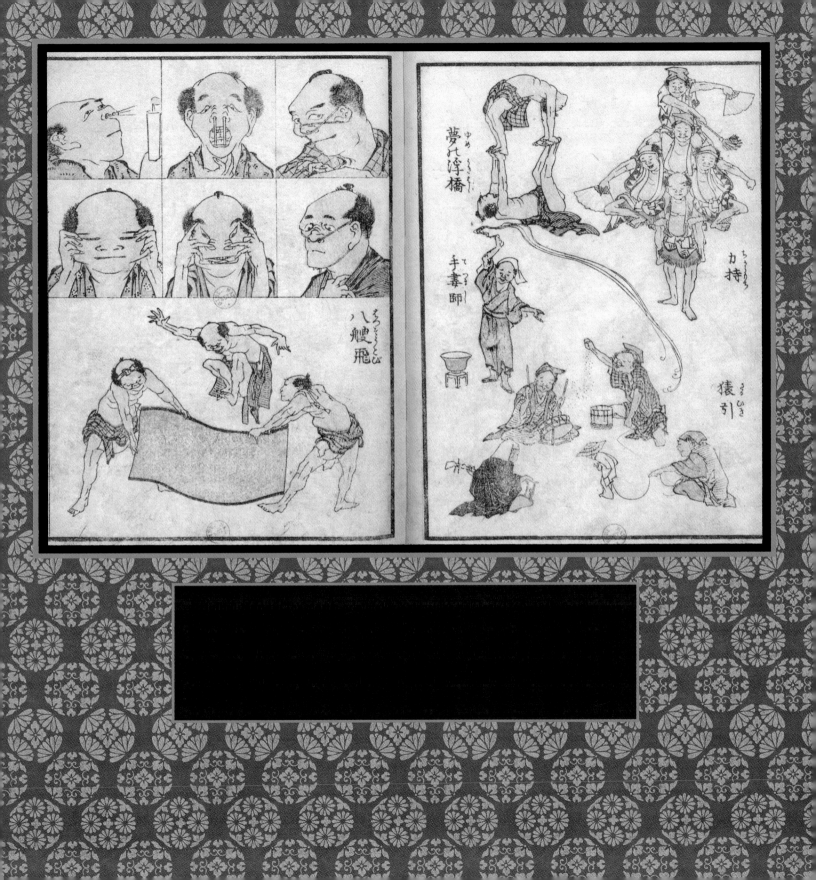

[redacted]

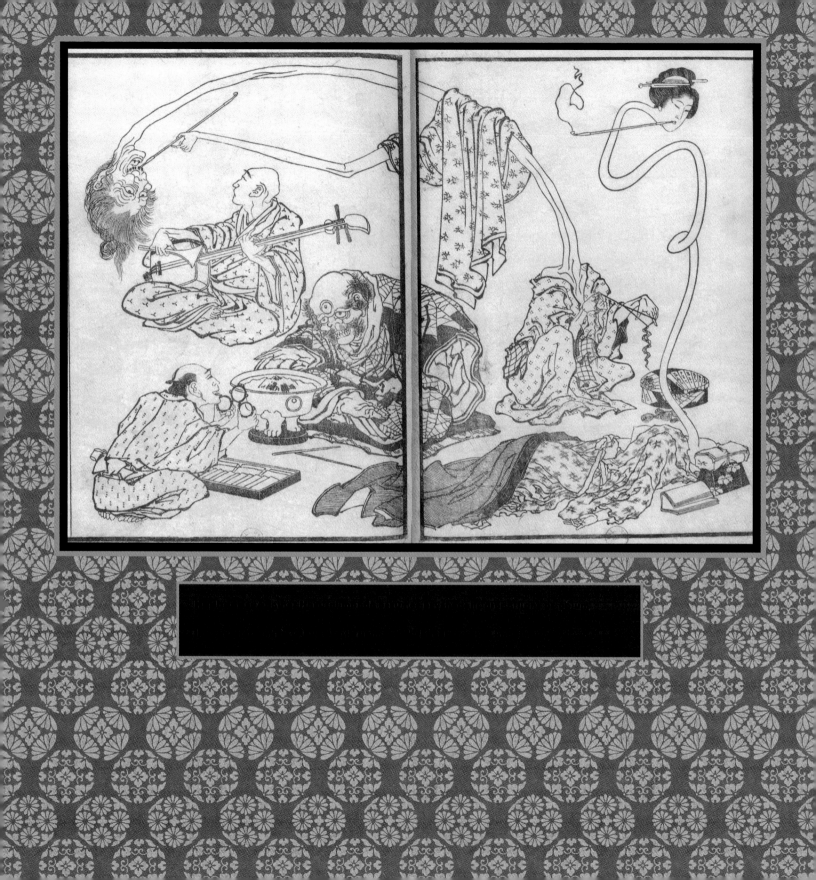

animation. In 1718 there was a fad for *nozoki megane*—a lensed contraption that appeared to give paintings depth and perspective like a stereopticon.

Etoki became popular in the late eighteenth century as itinerant story-tellers set up shop on the side of the road with an unrolled scroll hanging from a pole. In the Meiji period (1869–1914), *tachie* (literally, stand-up pictures) stories were told by performers who manipulated flat-paper-figure cutouts mounted on wooden poles, similar to shadow puppets in Indonesia and Burma. In the first of many police crackdowns on street-corner theater, *tachie* was driven out by the authorities in 1927, because the itinerant story-tellers were competing with local candy shops by peddling sweets to their audiences. At about the same time, a Zen priest named Nishimura is credited with using pictures during his sermons to entertain children—a precursor to the rise of *kamishibai*. Newly created newspapers, aimed at a working-class readership also popularized serial comic strips during the Depression.

The history of media in Japan and in the West followed divergent paths. Some observers theorize that different printing processes between the East and West in the late sixteenth century may account for the greater accep-tance of drawing as a means of communication among Asian nations. In the West, image and text gradually diverged because of the Gutenberg method of movable type. The Japanese language consists of kanji, which were more easily produced by the woodblock printing method imported from Korea following the military campaigns of 1592–93. Woodblock printing was more amenable to integrating words and pictures so that they carried equal weight on the page.

Likewise, Japan's history of film differs from the West's. Talkies did not immediately replace the silents in Japan as they did in America, because the English language was lost on Japanese audiences. In the silent era, Japan had a tradition of *benshi*—live actors who enacted dialogue and narration for the screen ghosts. *Benshi* actors had their own following, like movie stars. The earliest *kamishibai* are strikingly similar to silent films, with panels of intercut action and close-ups to express emotional intensity. Both media employ a narrator/actor just offstage who comments on the pictorial

action. When talkies finally came in, unemployed *benshi* actors turned to *kamishibai*.

Cinema was also influential on *kamishibai* because artists drew the likenesses of popular film and theater actors. *Kamishibai* artists borrowed the scarred, one-eyed, and one-armed samurai **Tange Sazen**, who originally appeared in a serialized newspaper novel in 1927, a silent film adaptation in 1928, and more than thirty *chambara* (swordfighting) sequels. Sazen was also rendered in a big-foot cartoon style by **Astro Boy** creator **Osamu Tezuka** in 1954, where his terrifying scarred eye was replaced with a Popeye-like **X**. One Tange Sazen episode uses a sophisticated flashback technique showing the samurai taking revenge on someone from his past, when he was in his full-bodied prime. *Chambara kamishibai* feature matinee-idol-handsome

Return of the Jidai: This *jidai geki*, a period drama set in feudal Japan (don't miss the wordplay of George Lucas's Jedi, who resemble medieval Japanese knights), is meant to convey the mood of long ago, but like Hollywood Westerns, it can be dated to the decade in which it was made. The main character in the foreground has the epicene prettiness of a 1930s matinee idol, while the framing of the group makes it look like a still from an old Toho Studios production.

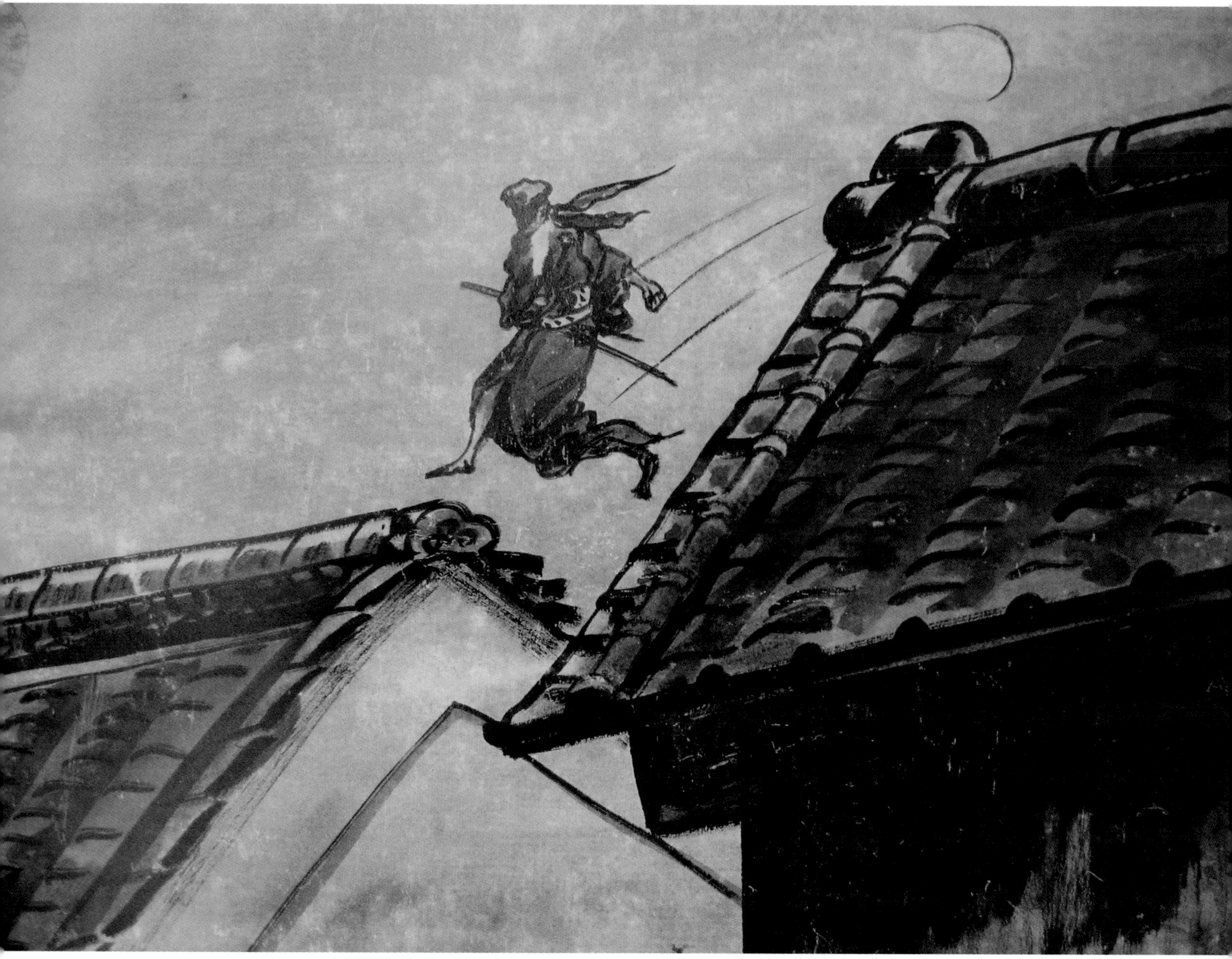

Moon River: A ninja skims the rooftops of what looks like a Toho Studios backlot, in this nocturne evocative of the high-wire acrobatics in *Crouching Tiger, Hidden Dragon* decades later. Ninja had their historical counterparts as spies for medieval warlords, but their powers have been embroidered over the centuries to include flight and invisibility. As much as Lolita Goth girls and Hello Kitty, ninja are one of Japan's chief exports to world popular culture.

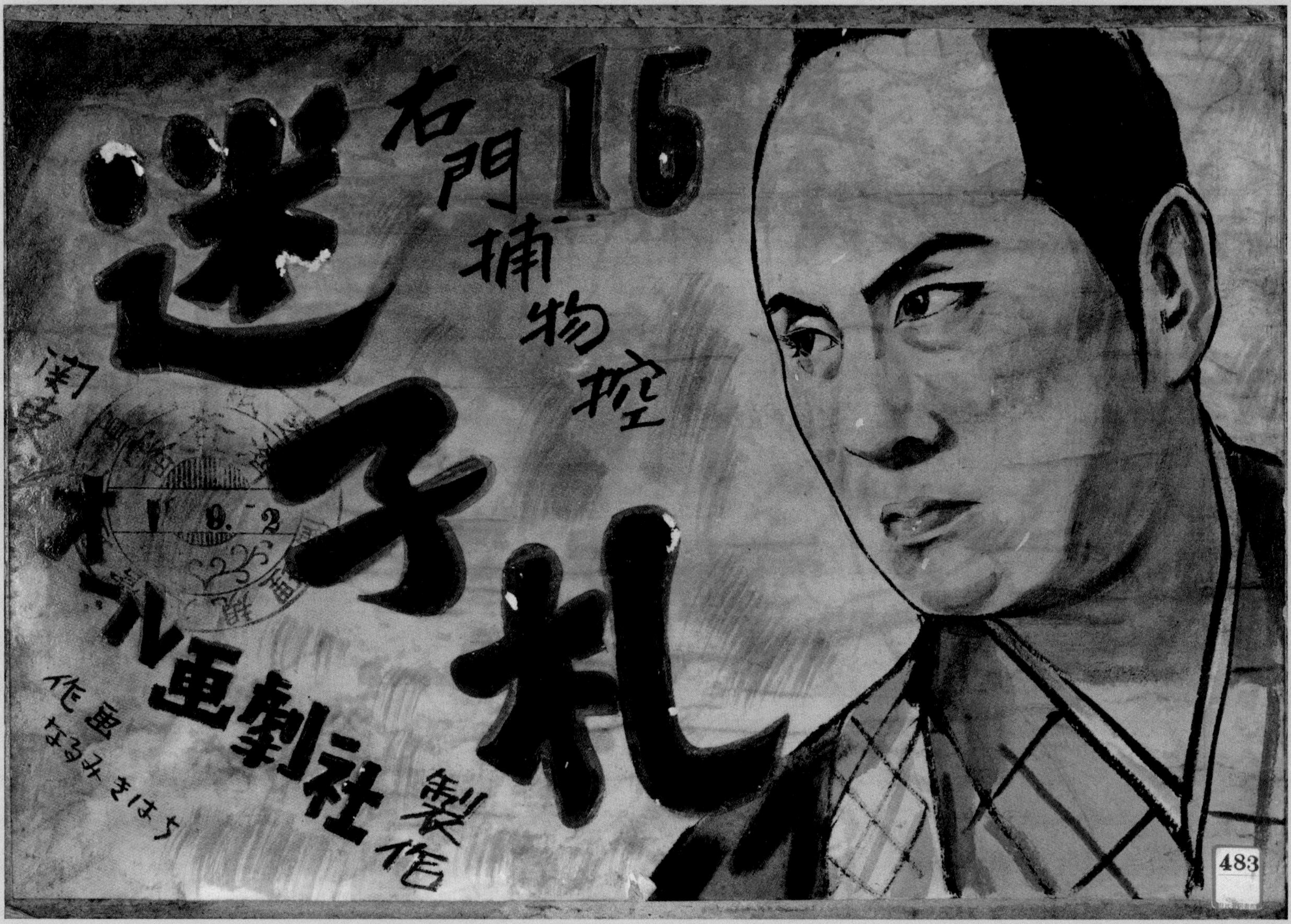
右門捕物控
16
迷子札
関東
画劇社製作
作画 なるみきはち
483

Samurai Detective: Based on the popular 1930 film *Umon Torimonocho: Rokuban Tegara Jinenji (Detective Umon's Diary)*, directed by Kumahiko Nishina and starring Kanjuro Arashi as the samurai detective Umon Kondo, this *kamishibai* case involves a search for a lost child.

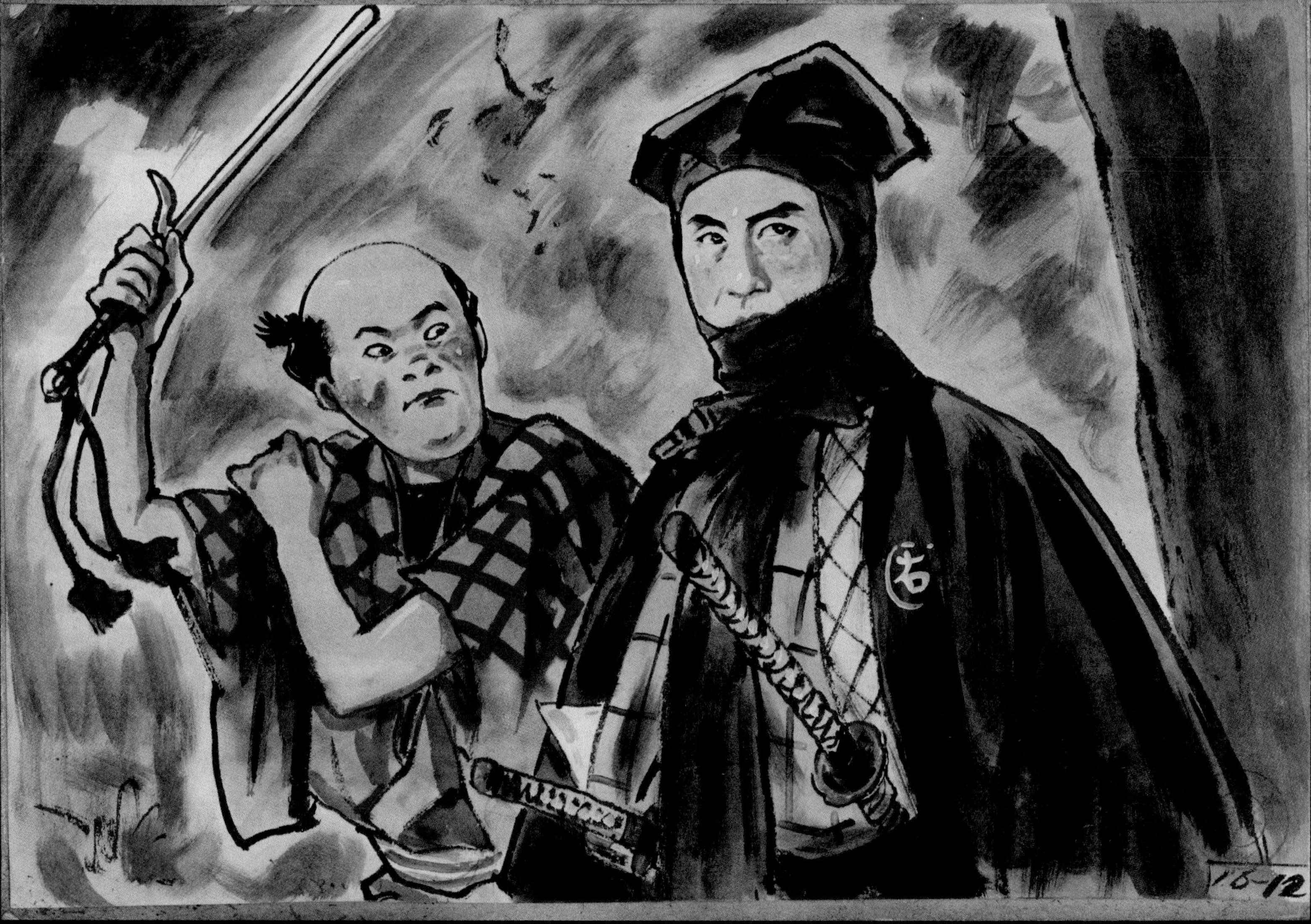
16-12

Samurai Sidekick: *Kamishibai* copied matinee idols and comic supporting characters. The samurai detective is portrayed with photographic realism, while his commoner sidekick is rendered in a looser, cartoonish style. The interplay of realistic and *chibi*, or miniaturized cartoon styles, is one of the pleasures of reading manga, as the characters bounce around according to where their moods take them.

Scar-Faced Samurai: The renowned actor Okochi Denjiro played the maimed, one-eyed, one-armed swordsman Tange Sazen in silent and sound films. The character has remained remarkably endurable, appearing in every medium short of a Pachinko game, including serialized newspaper novels, *kamishibai*, and manga.

samurai who look like they are working on a **Toho Studio** backlot, as well as more contemporary thrills like the rooftop-jumping nocturnal warriors in *Crouching Tiger, Hidden Dragon*.

Before Japanese animation became known as anime, it was simply called *manga eiga*, or moving manga. Early Japanese animation from the 1930s was heavily influenced by the American animation studios of Walt Disney and Max Fleischer, the latter best known for the wildly surrealistic Betty Boop cartoons. Put Betty Boop in a kimono, and presto! You have the first Japanese anime star. A number of early manga characters, notably Tagawa Suiho's popular Norakuro (Black Stray) in the 1930s, about the misadventures of a slacker puppy who enlists in the Imperial Army, made the leap from the printed page to the screen.

A fascinating parallel to *kamishibai* lies in the development of toy theater, also called paper theater, in nineteenth-century Europe. There is no direct evidence of cross-pollination with Japan, but there would have been many opportunities for British and Dutch colonialists to encounter shadow puppetry in Asia. Toy theater consists of small paper cutouts of actors in a tabletop proscenium stage. The miniature theaters were a popular home entertainment for middle-class families in England, Germany, and Denmark. Like *kamishibai*, toy theaters often featured images of actors from the legitimate theater and opera, as well as folktale characters. The first British toy theater was *Harlequin and Mother Goose* in 1811, and the art form lasted in Denmark as late as the 1940s, when it was equally influenced by cinema. There is a marvelous toy theater with candles for footlights in Bergman's *Fanny and Alexander*.

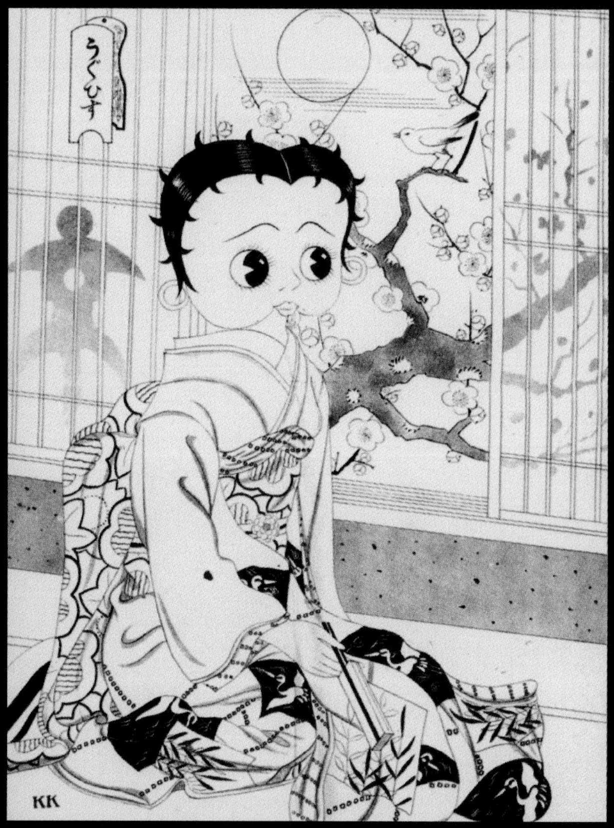

うぐひす
KK

Manga's Godmother: From out of the inkwell of the Fleischer Studios, jazz baby Betty Boop is the godmother of manga characters, whose most distinctive feature is their wide-awake pupils. When manga pioneer Osamu Tezuka created his best-known character Astro Boy (Atomu in Japan) more than fifty years ago, he was influenced by Boop's oversized eyes and delicate eyelashes as much as he was by Mickey Mouse. Round eyes are not simply used to make the characters appear more Caucasian; reflections of light and shadows make the eyes as emotionally expressive as possible. When Astro Boy first becomes sentient in the 1951 manga origin story, his flat black eyes alight with intraocular luminosity. Astro Boy set the paradigm for manga as Superman did for American comics.

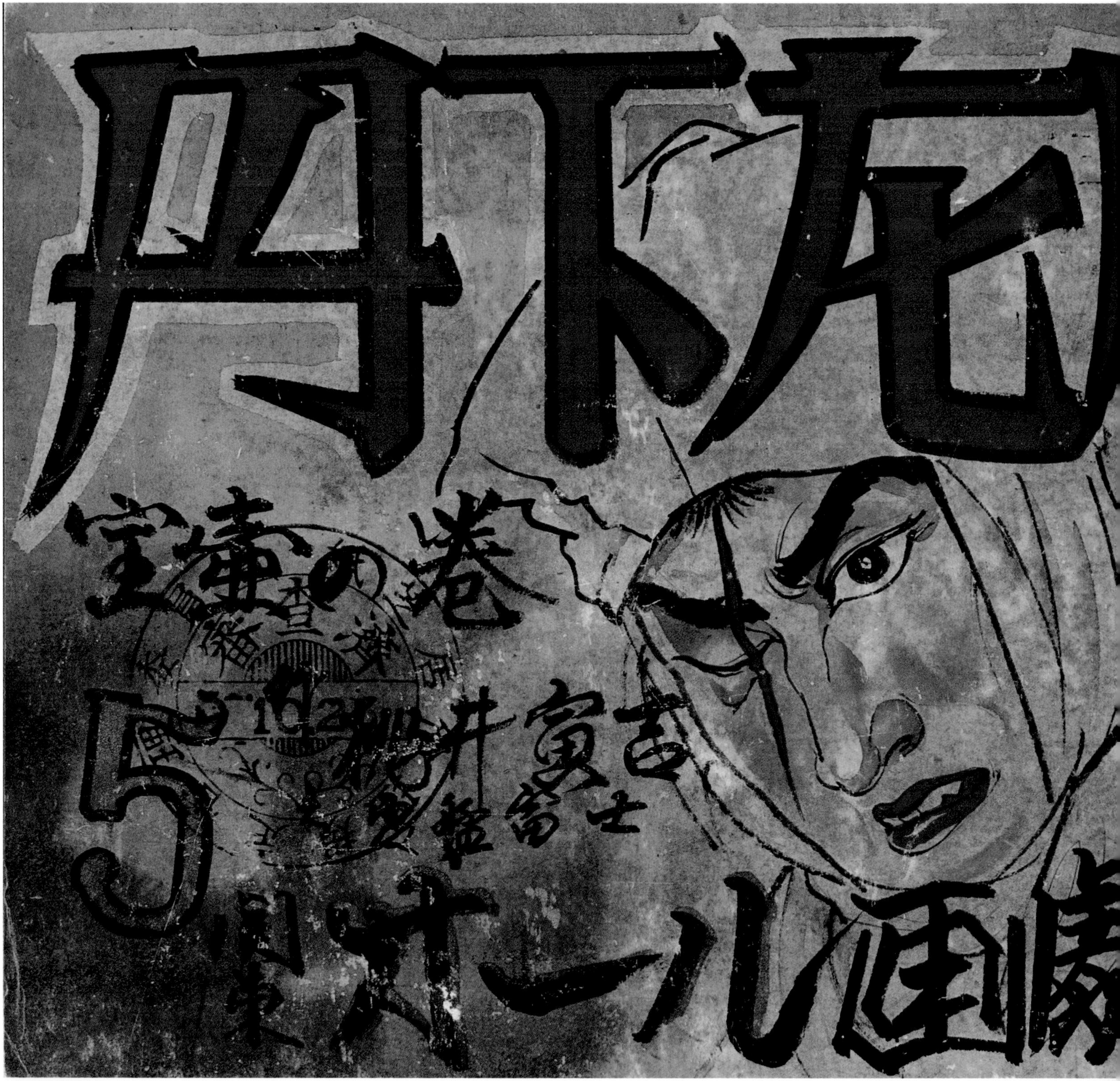
丹下左
宝庫の巻

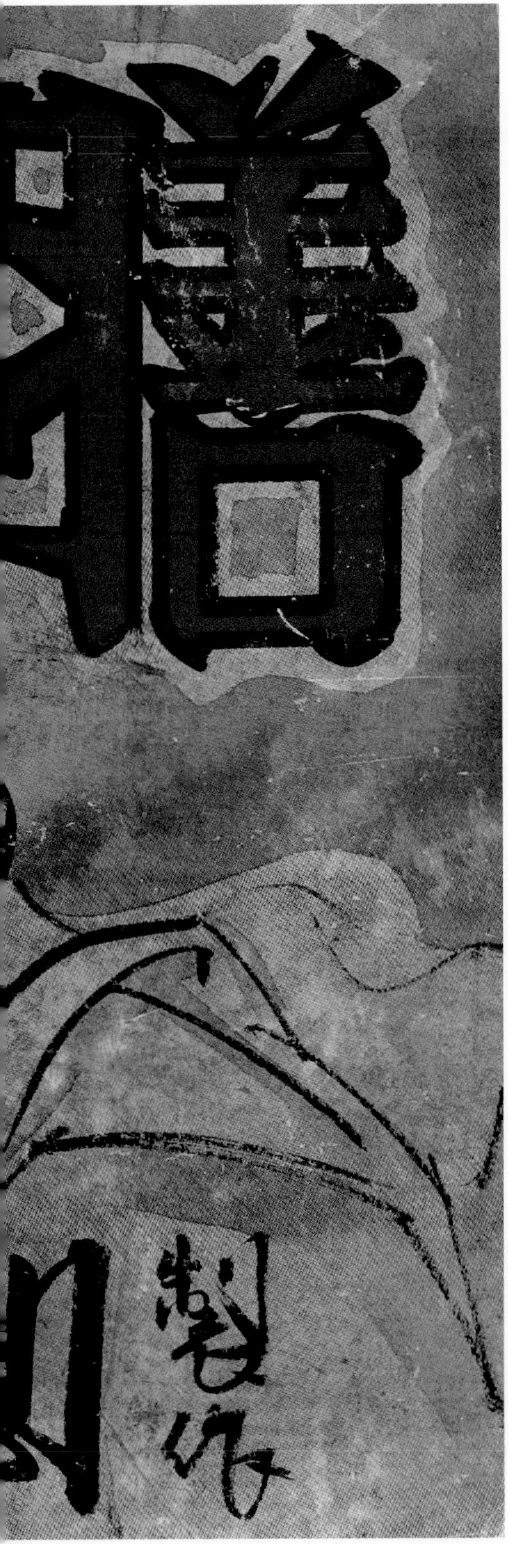

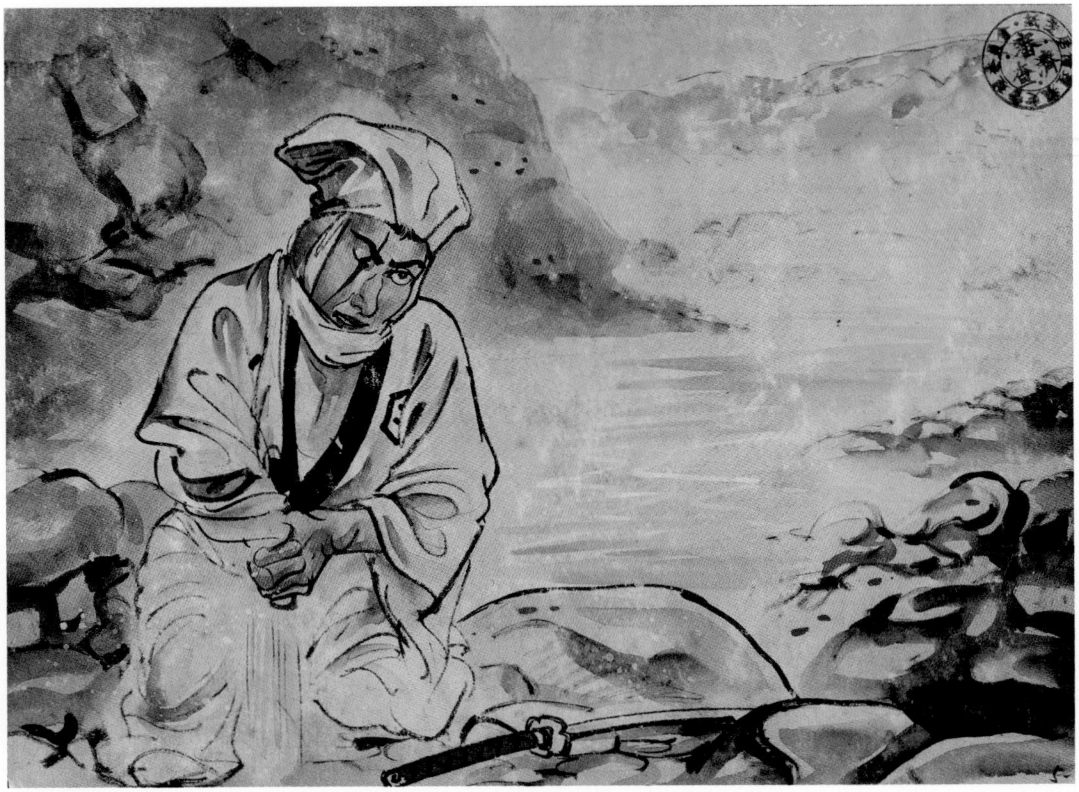

ABOVE Tange Sazen: The wounded *ronin* bathes in a stream as he recalls the events that led him here. *Kamishibai* creators were sophisticated in using cinematic devices including establishing shots, close-ups, montage, cross-cutting parallel action, and flashbacks.

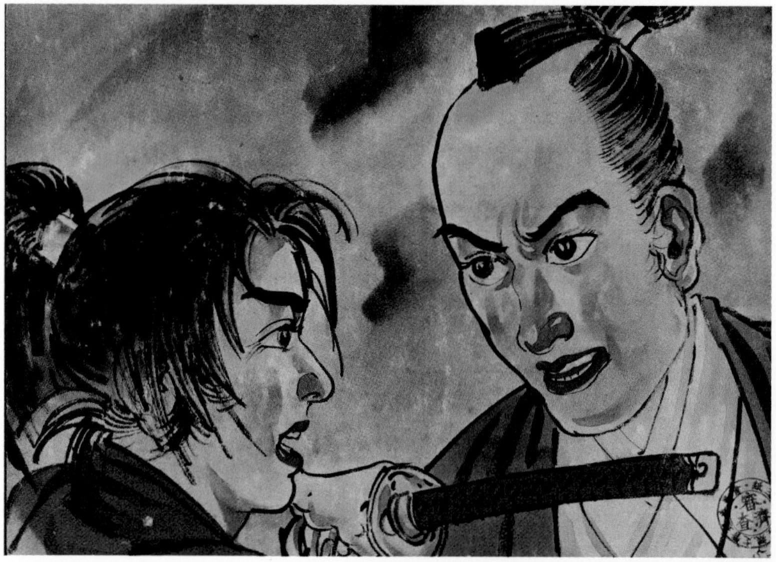

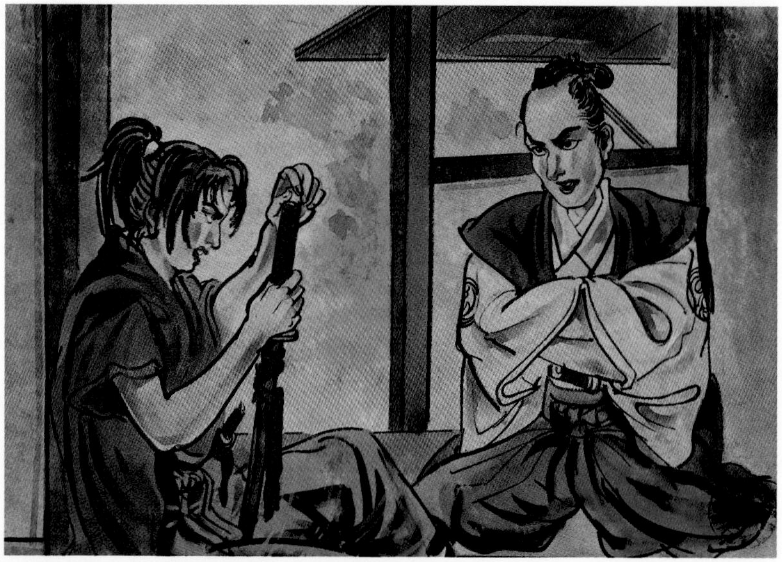

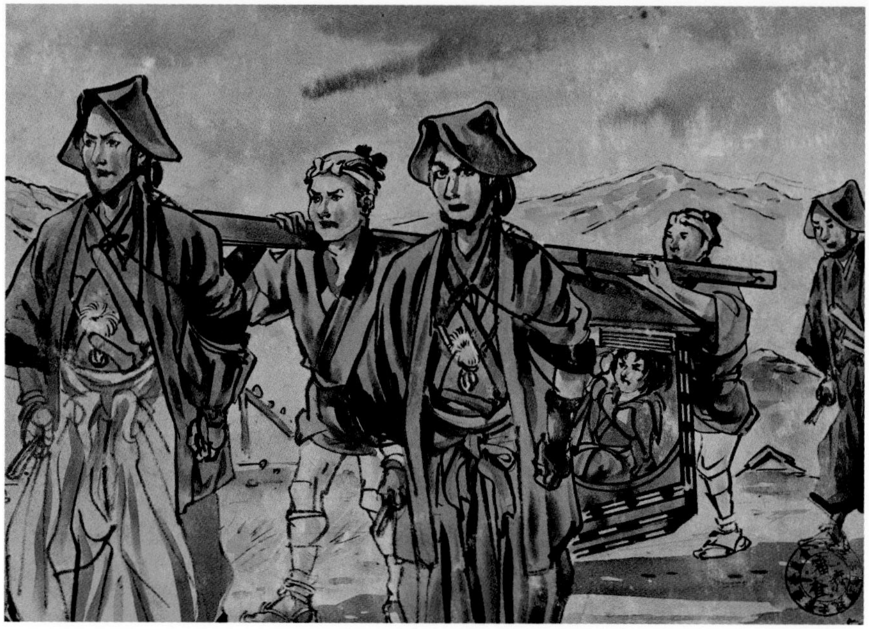

TOP LEFT Sazen flashes back to a time when he was unmarked and sound of limb. A young lord makes a casually threatening gesture, raising the hilt of his *katana* to Sazen's throat, an unpardonable rudeness, since swords are meant to be handled only if they are to be drawn.

TOP RIGHT Sazen coolly stares down his nemesis with a cross-armed gesture, but the young lord refuses to abandon his threatening posture.

BOTTOM A palanquin carrying the lord, now grown into manhood, passes along the road nearby the stream where Sazen watches. The imperiousness of the lord's retainers can be seen in their haughty expressions and the fact that their figures dominante the surrounding hillscape.

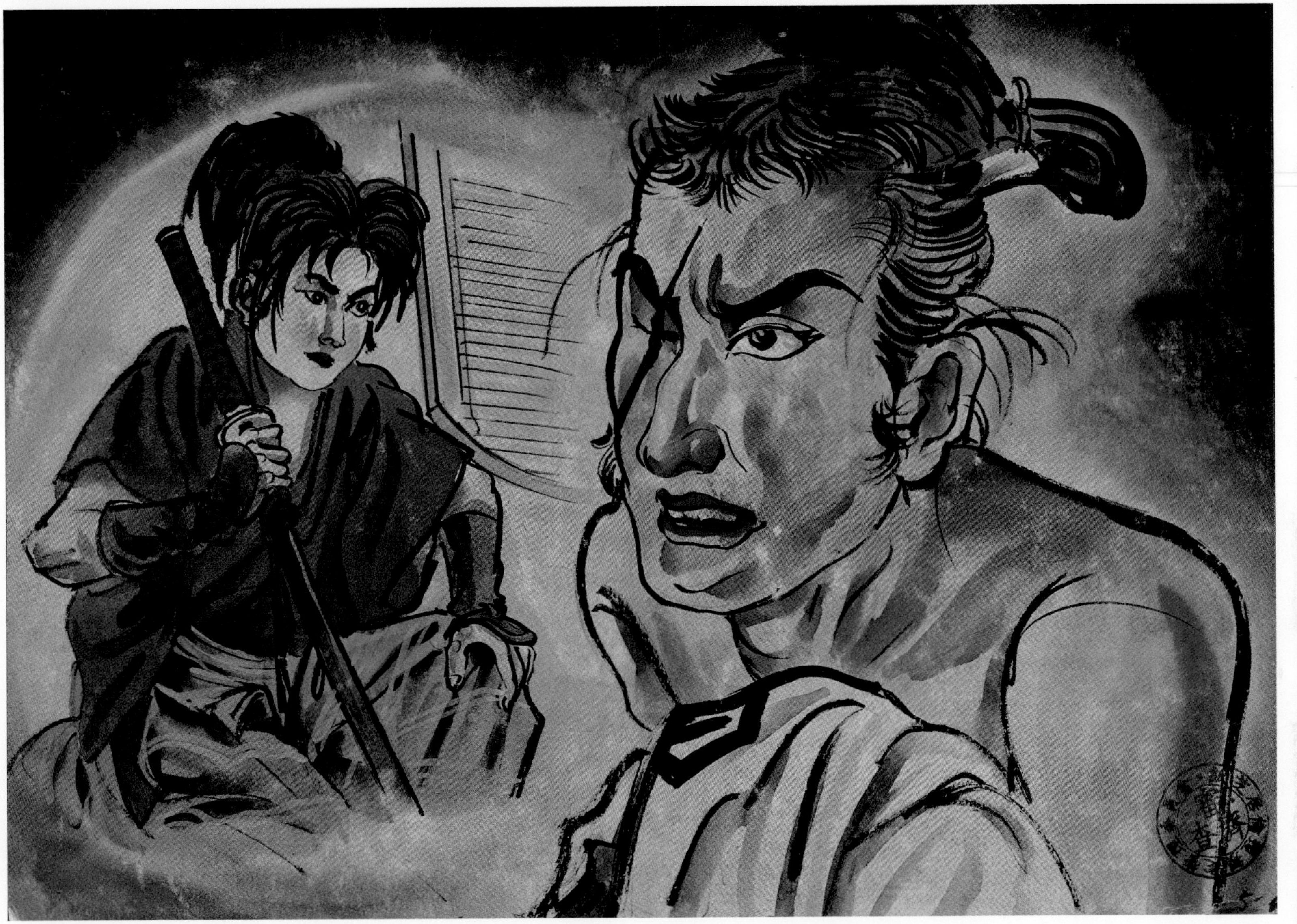

Flashback: Donning his kimono after bathing, Sazen recalls the disrespectful young lord. The hazy indigo of the frame is like the shimmering lines used to denote a flashback in old black-and-white films. Because of his wound, it appears as if Sazen is literally seeing the young lord in his mind's eye. Sazen's disheveled hair speaks to his fall as a *ronin*, compared to his tonsure when he was a younger samurai.

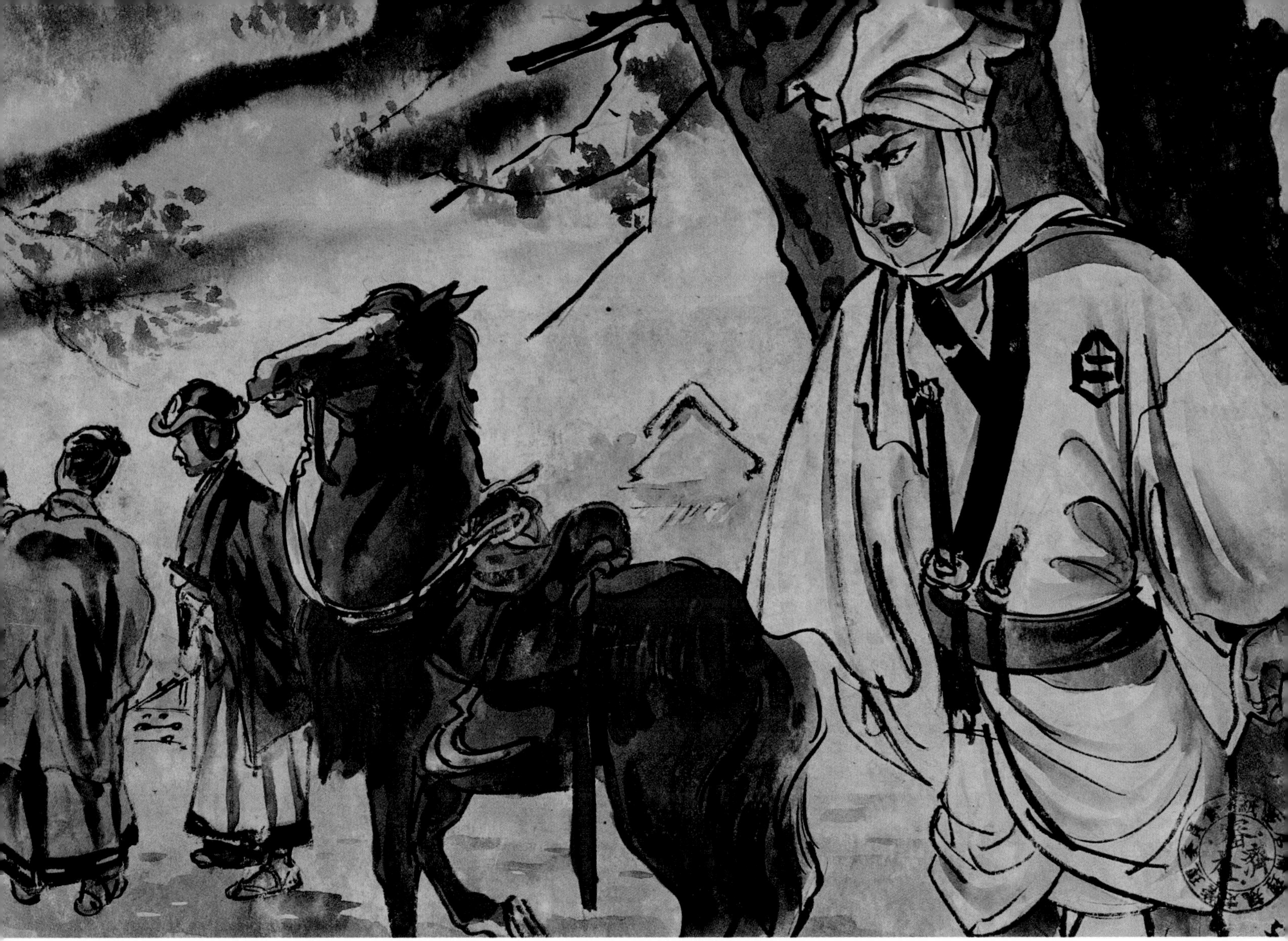

***Ronin* Rustler:** Hidden behind a tree, Sazen spots an unattended horse in the young lord's entourage, as the retainers stand with their backs to him. The roan horse and trees are rendered in an unusual combination of Oriental and Western techniques, with brush lines typical of Japanese ink painting, but molded volumetrically with color and shadow. This convergence may be due to *kamishibai* illustrators' familiarity with cinematic realism. The story has been building up with slow intensity to this point, concentrating on character development, and now it is time for . . .

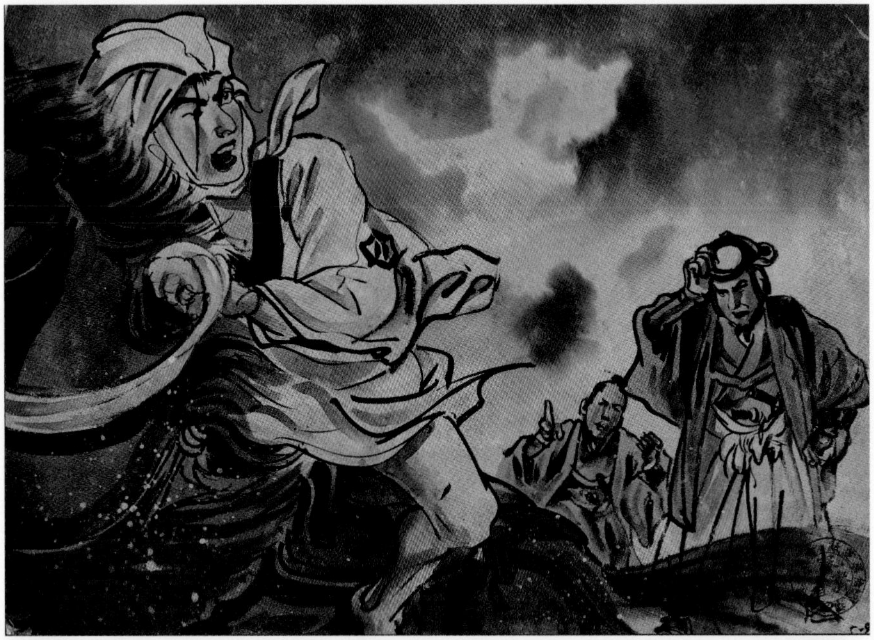

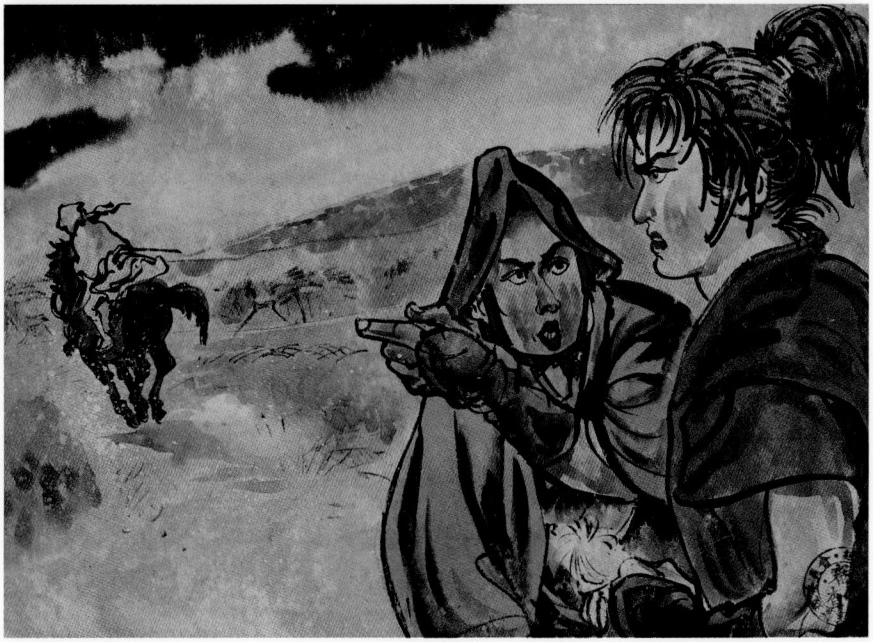

TOP . . . **ACTION!** Sazen straddles the horse and gallops off. The language of *kamishibai* is highly economical—just enough of the horse is shown to express the speed of escape, including the translucent red brushstrokes of the tail, but what advances the narrative is the provincial official's frustrated expression.

BOTTOM To Be Continued: The lord's retainer tells him that it was Sazen who took his horse. Depth of frame is used cinematically to convey motion, as the horse and rider take off into the distance. *Kamishibaiya* ended their presentations with words that have cast a spell over adventure lovers around the world, "Continued tomorrow!"

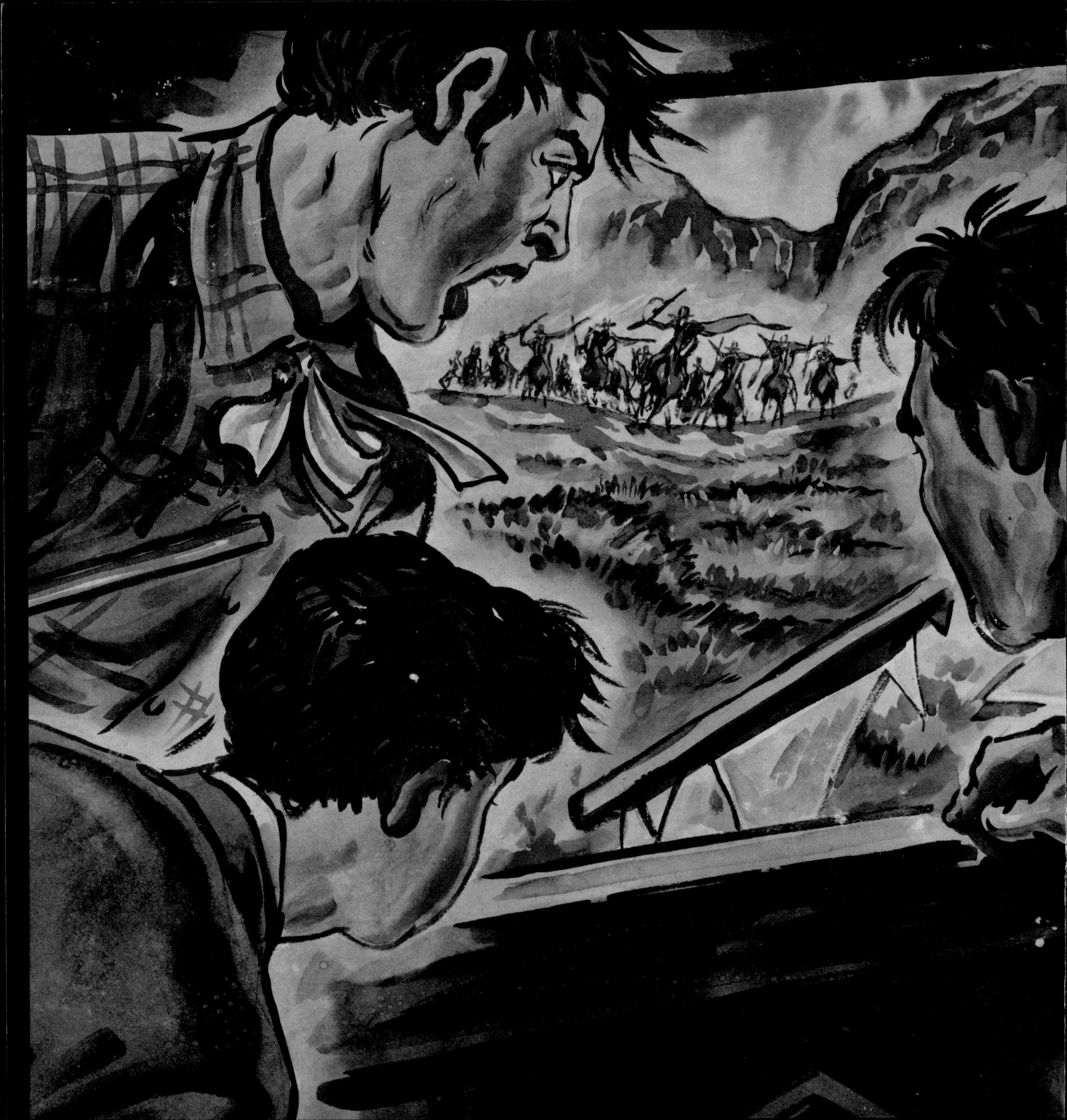

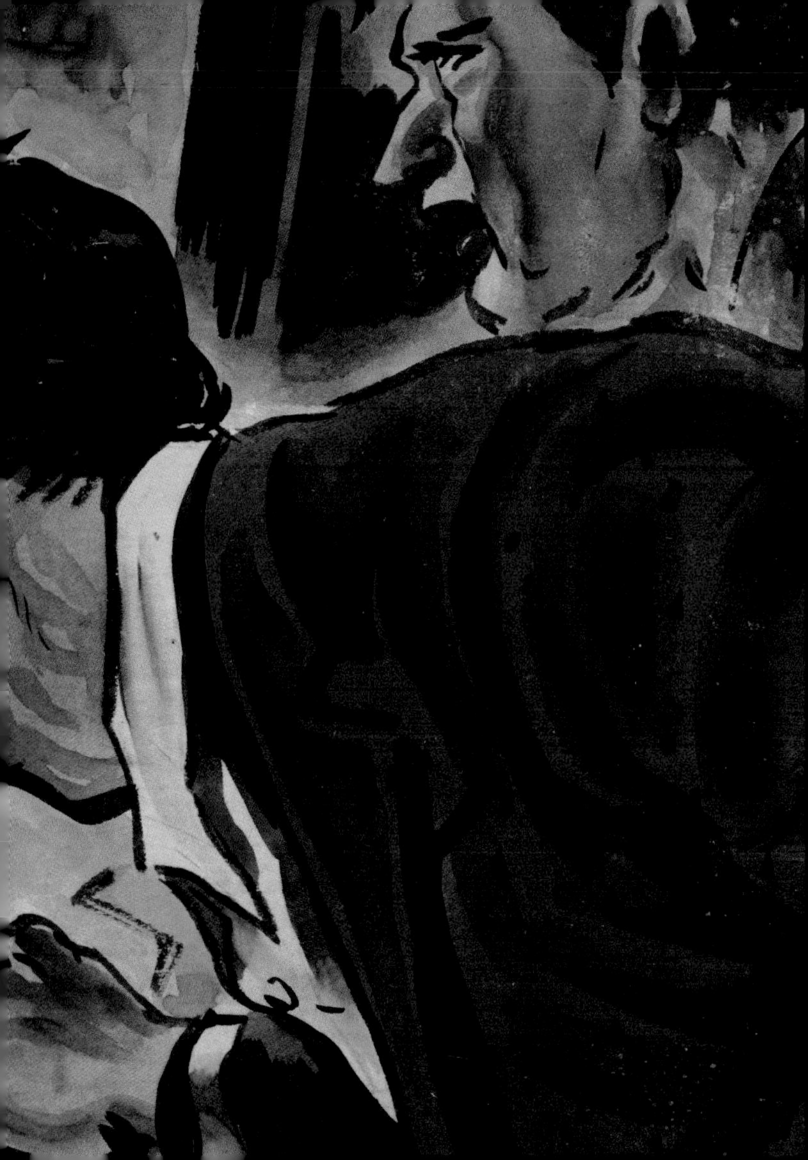

THE GOLDEN AGE OF KAMISHIBAI

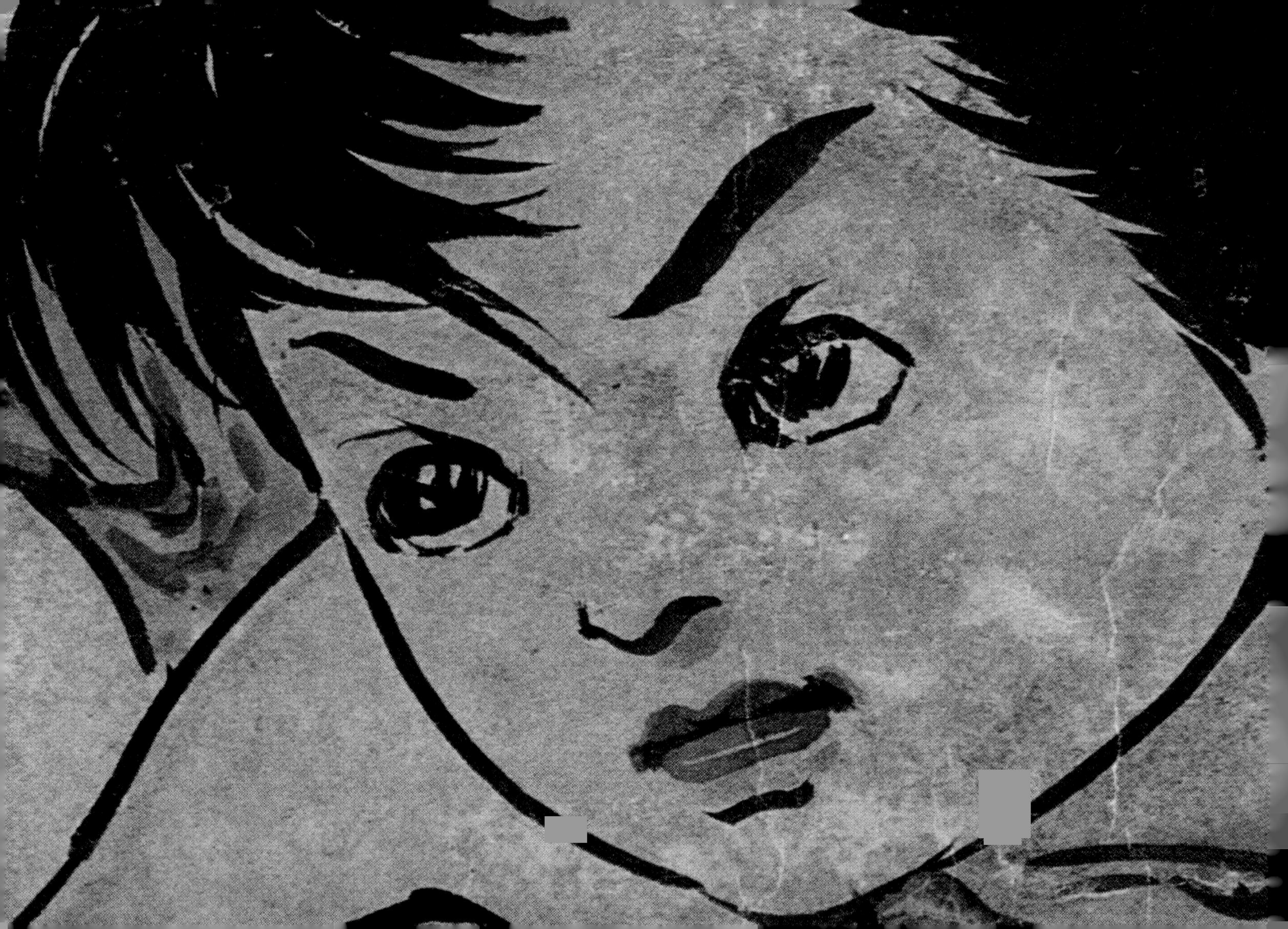

The Depression years were the most colorful for *kamishibai*, just as they were for pulp magazines in the United States. With 1.5 million unemployed in Tokyo in 1930, *kamishibai* storytelling offered creative job opportunities.

"The world looked down on *kamishibai* men as being partially unemployed, unable to work in the rain, with an unstable career," one *kamishibai* historian noted. "What made them continue was the love of the art, the fun of meeting kids, and the freedom of the life."

Kamishibai were told in a serial format with ten to twenty images daily, always ending with a cliff-hanger so that the breathless, sticky-fingered audience would return the following day to find out what happened. *Cry of the Andes*, set in what must have been the fabulously exotic land of Peru (the illustrated Andes Mountains are a delirious combination of movie Westerns and Chinese landscape painting), uses a John Ford–like rhythm of scenic long shots and intimate close-ups to tell the story of a boy battling a mysterious masked horseman in a quest for Inca gold, along with a literal cliff-hanger.

Artistic production was broken down somewhat along the lines of an American comic book company, with separate people doing the inking and coloring of a

Manga-Sized Eyes: A detail of Jungle Boy looks fresh and contemporary. Emotion is expressed with an economy of line, from the tilt of the eyebrows to the firm set of the mouth. Jungle Boy was one of the first characters to feature the oversized eyes with complex reflections that typify manga. Some observers criticize manga's use of large round eyes as a token of self-loathing and a Japanese desire to look Caucasian, yet the characters maintain distinctly Japanese traits. On a purely technical level, large eyes are used in manga as shorthand to convey emotion. Current manga, with their wildly colorful hairstyles and clothes, aim for a feeling of *mukokuseki* (statelessness), so that they are not identifiable with any one culture.

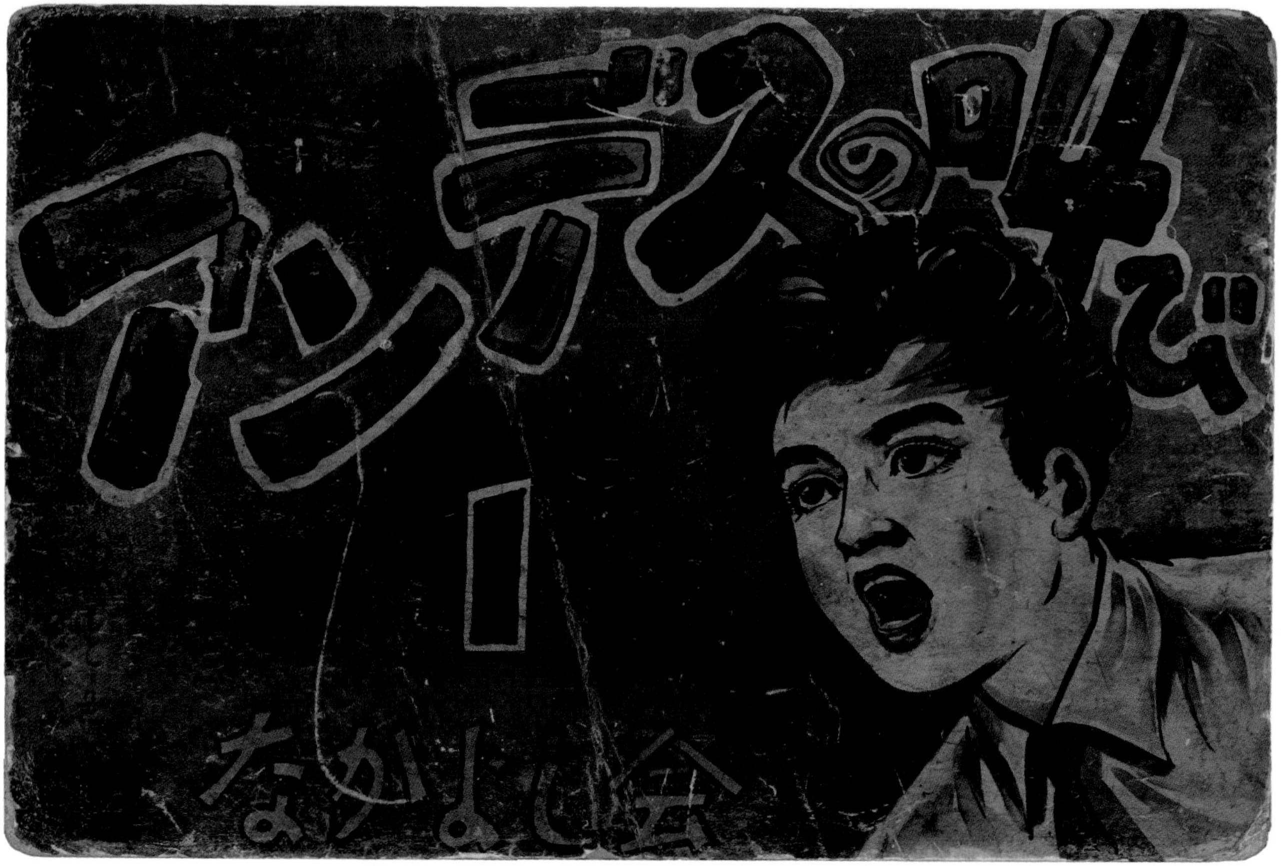
アンデスの叫び
なかよし会

Cry of the Andes: an adventure set in the exotic land of Peru.

panel. Aspiring artists often entered the field by serving as apprentices to a master. The principle illustrator made pencil sketches on heavy paper stock in a format of ten by fourteen inches, and then went over the drawing with a thick brush and India ink. Then watercolor paint was applied, building from the background to the foreground in eye-grabbing reds, blacks, whites, and golds. Opaque tempera paints were added on top, often to convey motion lines. Finally a coat of clear lacquer was applied to protect the watercolor hues, and make the images shine so that they would jump off the page. A layer of wax was often applied to the painted boards to protect them from rain. The boards were constantly being shuffled so that cracks and welts in the wax coating gave them the look of relics from an ancient civilization, albeit one familiar with giant robots.

Kamishibai were a departure from traditional Japanese painting, whose chief element is line art. Japanese art relies on the density and expressiveness of the ink brushstroke, and uses the relative boldness or faintness of line, rather than shading, to convey perspective. But *kamishibai* artists applied the Western style of chiaroscuro—contrasts of light and dark—to mold the masses of the figures and provide depth.

Street-corner *kamishibai* is a salty-sweet mix of trashy pop imagery and gorgeous artistry. Standard pulp fare like hard-boiled detective fiction is rendered with loving attention to details like teeth and reflections in the eye. Cartoon conventions like motion lines are conveyed with textured and feathered brushstrokes. *Kamishibai* are clearly in the cartoon tradition, but they are cartoons done by hand in ink, paint, and watercolors. Deep cinematic compositions reflect Hollywood's pervasive influence. Clean-edged lines, saturated colors, and filigreed articulation make pulp material like *Tiger Boy* look as fresh as contemporary imagery.

Top creators, like Kouji Kata, who worked on *Golden Bat*, could earn more than a high school principal, although they appeared to be working opposite sides of the educational fence. A writer could make up to two hundred yen for writing a series. In comparison, the average pay for a day laborer was 240 yen. Sweatshop conditions prevailed for apprentices and journeyman artists. Shigeru Mizuki, who later went on to pioneer horror manga and to create characters that are still popular, recollects producing up to ten pages a day in order to survive. Some artists labored over their brushes for up to fifteen hours a day for *kamishibai* companies. A good day's work was eleven pages, which took just over an hour each to produce, the equivalent of one new chapter, but artists like Nagamatsu recall pulling all-nighters and polishing off fifteen chapters. One illustrator remarked that he "would quit in a flash if there were other work."

Creators sold their original boards to *kamishibai* dealers (*kashimoto*), who in turn rented out the artwork to storytellers for a fee. Often a writer would approach a *kashimoto* with a story idea, and if the *kashimoto* liked it, he would hire the writer and illustrator. *Kamishibai* tellers could earn about four hundred to five hundred yen a day after paying the fifty-to-three-hundred-yen daily rental fee to the *kamishibai* dealer. A good *kamishibai*

Cover Story: The title card of a paper play was the equivalent of a cover or splash page in a comic book, highlighting the most exciting visual story point. In this chapter of *Golden Mask*, the Prince regains his rightful crown with the help of the beaked super hero. Golden Mask may have been inspired by the hawk-headed Egyptian deity Horus.

man could hope to earn up to one thousand yen a day, selling two pieces of candy for five yen and rice crackers with plum jam for one yen. Snacks for sale included pulls of corn-sugar candy served on disposable chopsticks, cinnamon sticks, and the delicacy: eels and ice cream. Prime locations in parks and on temple grounds were apportioned beforehand, with the best spots going to the more senior storytellers. Children associated *kamishibai* with sweets, the same way Americans recall the sugar-coated cereal rush of Saturday-morning cartoons. As in movie theaters and drive-ins, the real profit was in the concessions.

Kamishibai covered all styles, from Hitchcockian suspense featuring secretaries and stolen money, to "big foot" cartoony styles. Genres were mixed merrily, like *Golden Mask*, a serial about a whip-wielding character who wore a falcon's-head mask with an enormous ruff. *Golden Mask* combined Douglas Fairbanks' swashbuckling with *Prince and the Pauper* plotlines, another instance of Hollywood's global domination in the 1930s. Folklore and fairy tales, always a staple of street-corner *kamishibai*,

GOLDEN MASK

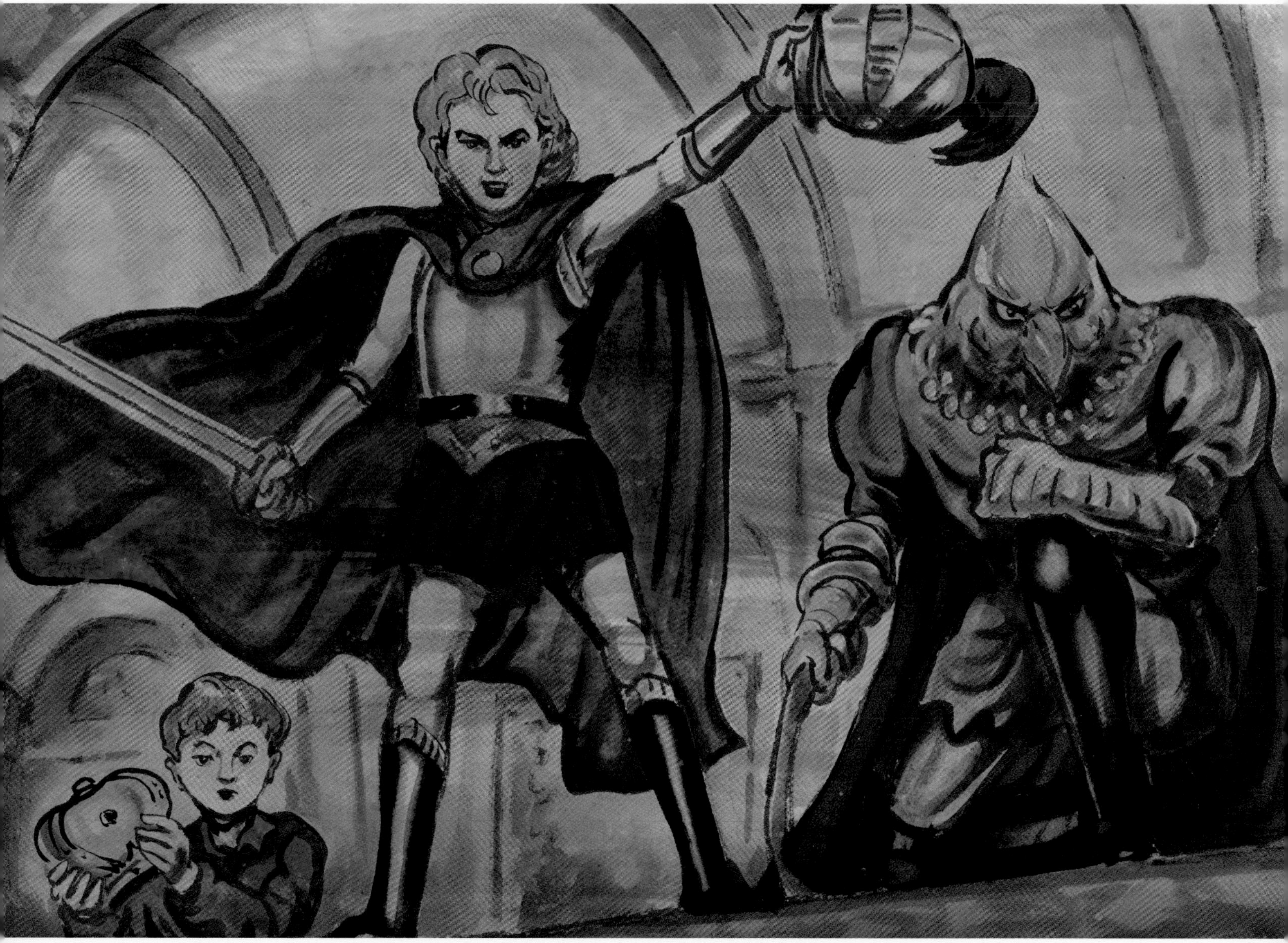

Falconhead: Golden Mask looks like Super Chicken on steroids but was another early masked super hero. This multipart story line borrows from *The Prince and The Pauper* as the true Prince doffs his knight's helmet to reveal his identity, and the pauper who has substituted for him removes his crown. *Golden Mask* is indicative of the rich variety of *kamishibai* genres, from knights in armor to Westerns like *Cry of the Andes* and out-of-this-world tales like *Prince of Gamma*.

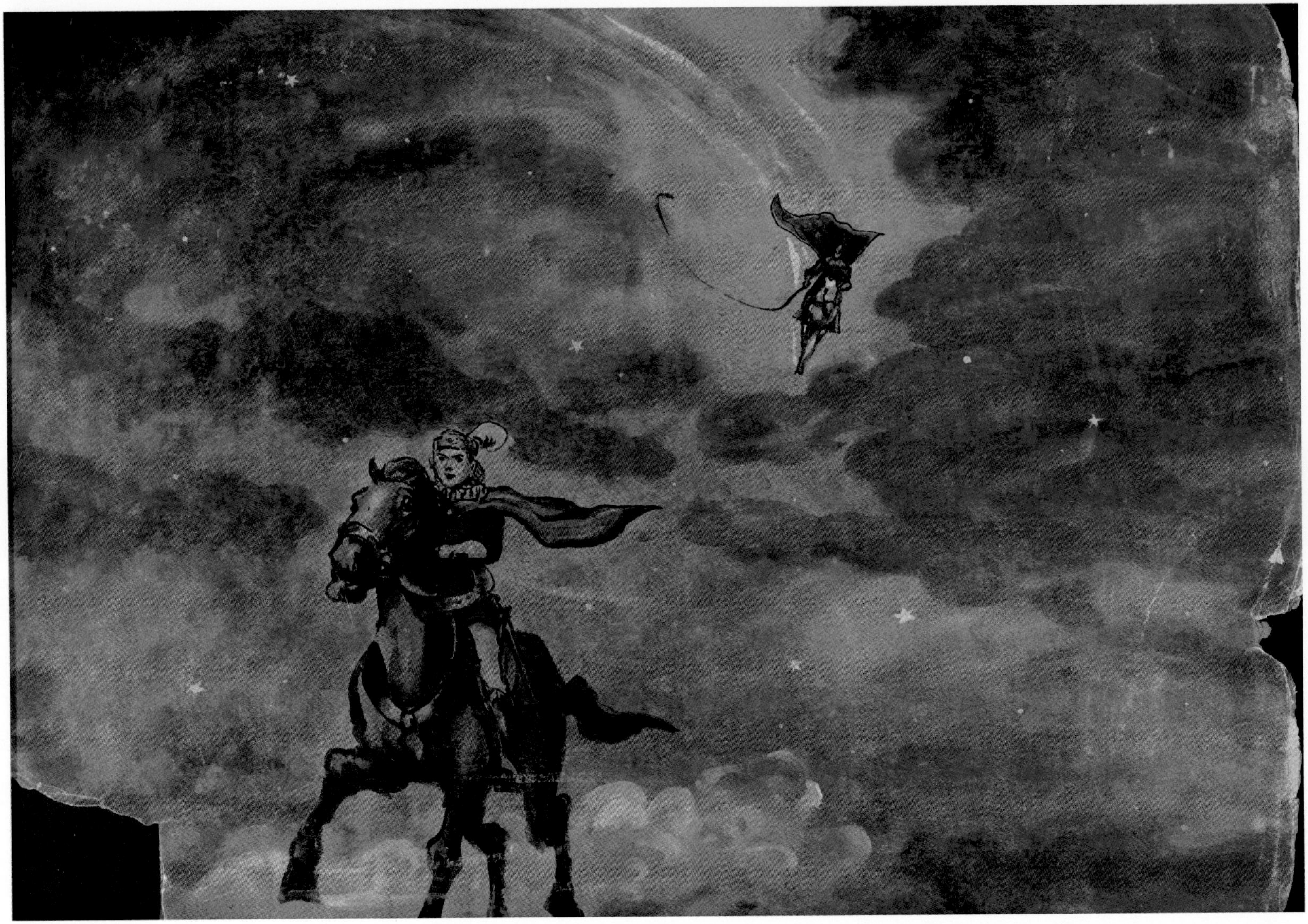

Starry Knight: This moody image of Golden Mask descending from a starry firmament has the mysterious quality of a medieval etching. A good *kamishibai* artist never wastes empty space—the night sky is textured with blue clouds flecked with white stars, the streak of Golden Mask's cape, and the cloud of dust from the horse's hooves.

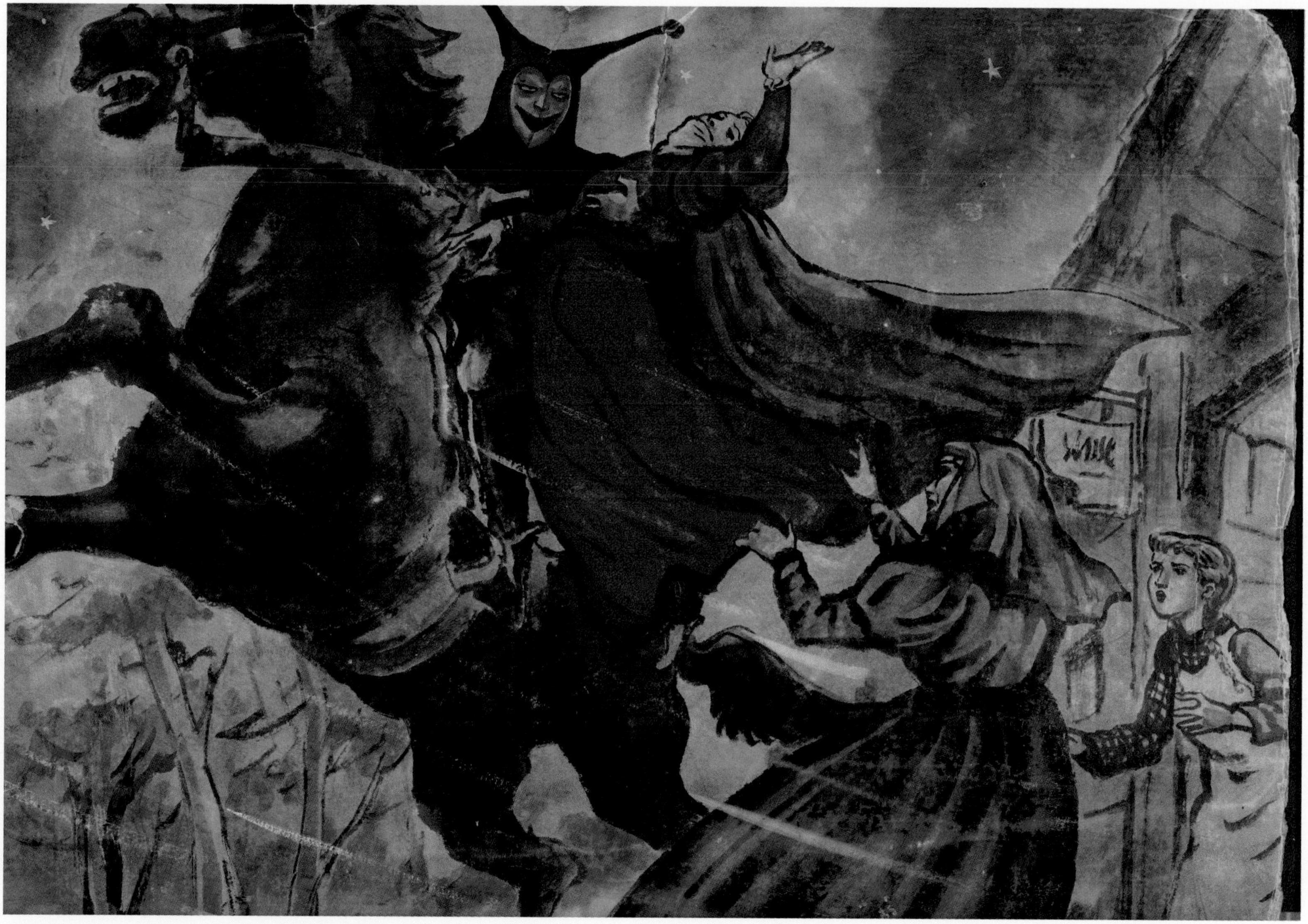

Costume Drama: In a virtuoso composition, the illustrator balances the finely rendered folds of the heroine's cloak with the body of the rearing horse. The villain in a jester's mask abducts the heroine from her mother and sister, who are wearing European garb, in this Japanese version of a Hollywood period piece.

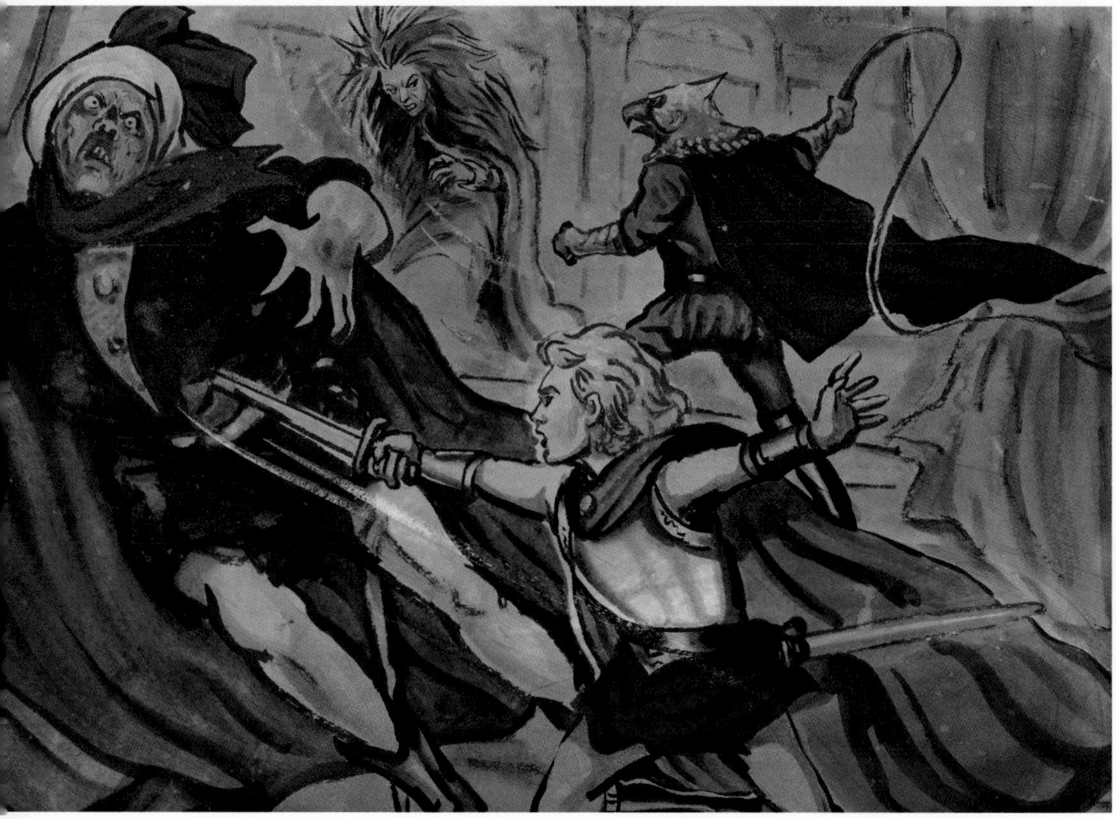

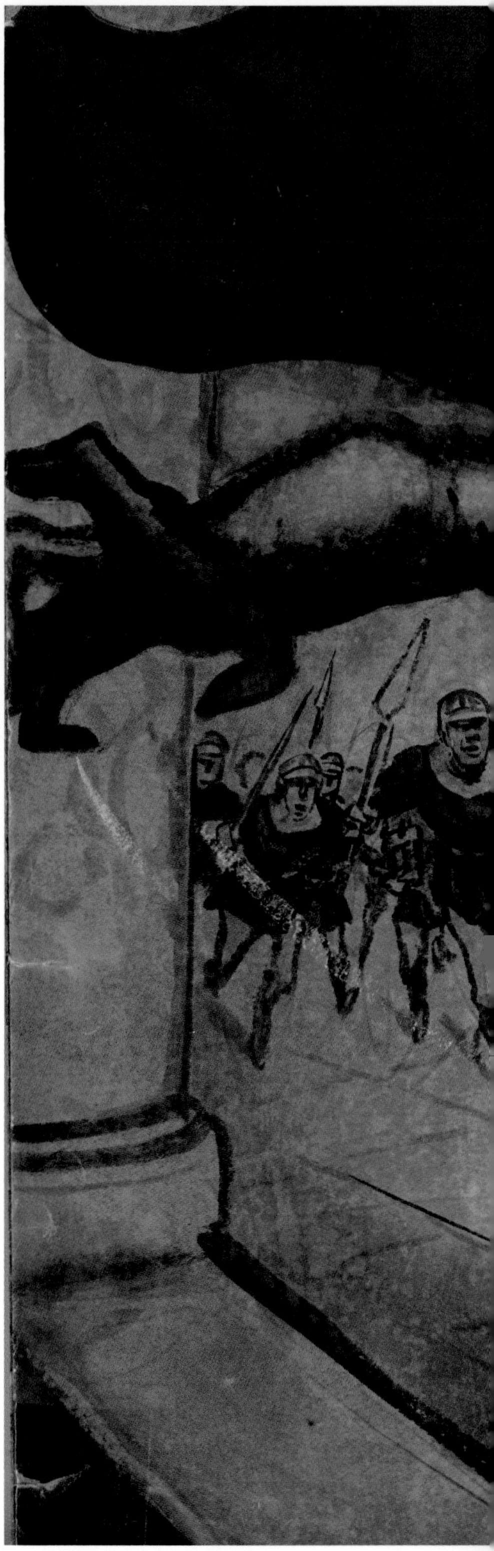

ABOVE Whippersnapper: The Prince skewers the traitor while Golden Mask, à la Indiana Jones, lashes a frazzled witchy character. The entire scene is composed with Renaissance-style drapery: the unbalanced pose of the fallen traitor is set against a river of blue in the superimposed cloaks, Golden Mask's flying scarlet cape is offset by the folds of the wall hanging, and the witch's green cape provides a focal point deep within the frame. The tableau provides a rich cast of characters for the *kamishibaiya* to vocalize: the muffled basso of Golden Mask, the chipper voice of the Prince, the traitor's curses, and the witch's cackle.

RIGHT Skeleton Crew: The masked villain in an eerie skeleton costume evades the royal guard to fight another day. The figure is foreshortened, another development of Renaissance art, to make him look as if he is reaching out of the picture plane into the viewer's space like a Caravaggio painting. The villian's ghostly mask is unmistakably Oriental, like a Kabuki character's, but the rest of the scene suggests a European setting. The villain's voluminous cloak settles like a curtain, marking the end of the episode.

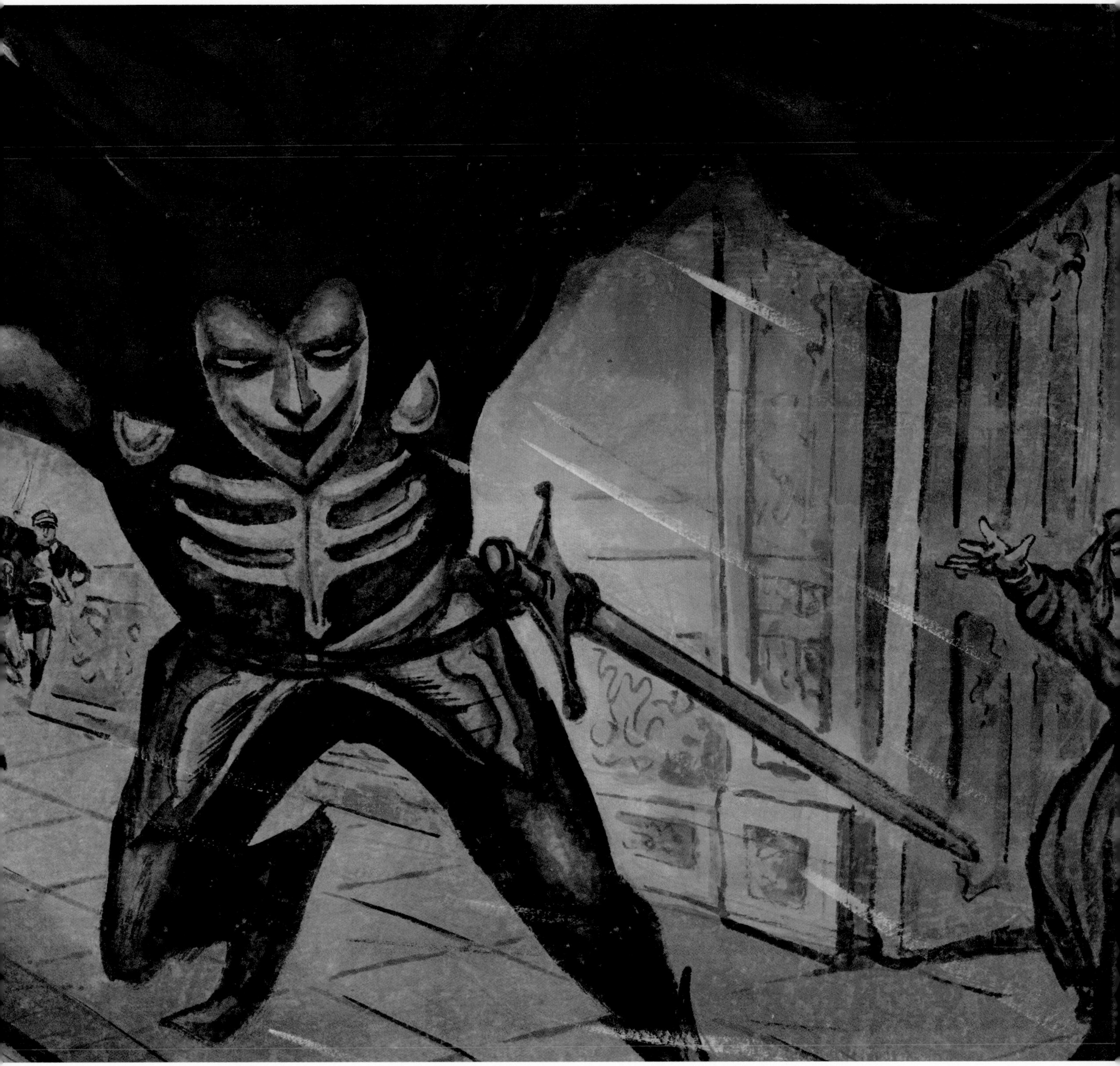

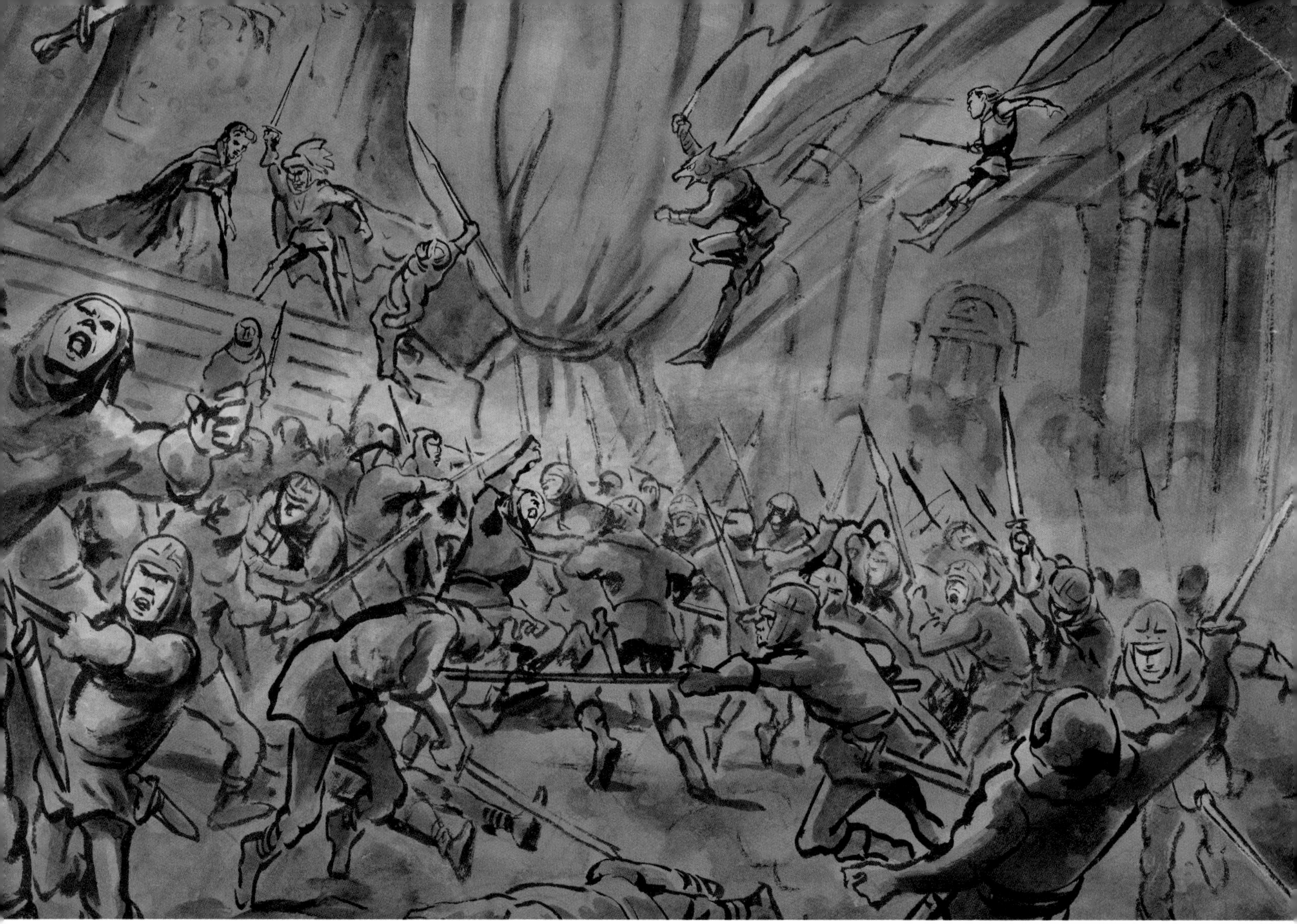

continued on into educational *kamishibai*. Animals are often portrayed engaging in entirely human activities, like kimono-clad foxes picnicking during cherry blossom season.

Reform-minded educators called for an investigation into *gaito kamishibai* in the mid-1930s, much like the witch hunt against comic books by the Kefauver Senate committee in 1955–56 in the United States. One critic in America called comic books "the marijuana of the nursery." The Japanese government wanted to regulate the grisly, pulp horrors that have always

Swashbucklers: This crowded action scene from Golden Mask recalls both a medieval tapestry and a Depression-era Hollywood epic with the swashbuckling swoop of the prince and Golden Hawk.

appealed to young fans. In one horror *kamishibai*, a doctor implants the heart of a gorilla into the body of a mortally wounded man who proceeds to metamorphose into a blood-thirsty Frankenstein monster lookalike, with one neat Japanese detail—he wears a peasant's straw winter coat. The monster proceeds to eat the live entrails of animals and dies in a fusillade of police bullets in the fiery wreckage of a pier. E.C. Comics had nothing on this!

Tokyo government investigators questioned the wholesomeness of *kamishibai* for young minds in the same way they were alarmed about the health risk of homemade street candy. The top-selling *kamishibai* at the time were *Golden Bat* and *Tiger Boy* for boys, and *Snow White* for girls. A city government survey of 1,943 eight-year-old elementary schoolboys found that 515 watched *kamishibai* shows more than twice a day, proof of *kamishibai*'s pernicious influence. *Kamishibai* were banned in many schools and neighborhoods. Officials claimed that *kamishibai* caused traffic problems because of the crowds of kids, that it was unhygienic because candy was passed along by dirty hands, and that the riotous compositions and colors were "too stimulating" to young minds.

Following the investigations, some *kamishibai* companies took remedial steps. By 1935 a teacher named Yone Imai was producing Christian-themed stories. Her first character was Young David from the Bible. She went on to create eighteen *kamishibai* in 1933–34 and published fifty in her lifetime. Bible stories like Daniel in the Lion's Den still provided thrilling action scenes suited to the appetites of *kamishibai* audiences. Another creator named Gozan Takahashi produced kindergarten *kamishibai*. Religious and educational *kamishibai* tended to be printed on paper rather than hand-painted because they were more broadly distributed. Kenya Matsunaga cofounded the Japan Educational *Kamishibai* Association in the mid-1930s to combat the scurrilous reputation of street-corner *kamishibai*.

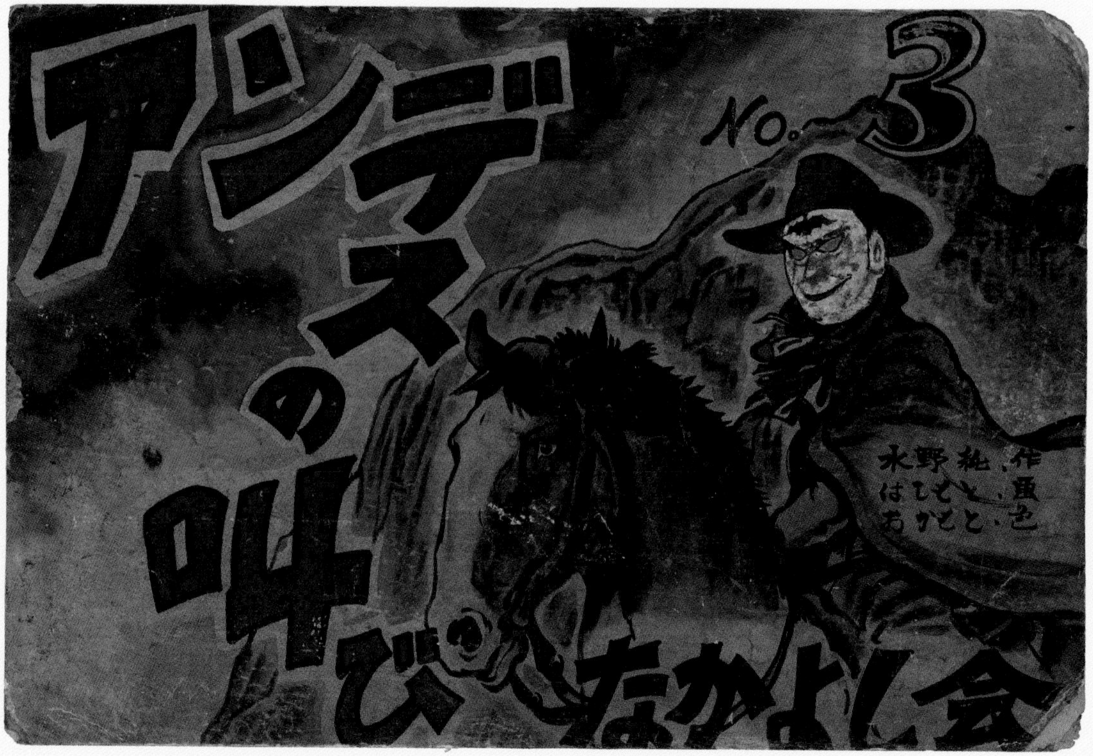
アンデスの叫び
No. 3
なかよし会

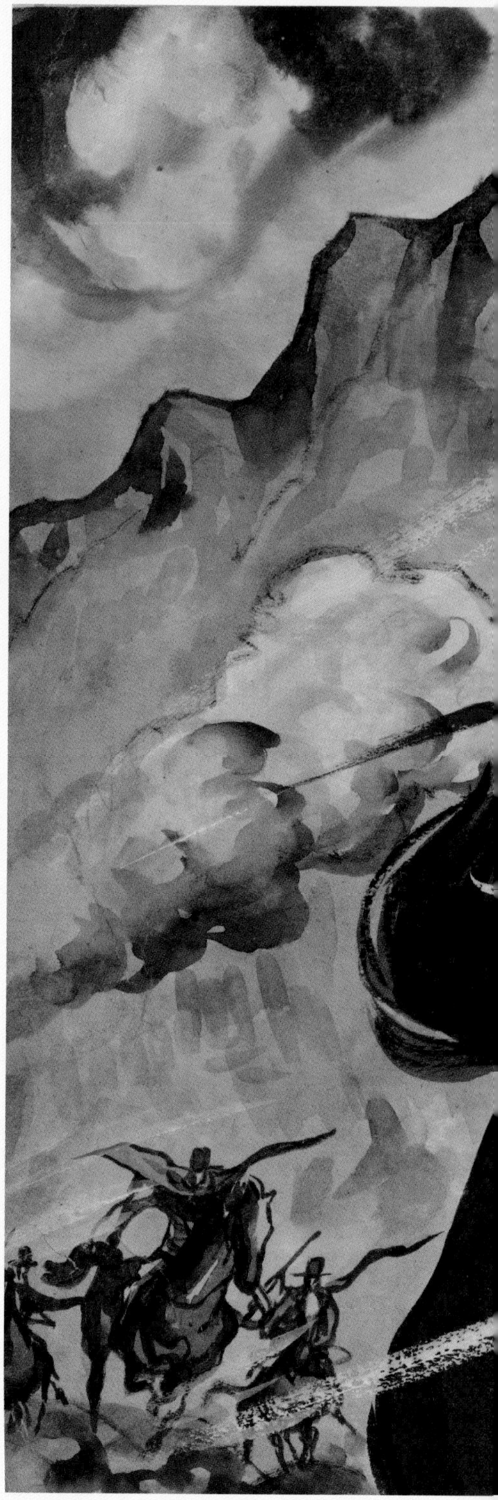

ABOVE Kabuki Cowboy: Chapter 3 of *Cry of the Andes* features a weirdly disguised villain with a bat emblazoned on his forehead and his mask set in a cruel grin like a Kabuki character.

RIGHT A Cloud of Dust: The opening panel begins with a bang and a puff of smoke as the boy hero shoots back at his pursuers under a blazing sky. His roan horse, the foliage, and the mountain peaks have their roots in Japanese painting, but the perspective is pure Hollywood with the horse's head prominent in the foreground and the bandits on a distant diagonal in the background, like a tracking shot in a Western.

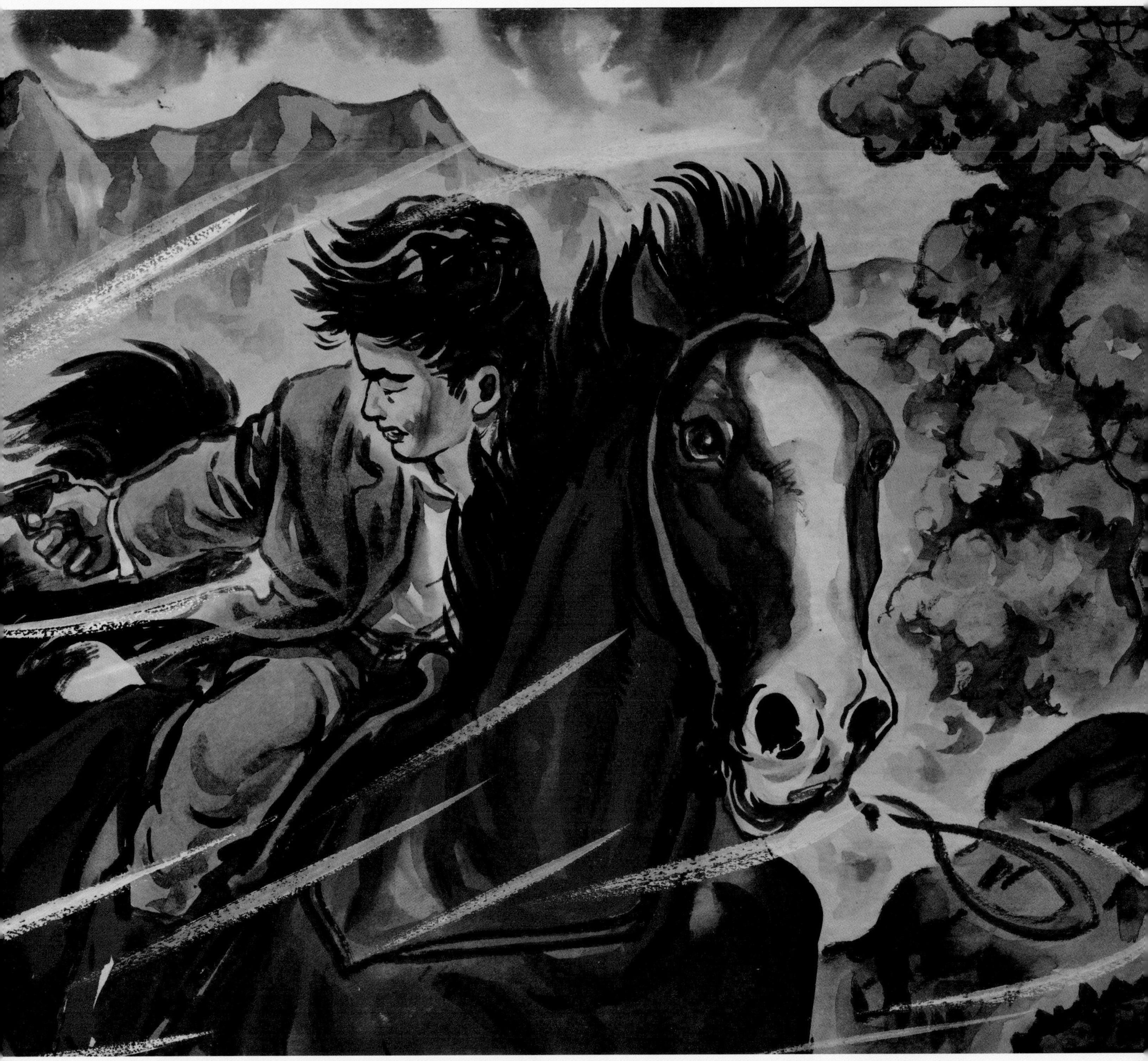

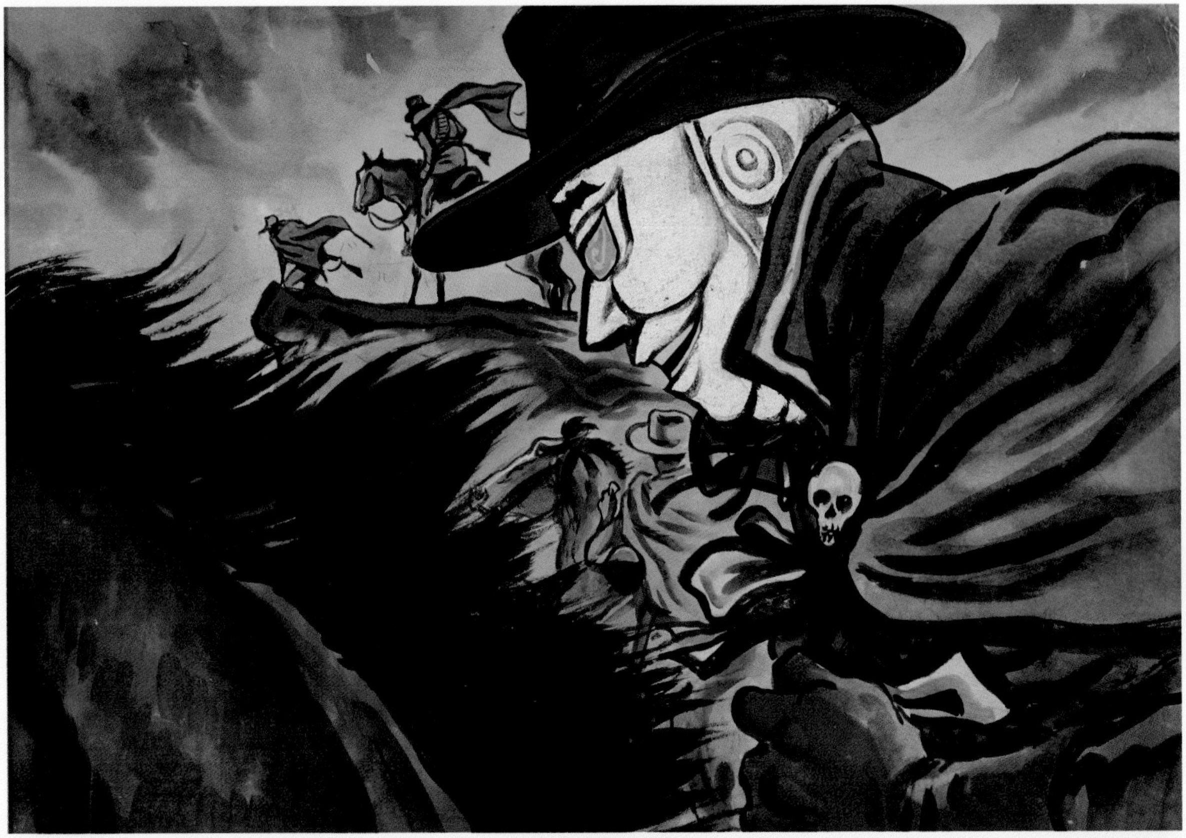

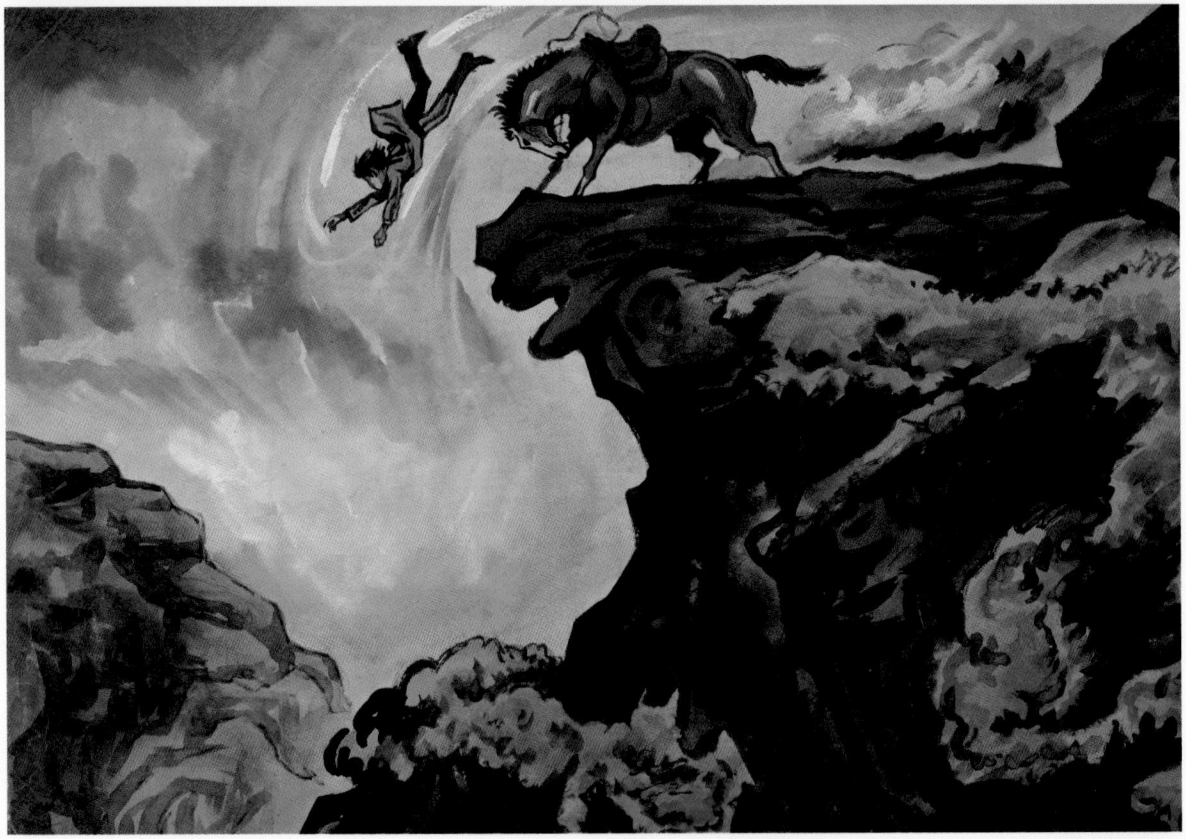

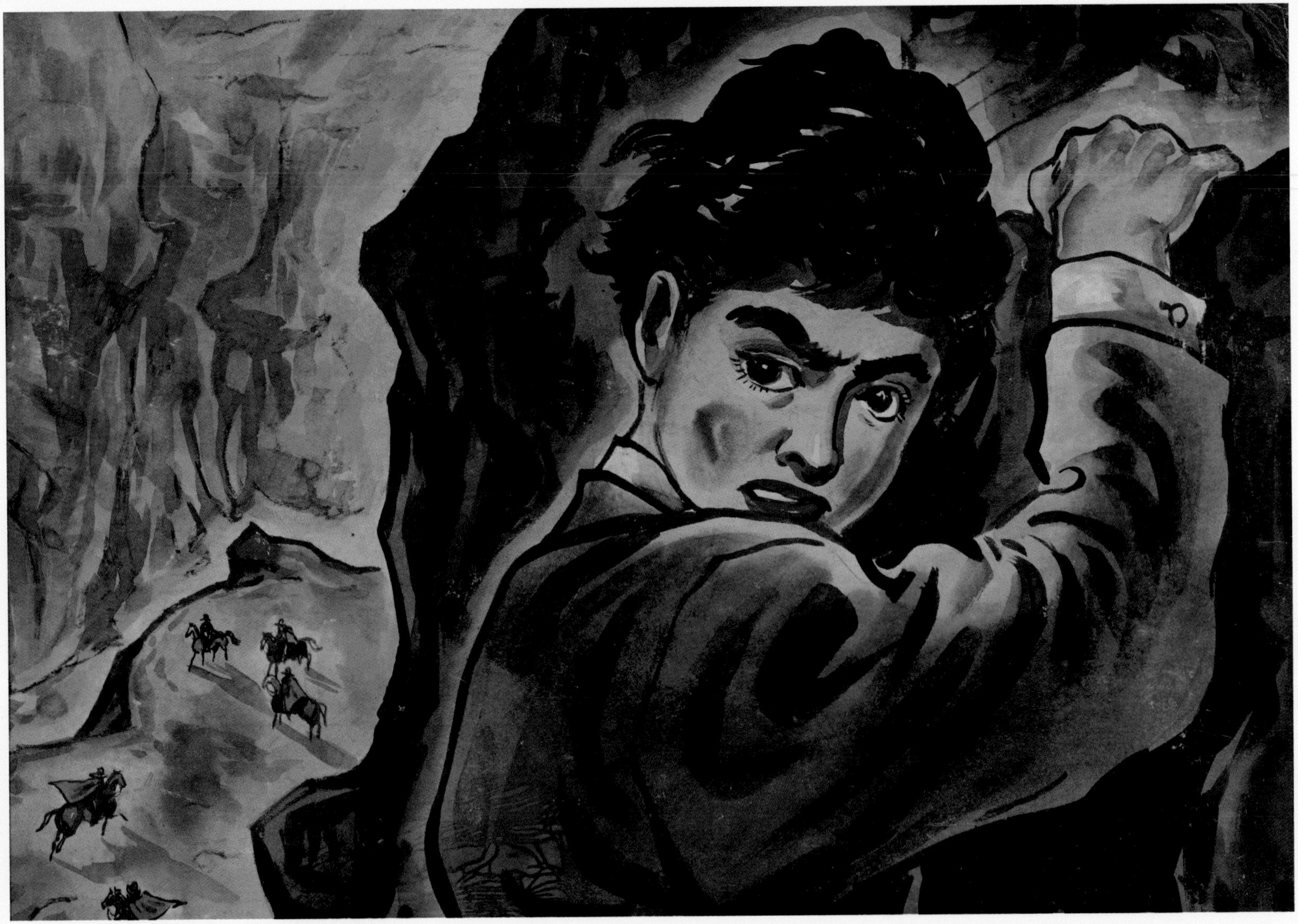

OPPOSITE, TOP Eastern Western: *Kamishibai* scenes paralleled film editing. This close-up is imbued with kineticism, from the cords of the horse's neck to its flying mane and the ghost rider's flowing blue cloak. The villain grins as the boy's horse is cornered at a cliff.

OPPOSITE, BOTTOM The Buck Stops Here: The hero's horse balks at the last step and bucks him headlong into the abyss! Reference sources were scarce in Japan as to what the Andes really looked like, so the artist depicted the mountain range as a fantasia of Chinese landscape painting and backgrounds cribbed from American cowboy movies.

ABOVE Cliffhanger: The boy manages to hold onto the rock face in the foreground while the bandits gather far below. This kind of split focus is typical in film but not seen in the Japanese classical tradition. The painting contains three narrative elements, reading from right to left: the boy's handhold on the rock provides a solution to the predicament in the previous panel, his determined expression as he tries to see what the bandits are up to, and the mystery of why they are gathering at the cliff.

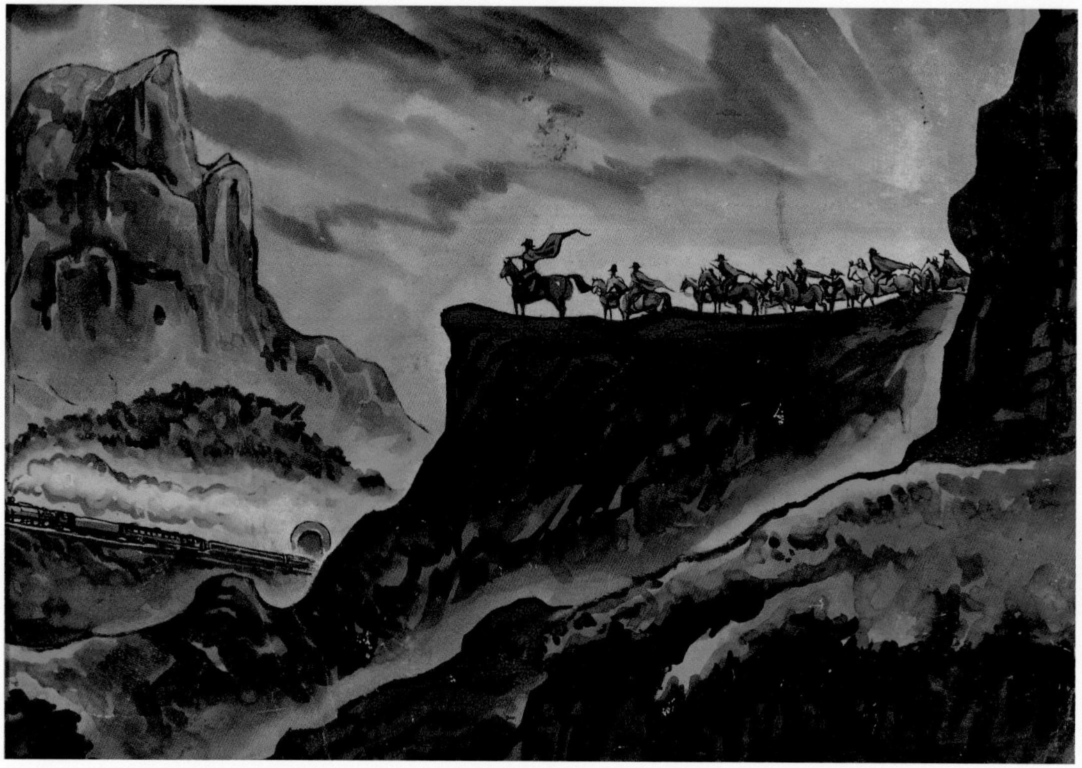

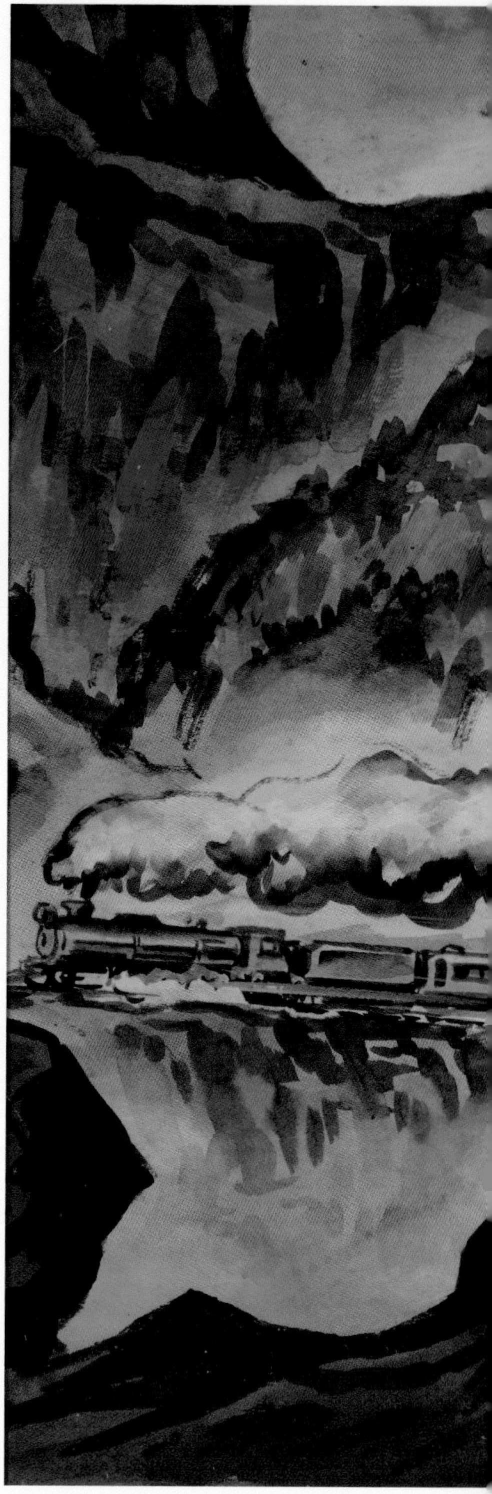

ABOVE Smokey and the Bandit: In a long shot, the bandit chief looks out from the cliff as a plume of smoke appears in the center of the scene. The composition reflects traditional landscape painting, where the viewer looks down on the human-scaled foreground, out at the middle distance and up at the distant peaks. The narrative virtually forces the next panel to be revealed so the audience can find out what the cloud means and what the bandits are planning.

RIGHT Trainspotting: A locomotive hurtles across the horizon of the picture as the bandit chief, cloak flying straight in the air, waits with his gang.

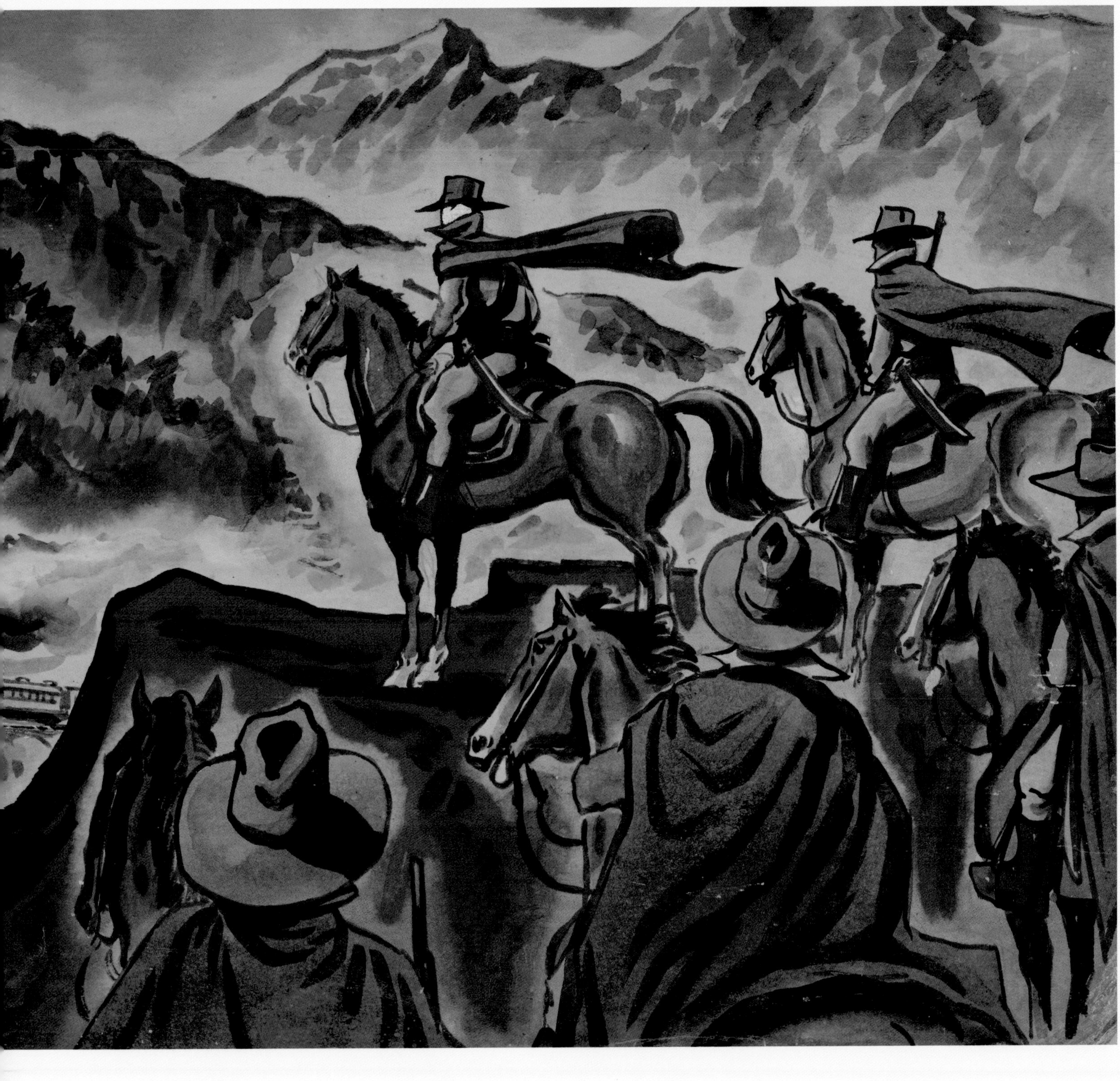

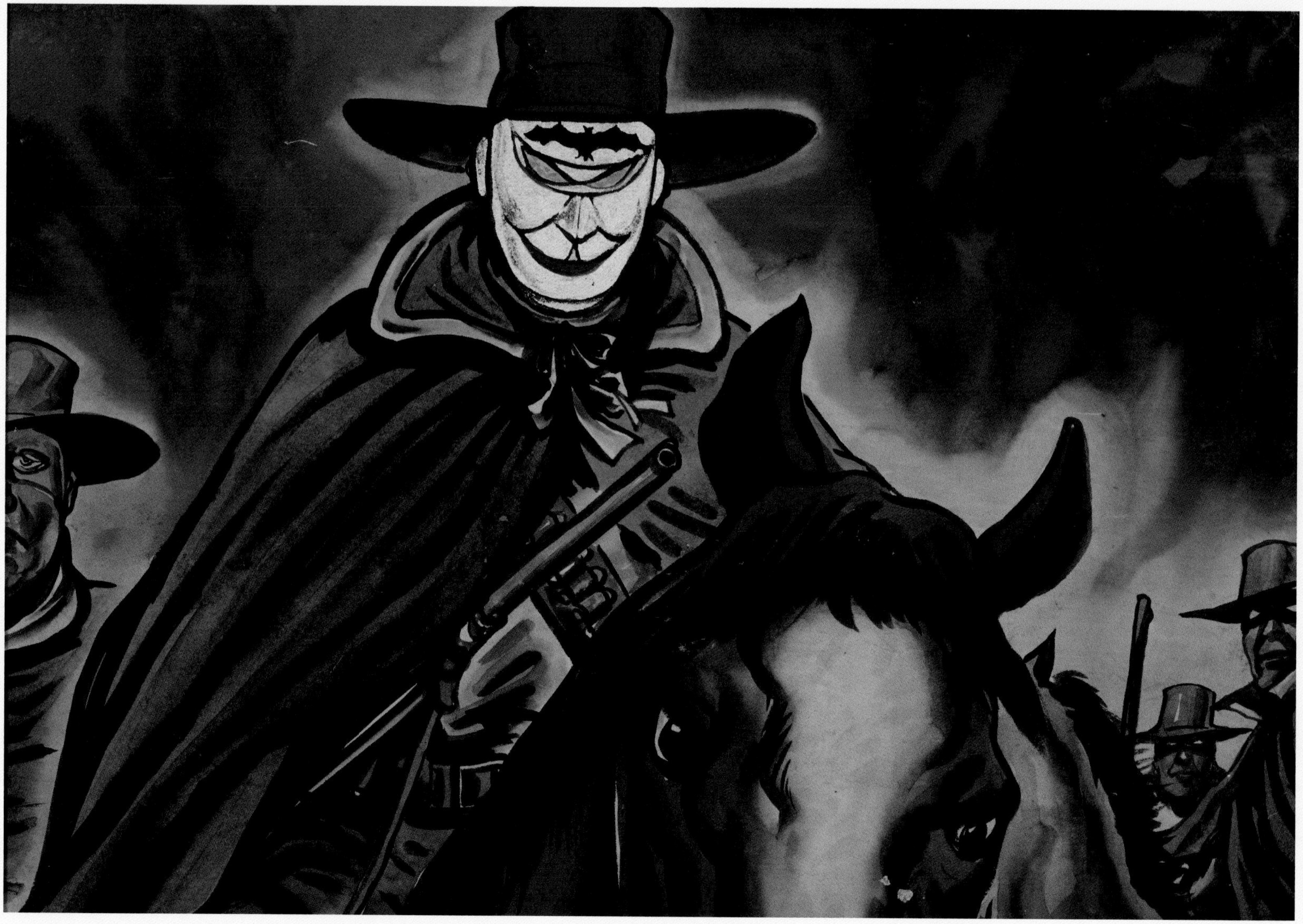

ABOVE **Pale Rider:** Every great serial needs a great villain. The bandit chief's mask looks like a cross between Batman's symbol and the Joker's grin. With a rifle beneath his cloak, the chief gives the signal to his masked gang to ride down on the gold-laden train.

OPPOSITE **Going for the Gold:** The bandits swarm down on the gold train in a strong diagonal like the composition of a John Ford Western, yet at the same time they echo the tiny figures typical of Chinese and Japanese landscape painting.

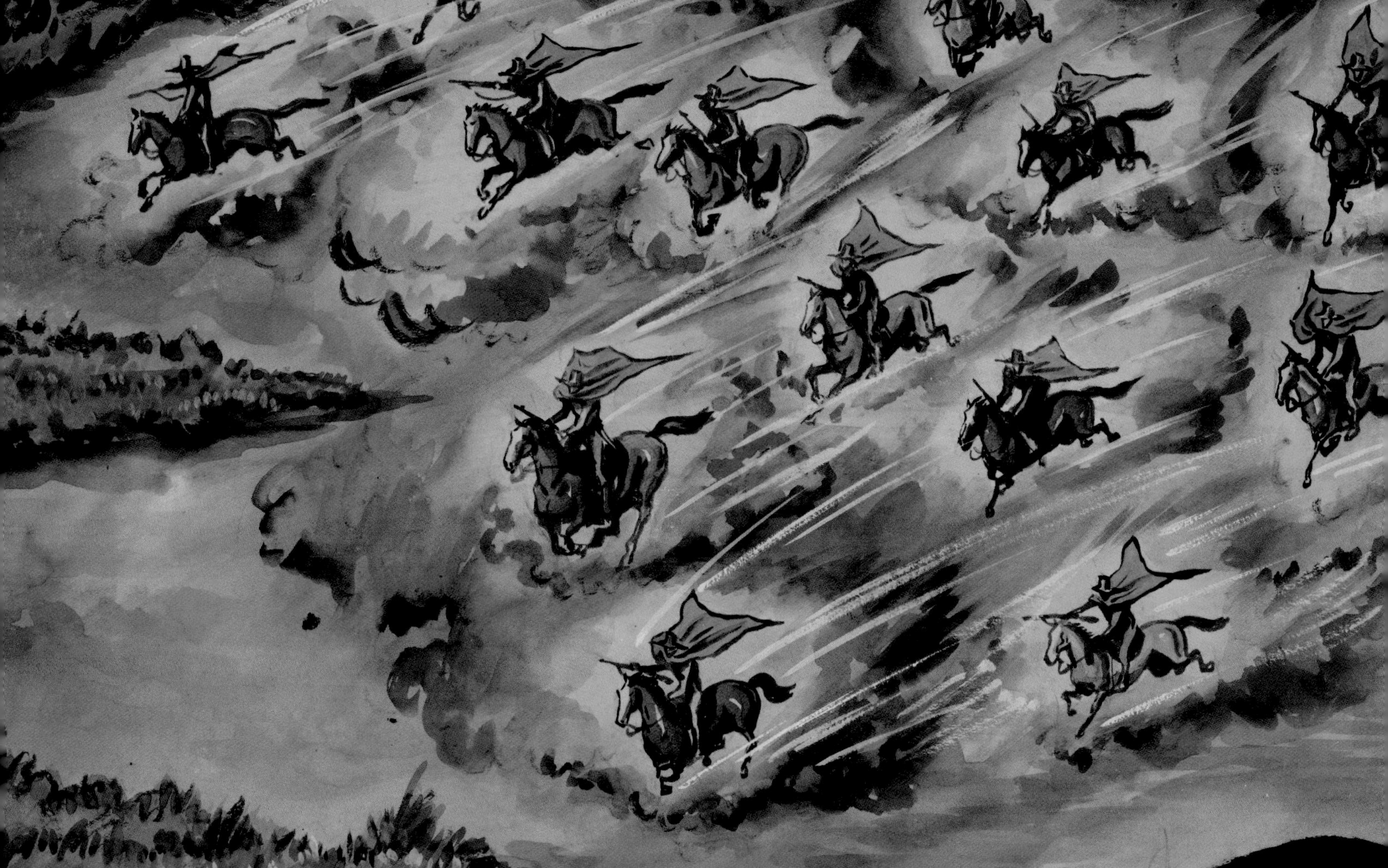

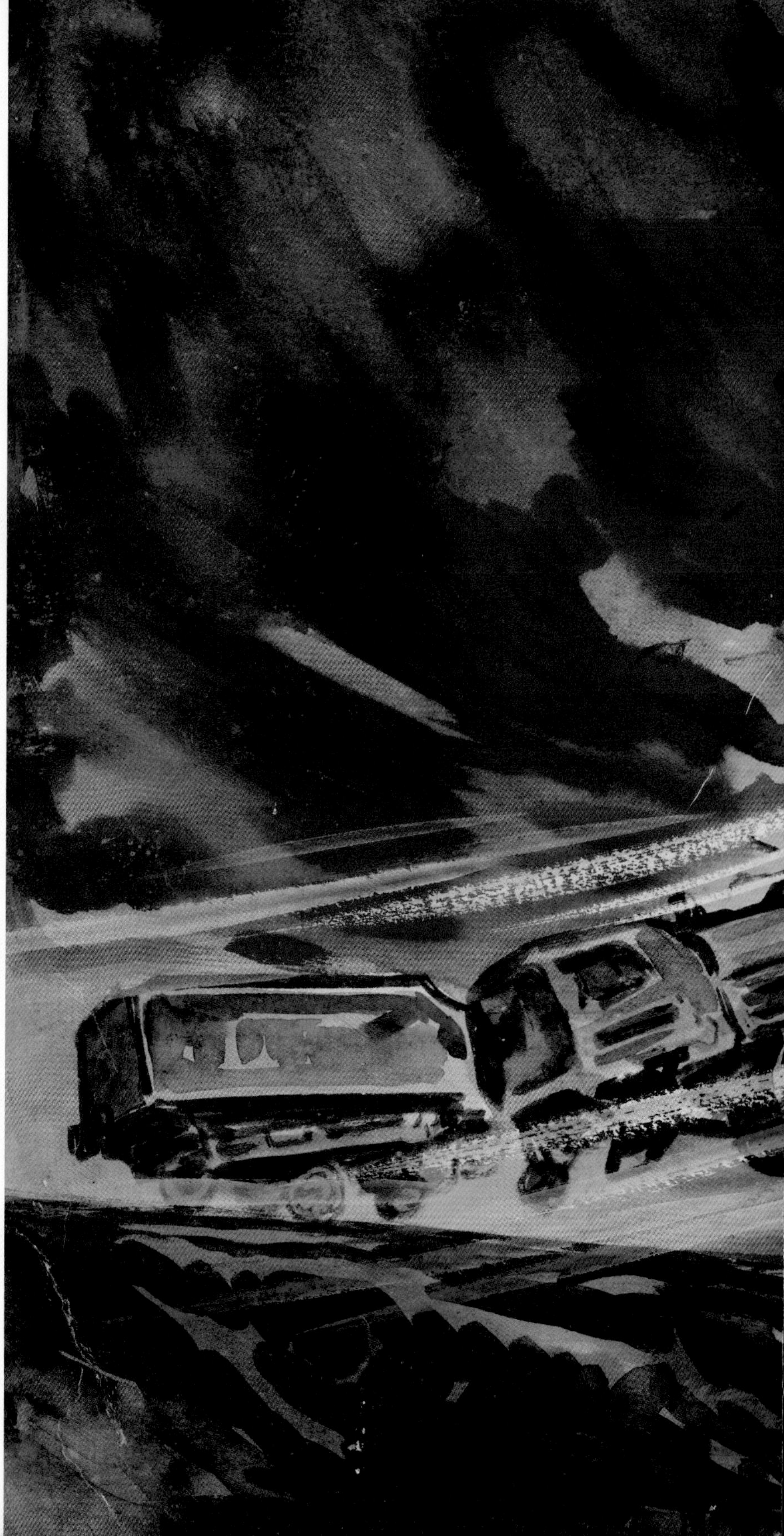

Blood on the Tracks: The gold train is dynamited in an abstract explosion of red and orange flame as the chapter ends on a suspenseful highpoint. The masses of the train and the blue motion lines collide in the center of the frame, while the red flames radiate outward, creating a dynamic push-pull dimension.

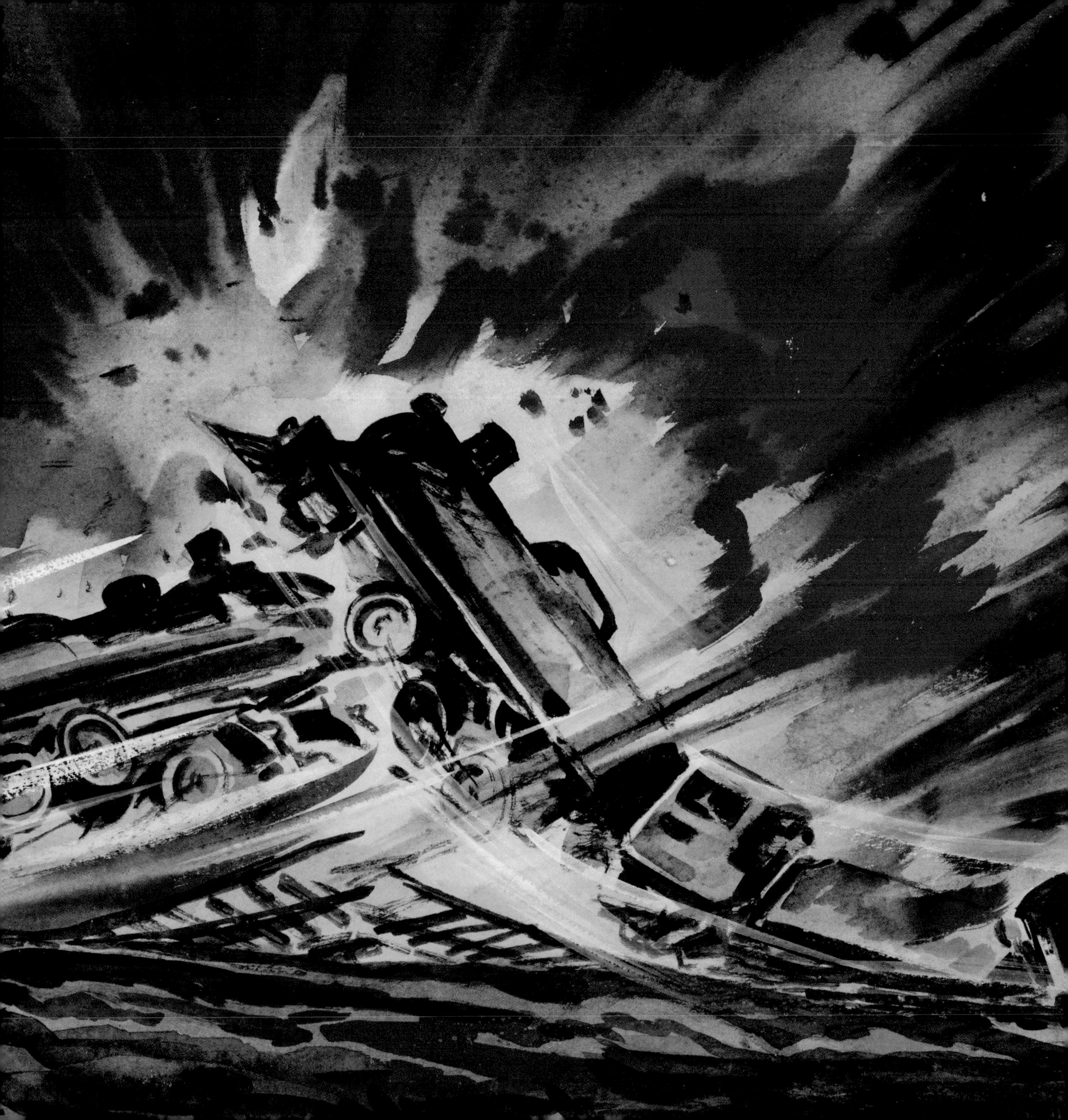

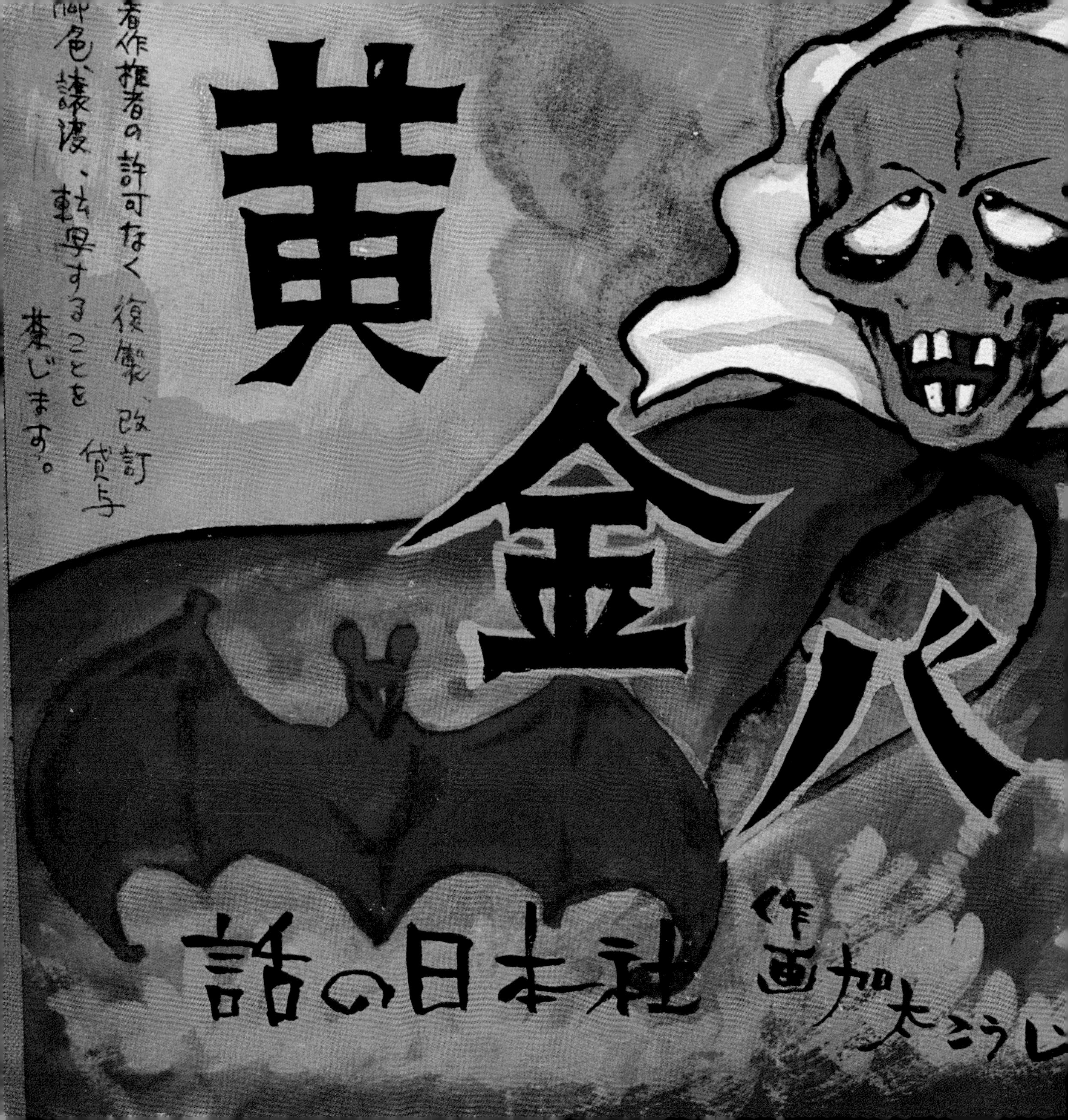
著作権者の許可なく複製、改訂
脚色、譲渡、転写することを 貸与
禁じます。
黄
金
話の日本社
作画 加太こうじ

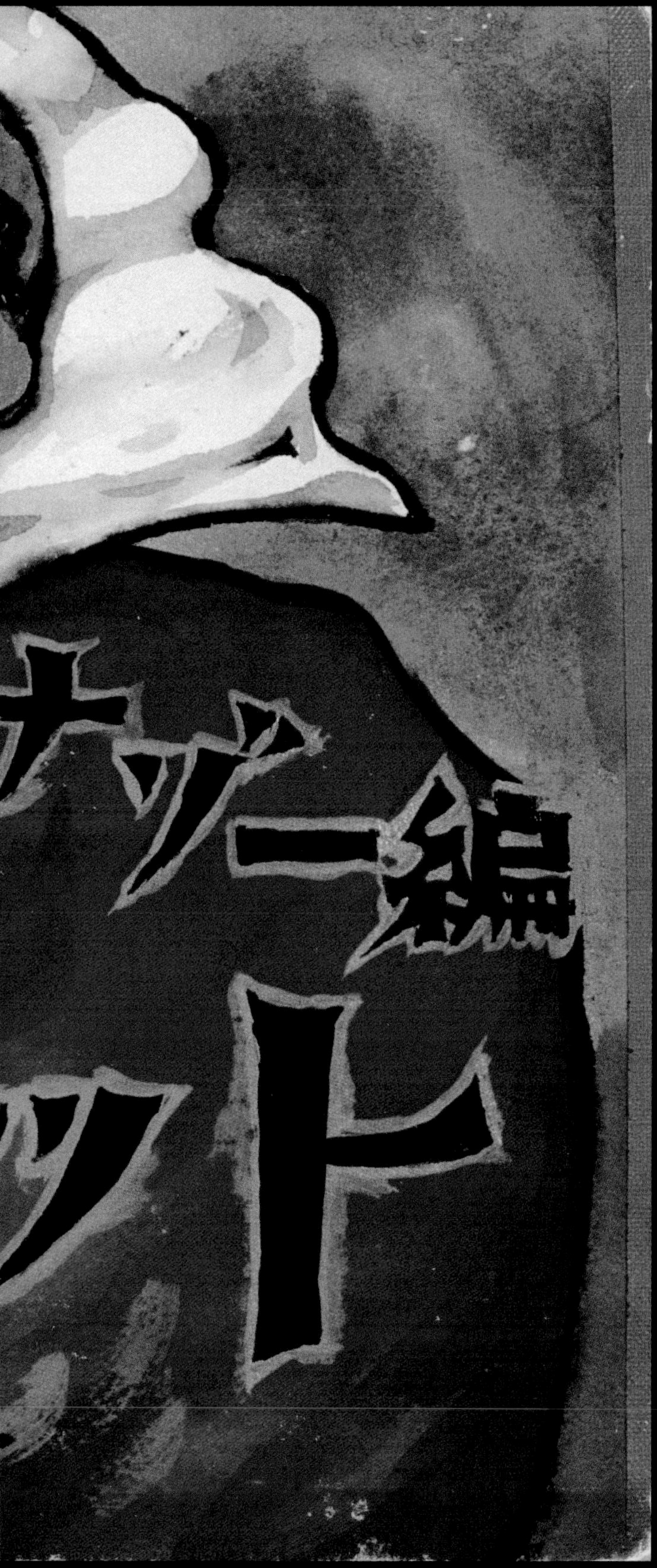
サツー編
ット

AND

CREATURES

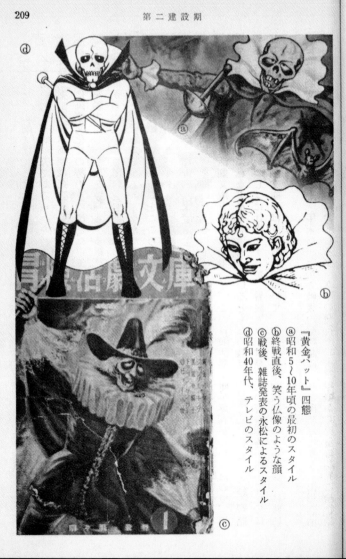

また児童雑誌における絵物語ブームを作りだすきっかけにもなった。

山川よりも先に永松武雄は旧知の出版関係者がはじめた明々社の『冒険活劇文庫』に仲間をさそって絵物語を掲載した。掲載したというよりは、昭和二十一年初頭からはじまった紙芝居がどこでも大人気だったので、それをそっくり雑誌へ持ってくるかたちで『冒険活劇文庫』は発刊されたのである。永松は永松スタイルの『黄金バット』を描いた。私の描いた黄金バットは、はじめは昭和六、七年頃の黄金の骸骨のマスクで検閲に提出した。すると連合軍側の担当者が、欧米では骸骨は悪のシンボルになっているから、子ども向きのやさしげな顔に直せといった。いくら話しても向こうは直せといって検閲印を押さない。仕方がないので骸骨マスクを仏像のような黄金の顔にした。すると、そんなかたちのウェーブ頭はやや長めの髪でパーマネントウェーブをかけたようにした。すると、そんなかたちのウェーブをかけた女性が街をいくたびに、紙芝居ファンの子どもたちから〈黄金バットのおねえさんだ〉などといわれた。それほどに黄金バットは人気があった。

永松は〈紙芝居ではきみが黄金バットをやれ、ぼくは創刊された冒険活劇文庫へ黄金バットを発表する〉と私にいって、自作の台本でスタイルも骸骨マスクに大きな帽子をかぶせたものにして冒険活劇文庫へ連載した。これはこれで非常な人気を得た。それゆえ、黄金バットには三つの顔ができた。かつての紙芝居でおぼえた者は黄金のガイコツと記憶している。昭和二十一年以後、はじめて紙芝居で見た者はパーマネントのような黄金の頭髪を持つ黄金の仏像の顔、他は永松の帽子に冬服スタイルの絵物語のものである。

冒険活劇文庫は書店で売るほかに、画劇文化社という紙芝居製作所の手を通して紙芝居屋が売る

ⓓ
ⓐ
ⓑ
ⓒ
冒険活劇文庫

『黄金バット』四態
ⓐ昭和5〜10年頃の最初のスタイル
ⓑ終戦直後、笑う仏像のような顔
ⓒ戦後、雑誌発表の永松によるスタイル
ⓓ昭和40年代、テレビのスタイル

Major manga figures who got their start in *kamishibai* include **Takeo Nagamatsu**, who created *Golden Bat*; **Sanpei Shirato**, who pioneered *gekiga* manga with his tale of the rogue ninja *Kamui-dan* (*The Legend of Kamui*); **Shigeru Mizuki**, known for his horror comics and the whimsical one-eyed monster **GeGeGe no Kitaro**; and **Kazuo Koike**, who went on to write one of the landmarks of world comics, the epic, twenty-five-volume, eight thousand–page series *Lone Wolf and Cub*, illustrated by **Goseki Koujima**.

Appearing in 1931, **Golden Bat** is one of the world's first illustrated super heroes, even earlier than what was considered the record holder—Lee Falk's classic newspaper strip *The Phantom* from 1936. The masked swordsman Zorro, who appeared in American pulps in 1919 may be the granddaddy of super heroes with a mask and secret identity, but **Golden Bat** with his cape, European-style ruff collar, pantaloons, and skull-faced visage is a true comic book character. He has crossed eyes, shorthand for emotional paroxysm in *ukiyo-e* prints, but used here for comic effect. Scriptwriter **Ichiro Suzuki** was twenty-five at the time, and illustrator **Takeo Nagamatsu** was a tender sixteen. Nagamatsu set up shop in **Shimoya** in the Ueno district of Tokyo. **Kouji Kata** later took over as writer and illustrator when **Golden Bat** made the leap to manga form in the postwar era. **Golden Bat**, also called **Ogun Batto** in Japanese, still resonates with a musty

Skullduggery: Golden Bat is one of the world's first illustrated costumed super heroes. An early model sheet suggests the influence of Lon Chaney's *The Phantom of the Opera* in the skull-like visage and opera cape. "When I look at his work it really makes me wonder what influenced him," Nagamatsu's daughter Yoko Taniguchi recalls. "I think that's where his genius was, considering the lack of influence at the time. You can't even picture the way it used to be."

sense of nostalgia for both old and young Japanese, much the way the Lone Ranger or Flash Gordon does for Americans.

Its origins uncertain, the character may have been named after a brand of cigarettes, Golden Bat, introduced in Japan in 1906, featuring two fluttering art nouveau bats on the package. Still sold in Japan today, the cigarettes were known as *kinshi*, or flying kite, during World War II, when the use of English-language words was prohibited. Golden Bat's *kamishibai* peak years were 1931–32 and 1946–47. After the war, copyright for the character was awarded to Koji Kata, who also created a character called the Punishing Spider.

Something of a showboat, Takeo Nagamatsu wore a jaunty hat for photographers and appeared in youth-oriented magazines. Like many dedicated American comics creators, Nagamatsu wasn't in *kamishibai* for the money. "I had a million chances to get off this path and do something else," Nagamatsu recalled, "but I stayed though many others strayed.

"Pictures that would look nice in someone's house are great," he said, "but *kamishibai* are loved by many children and cheer them up. When I think of these children later growing up to be honorable Japanese adults, it makes me realize the significance of creating *kamishibai*."

About the role of *kamishibai* in Japan's reconstruction, he said, "I didn't set out to make it educational, but first and foremost to entertain

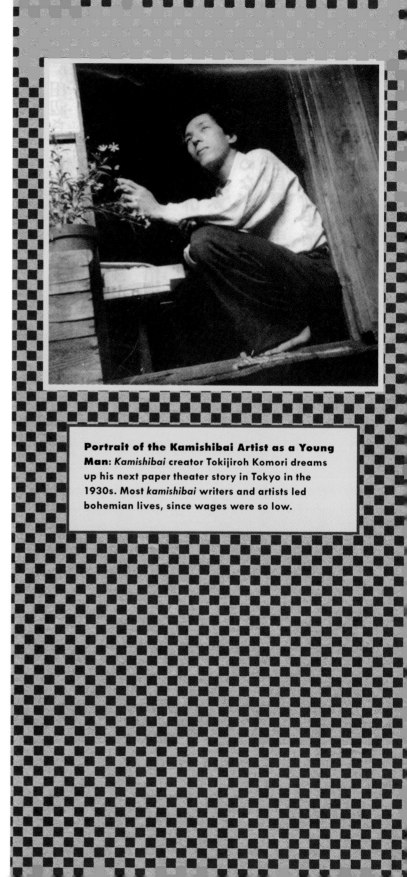

Portrait of the Kamishibai Artist as a Young Man: *Kamishibai* creator Tokijiroh Komori dreams up his next paper theater story in Tokyo in the 1930s. Most *kamishibai* writers and artists led bohemian lives, since wages were so low.

kids, and hopefully they would pick up values along the way.

"Especially in postwar Japan, many struggled in the face of difficulty. People had to overcome this, and with a peaceful and just spirit rebuild Japan. In light of this, the theme of struggle naturally came out of my work."

Nagamatsu's daughter Yoko Taniguchi recalls her childhood home in the Adachi section of Tokyo in the late 1950s as a hub of *kamishibai* and manga activity. "The second floor of our house was my father's atelier," she says. "It was in the back and he always worked there alone. He had a couple of apprentices who would draw crowded around a table in the front.

"When I came home from school or playing, he would be sharpening many pencils, which he gave to his apprentices. Then he took what was called a *maru* (crow-quill) pen and continuously drew using this ink pen."

Some of the apprentices were young men getting their start, but there were also manga veterans and *kamishibai* creators. Manga writers would wait downstairs for finished pages, often until the middle of the night. Other young *kamishibai* creators rented apartments nearby to work with their mentor.

"He felt that *kamishibai* was a mass art form, but that good work could be done for children and that it was worthwhile pursuing," Taniguchi says. "His view was that Japan has many different kinds of wonderful art, and that *kamishibai* was one of

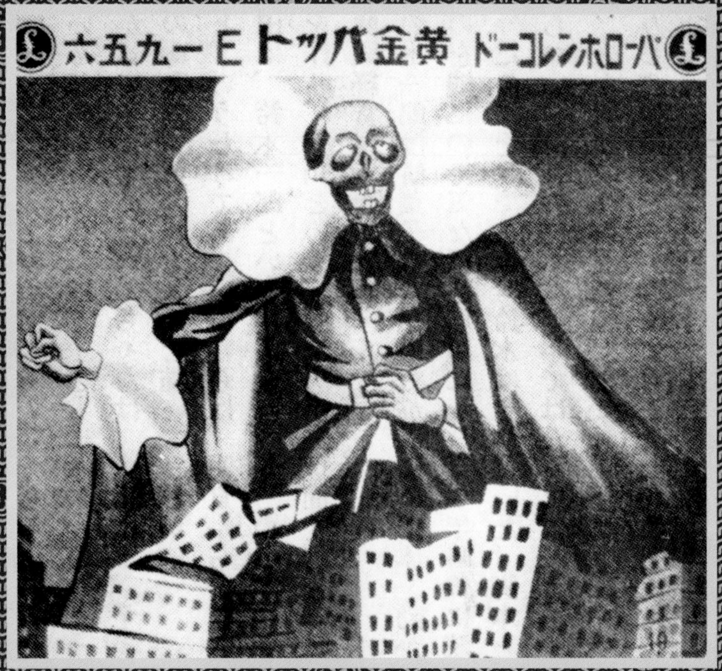
黄金バットE一九五六

First at Bat: In one of his earliest incarnations, Golden Bat looms over an Expressionist cityscape of toppling towers.

them, an outstanding one," Taniguchi says. "He said that *kamishibai* was a noble profession and that as creators they should be proud of it."

Nagamatsu studied design in college and worked as a designer for a necktie company before pursuing a career as a *kamishibai* artist. "*Kamishibai* artists were in demand, and after applying, he and one other person were selected out of hundreds of people for a part-time job drawing *kamishibai*," Taniguchi says. "This was the Golden Age of *kamishibai*. Although it was not viewed favorably by society, there was a lot of work available and you were able to make money."

At first, Nagamatsu had trouble breaking into the industry. "His drawing was very precise and refined, and not necessarily what they were looking for to appeal to the masses," his daughter says. "Compared to other *kamishibai* creators at the time, his work was more artistic because of his training. He wasn't able to produce in the large amounts that were required, and his office would get angry at him for this. Because my father wasn't able to meet their demand, they had other people draw Golden Bat as well. But it turned out that the kids didn't like anyone else's drawings, and they would say, 'This is a fake Golden Bat!' The kids knew right away when it wasn't my father's work."

Kids were thrilled by the adventures of Golden Bat, a mysterious figure sent from ten thousand years in the future to combat the evil Nazo, a self-styled Emperor of the Universe. (The name Nazo may be a stand-in for Nazis, who were often portrayed as villains in Japanese fiction, despite the Axis alliance.) An early Golden Bat installment is paced like a silent two-reeler: In one *Perils of Pauline* predicament the hero is tied down in front of an onrushing train, intercut with scenes of the heroine held captive by Nazo, and Golden Bat flying to the rescue. The faces of the characters in this paper theater actually look like the expressions of silent screen actors.

Nazo, a sinister being from another planet, menaces the heroine, while a black-hooded henchman with a skull and crossbones symbol on his chest stands guard. Cut to the brilliantined hero in jodhpurs lashed to the tracks. In watercolor shades of vermillion and ink wash, the train roars through a tunnel. **MEANWHILE** . . . as American strips and serials are so fond of saying, back at a ranch high in the Japanese alps, an old man is menaced by hooded thugs who look as if they had stepped straight out of *Birth of a Nation*. The old man and Nazo's henchmen fall victim to a landslide, just as a sepulchral, dandified Golden Bat arrives on the scene. In another instance of the parallel editing that D. W. Griffith used to such rousing effect, the scene cuts back to Nazo's lair, where the hot-eyed heroine refuses to disclose Golden Bat's whereabouts. The train rushes pell-mell toward the hero. Who can save him? Golden Bat to the rescue! Golden Bat unleashes his top-secret bat bomb to take out the train. The bomb collides with the train, and the steel tracks ripple like ramen. The hero thanks Golden Bat and tearfully asks him to save his sweetie. Nazo's henchmen take cover behind the overturned train and lay down a deadly fusillade. Can Golden Bat save the heroine in time? Tune in tomorrow—same Golden Bat time, same Golden Bat street corner!

Silent Screen: The pacing and facial expressions in this early *Golden Bat* serial are delightfully reminiscent of a silent two-reeler from D. W. Griffith's Biograph studios. Griffith was the first to make generous use of close-ups of faces to convey emotion in a story. Here, the hot-eyed heroine angrily defies Nazo. You can almost hear a player piano as the scenes shift.

Nagamatsu drew inspiration from silent classics like *The Phantom of the Opera*, and kept up with scarce foreign magazines like *Life*, but in general Taniguchi says there was not a lot of exposure to cultural sources when her father was creating Golden Bat. Nagamatsu created *Golden Bat* for a mass audience and drew his inspiration from an unlikely source, visiting the Ueno Royal Art Museum with his daughter to see folding screens, old monochrome drawings, and landscapes.

"One thing I think is amazing about his *kamishibai* is the machines that show up in them," Taniguchi says. "At that time, there was nothing you ride like rockets, yet these fanciful pictures are in my father's work and they're beautiful.

STREET OF DREAMS

Dream Mother: An orphan in a peasant's straw winter cape makes his way through a snowstorm in a heartrending story by Gosei Yamamoto, much like *The Little Match Girl*.

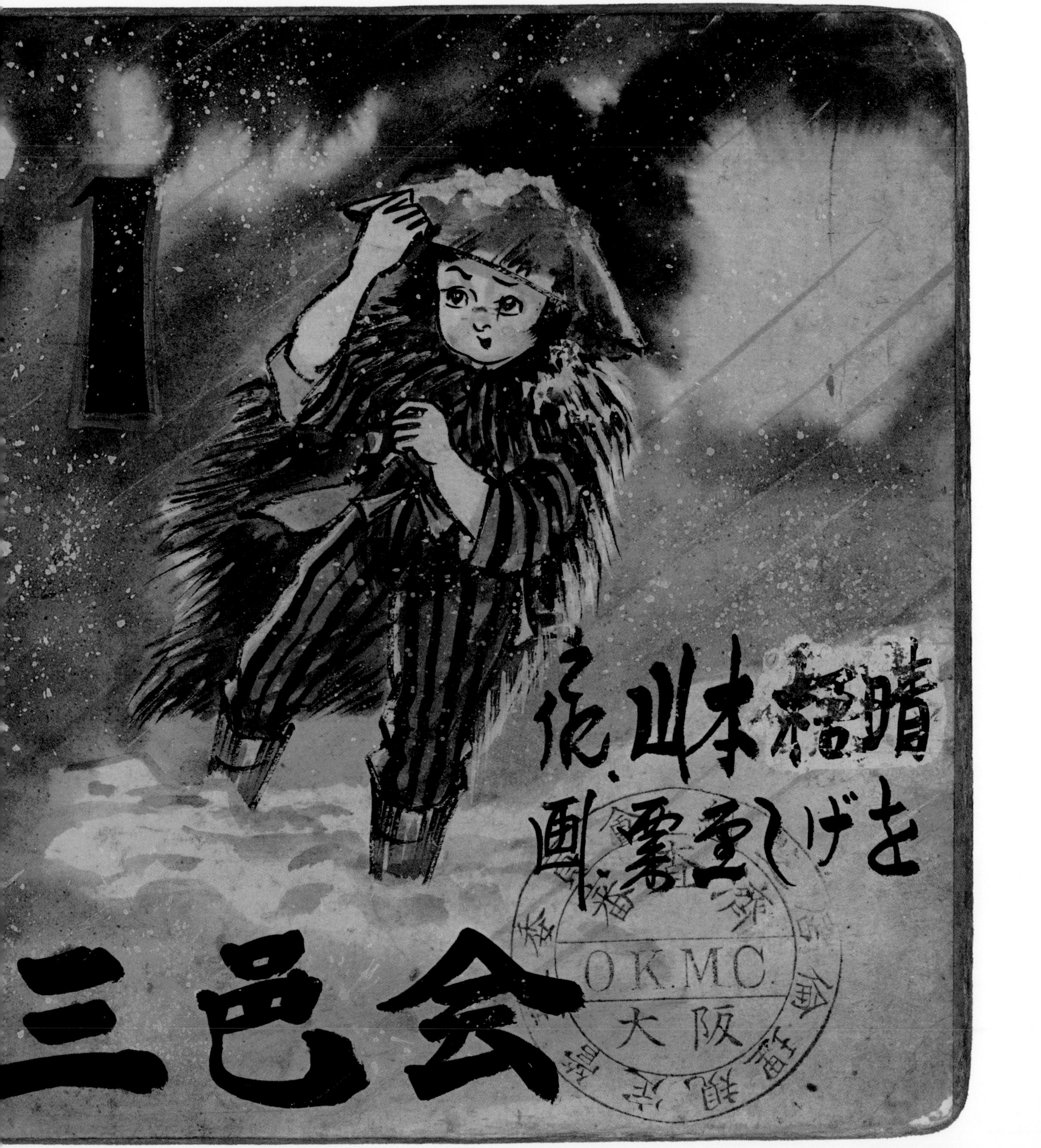

1
O.K.M.C.
大阪
三邑会

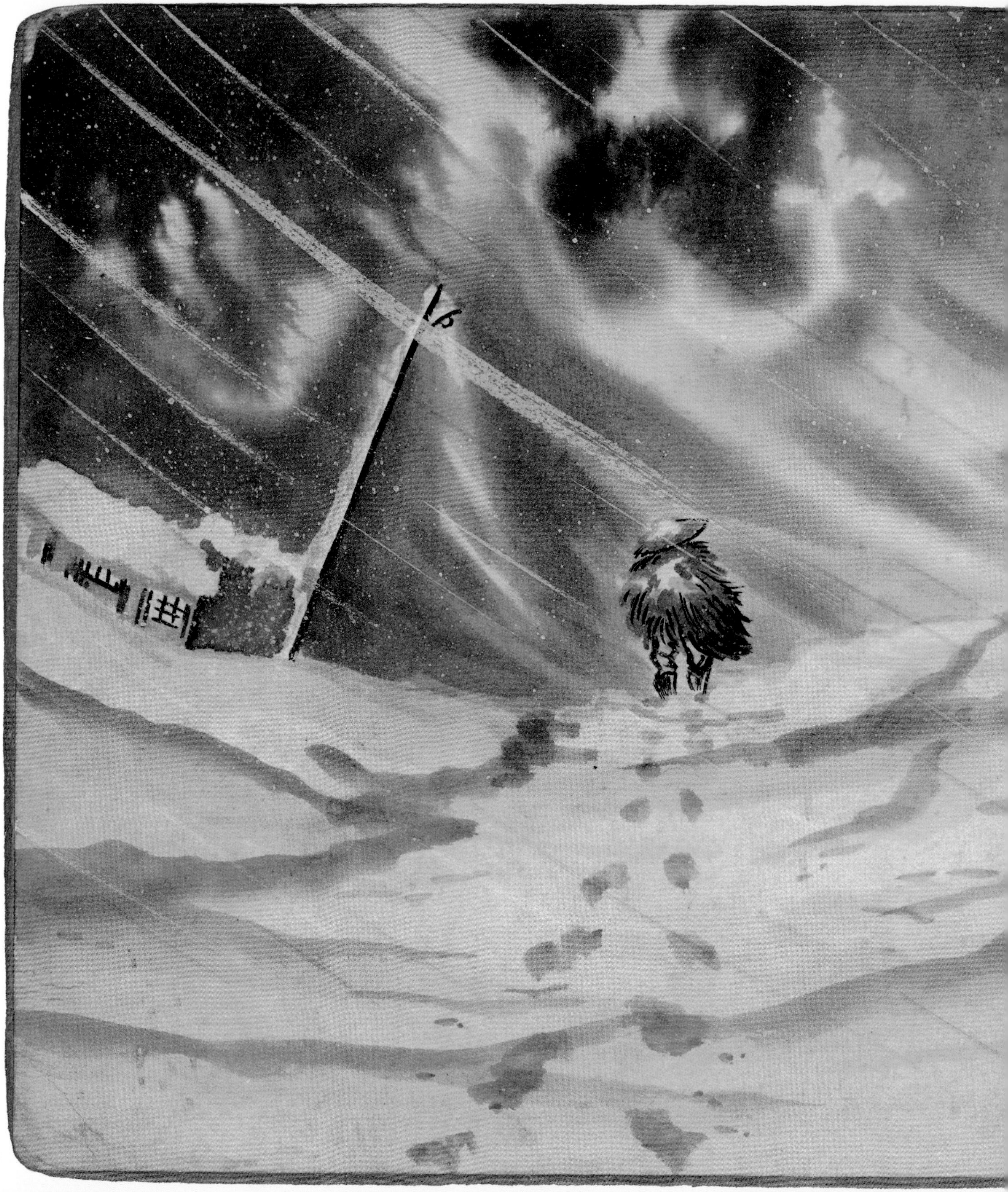

Set Design: The boy's tracks recede deep into the frame in a panel that has the feel of a Hollywood set design, rather than a scene observed from nature, with the crooked fence leaning into the foreground and the stormy sky like a theatrical scrim in the background.

"When I look at his work it really makes me wonder what influenced him," she says. "I think that's where his genius was, considering the lack of influence at the time. You can't even picture the way it used to be. Currently dinosaurs and things flying in the sky appear often in manga, but my father was drawing those things since his *kamishibai* days. There were many dinosaurs in *Golden Bat*. Golden Bat was the first super hero."

A later *Golden Bat* episode features a more confident style, a brash chromatic palette, and a playful protagonist. The ingenue Emily is held hostage by Nazo (again). High in his mountain retreat in the Japanese Alps, Golden Bat hears her plea and flies to the rescue, trashing a cat-eyed giant robot on the way.

Golden Bat was the most successful character in making the leap from the street-corner *kamishibai* to manga, anime, toy merchandising, and film. *Golden Bat* first appeared in manga form in 1948, during a time when Japan was still very poor but economic expectations were rising. One child would buy a copy of the manga and it would circulate through many hands.

Golden Bat also starred in a 1966 cheapie *Ogon Batto Ga Yattekuru* or *Golden Bat Is Here*. The widescreen Toei Studio picture in living black and white is faithful to its street-corner origins, from the theme song, "Golden Bat! Where, where, where does he come from? Only the bats know" to the pimped-out super hero with his cloak, baton of destiny, and kooky cackle. His nemesis Nazo is a four-eyed, donkey-eared alien with a claw hand, just like in the *kamishibai*, except he is wearing a terrycloth suit with a distractingly obvious zipper in the back.

Every pulp trope is duly followed: Golden Bat is resurrected in a temple of Lost Atlantis, tastefully decorated in an Egypto-Aztec style. The dialogue is classically stilted: "I am Golden Bat," he declares as he rises from his sarcophagus. "I have awakened from a ten-thousand-year sleep and will now fight for you. I fight for justice alone." When thwarted, the villains swear, "Damn you, Golden Bat!"

A young, goateed Sonny Chiba plays the head of a top-secret UN team who favor white boots and turtlenecks and are out to save the world with their nifty Super Destruction Beam Cannon. In the *kamishibai*, Emily is a schoolgirl in a tab collar; in the film she is reoutfitted in a Jiffy Pop silver spacesuit and white crash helmet. After saving the planet once again, Golden Bat flits off to his secret headquarters. The feature was followed in 1967 by a fifty-two-part anime series with Doc Savage titles like *Man-Eating Plants* and *The Mystery of the Exhilarating Mushrooms*.

Good Vibrations: The vibratory background of this portrait appears to be influenced by the golden hues of van Gogh's textured *Sunflowers* series. Emily sheds silent tears of defiance.

Known as Mr. *Kamishibai* or just boss, Koji Kata started in *kamishibai* at the age of fourteen, painting sixteen pages a day to support his family after his father, a businessman, became ill. In 1932 he joined the *Golden Bat* team as an illustrator. He was almost let go because his pictures weren't faithful to Nagamatsu's style, but his work became widely popular after he introduced a romantic element to the story in 1934. After the war, he did his own writing and illustration.

"For the most part, I didn't use other people's work, but created all my own," Kata recalled in an interview. "Also, I was the only creator to study montage theory."

After a friend recommended that he study cinema theory to improve his stories, Kata read up on Russian director Sergei Eisenstein's theory of film editing to create contradiction, opposition, and conflict in the images on screen. Kata introduced cinematic devices into *kamishibai* including the use of close-up reaction shots and flashbacks. Both *kamishibai* and manga rely more on Eisensteinian montage than American comics, contrasting action with shots of facial expressions to heighten the emotionality of a sequence.

Manga is chockfull of Sergio Leone–style stare-downs between combatants, even over a game of Go, as in the popular series *Hikaru no Go*, credited with reviving the popularity of the game in Japan.

Even in a relatively static medium of about twenty still pictures, *kamishibai* relies heavily on reaction shots. The *kamishibai Children of the Bomb* (*Genbaku no Ko*), about a young woman who survives Hiroshima with radiation-burn scars on her face only to be mocked by callow schoolchildren, is essentially told through reaction shots.

Kamishibai took on the tragedy of the atomic bomb decades before Keiji Nakazawa's powerful, autobiographical manga *Barefoot Gen* in 1972. Postwar stories about the war, from *kamishibai* to anime like *Graveyard of the Fireflies*, tend to portray the Japanese people at their most innocent and pitiable in the suffering of a young girl.

Koji Kata did not serve in the military because of a childhood injury to an eardrum. After the war, he was fortunate to be awarded the copyright to *Golden Bat* as well as approval from **SCAP** censors. Kata had a long and successful career in *kamishibai*, but in the early 1950s when improvements ranging from television to better roads conspired against the art form, he switched over to writing criticism about the popular arts and subjects like sexuality in Edo Japan.

For those who prefer their blade-wielding with a leftist political slant, former *kamishibai* creator Sanpei Shirato published the adventures of the rogue ninja Kamui in the legendary underground comix magazine *Garo*. His epic *Kamui-dan* (*The Legend of Kamui*) challenged feudal and militaristic aspects of Japanese society, and Kamui was adopted as a mascot by the radical student movement of the late 1960s. Shirato's trademark slow-motion buildup to action sequences can be traced to the timing and tension-raising techniques of *kamishibai* performance.

The son of a prominent leftist painter, Shirato finished high school at the age of eighteen, and worked in *kamishibai* and the *kashihon* (lending-library system for manga) before becoming part of the great ninja revival of the 1960s. Ninjas had been popular characters in *kamishibai* and prewar pulp

A silhouetted figure representing Everyman runs in despair through the devastation of Hiroshima seconds after the atomic bomb code-named Little Boy explodes at seventeen seconds after 8:15 A.M. on August 6, 1945. The explosion is often referred to as a mushroom cloud, but it was a pillar of fire in the heart of the city, with temperatures reaching over seven thousand degrees Fahrenheit, twice the temperature of molten steel. In Japanese, the bomb was referred to as *pika-don, pika* meaning white flash, and *don* an onomatopoeic word for the explosion.

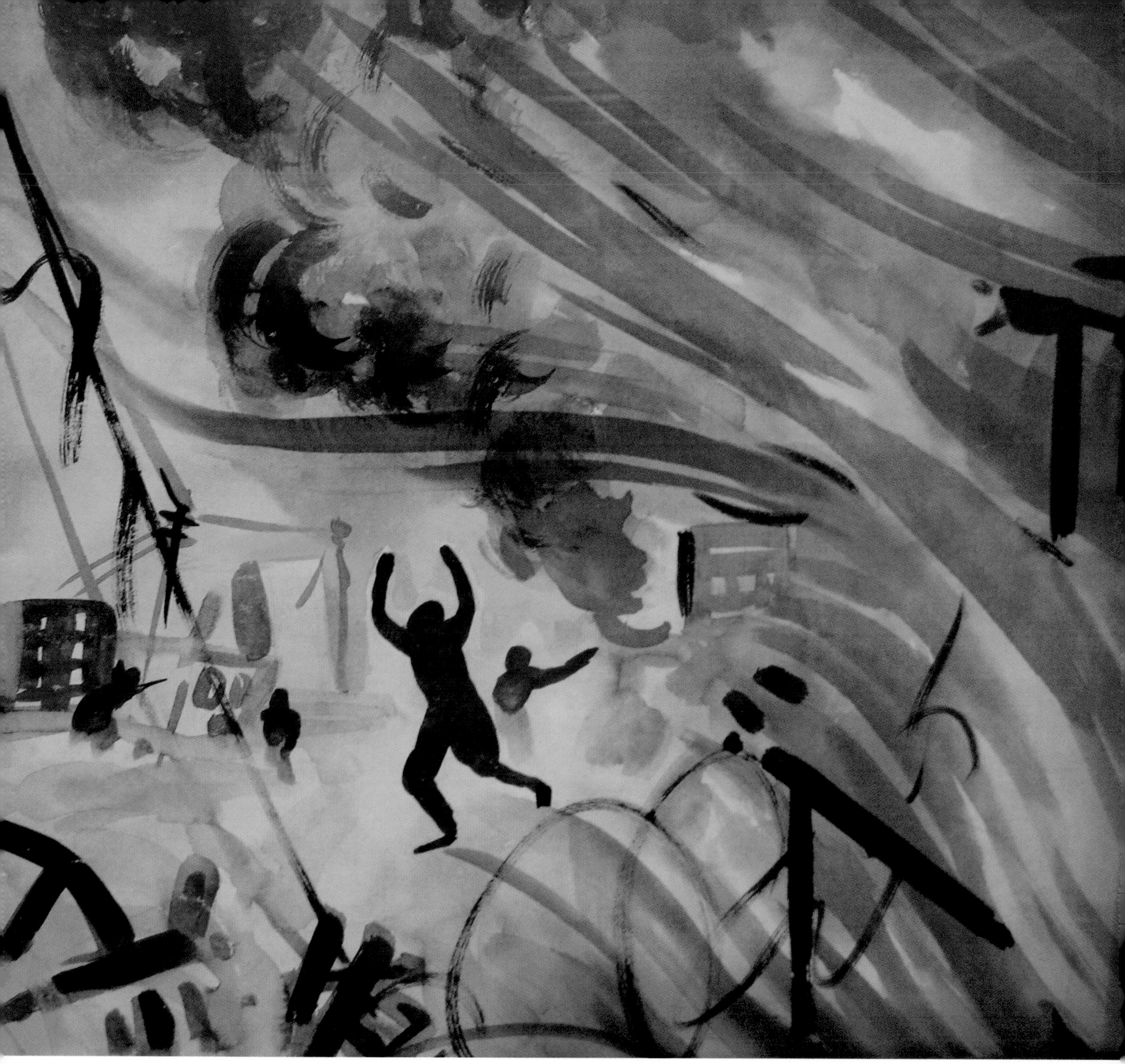

Shigeru Mizuki (middle row, fourth from left) and his troop from Tottori Prefecture.

novels, but disappeared for decades during the war and subsequent censorship under the American occupation. Turning the pages of Shirato's epic, you can almost trace the evolution of manga from the highly stylized cartoons of Osamu Tezuka to the more realistic approach of Goseki Koujima.

Another *kamishibai* creator who switched to manga in the postwar period is Shigeru Mizuki, known for his horror comics, and creator of the whimsical eyeball monster in GeGeGe no Kitaro (Cackling Kitaro), popular today in manga and toy merchandising. Born in 1922, Mizuki spent much of his childhood at a local Buddhist temple, where he studied paintings of heaven and hell, and the temple housekeeper supplemented his education with tales of the shadow world. Mizuki's first original character Kitaro, appeared in the *kamishibai Kitaro of the Graveyard* in the 1960s, and then in the *Akabon* (comic publications with red covers) market before it was serialized in *Shonen Magazine*. Kitaro's father, a disembodied eyeba ll who looks like underground cartoonist Rick Griffin's winged eye, is known for human antics like relaxing in a cup of warm sake. The character appeared in a television cartoon in 1968, and is still popular today. Mizuki also influenced Osamu Tezuka's darker works, like his novel-length werewolf tale *Ode to Kirihito*. The influence of Mizuki's spirit world, richly populated with demons and anthropomorphic animals, can also be seen in breakthrough feature animation like Hayao Miyazaki's *Spirited Away* (2001).

Shigeru Mizuki lost his left arm in the battlefields of New Guinea. As a returnee from the war, Mizuki struggled as a commercial fisherman, a rice vendor on the black market, and an amputee beggar before he serendipitously started out in *kamishibai* when he rented a room from a *kamishibai* maker.

"Life was very poor after the war," Mizuki says, "and *kamishibai* was a way to make a living." Later, he worked alone from home, so he says, "I only had a slight association with other creators."

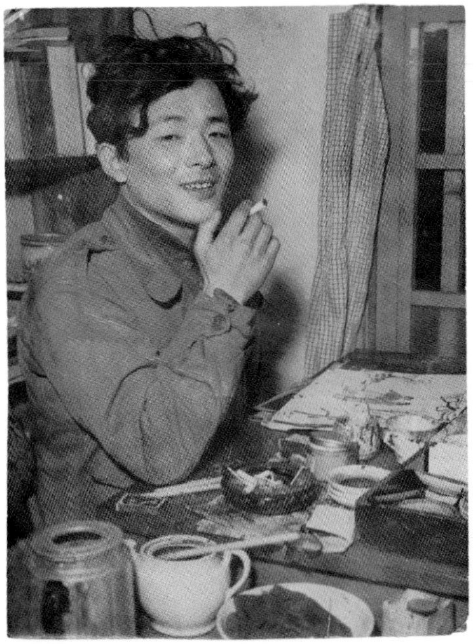

Shigeru Mizuki at work with ink and brushes.

BELOW Inked sketches for Mizoguchi's *kamishibai*.

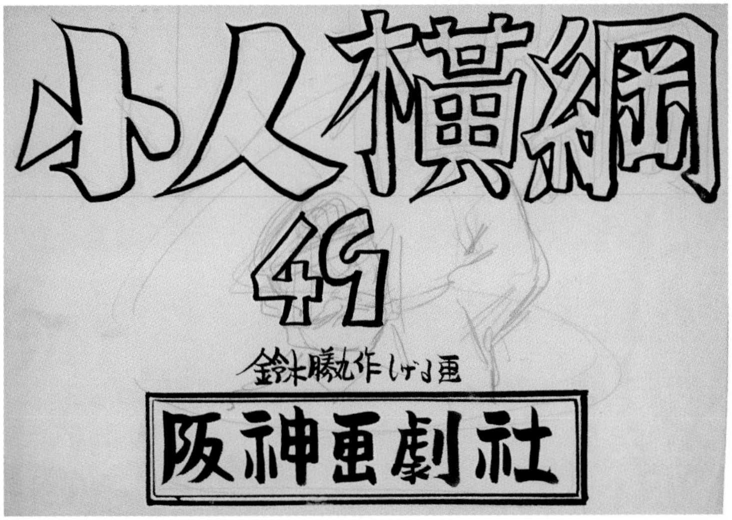
小人横綱
49
鈴木勝丸作しげる画
阪神画劇社

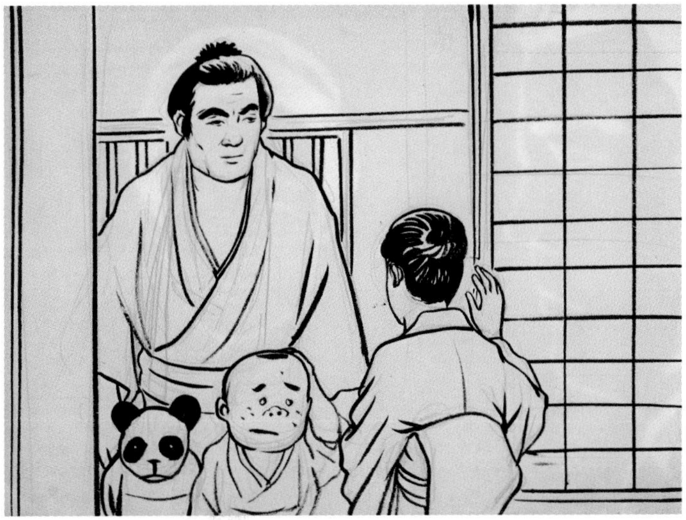

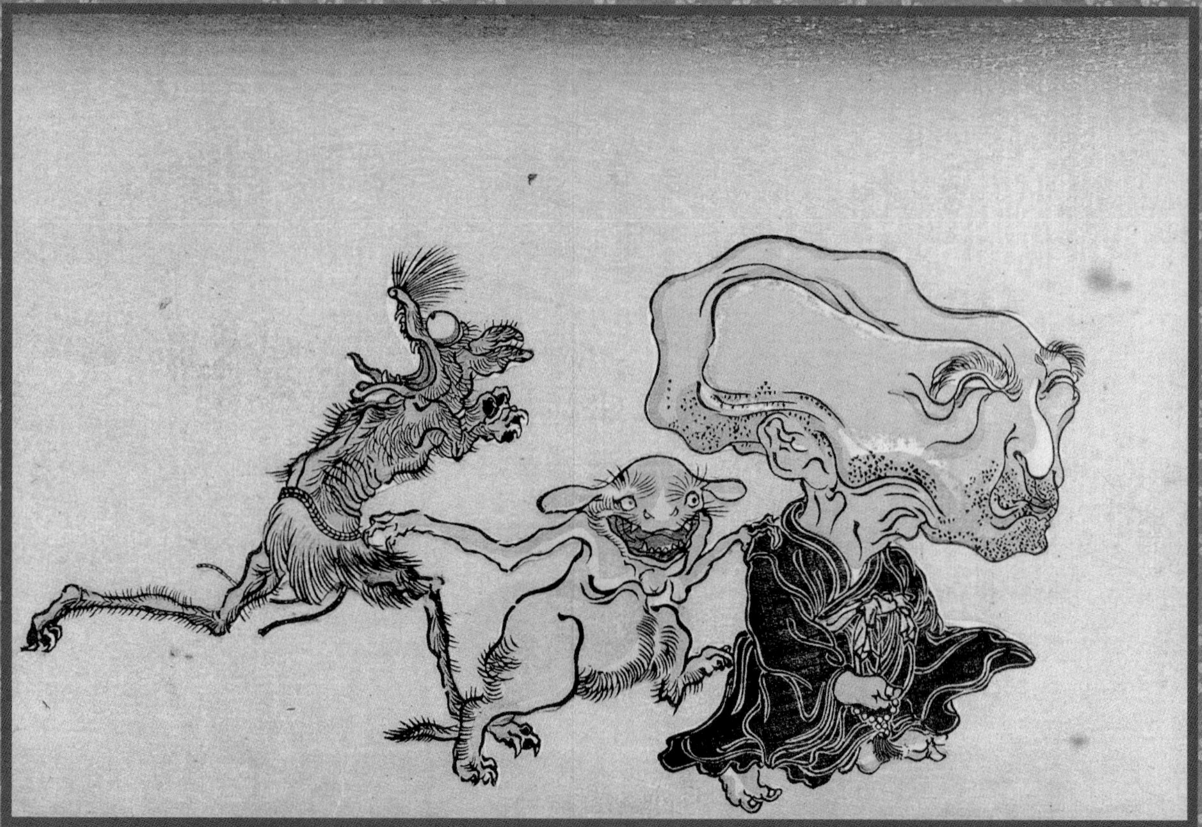

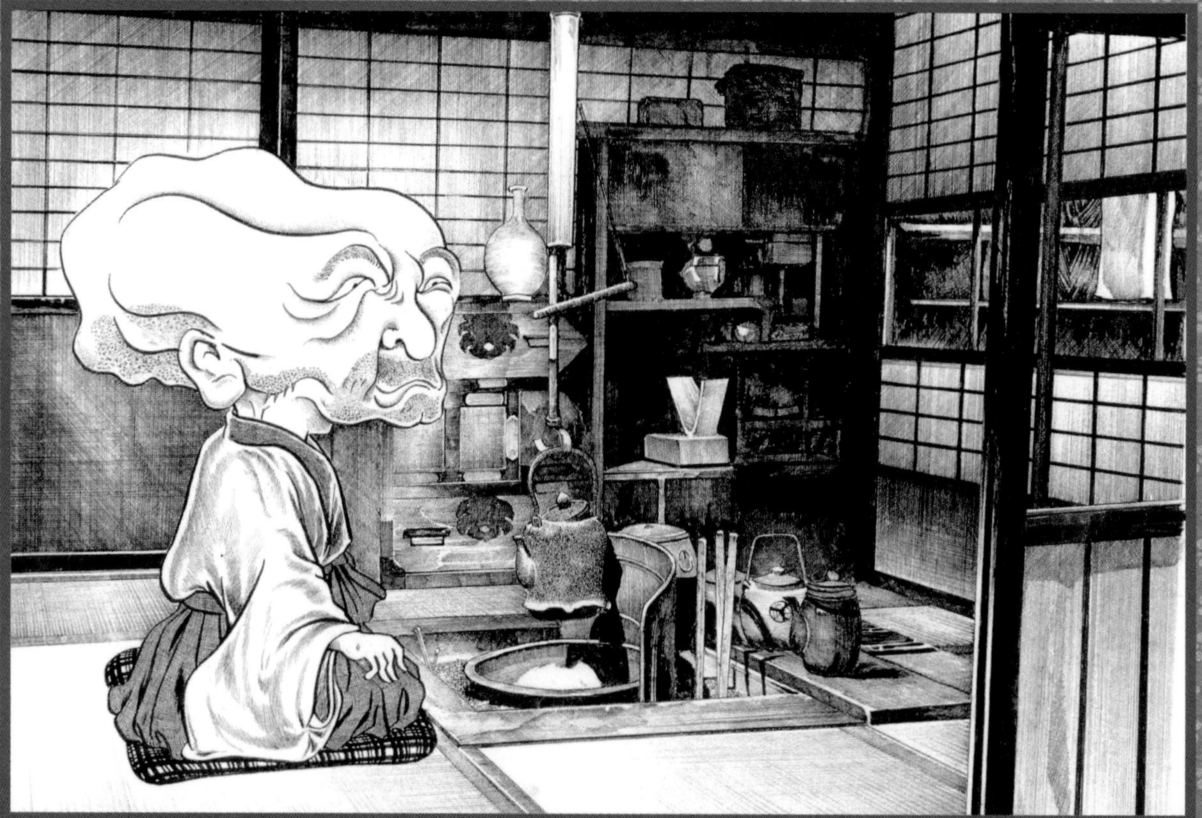

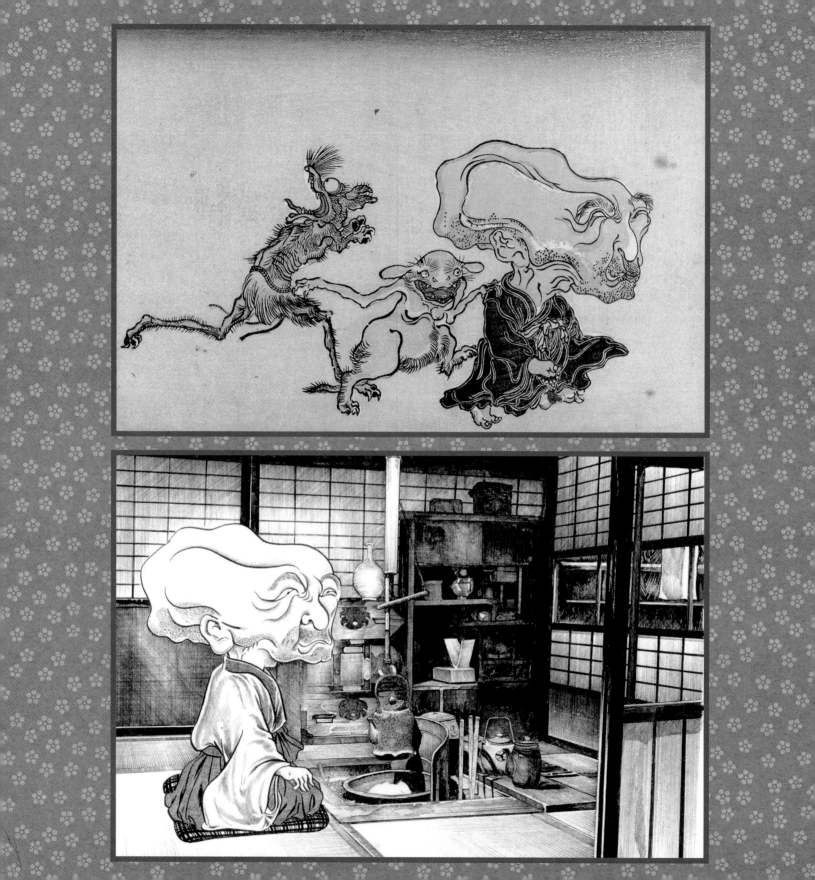

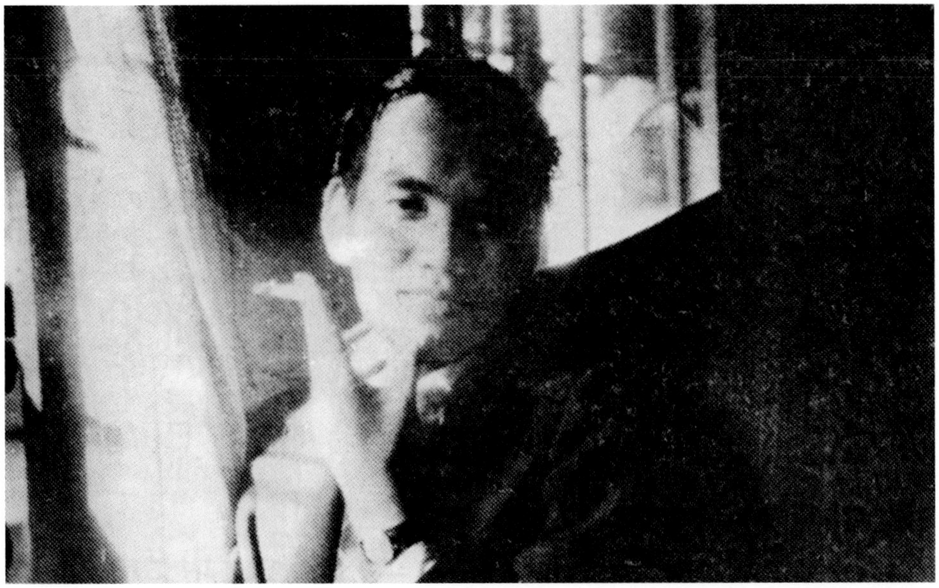

Golden Years: Koji Kato, one of the first kamishibai writers, at the age of 20.

"There was no particular relation between my *kamishibai* and manga," he continues. Surprisingly he chose to work in a naturalistic style, with characters in simple domestic dramas. In one wistful story, a brutish father forbids his daughter to take in a stray kitten, but she smuggles it under the covers as he snores drunkenly.

Mizuki is a scholar of the occult, and wrote a number of serious books on the subject. Traditional ghost characters were often employed in Muzuki's storytelling, like Sunakake Baba (Old Sand Woman), Neko Musume (Cat Girl), and Konaki Jiji (Crying Old Man), mostly in a humorous context. His characters like the hydrocephalic horror *Yokai Nuraikyon of the Night Procession of the Hundred Demons* were often drawn directly from historical prints. A long-legged rat from the same classic print looks like a refugee from an Ed Roth Big Daddy cartoon.

Rat Fink: Mizuki uses monsters from Japanese mythology in his manga like this hydrocephalic horror. The character on the left in the original painting looks like the ancestor of a "Big Daddy" Ed Roth Rat Fink cartoon.

After six years of work in the field, Mizuki found his audience drifting toward manga and television. His first manga for the rental-book market in 1957 was an *Astro Boy* clone called *Rocket Man*, the cover of which looks distinctly like Jerry Siegel and Joe Shuster's Superman in a different-colored

KURUMA THE CAT

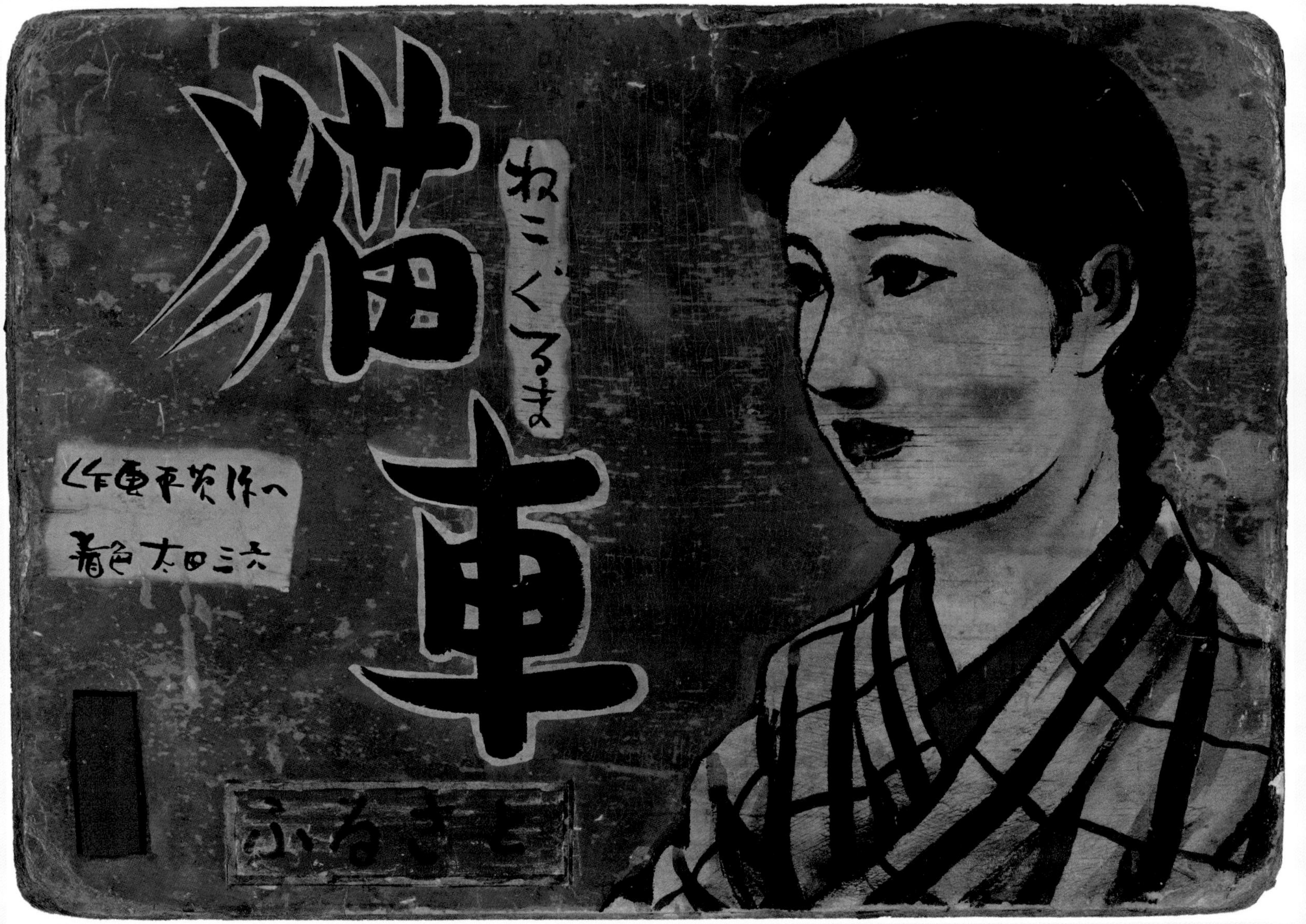
猫車
ねこぐるま
ふるさと

***Kuruma the Cat*:** In contrast to his later phantasmagoric manga style, Shigeru Mizuki's *kamishibai* paintings are a model of naturalism.

Chamber Play: *Shojo* stories were more likely to be domestic dramas about everyday people rather than super heroic antics, although there was an occasional *shojo* ninja story for the more adventurous. In this one set in a wintery nighttime cityscape, a young woman finds happiness in the warmth of a very human-looking ginger kitten.

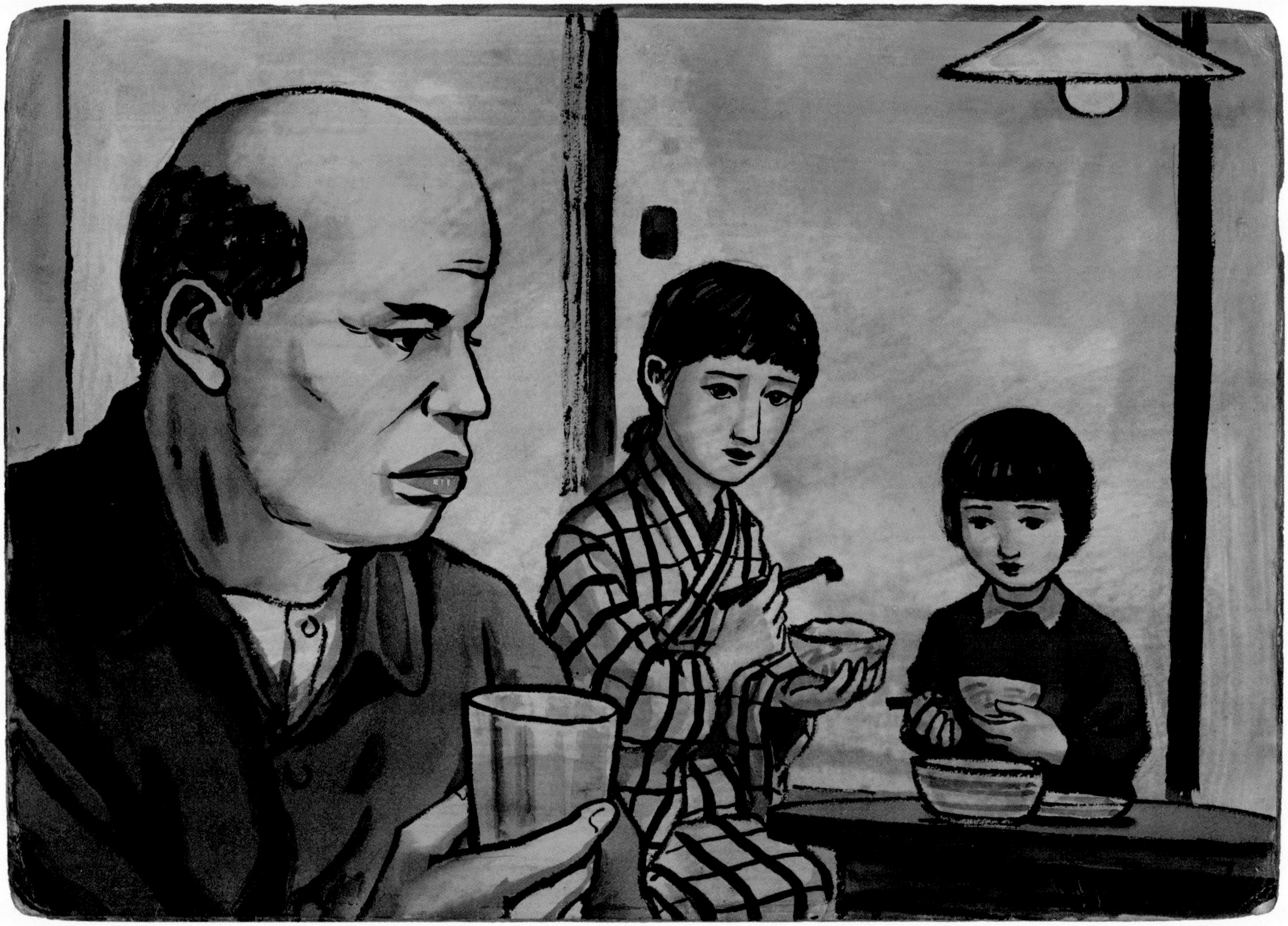

Family Feudalism: The girls' drunken, boorish father forbids them to have any pets, as the saddened girls cast down their eyes. The story is told in quietly paced medium shots like Yasujiro Ozu's domestic dramas. The images have a static feel, like a camera on a tripod, compared with the tracking shots of the boy on horseback in *Cry of the Andes*, where the viewpoint seems to be in motion along with its subject.

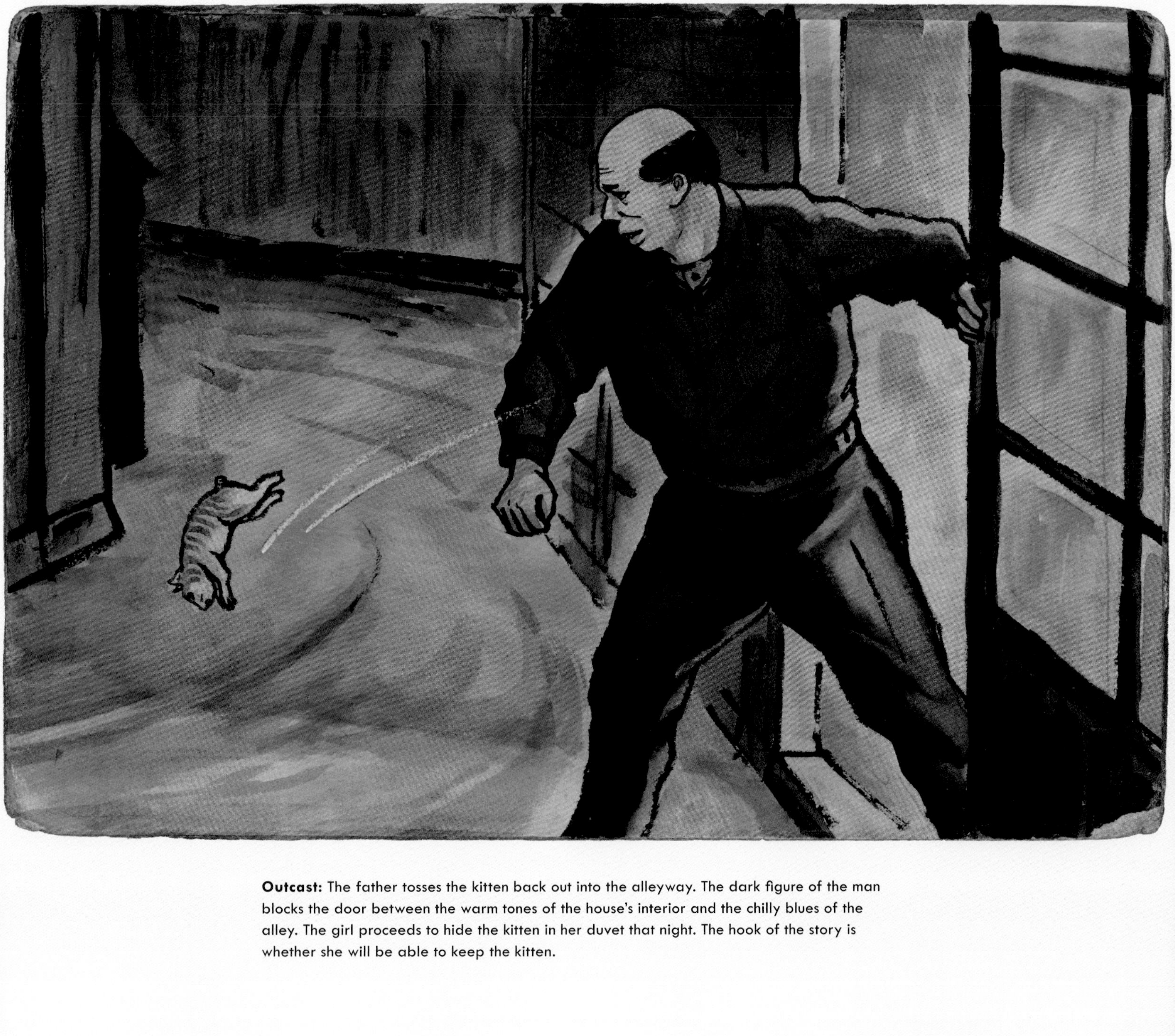

Outcast: The father tosses the kitten back out into the alleyway. The dark figure of the man blocks the door between the warm tones of the house's interior and the chilly blues of the alley. The girl proceeds to hide the kitten in her duvet that night. The hook of the story is whether she will be able to keep the kitten.

uniform. Mizuki continued to create manga, and later became famous for atmospheric horror comics like *Akumakun* (*Devil Boy*).

Soji Yamakawa, who had a long career as an illustrator of *emonogatari* (illustrated storybooks) got his start in *kamishibai* after working at a printing press at age fifteen and studying illustration in night school. His best known *kamishibai* character was Shonen Tiger (Tiger Boy), who, in the tradition of Mowgli and Tarzan, was raised by a tiger after a villain killed his father. Painted in flat, poster colors, Tiger Boy looks remarkably contemporary with the wide eyes of a manga character. Yamakawa also produced two *kamishibai* volumes that came with recorded narration and music, making them even more of an interstitial medium between manga and a nime. Published after the war in 1947, his *emonogatari Shonen Oja* (*Boy King*) was a huge hit, selling five hundred thousand copies in its first six months. Shonen Oja books appeared until 1954. The complexity and detail of Yamakawa's drawings of tropical climes and rare animals is seen as a forerunner of today's *gekiga*.

Lone Writer: Kazuo Koike, who co-created *Lone Wolf and Cub*, one of the masterworks of world comics, began his career as a *kamishibai* writer.

The writer Kazuo Koike was another major *gekiga manga-ka* who started out in *kamishibai*. Along with the artist Goseki Kojima, Koike created the sweeping, multivolume epics *Lone Wolf and Cub*, *Path of the Assassin*, and *Samurai Executioner*. Born on November 3, 1928, the same day as Osamu Tezuka, Koike moved to Tokyo in 1950, in the waning years of the *kamishibai* scene. He later broke into the *kashihon* market.

The template for Koike and Kojima's serials was *Musashi*, by Eiji

Yoshikawa, a saga about the life of legendary sixteenth-century swordsman Miyamoto Musashi that was serialized in *The Asahi Shimbun* in the 1930s, and went on to sell more than 120 million copies in Japan. Adventures set in the sword-wielding samurai era before the Meiji Restoration are known as *jidai geki*. Redolent with atmosphere like many *kamishibai jidai geki*, Koike and Kojima's manga are a cinematic experience, with an alternating rhythm of widescreen compositions and close-ups that parallels film editing. You can almost hear the soundtrack as you turn the pages. It's hard not to hear the homonym of jidai in those other *mukashi mukashi* warriors ("a long, long time ago," as Japanese fairy tales begin), the Jedi in George Lucas's *Star Wars*.

Another early adventurer, Gekkou Kamen (Moonlight Mask) looks quite up to date in his all-white outfit with shades, white boots, and turban with a crescent. The character went on to star in manga and anime, and become Japan's first live-action television super hero in 1958, astride a white motorscooter wearing oversized cat's-eye sunglasses that would not look out of place on a mah-jongg lady. (The character is not to be confused with the 1991 soft-core spoof *Kekko Kamen*, based on the eponymous manga series by Go Nagai, in which a nude heroine "streaks to the rescue" in a mask, cape, and little else.) In a charming tin rendition, Moonlight Mask was one of the first characters to cross over into the multimillion-dollar toy industry.

According to a 1933 survey of the industry, there were ninety-three production companies and 1,265 *kamishibaiya* in Tokyo. Of the companies, fifty-three were small shops employing one to eight people, but the larger companies had as many as two hundred employees.

The coming war with China would change everything.

Moonlighting: This pressed-tin toy of the Moonlight Mask is one of the earliest examples of a *kamishibai* character crossing over into lucrative merchandising. Shigeru Mizuki's GeGeGe no Kitaro is another long-lasting character in the toy market. In the prosperous and productive 1950s, Japan began exporting toy friction cars and walking, sparking robots that ran on bulky D-cell batteries. Walt Disney showed the way, but Japanese toymakers quickly caught up with the *figyura* (figurine) industry.

GOLDEN BAT TO THE RESCUE

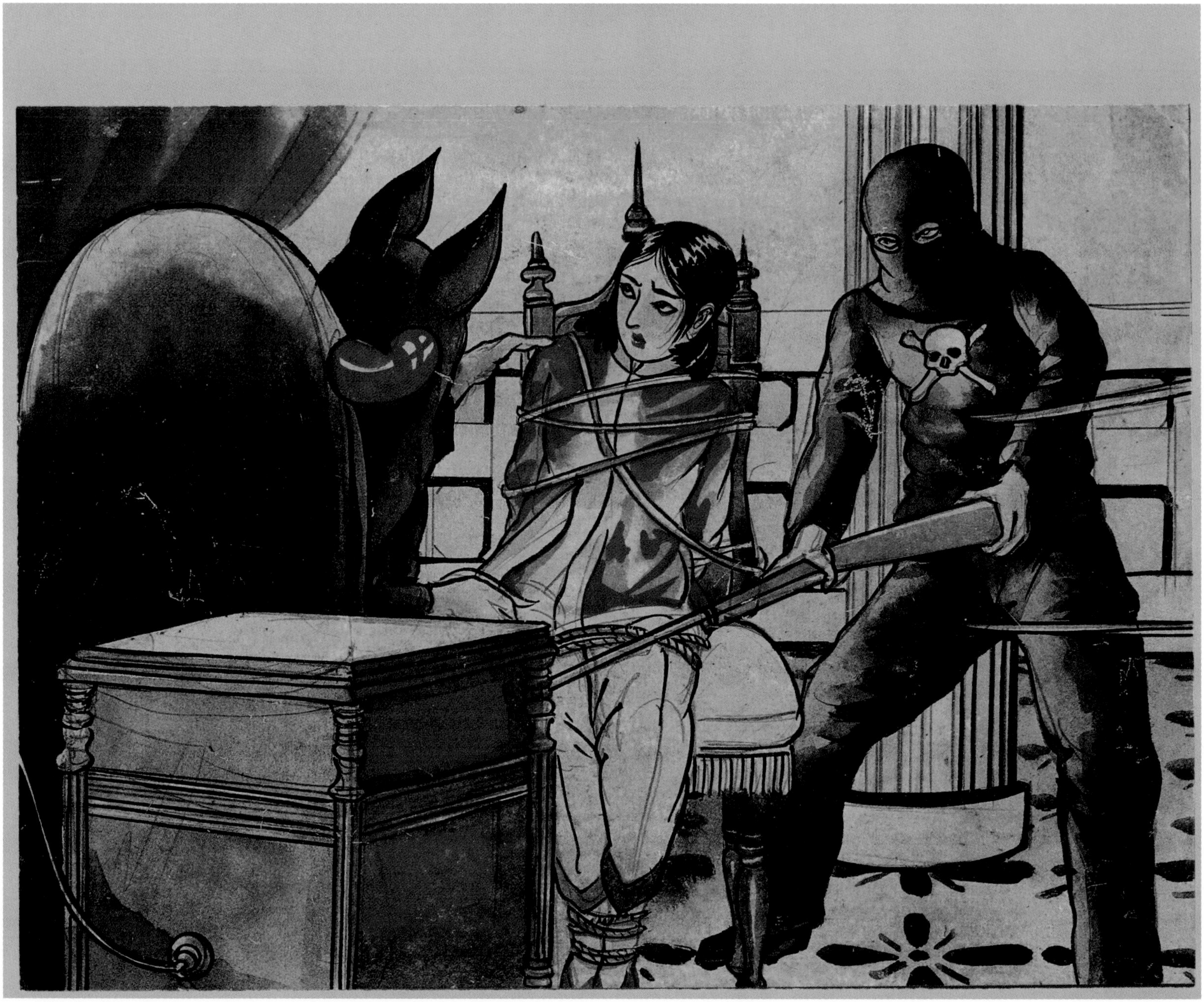

Perils of Pauline-chan: An establishing shot places the heroine held hostage in the lair of the donkey-eared alien Nazo, Emperor of the Universe. His hooded henchman, with a skull and crossbones emblazoned on his chest, stands guard with a bayoneted rifle. Nazo commands the heroine to reveal the hideout of Golden Bat, or else her boyfriend, who is tied to the tracks, will be killed by an onrushing train.

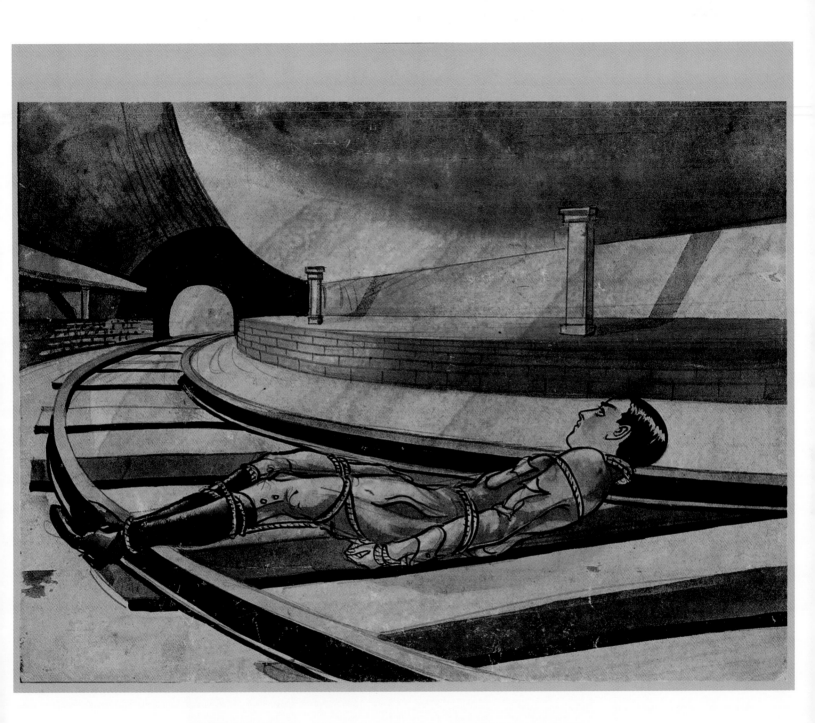

Tie Me Up, Tie Me Down: Lashed to the tracks, the hero listens for the approach of the train that will mean his doom. He is dressed like a matinee idol of the era, in jodhpurs and brilliantined hair. The colorful ties of the curving track lead the eye back to the arch of the tunnel in the background, a reflection of the rigorous geometries of the contemporaneous Constructivist school.

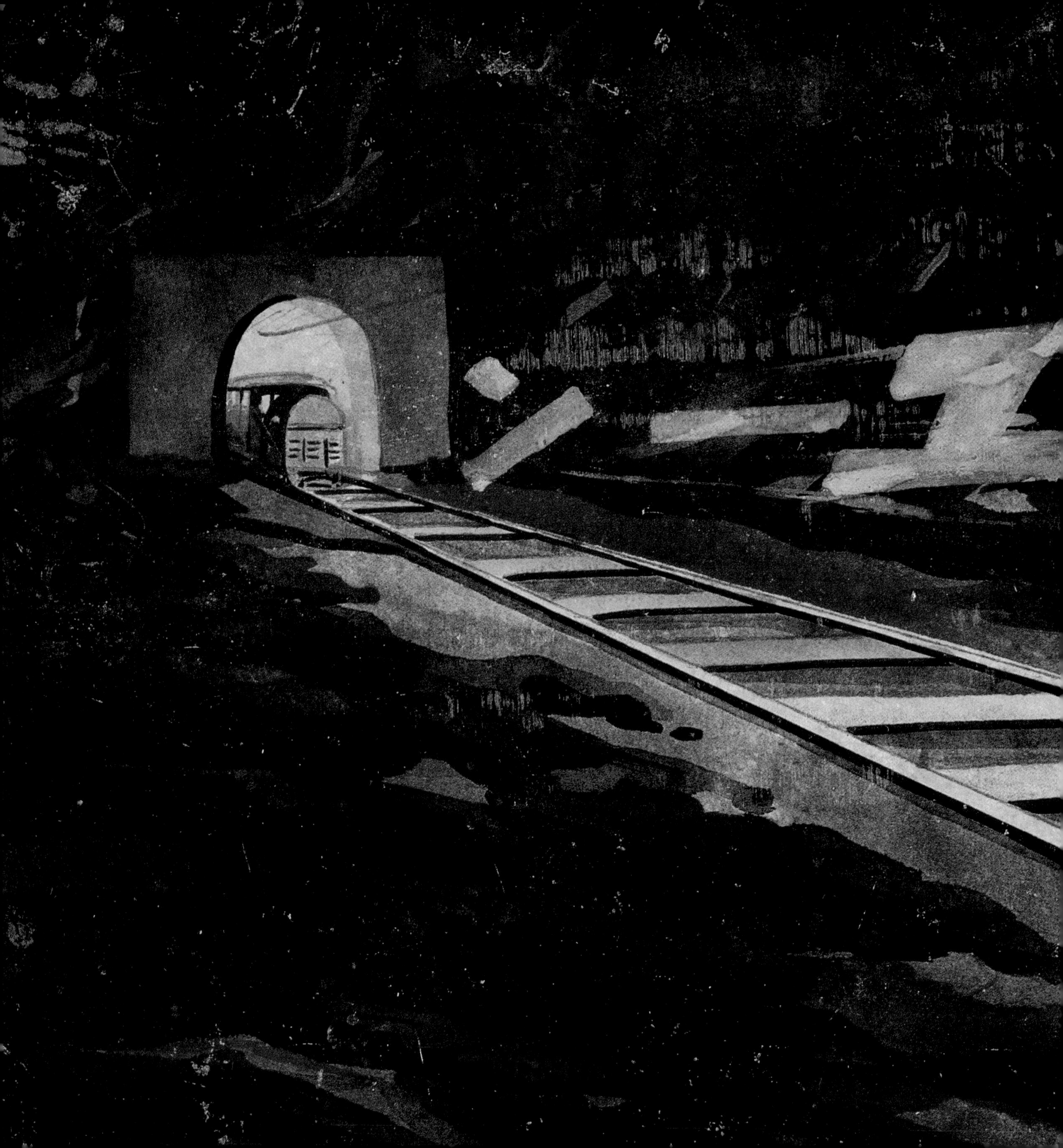

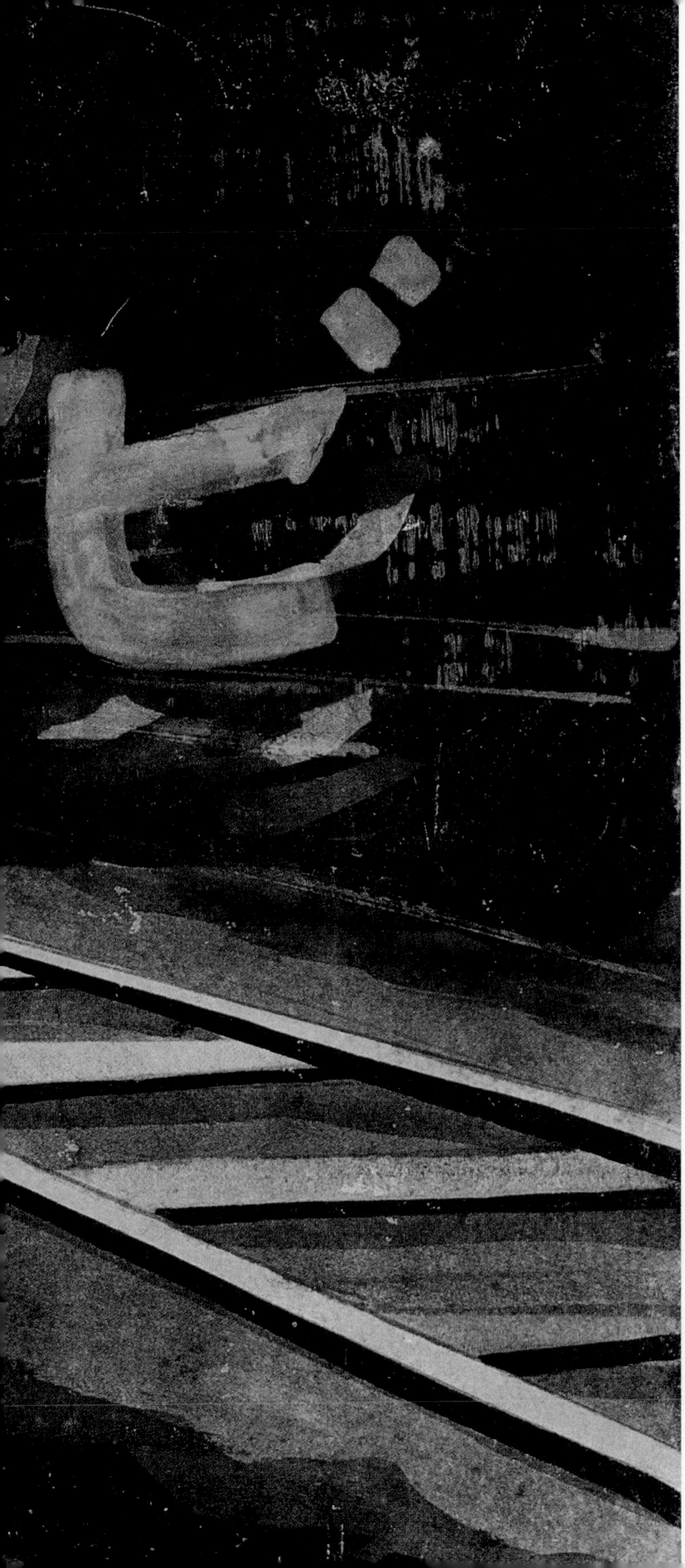

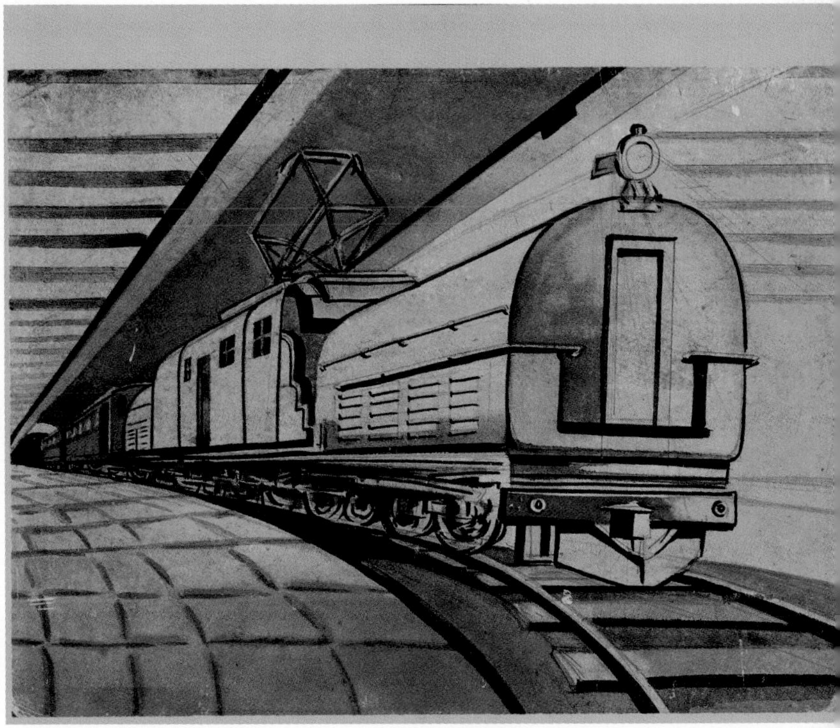

LEFT Sign Language: The *kanji* for the sound effect of the train's whistle are visually integrated into the picture. Eskimos do not really have twenty words for snow, but Japanese have dozens of onomatopoeic words for rainfall and footsteps.

ABOVE Railroaded: The train clatters along the tracks. With only seconds left, how will the hero survive?

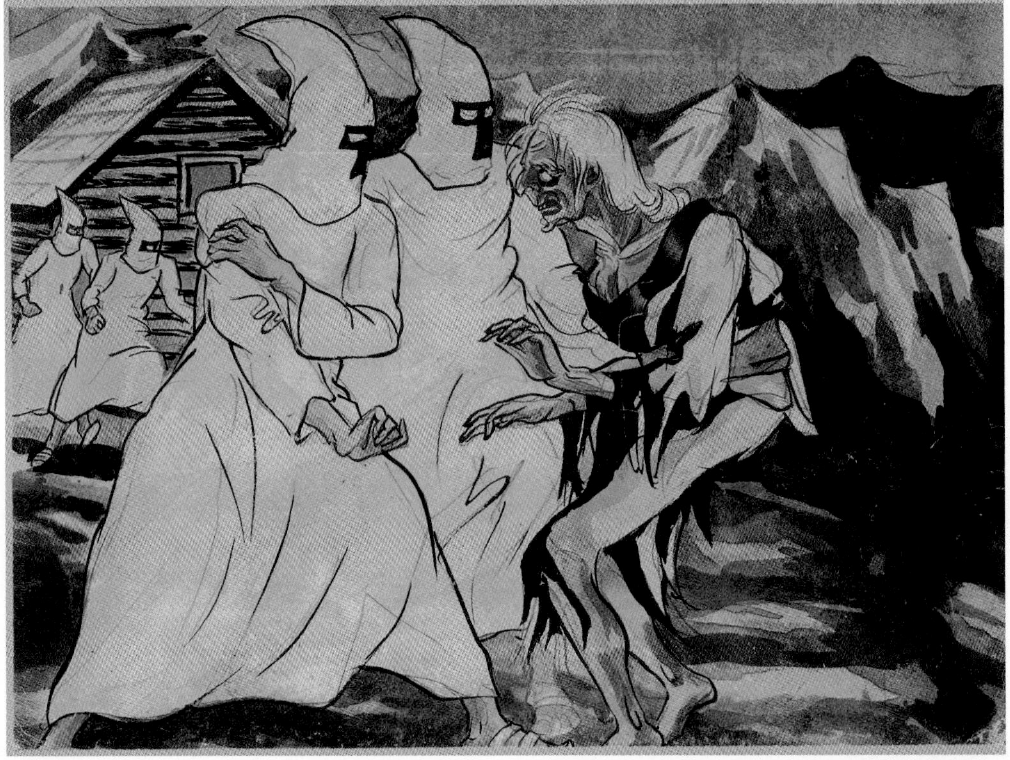

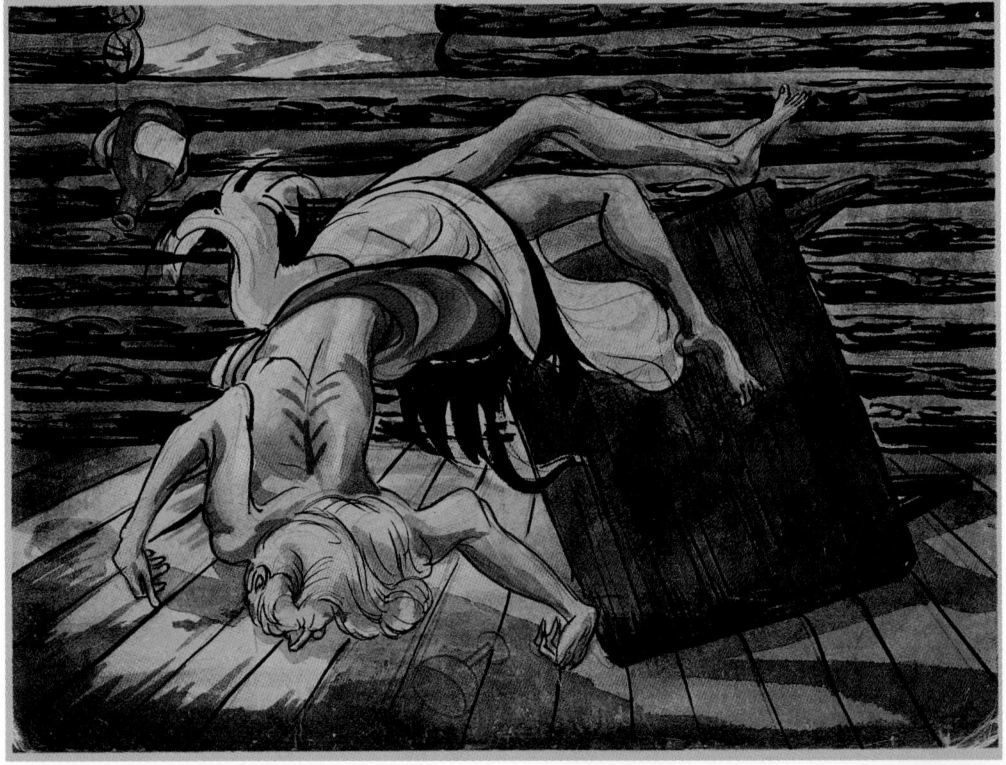

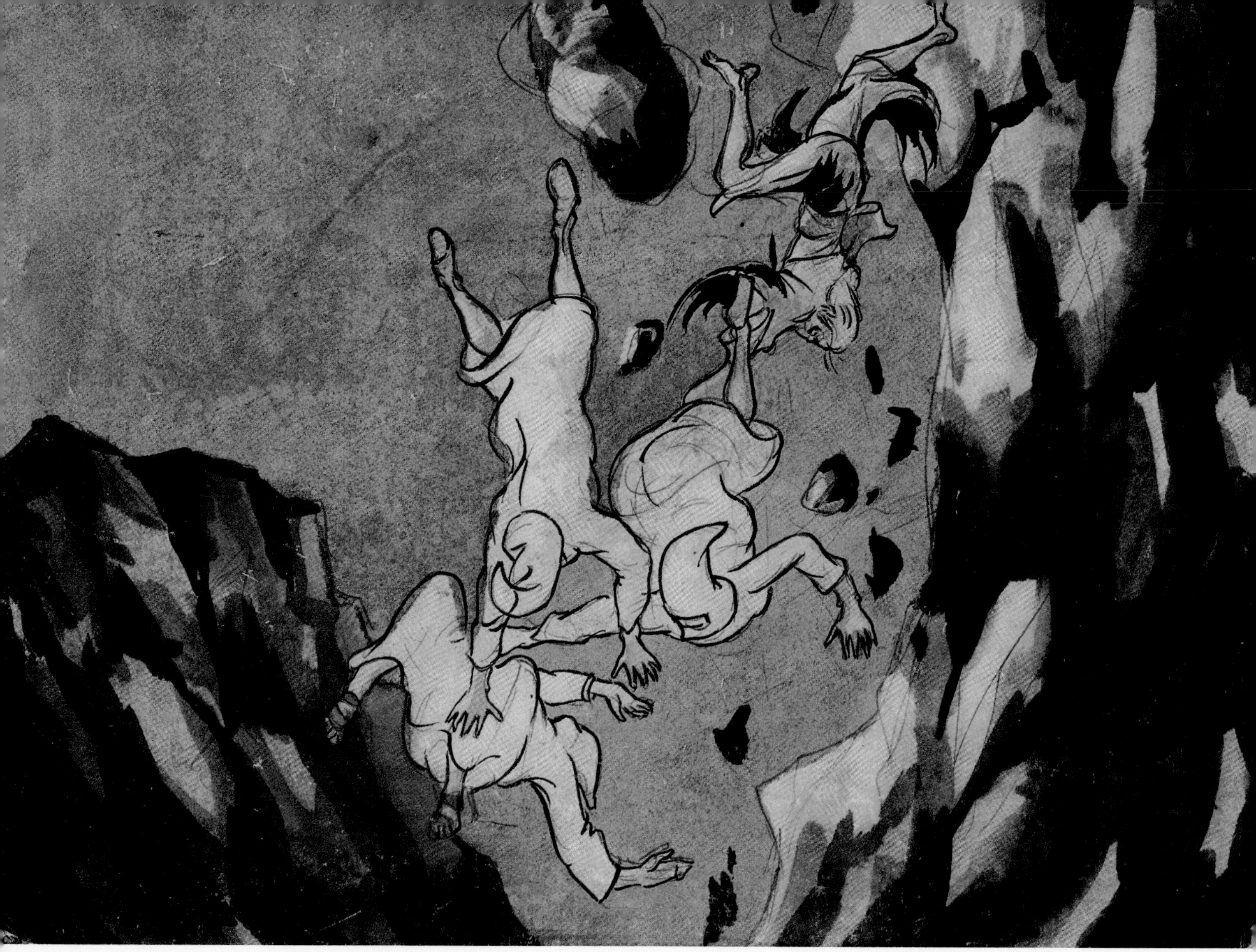

OPPOSITE, TOP MEANWHILE . . . just to ratchet up the suspense, Nazo's white-robed goons conspire with an old man who knows of Golden Bat's hideout in the mountains.

OPPOSITE, BOTTOM **Rocking the House:** Golden Bat sends the old man sprawling. The character's corybantic pose recalls *ukiyo*-e woodblock prints of the Edo era.

ABOVE **Fall Guys:** Golden Bat drops the crew of conspirators down the mountainside.

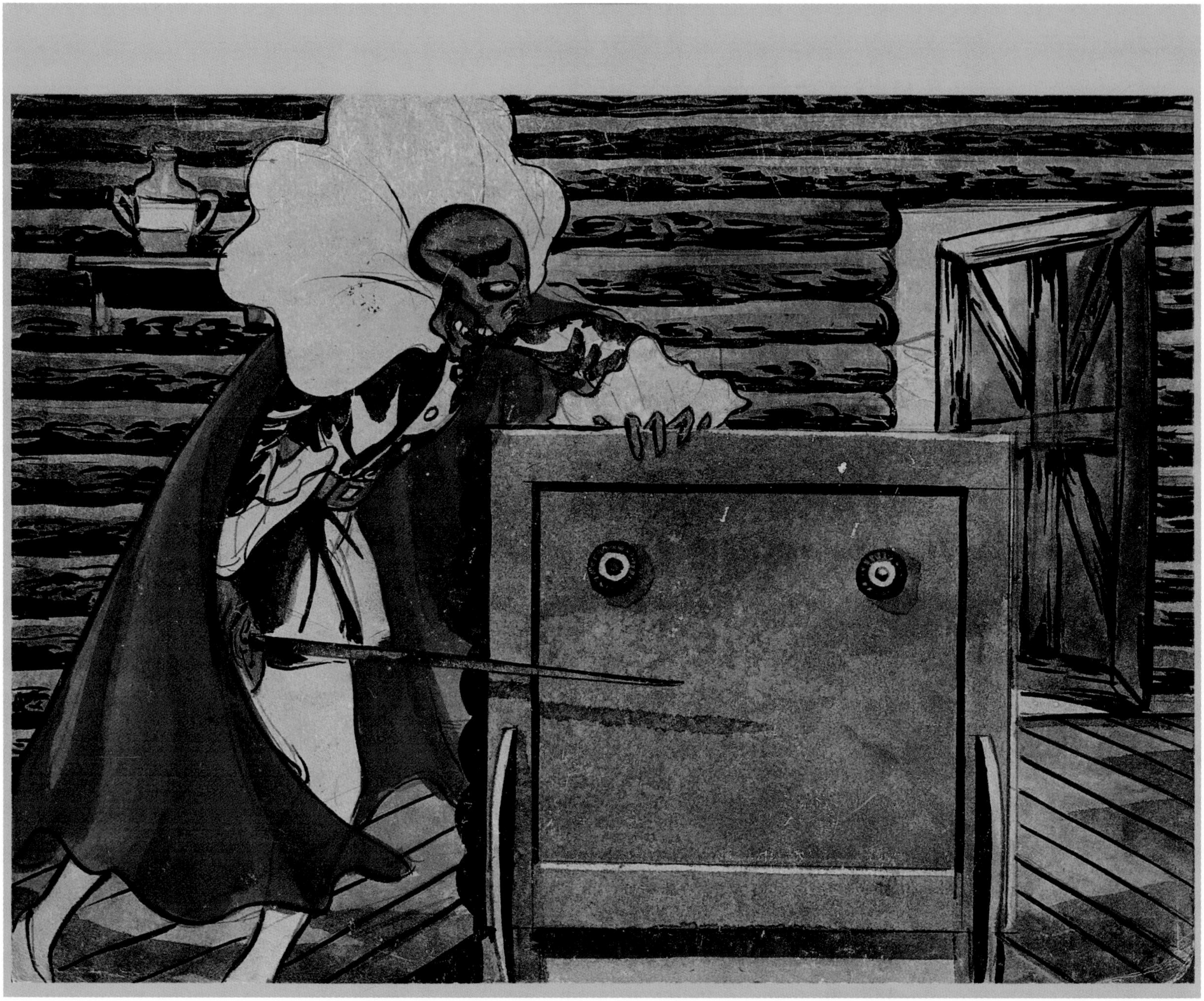

Safehouse: Inside the cabin, heavily delineated with horizontal lines, Golden Bat searches for clues to the heroine's whereabouts. This early version of the long-running character series uses delicate tints of watercolor and thin ink lines, compared with the bold outlines and primary colors of later episodes.

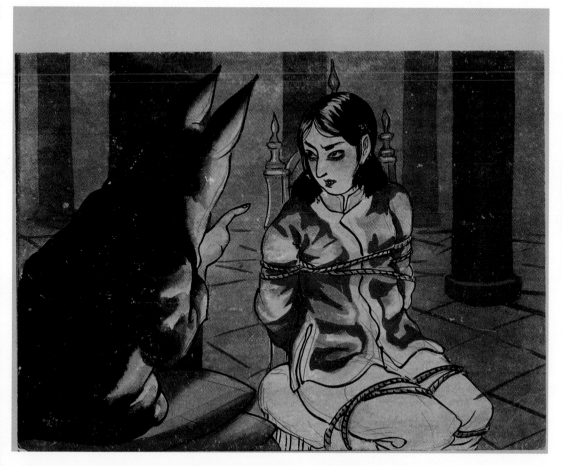

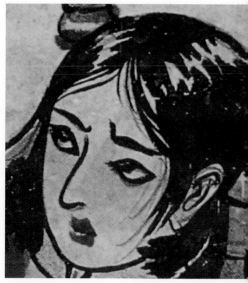

Paper Player: The ingenue's expression changes in response to a browbeating. *Kamishibaiya* were expert at vocalizing villainous growls and high-pitched women's voices.

Making a Point: In Popsicle tones of mauve and vermillion, Nazo gives his ultimatum to the helpless heroine. She can still save the life of her boyfriend, if only she will reveal Golden Bat's secret.

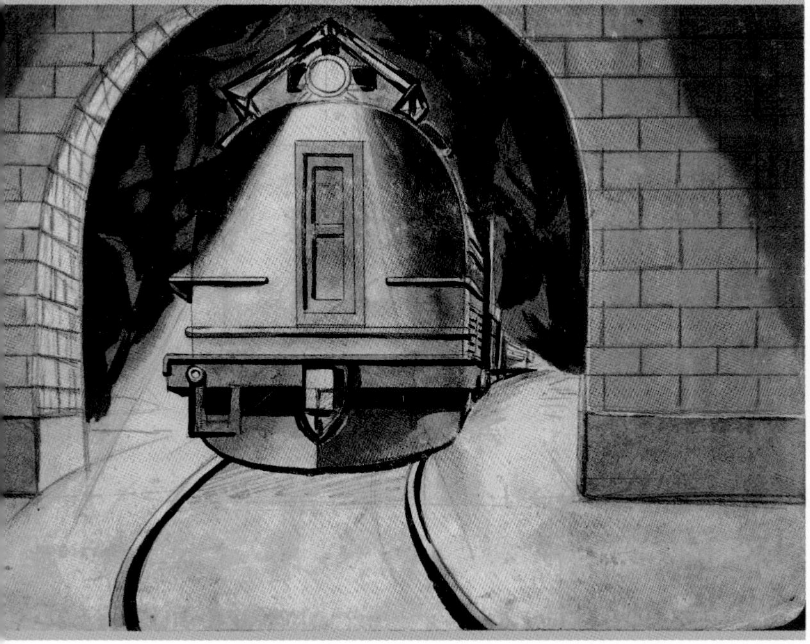

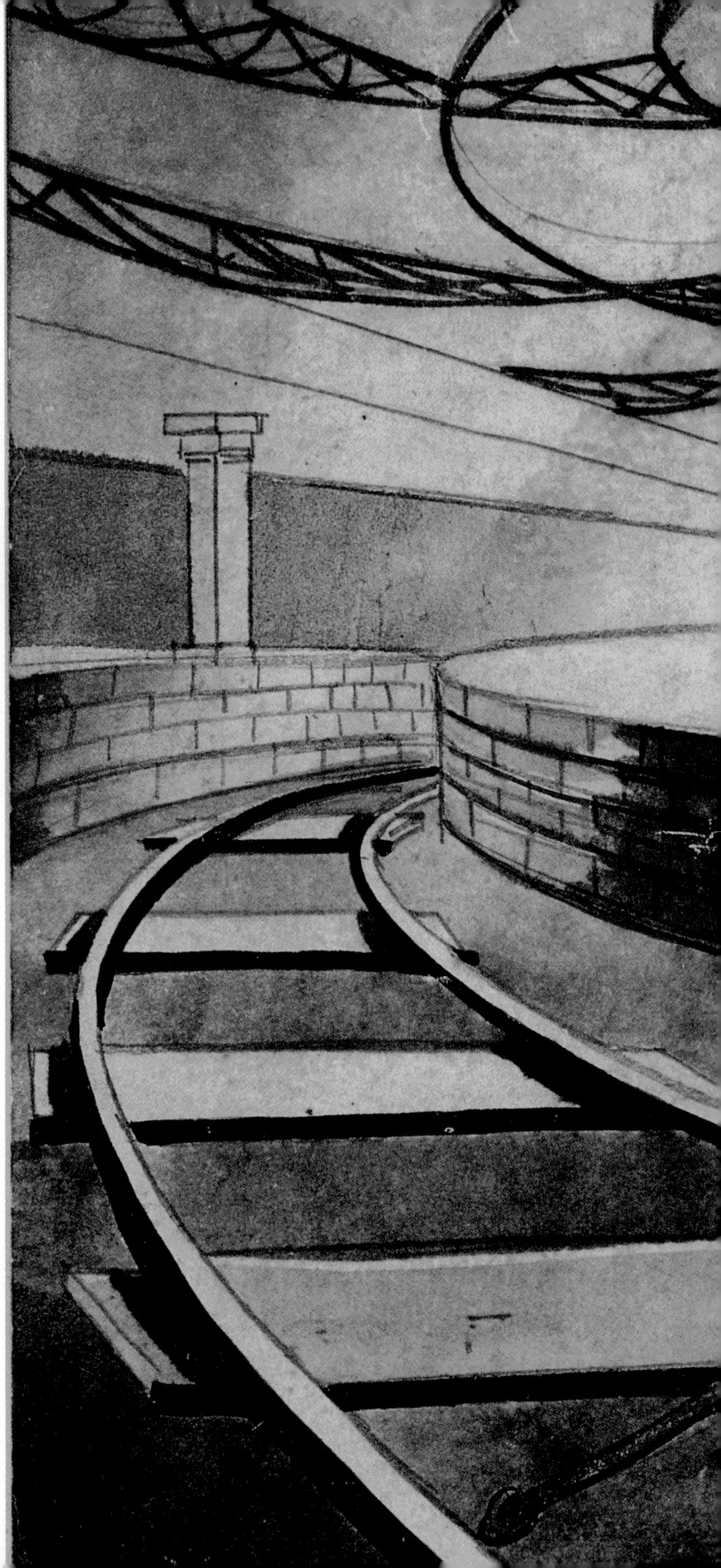

ABOVE **Highballing:** The train emerges from the tunnel, its headlight bearing down.

RIGHT **The Last Laugh:** In the nick of time, Golden Bat appears on the scene, still bearing his maniacal grin.

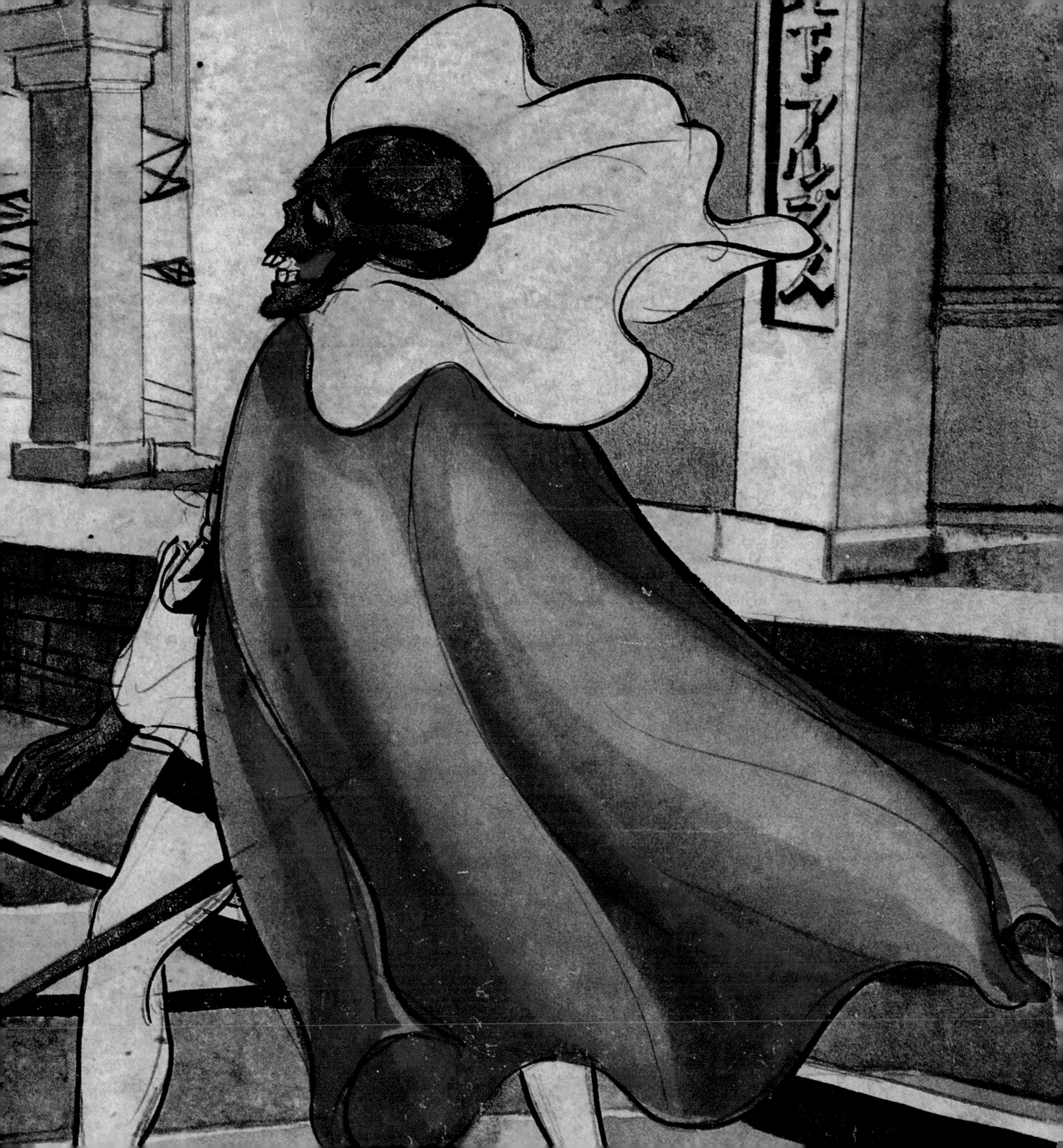

Bat Bomb: Golden Bat sets his handy, self-propelled rocket bomb in motion. The creator's daughter, Yoko Taniguchi, recalls: "One thing I think is amazing about his *kamishibai* is the machines that show up in them. At that time, there was nothing you ride like rockets, yet these fanciful pictures are in my father's work and they're beautiful."

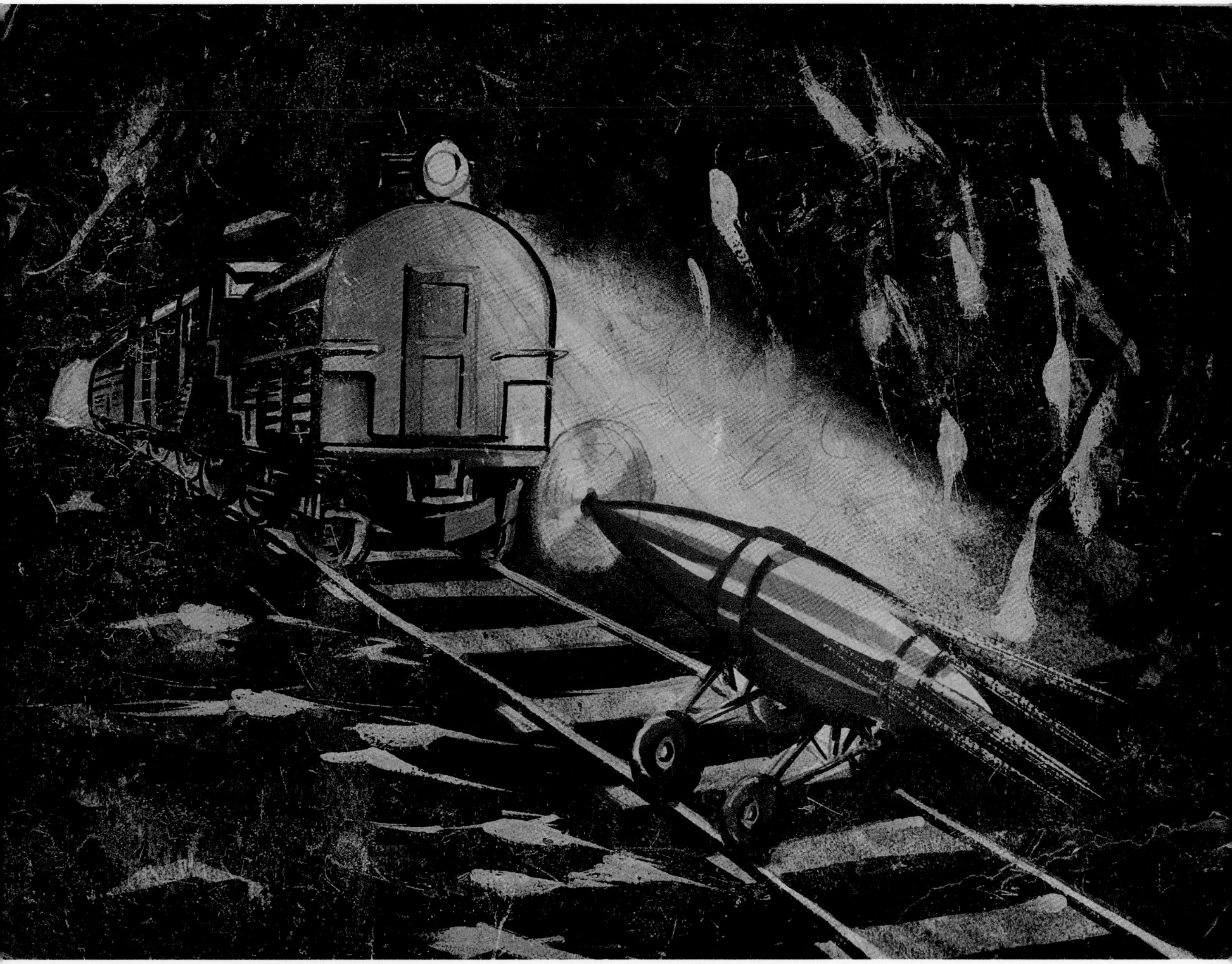

Tunnel Vision: The propeller-driven rocket bomb is about to collide with the train, highlighted in a rainbow wash of color from its lantern within the dark recesses of the tunnel. Lighting from a source within the picture is more typical of Rembrandt lighting than Japanese painting. *Kamishibai* artists were conversant with the history of Western art, at least through art books, as well as cinema.

Offtrack Betting: The train jumps the tracks as it explodes entering the station, turning steel rails into tangled ramen. The rails and billowing plumes of smoke contrast with the orderly geometry of the arced platform, leading the eye into the background of the frame in classic Renaissance perspective.

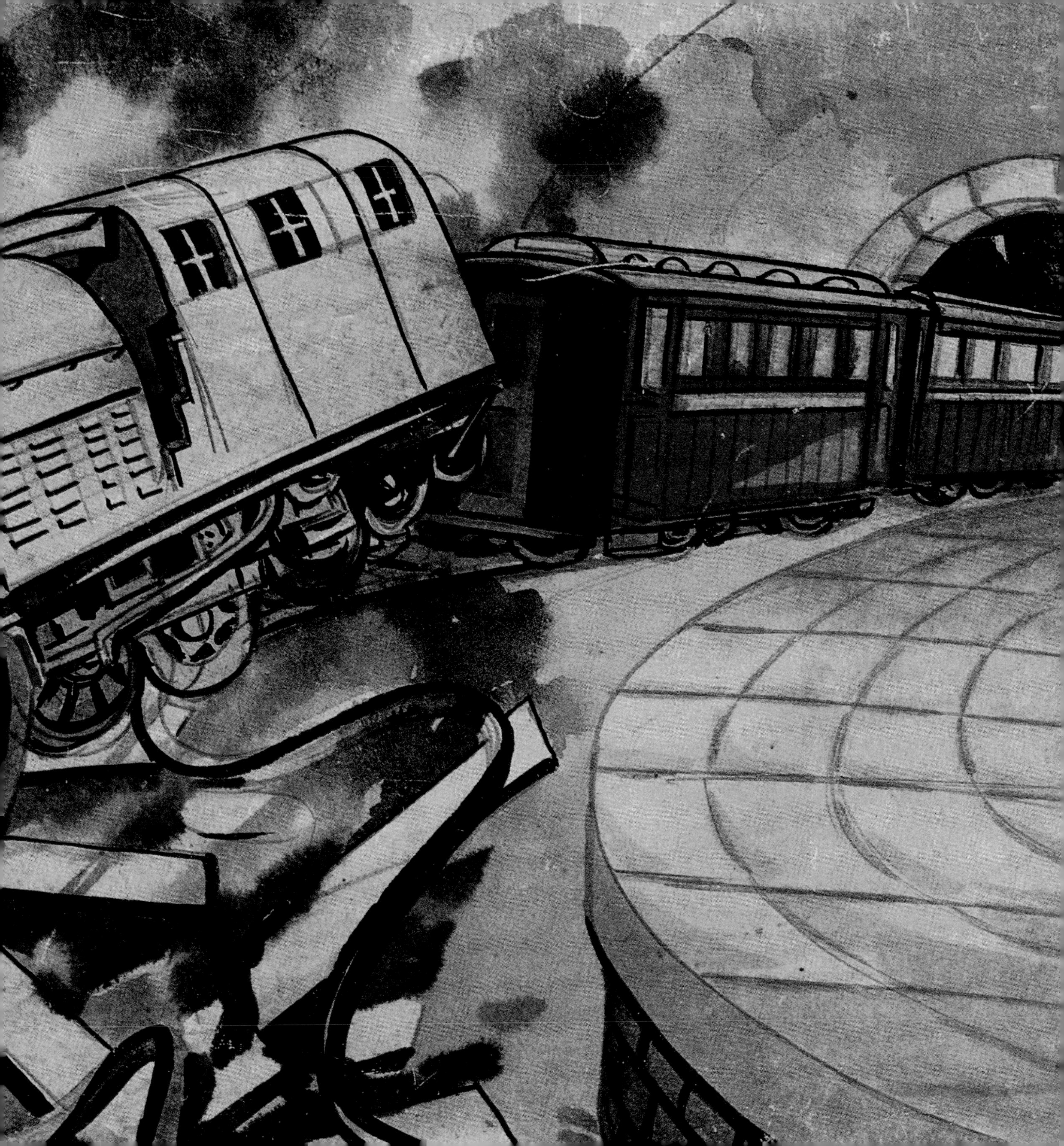

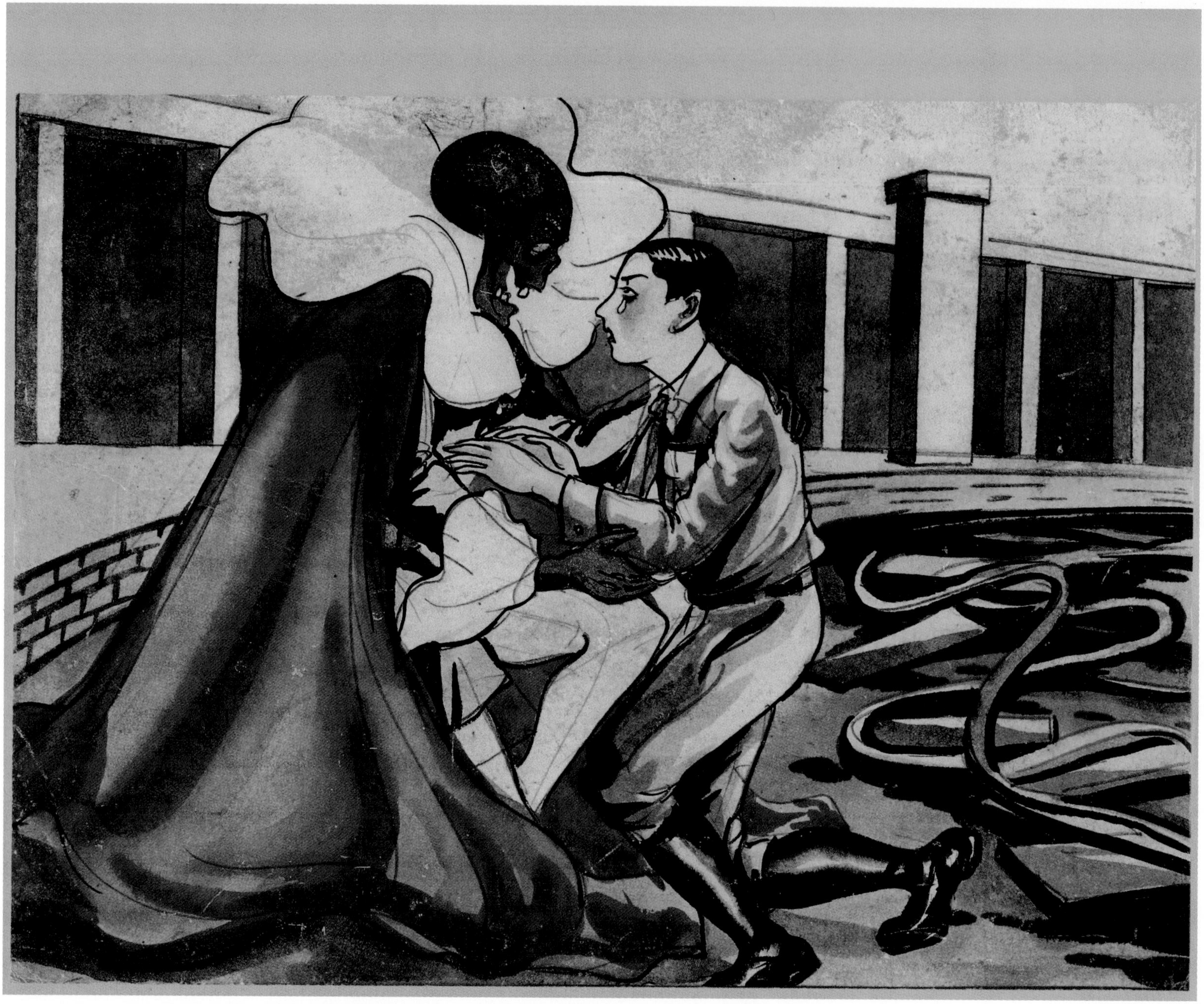

Tracks of my Tears: The youthful hero tearfully thanks his skeletal rescuer. Tears are not an indication of weakness in Japanese culture, but rather a symbol of overwhelming emotion that cannot be expressed in words. The panel has a strong rhythmic composition with the super hero's flowing cape and collar, the twisted rails and orderly colonnade in the background. The exchange of glances between the two characters forms the central focus and emotional core of the picture. Golden Bat appears as a macabre disembodied skull set against his petal-like yellow collar. As the creators became more confident, Golden Bat emerged as a more comical figure.

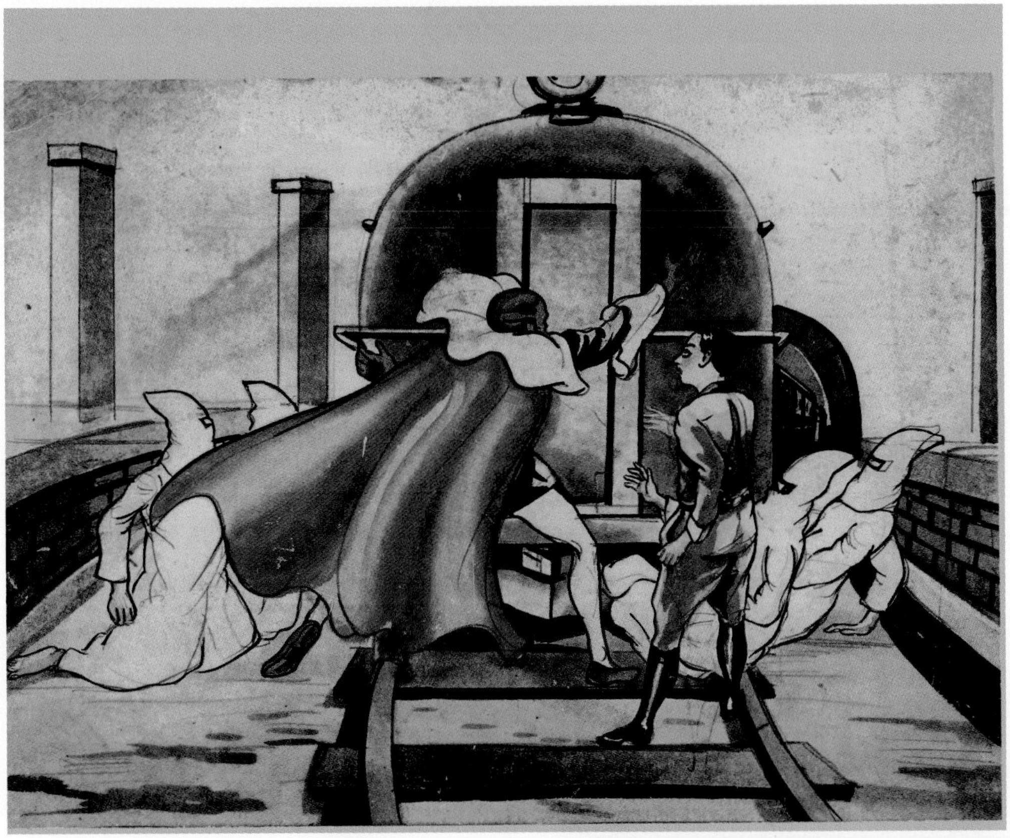

LEFT Trainswitch: Golden Bat frees the hero from the tracks and halts the locomotive as the hooded henchmen appear.

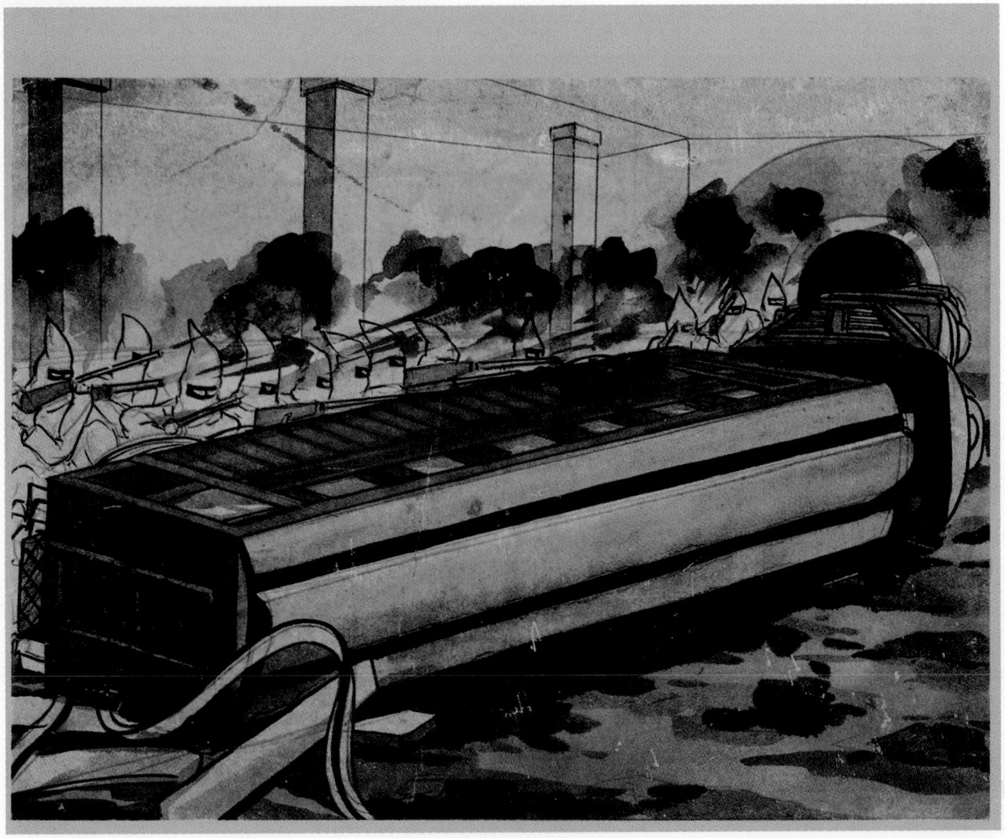

RIGHT Line of Fire: The bad guys lay down a fusillade, protected by the overturned railway car. Puffs of smoke and rifle fire crackle along the line. How will Golden Bat defend himself? Tune in tomorrow and don't forget to bring a one-yen coin for candy to get the best coign of vantage.

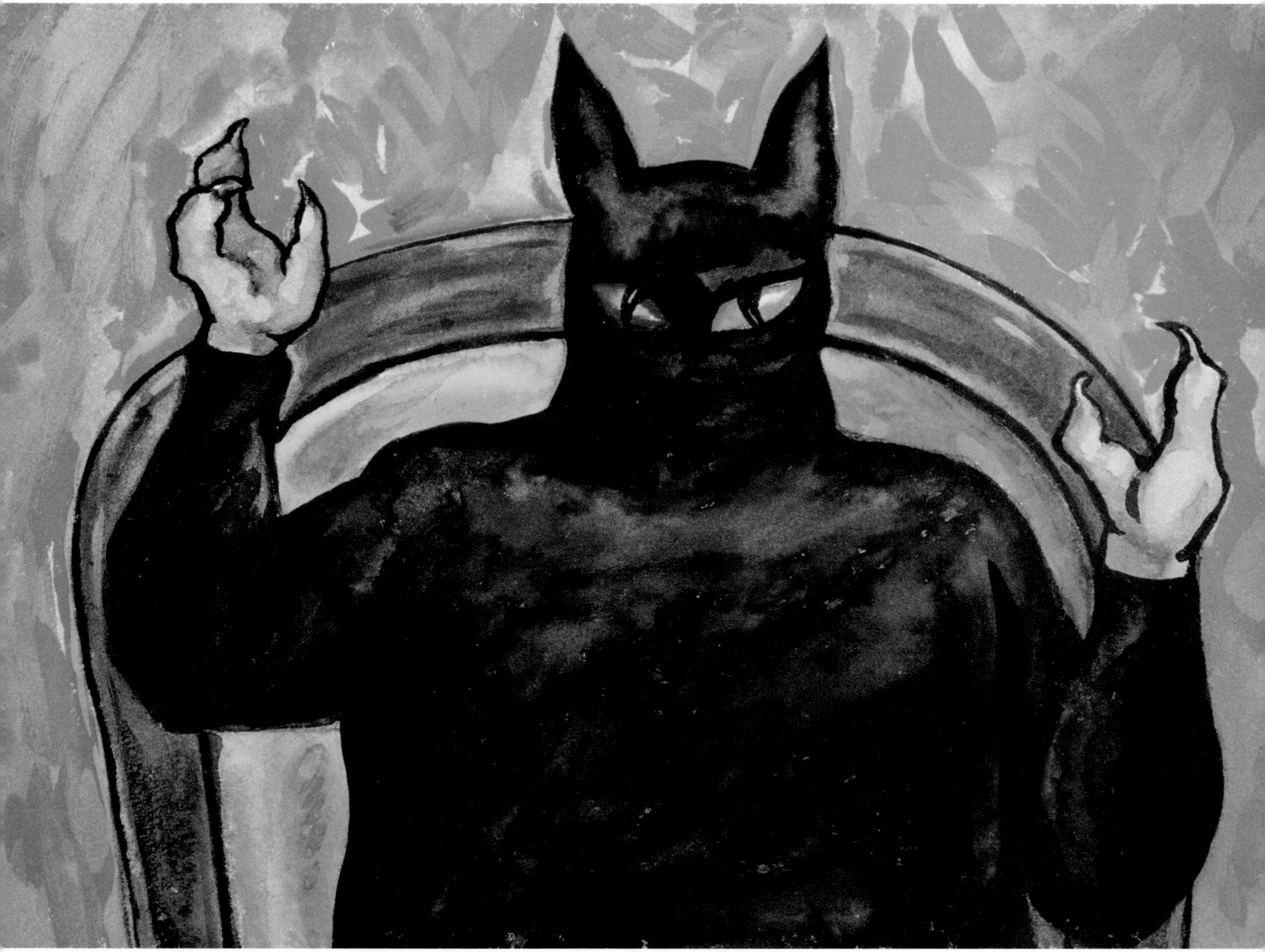

Emperor of the Universe: A postwar *Golden Bat* reveals a bolder palette of deeply saturated reds and blues and a more naturalistic style, seemingly influenced by van Gogh's portraits. The artist Takeo Nagamatsu's favorite pastime was viewing paintings in Tokyo's Ueno Museum of Art. Nazo's heterochromial red and blue eyes stare out hypnotically at the viewer.

Replay: The scene is familiar—the ingenue Emily is held hostage by Nazo, but the composition, chromaticism, and posing of the figures is freshly updated. Hand gestures tell the story, like those in a Poussin painting: Nazo's threatening right arm, his left hand egocentrically pointing to himself, the guards' heavy hands on the girl's shoulders, and the girl's own unpictured hands, connoting powerlessness.

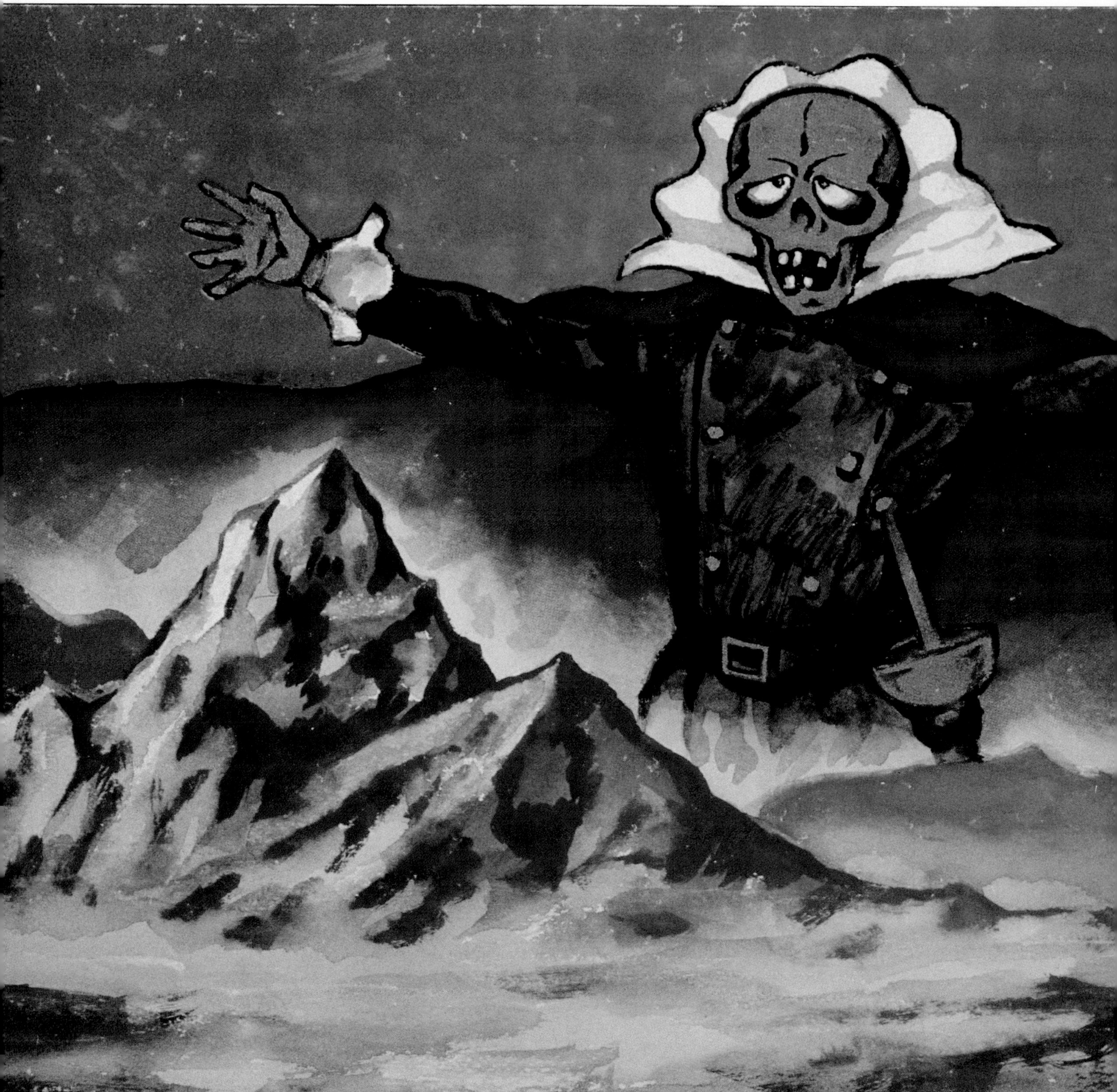

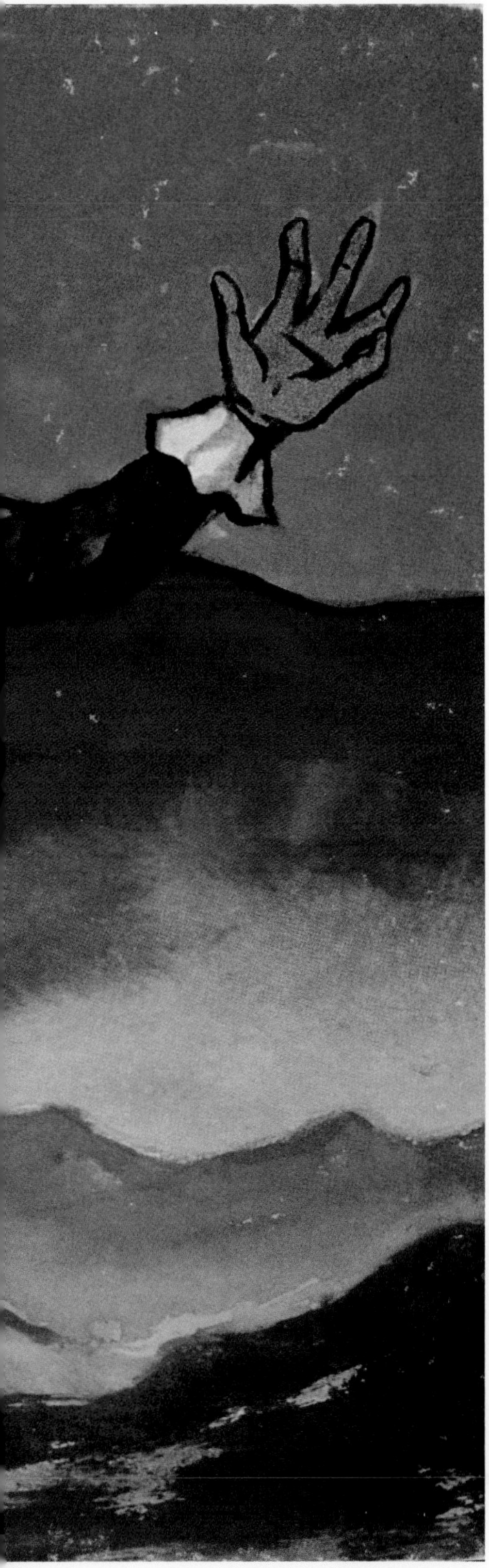

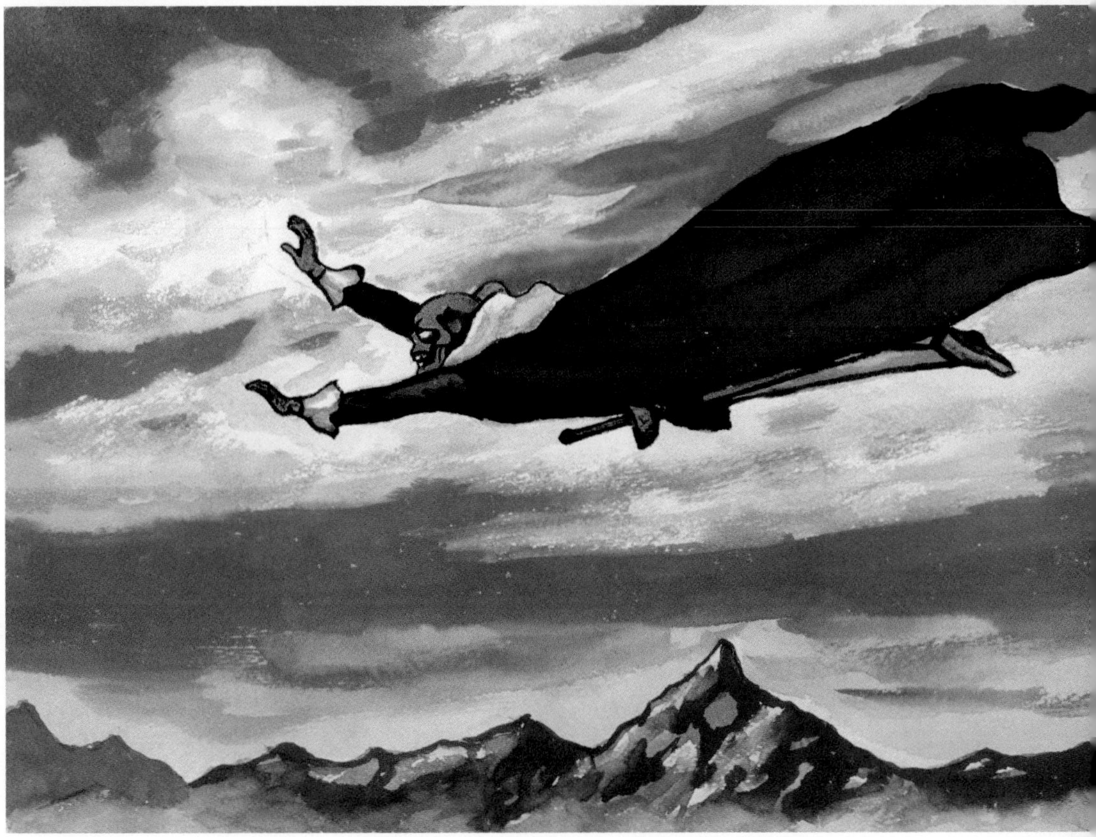

LEFT Golden Bat Signal: From his Fortress of Solitude high in the Japanese alps, Golden Bat is telepathically attuned to Emily's silent plea. The snow-capped peaks are rendered naturalistically in tones of blue and white, while Golden Bat is a cartoon character with a snaggletoothed grin and crossed eyes in hollowed-out sockets. Audiences would be amused and thrilled by the combination of his comical face and dashing costume complete with a European-style rapier at his waist. His scarlet cloak extends from border to border of the panel, emphasizing his role as global protector.

ABOVE Bone Voyage: Golden Bat flits high above the mountaintops. Perhaps as a product of some collective unconscious, *Golden Bat* contains a remarkable number of super hero tropes: a Fortress of Solitude in an arctic region, cape, superstrength, and the power of flight.

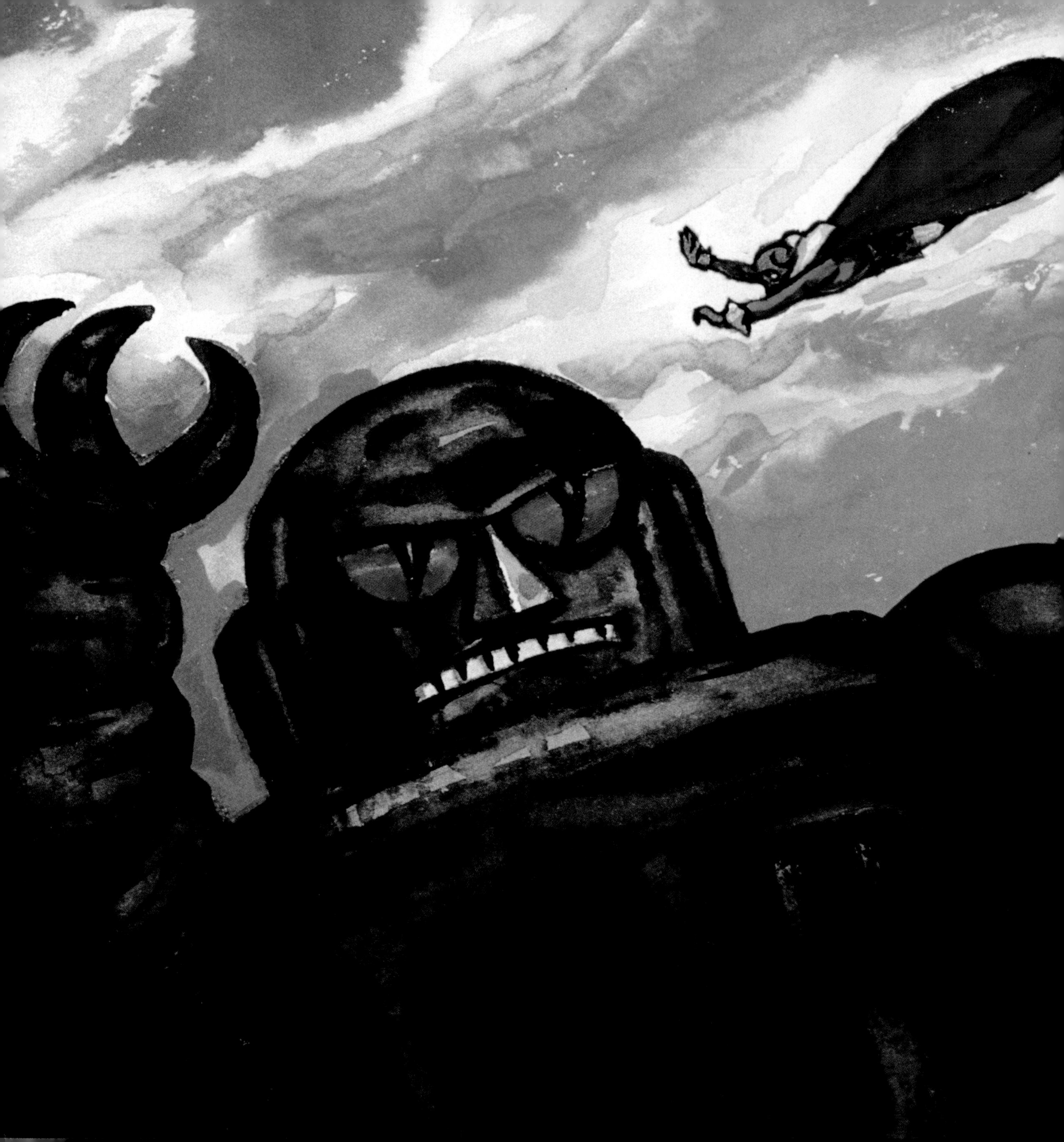

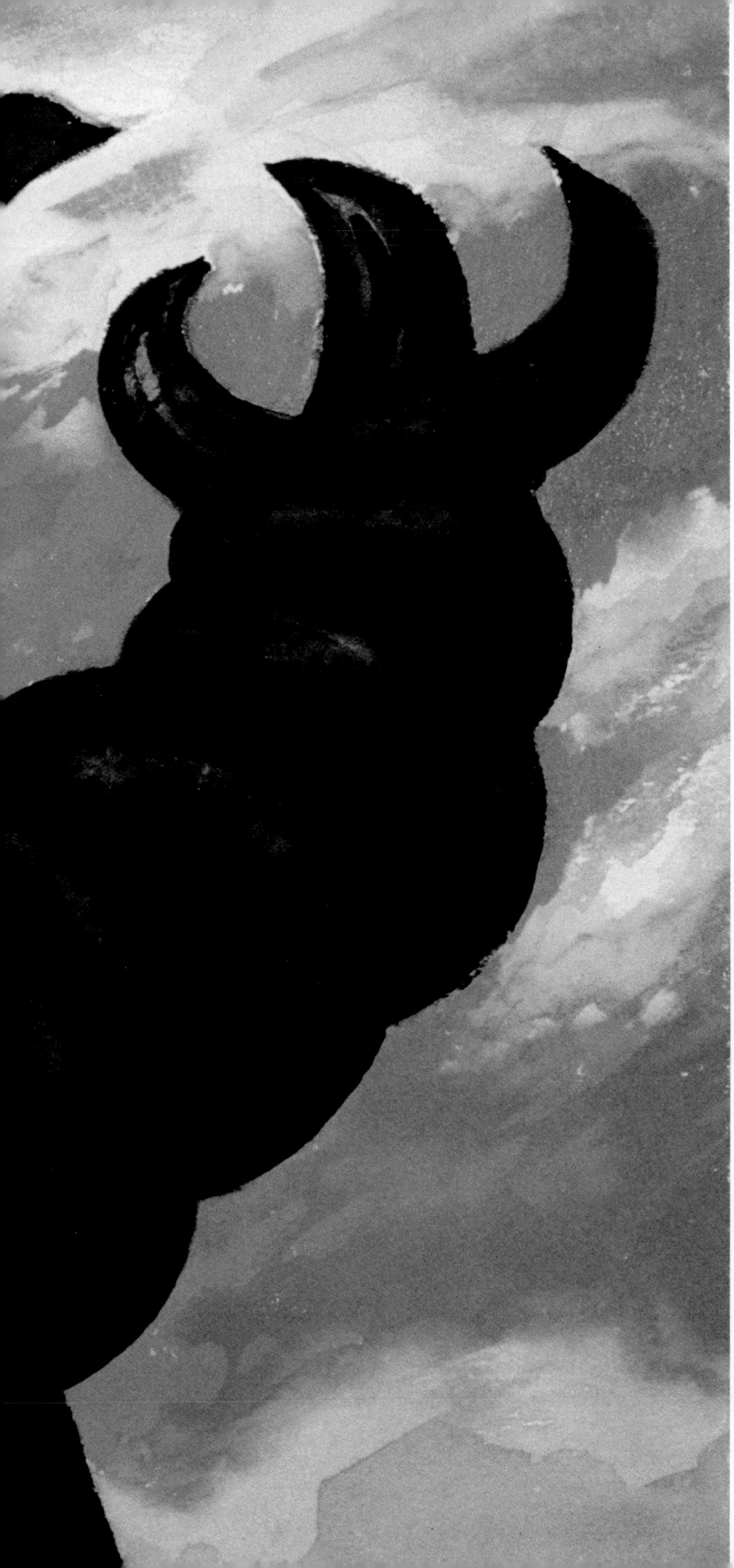

Giant Robot: Before Astro Boy (1952); Gigantor (1956); and one of the very first cyborgs, Tobor the 8th Man (1963)—all of whom were part of the first wave of Japanese animation in the early 1960s—Golden Bat dueled with mechanized monsters. This tubby fellow looks like a mean Michelin Man, with radial-tire arms, a bullet head, and a permanent scowl. Scale is cinematically displayed by taking the figure that fills the previous panel and showing it in miniature against the robot.

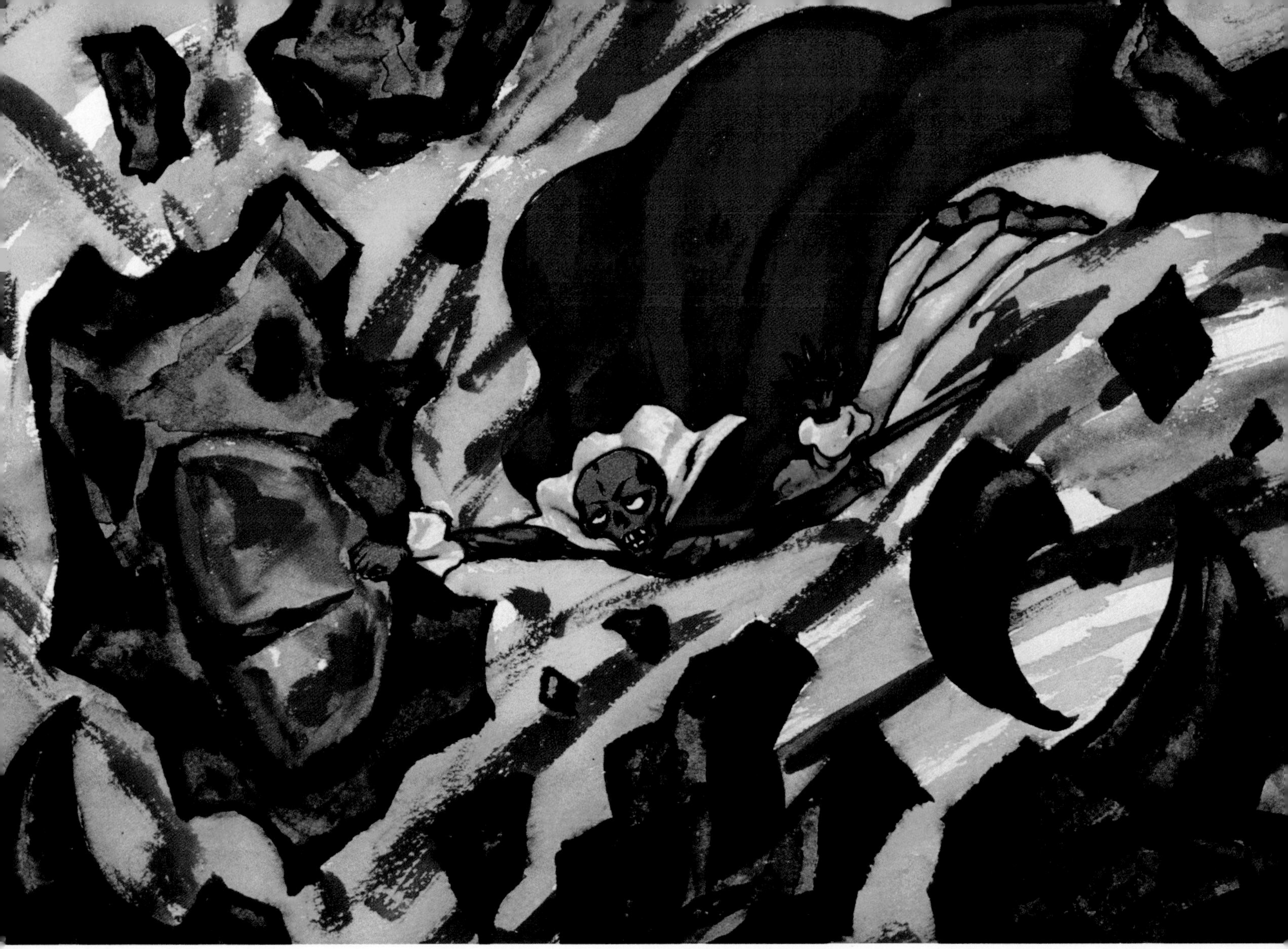

Cape Fear: Golden Bat renders the giant robot into a scrapheap of scattered pincers and glass eyeballs. The deep crimson of Golden Bat's cape leaps from the page and offsets the flying mechanical pieces.

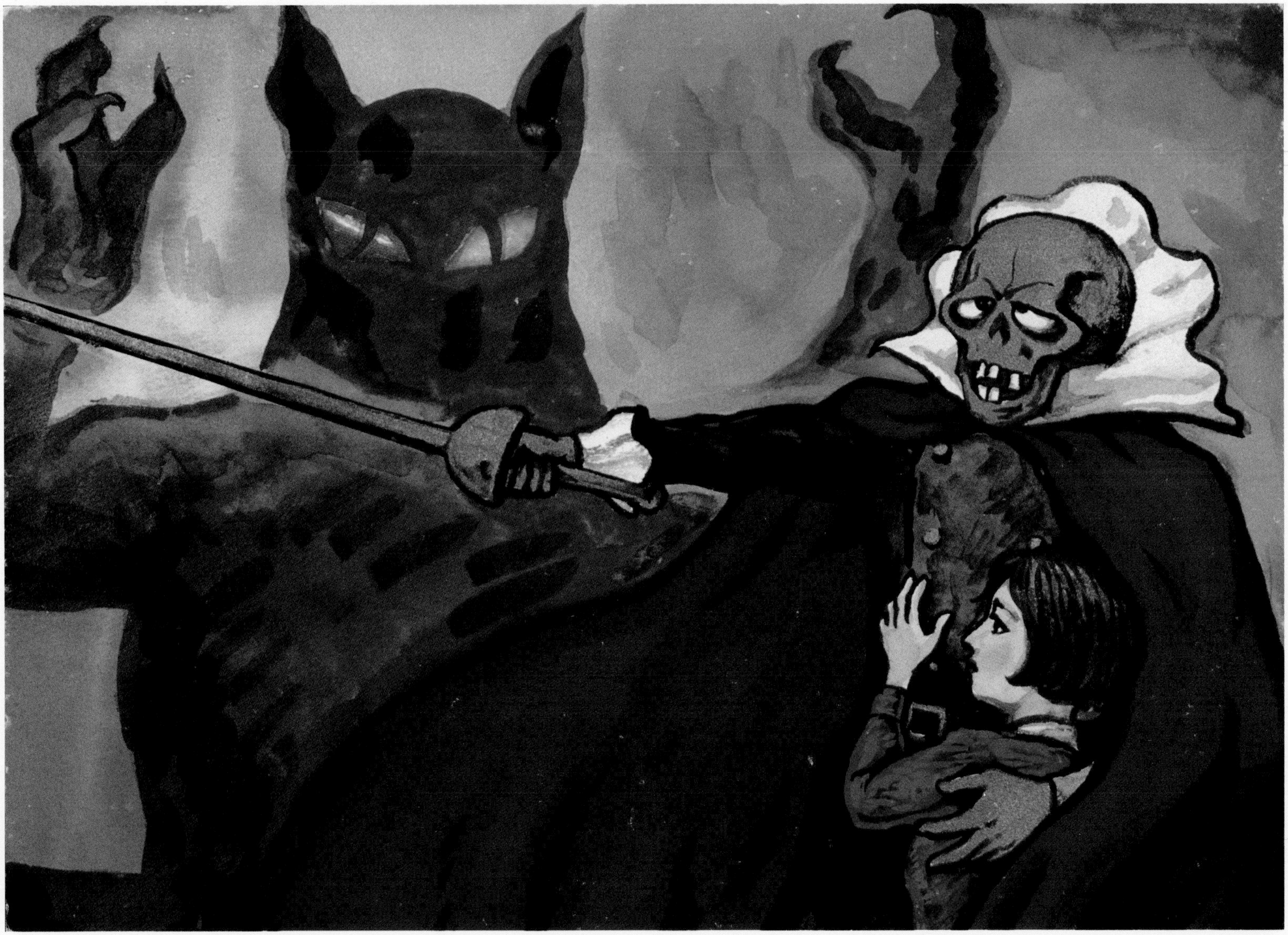

Rapier Wit: Protecting Emily within the folds of his cloak, the strabismic super hero strikes a defiant pose against his looming nemesis Nazo. To be continued!

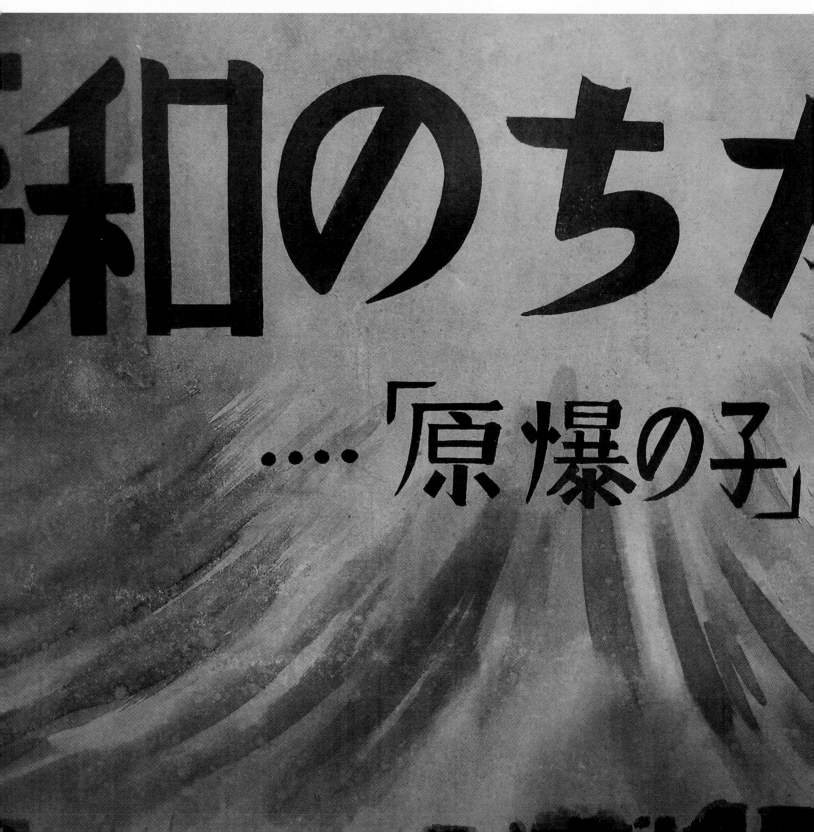

和のちね

....「原爆の子」

ぶん

より‥‥

Pledge of Peace from Children of the Bomb: After the censorship of the American occupation was lifted, *kamishibai* creators were able to confront the forbidden subject of the atom bomb and its aftermath. This *kamishibai* demonstrates the range of the art form in taking on serious subjects. The hecatomb of Hiroshima is presented in sober medium shots and moving close-ups. Child survivors are known as *genbaku no ko*—children of the bomb.

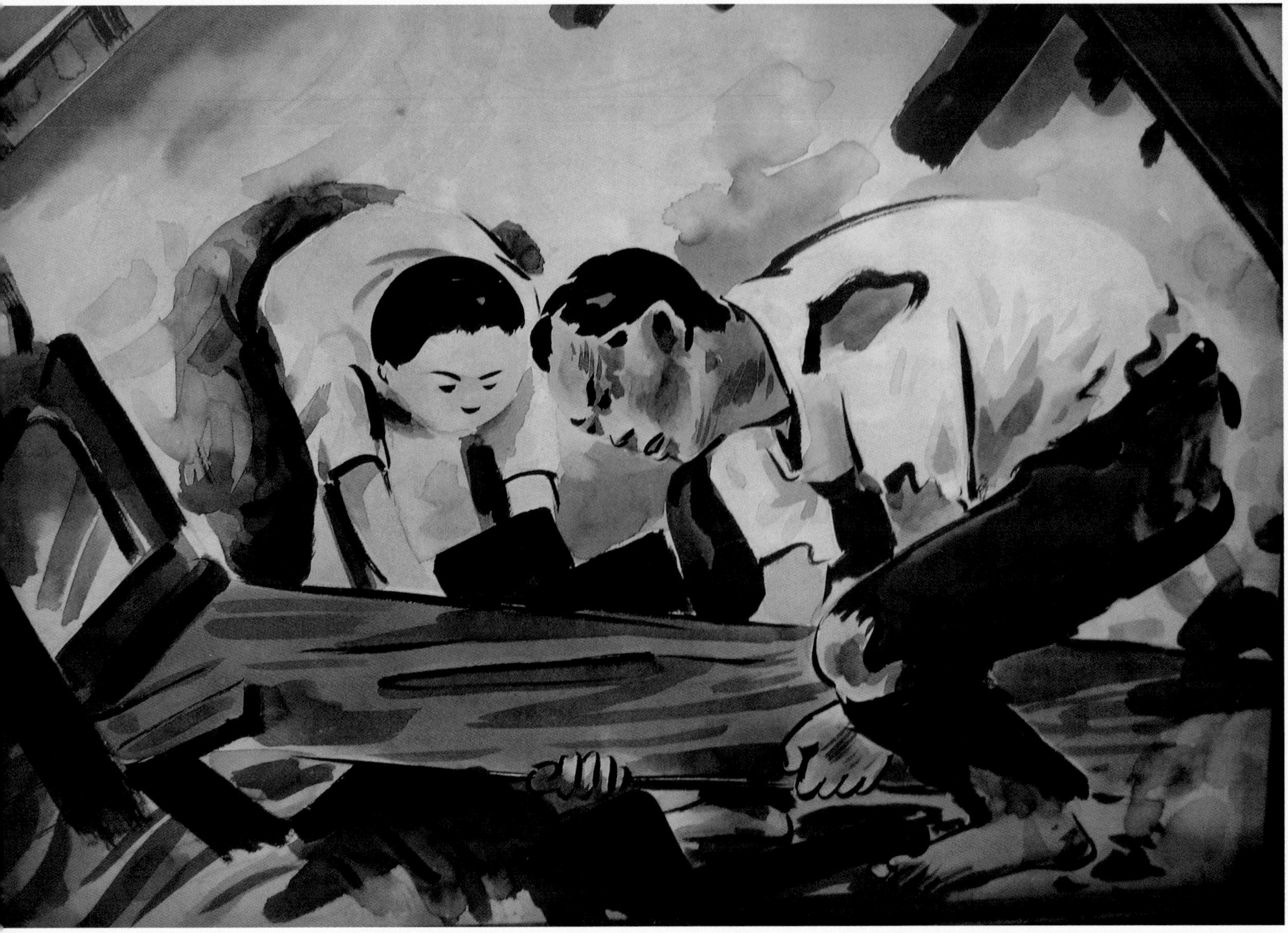

A father trying to rescue his family from the ruins of their home is helped by a young boy, but the wooden beam is too heavy to lift. Midshots focus on the human element rather than the wider devastation.

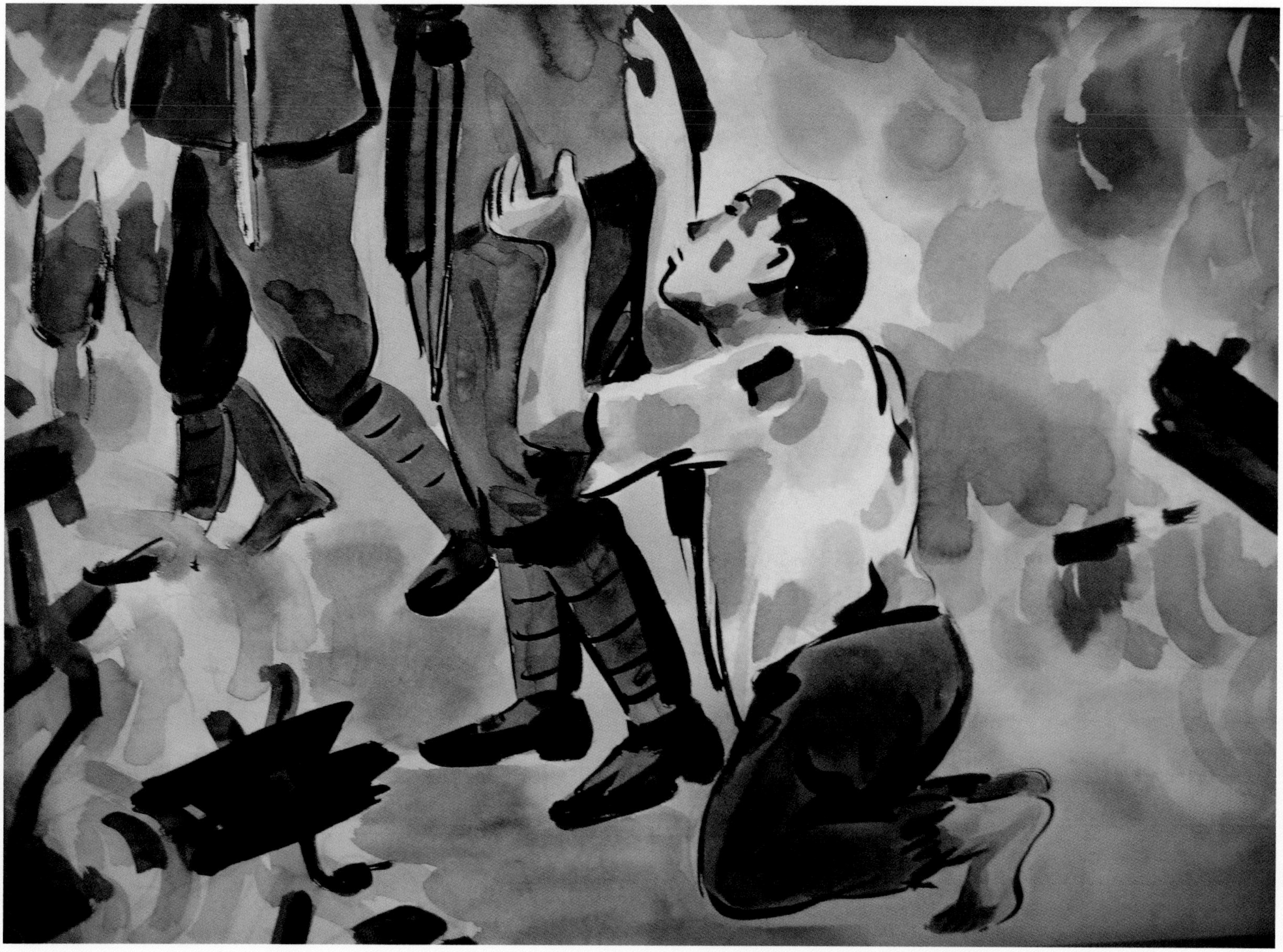

The man pleads for help at the feet of Japanese soldiers, but they have no time for him. The upward angle showing only the soldiers' puttee leggings highlights the man's abasement and the indifference of the troops. It took decades for victims of the bomb to make their case that the Japanese government was responsible for the bombing and owed them compensation.

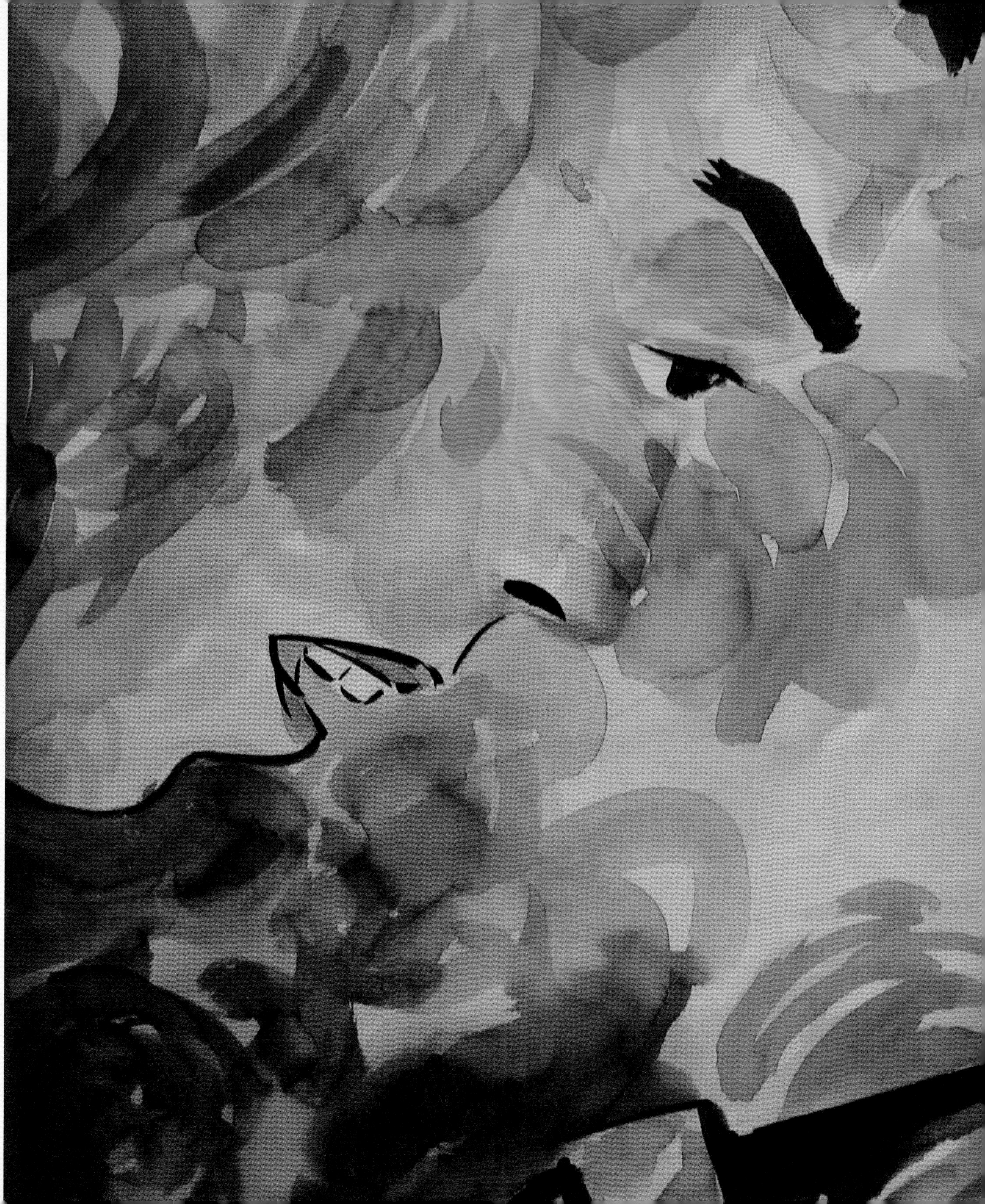

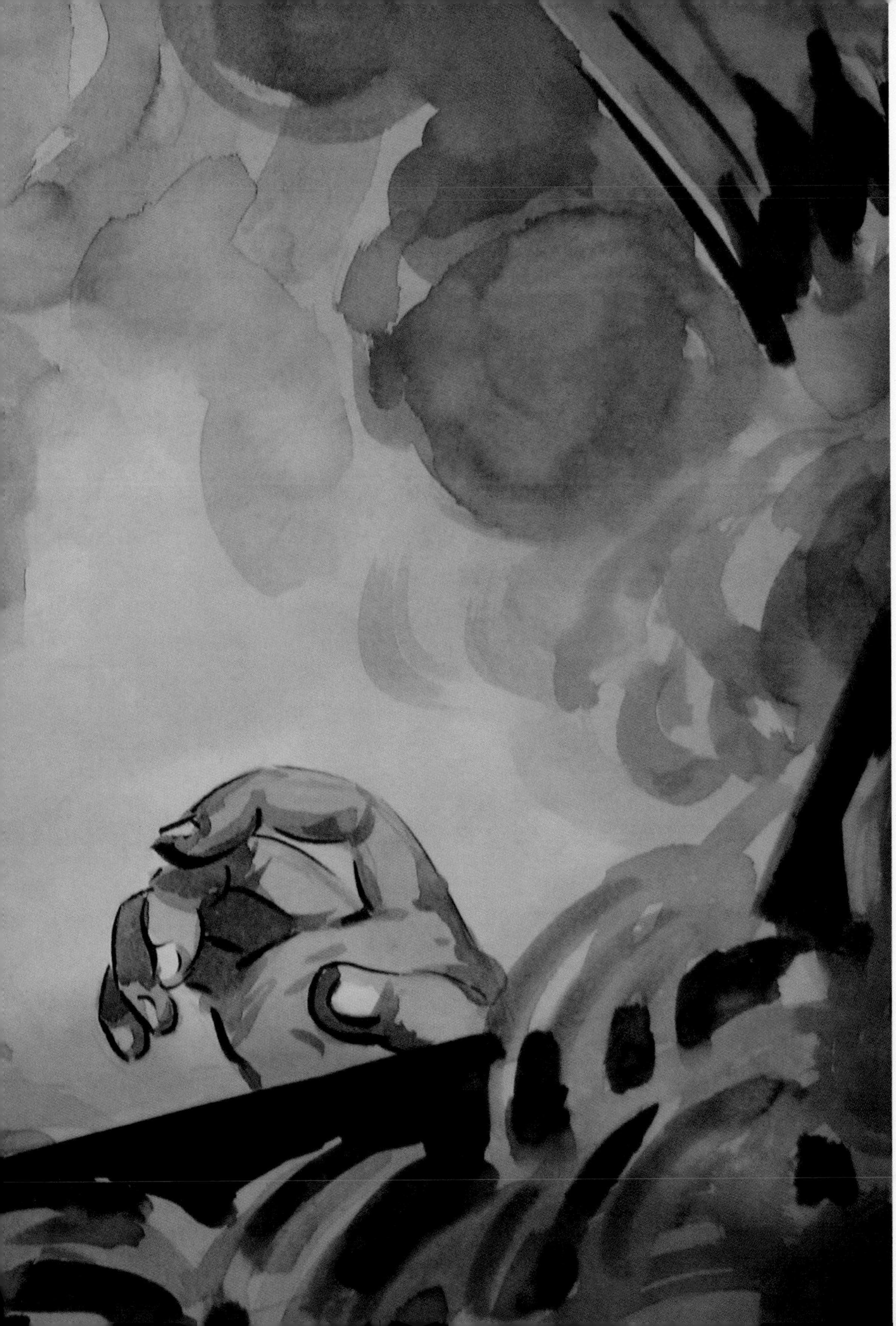

A faint voice pleads, and a ghastly greenish hand emerges from the rubble as the man looks on, unable to help. Most of the burn victims simply asked for water. The hand's chlorotic hue hints at a problem that would become even more frightening than the initial bomb blast: *genbaku sho*, "atomic-bomb disease" (i.e., radiation sickness), whose genetic effects could show up decades later. Survivors of the bomb, known as *hibakusha* (explosion-affected people), were often discriminated against in Japan because of this fear.

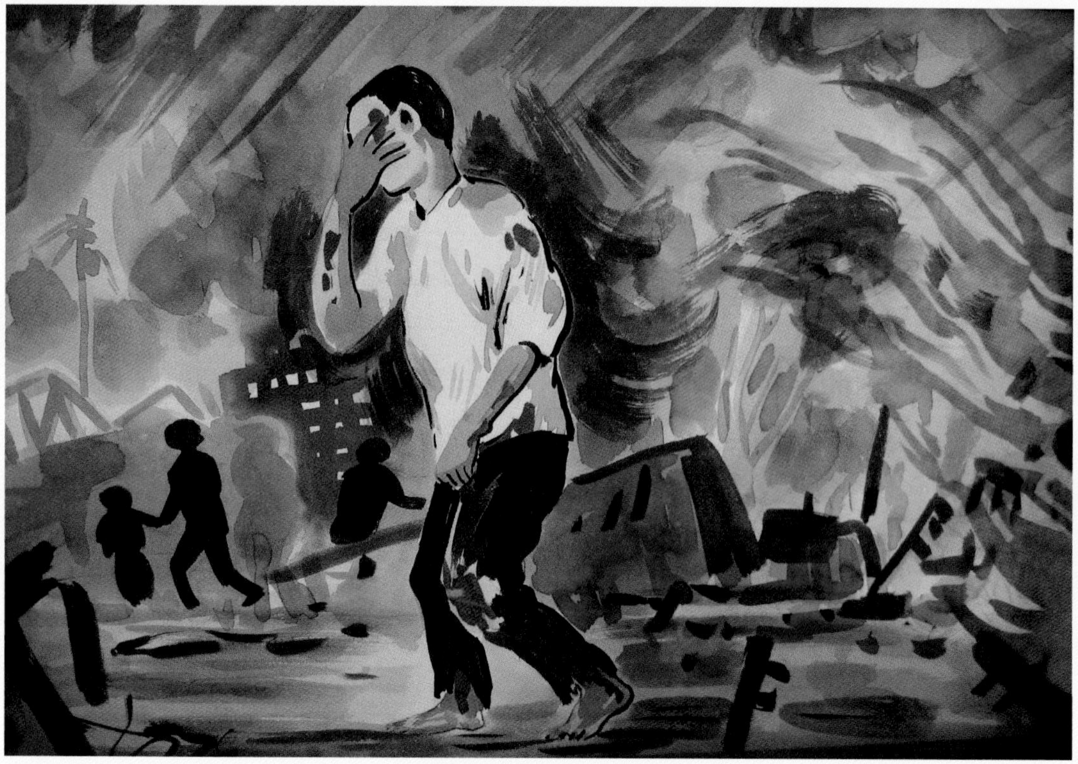

ABOVE Barefoot and bloodied, the man shuffles aimlessly through the silhouetted crowds and shattered buildings. The panel is filled with detail, yet the man is isolated in the foreground. His disorientation is conveyed by his hand covering his face.

RIGHT Burned raw, people emerge in a ghostlike herd from the smoking ruins. This *kamishibai* was meant as an educational tool for children who grew up after the bomb.

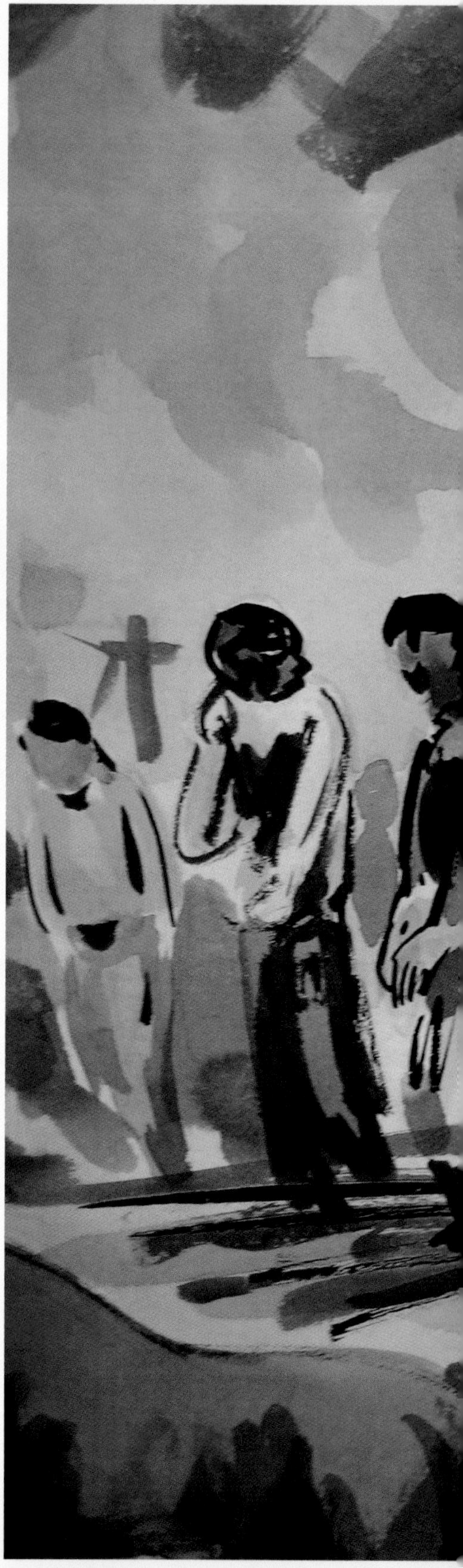

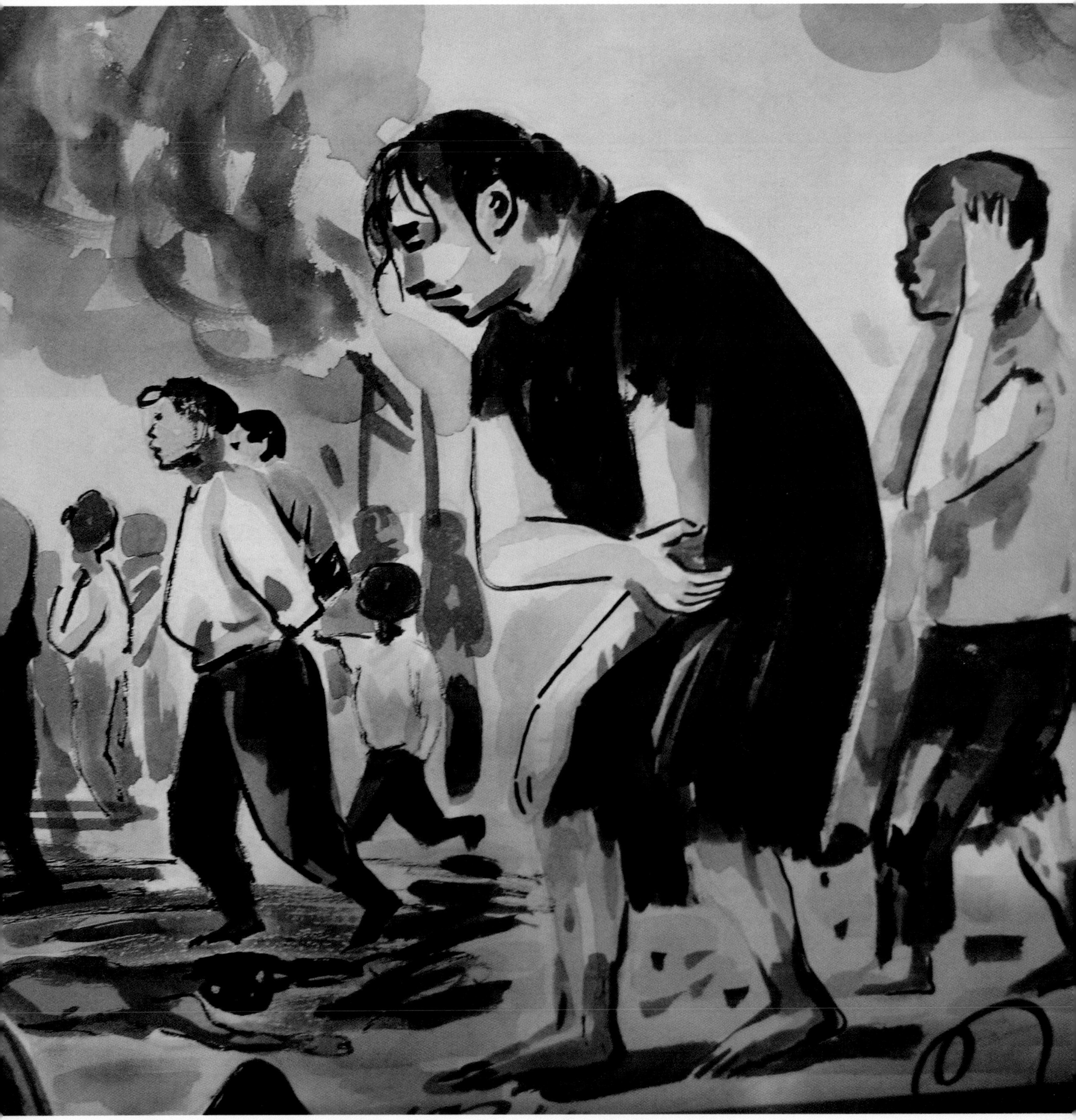

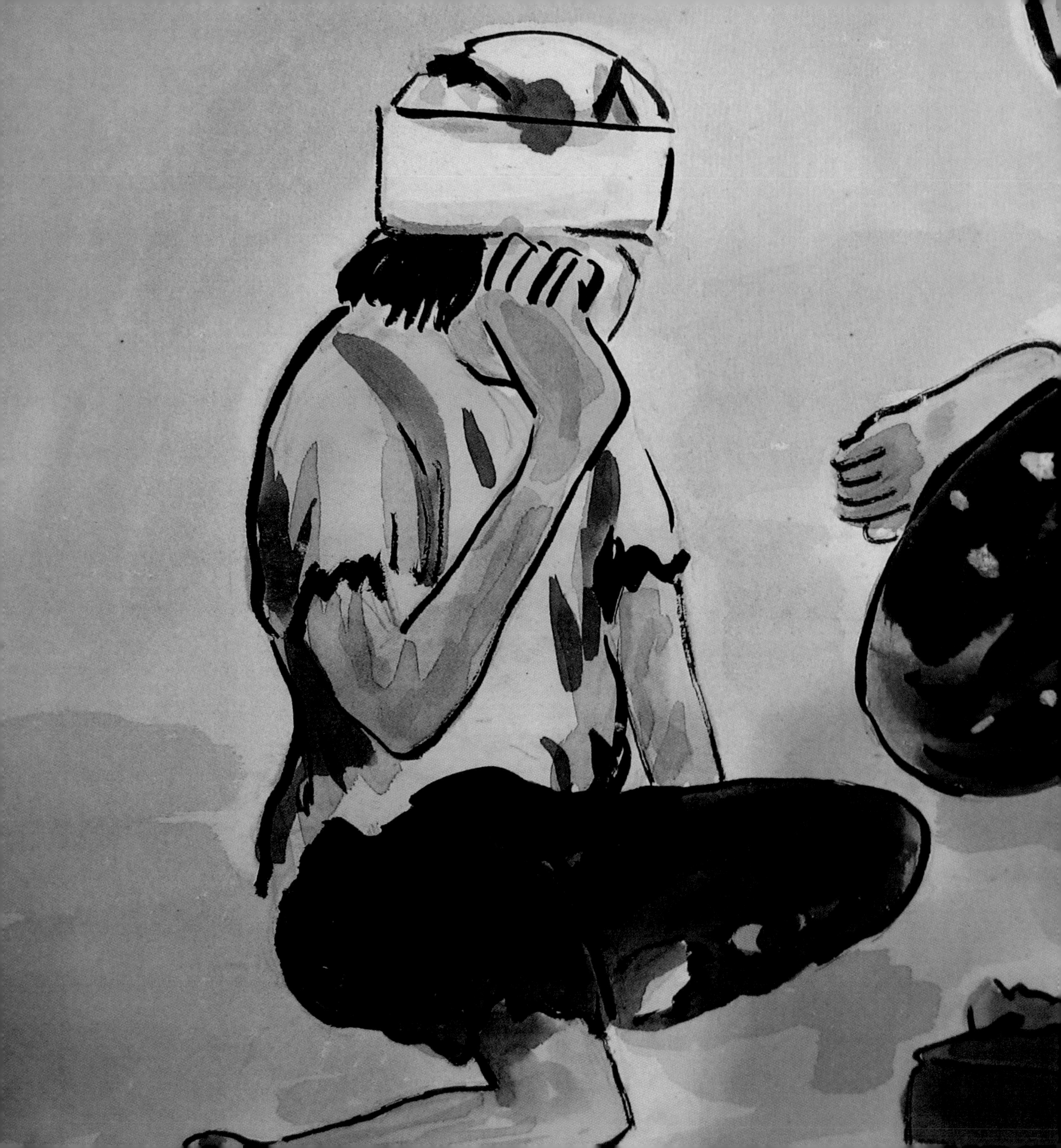

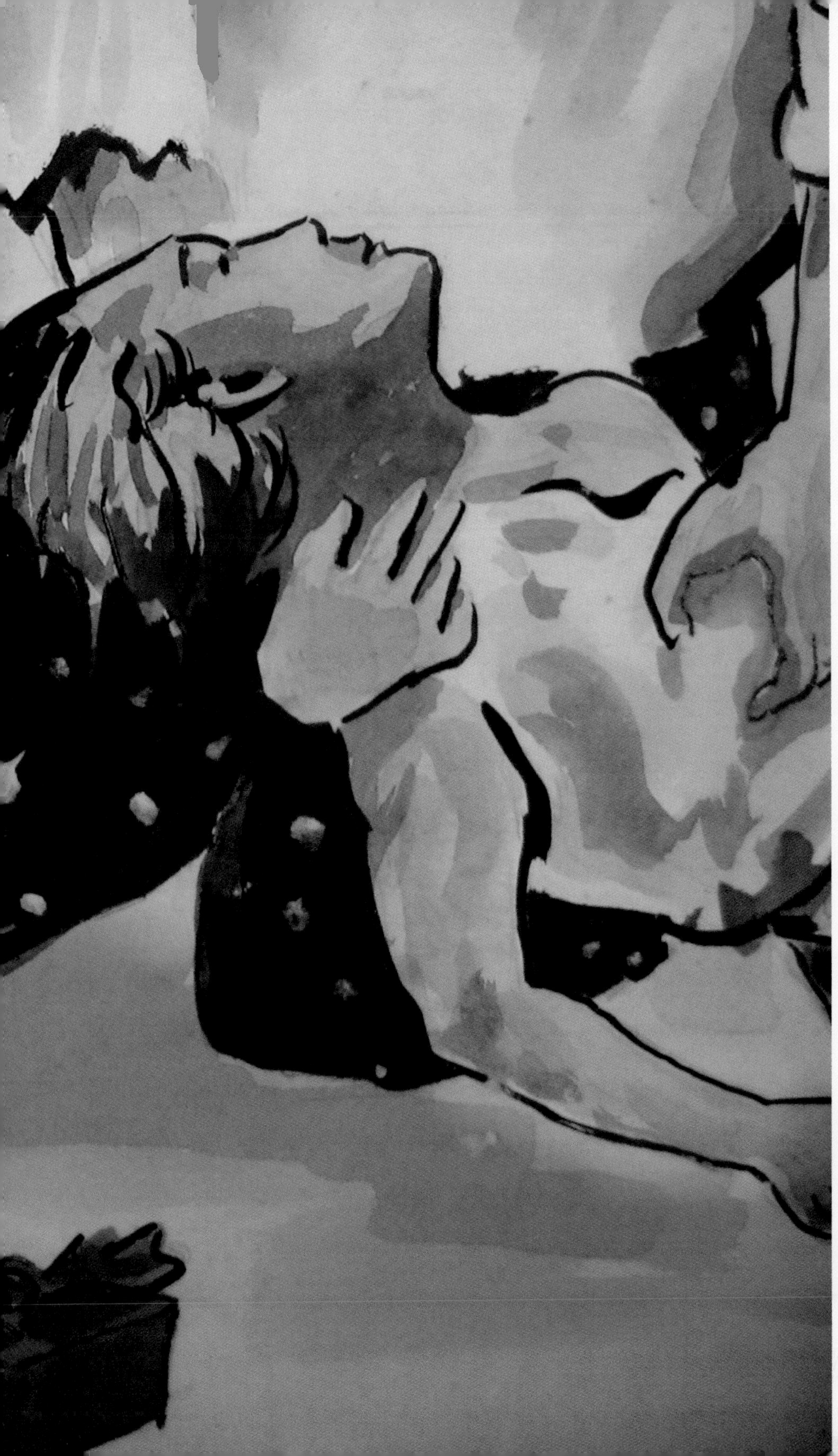

An orphaned girl with a bandaged head weeps as a woman dies in the arms of a stranger. There is a touch of humanity even amid the devastation—the dying woman gives her neatly wrapped *bento* box (wooden lunchbox) to the girl.

Years later, the young woman returns to the site of the Genbaku Dome in Hiroshima, the only structure left standing at the hypocenter of the bomb.

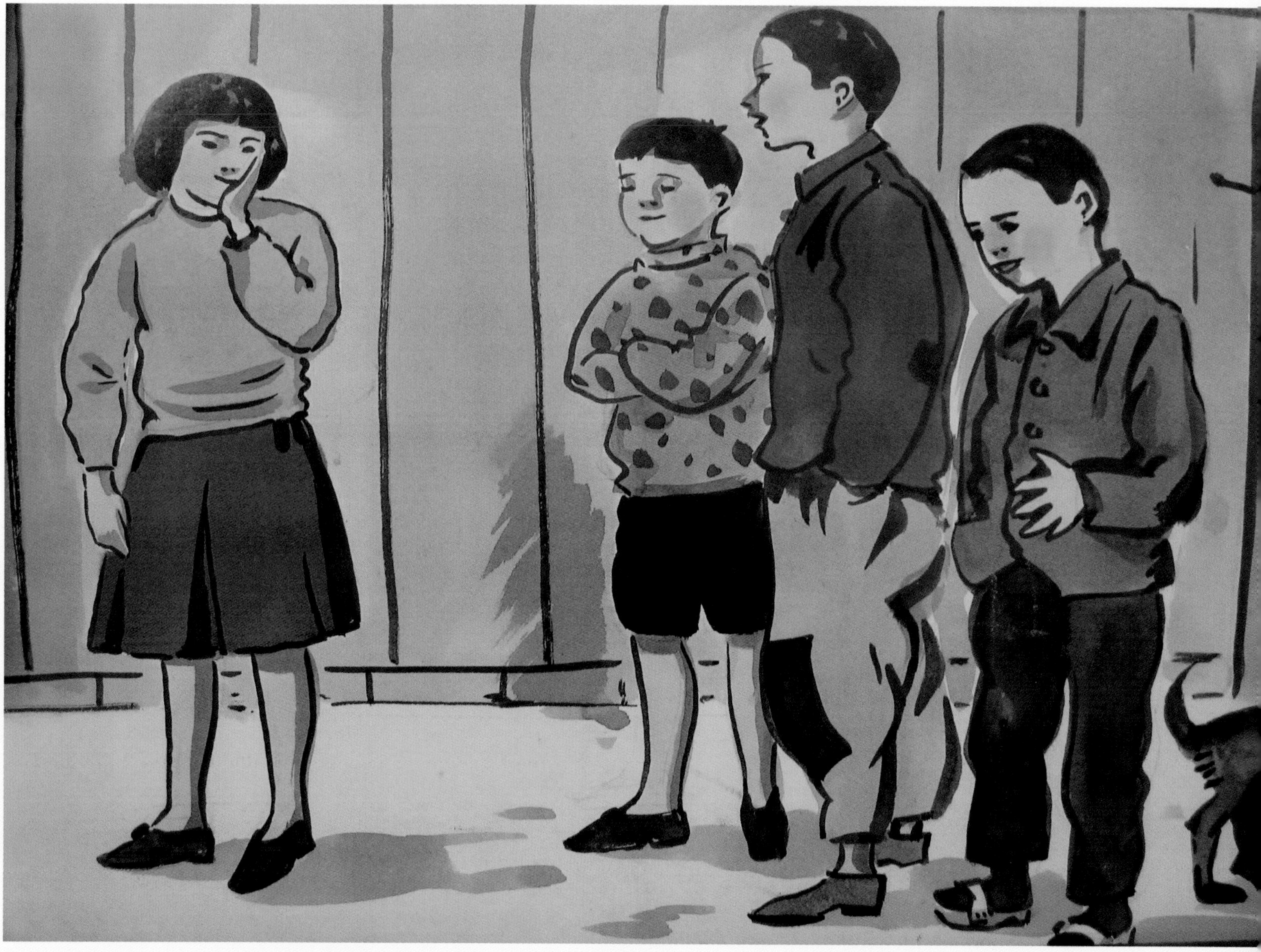

A group of schoolkids who grew up after the bomb taunts the woman, who hides her face in shame. Clearly, this is the prosperous Tokyo of the postoccupation era—the children are well shod and dressed in Western style, and the streets are clean.

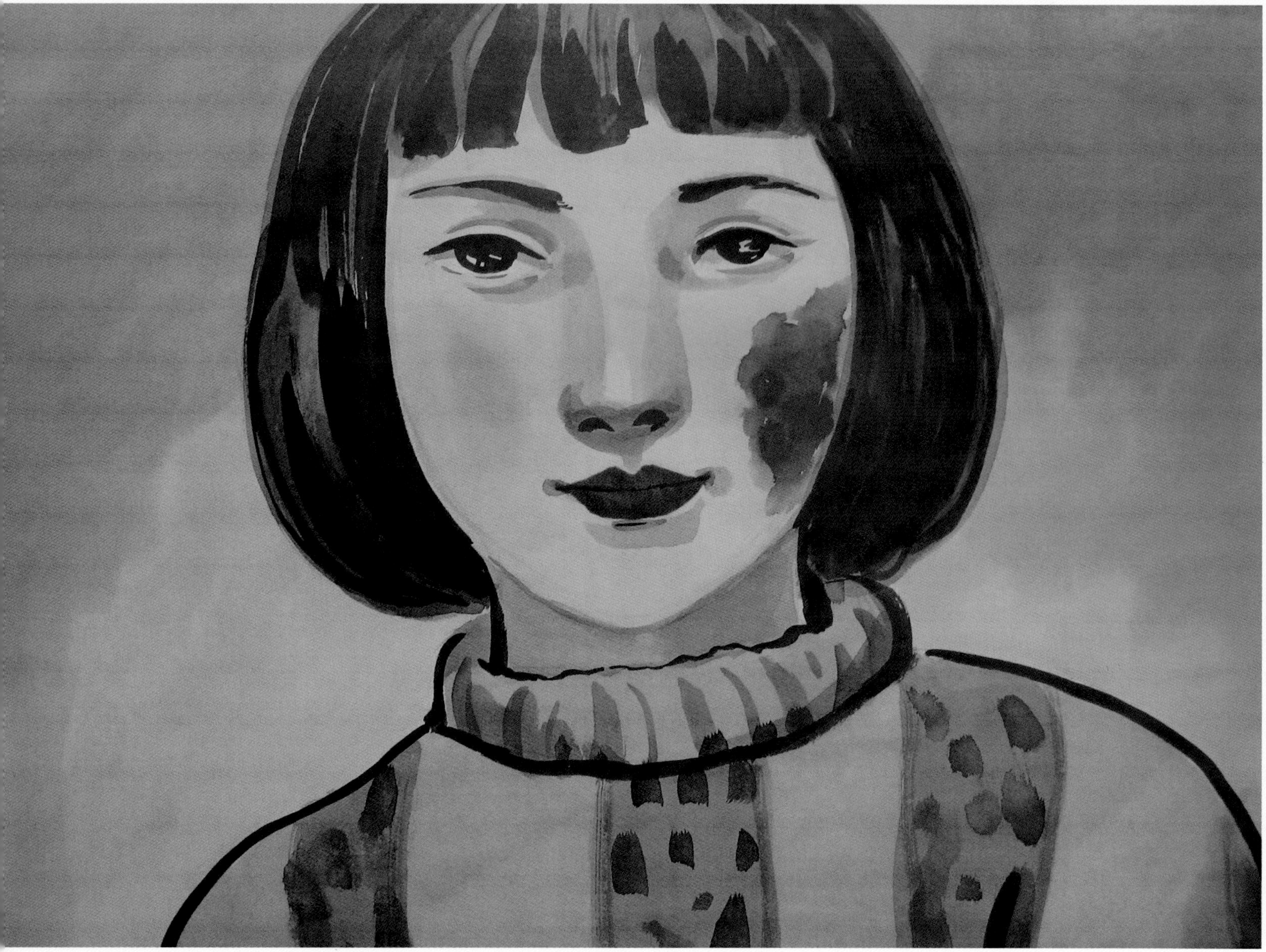

With a calm expression, the woman reveals the keloid radiation scars on her face.

A uniformed middle-school student explains that the woman is a *genbaku no ko*, a child of the bomb, and admonishes them for mocking her—an object lesson for young *kamishibai* viewers.

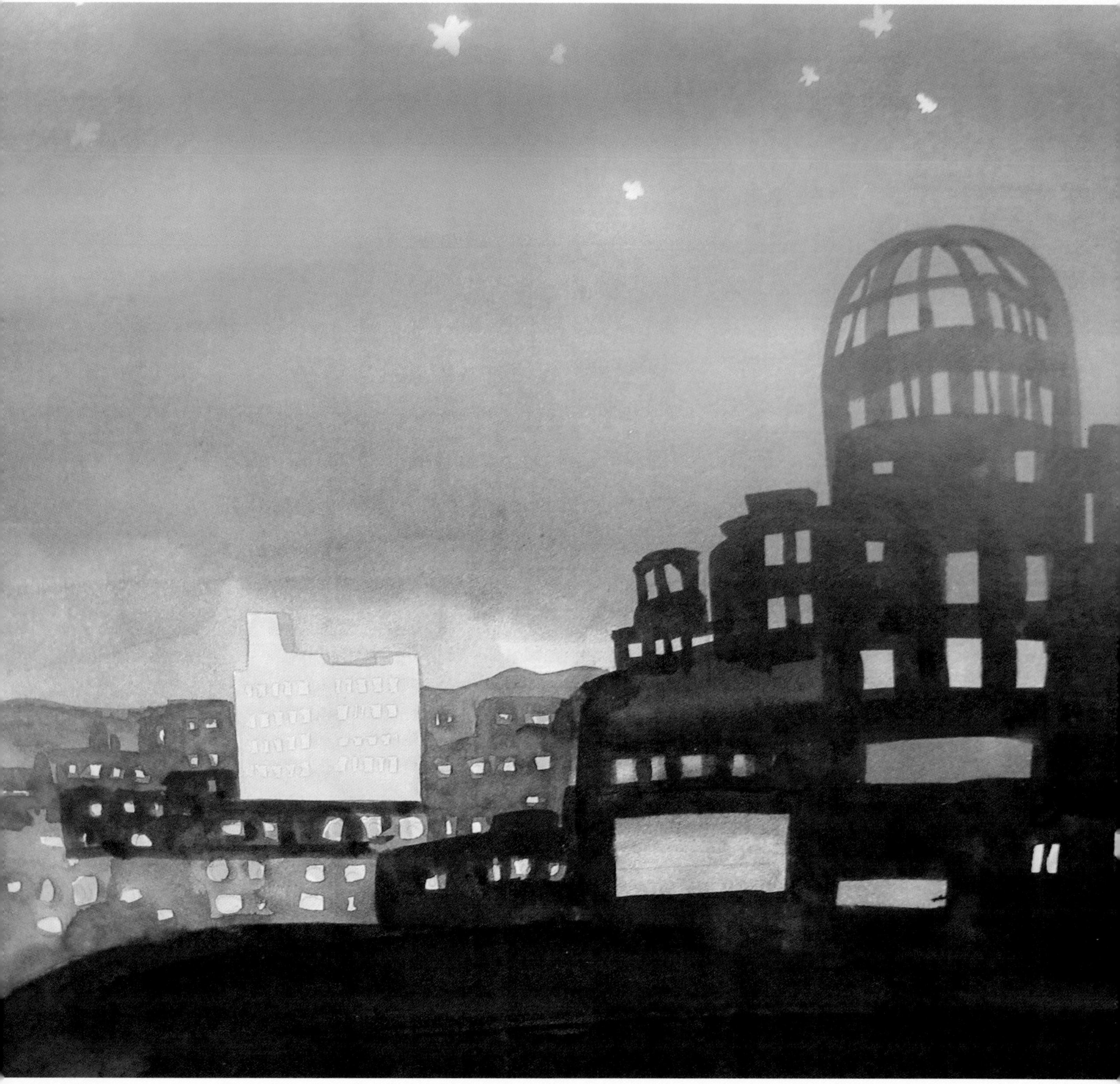

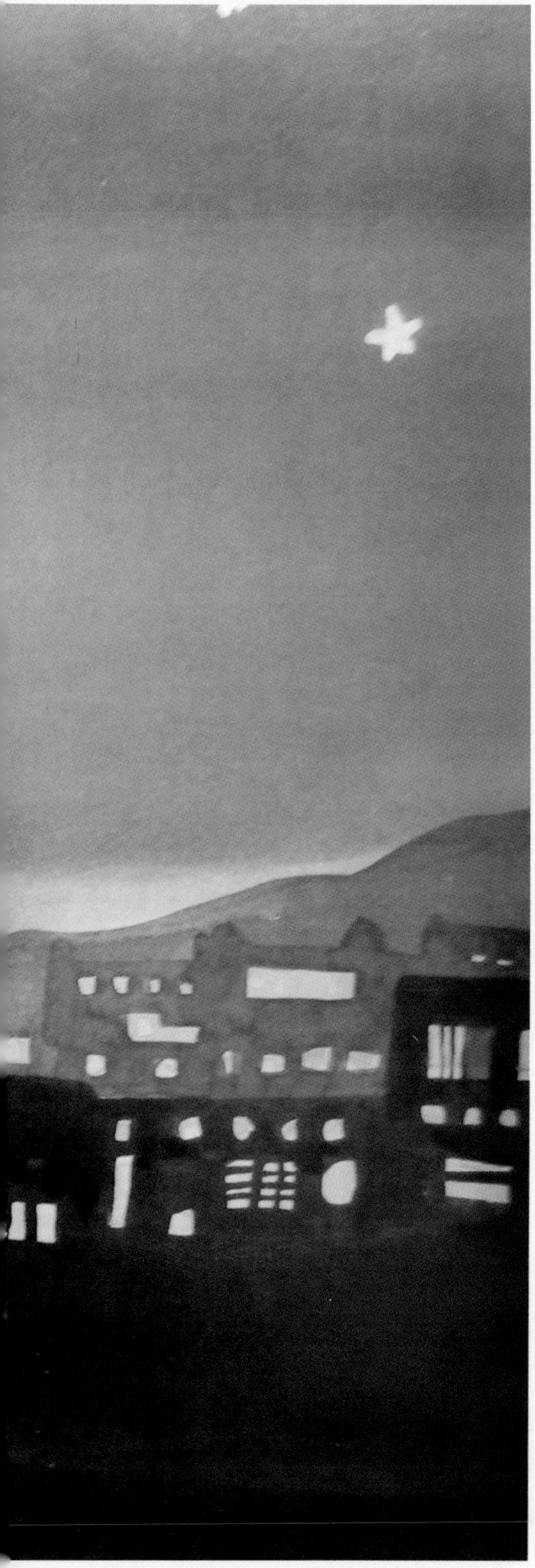

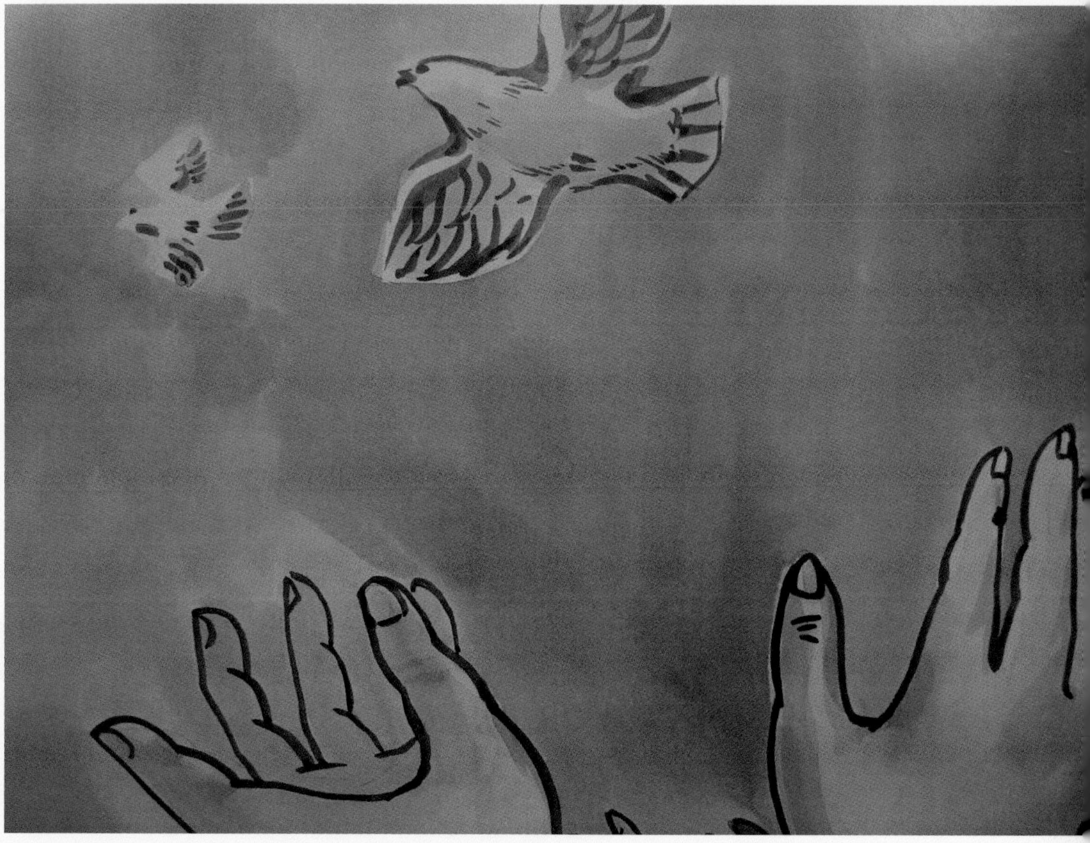

LEFT The skeletal dome stands out against the starry night sky. The lit windows of the city are a sign of renewed hope, but they glow tentatively like fireflies, a Japanese symbol of the transience of life, as seen in Isao Takahata's masterful 1988 anime *Graveyard of the Fireflies*, about an orphaned brother and sister who survive the firebombing of Kobe. Many postwar Japanese stories about the war years are told from the point of view of children, in part to evoke sympathy, but also to avoid the more complicated question of Japanese complicity in causing the war.

ABOVE A pair of hands lets fly a pair of doves in a universal message of peace. As the only people to have survived an atom-bomb attack, the Japanese are involved in the international nuclear disarmament movement.

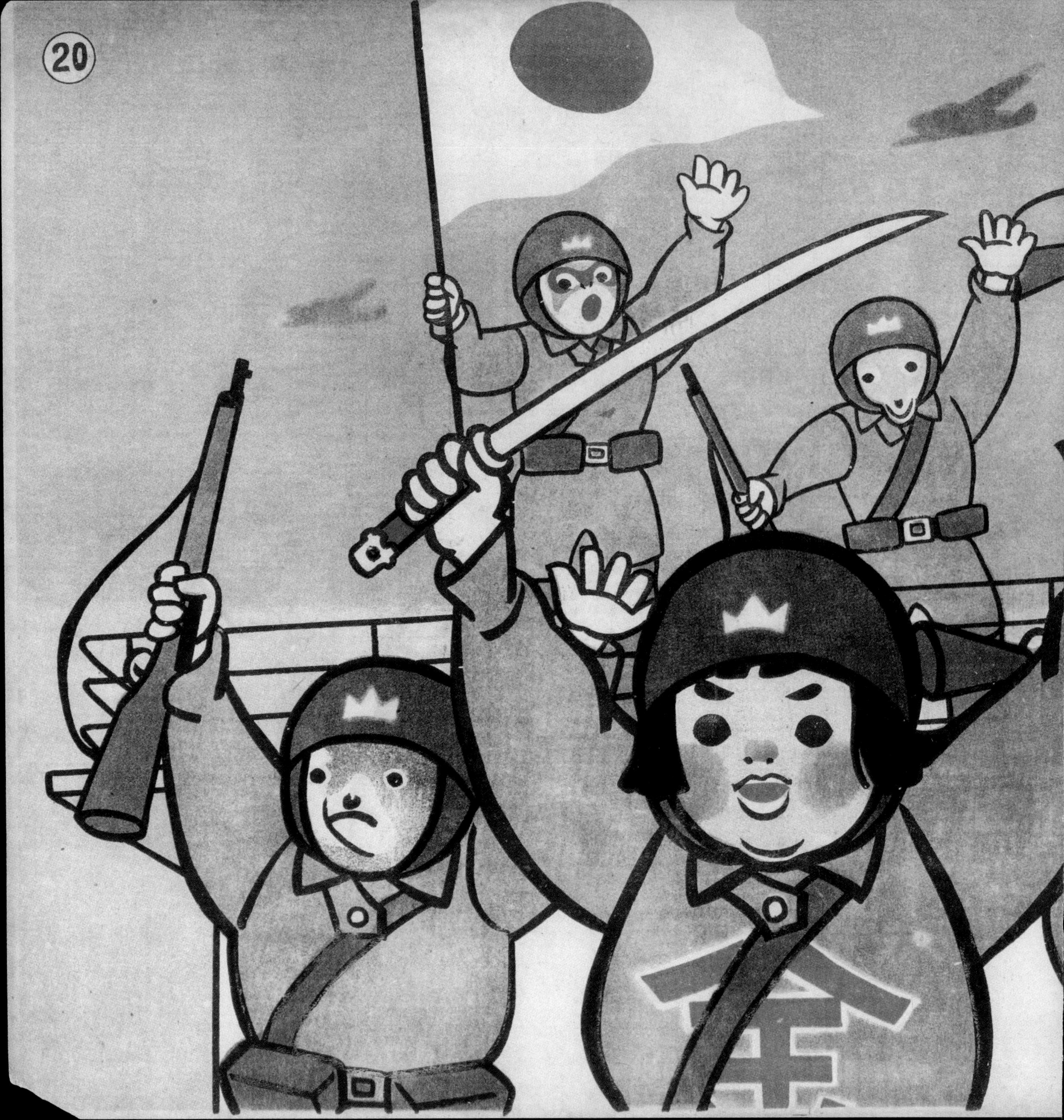
20

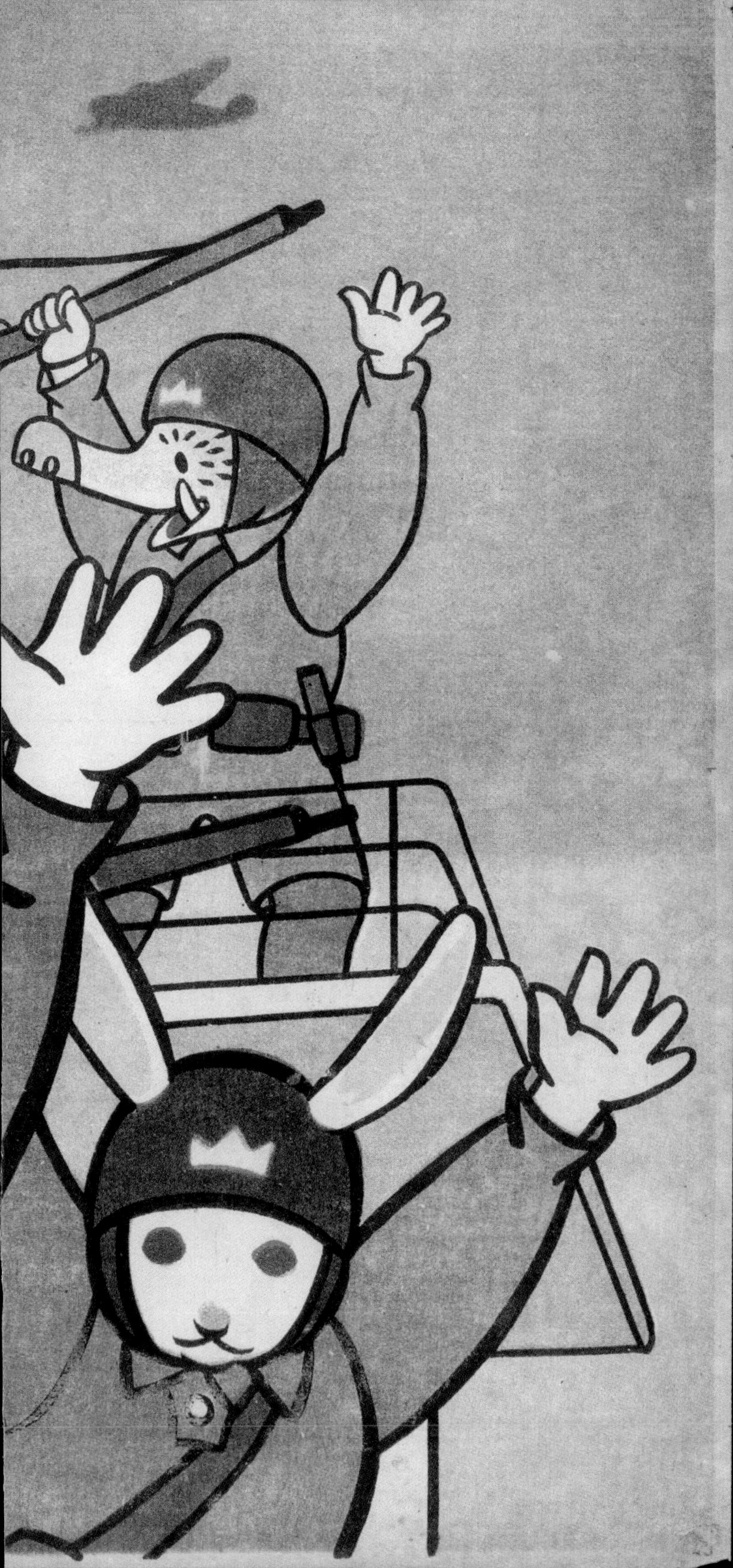

BANZAI FOR BUNNY RABBITS

◂ **Boy Soldier**: Children's *kamishibai* were used for propaganda during World War II.

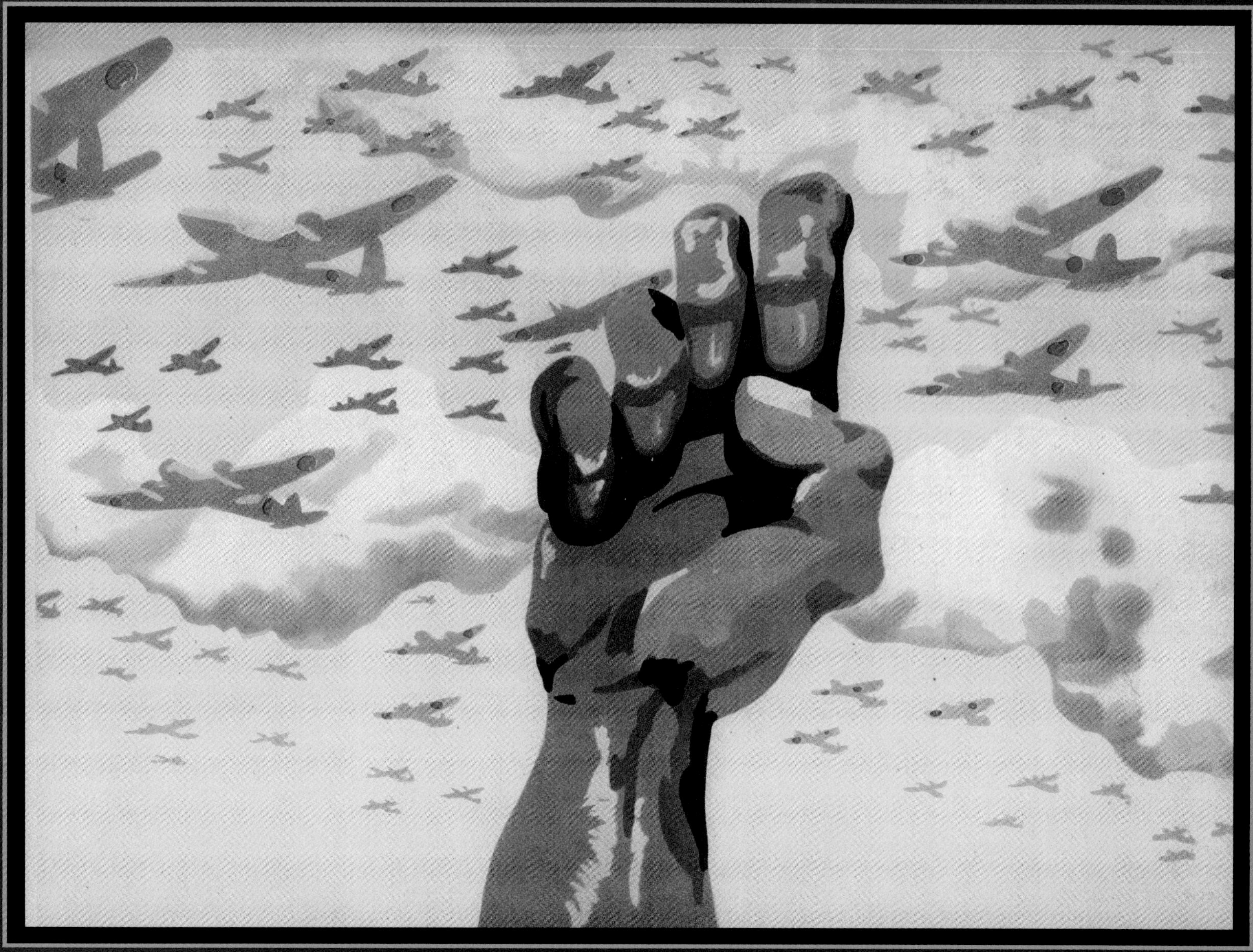

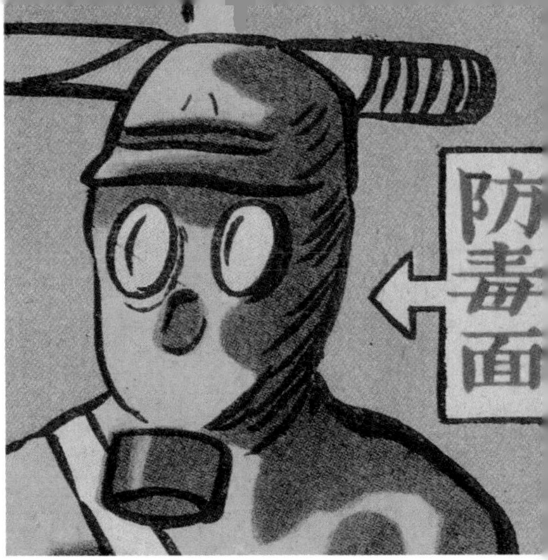
防毒面

At the same time as the crackdown on street-corner *kamishibai* in the mid-1930s, the Japanese government was waging its infamous war on mainland China. Just after the China Incident in 1937, the Home Ministry declared:

> As can be seen recently in drama, musical revues, *manzai* (comedy duos), *raguko* (comedy sketches) and *kamishibai* and other diversions, amusements for the masses are debasing themselves to the lowest common denominator. The actual quality of entertainment is plummeting toward the crude, and social morals are not being heeded. Moreover, while it is true that many of the diversions are treating the China Incident, the content is usually unpolished.

In 1938 Takeo Nagamatsu founded the Educational *Kamishibai* Association, a propaganda wing of the government that produced 450 prowar *kamishibai* works.

Nagamatsu and other *kamishibai* creators were shipped to Manchukuo, the Japanese name for the conquered Chinese state of Manchuria, where they produced propaganda to legitimize the puppet government

Fist of Fury: A vengeful fist set against a sky swarming with Zeroes bearing the red ball insignia on their gray underwings and fuselages demonstrates the persuasive power of *kamishibai* propaganda. The announcer would read from the back of the placard: "It's time for us ten million Japanese to take up our weapons!"

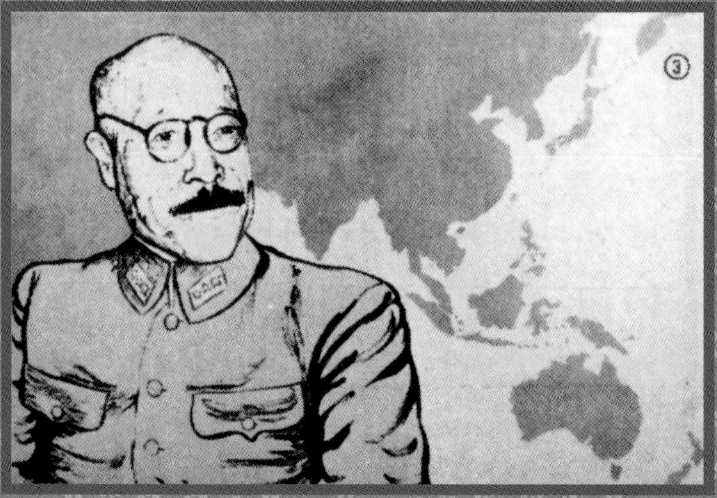
③

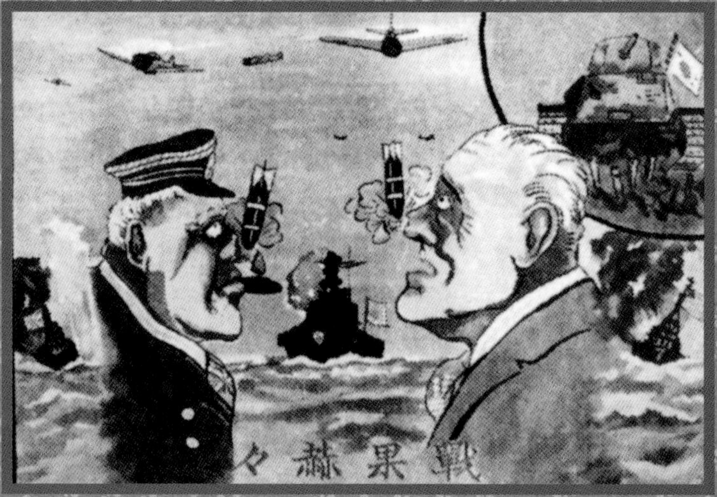
戰果赫々

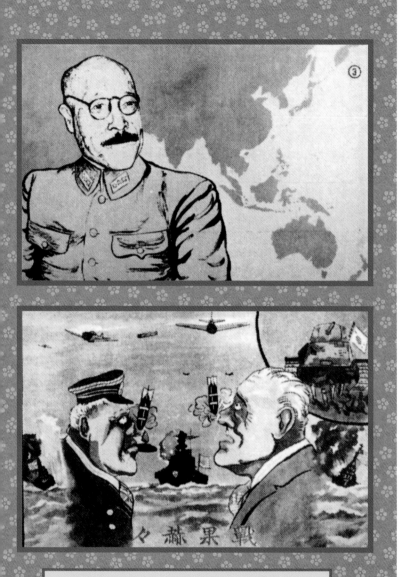

Nightly News: *Kamishibai* during wartime often functioned as a news source for a populace too poor to afford radio. Real photos were printed, like this one of Prime Minister Hideki Tojo superimposed over the Empire of Japan. Realistic airplanes and battleships are victorious over caricatures of Churchill and Roosevelt.

manipulated by Japan, with Pu Yi, China's last emperor, as figurehead. Once suppressed by local governments, *kamishibai* now became an arm of the state. Under the aegis of the Imperial army public relations department, *kamishibai* like *Peaceful Savior* were published in Japanese and Chinese to promote pacification. For Japanese enlisted men in occupied areas, *kamishibai* like *Babies and Soldiers*, about army life in the colonies, were performed for capacity crowds in huge theaters.

Kokusaku (war-boostering) *kamishibai* served to lift morale and entertain troops at the front, to instruct conquered civilian populations in China and Southeast Asia in Japanese ways, and to be an informal news network for a home-front population too poor to afford radio or newspapers. During the Sino-Japanese War, *kamishibai* functioned on the home front as a poor man's evening news, with actual photographs from the Asahi news service pasted into the miniature prosceniums. Later *kamishibai* featured photographs of Prime Minister Tojo and caustic caricatures of Roosevelt and Churchill.

War crimes like the atrocities committed in the Rape of Nanking in 1937, when three hundred thousand Chinese civilians within the ancient walled city were raped and brutally dispatched, were censored in favor of sympathetic portrayals of a young cadet's self-sacrifice in Manchukuo in the 1941 *kamishibai Distinguished Service with Tears*. *Kokusaku kamishibai* encouraged those on the home front to support their fighting men, featuring stories about Japanese history and legendary

heroes as well as news about the war and world events. The Japan National Culture Association was founded in 1941 with a *kamishibai* branch, whose mission was to send professional *kamishibai* men into remote prefectures to train local performers. Particular emphasis was placed on tales of youth dying violent but beautiful deaths for their country, like the ten soldiers sent to Pearl Harbor on suicide missions in two-man submarines. The essence of the *kokusaku kamishibai* message was group sacrifice, so the medium of a shared group experience was powerfully persuasive.

Kamishibai experts often speak of *kyokan*, the formation of a unified group mind that audiences experience as the world of the story envelops

Figures of Speech: British prime minister Winston Churchill and U.S. president Franklin D. Roosevelt were targets of satire in *kamishibai* and political cartoons, often portrayed as decadent old men or horned demons. Roosevelt's promise was fulfilled: "We shall carry the attack to the enemy. We shall hit him and hit him again, wherever and whenever we can reach him, for we intend to bring this battle back to him on his own homeground."

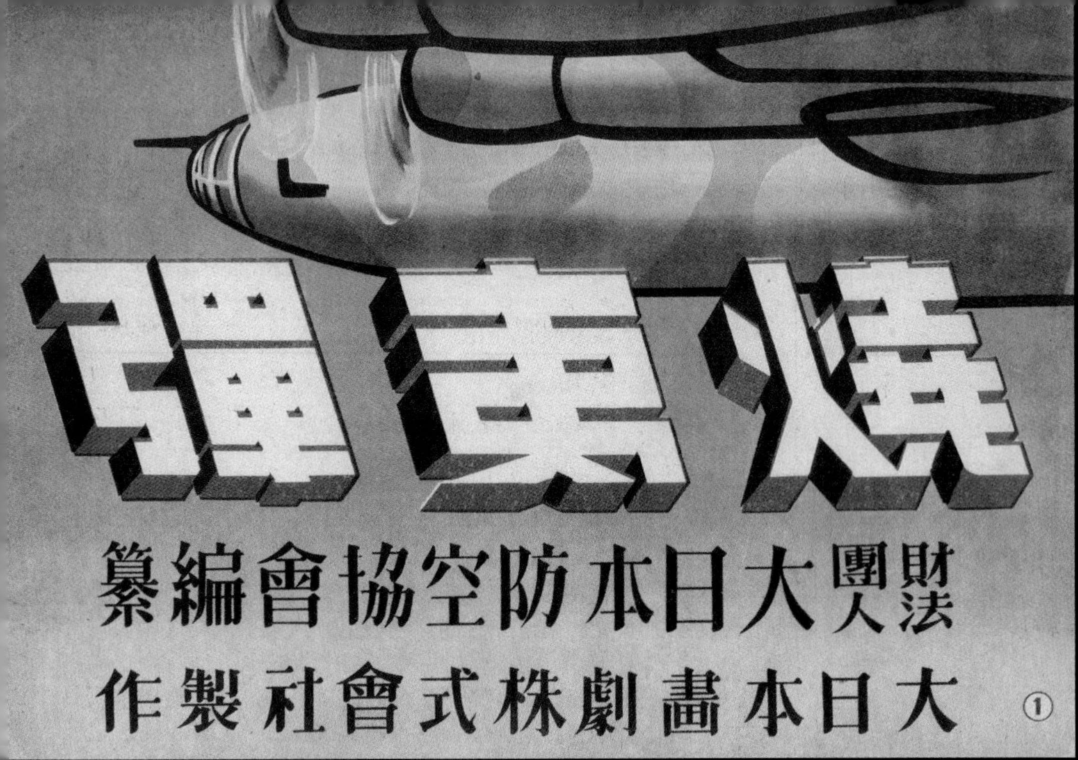
燒夷彈
財團法人大日本防空協會編纂
大日本畫劇株式會社製作
①

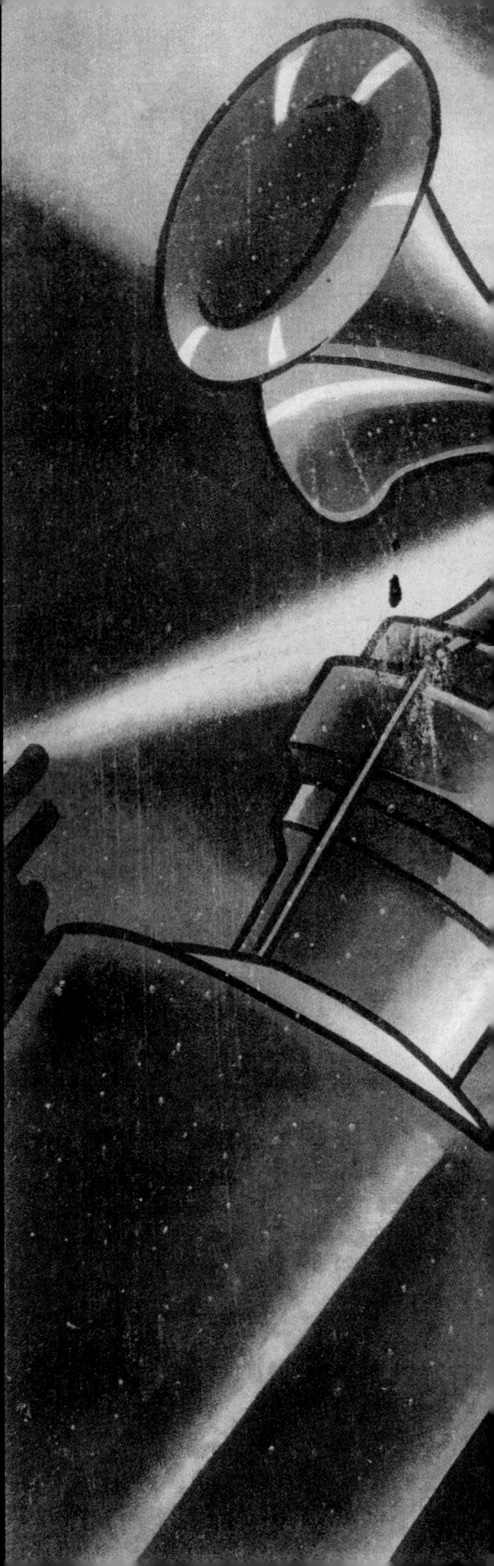

Electronic Incendiary Bomb: English words written in Japanese letters are used to describe the mechanism of this fire bomb. American B-29s flew low-altitude nighttime saturation bombing raids with incendiary bombs. Napalm, a form of gelled petroleum that stuck like lava to the victim's skin and burned even in water, was developed at Harvard in 1942 and first used on Japanese civilians.

Air-raid sirens wail as searchlights lance through the skies over the blacked-out city to herald another predawn bombing raid. The skewed perspective and strong diagonals

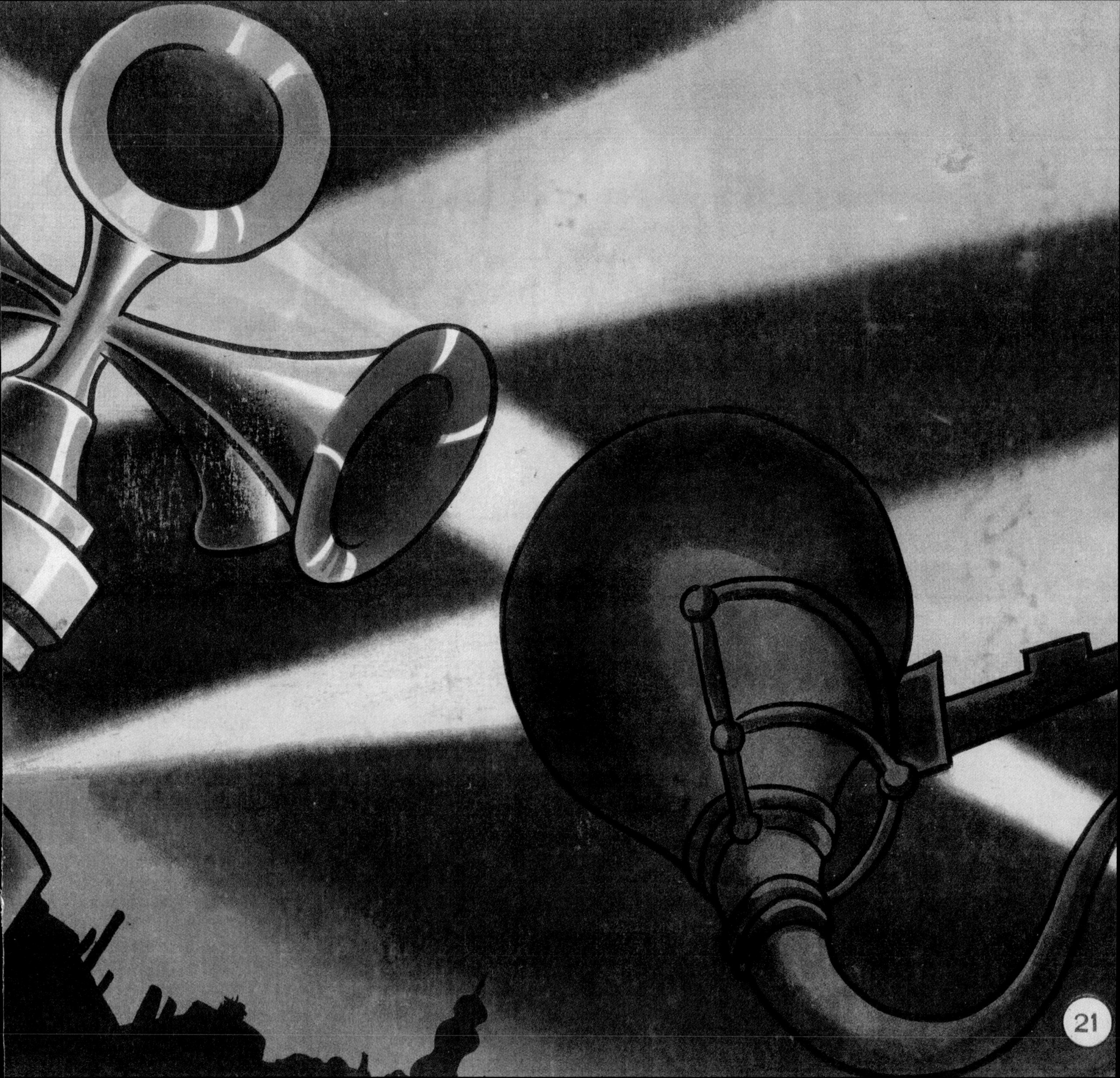

them, much the way an audience absorbs the live performance of a play or a concert. Kyokan helped make *kamishibai* an effective propaganda tool.

Some Chinese audiences found *kamishibai* childish, but Japanese authorities felt it was essential in unnerving members of the Chinese guerilla underground who saw the consequences of opposition to the Japanese. Like the notorious Tokyo Rose broadcasts aimed at the homesickness of U.S. troops during World War II, *kamishibai* extolled the pleasures of life if only the population surrendered. In 1939 the Japanese colonial government in Taiwan banned traditional Chinese puppet shows, when they were found lampooning the military rulers. Puppet shows were replaced with *kamishibai*, which the government had once tried to ban at home.

Demand for *kokusaku kamishibai* increased with the entry of the United States into the Pacific War following Pearl Harbor on December 7, 1941. Funding was provided by the Asahi Shimbun to churn out *kokusaku kamishibai* on flimsy, war-rationed paper. The numbers are staggering: In 1943, when paper production was placed under government control, 830,000 *kamishibai* copies were printed. One especially popular series *Gunshin no Haha* (*Mother of a Fallen Hero*), written by a woman, Noriko Suzuki, struck at the core psychical connection in Japanese society and was seen by more than 18 million people, even in the hinterlands of the island empire.

Kamishibai were wildly popular on the home front at munitions factories, schools, and army bases. Titles of the time include *Bravery and Sadness* and *Chocolate and Soldiers*, the latter is the story of a soldier who sends his wife and children a chocolate bar from the front and then dies in combat. His son says, "Now Dad's at Yasukuni Shrine," dedicated to the fallen. The last scene is at a beach where the family used to play. Government regulations required that stories be told exactly according to the script rather than ad-libbed, as early *kamishibai* were. Final placards of fists raised in victory or defiance attest to the propaganda power of *kamishibai*.

Kokusaku kamishibai are a sometimes shocking window into the Japanese view of the Pacific

Defend the Home Front: A boldly graphic banner was designed to inspire patriotism and sacrifice.

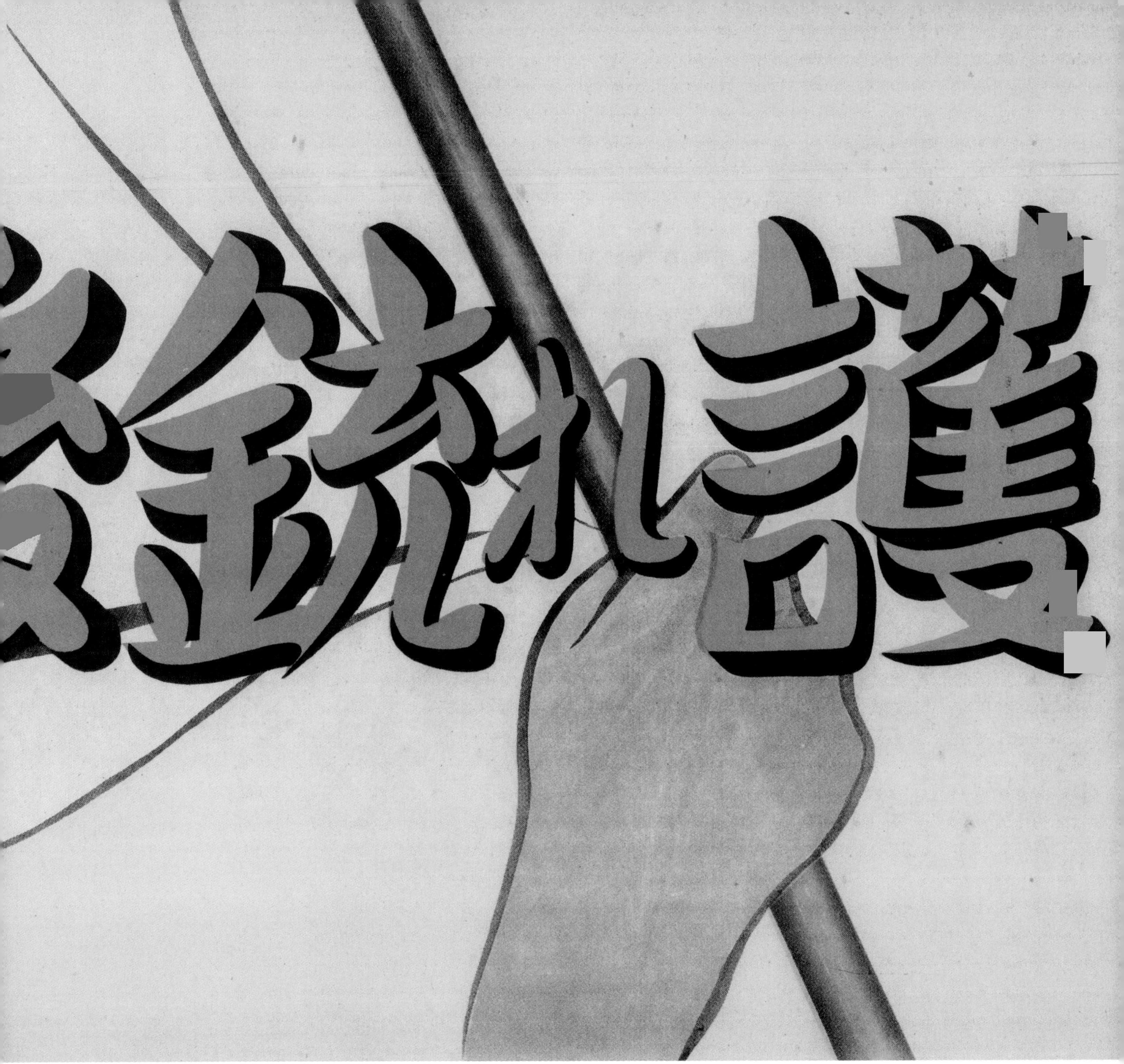

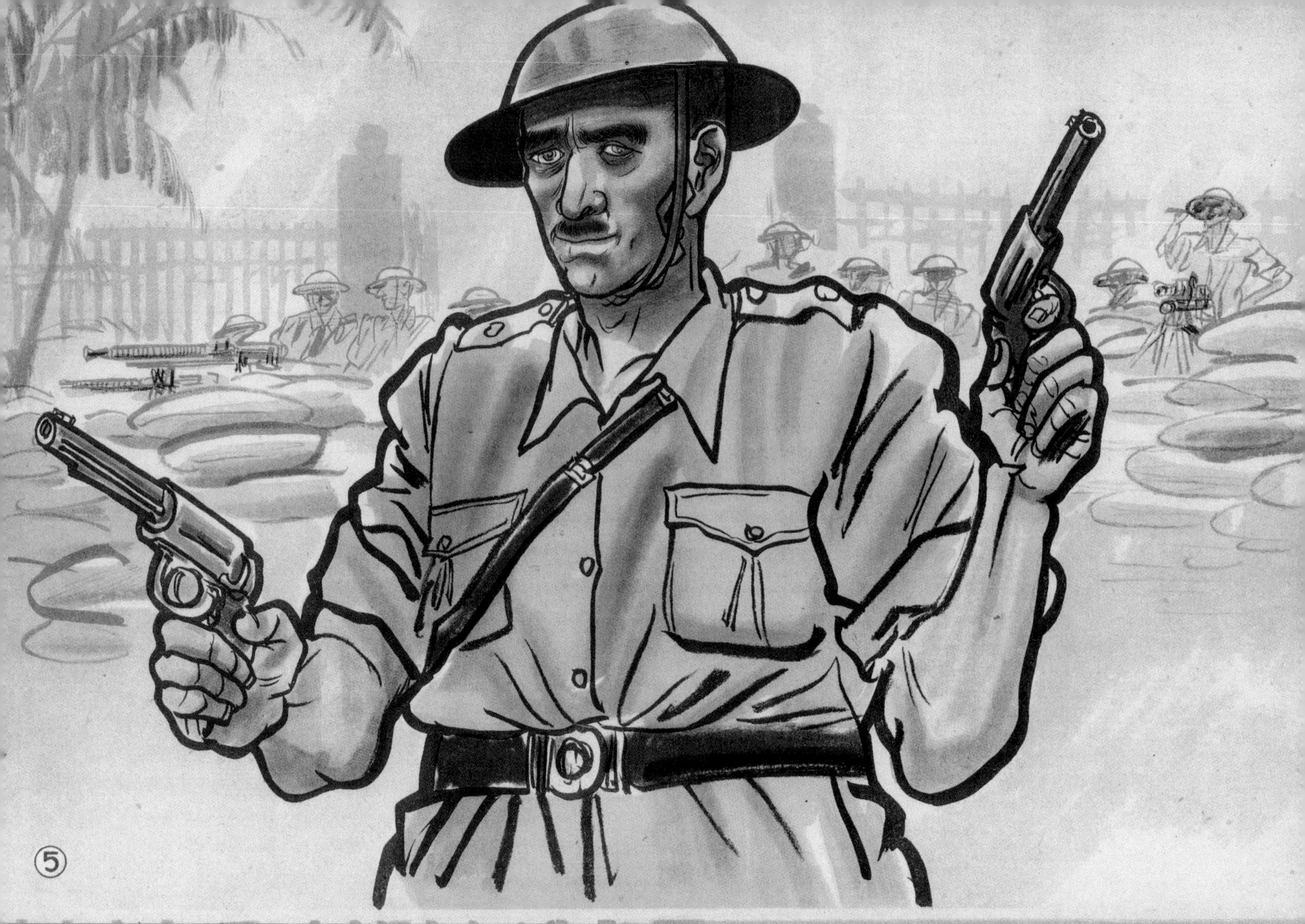

ABOVE **Red-Faced Sadist**: Japanese and American propaganda were reflections of each other in funhouse mirrors. Just as Japanese officers were depicted as sadists by the Allies, this image is a fascinating insight into the Japanese point of view. A gangly, gorillalike American officer with a red face and cruel blue eyes brandishes two pistols. He is wearing a World War I doughboy "soup-plate" helmet, worn by some U.S. troops through 1942.

OPPOSITE, TOP **Through the Looking Glass**: In this cautionary tale about the consequences of being captured by the Americans, Japanese civilian POWs toil in the noonday sun, a reverse view of conditions where Allied POWs were starved, tortured, and executed.

OPPOSITE, BOTTOM **Tied to the Whipping Pole**: Gloating American soldiers flay an innocent civilian. During the war, much was made of Japanese torture of prisoners. An image like this was used to counteract perceptions and justify harsh treatment of Allied captives. At the same time, it instilled a dread of being captured by the Americans, so that Japanese soldiers would choose death over capture.

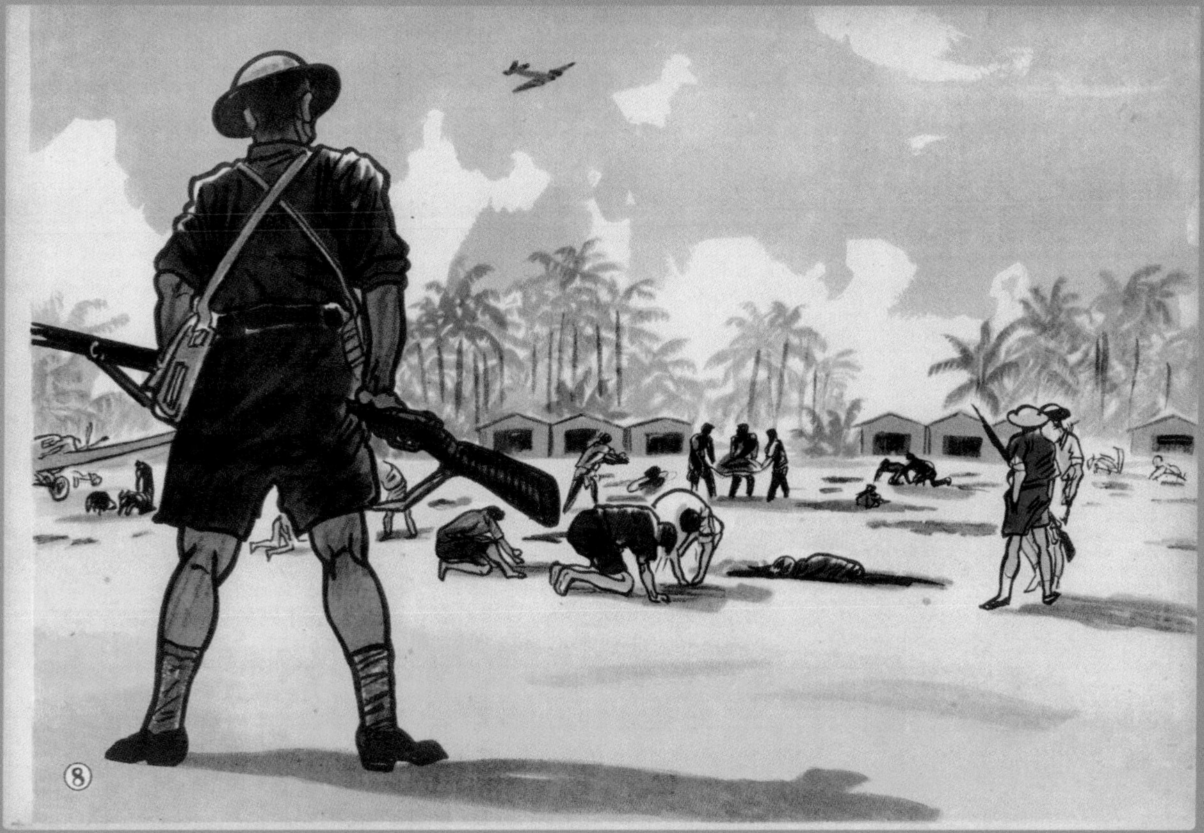
⑧

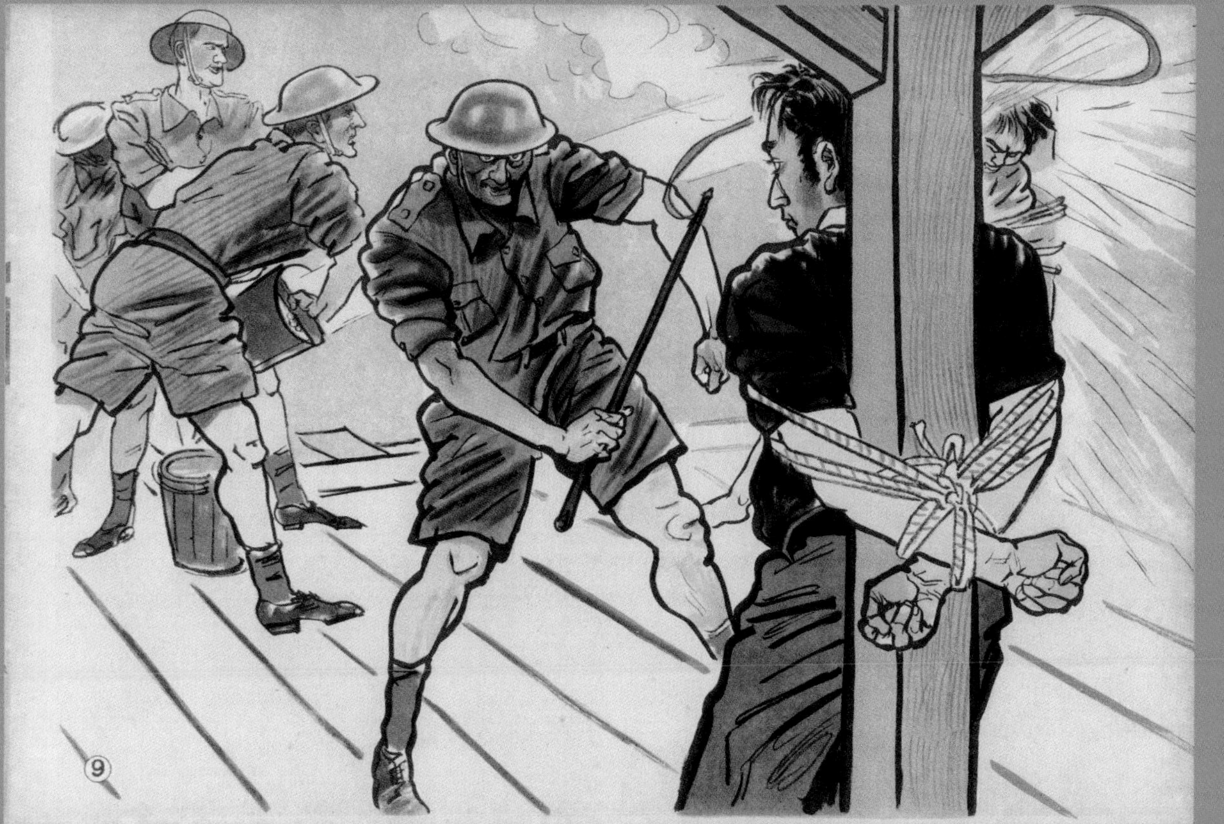
⑨

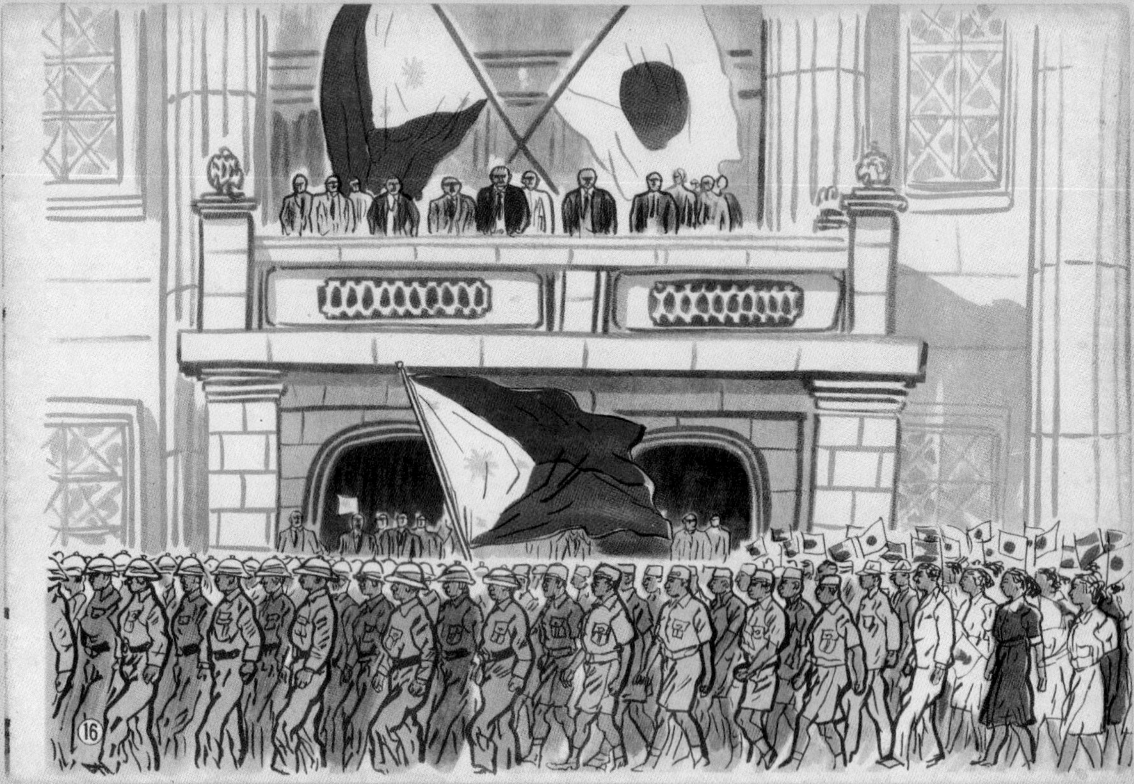
16

RIGHT **Marching Through Manila**: The Philippines fell to the Japanese in a weeklong battle ending February 15, 1942. This scene depicts the victory march through Manila, beneath the nations' paired flags (the Philippine flag is flown with the blue field on top in times of peace, and the red field on top in times of war). Japanese forces claimed to be liberating countries from colonial rule under the banner of "Asia for the Asiatics" but turned out to be much harsher masters. In a month-long rampage ending March 3, 1945, Japanese soldiers randomly killed one hundred thousand residents of Manila, or one in ten.

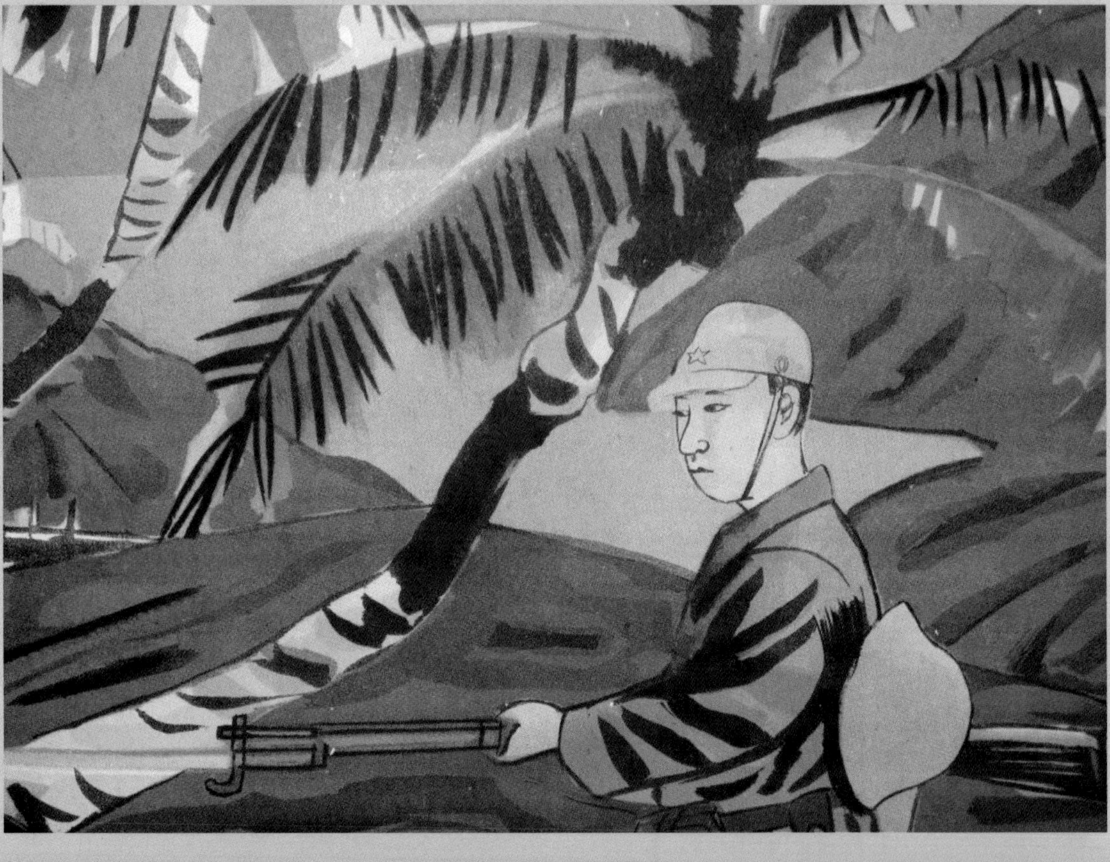

LEFT **Lightning War**: A foot soldier patrols with a bayonet under the jungle canopy as the Japanese Imperial Army advances on the capital city, low on the horizon against the Bay of Manila. As in the Nazi blitzkrieg, the Imperial Japanese Army rolled up lightning victories in Singapore, Hong Kong, the Philippines, Indonesia, and Burma. The Japanese invaded Malaya by bicycle. After the pivotal battle of Midway in June 1942 and the months-long campaign of Guadalcanal in 1943, Japanese forces were on the defensive.

OPPOSITE **Palm Reading**: A highly stylized palm tree in this detail shows how the jungle foliage is delineated in simple, bold strokes with a collagelike technique of abstract patches of color.

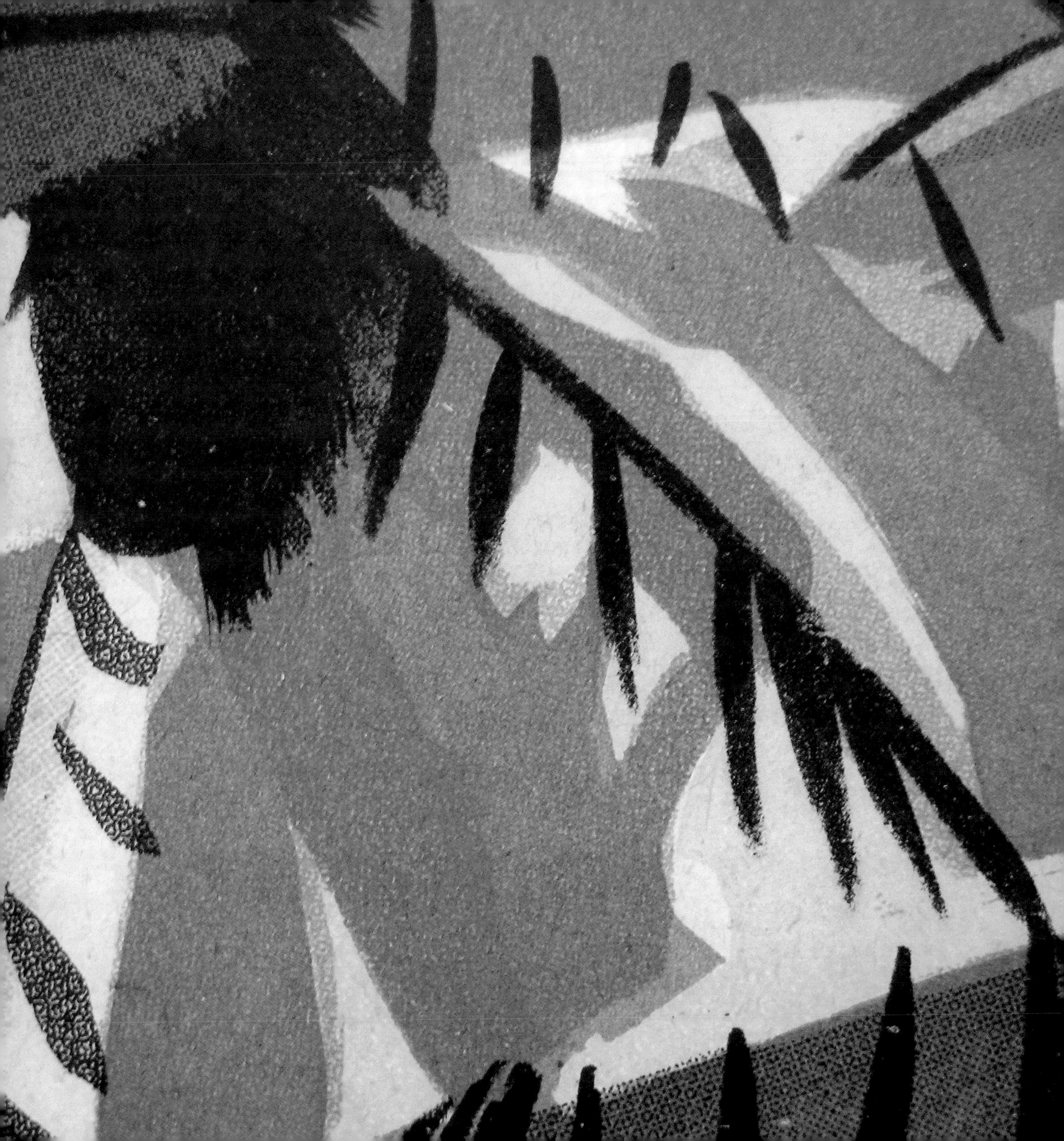

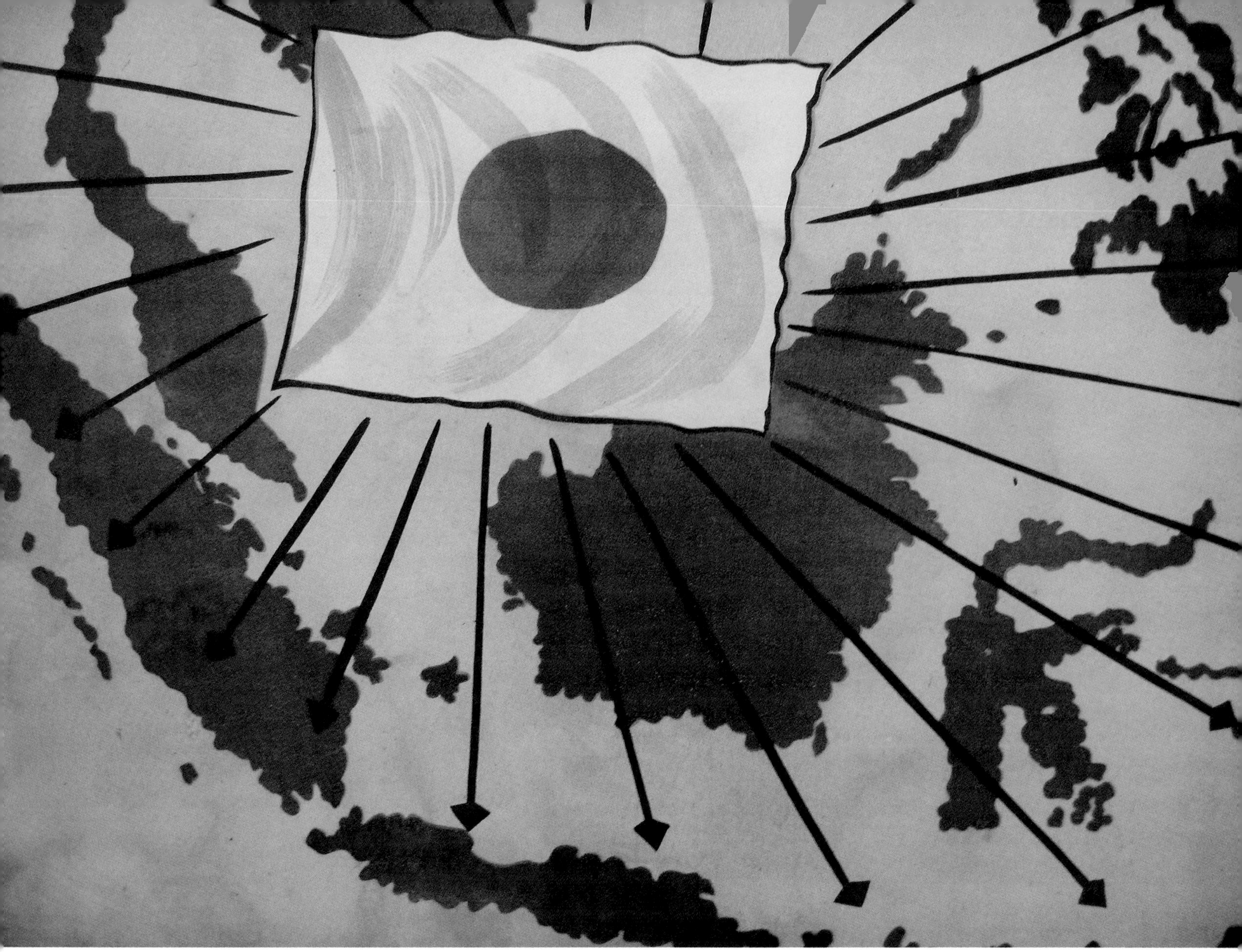

theater of war. Americans and Japanese regarded each other in distorted funhouse mirrors. American GIs are portrayed as red-faced sadists. An American officer's cruel blue eyes gleam as he brandishes two pistols. Japanese POWs collapse in the midday sun, only to be tied to a cross and whipped.

Fevered *kamishibai* images from Imperial Japan record the glorious conquest of Singapore in 1942, and depict the dreaded rising-sun flag of the

Under a Red Sun: The dreaded flag of the rising sun extends over conquered territories, the large island of Borneo in the center, beyond the equator to the Netherlands Antilles. At its zenith, the Empire of the Sun spanned one sixteenth of the globe's surface.

Hitler Salute: In this fever dream of propaganda, Hitler stands atop a giant black falcon under the Nazi flag. Curiously, Hitler is portrayed with a handlebar mustache rather than his trademark toothbrush bristle. The handlebar mustache had been shorthand for portraying Anglo-Saxons ever since Commander Matthew Perry's gunboats opened Japan to the West in 1854, after centuries of isolation.

Greater East Asia Co-Prosperity Sphere extending its tentacles over all of the island Pacific. Hitler is shown standing atop a giant flying eagle bearing a swastika. (Standing on an eagle's back is also Golden Mask's preferred means of transportation.) Curiously, Hitler's trademark toothbrush moustache resembles that of a nineteenth-century gentleman, like a member of Admiral Perry's crew, who opened Japan to the West in 1854.

The Japanese perspective emphasizes the heroism, humanity, and sacrifice of the common soldier. In one drawing, a bandaged Japanese soldier plays a melancholy air on a *shakuhachi* (wooden flute) in a field hospital. Another panel shows Japanese troops trampling on the American flag. The *kamishibai Scratched in Stone* reveals a doomed unit's last sentiments etched into the side of a boulder: Long Live the Emperor.

Japanese propaganda, including *kamishibai*, portrayed fighting men as following the ancient samurai code of *Bushido* that valued loyalty, courage, and death before dishonor. In one panel soldiers on the deck of a carrier ship practice *kendo*, the art of fighting with *bokken* (wooden swords), in

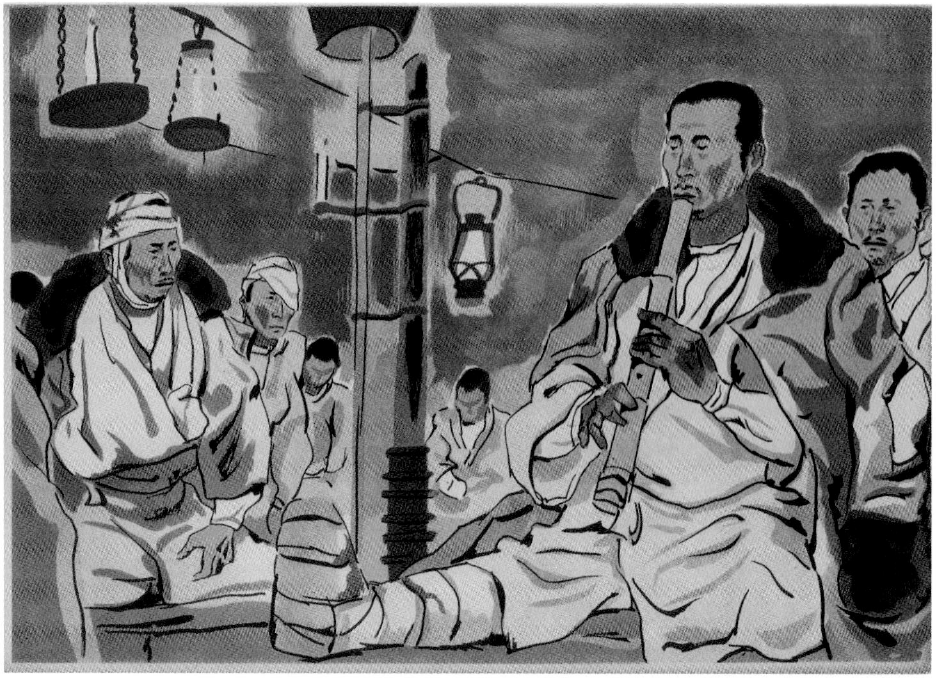

Hors de Combat: A wounded soldier in a field hospital plays a mournful tune on a *shakuhachi* wooden flute as his fellow soldiers think of family and home. As the tide of war in the Pacific turned against Japan, the focus was increasingly on the courage of the doomed warriors. Soldiers were shown dying a glorious death in service of country, like samurai of old. Modern historians have written that soldiers were equally motivated by a sense of collective shame about failure.

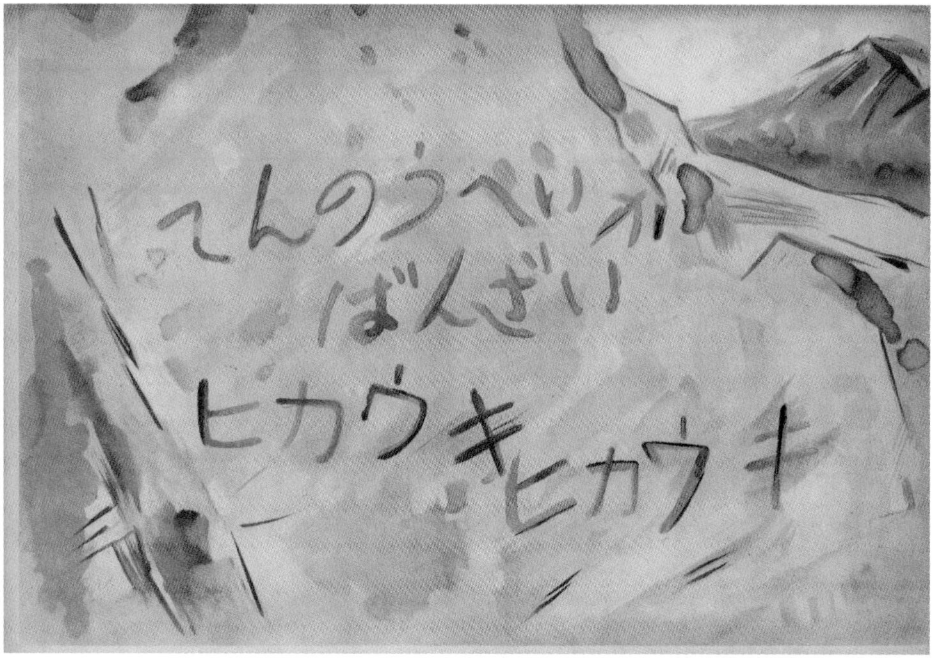
てんのうへい
ばんざい
ヒカウキ
ヒカウキ

Scratched Letters: An air crew leaves its dying message scratched into a rock face—"Long Live the Emperor"—in this 1943 *kokusaku kamishibai* by Shigeru Nonoguchi. By the time U.S. Marines landed on Iwo Jima and Okinawa, Japanese soldiers were falling on their own grenades rather than face surrender.

traditional protective gear. *Kokusaku kamishibai* feature scenes of bloody hand-to-hand combat, where Japanese soldiers wield traditional bladed weapons of *katana* (Japanese swords) and bayonets, like twentieth-century samurai. A romantic kamikaze cadet inspired by *Yamato damashii* (the spirit of Japan) gazes at Mount Fuji as he prepares to fall like a cherry blossom for his country. The sway of Bushido in Japanese society was a primary reason why General Douglas MacArthur as Supreme Commander of the Allied Pacific (SCAP) banned presentations of historical stories in the postwar occupation period. The man and the office of SCAP were indistinguishable.

Under the Volcano: Inspired by Yamato *damashii*, the spirit of Yamato, the ancient name for Japan, a romantic cadet gazes at Mount Fuji in the mist for the last time. Young soldiers were indoctrinated to lay down their lives in service of their country, like samurai whose lives were said to be as transient as cherry blossoms dropping from a tree. Under the spell of patriotism, young recruits were shipped off by the trainload to a sea of cheering crowds waving miniature rising-sun flags. While movie-mad America watched War Department–approved propaganda films about the efficacy of the Norton Bombsight and endless production lines of Flying Fortresses like *Air Force* (1943) with John Garfield (100 million people, two-thirds of the population, went to the movies weekly), Japanese audiences subsisted on cheaper fare.

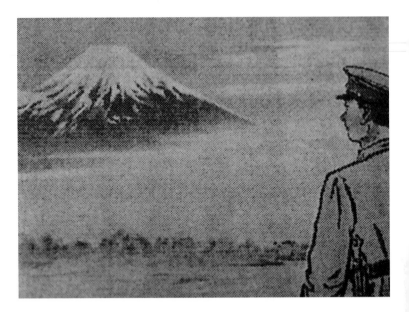

Although 70 percent of *kokusaku kamishibai* was directed at adults, there were also war stories for children. One juvenile *kamishibai* in primary colors featured the adventures of a canine corps as they carry messages between units under mortar fire. One dog has his wounds dressed like a soldier and is given a hero's *banzai* (a cheer or salute meaning "may you live 10,000 years") as he holds an Imperial flag in his mouth. *Kintaro the Paratrooper*, one of the most surreal examples in a country known for the efficacy of its *Tokko* (thought police), combines folktales and propaganda in the story of the boy soldier Kintaro, who bears a strong resemblance to the traditional folk hero Momotaro (Peach Boy), in modern military dress. *Momotaro* is the tale of a boy samurai miraculously born from a peach, who defends the homeland from marauding demons with the help of a dog, a monkey, and a pheasant. Kintaro parachutes from an airplane alongside his comrades rabbit, fox, and boar. The multispecies commandos defeat enemy tanks with flamethrowers and grenades, and then celebrate with a cry of "Banzai!" The breakdown of panels is remarkably faithful to a documentary-style *kamishibai* about paratroopers, down to the details of their webbed parachute packs as they huddle in the cargo bay, then leap free of the airplane. The graphic impact of

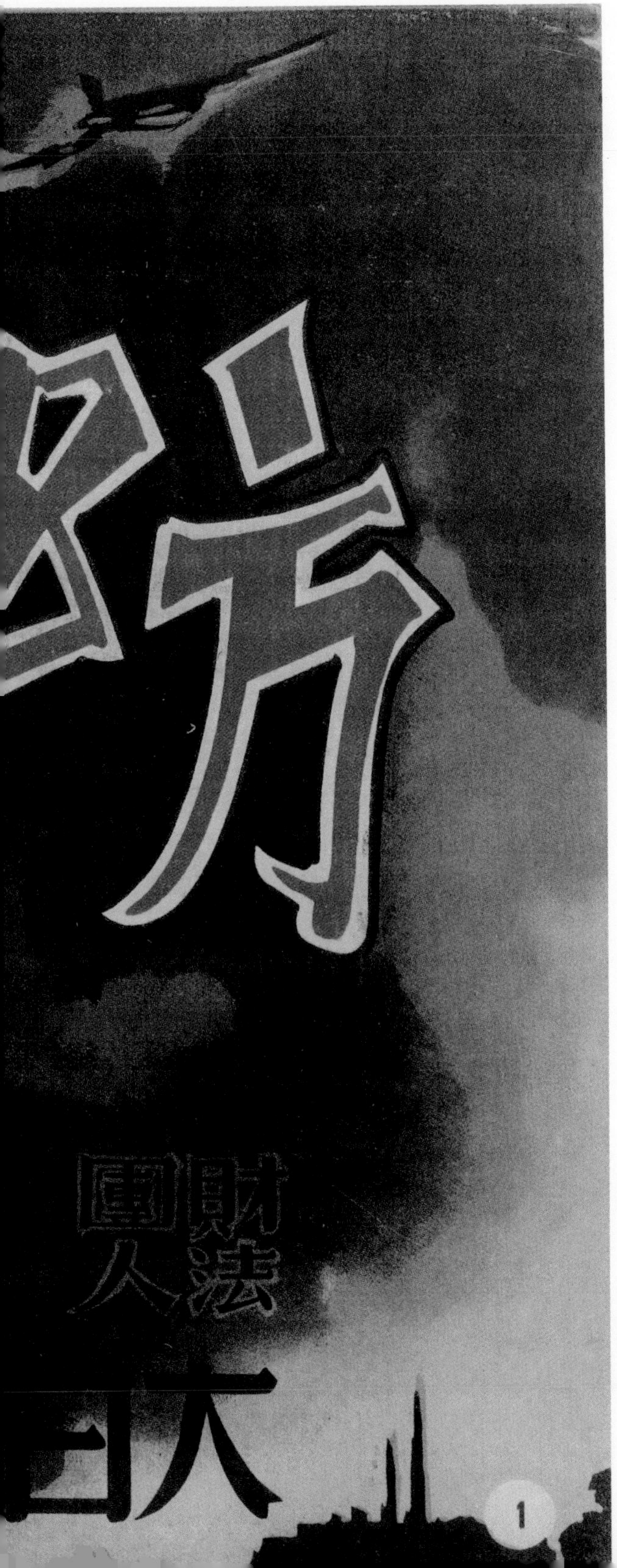
財團法人
大
1

***Air Raid Shelter*:** Produced by The Great Japan Air Defense Society, this *kamishibai* instructs civilians on how to build home bomb shelters, which proved to be largely useless and lethal because Japan's major cities were made of wood. "Properly kindled," *Time* magazine crowed about the March 1945 fire-bombing raids on Tokyo and Nagoya, "Japanese cities will burn like autumn leaves."

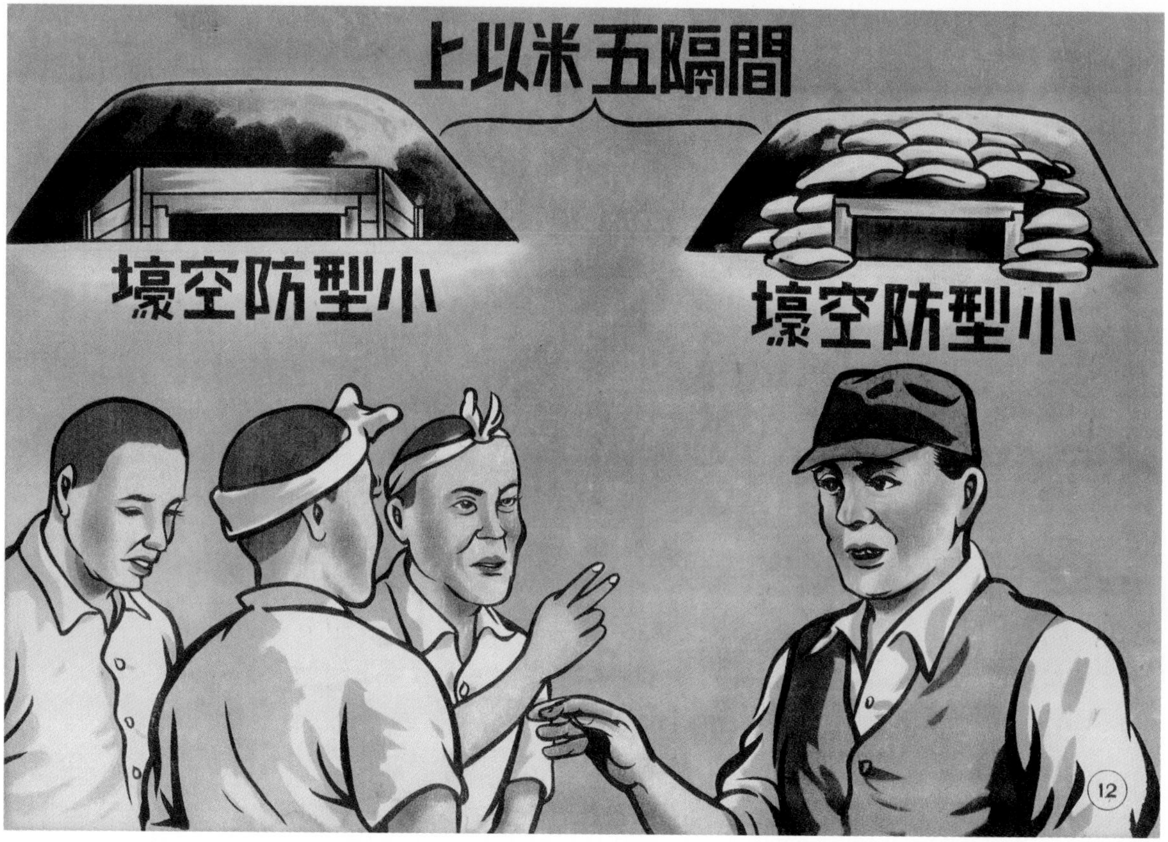
間隔五米以上
小型防空壕
小型防空壕
12

ABOVE Useless Measures: A civil defense leader tells civilians to build home bomb shelters at least five meters apart, but this accomplished next to nothing in face of the American onslaught. In one night on March 9, 1945, sixteen square miles of Tokyo burned to the ground in two hours. The fire-bombing raids on Tokyo claimed one hundred thousand victims, more than the immediate deaths at Hiroshima, paying Japan back for Pearl Harbor a thousandfold. Seemingly out of sheer vindictiveness and just to make the rubble bounce, General Curtis LeMay launched a one thousand–plane bombing run over the crippled nation of Japan five days after the plutonium bomb was dropped on Nagasaki on August 9, as part of what President Harry Truman promised would be a "rain of ruin" if Japan did not surrender unconditionally.

OPPOSITE, TOP Backyard Bomb Shelter: The civil defense leader shows the dimensions for a single and two-person bomb shelter. The shelters were incredibly small and shallow, just over three feet deep. The pit for the shelter resembles a freshly dug grave. By the end of the war, the home island had virtually no air cover or anti-aircraft guns. The Allies dropped one bomb for every fifteen people in Japan.

OPPOSITE, BOTTOM The Last Ditch: Civil defense was left to children and old men. A civil defense officer gives instructions to a young girl, a boy, and a carpenter (identified by the guild symbol on the back of his kimono) on how to build a backyard bomb shelter with a shovel and measuring tape.

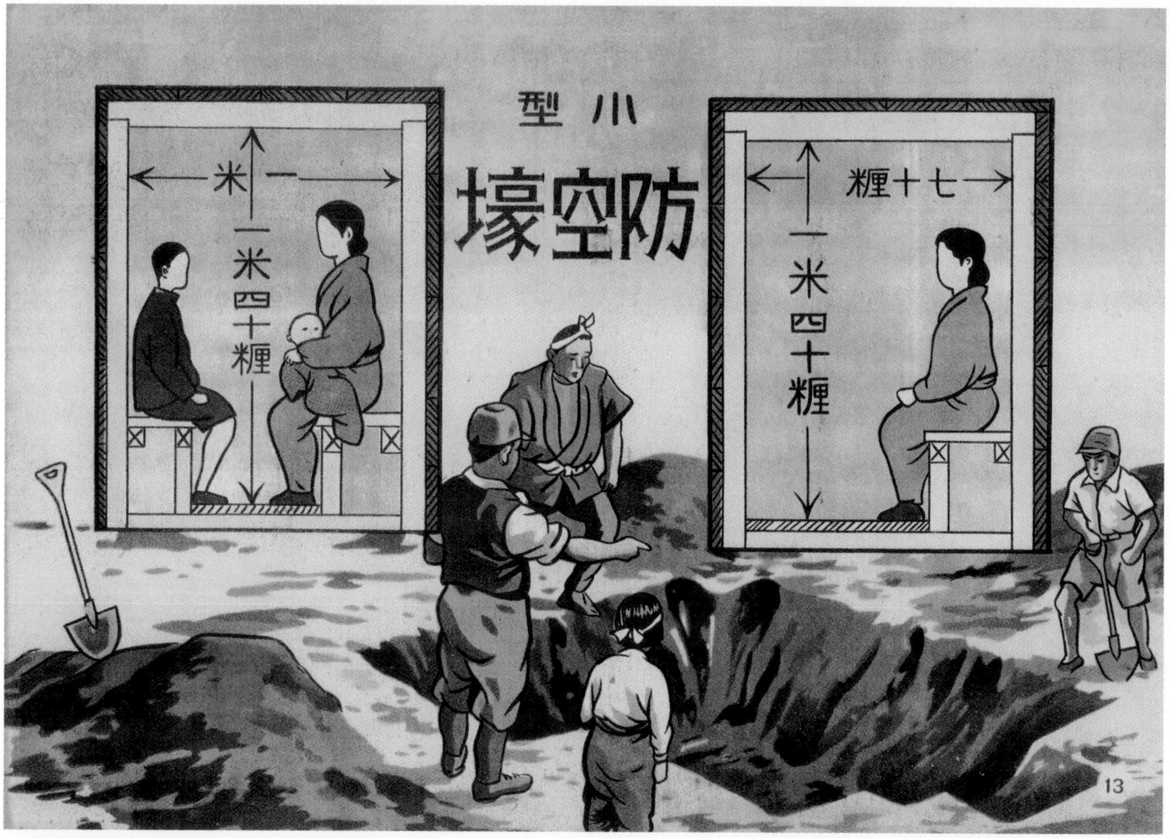
小型
防空壕
一米
一米四十糎
七十糎
一米四十糎
13

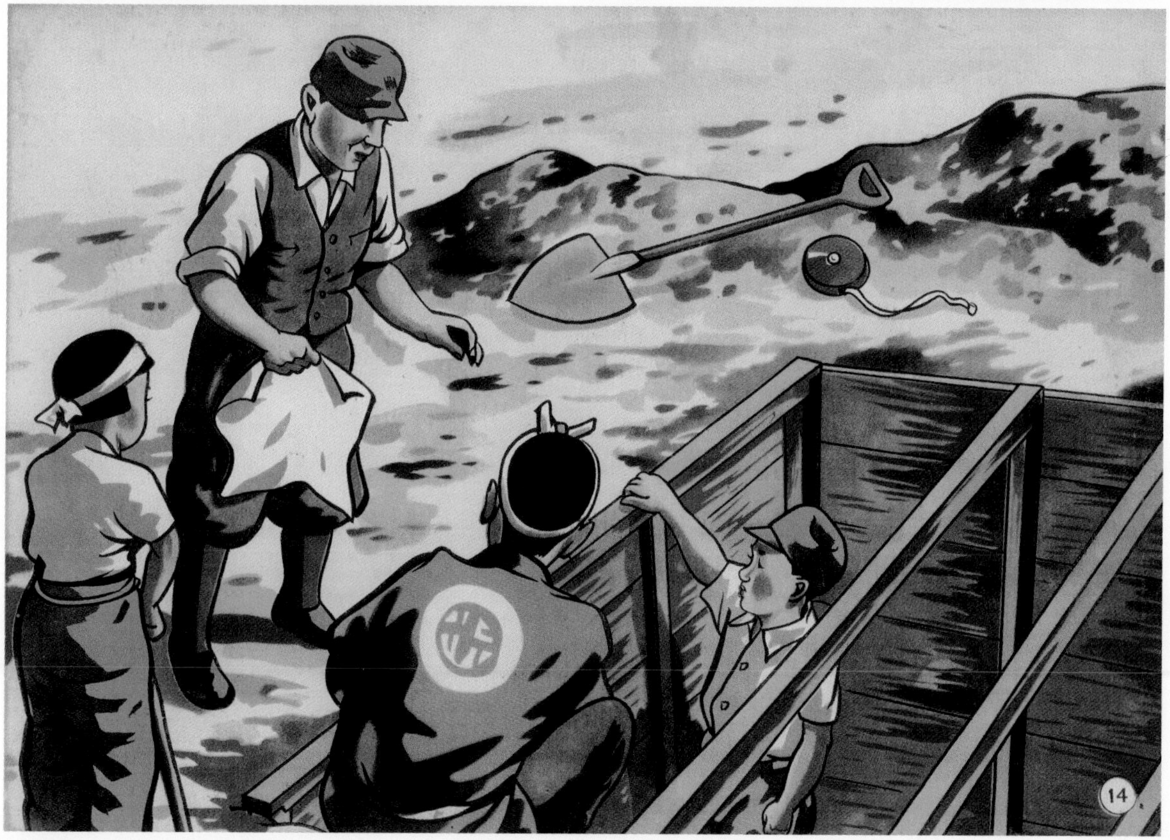
14

Monkey Business: Children had their own idylls from war, like this charming tale *Banana Train* by Taneomi Utagawa in 1942, about monkeys who organize a railroad to bring bananas out of the jungle. The image has a strong graphic feel in the clean contour of line and purity of form, like the simplified outline of the black telephone against the yellow table. The artist has absorbed the lessons of Cubism, placing objects in a plane, from artists like Georges Braque and Stuart Davis.

kamishibai can be seen in the strong diagonals as a paratrooper hits the silk and drops behind enemy lines.

Children had their own idylls from war. *Cicada*, a *kamishibai* from 1941, is a primer on collecting insects, a cost-free pastime for a rural audience. *Banana Train* is a charming Curious George–like tale of monkeys who organize a rail shipping system for bananas to make Japanese children happy. Some *kamishibai* featured moving panels like a pop-up book for the further delight of children. A coloring book of the time features Betty Boop in a print kimono of Imperial sun flags and swastikas (the swastika, an ancient Buddhist symbol, called *manji* in Japan, was frequently used to decorate temples and clothing, therefore it did not have the same meaning as the German swastika in this context).

Akio Saki, president of the Nihon *Kamishibai* Association, wrote in 1943 that *kamishibai* were essential in inculcating a "cultural work ethic" in wartime Japan and its colonies. *Kamishibai* was a valuable method of communication in Indonesia and other conquered countries in Southeast Asia because of high illiteracy rates among rural populations. *Kokusai kamishibai* were

Swiped Swastika: The swastika is an ancient Buddhist symbol of harmony and stability that was appropriated by Adolf Hitler. The Nazi swastika was tilted on its axis, which could be interpreted as upsetting the world order. This gilded *manji* is prominently displayed at the apex of a seventeenth-century temple in Tokyo's Ueno Park.

also used to make native populations cooperate with the Japanese military. After the Imperial Army conquered Indonesia in 1942, an eight-panel *kamishibai* entitled *Harmony Brings Forth Tranquility* was brought to villages to legitimize the Japanese administration. The *kamishibai* presented daily life organized by neighborhood associations answerable to Japanese rule as a return to traditional Japanese values that had been lost to the individualism and liberalism of the West. One panel depicts young Indonesian boys smiling and saluting a benevolent Japanese officer.

Another *kokusaku kamishibai* shows Japanese soldiers routing the British in Burma. Heavily camouflaged tanks prowl the jungle in the title card. A young native scout in a bush hat guides the Imperial tank cavalry to the enemy's hidden position. Astride a water buffalo, he leads villagers, and the soldiers give a victory cheer to the shaven-headed Burmese boy.

When Japan's string of victories in Burma, the Philippines, Indochina, and Indonesia ended with the battle of Midway in 1942, news of the war became ever grimmer. *Kamishibai* story lines changed from over-optimistic projections of Japan's hegemony in the South Pacific to stories of mothers losing their young sons in battle. One *kamishibai* solicited by the army intelligence office was entitled *Heroic Soldiers Who Accept Honorable Death*. *Kamishibai* that once documented victories, now depicted the total defeat of the Japanese Army on Attu Island, with an emphasis on the bravery of the fallen.

Axis Accessories: This wartime image from a children's coloring book shows Betty Boop dressed in a kimono decorated with rising-sun emblems and swastikas. The images would not necessarily have the same fascist impact at home because the swastika, *manji*, was an ancient symbol of good fortune that migrated to Japan by way of Buddhism from India.

THE BURMESE BOY AND THE TANKS

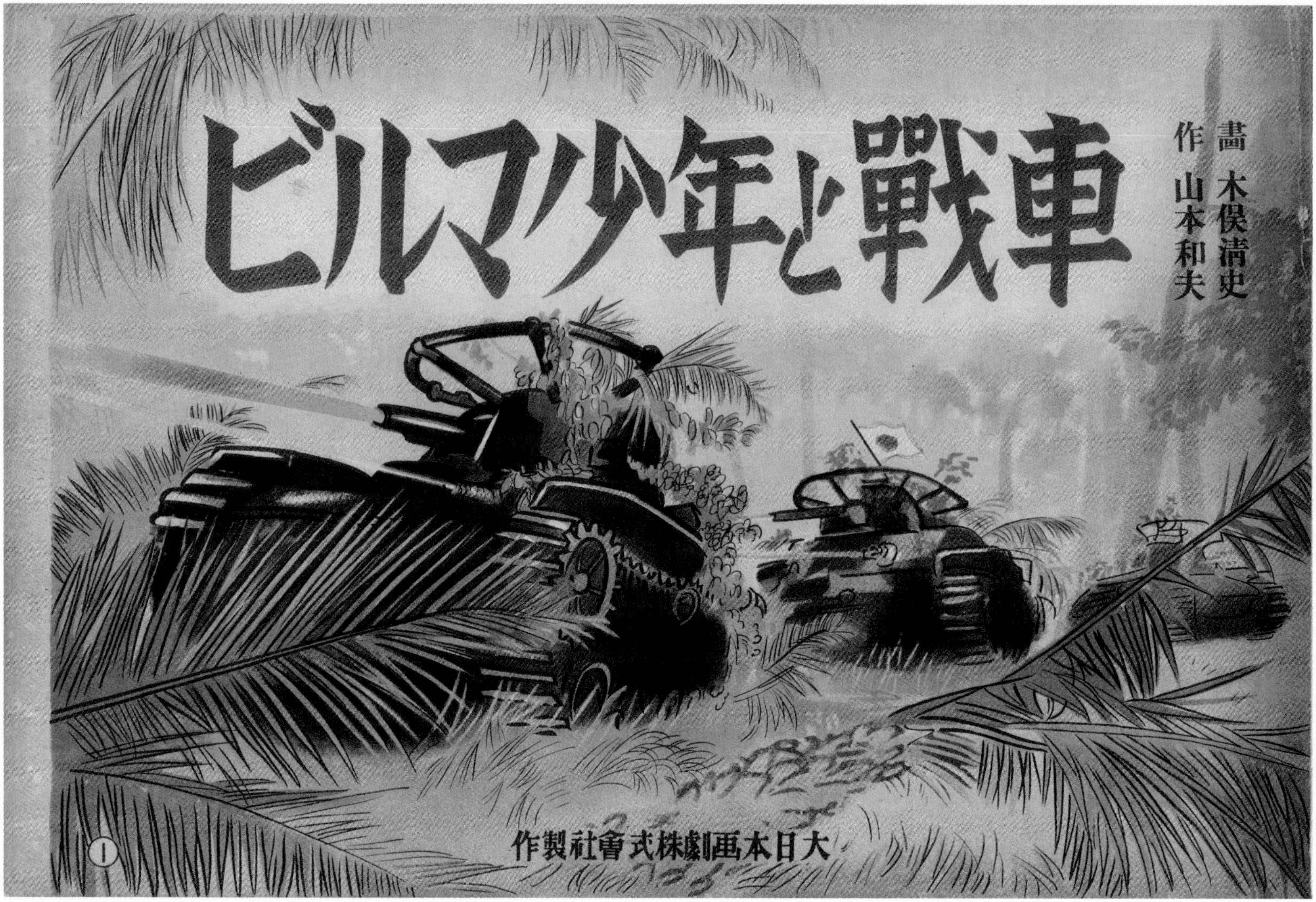
ビルマ少年と戰車
畫 木俣清史
作 山本和夫
1
大日本画劇株式會社製作

The Burmese Boy and the Tanks: *Kamishibai* from the Pacific war are filled with scenes of military glory. The Imperial Japanese Army handily routed the British in Burma in this 1944 *kamishibai* by Kimata Kiyoshi. The capital of Rangoon fell in March 1942, and Japan's three hundred thousand–strong troops were greeted as liberators from British colonialism, aided by the twelve thousand soldiers of the Burmese Independence Army. Wounded British soldiers were put to death by bayonet.

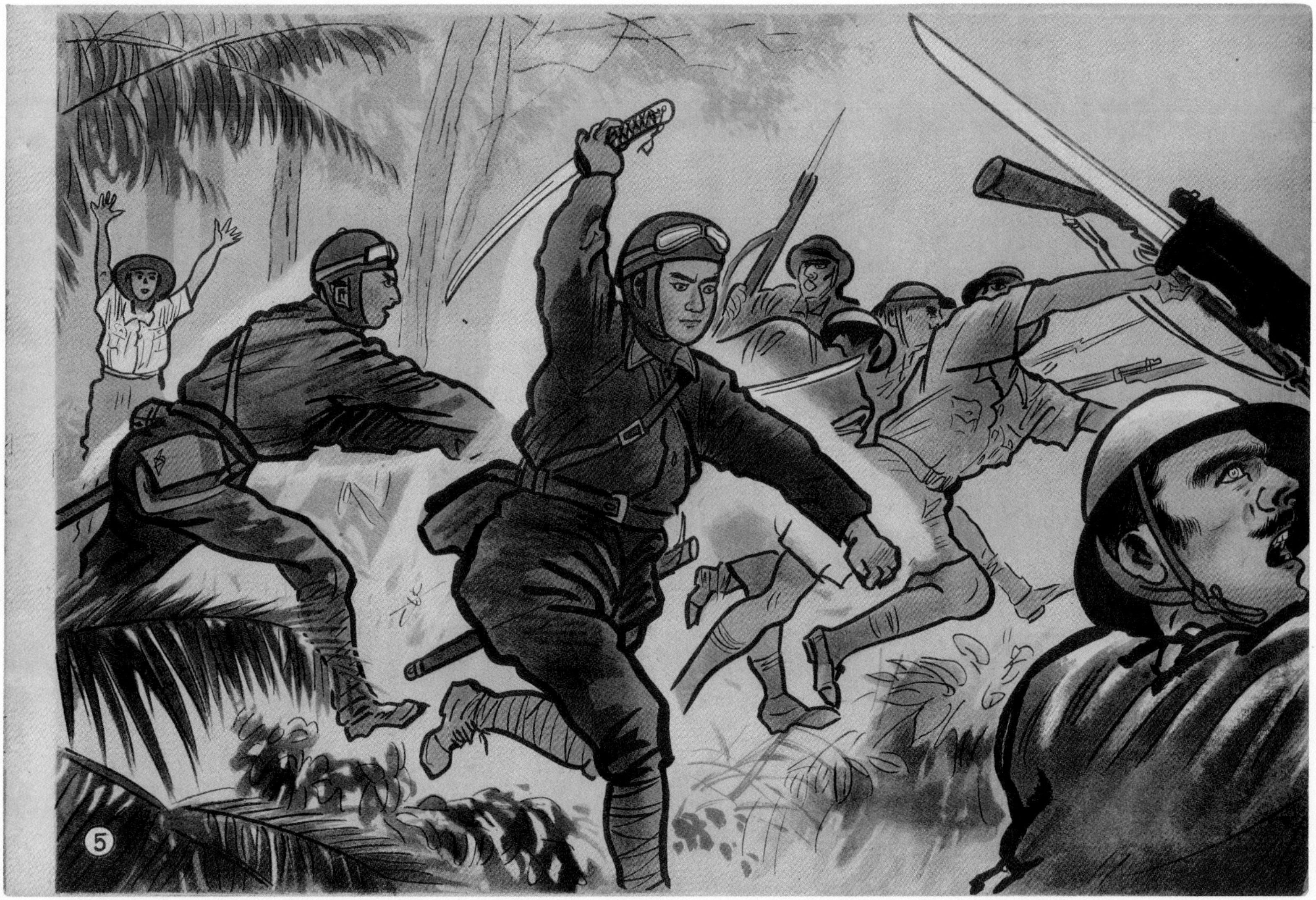
5

Soul of the Samurai: At left, a young Burmese scout leads Japanese invaders to a jungle ambush on British soldiers. Like twentieth-century samurai, Japanese soldiers are frequently portrayed using traditional, edged weapons such as swords and bayonets, considered more honorable than machines that kill from a distance. In an example of Shintoist hylozoism, some inanimate objects are believed to posses a spirit to be revered. The sword is said to be the soul of the samurai.

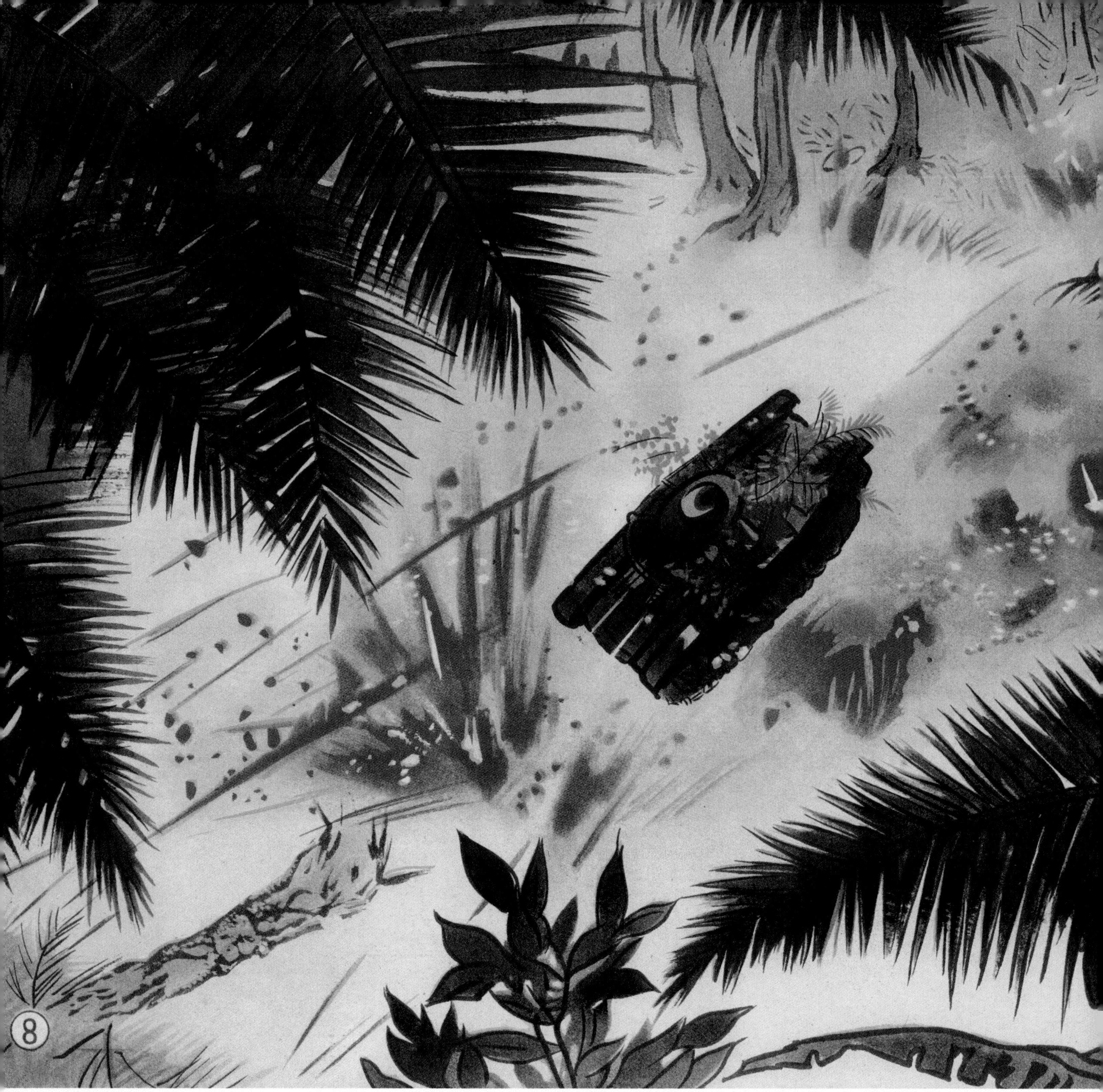

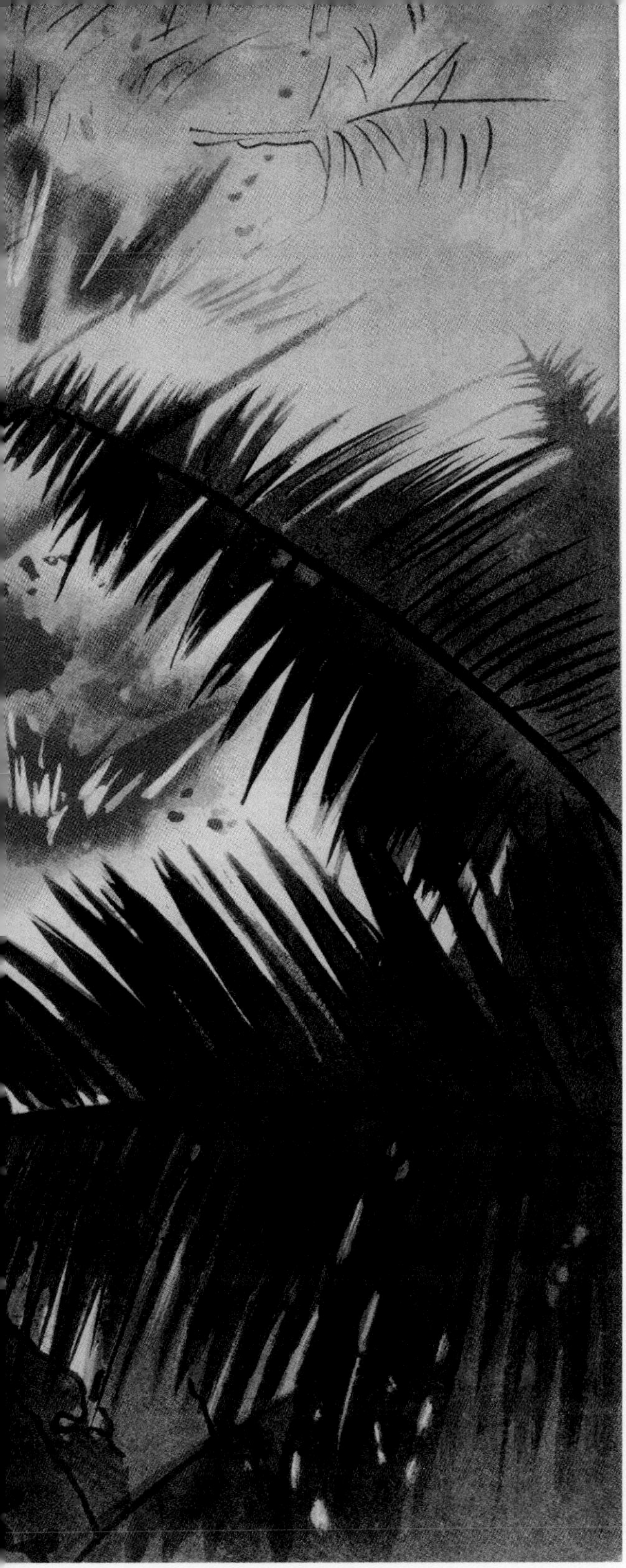

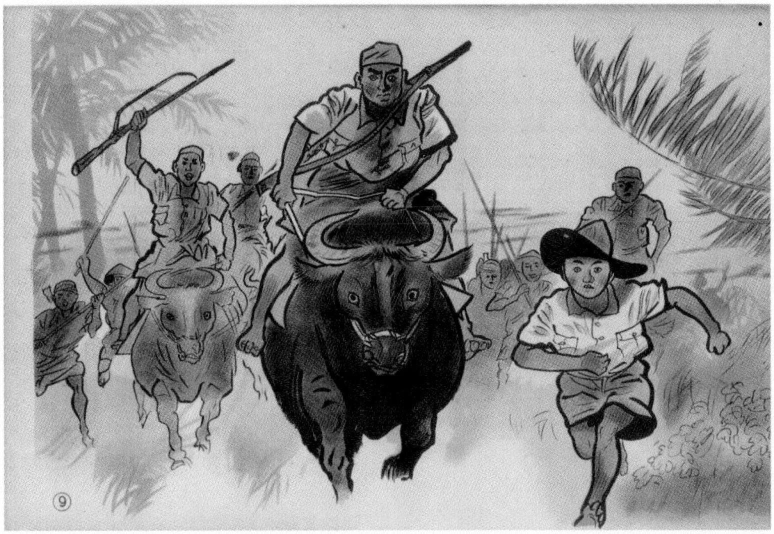
9

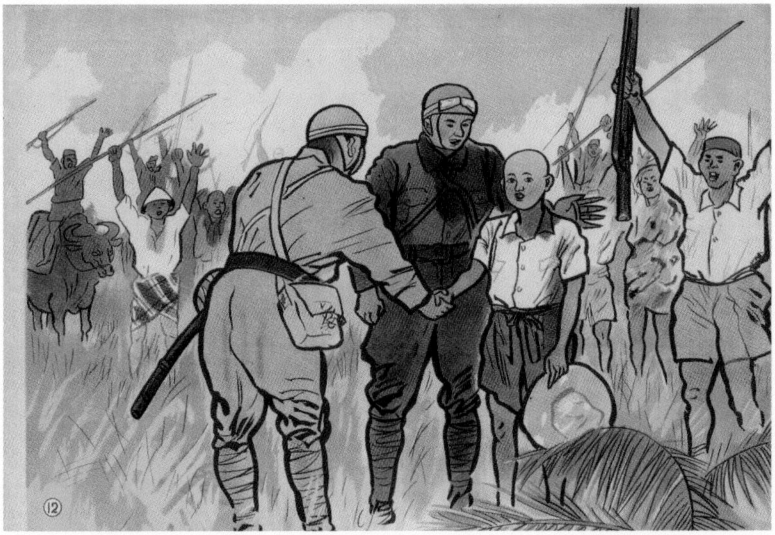
12

LEFT Tracking Shot: A Japanese tank crawls through a lush Burmese jungle amid crimson artillery-fire flashes. The scene is impressionistic, with the tank at the center of splattered strokes of flame and brushy palm trees. Compared with American juggernauts, Japanese tanks were little more than thinly armored personnel carriers.

ABOVE, TOP Buffalo Soldiers: The young scout leads a cavalry charge of armed villagers astride water buffalo. The role of the boy was intended to inspire patriotism among children on the home front and cooperation of the native population in conquered lands. The Japanese Army excelled at lightninglike advances, but logistics were medieval—in the failed invasion of neighboring India, the army relied on thirty thousand oxen and one thousand elephants. Only a few elephants survived.

ABOVE, BOTTOM Hearts and Minds: Officers congratulate the boy for his help, while Burmese villagers give a *banzai* cheer.

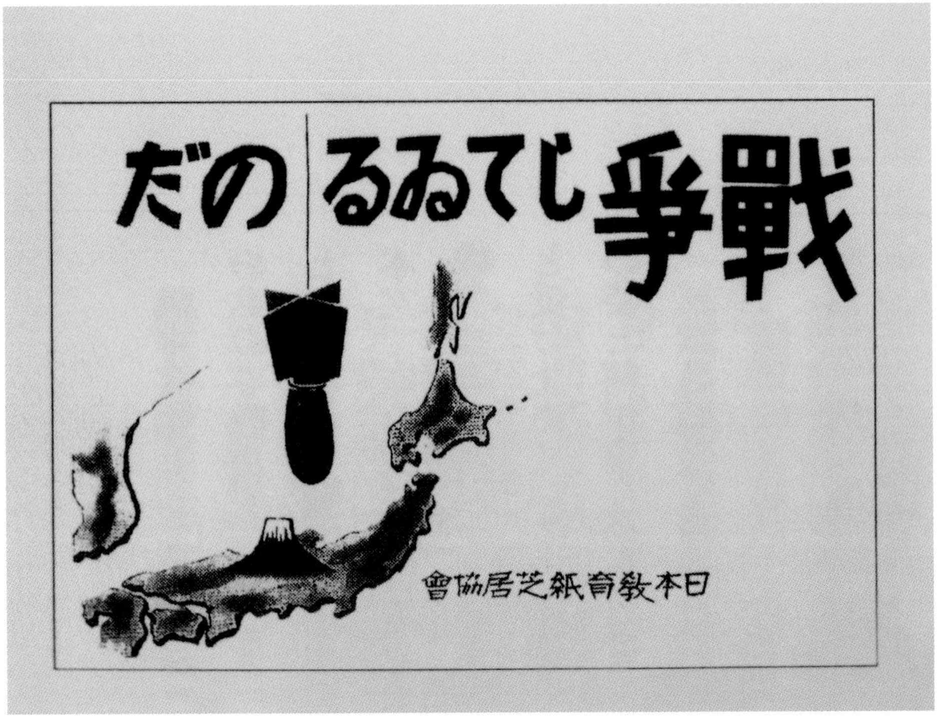
戰爭してゐるのだ
日本教育紙芝居協會

We Are Fighting a War: A giant bomb threatens the symmetrical volcanic cone of Mount Fuji, the symbol of Japan itself, a significant departure from the Imperial flag spreading over the Pacific. Once American bombers were in range after the Marianas were captured, Japanese cities were virtually defenseless.

Living in an earthquake-prone land in wood and paper houses susceptible to fire, the Japanese people must have felt that the Allied bombing was a form of divine retribution. Not only had it been a fatal miscalculation of America's mechanized might and willingness to fight back after Pearl Harbor, but the Allies had adopted a strategy of total war by bombing civilian populations. (Cartoons were also influential propaganda in the United States: Disney's animated *Victory Through Air Power* (1943) is credited with helping to persuade American chiefs of staff to prosecute a total war that ultimately left the cities of Hiroshima and Nagasaki as radioactive crematoria.)

Island Japan's vulnerability was reflected in *kamishibai*: The title card of *We Are Fighting a War* presents an aerial view of a bomb overshadowing Mount Fuji. Another *kamishibai* title page shows an American dropping bombs on a darkened city skyline. In one panel, a civil defense officer discusses the merits of building a bomb shelter with an earthen berm (sandbags covered in soil). Depth and width measurements are given for one- and two-person shelters. The freshly dug shelter looks like an open grave. Tellingly, the diggers include a schoolboy and schoolgirl, Japan's last feeble line of defense as the predawn air-raid sirens wailed.

Another civil-defense *kamishibai, Incendiary Bomb*, details the havoc different types of bombshells can wreak. In a fascinating historical twist, the British use of communal air-raid shelters to protect themselves from Japan's ally in the Blitz seems to have inspired Tokyo residents. In one panel, Londoners, all blond and the women looking as manly as the men folk, are shown lining up to enter a group shelter. A panel illustrates what to do when the klaxons sound—extinguish hearth fires, unplug irons, and turn off gas lines. One particularly chilling panel shows how far *kamishibai* evolved from being children's entertainment: a well-equipped couple stands ready in full body suits and gas masks with water barrels, large dipper, bucket, and shovel. The couple pose with their belongings like a hellish version of van Eyck's *Marriage of Giovanni Arnolfini and His Wife Giovanna Cenami*. The gas mask is an eerie echo of all the earlier masked characters in *kamishibai*. The story also extols the dedication and bravery of Tokyo firefighters. The Japanese civil-defense system is heartbreakingly homemade in the face of the tonnage dropped on their cities: A civil-defense officer on a bicycle announces an incoming raid with a megaphone.

Air raids in 1945 destroyed a section of central Tokyo where many *kamishibai* companies were located. The sole officially approved comics magazine, *Manga*, survived until 1944, when the company building burned in an Allied bombing raid. Like weeds pushing through concrete, portable *kamishibai* were easy to stage in ruined neighborhoods and even in bomb shelters.

When the American occupation ended, *kamishibai* stories would deal with the atomic bomb and its aftermath.

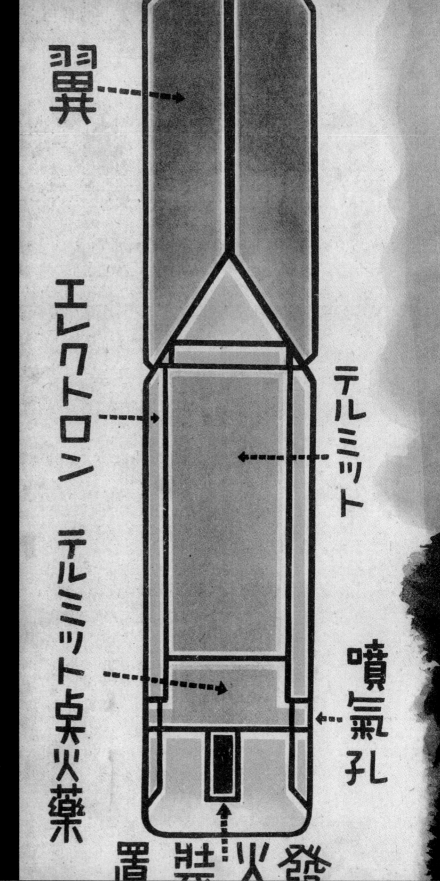

Incendiary Bomb: Japanese propaganda was silent about losses, so the ability of aircraft-carrier-launched American medium-range B-25 bombers to reach Tokyo and other cities in Doolittle's daring daylight raid in April 1942 came as a shock to the populace and a psychological boost to the Americans.

翼

エレクトロン

テルミット点火薬

テルミット

噴氣孔

發火裝置

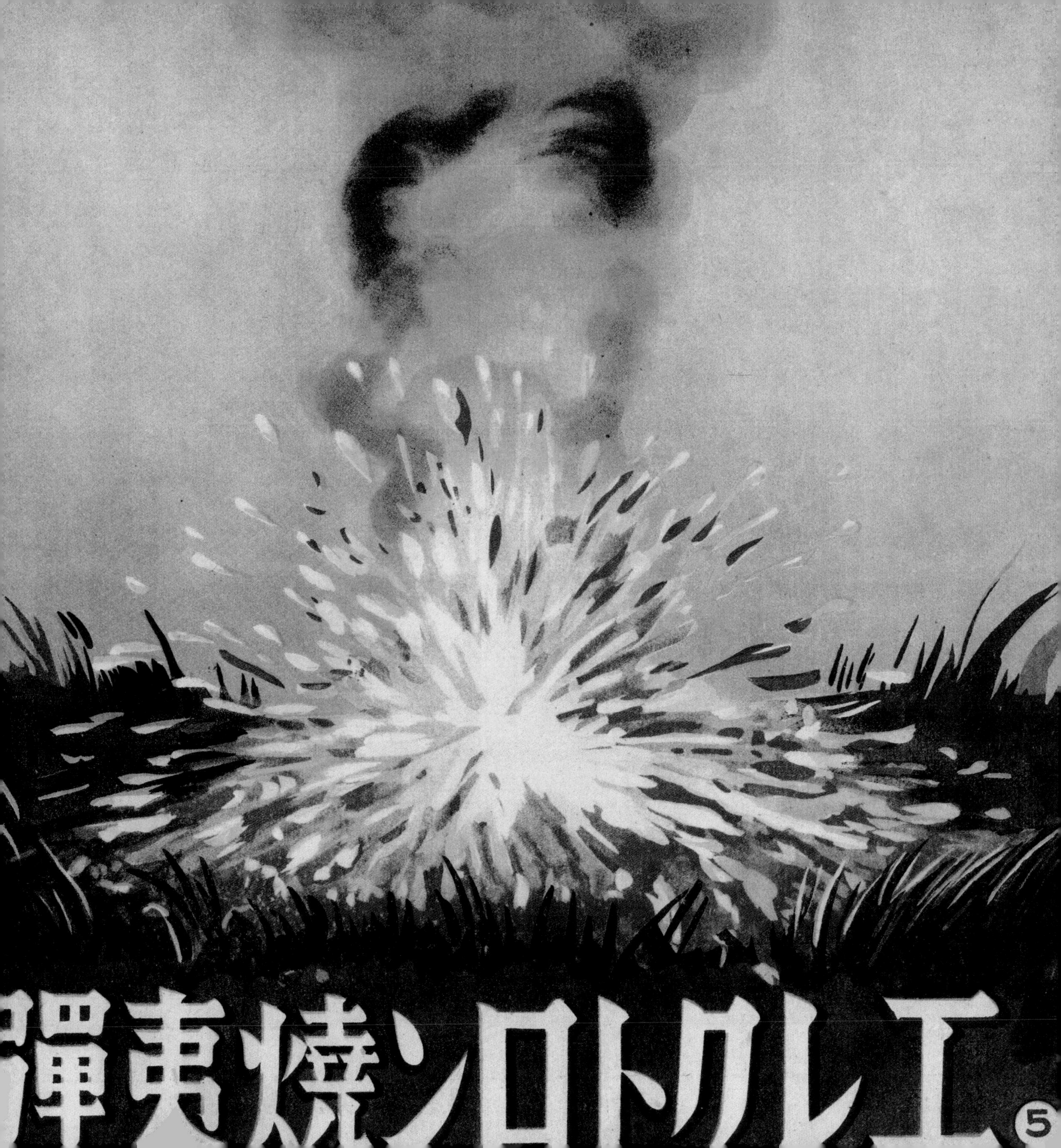

⑤
エレクトロン焼夷弾

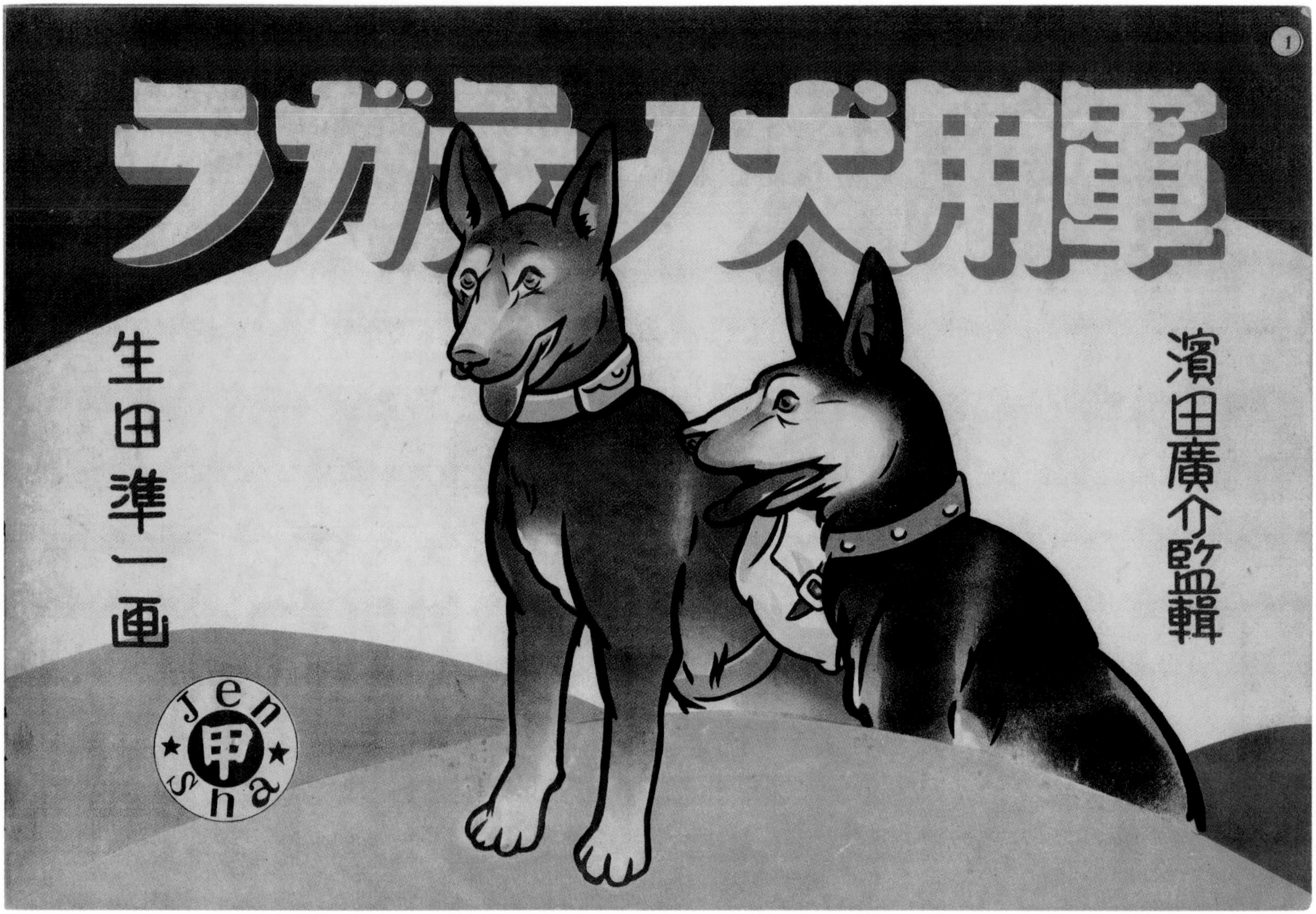
1
軍用犬ノテガラ
濱田廣介監輯
生田準一画
Jen 甲 sha

ABOVE Exploits of Military Dogs: Wartime *kamishibai* were mass produced on flimsy, rationed paper, but this one makes the most of the four-color printing process.

OPPOSITE, TOP Dog Soldiers: This *kamishibai* relies on children's natural love of animals to draw them into a prowar story. As an officer in the background calls for a charge with his raised sword, the dogs, like happy warriors, strain at the leash. The coloring of the dogs' coats is highly anthropomorphized, with khaki colors similar to the uniform of the Imperial Japanese Army and the black dog matching the soldier's stubble.

OPPOSITE, BOTTOM Dogs of War: Under fire, the dogs await directives written by the soldiers. The dogs' poses closely match those of the soldiers, emphasizing their commonality: one dog sits as the soldier kneels beside him to put the message in his collar, and the other dog kneels on its forelegs in a copy of the soldier's prone position propped up on his forearms.

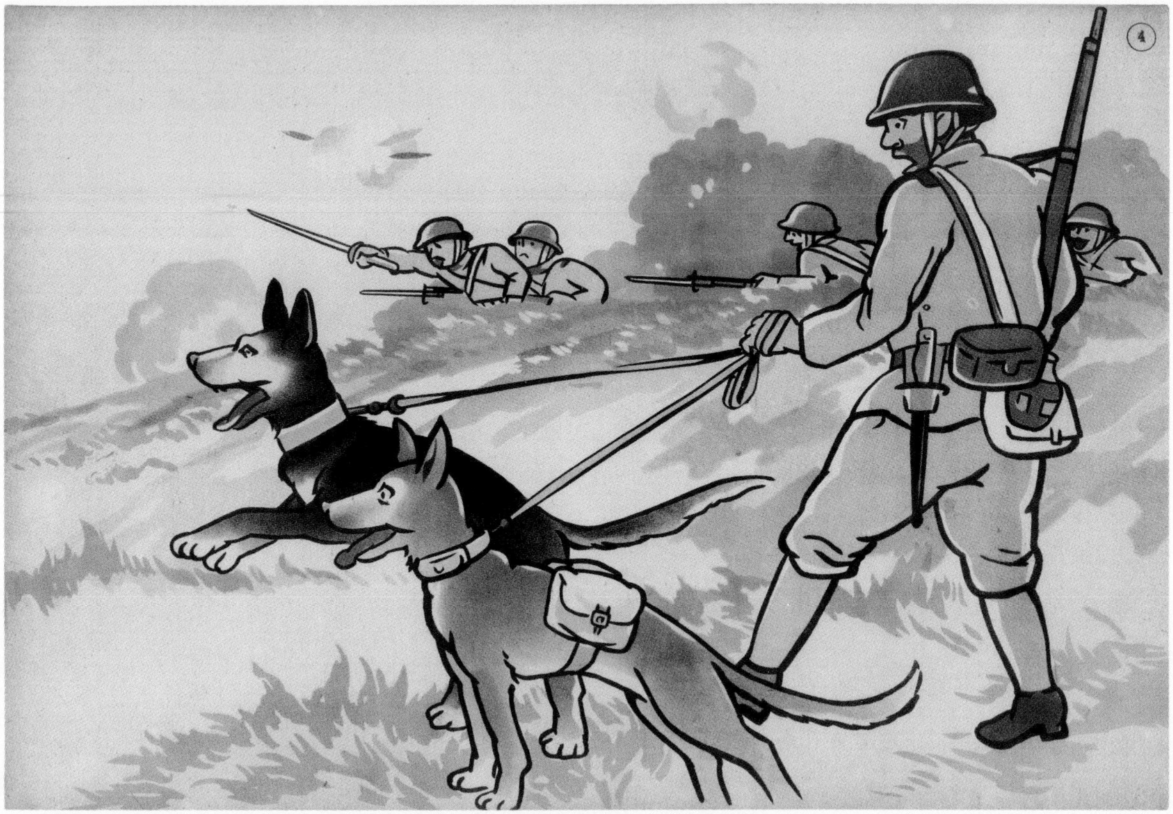
4

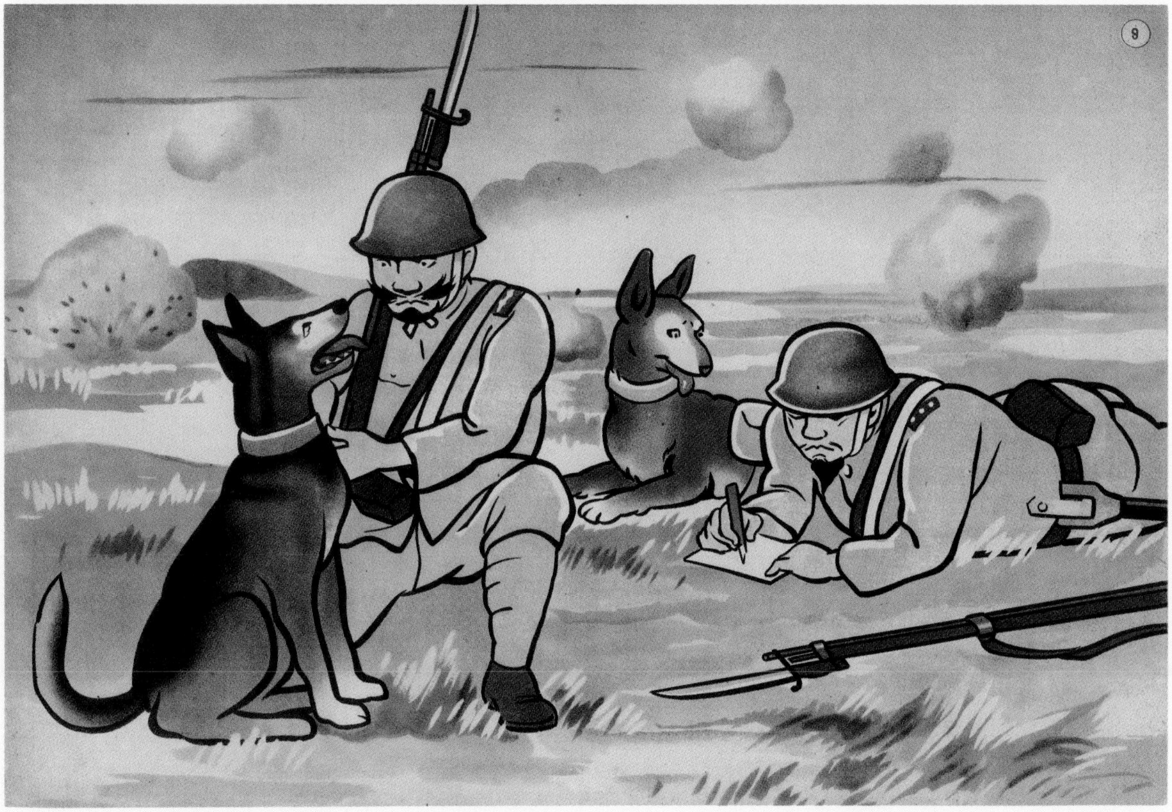

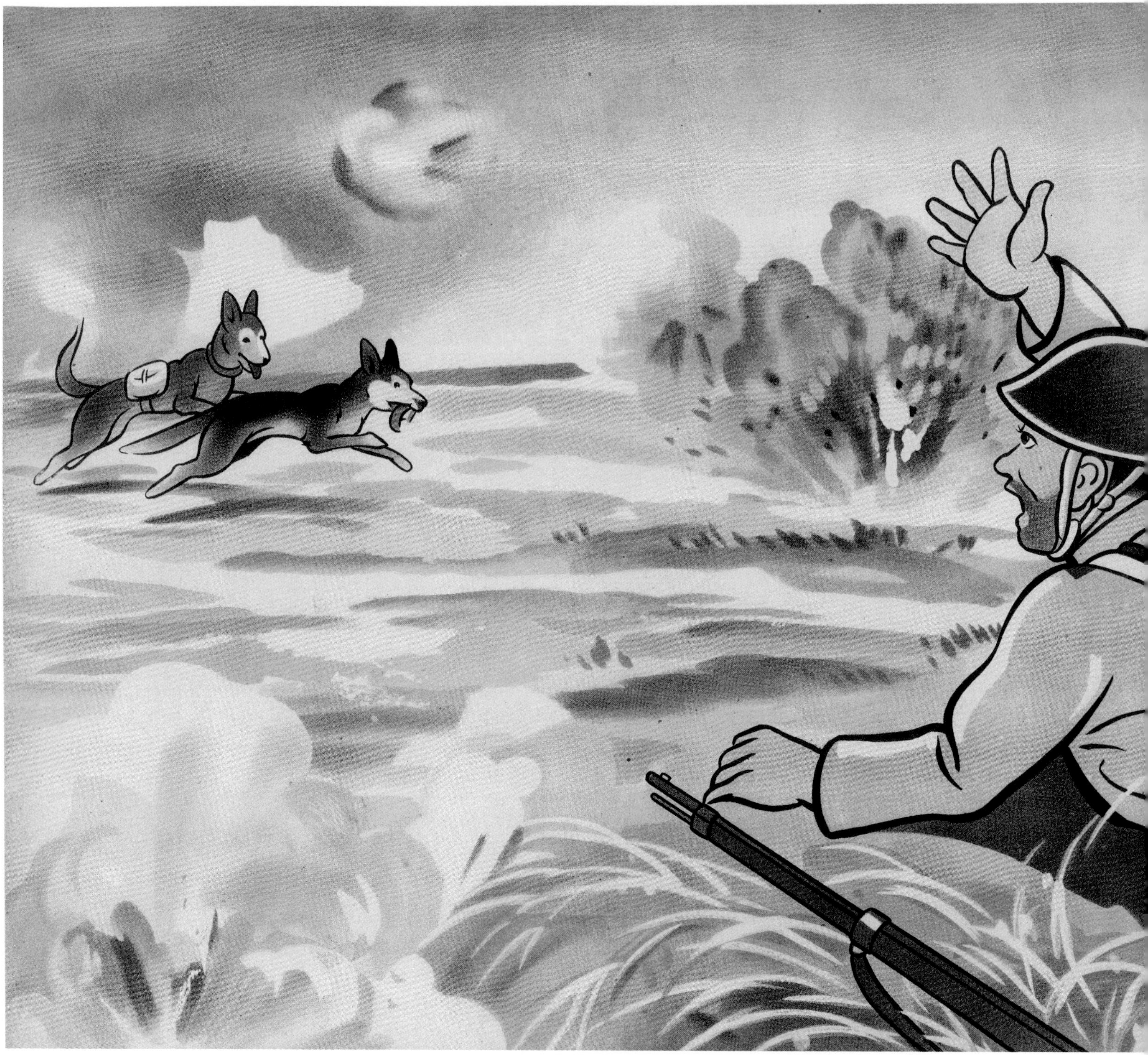

Muzzle Velocity: An officer in another foxhole hails the dogs. The bright colors of this sanitized version of warfare are also meant to appeal to children. The Japanese language contains many similar-sounding words with wildly varying meanings, so written messages were still an important means of communication in combat.

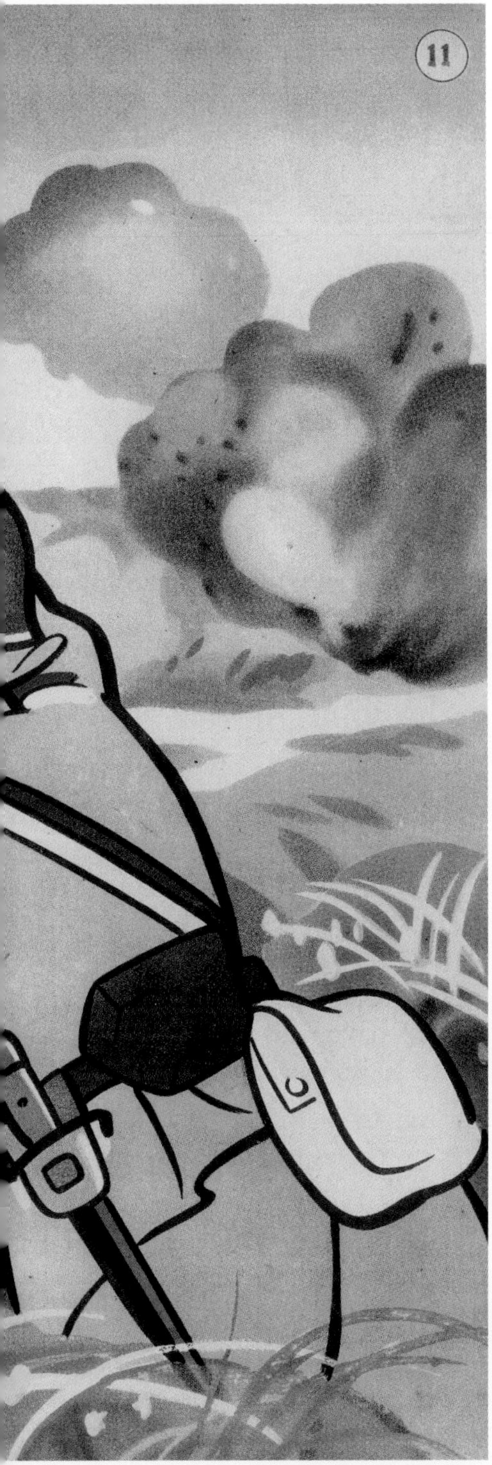
11

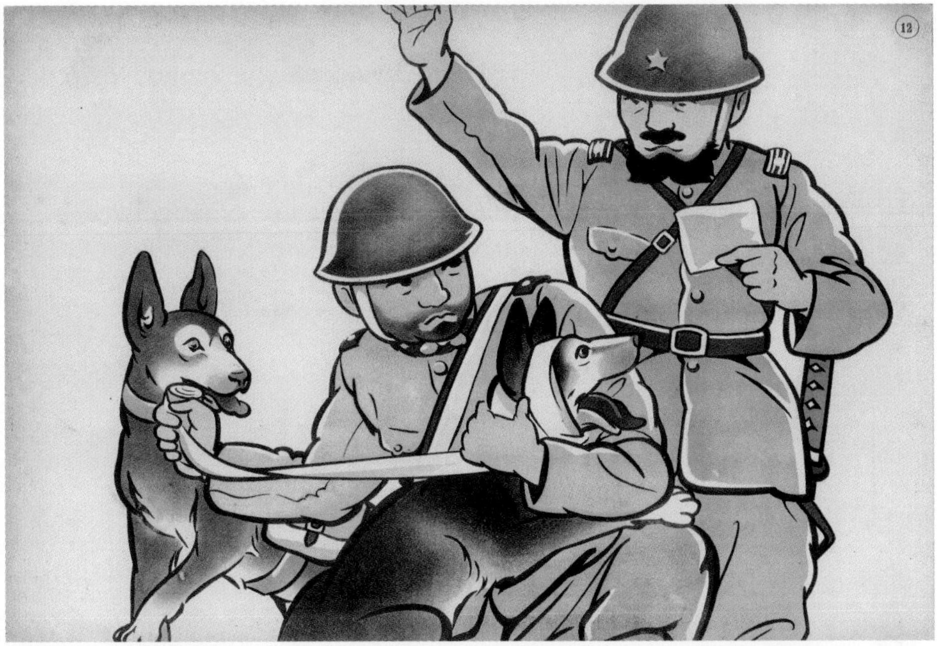
12

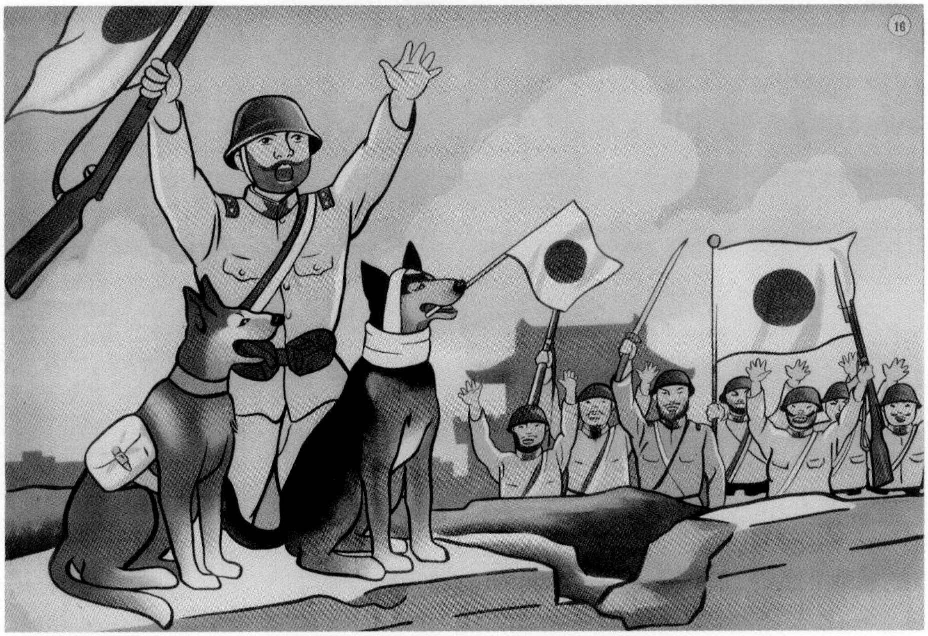
16

TOP Canine Corpsman: The commanding officer is cheered by the message from the front that leads to victory. The black dog has been wounded in the mission and is given medical care as if he were a human soldier.

BOTTOM Howling Commandos: Like the troops shouting *banzai* and waving the rising-sun flag, the courageous wounded dog waves a flag in his mouth. *Kamishibai* from early in the war are about bravery and victory on the battlefield. The enemy is not even present in this tale.

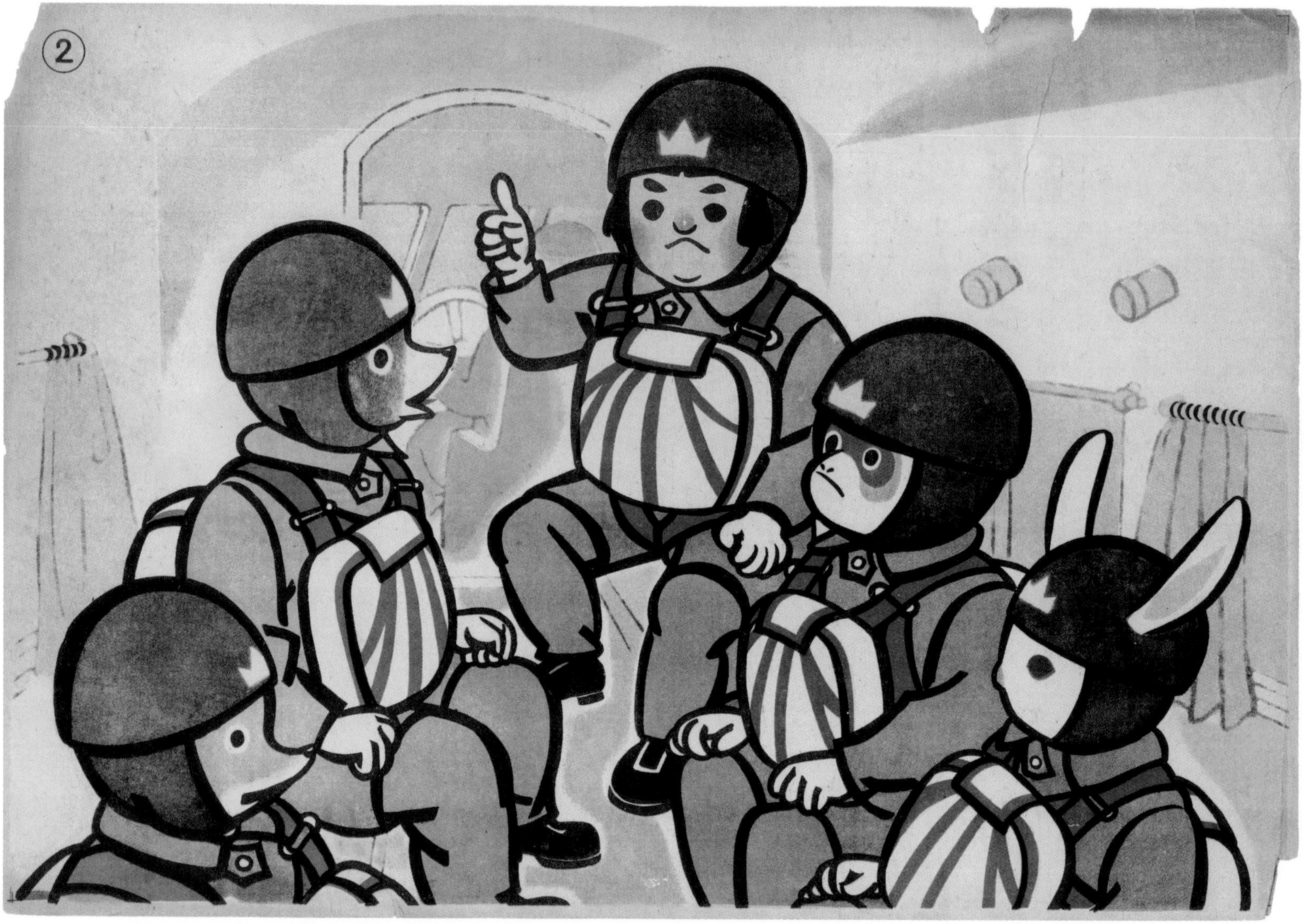
2

Totemic Paratroopers: This *kamishibai* of Kintaro, the boy paratrooper, updates the tale of Momotaro, the Peach Boy, a folkloric figure who defends Japan from foreign demons with the help of a dog, monkey, and pheasant. In the hold of an aircraft, Kintaro lectures his fellow commandos Badger, Fox, and Bunny on the finer points of parachuting. The webbing on their parachute bags is a stylized but accurate image of the real thing.

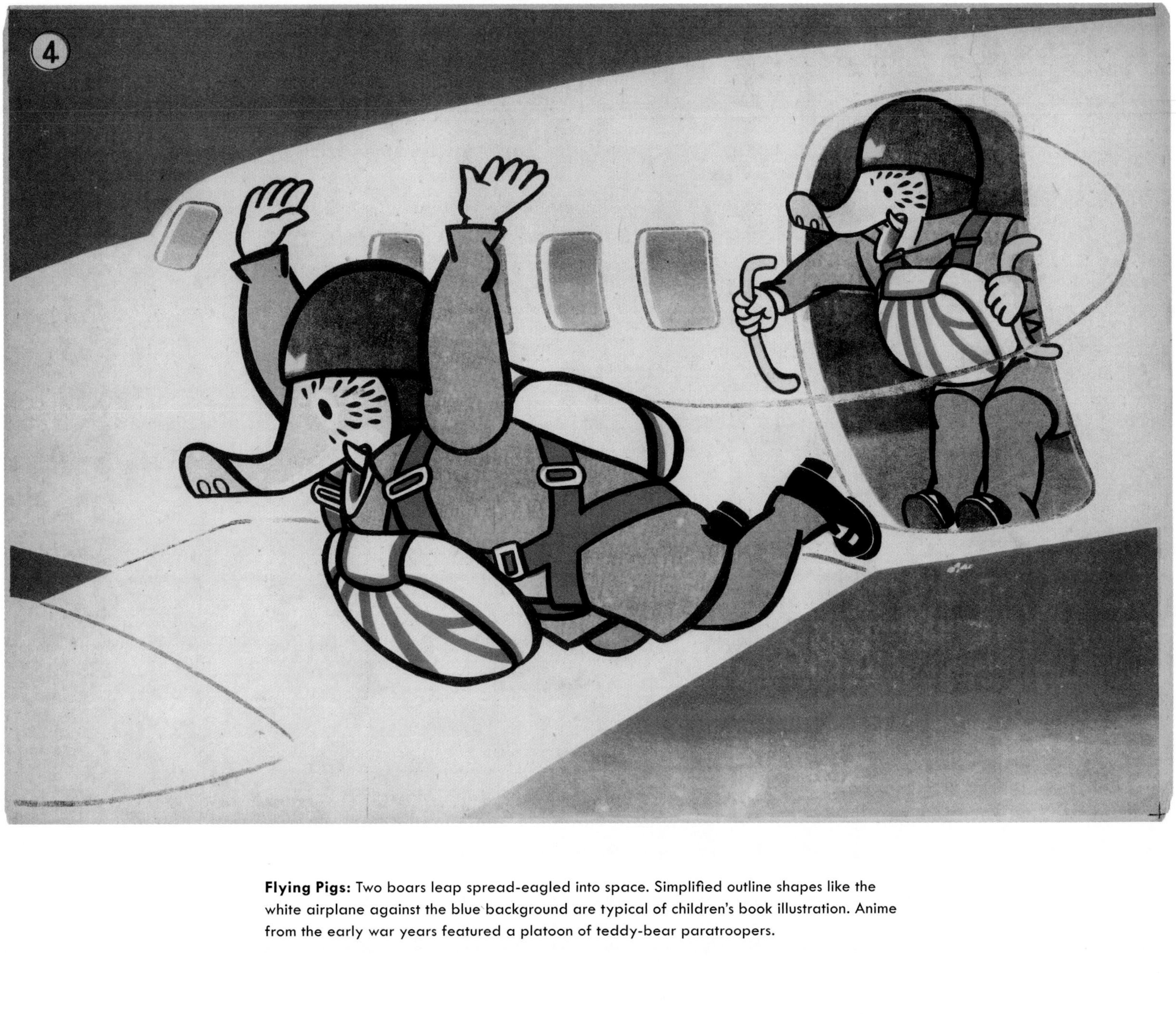
4

Flying Pigs: Two boars leap spread-eagled into space. Simplified outline shapes like the white airplane against the blue background are typical of children's book illustration. Anime from the early war years featured a platoon of teddy-bear paratroopers.

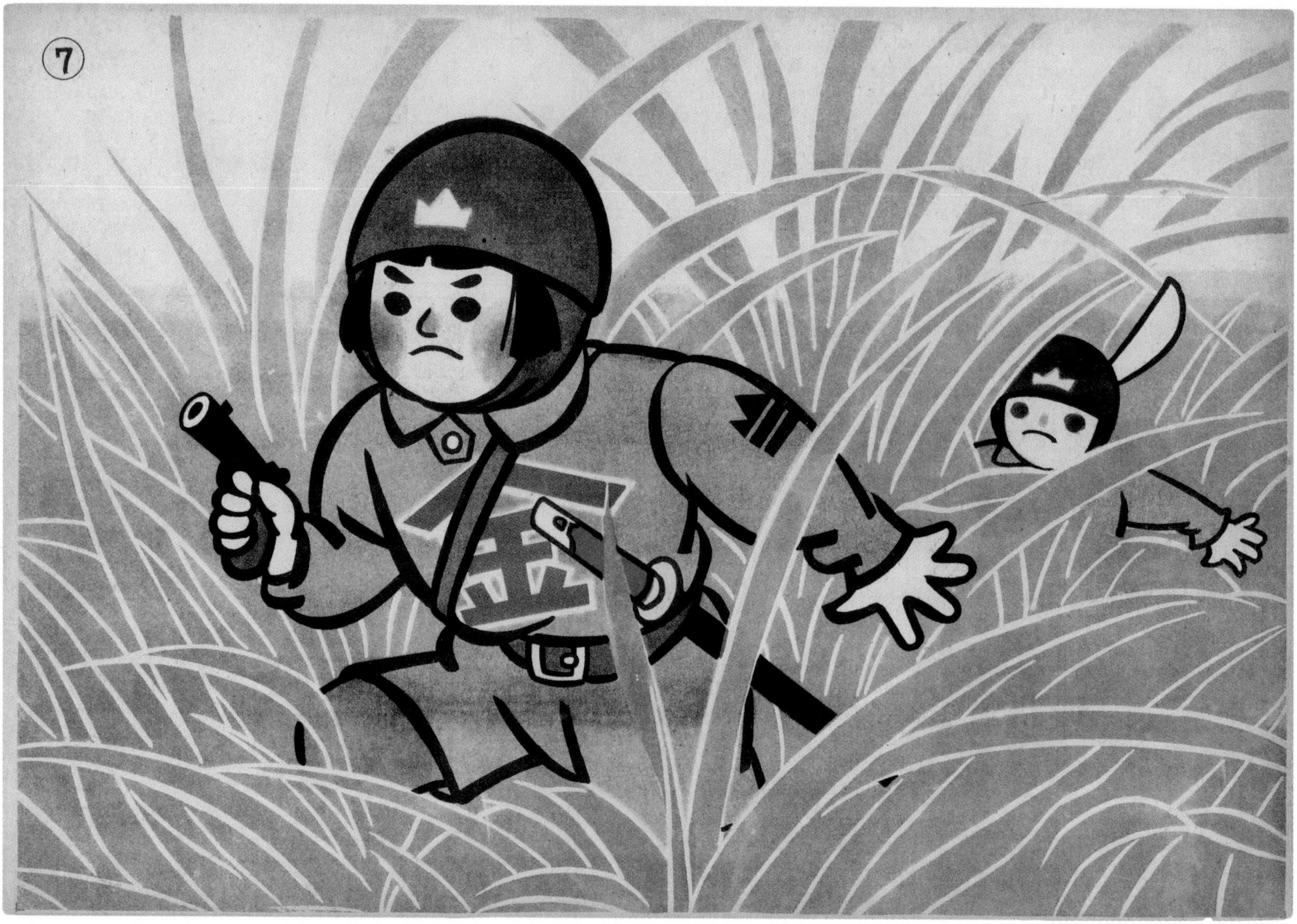
7

ABOVE Bunny Bushido: With an officer's pistol and *katana* (sword) at the ready, and his name emblazoned across his chest, commando leader Kintaro makes his way through a highly stylized jungle followed by his compatriot Bunny. The disconnect between the child-friendly style and the startling war imagery typifies the national psyche, where every person's will was directed toward victory. The fanaticism of the Japanese military knew no limits: by war's end, when Japan was bracing for an Allied invasion of the mainland, young women trained with spears made of bamboo.

OPPOSITE, TOP Cartoon Cavalry: British soldiers with sunburned noses and ears appear in a phalanx protected by a tank. Caucasians are rendered as stock characters with long noses and blond hair.

OPPOSITE, BOTTOM Grade-school Grenadier: Kintaro pulls the pin and lobs a grenade at the tanks. The three animal characters form an active combat group, looking in all directions. Bunny points offscreen, anticipating the next panel.

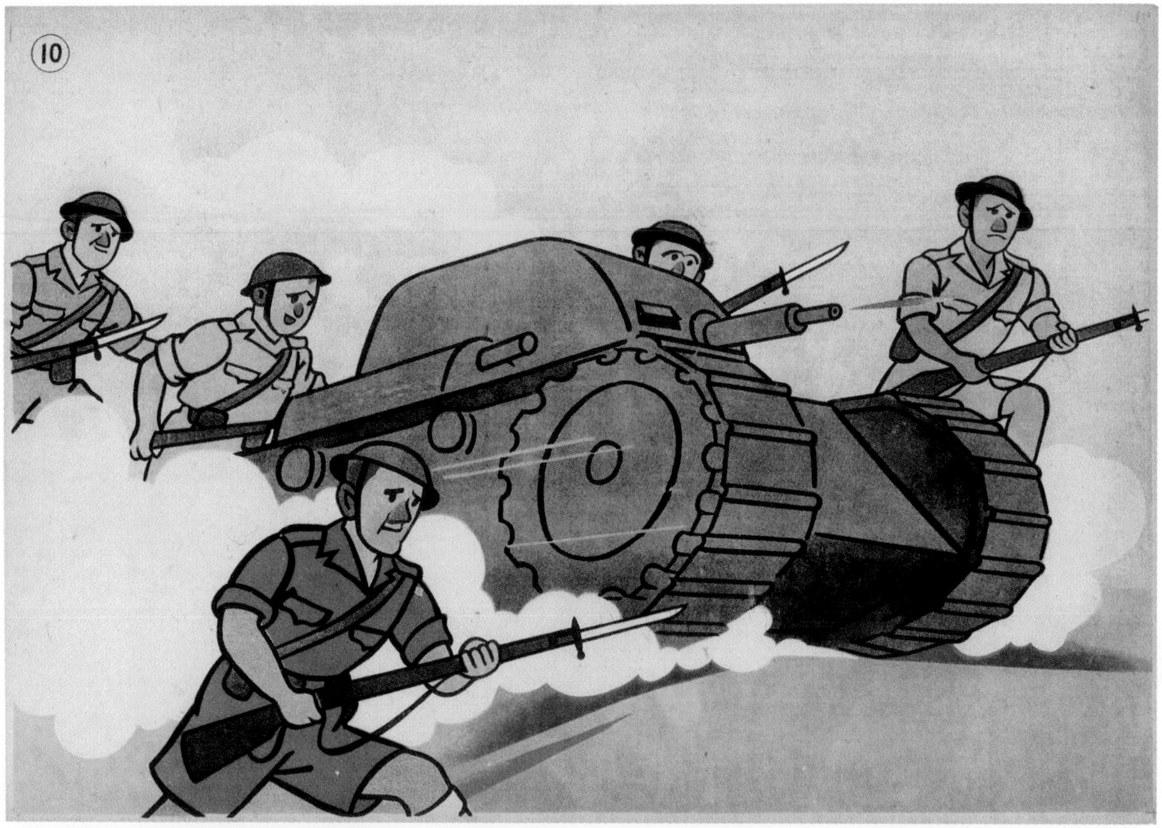
10

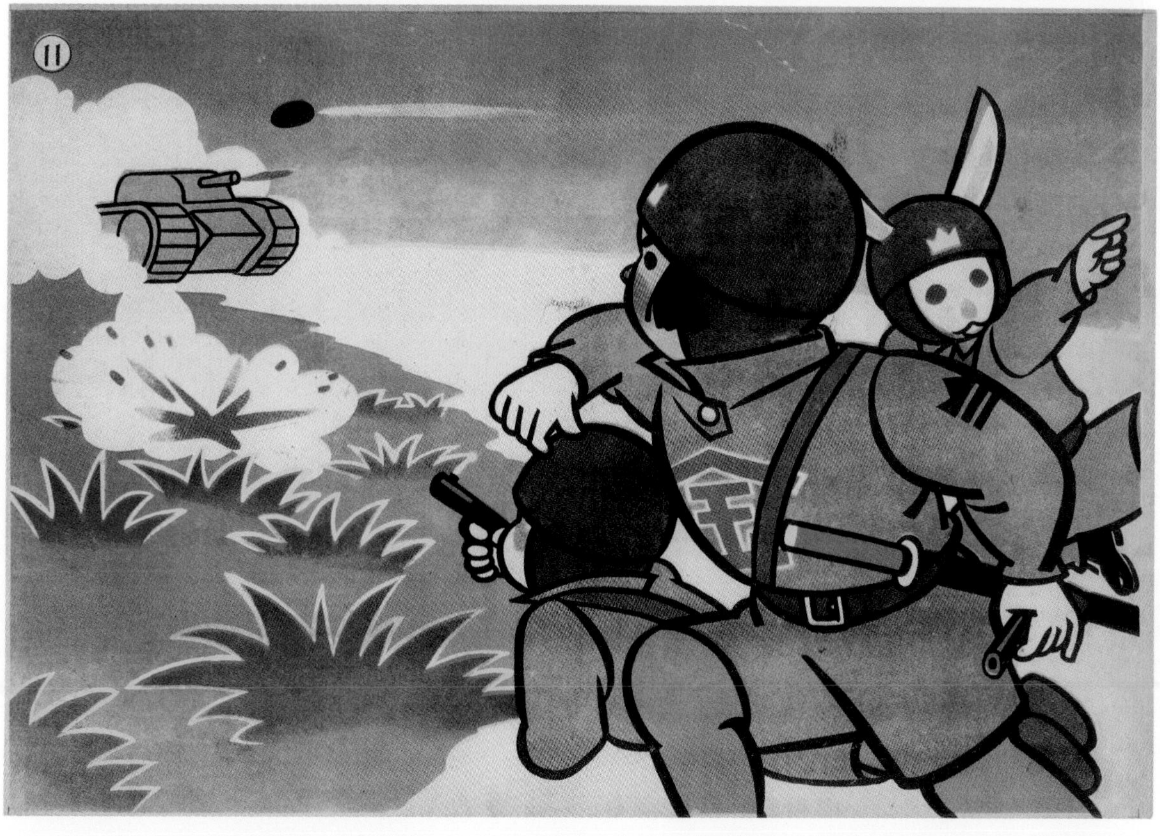
11

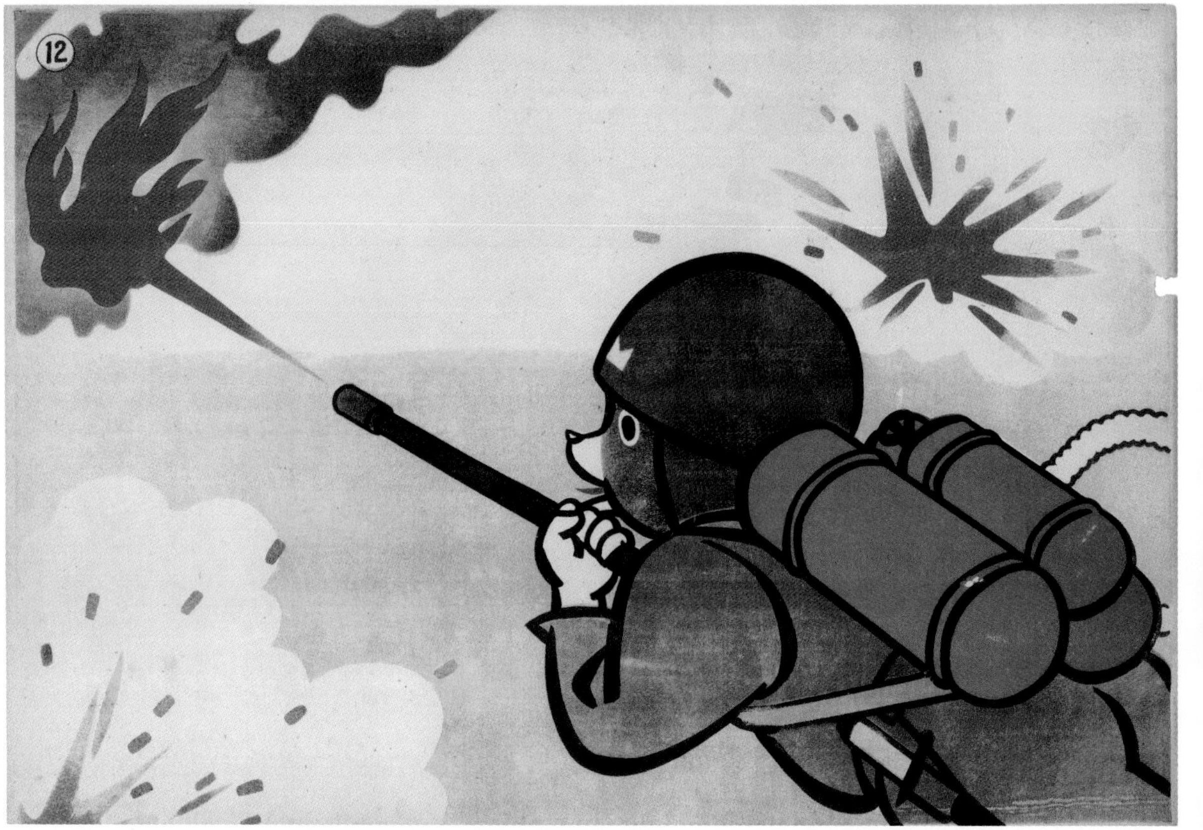
12

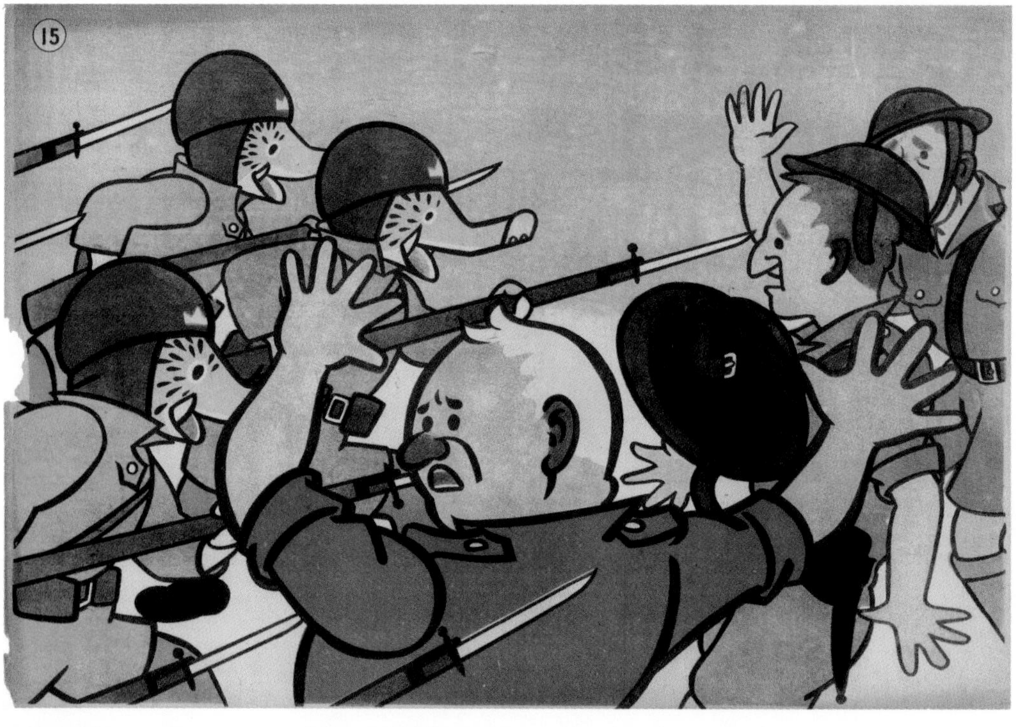
15

ABOVE Pyrotechnic Tanuki: Badger ignites a flamethrower in a burst of red. The Japanese used flamethrowers in battles like Bataan to clear out American pillboxes, but toward the end of the war they fell into disuse because the army was on the defensive.

LEFT Boar War: In a bayonet charge, the boars overrun the hapless British troops. Japanese soldiers were most often shown using the bayonet as the twentieth-century equivalent of the pure samurai sword.

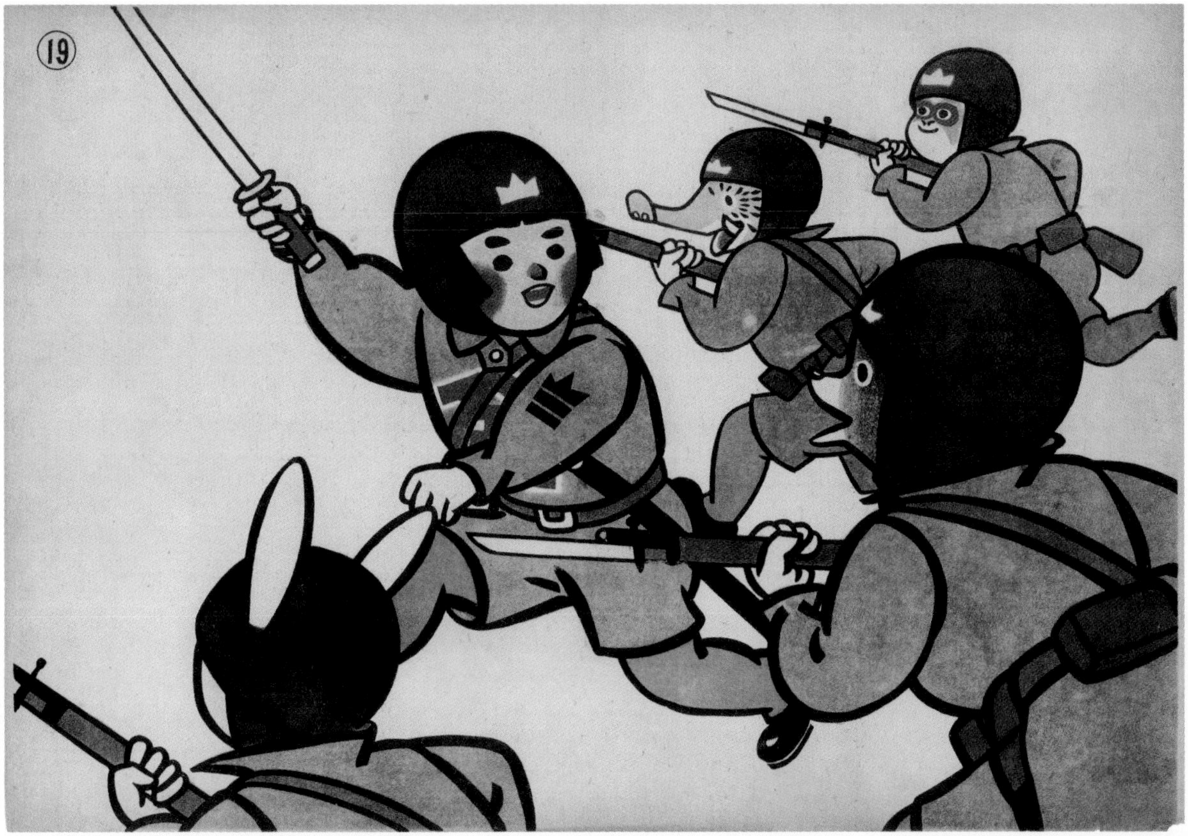
19

ABOVE Commander Kintaro: With his sword raised high, Kintaro leads a bayonet charge to victory. The bloodshed of real warfare has been neatly excised from this children's tale.

RIGHT *Banzai* for Bunny Rabbits: Flags, swords, and rifles are raised in a *banzai* shout celebrating victory, as the commandos are returned to their ship with Zeroes flying overhead.

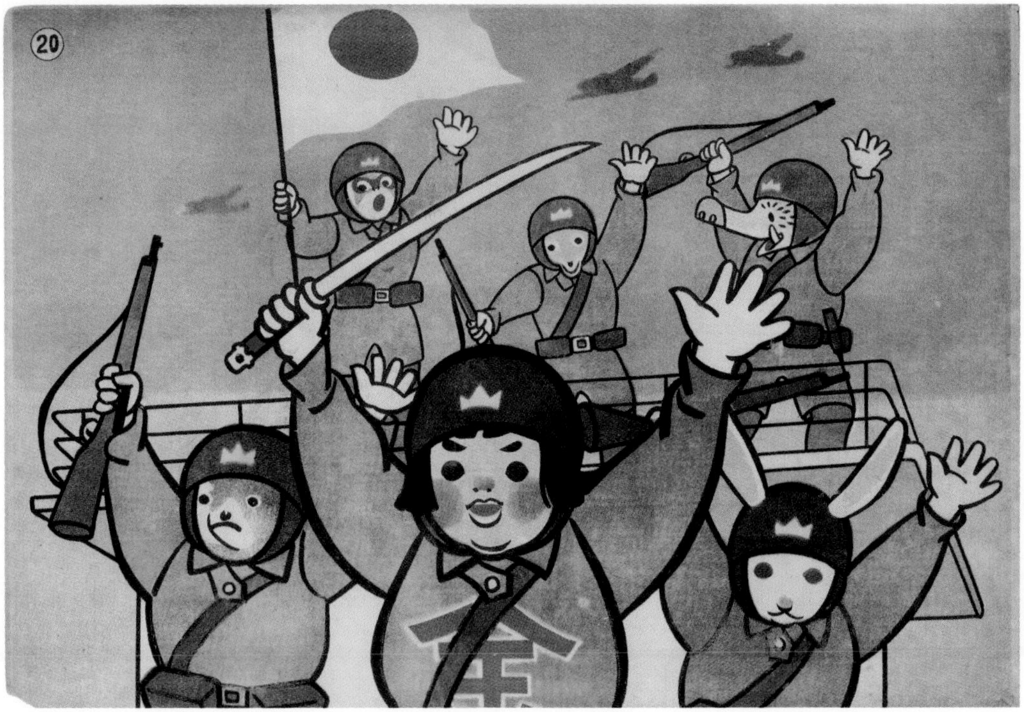
20

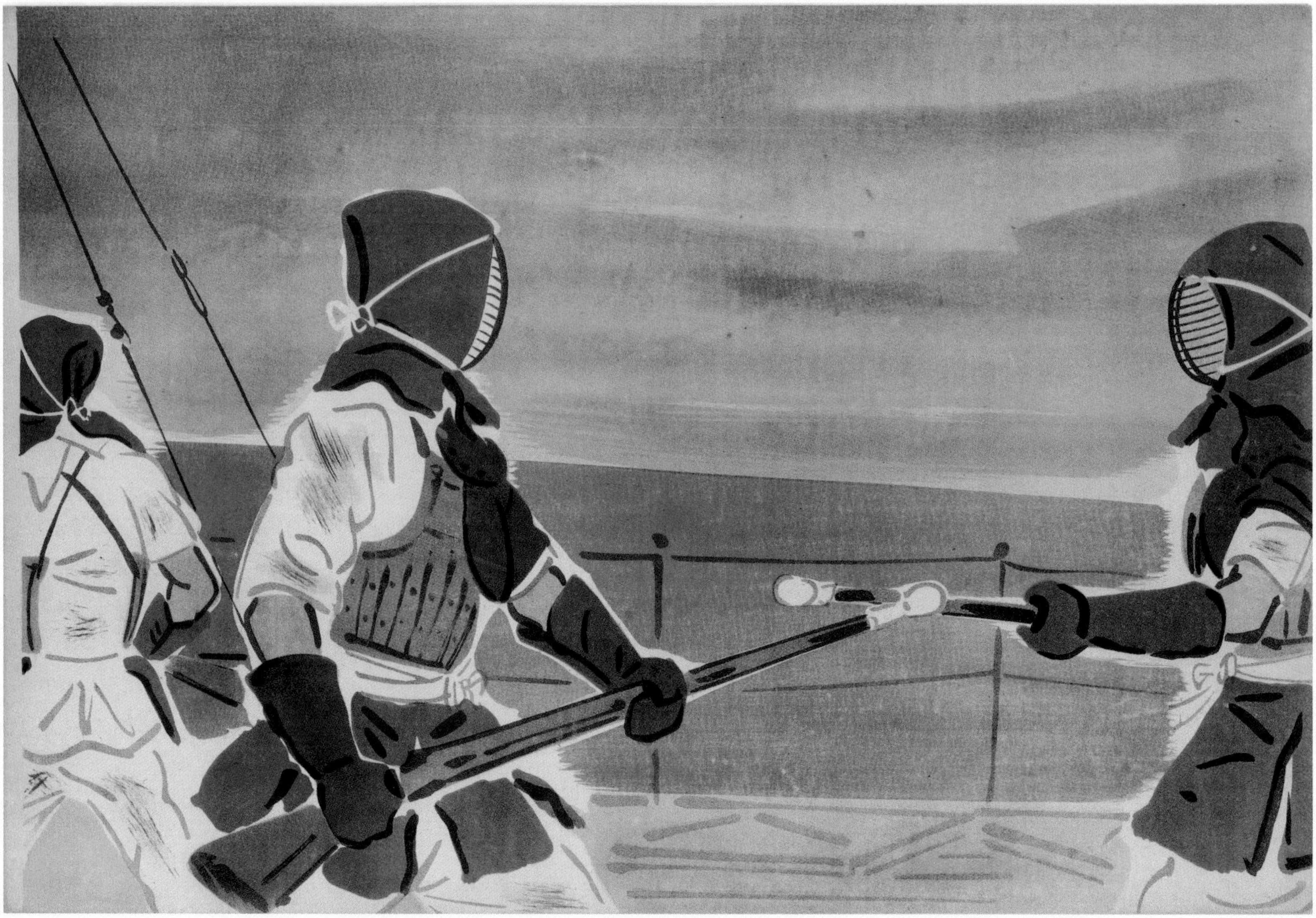

Twentieth-Century Samurai: On the carrier ship bringing them to their mission, commandos wearing wicker helmets and padding for *kendo* sword fighting take part in bayonet practice with wooden rifles.

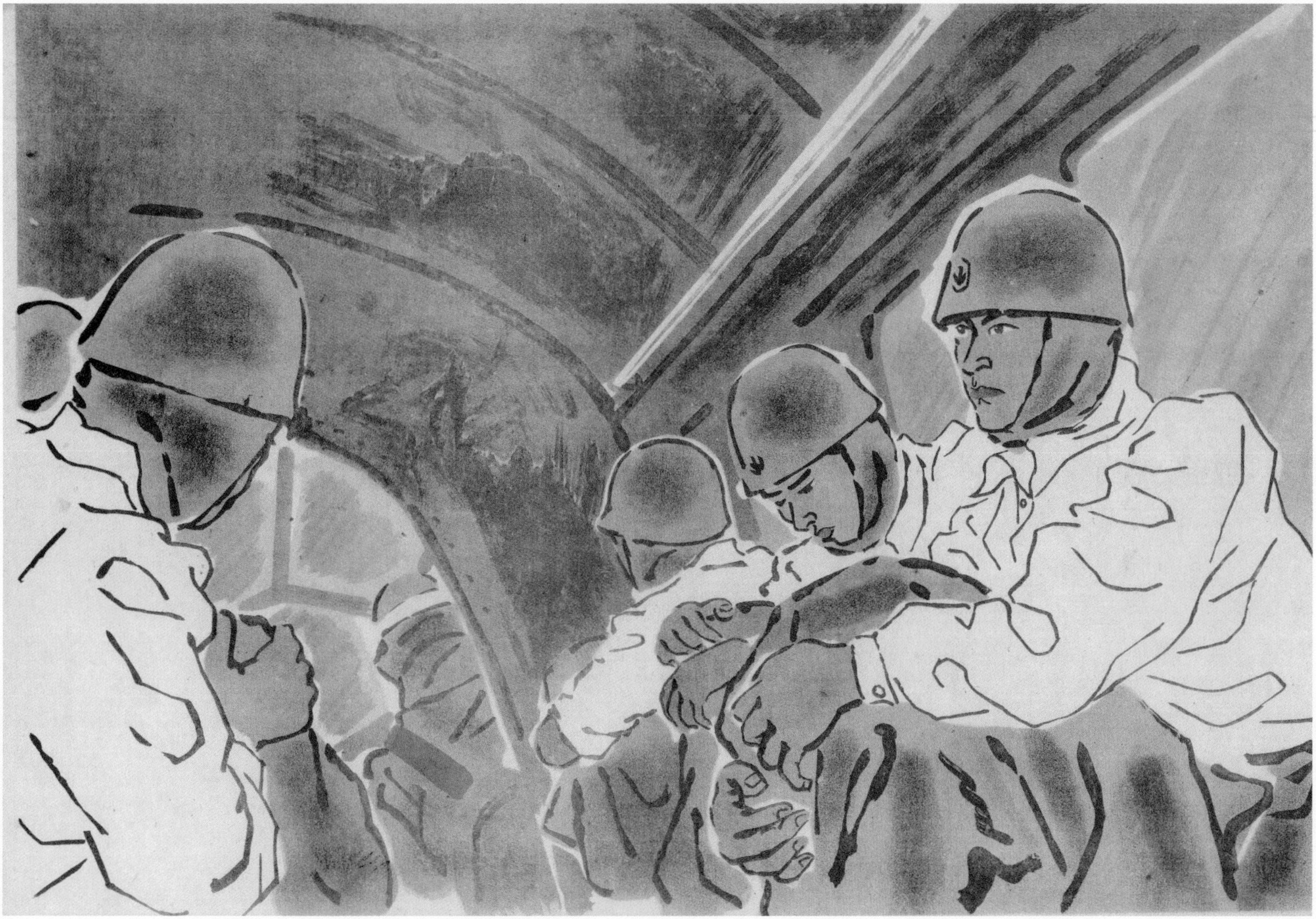

***Shonen* Jump:** Paratroopers huddle in the freezing bay in the suspenseful moments before a jump. With determined faces, the commandos are lost in private thoughts of mortality and home.

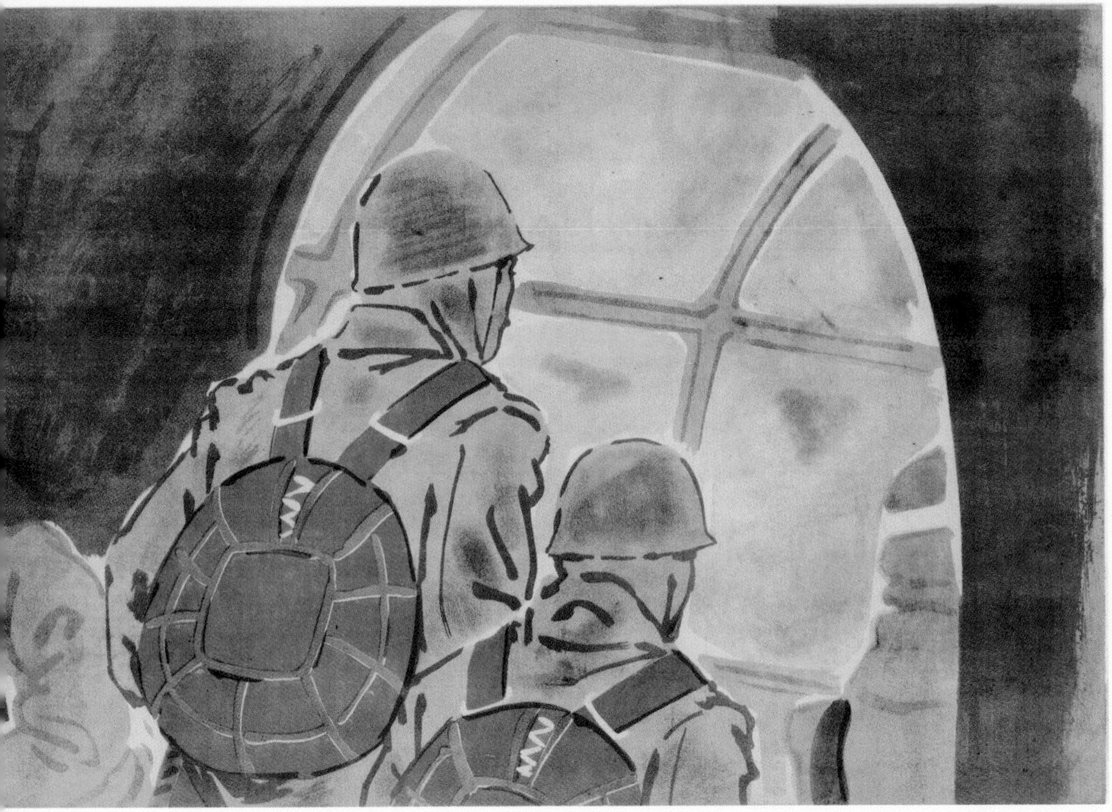

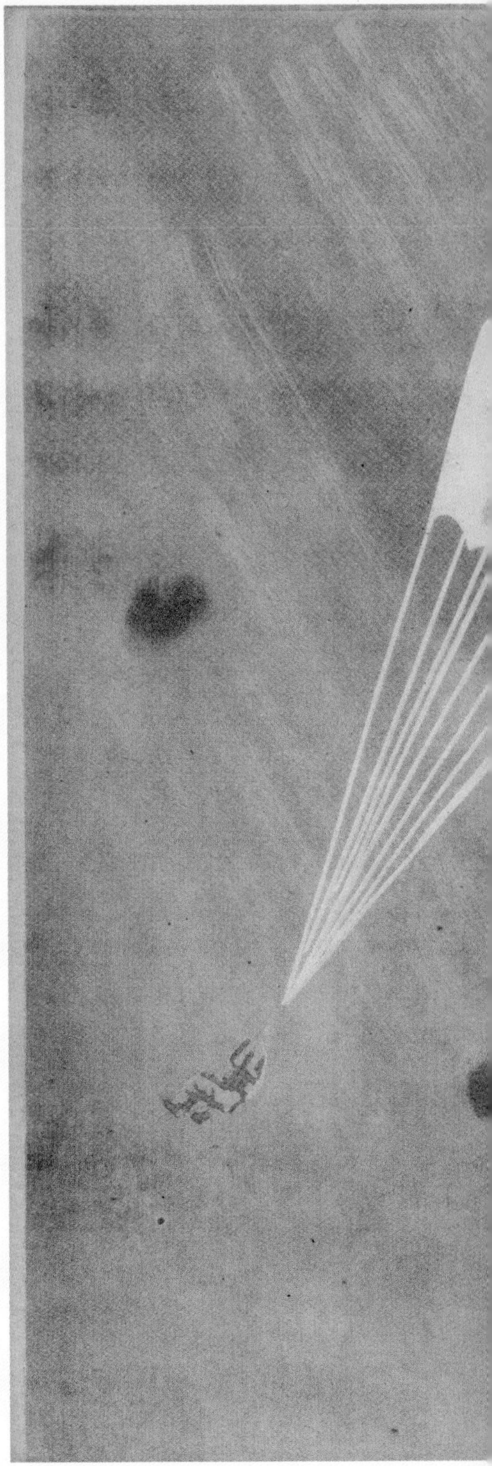

ABOVE Hitting the Silk: Paratroopers' chutes open automatically as they jump into a flak-filled sky.

RIGHT Stand and Deliver: A paratrooper stands in the door. Like manga, *kamishibai* often pause at the moment just before action, like in a duel between swordsmen.

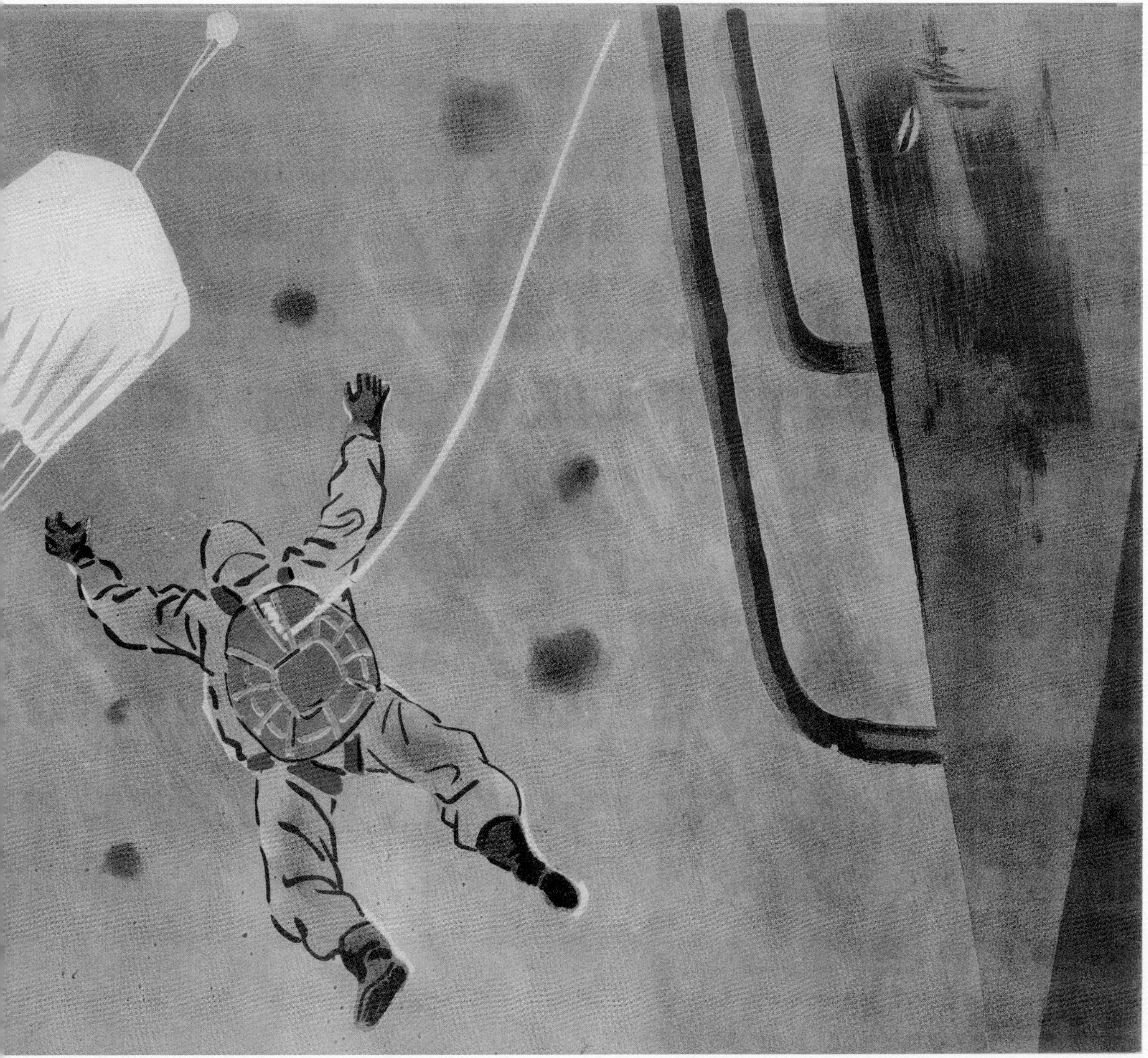

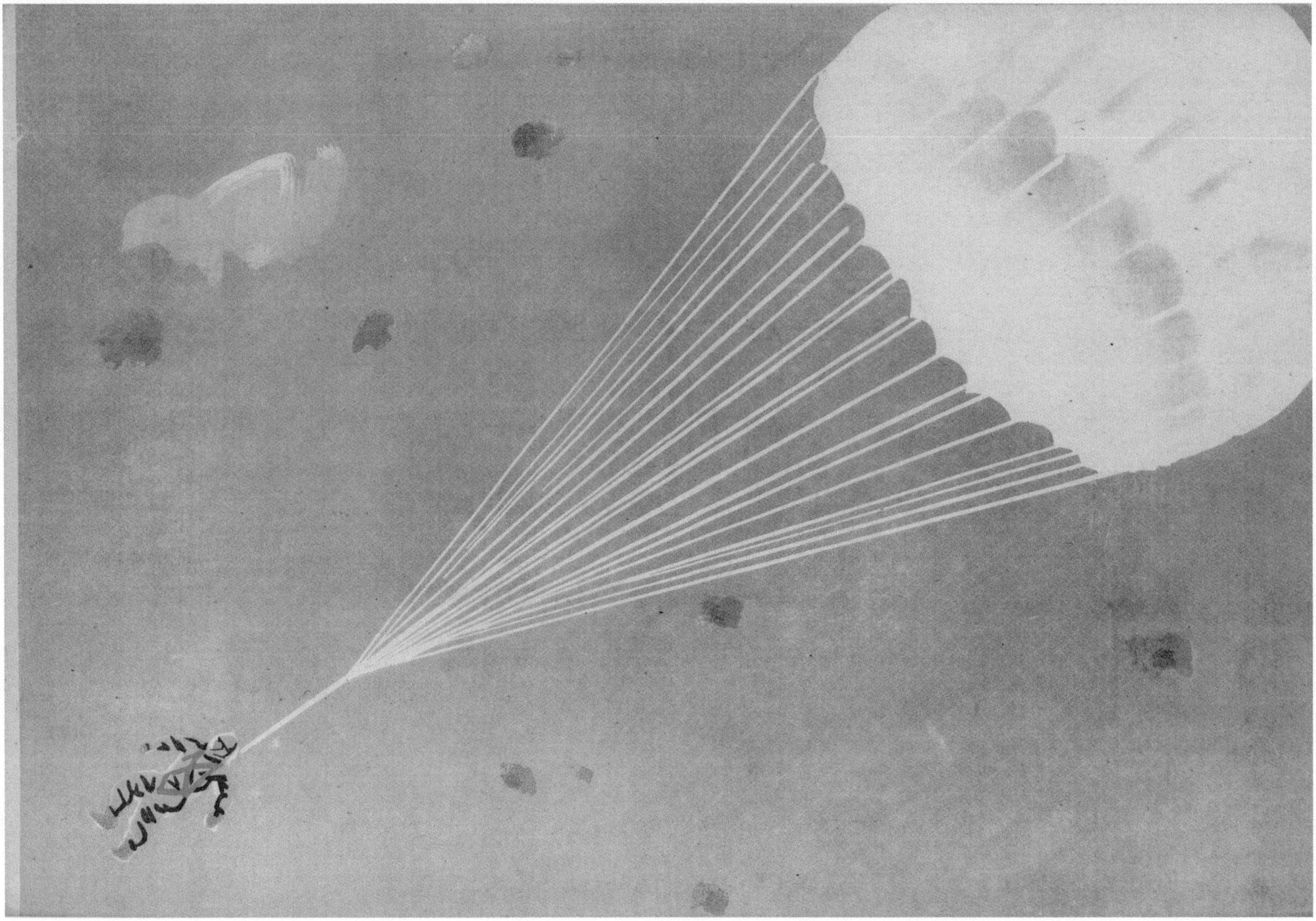

Silk Screen: The *kamishibai* is presented in a documentary style, yet the artist adds graphic impact in the lines of the parachute radiating diagonally from corner to corner, contrasting with the tiny figure of the man. The editing of the panels is paced cinematically from medium to increasingly long shots.

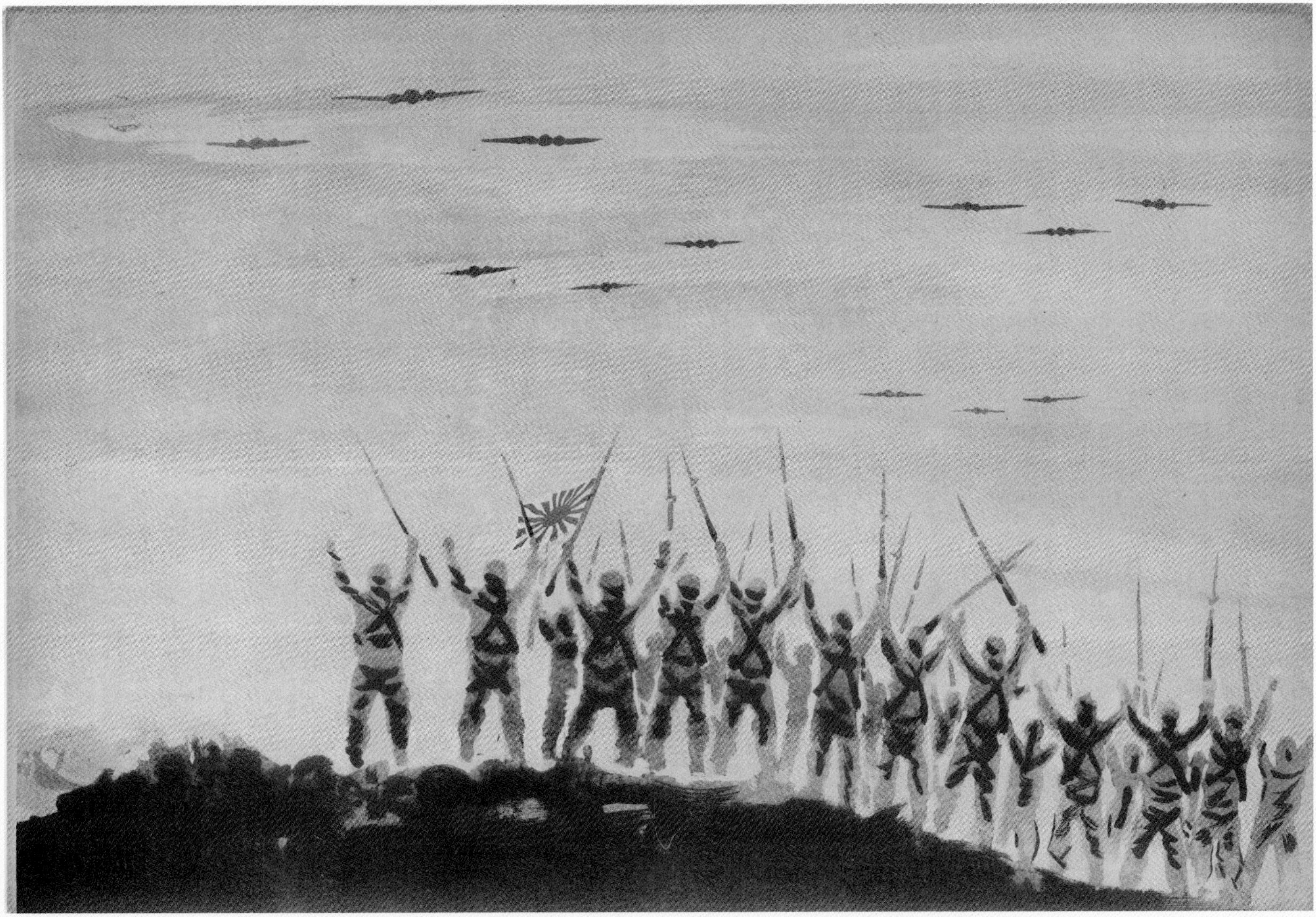

"May You Live Ten Thousand Years": As in the last frame of *Kintaro*, which parallels the action of this realistic *kamishibai* in a children's format, the group of soldiers raises the flag in a *banzai* shout as victorious planes fly overhead. Japanese propaganda emphasized the soldiers' *bushido* (warrior) spirit over mechanized might, while American propaganda displayed industrial strength as well as the will of workers in images like Rosie the Riveter and Disney's *Victory Through Air Power*, which helped convince the chiefs of staff to launch air attacks on Japanese civilians.

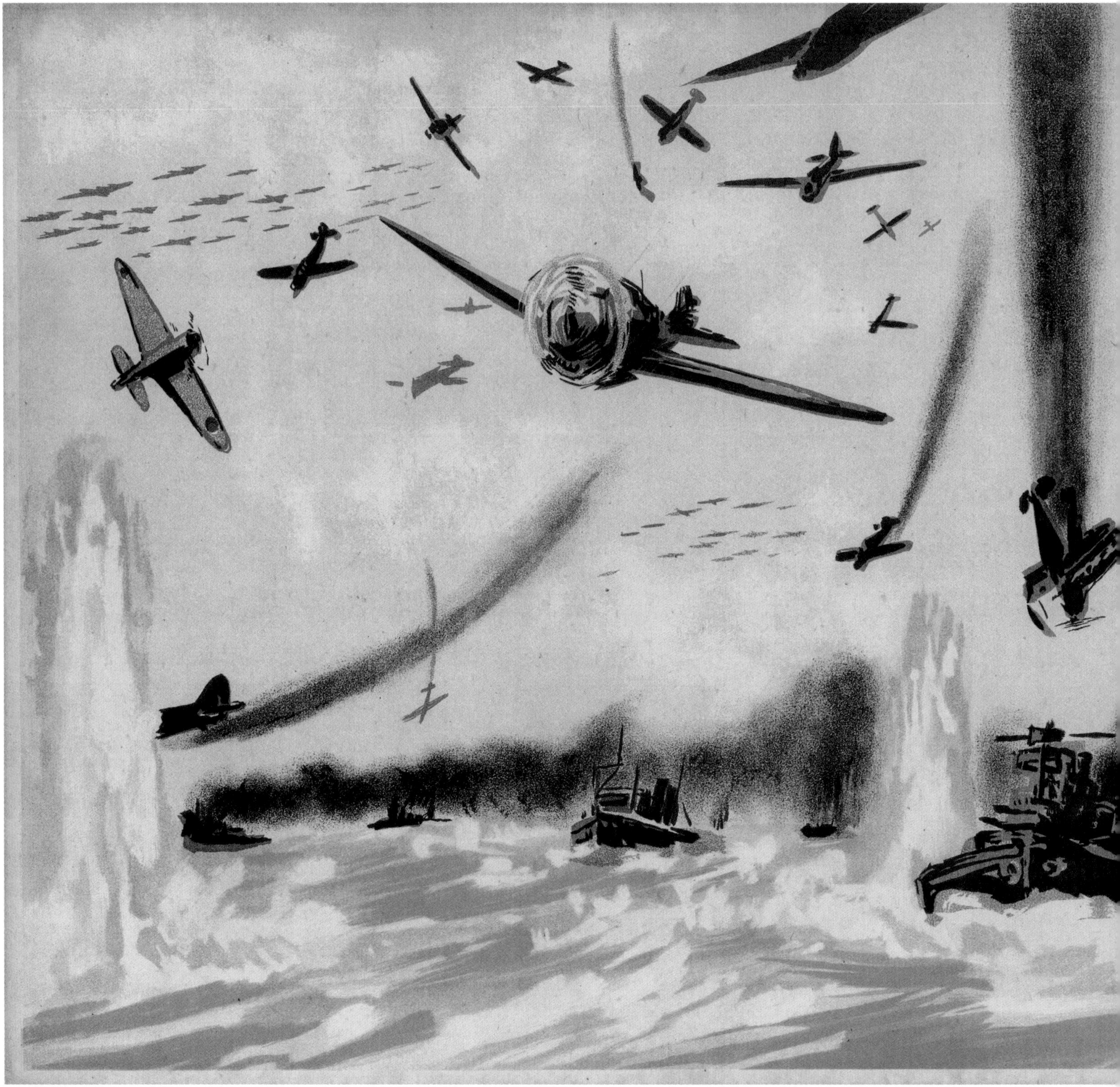

LEFT Paper Newsreel: This scene of Japanese fliers attacking an American flotilla is presented in the documentary style of combat newsreel footage. Even when using machines, the Japanese military followed the hand-to-hand code of *bushido*: a downed pilot directs his flaming aircraft at an American ship. The Japanese set up garrisons like a global game of Go until the Americans switched their strategy to island hopping, skipping the marcescent Japanese strongholds and carving their own landing strips out of jungle atolls to bomb the homeland. The war was essentially lost when Saipan in the Marianas fell in July 1944, allowing Americans to bomb Japan around the clock. In the next year, three-quarters of the homes in three-quarters of the major Japanese cities were destroyed. Outmanned and outgunned, the Japanese adopted the "Special Tactics" of kamikaze missions.

ABOVE Surfacing Sun: A Japanese submarine flies the sixteen-rayed naval ensign. Japan was proud of its navy: when the *Yamato* and *Musashi*, sister battleships bristling with one thousand guns, were built in 1937 they were the largest and most heavily armed ships in history. Rather than using their submarine fleet as hunter-killers as the Americans did, the Japanese Navy used them ineffectively as transport ships. Article 9 of the postwar Japanese constitution declared that "land, sea, and air forces, as well as other war potential, will never be maintained." Cryptofascist tendencies can be read into anime like *Silent Service*, where a rebel Japanese admiral takes command of a nuclear sub. Suehiro Maruo imagines an alternative history of Japan winning the war and ritually beheading General Douglas MacArthur in his manga *Planet of the Jap*.

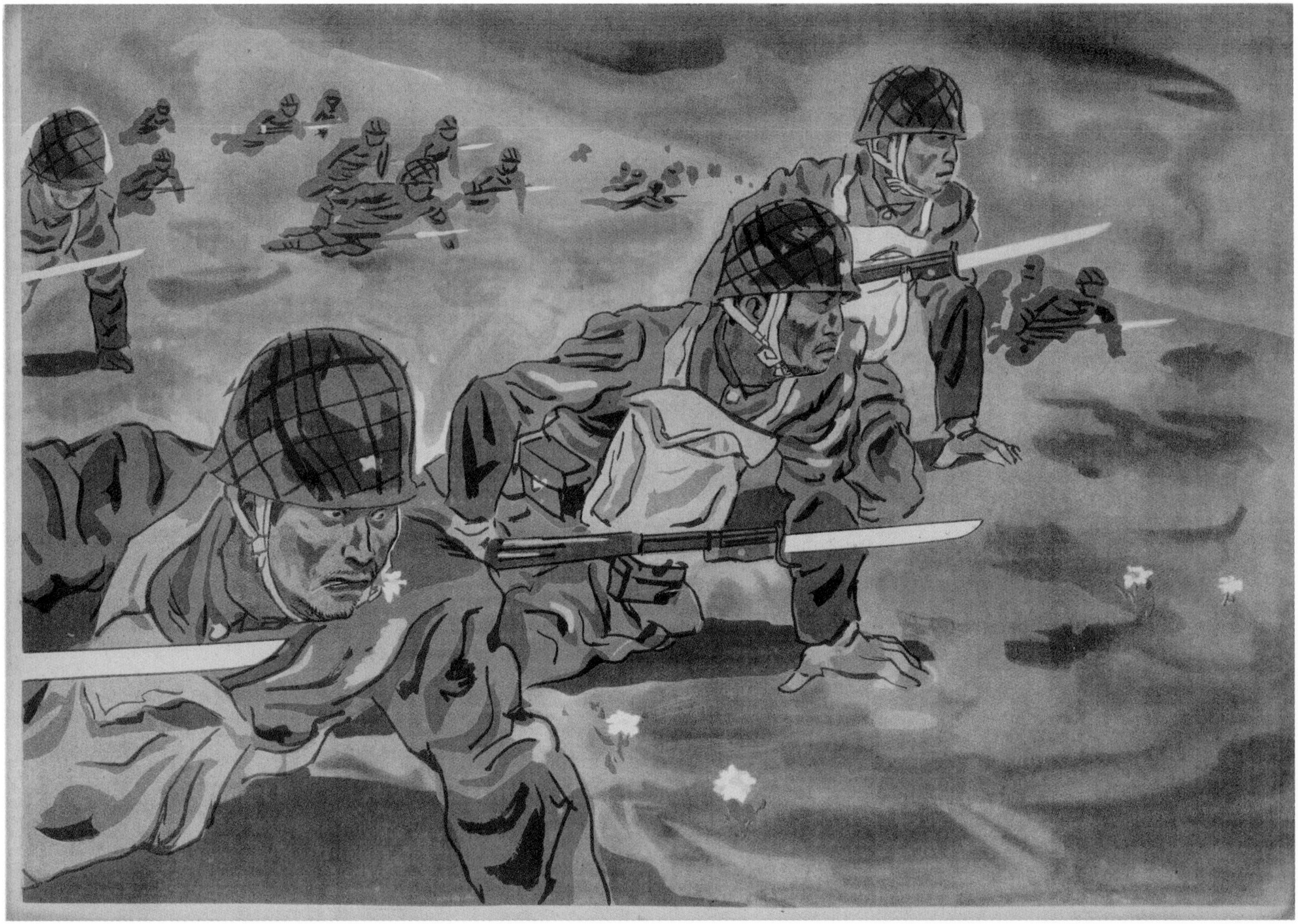

Fixed Bayonets: A line of Japanese soldiers prepares to charge in one of the more documentary depictions of combat, directed at an adult audience as well. Despite the depiction of heroics, this *kamishibai* is about the total destruction of Japanese forces at Attu Island in the icy Aleutians. The soldier in the foreground holds a flower in his teeth as a symbol of his imminent death.

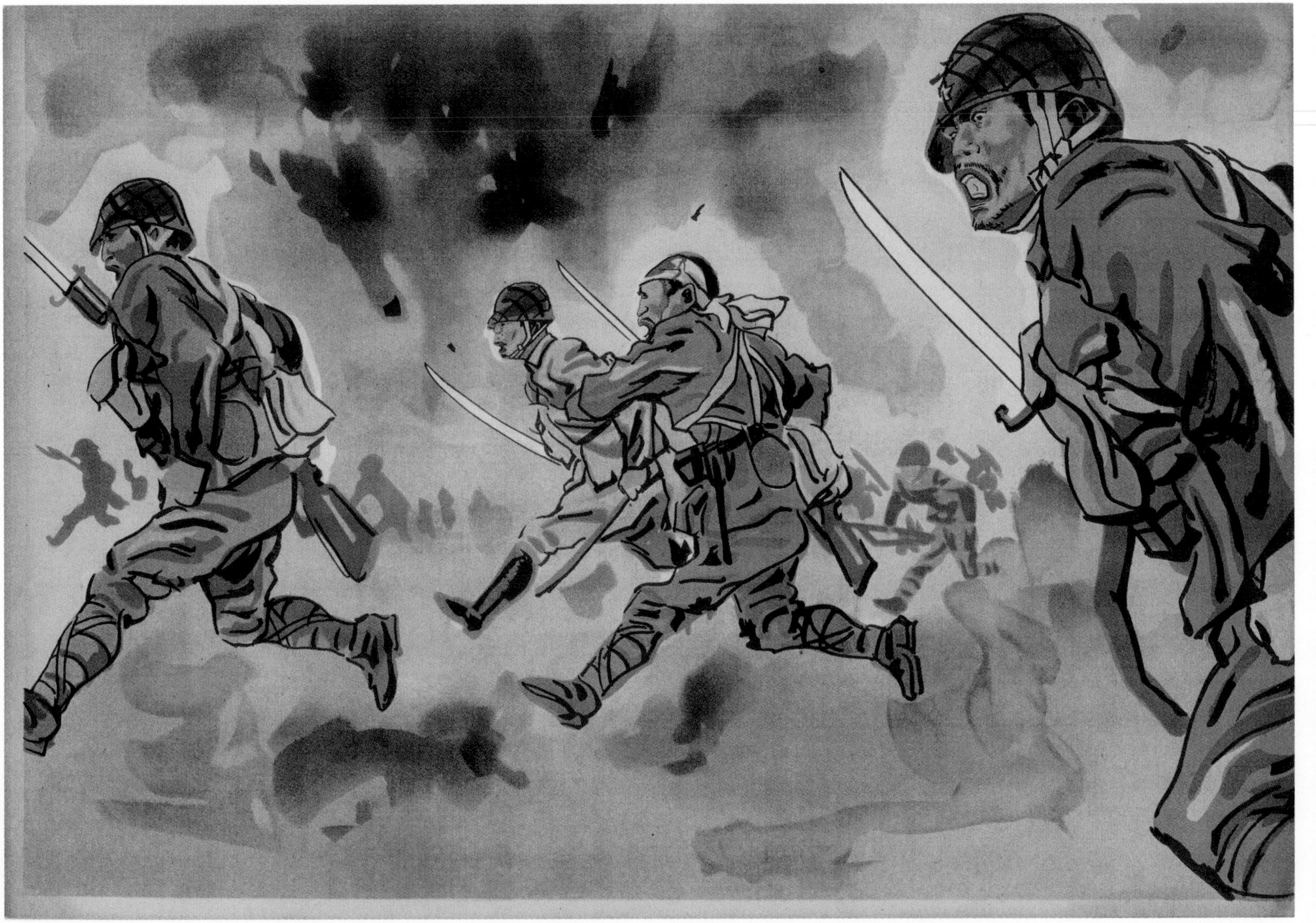

***Banzai* Charge:** In one of the largest *banzai* charges in the Pacific War, Japanese infantrymen charged American lines under a salvo of artillery fire, portrayed here as an impressionistic wash of color.

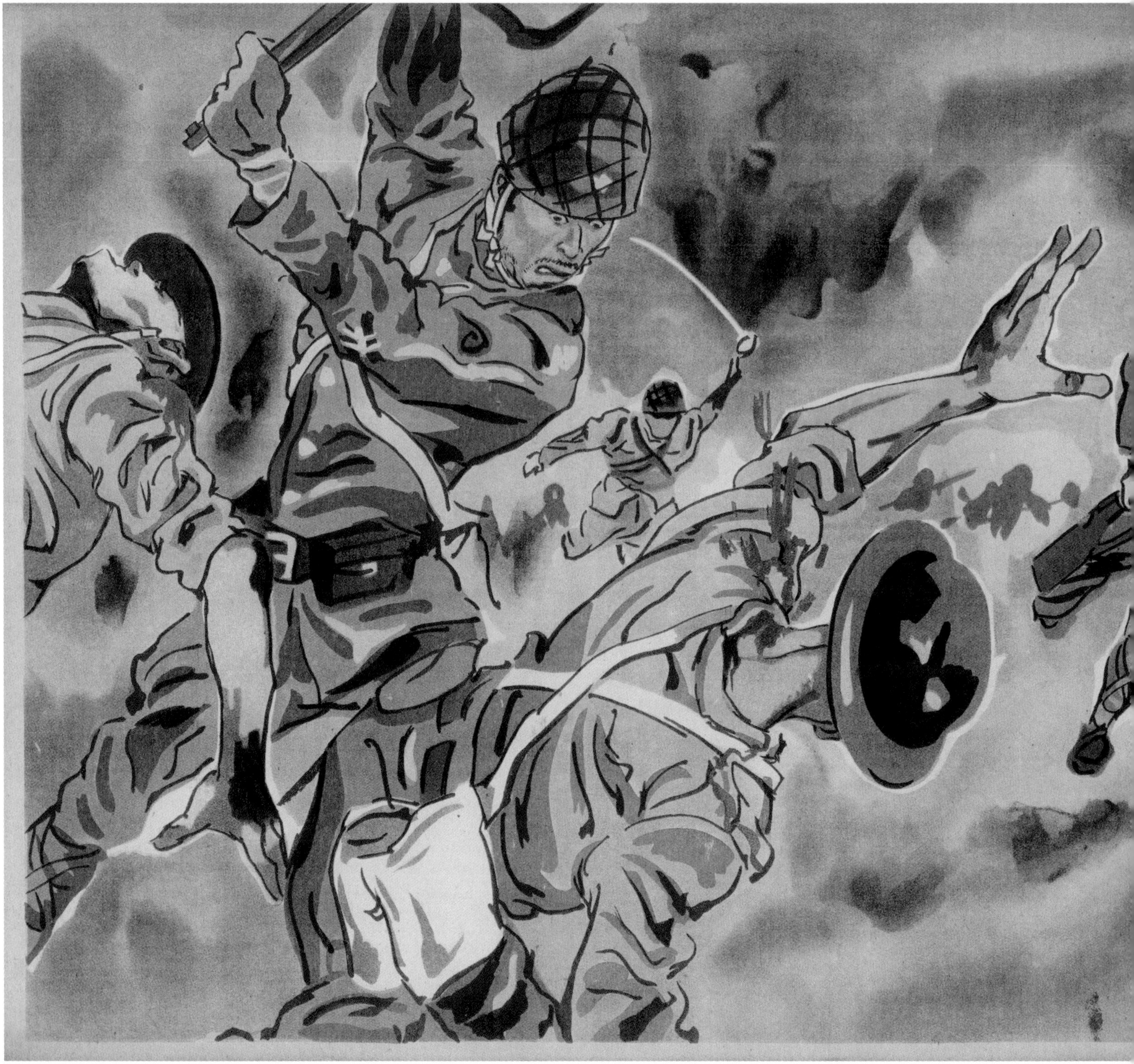

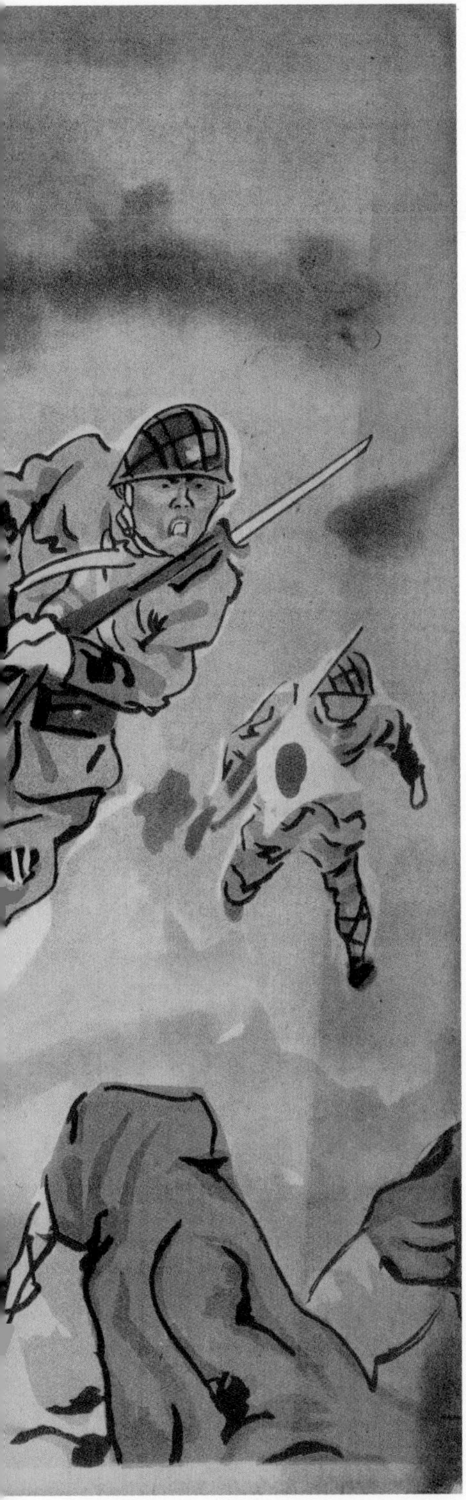

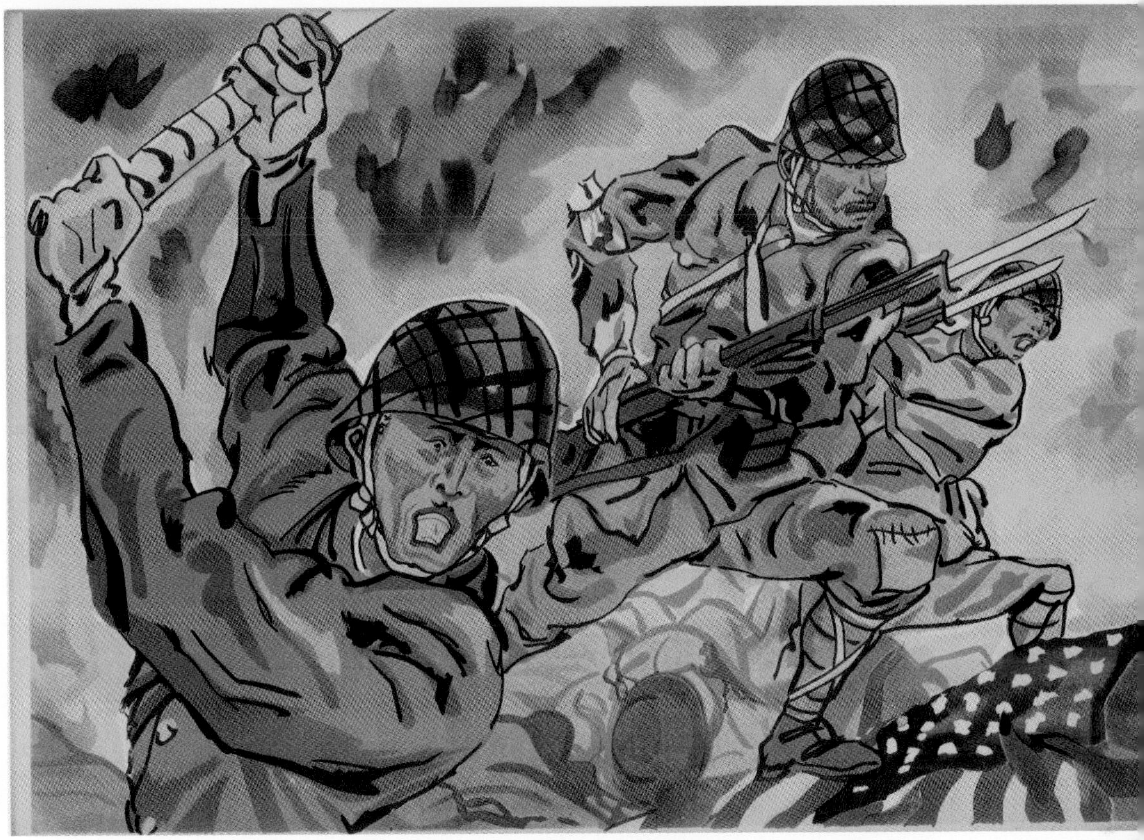

LEFT Drawing Blood: The specialty of the Japanese soldier was close combat. Here a combatant wields his rifle like a samurai sword as he slices through two American soldiers. The image was not cleaned up for children—the thread of blood adds to the intensity.

ABOVE Flag Underfoot: *Banzai* chargers penetrate to the rear echelons of the U.S. forces on Attu as Japanese soldiers trample an American flag. Of more than two thousand Japanese soldiers, only twenty-eight survived. The soldiers' tattered uniforms show they are veteran fighters.

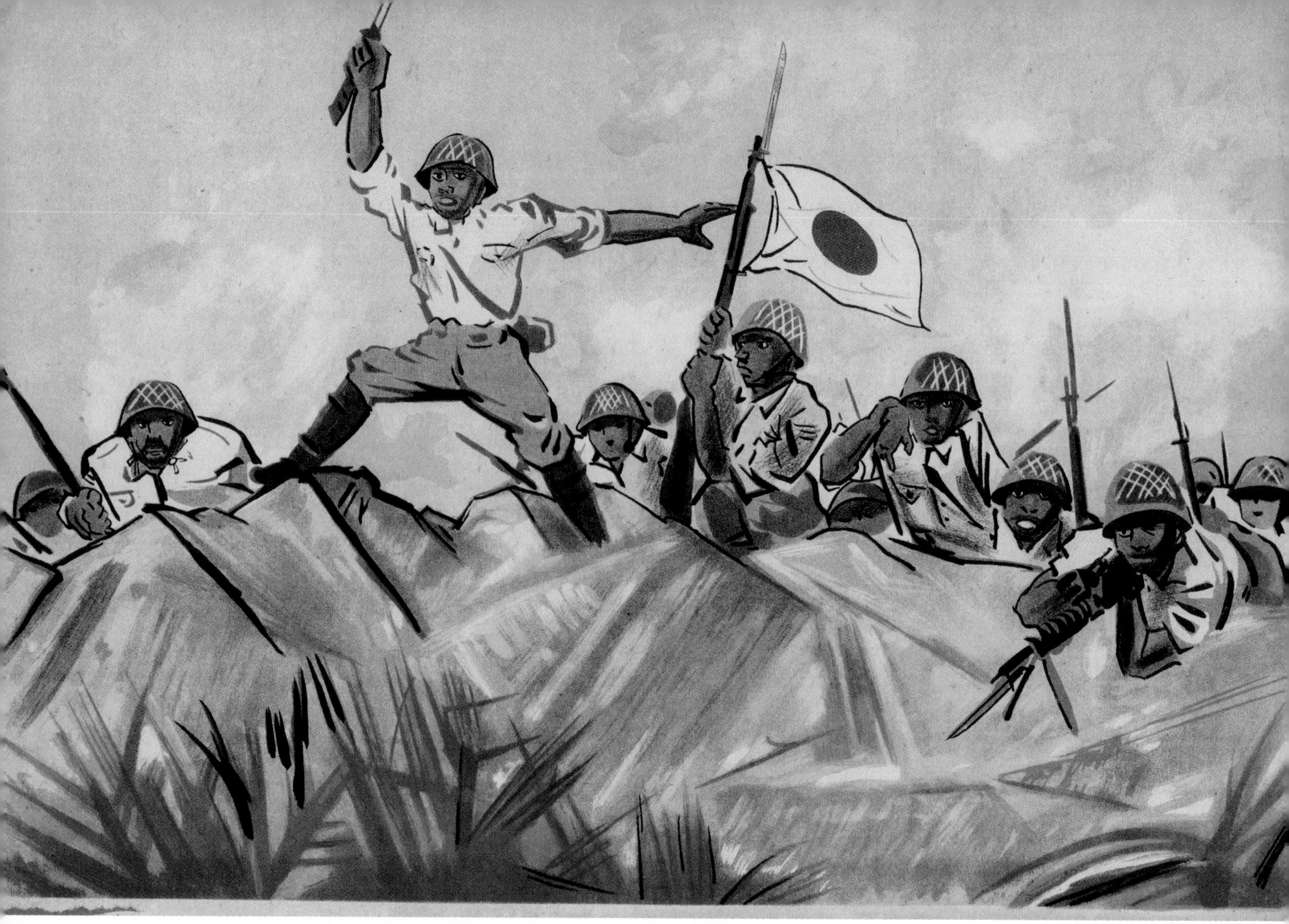

Spell of the Samurai: Japanese soldiers raise the rising-sun flag in victory after taking a hill. A rifleman at the right of the picture lays down cover fire, but the focus is on the soldiers brandishing bladed weapons, as in a painting of a feudal battle scene. General MacArthur wrote of his foe in his reports on the Southwest Pacific campaign that it was "an Army that was steeped in medieval cruelty, but fought with the most modern technical skill and savage valor, until superior skill and equal valor broke the spell of the Samurai and the legend of an invincible Empire."

Armies of the Night: After battle, a wounded soldier regales his comrades with stories of the day's heroism. The nocturnal bamboo forest is suggested with just a few brushstrokes. Japanese soldiers were feared as fierce night fighters. One training slogan was, "The night is a million reinforcements." A racial myth held that dark Japanese eyes were superior to the fair eyes of the enemy for night fighting.

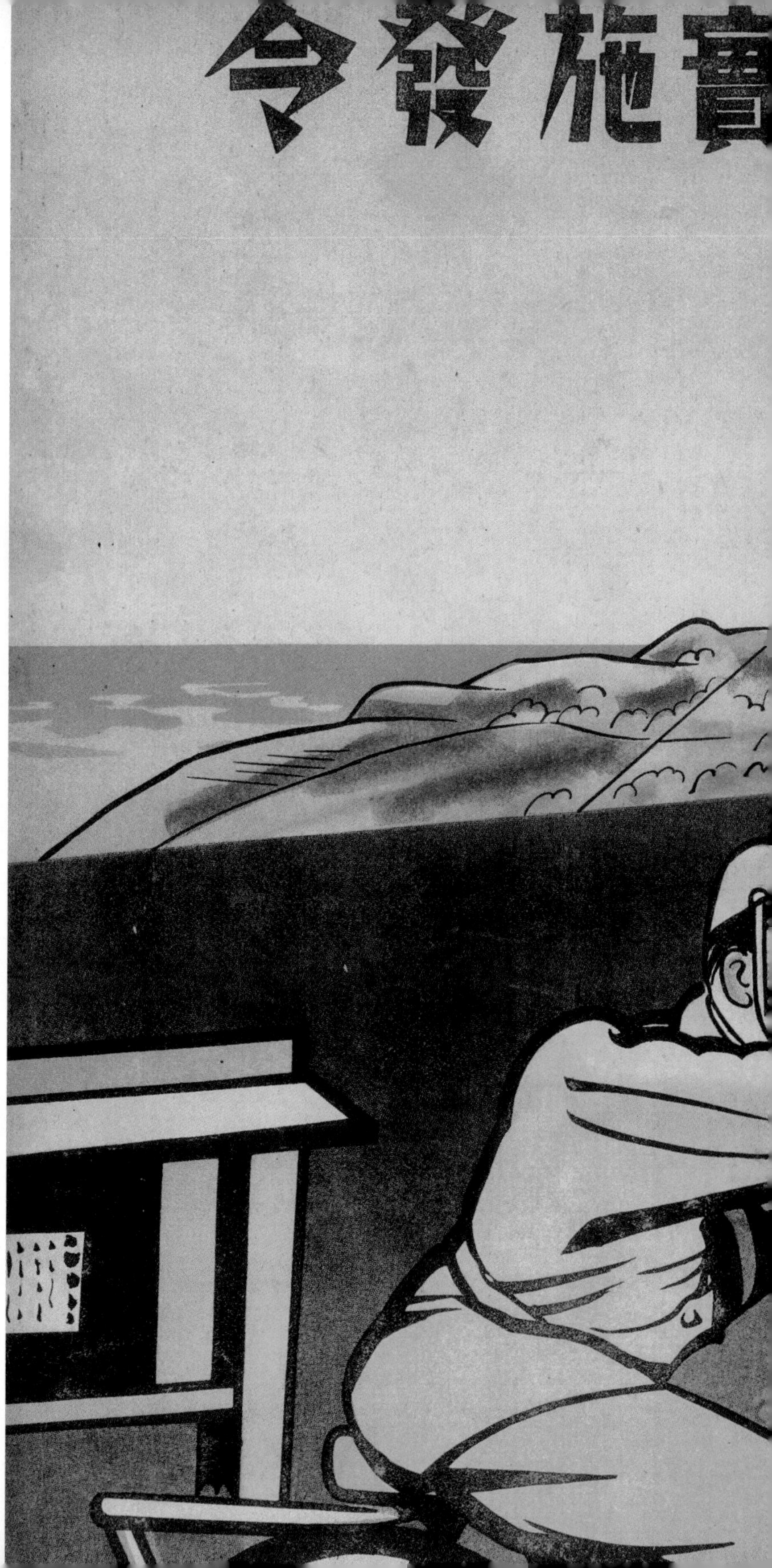
實施發令

***Order for Air Defense*:** Japanese civil defense was pitiably homemade in the face of America's winged might. In a cinematic split screen, spotters on the shoreline give an early warning without benefit of radar. A civil defense announcer with only a bicycle and a megaphone calls out, "An air-defense alert has been issued." American bombing raids took advantage of night skies to avoid early warnings.

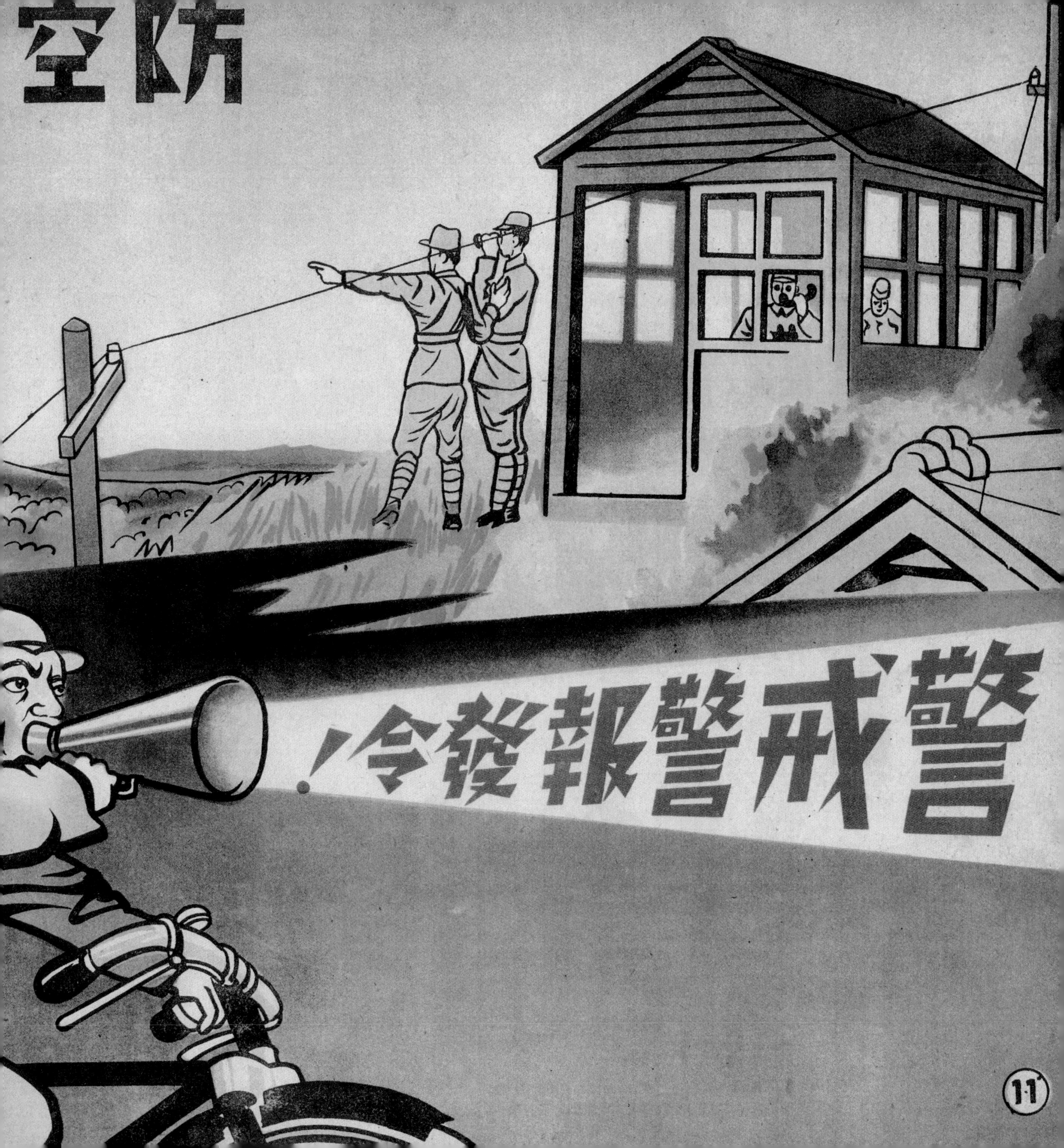
防空
警戒警報發令!
11

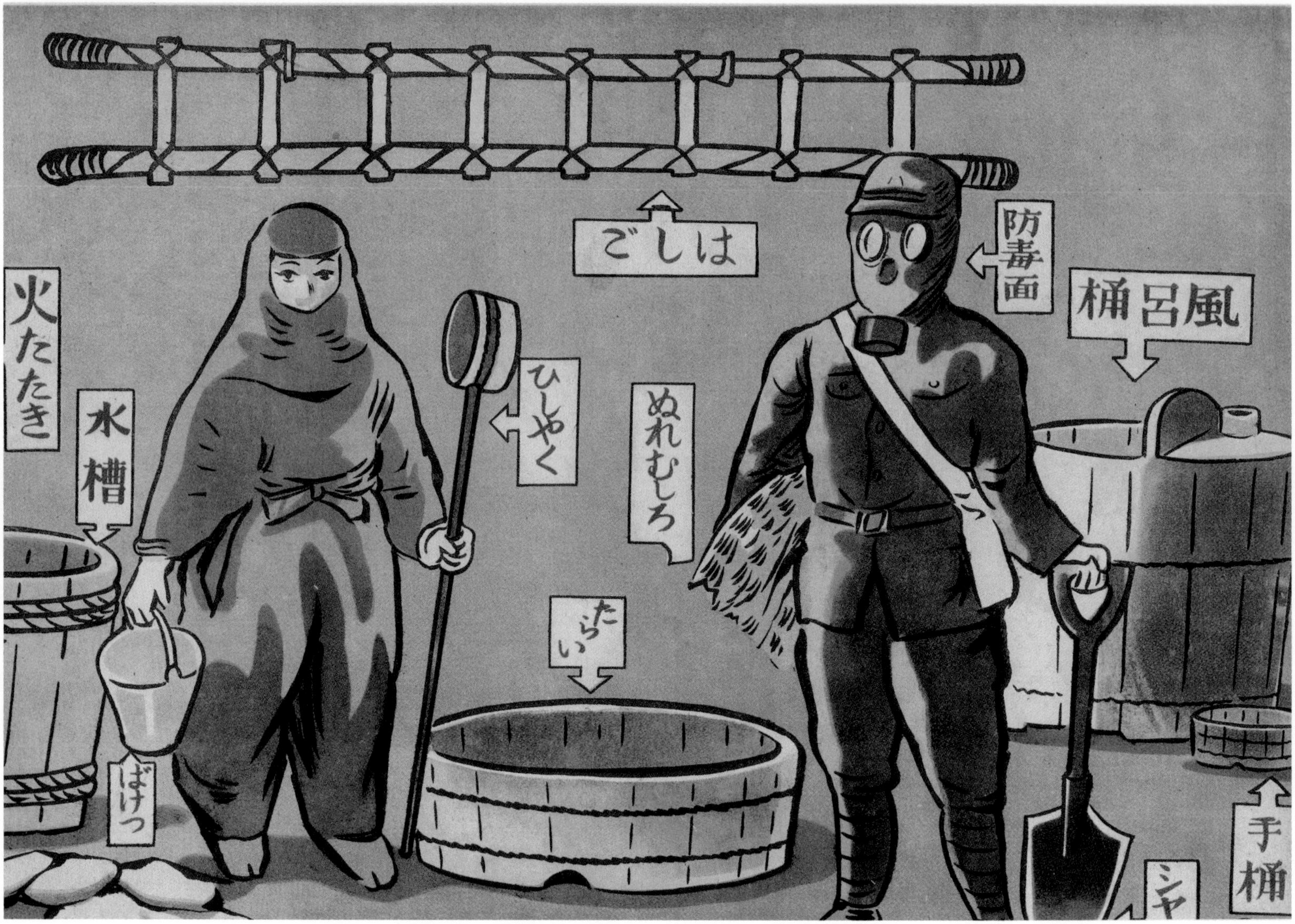

はしご
防毒面
風呂桶
火たたき
水槽
ひしやく
ぬれむしろ
たらい
ばけつ
手桶

Fireproof Fashion: A couple shows the proper firefighting equipment—rudimentary household items like a water-filled bathtub, a ladle and bucket, a bamboo ladder, and a wet blanket, held by the man. Few civilians were fortunate enough to have gas masks. *Kamishibai*, once used just for entertainment, were now directed at survival; the masked figure here is an eerie echo of pulp heroes in *kamishibai*'s formative years.

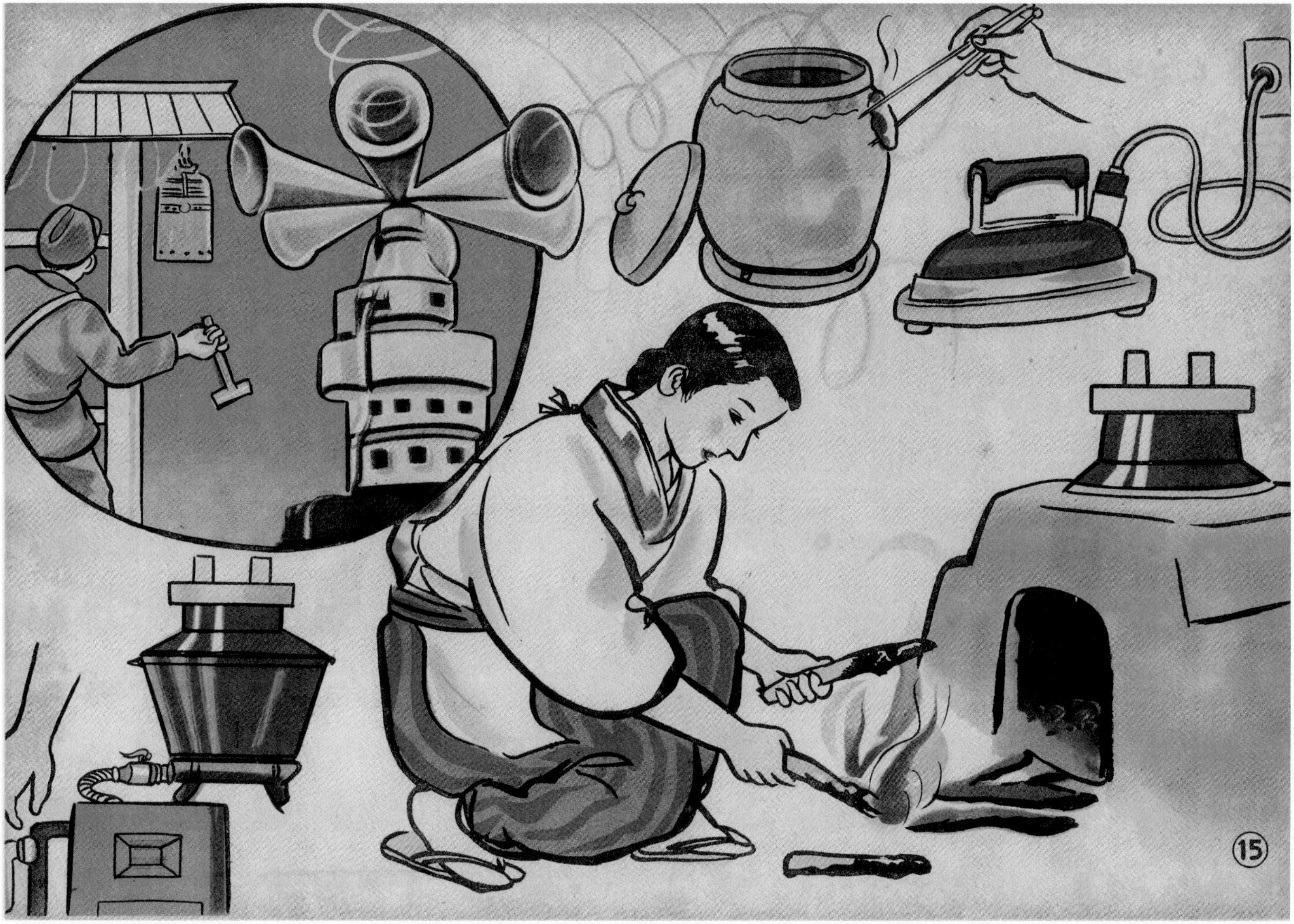
15

Hearth Attack: A primer on what to do when the air raid sirens sound: to reduce the risk of fire, turn off rice cookers, unplug irons, douse hearth fires (even modern kitchens used coal-fired ovens), and turn off hot-water heaters. The mother is the tutelary spirit of the household. In the circular inset, ancient bells and hammers are shown being used for fire alarms.

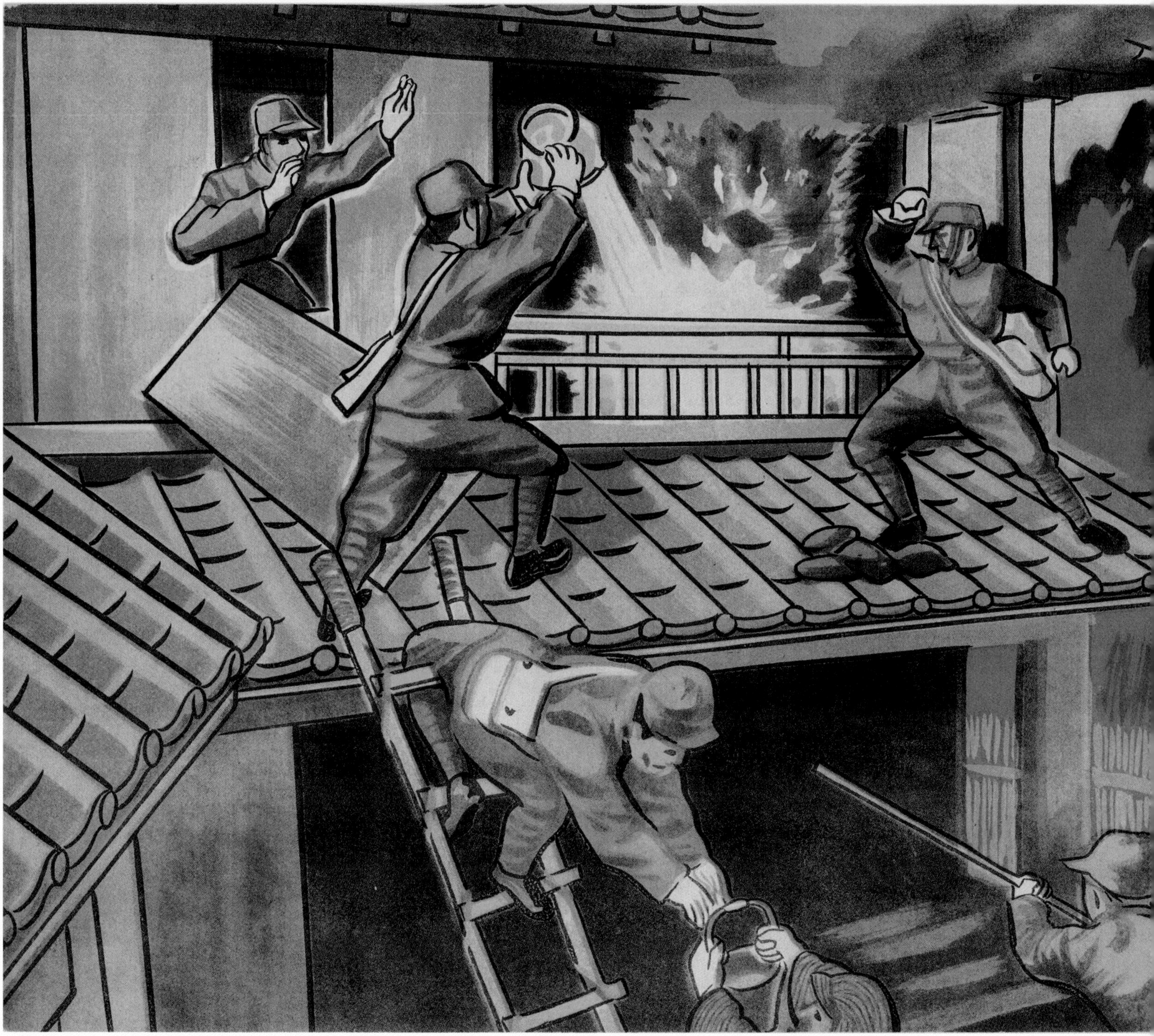

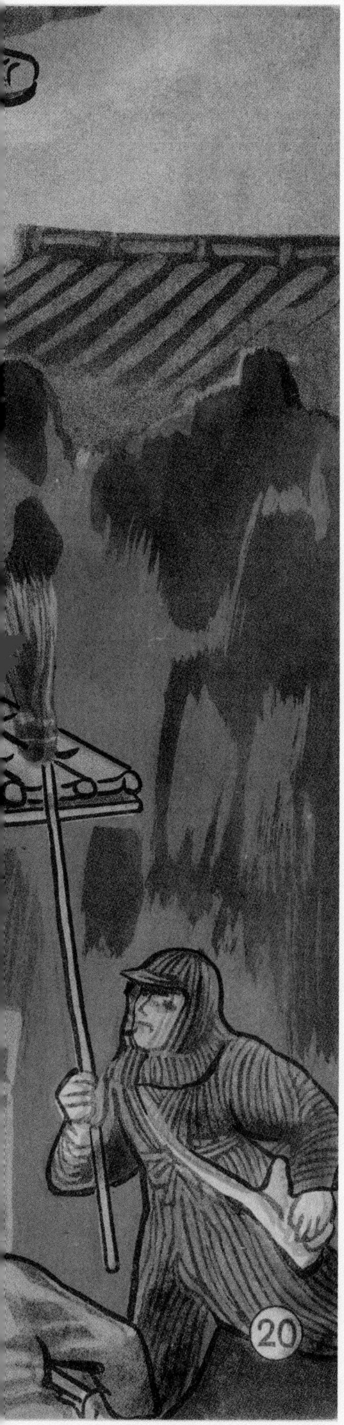

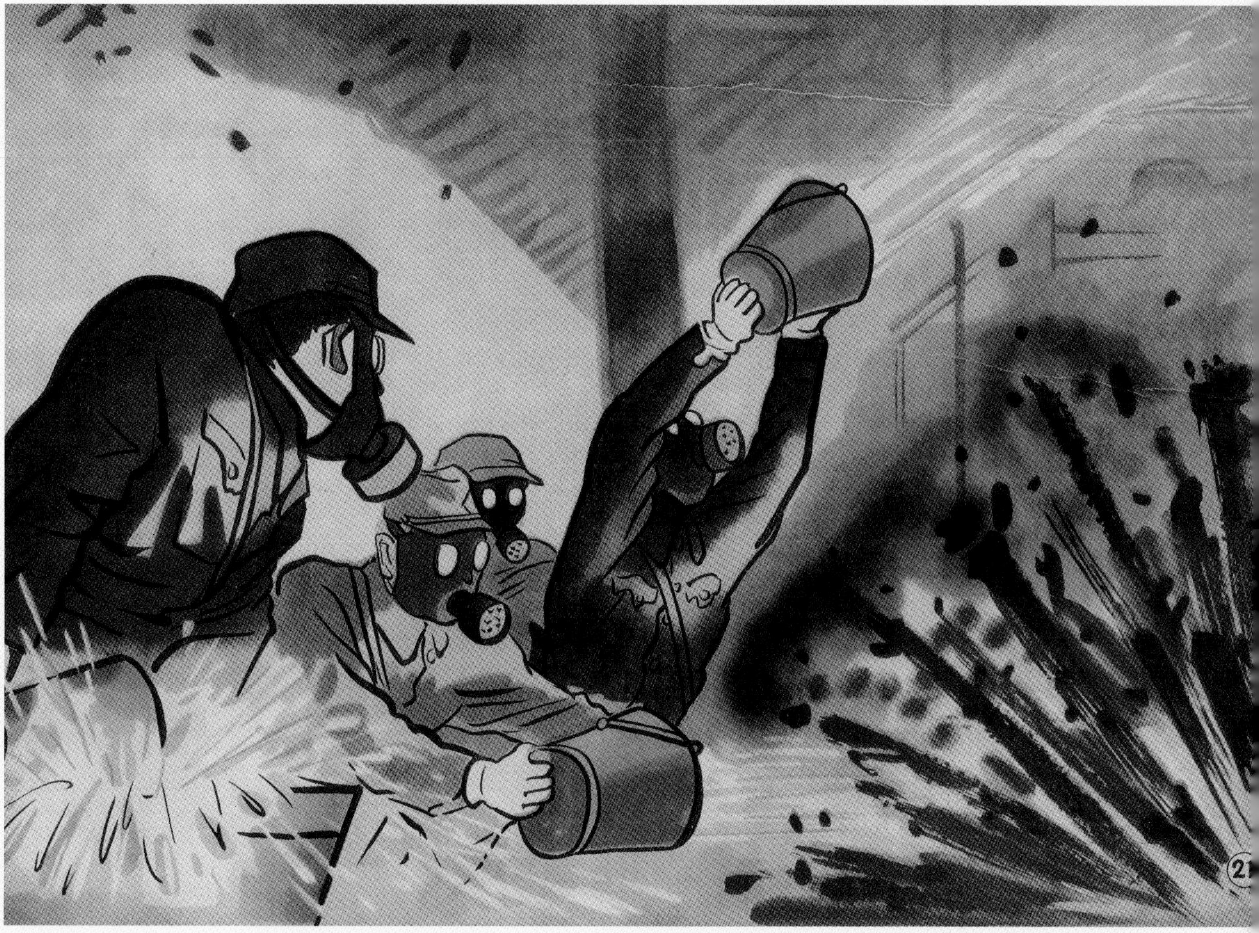

LEFT Bucket Brigade: Civil-defense workers in khaki uniforms help a city firefighter, wearing capelike protection and carrying a broom, put out a second-story fire.

ABOVE Inferno: Wearing gas masks against the smoke, a team of civil-defense workers throws buckets of water on a fire, the same way fires were put out for centuries. Burns from fires caused by bombing were the chief cause of fatalities among civilians.

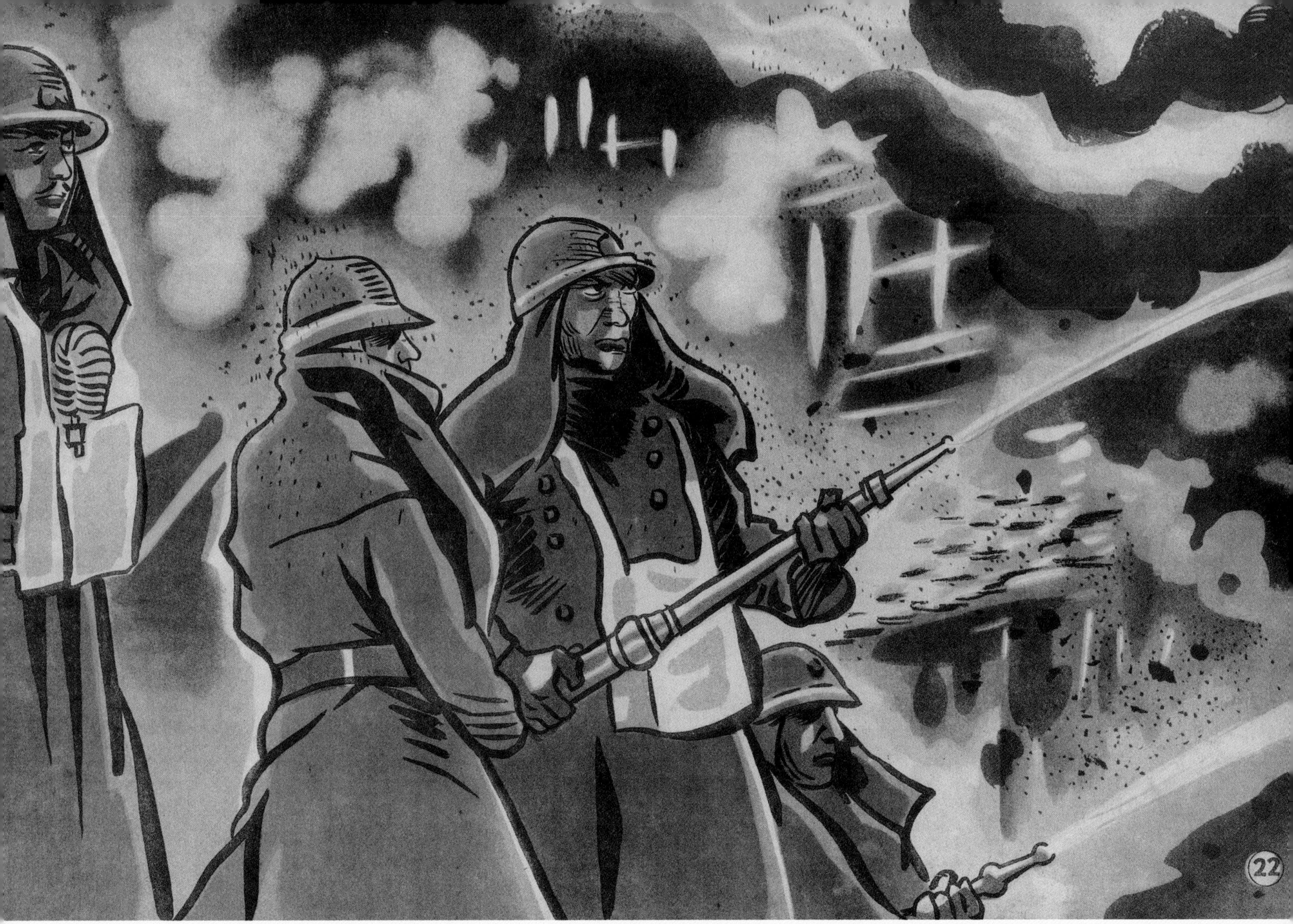
22

Tinderbox Tokyo: Heroically posed hooded firefighters in lacquered leather helmets douse flames with water hoses. Firefighting equipment was primitive—some teams still used hand-drawn water pumps, and trucks were powered by charcoal-burning furnaces because gasoline was scarce. Young women, too, served as firefighters.

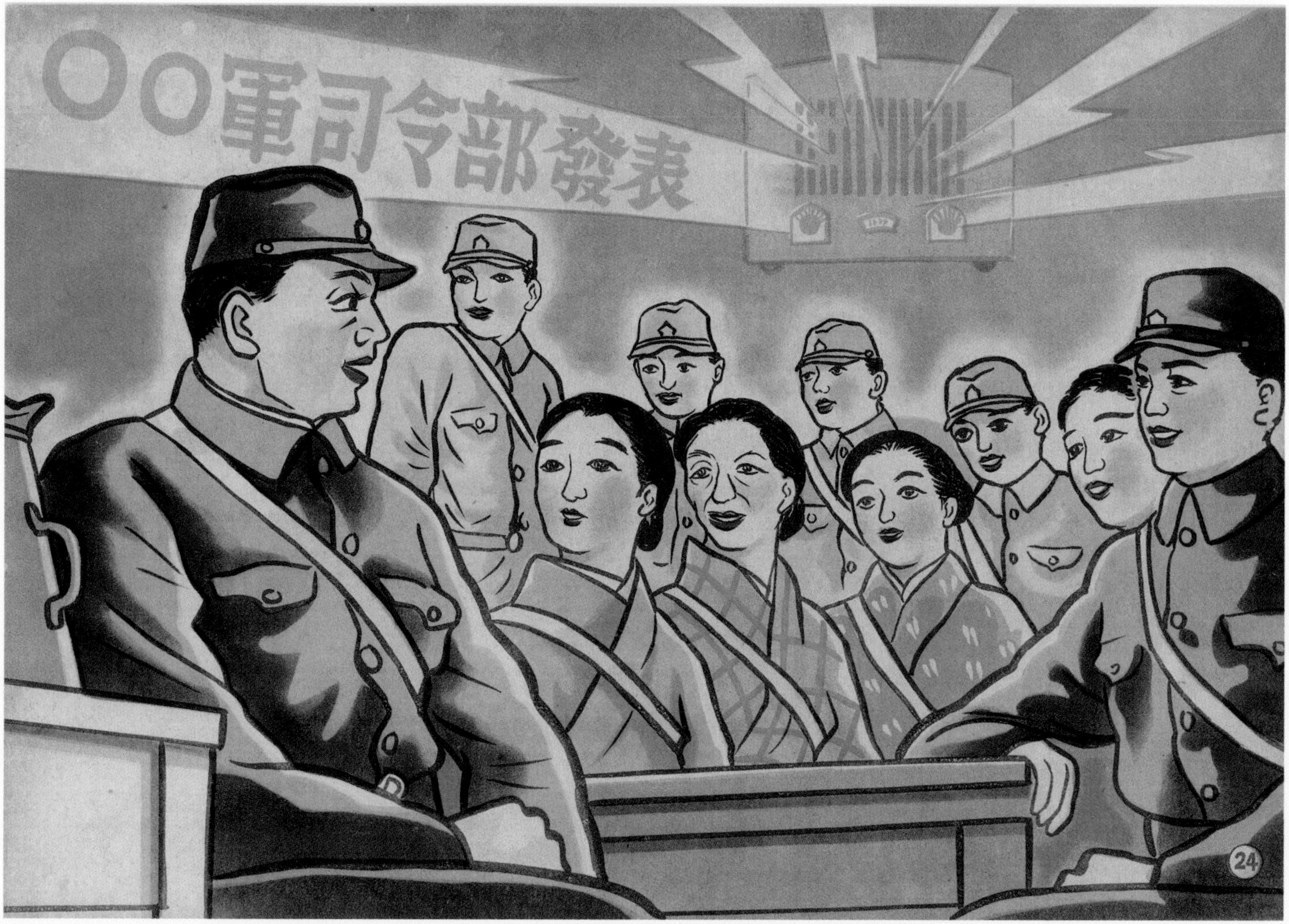
○○軍司令部發表
24

All Clear: A radio announcer calls the end of the air raid. The communal bomb shelter is occupied by women and boys.

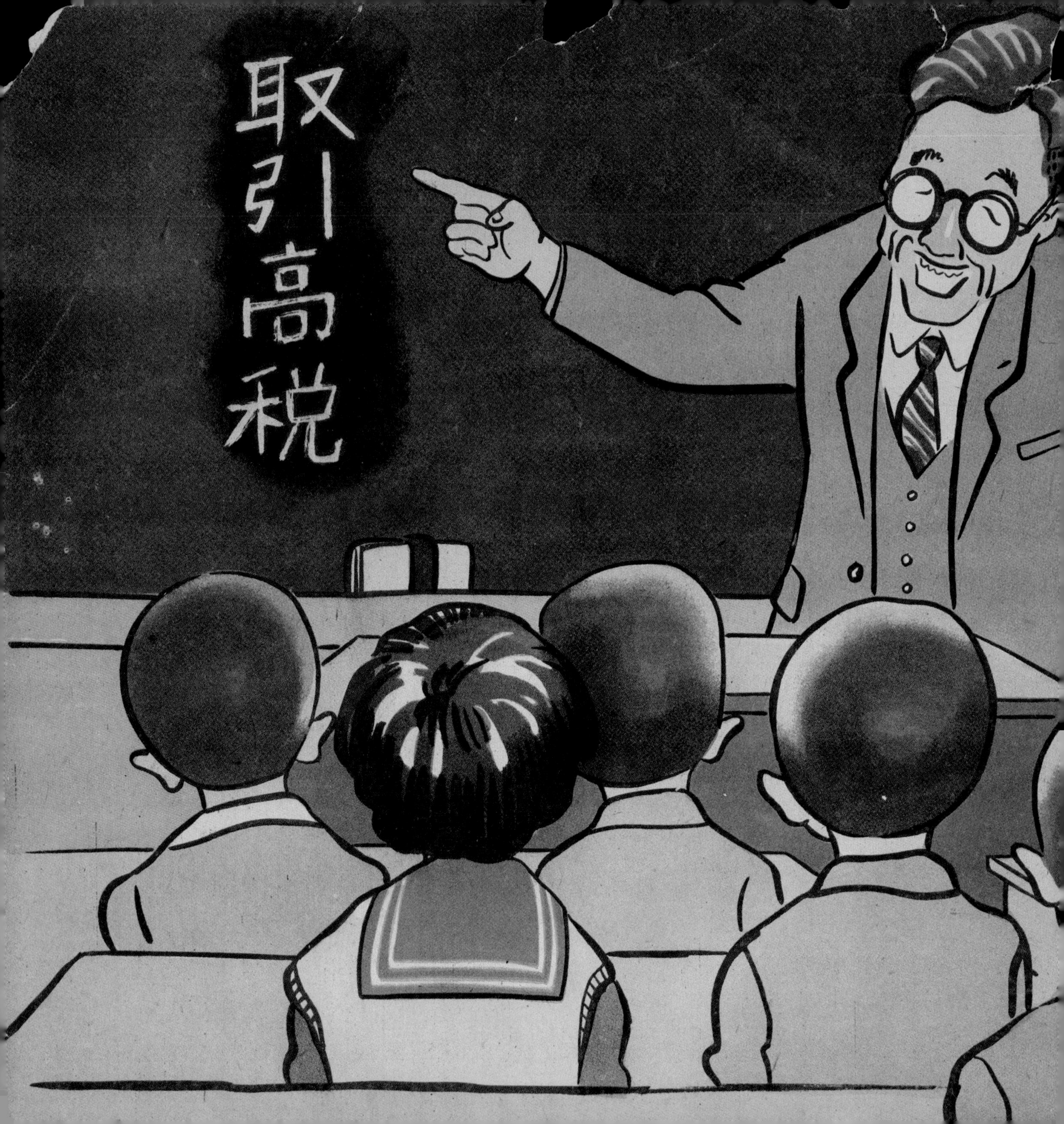
取引高税

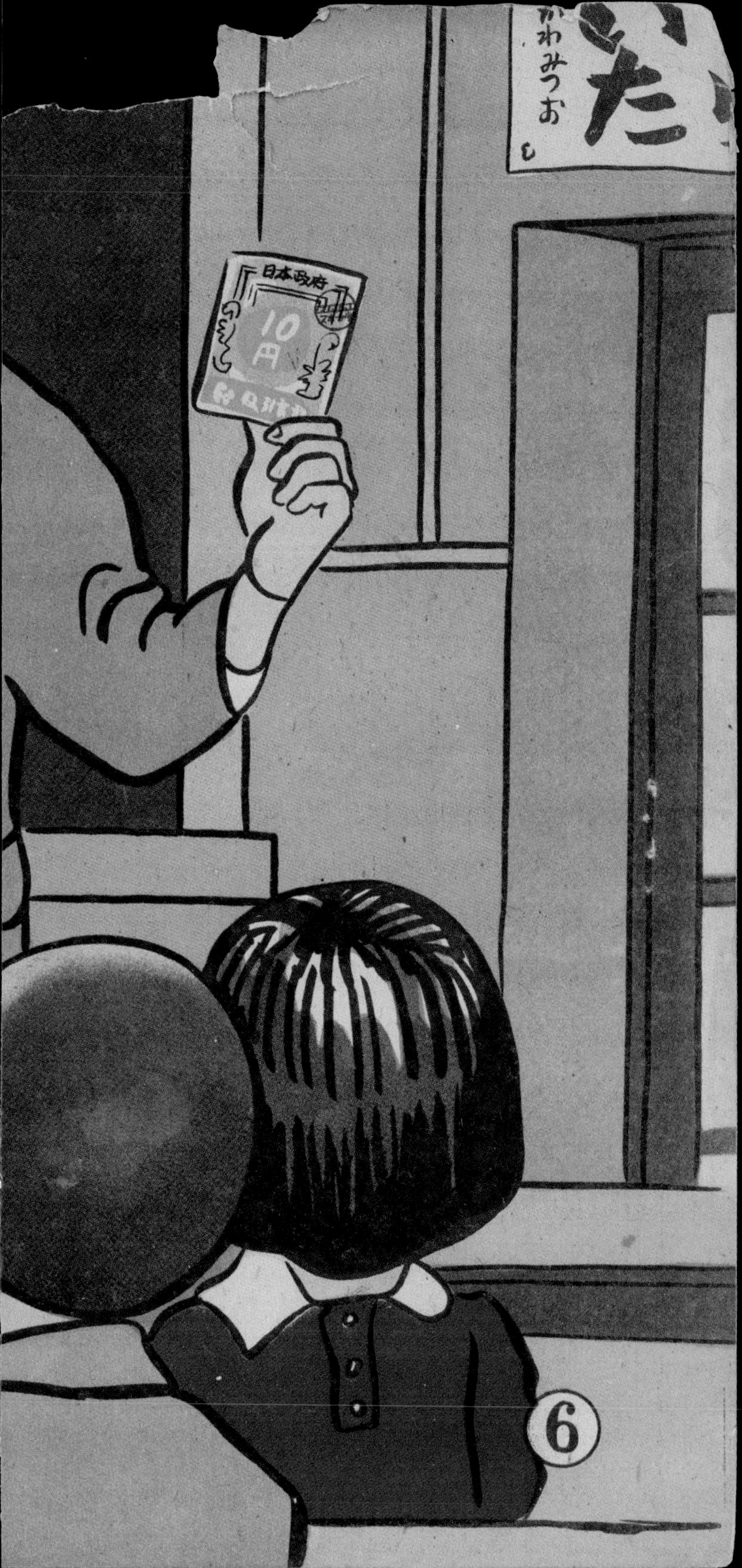
かわみつお
日本政府
10円
6

MADE IN OCCUPIED JAPAN

◀ **Lessons in Democracy:** *Kamishibai* during the American occupation were controlled to instill democratic values in the population.

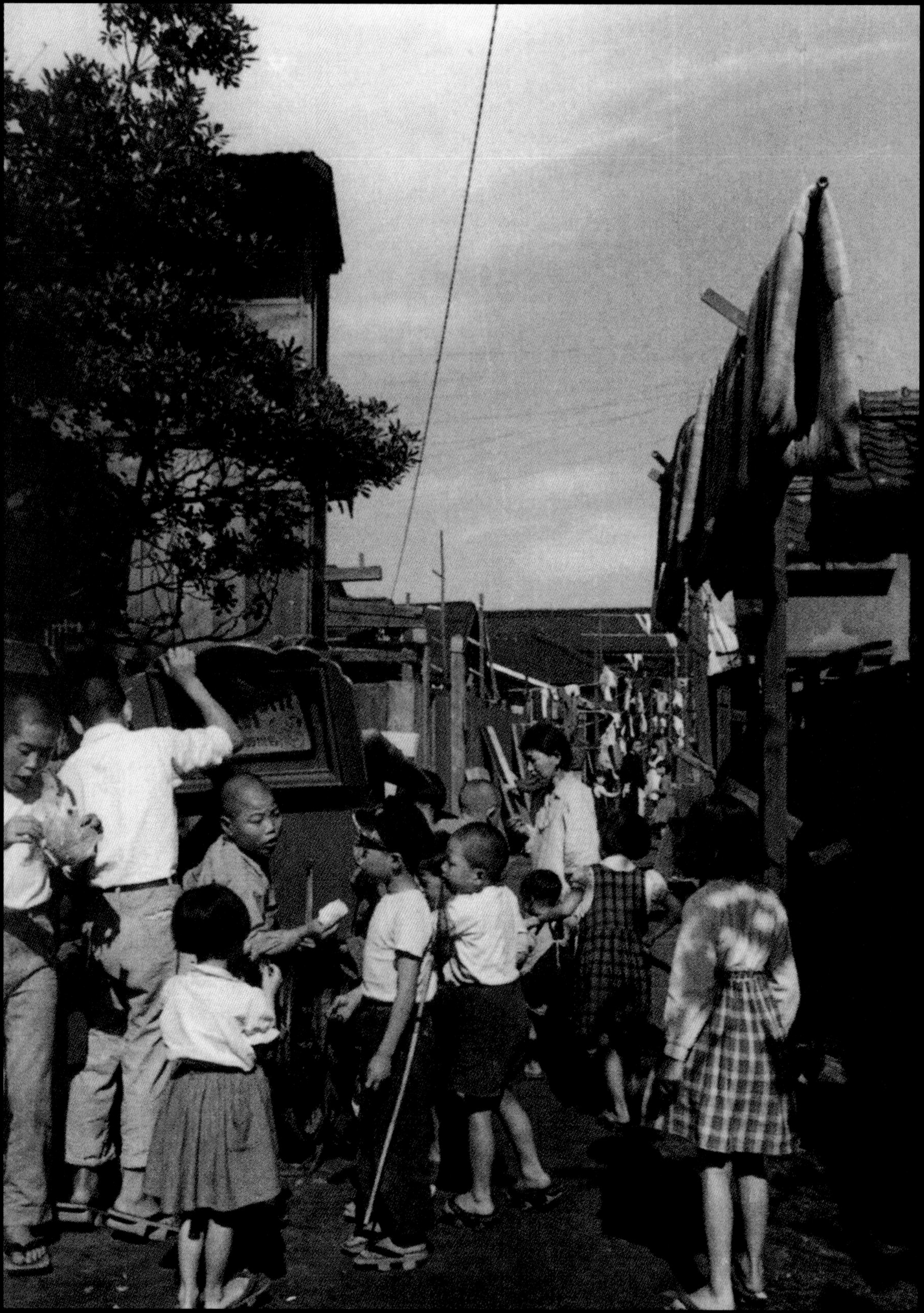

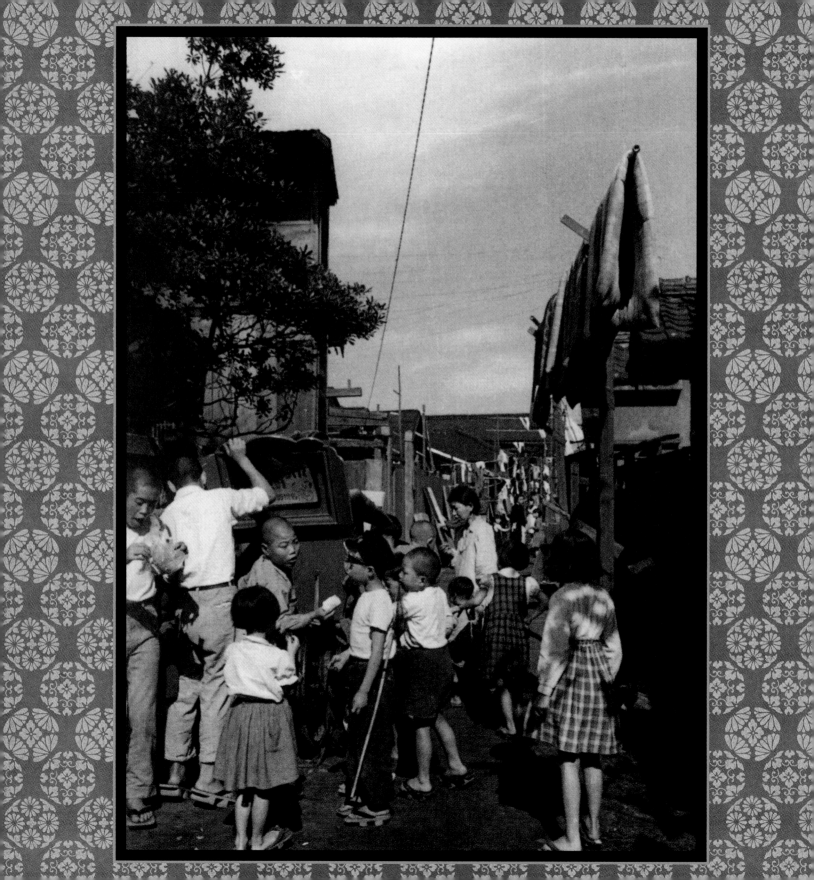

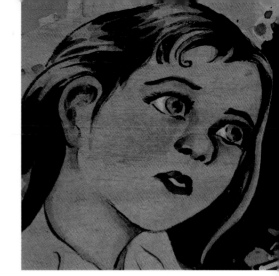

The *kamishibai* industry crawled out from under the ruins of postwar Tokyo. It is hard to imagine the abject poverty of a proud nation where after the bombing anything from a woman to an acre of land could be had for a carton of Luckies. The Supreme Commander for the Allied Pacific, General Douglas MacArthur, recalled his entry into Tokyo as "twenty-two miles of devastation and vast piles of charred rubble."

As the American flag flew over the rusty, corrugated-iron roofs of Tokyo's slums, SCAP's censors banned many topics of popular entertainment to tame Japan's warlike nature. This included *jidai geki*, as well as depictions of martial arts including judo, kendo, and karate, which were replaced with more acceptable pursuits like baseball and science fiction. A defeated populace eagerly embraced imported American novelties like Coca-Cola, chewing gum, and the jitterbug.

The first concern of SCAP was to stamp out all traces of Japan's militarism and nationalism. MacArthur referred to Japan's military as "an army that was steeped in medieval cruelty, but fought with the most modern technical skill and savage valor, until superior skill and equal valor broke the spell of the samurai and the legend of an invincible empire."

A 1952 photo of a *kamishibaiya* during the American occupation, when paper theater was at its peak, with an audience of 5 million daily, and Tokyo was a city of street stalls and open cesspools.

Kamishibai approved by SCAP promoted high-minded ideals such as freedom of the press, public

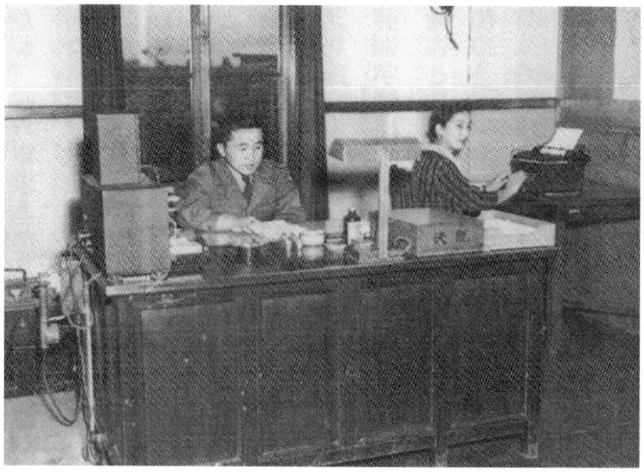
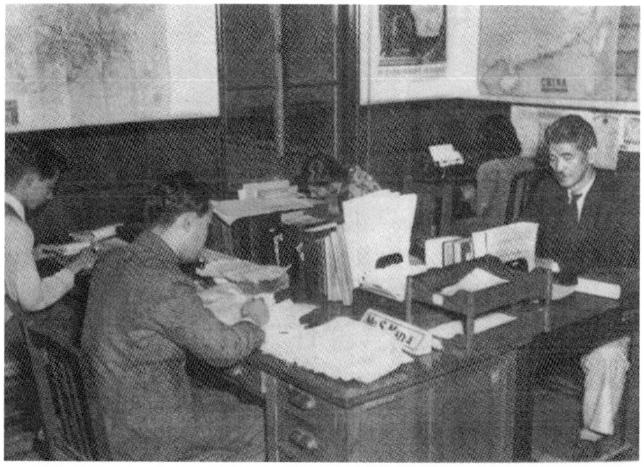

health, overthrowing feudalistic attitudes, and countering pickpockets. SCAP put its long eagle beak into everything, including cinema, radio broadcasts, public posters, magazines, kabuki, *kamishibai*, even erotica.

In answer to the question "What is *kamishibai*?" a reporter to SCAP wrote, "Generally speaking, Japanese people are good at painting small pictures. Though '*kamishibai*' painters are not all high class ones, they paint very expressive and impressive pictures with bold lines in bright colors. Both Japanese and Western paintings are used; in historical plays Japanese painting is preferred and in modern ones, Western painting. They may be called special painters of *kamishibai*, and their strong point is in speedy painting with poor materials."

The writer also gave a similar assessment of *kamishibai* content as the one critics offered of crime comics when they appeared before the United States Senate in 1954: "Nearly all street '*kamishibai*' stories are filled with struggles between the good and the evil, and though at the end the good defeats the evil, the exploits of the evil in the process are too minutely explained, so that children are more deeply impressed with outrageous or immoral acts rather than the fact that the evil are conquered at last. This is the weak point quite different from American comics such as the *Superman* in which as soon as the evil are prosperous, they will be suppressed."

SCAP Censors: Japanese censors working for the office of the Supreme Commander for the Allied Powers (SCAP) review *kamishibai*. General Douglas MacArthur, who acted with the impunity of a twentieth-century shogun, forbade representations of martial themes in popular arts. Tales of samurai and ninja were replaced with more wholesome activities like baseball, science fiction, and funny comic strips. MacArthur himself preferred the clear-cut morality of Hollywood Westerns.

Kamishibai again became a subject of investigation at the International Military Tribunal for the Far East, also known as the Tokyo Trials, for its role in contributing to the war effort. Akio Saki, president of the Nihon *Kamishibai* Association, was called to testify before the tribunal.

"Following the China Incident," Saki told the tribunal about the 1937 battle that touched off the major Japanese offensive against mainland China, "card sets and stories to match became popular . . . gradually of an ultranationalistic and militarist nature, sets of this type being manufactured upon instruction from the government."

Saki read from a *kamishibai* produced by his company in July 1941, entitled *Japan Is Now Fighting*. Thousands of copies were made of this set depicting the United States and Great Britain as responsible for the Sino-Japanese War.

"Japanese and Chinese are close brothers," the *kamishibai* set read. "If one pushes the other off the mountain, the other will fall off the mountain together [*sic*]." The script continued, saying that the United States and Britain "want to drink sweet wine out of the result of Japan and China's fatigue" portraying acts of heroism in the conquest of Manchuria: "Their belief in absolute victory is what made these human beings do such a wonder."

Summing up the case against *kamishibai*, the prosecution said, "Even picture cards or *kamishibai*, which traditionally were used mostly for the entertainment of children, were utilized to spread inflammatory ideas."

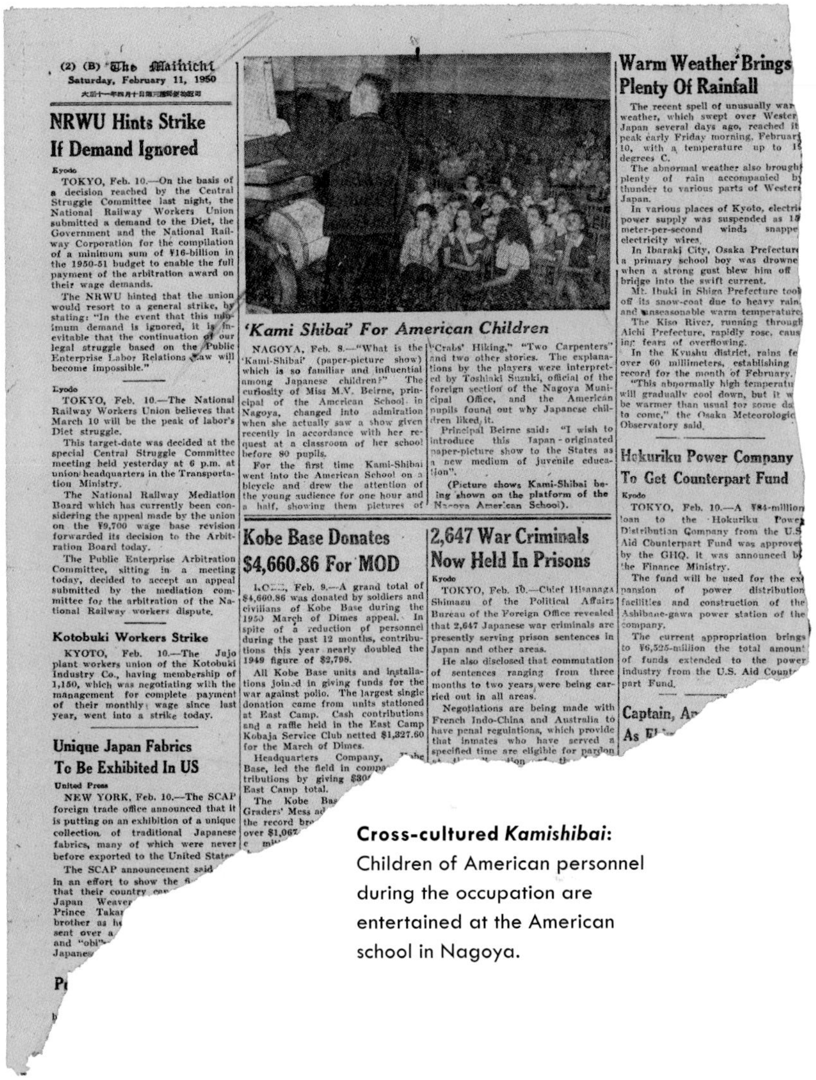

(2) (B) The Mainichi
Saturday, February 11, 1950

NRWU Hints Strike If Demand Ignored

Kyodo

TOKYO, Feb. 10.—On the basis of a decision reached by the Central Struggle Committee last night, the National Railway Workers Union submitted a demand to the Diet, the Government and the National Railway Corporation for the compilation of a minimum sum of ¥16-billion in the 1950-51 budget to enable the full payment of the arbitration award on their wage demands.

The NRWU hinted that the union would resort to a general strike, by stating: "In the event that this minimum demand is ignored, it is inevitable that the continuation of our legal struggle based on the Public Enterprise Labor Relations Law will become impossible."

Kyodo

TOKYO, Feb. 10.—The National Railway Workers Union believes that March 10 will be the peak of labor's Diet struggle.

This target-date was decided at the special Central Struggle Committee meeting held yesterday at 6 p.m. at union headquarters in the Transportation Ministry.

The National Railway Mediation Board which has currently been considering the appeal made by the union on the ¥9,700 wage base revision forwarded its decision to the Arbitration Board today.

The Public Enterprise Arbitration Committee, sitting in a meeting today, decided to accept an appeal submitted by the mediation committee for the arbitration of the National Railway workers dispute.

Kotobuki Workers Strike

KYOTO, Feb. 10.—The Jujo plant workers union of the Kotobuki Industry Co., having membership of 1,150, which was negotiating with the management for complete payment of their monthly wage since last year, went into a strike today.

Unique Japan Fabrics To Be Exhibited In US

United Press

NEW YORK, Feb. 10.—The SCAP foreign trade office announced that it is putting on an exhibition of a unique collection of traditional Japanese fabrics, many of which were never before exported to the United State…

The SCAP announcement said … in an effort to show the … that their country … Japan Weaver… Prince Takar… brother as h… sent over a… and "obi"… Japanes…

P…

'Kami Shibai' For American Children

NAGOYA, Feb. 8.—"What is the 'Kami-Shibai' (paper-picture show) which is so familiar and influential among Japanese children?" The curiosity of Miss M.V. Beirne, principal of the American School in Nagoya, changed into admiration when she actually saw a show given recently in accordance with her request at a classroom of her school before 80 pupils.

For the first time Kami-Shibai went into the American School on a bicycle and drew the attention of the young audience for one hour and a half, showing them pictures of "Crabs' Hiking," "Two Carpenters" and two other stories. The explanations by the players were interpreted by Toshiaki Suzuki, official of the foreign section of the Nagoya Municipal Office, and the American pupils found out why Japanese children liked it.

Principal Beirne said: "I wish to introduce this Japan-originated paper-picture show to the States as a new medium of juvenile education".

(Picture shows Kami-Shibai being shown on the platform of the Nagoya American School).

Kobe Base Donates $4,660.86 For MOD

K…, Feb. 9.—A grand total of $4,660.86 was donated by soldiers and civilians of Kobe Base during the 1950 March of Dimes appeal. In spite of a reduction of personnel during the past 12 months, contributions this year nearly doubled the 1949 figure of $2,798.

All Kobe Base units and installations joined in giving funds for the war against polio. The largest single donation came from units stationed at East Camp. Cash contributions and a raffle held in the East Camp Kobaja Service Club netted $1,327.60 for the March of Dimes.

Headquarters Company, … Base, led the field in compa… tributions by giving $30… East Camp total.

The Kobe Ba… Graders' Mess a… the record br… over $1,067…

2,647 War Criminals Now Held In Prisons

Kyodo

TOKYO, Feb. 10.—Chief Hisanaga Shimazu of the Political Affairs Bureau of the Foreign Office revealed that 2,647 Japanese war criminals are presently serving prison sentences in Japan and other areas.

He also disclosed that commutation of sentences ranging from three months to two years were being carried out in all areas.

Negotiations are being made with French Indo-China and Australia to have penal regulations, which provide that inmates who have served a specified time are eligible for pardon …

Warm Weather Brings Plenty Of Rainfall

The recent spell of unusually war… weather, which swept over Wester… Japan several days ago, reached it… peak early Friday morning, Februar… 10, with a temperature up to 1… degrees C.

The abnormal weather also brough… plenty of rain accompanied b… thunder to various parts of Wester… Japan.

In various places of Kyoto, electri… power supply was suspended as 1… meter-per-second winds snappe… electricity wires.

In Ibaraki City, Osaka Prefectur… a primary school boy was drowne… when a strong gust blew him off … bridge into the swift current.

Mt. Ibuki in Shiga Prefecture too… off its snow-coat due to heavy rain and unseasonable warm temperature.

The Kiso River, running throug… Aichi Prefecture, rapidly rose, caus… ing fears of overflowing.

In the Kyushu district, rains fe… over 60 millimeters, establishing … record for the month of February.

"This abnormally high temperatu… will gradually cool down, but it w… be warmer than usual for some da… to come," the Osaka Meteorologic… Observatory said.

Hokuriku Power Company To Get Counterpart Fund

Kyodo

TOKYO, Feb. 10.—A ¥84-million loan to the Hokuriku Powe… Distribution Company from the U.S… Aid Counterpart Fund was approve… by the GHQ. It was announced b… the Finance Ministry.

The fund will be used for the ex… pansion of power distribution facilities and construction of the Ashibane-gawa power station of the company.

The current appropriation brings to ¥6,525-million the total amount of funds extended to the power industry from the U.S. Aid Count… part Fund.

Captain, A… As E…

Cross-cultured *Kamishibai*: Children of American personnel during the occupation are entertained at the American school in Nagoya.

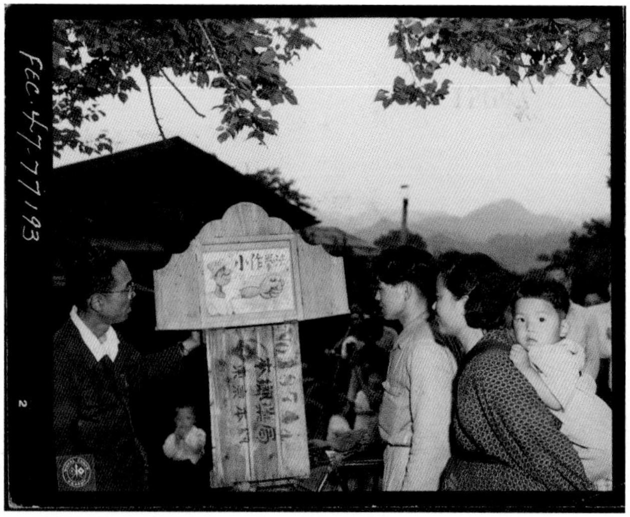
FEC-47-77193

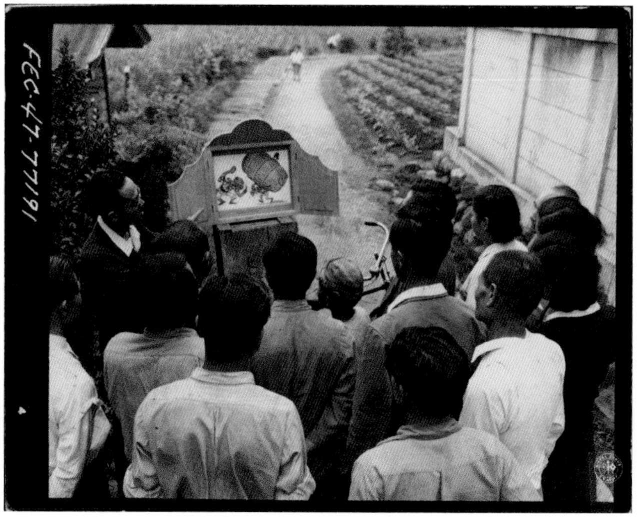
FEC-47-77191

Land Reform: The U.S. occupation sent *kamishibaiya* to villages to explain changes in land ownership under feudal and democratic systems, but it was difficult to uproot patterns of behavior ingrained in the Japanese culture over thousands of years.

In contrast, the defense said, "The prosecution attempted to make much ado about the sale of such items as candy, ice cream, popsicles, and many other such items as would appeal to children. Their contention was that the government of Japan, particularly when [Sadao] Araki was War Minister, was sponsoring sales talks by the vendors of these items for the purpose of instilling in the minds of the aforementioned children ideas of aggression."

The defense compared *kamishibai* tales to promotional cards of "famous prizefighters, movie stars, battleships, famous historians, writers, philosophers, etc." used as incentives to buy candy or tobacco, but may have overstated the case by saying, "There is not a scintilla of proof that the government of Japan or Araki ever sponsored any such program for aggressive or nationalistic purposes."

In the years after the war, up to 5 million people a day, including adults but mainly children, watched *kamishibai* shows. With the high rate of unemployment, many demobilized servicemen became *kamishibaiya*. There were forty production houses and fifty thousand *kamishibai* storytellers in Tokyo and Kansai, the western region of Japan. Manga production also boomed: in the first eight months of the occupation the number of book and manga publishers increased exponentially from three hundred to more than two thousand.

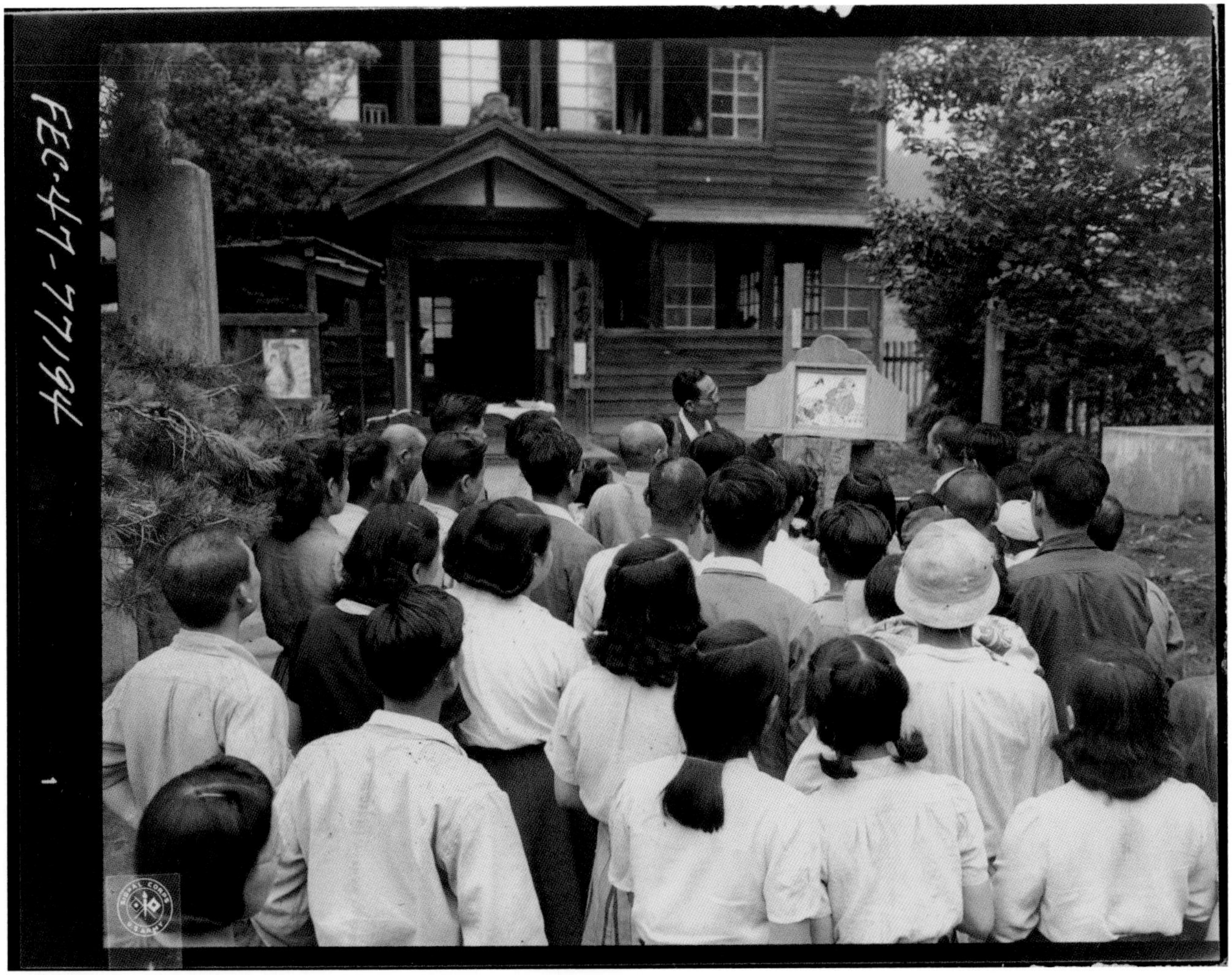
FEC-47-77194

Despite the ban on *jidai geki*, historical Kabuki drama thrived during the occupation and was enthusiastically attended by Americans, including Faubion Bowers, who is credited with saving the art form. There was also a true guerilla theater called *taishu engeki*, where small itinerant theatrical companies put on period dramas centering on swordfights and feudal loyalty—despite the ban by the nation's enigmatic, blue-eyed shogun, MacArthur. The troupes were fleet-footed enough to put on plays in provinces

Demokrashi on Display: Well-scrubbed villagers in Western attire listen to a *kamishibaiya*'s explanation of the new democratic system of land reform. Japanese had to use an imported term for the concept of demokrashi.

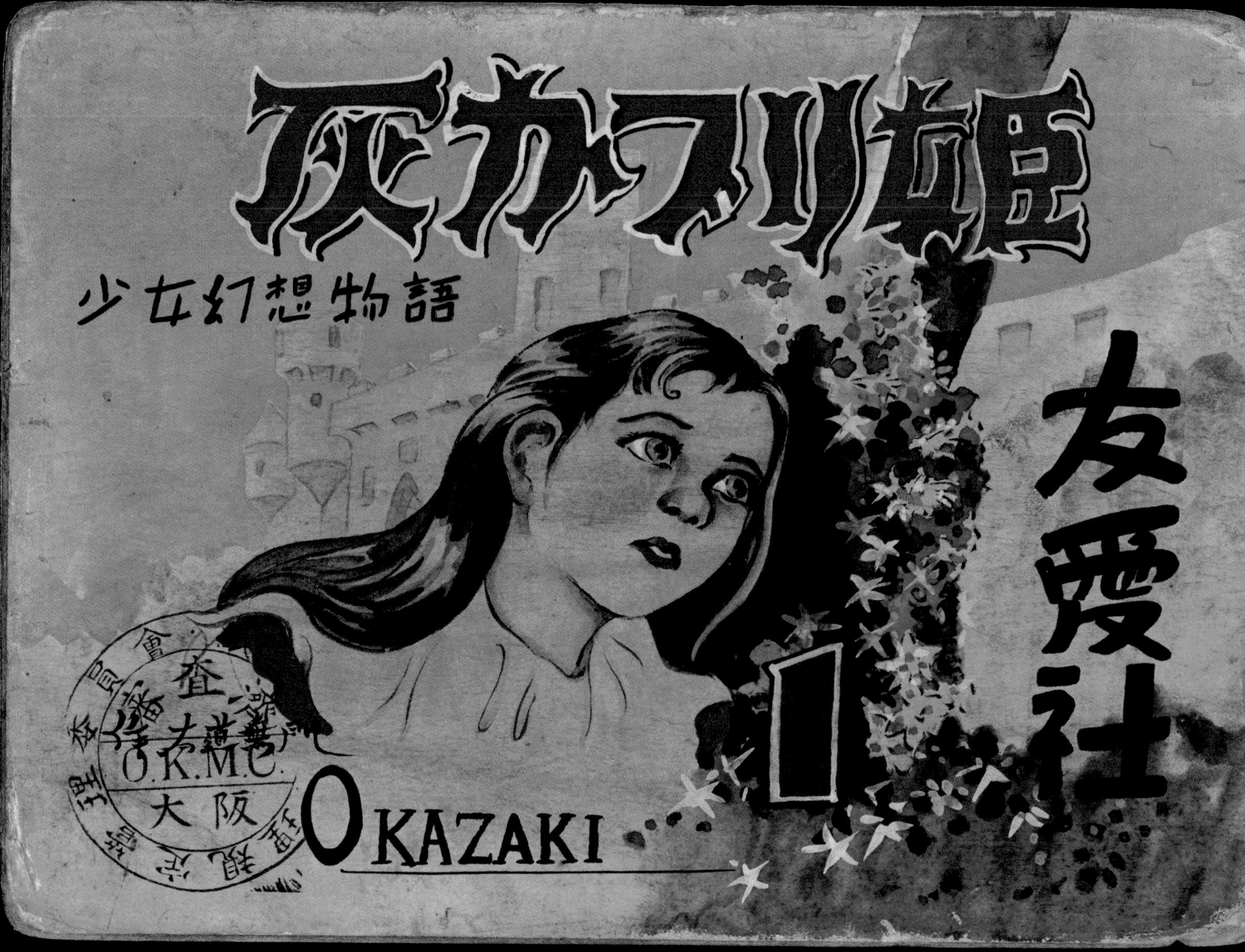
灰カブリ姫
少女幻想物語
友愛社
1
審査
O.K.M.C
大阪
OKAZAKI

Ash-Covered Princess, better known as *Cinderella*, came out in 1953, a year after the Disney version in 1952. Disney had a profound influence on manga, like Osamu Tezuka's *Astro Boy*. This paper play is billed forthrightly as a "girls' fantasy story."

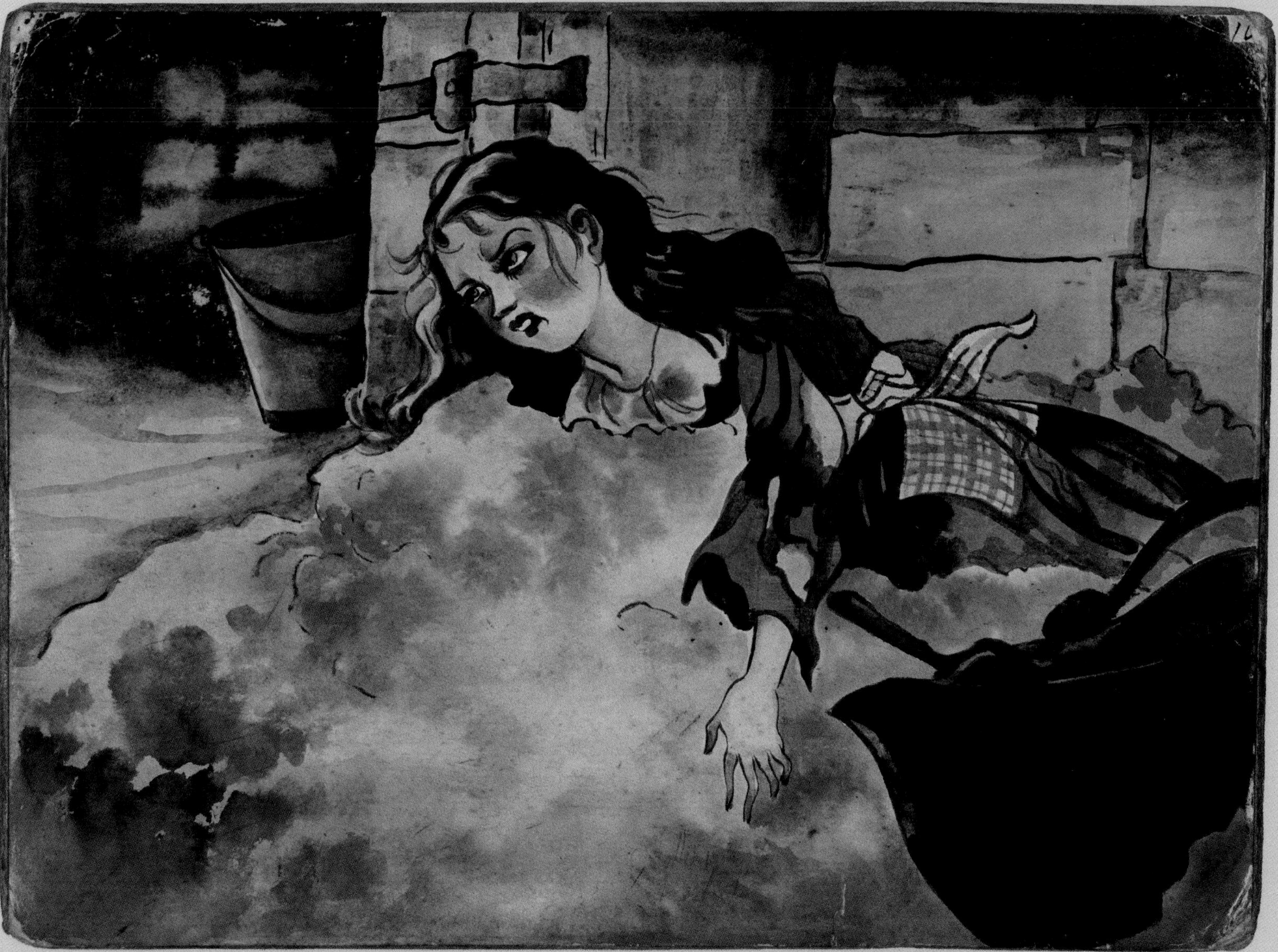

Kabuki Cinderella: Though inspired by Disney, this version of Cinderella has a distinctly Japanese flavor in the heroine's Kabuki-like despair, as she throws herself on a dust heap that threatens to overwhelm her. Her eyes are crossed and unfocused in Kabuki style and signify peak emotion.

赤ずきん

グリム童話

like Kyushu, where they were enthusiastically received, and leave town before they brought the attention of the censors. This popular theater form was also known as *sanryu* (third-rate) Kabuki.

The Adachi section of Tokyo became the center of postwar *kamishibai* when top creators, including Takeo Nagamatsu and Kouji Kata, moved there. Kouji Kata was always generous and found *kamishibai* work for his unemployed friends. A *kamishibai* union was formed in 1953.

Kamishibai was under particular scrutiny because of its popularity. The demotic street art form was viewed as subversive, because it was well suited

Slide Show: Audio-visual slides also appeared under the occupation, approved by censors. This version of *Little Red Riding Hood* seems to be heavily influenced by American animators Bob Clampett and Tex Avery.

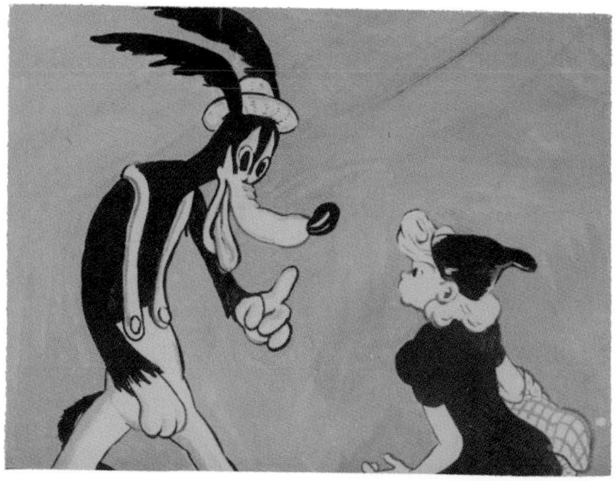

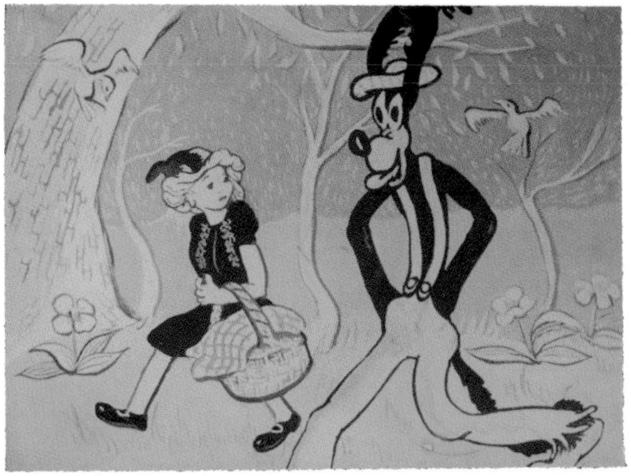

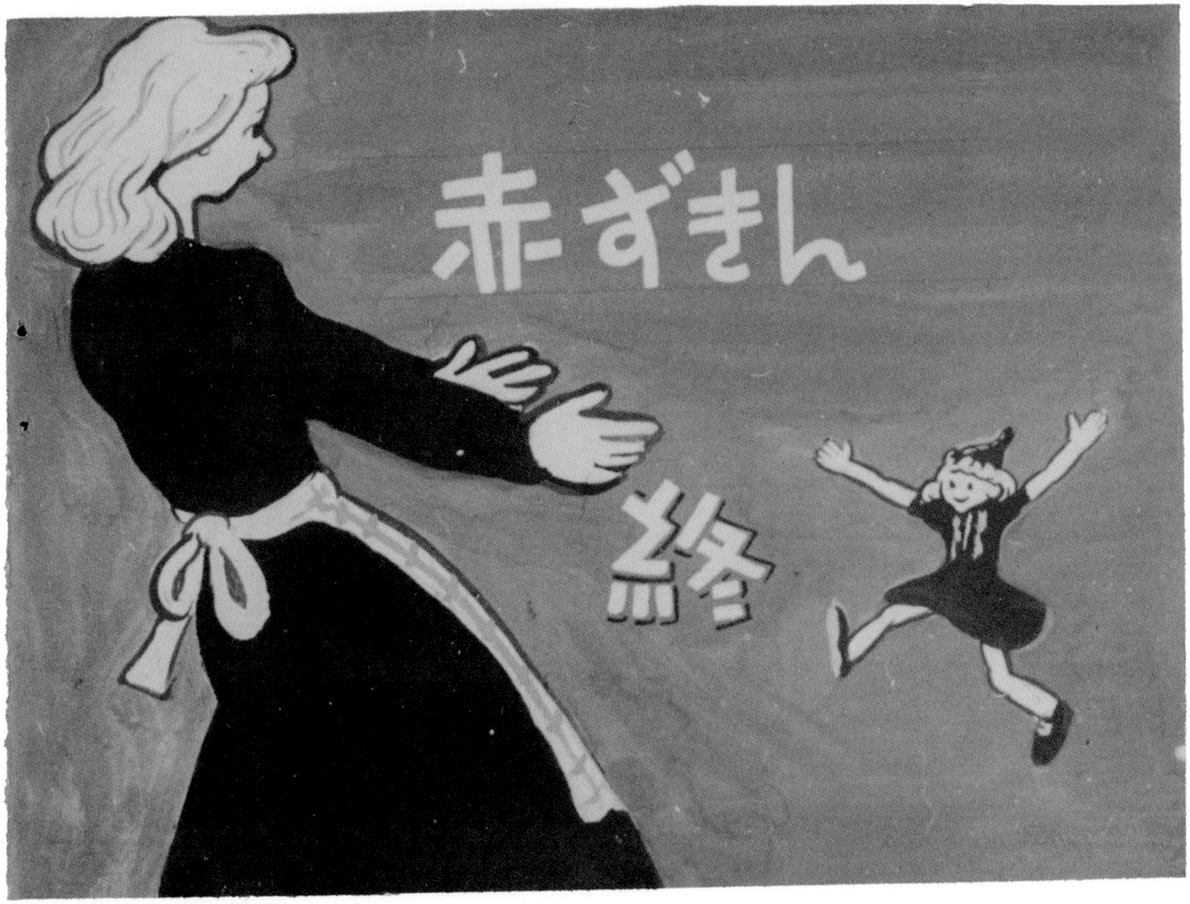
赤ずきん
終

MYSTERY TRAIN

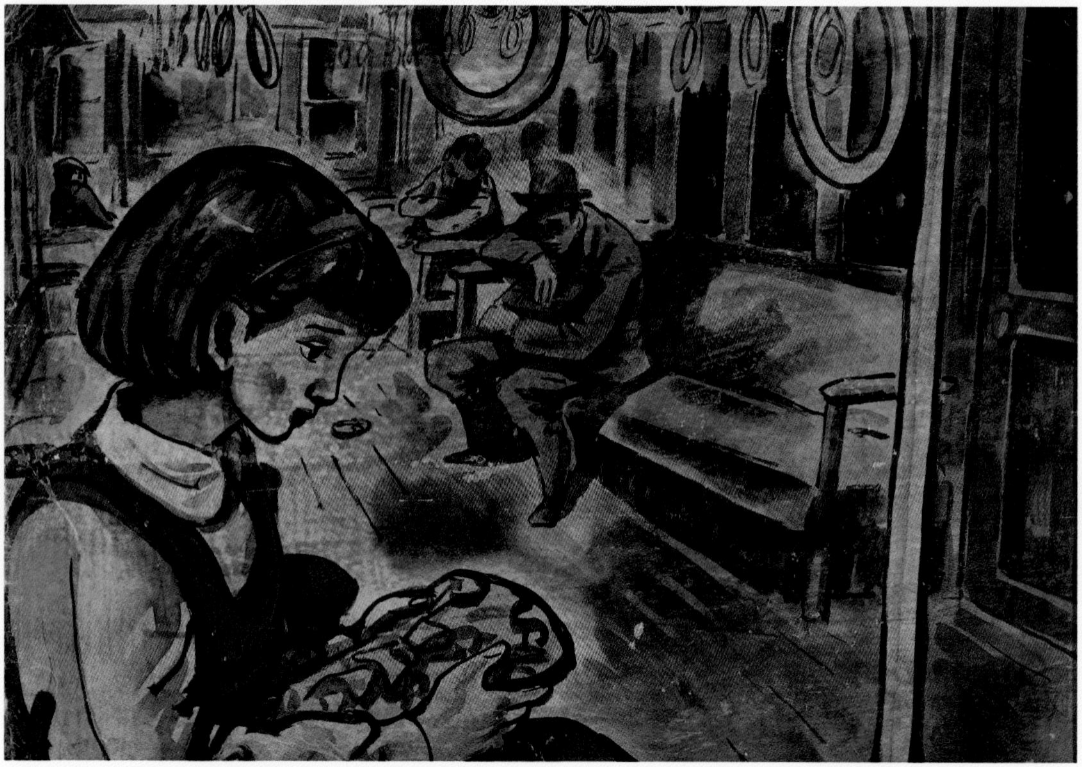

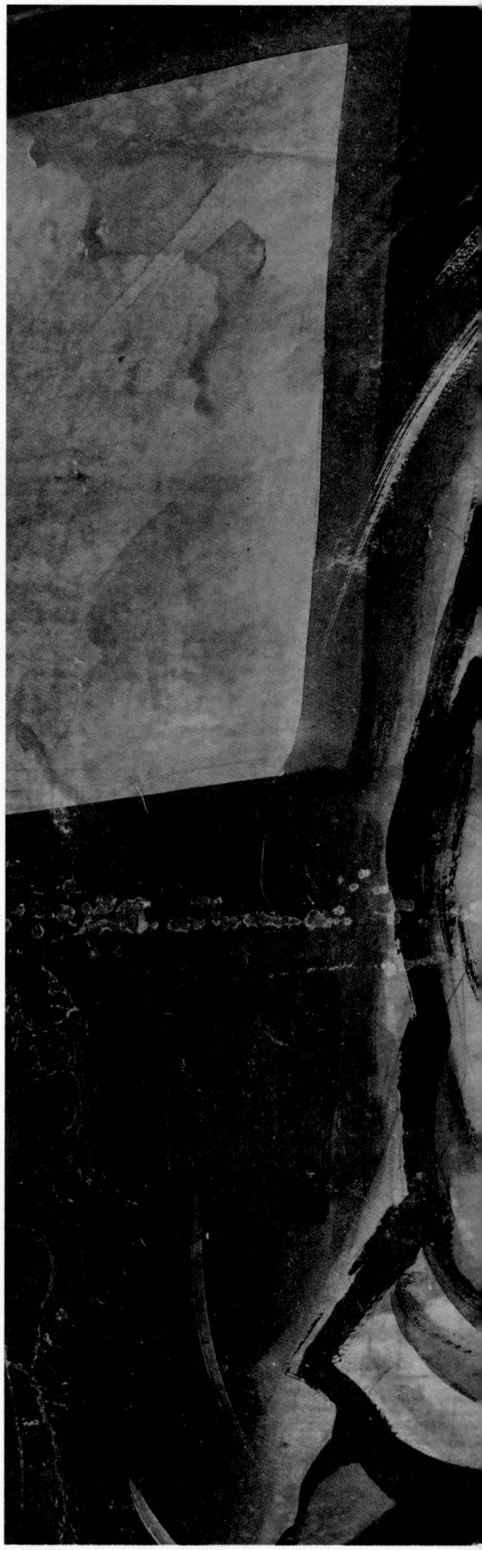

ABOVE Next Stop, the Twilight Zone: Under the American occupation, *kamishibai* had to pass the review of censors, so the stories were frequently about fantasy and science fiction. In a *Twilight Zone*—like episode, a young girl dozes on a late-night commuter train, a fascinating look at the shadowy, wooden-floored trains of old Tokyo. Perhaps in a case of cultural amnesia about the war, Tokyo today is a city of bright lights and spotless surfaces.

RIGHT An improbable monster in the shape of a giant hand wearing a glove enters the car.

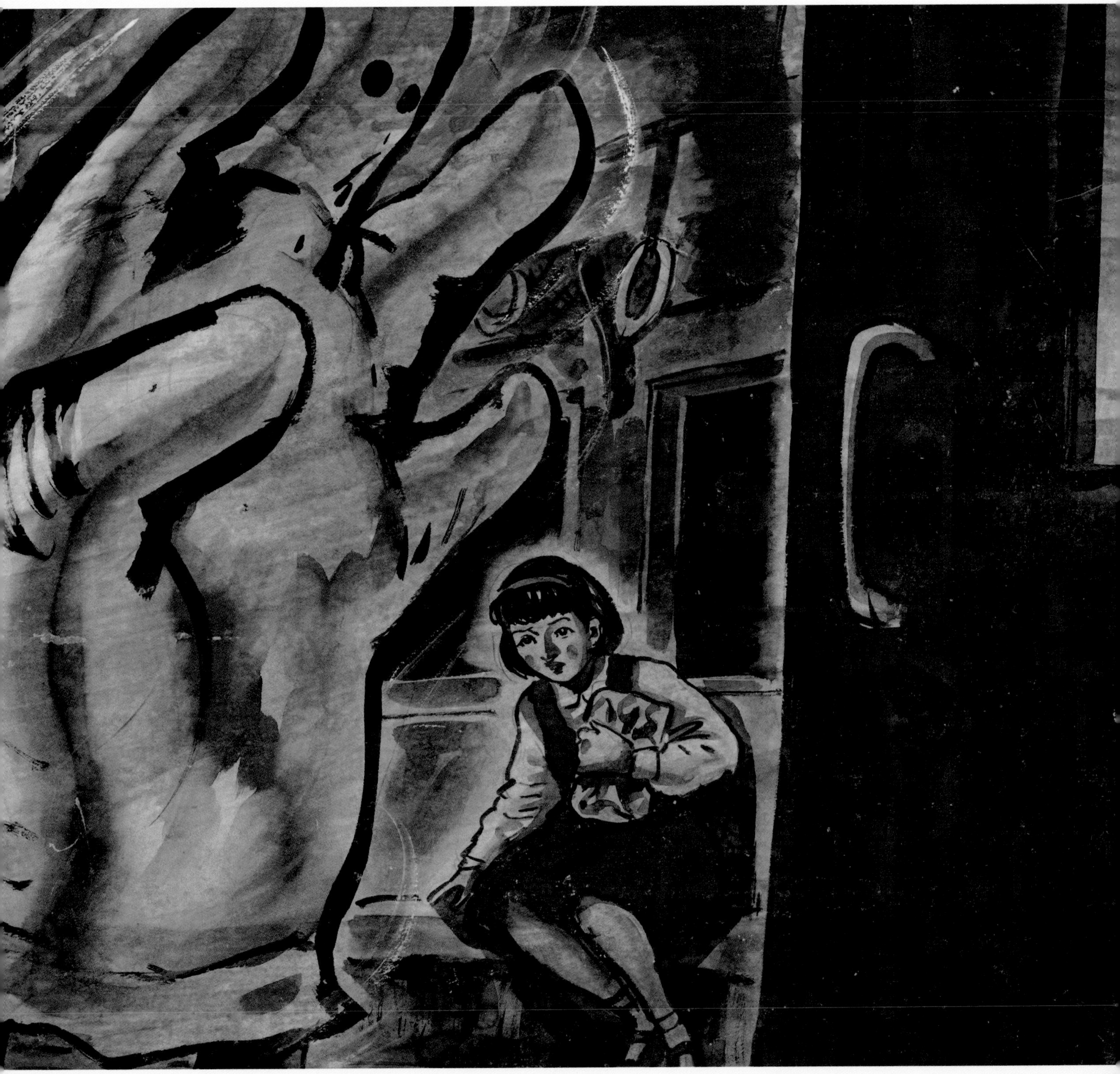

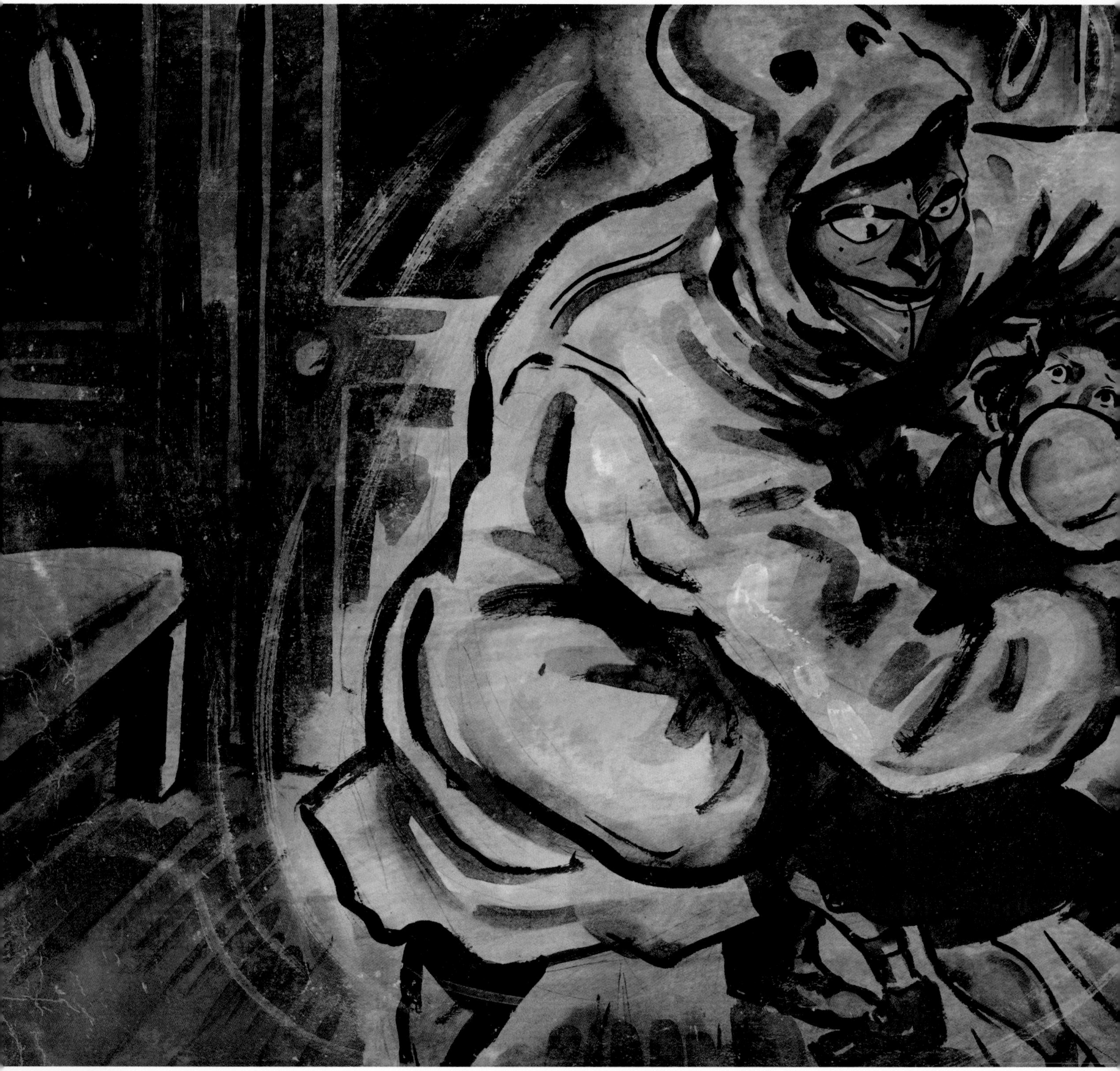

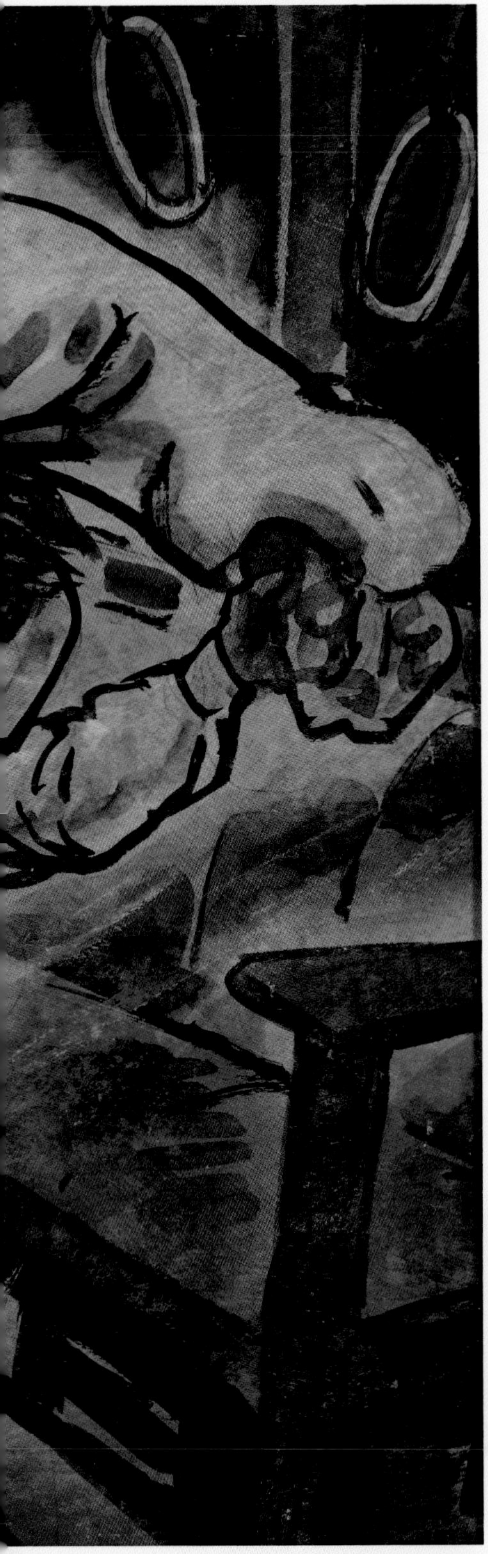

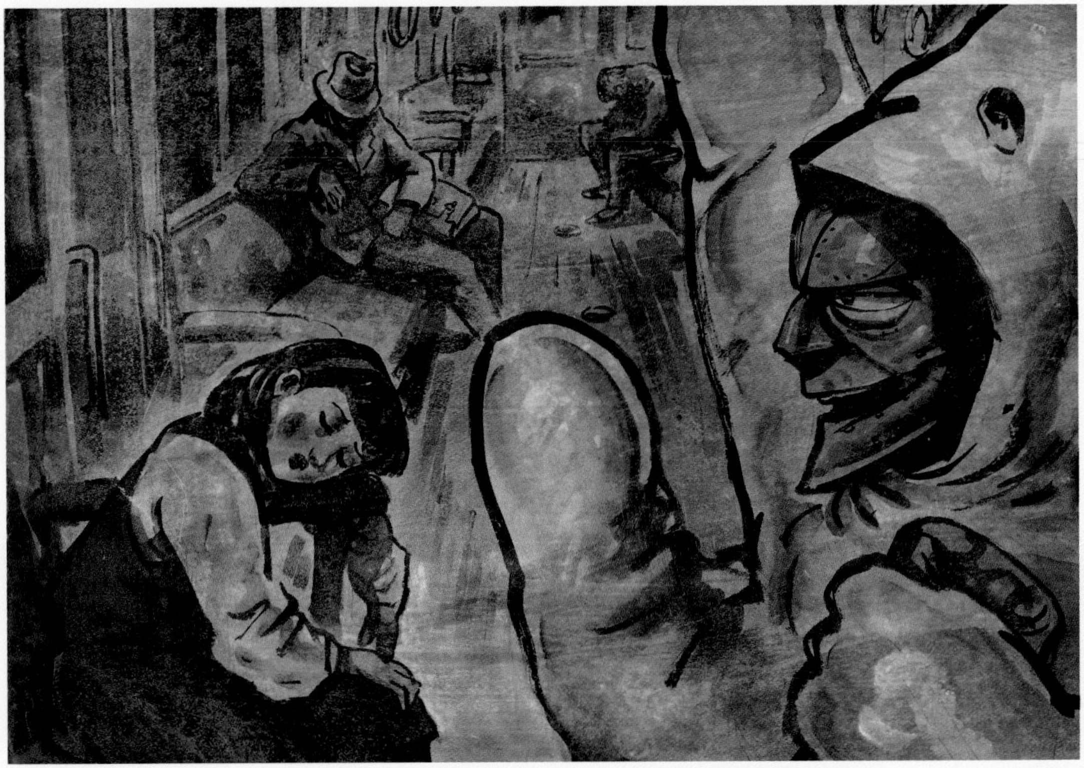

LEFT The monster's hood slips to reveal a grotesque green face as he is about to crush the girl.

ABOVE The girl faints dead away as the giant hand waves good-bye.

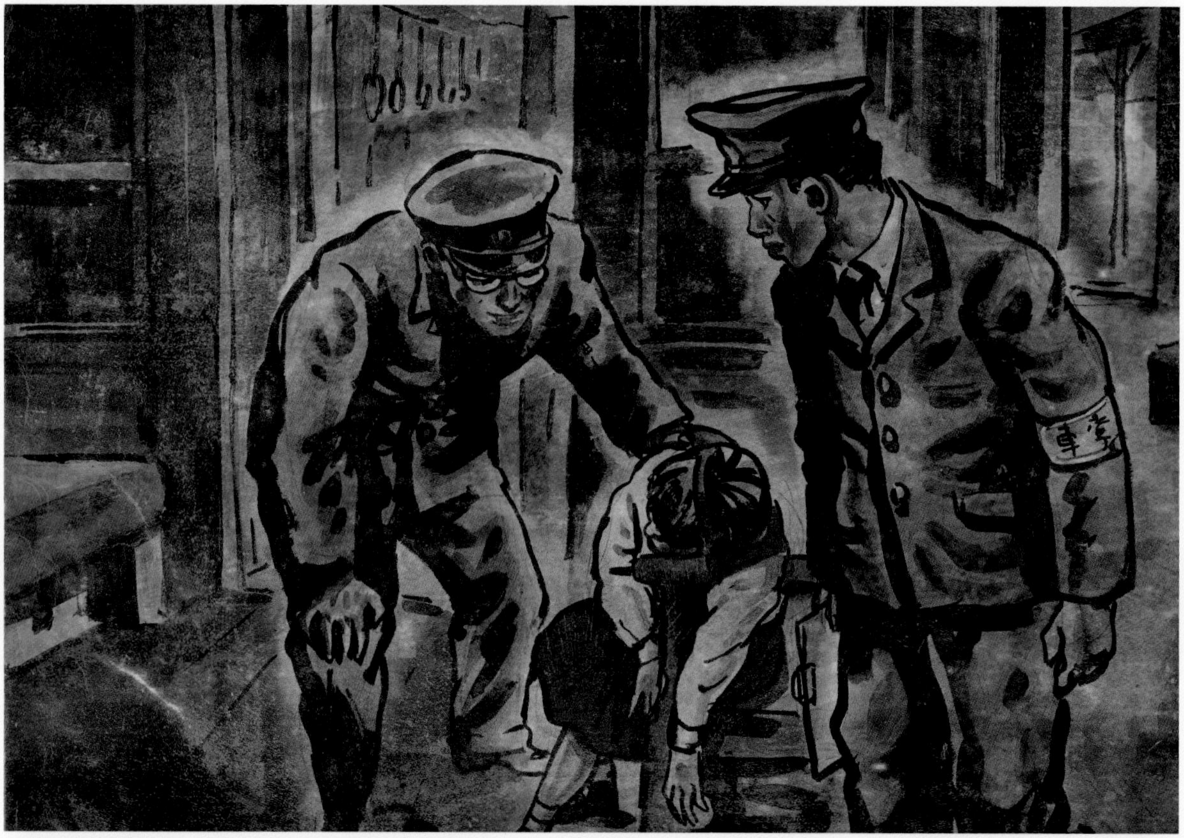

車

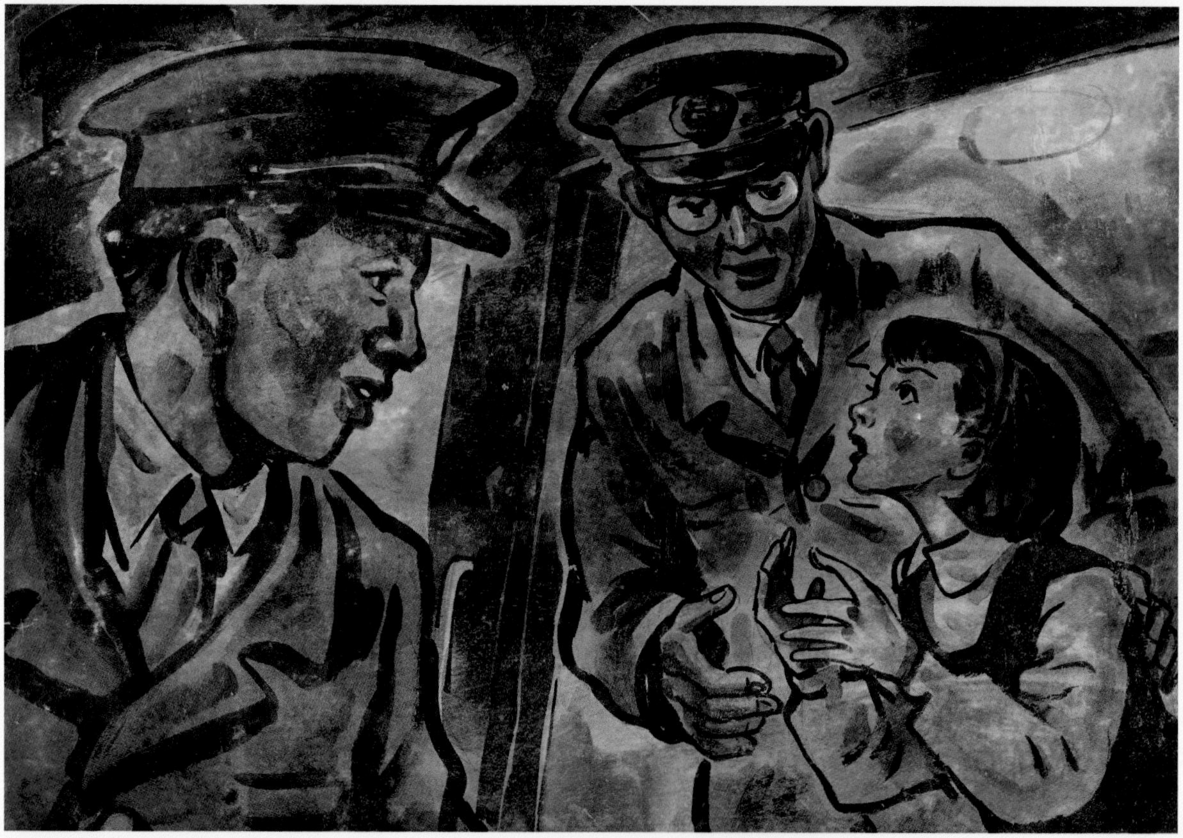

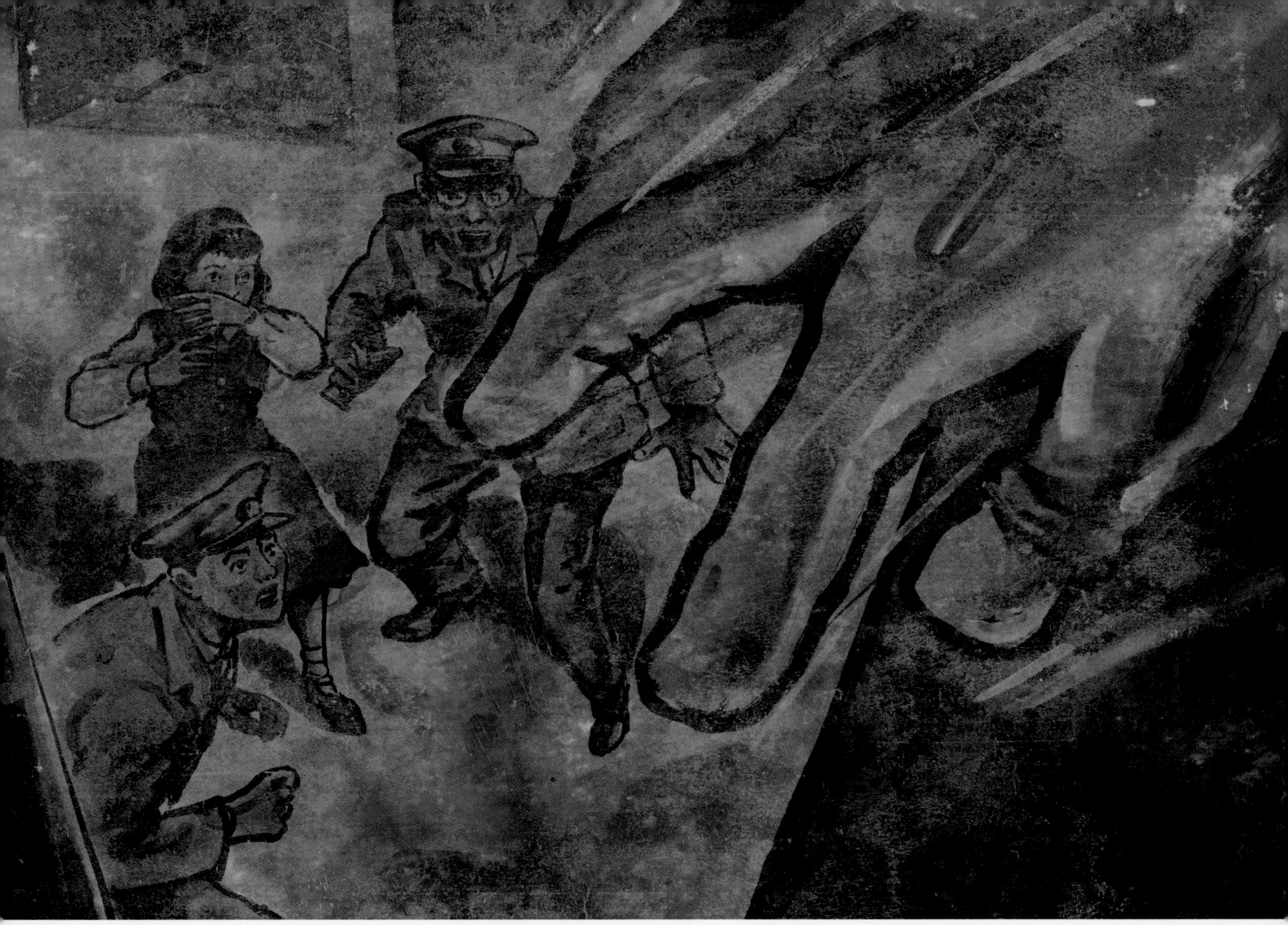

OPPOSITE, TOP At the last stop, the conductors rouse the unconscious girl. Postwar Japan has long been a safe, well-run society where a child can travel alone, but science-fiction monsters like Godzilla and this giant hand express subconscious fears about the war.

OPPOSITE, BOTTOM The conductors smile indulgently as the girl tries to describe the horrible hand monster. They assure her it was only a bad dream.

ABOVE The hand suddenly reappears, looming over the small human figures. What could possibly happen next? Come back tomorrow!

to grassroots radical social criticism. A stamp was required on the back of *kamishibai* works to show that they had been approved by censors. Between November 1945 and February 1947, censors from the Press, Pictorial, and Broadcast Division in District I, which covered Tokyo and its northern prefectures, reviewed 8,821 *kamishibai* shows.

As soon as right-wing nationalistic propaganda was suppressed, SCAP turned its attention to left-wing communist influences. *Golden Bat* illustrator Kata Kouji was censored for his *Hataraku Mono no Kuni* (*The Land of the Workers*), an outright piece of agitprop *kamishibai* that SCAP censors said "attempts to paint Russia as a workman's utopia." Both Kouji and Takeo Nagamatsu were members of the Democratic Illustrated Story Teller's group, a *kamishibai* association that was suspected because "it attempts to utilize *kamishibai* for the best interest of the communist movements and not for the development of democracy in the *kamishibai* field."

ソヴエット勞働者の生活
働くものの國

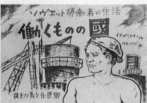

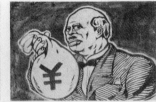

Suppressed Communist Kami-shibai
"The Land of the Workers"

1. "The USSR is the only country of workers and farmers in the world."

2. "There is the capitalist who is unsatisfied unless he makes a profit."

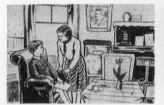

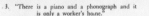

3. "There is a piano and a phonograph and it is only a worker's home."

4. "Hunger, sickness, unemployment! Yes, we Japanese are always afraid."

ABOVE Red Scare: SCAP censors said Kata Kouji's pro-Soviet *Land of the Workers* "attempts to paint Russia as a workman's utopia."

OPPOSITE Red Ink: Kouji's *kamishibai* compared the slum conditions of Tokyo with an idealized version of Russia.

Kamishibai men were often at odds with GHQ censors. Production of new *kamishibai* stories that passed the censors slowed to a trickle. In 1949 GHQ pressured prefectural offices to crack down on *kamishibai*; the first ban was in Kanagawa prefecture in March 1949. Bans followed in Chiba and Osaka. Despite the crackdowns, the industry continued to grow. By 1949, Osaka had ten *kamishibai* dealers and fifteen hundred storytellers. Creators outfoxed the censors by producing stories with historical merit, like biographies of Alfred Nobel and Florence Nightingale. *Kamishibai* tales produced in Osaka were known for having a slower pace than Tokyo stories,

Suppressed Communist Kami-shibai

5. "These are the workers' houses. They are all clean and complete with every convenience."

6. "Think of our noisy tenements full of rubbish and dirt."

7. "Only we the workers can revive once more this pitiful and sorrowful Japan."

8. "The capitalist says labor is cheaper than capital."

"The Land of the Workers" (Hataraku Mono No Kuni) was produced by the Democratic Culture League (Bunren).

fitting the stereotype that Kansai residents were more countrified than their city kin.

The authorities' aversion to the content of street-corner *kamishibai* was masked as concern for the health of the children. *Kamishibai* licenses were forbidden to be given to the mentally ill and people with contagious diseases. In 1950 **GHQ** posted an ordinance in **Osaka** that required *kamishibaiya* to take a government course and pass a licensing exam on children's welfare, public hygiene, and safe transportation. In **Shikoku** a group was formed to regulate food sold by *kamishibaiya*. **Osaka** was the last region to repeal the ordinances as late as 1984.

Like participants in the **American comic book industry** who voluntarily joined to form the **Comics Code Authority**, with its **Seal of Approval** prominently pasted on comic book covers in the wake of the **Kefauver hearings** of the 1950s, *kamishibai* producers formed a **Regulation Committee** in 1951. The committee received submissions at the rate of four new *kamishibai* a day.

Kamishibai and manga were dragooned to support another propaganda purpose, the word for which the Japanese had to import: *demokrashi*. To help acculturate the Japanese people to democratic values, **Chic Young's** *Blondie*, at the time the most widely read comic strip in the world, appeared in the daily *Tokyo Asahi* in 1946. Also at this time, local civic groups sponsored the **Tokyo City** *Kamishibai* Contest for both street-corner and printed *kamishibai*. With the support of school boards, such contests were held until 1960.

The postwar period also saw the rise of *akabon* (red books). So named for their gaudy red covers, they were sold in candy stores and street fairs rather than at newsstands. Many of the great *manga-ka*, including **Osamu Tezuka**, got their start in red books. Tezuka's 1947 red book, *New Treasure Island*, established the long-story format for manga and sold nearly half a million copies. **Osaka** was the center of *akabon* activity, and **Kansai** was flooded with comics. The cheaply printed red-book manga made a virtue of the black-and-white printing process, as seen in the luscious blacks of **Astro Boy** and **Sanpei Shirato's** naturalistic crosshatching.

Red books have the handcrafted modesty of toys made during the occupation, which were among the first objects to be manufactured in Japan's scrapheap economy. One toy, a humble metal Jeep made from recycled beer cans and sold in Ginza stalls seems to embody the Japanese spirit: with a painted American star, the little "Jeepu" is heartbreaking as the product of a broken nation, in its modest ingenuity and resourcefulness combined with a simple desire to make something to cheer up children. Just as the craze for Japanese toy friction cars in the early 1960s hinted at the ascendancy of their auto industry, disposable red books foreshadowed the rise of manga and anime.

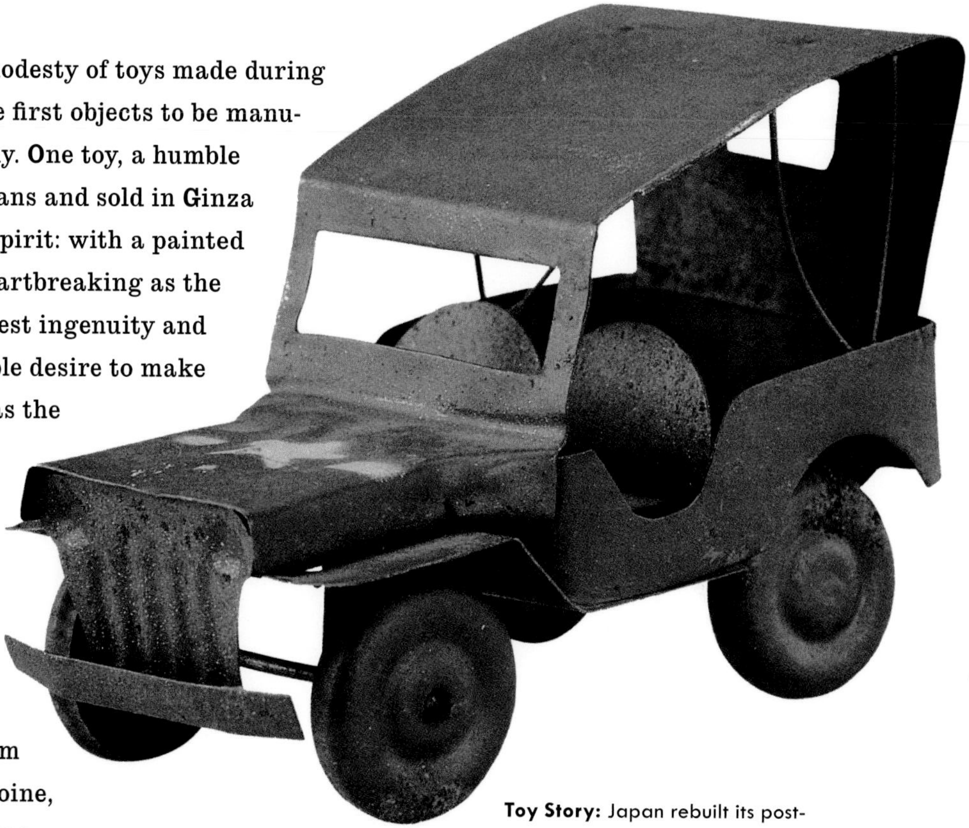

Toy Story: Japan rebuilt its postwar economy from the scrapheap. This ingenious "Jeepu," made from recycled beer cans, was one of the first toys exported to the United States. In just a few decades, Japan would grow to dominate the U.S. car industry.

Disney continued to be a pervasive influence in every decade of *kamishibai*. One *kamishibai* serial from the 1950s featured Cinderella as a heroine, although her disheveled despair at being left at home on the night of the ball reaches kabuki-like intensity.

Fifties science-fiction *kamishibai* also feature ***Twilight Zone*** reversals: A little girl on a late-night train sees a monster in the form of a gigantic hand, only to be told that she is dreaming. In the last panel, the hand looms over the train police.

GHQ restrictions on *kamishibai* and other popular art forms were enforced until the San Francisco peace accord of 1952 ended the occupation. America's cultural dominance did not end with the occupation, because the United States continued to use Japan as a permanent aircraft base in the Korean War, a major factor behind the Japanese miracle economy of the 1960s.

But soon *kamishibai* would grapple with the biggest robot monster of them all: television.

YOSHIO'S GLOVE

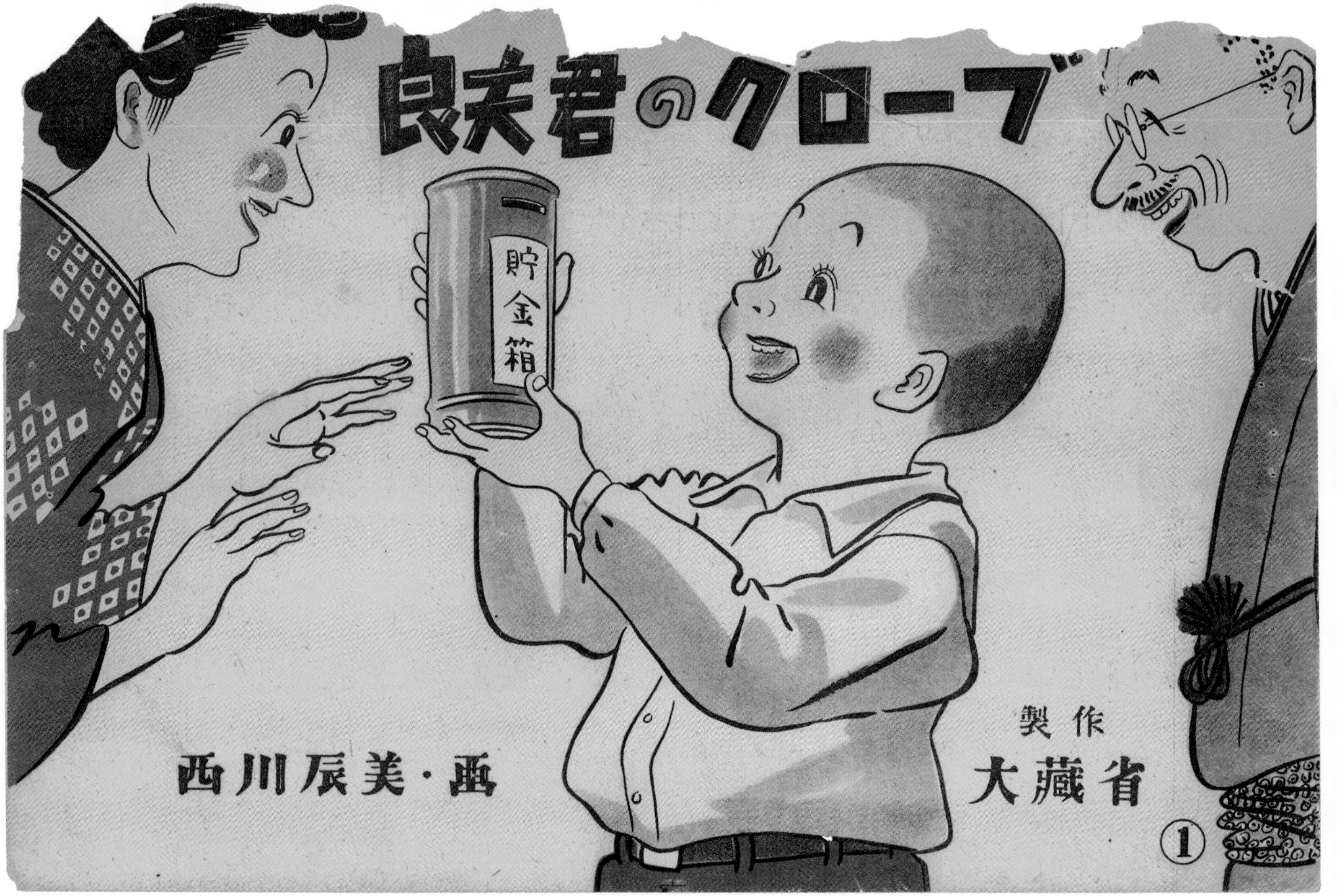
良夫君のグローブ
貯金箱
西川辰美・画
製作
大藏省
①

ABOVE ***Yoshio's Glove*****:** A *kamishibai* produced under the occupation attempts to instill the value of thrift in the rising generation through the story of a boy who saves up for a new baseball glove. The older generation is shown in traditional Japanese clothing while the boy appears thoroughly Westernized.

OPPOSITE, TOP **Home Run:** Wearing an American-style baseball cap, Yoshio runs to the sporting goods store to buy his new glove. The content and style are reminiscent of small-town America.

OPPOSITE, BOTTOM **All-American:** *Kamishibai* during the occupation attempted to impart the same sense of optimism and looking toward the future as was prevalent in postwar America by importing American values.

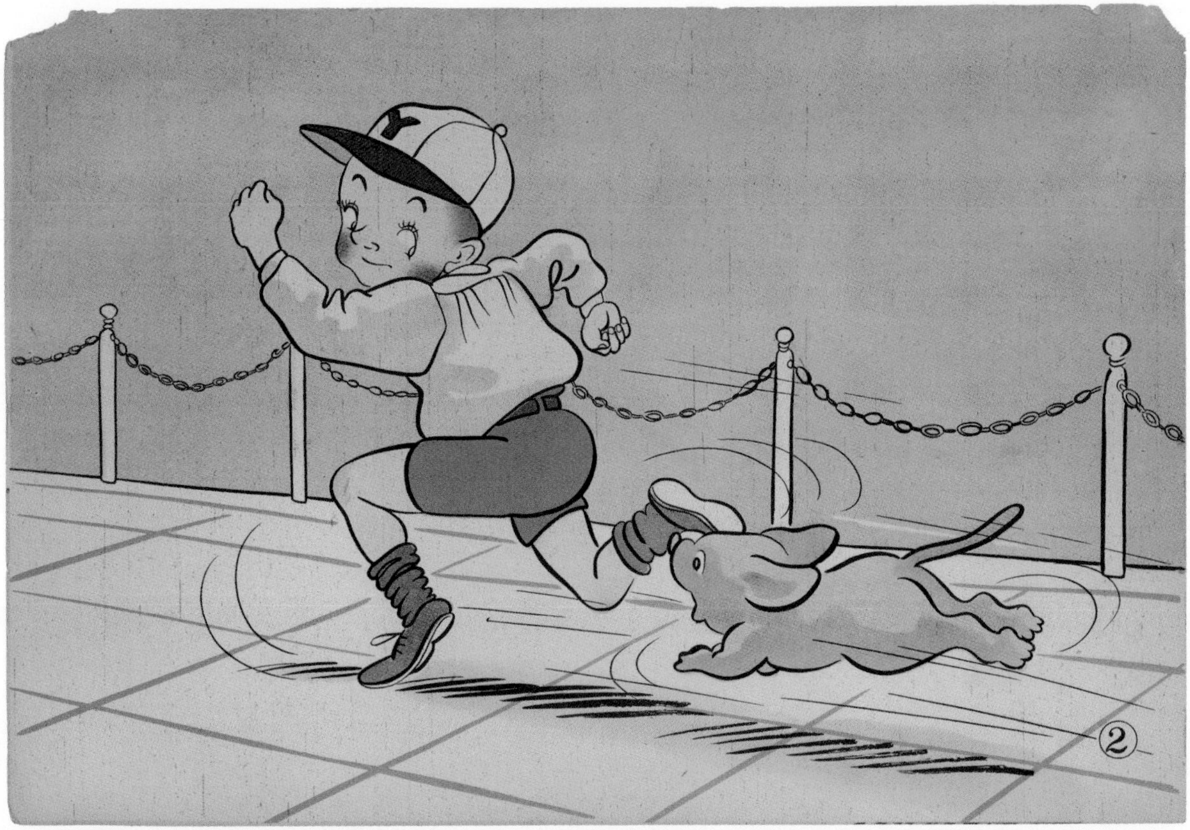
②

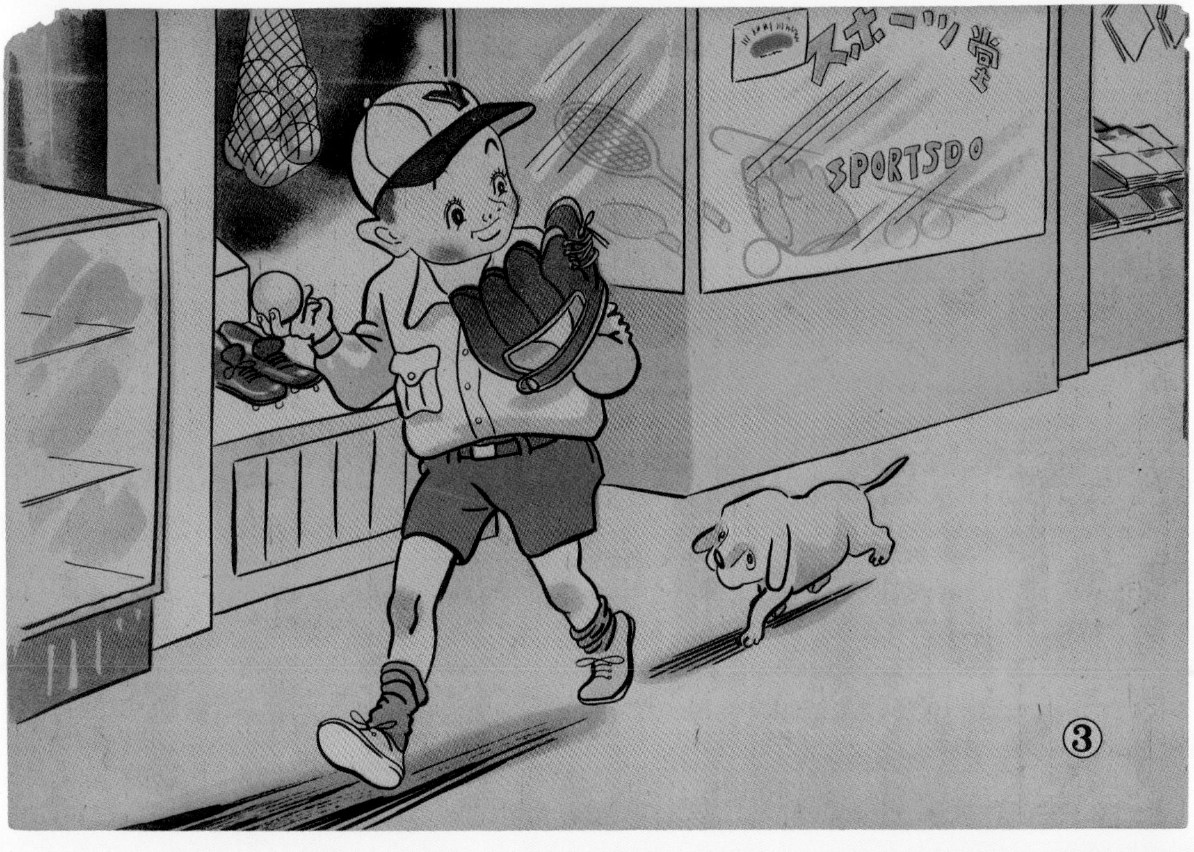
スポーツ堂
SPORTSDO
③

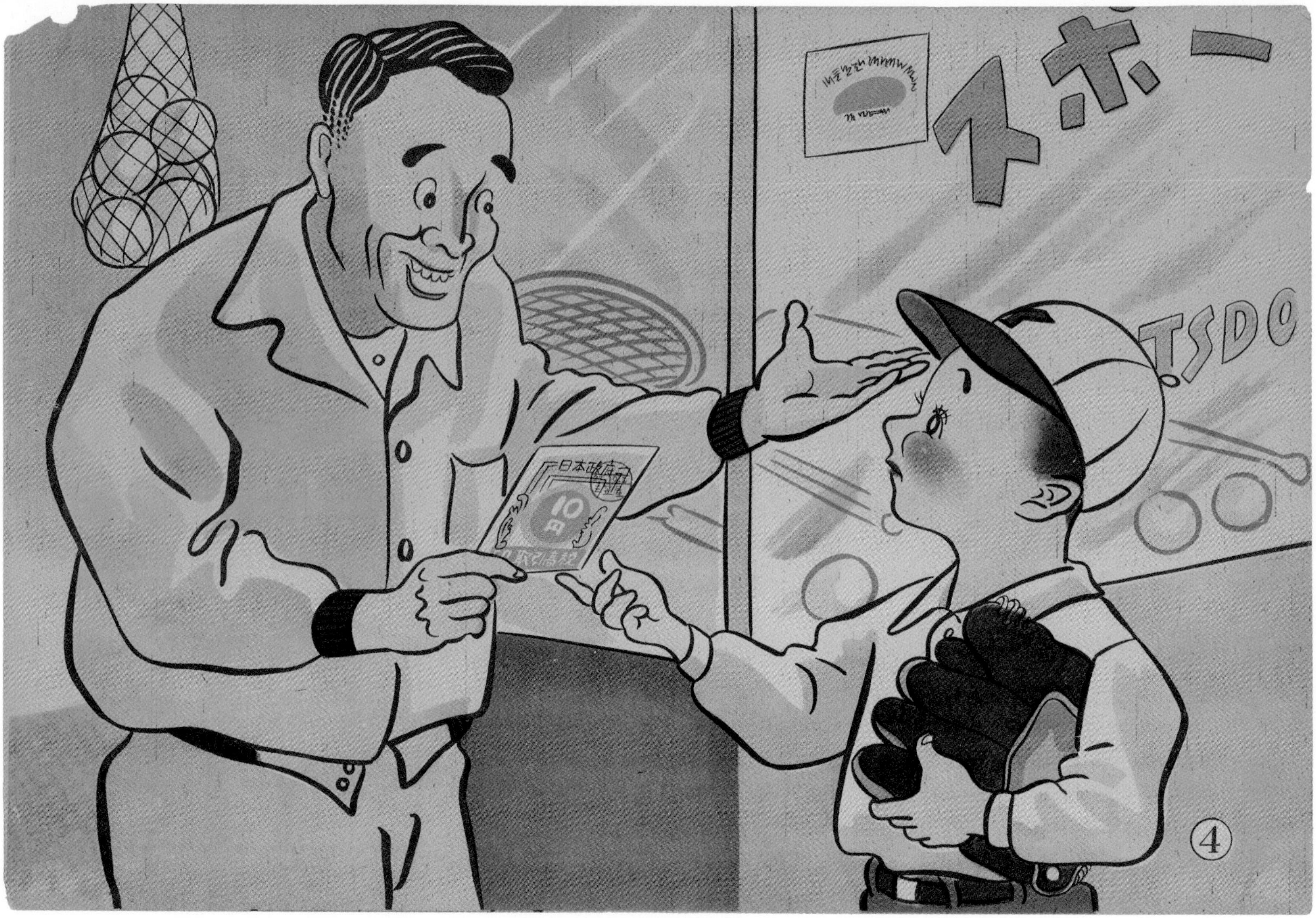
スポー
TSDO
④

Good Sport: The store owner explains that Yoshio can save up coupons to buy uniforms for a baseball team. The Japanese passion for baseball dates to the turn of the last century, when the Tokyo University team beat a visiting American team.

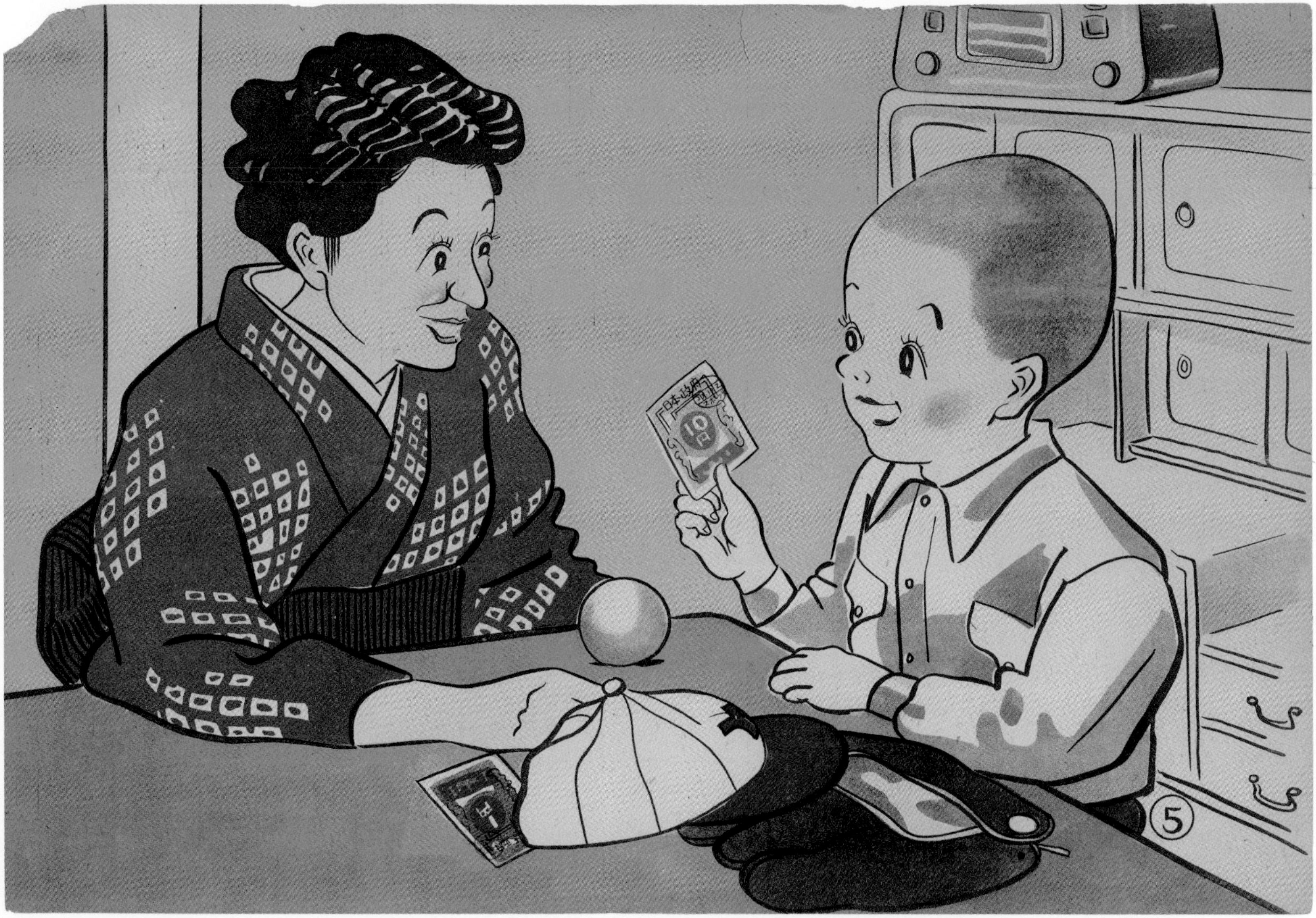
5

Consumer Culture: Yoshio explains his plan to his mother. This was a new, prosperous Japan that could afford consumer items like the radio in the background. SCAP hoped to reform Japanese culture by having the younger generation teach new values to the old.

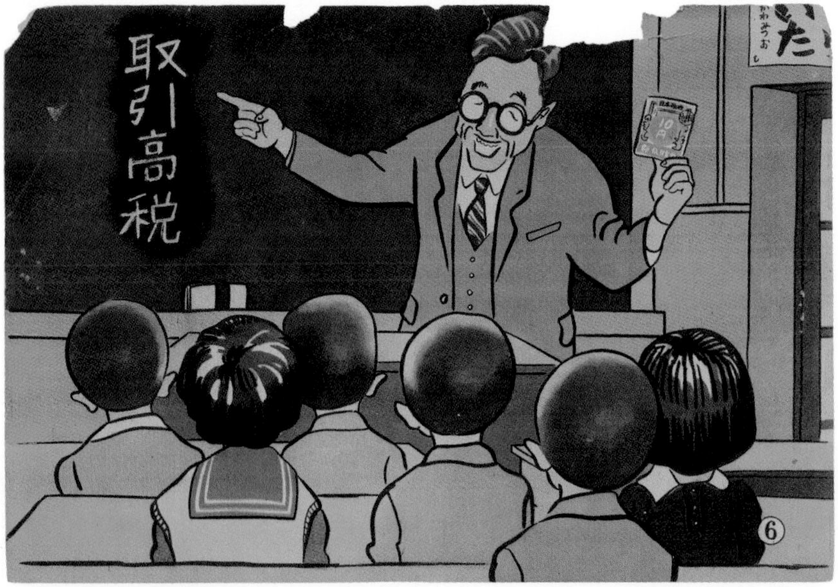
取引高税
⑥

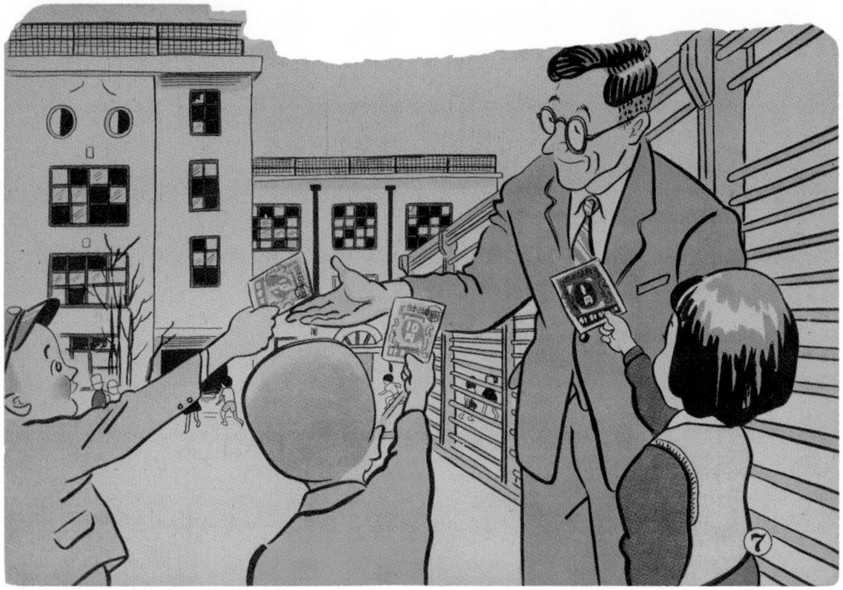
⑦

Team Spirit: The schoolteacher (top left) points out that if all the children save coupons, the team can buy baseball and basketball equipment. The children (above), including a little girl, hand in their coupons. The boys play baseball (right) and the girls play basketball in their new, hygienic playground with a water fountain and a surreally smiling building in the background.

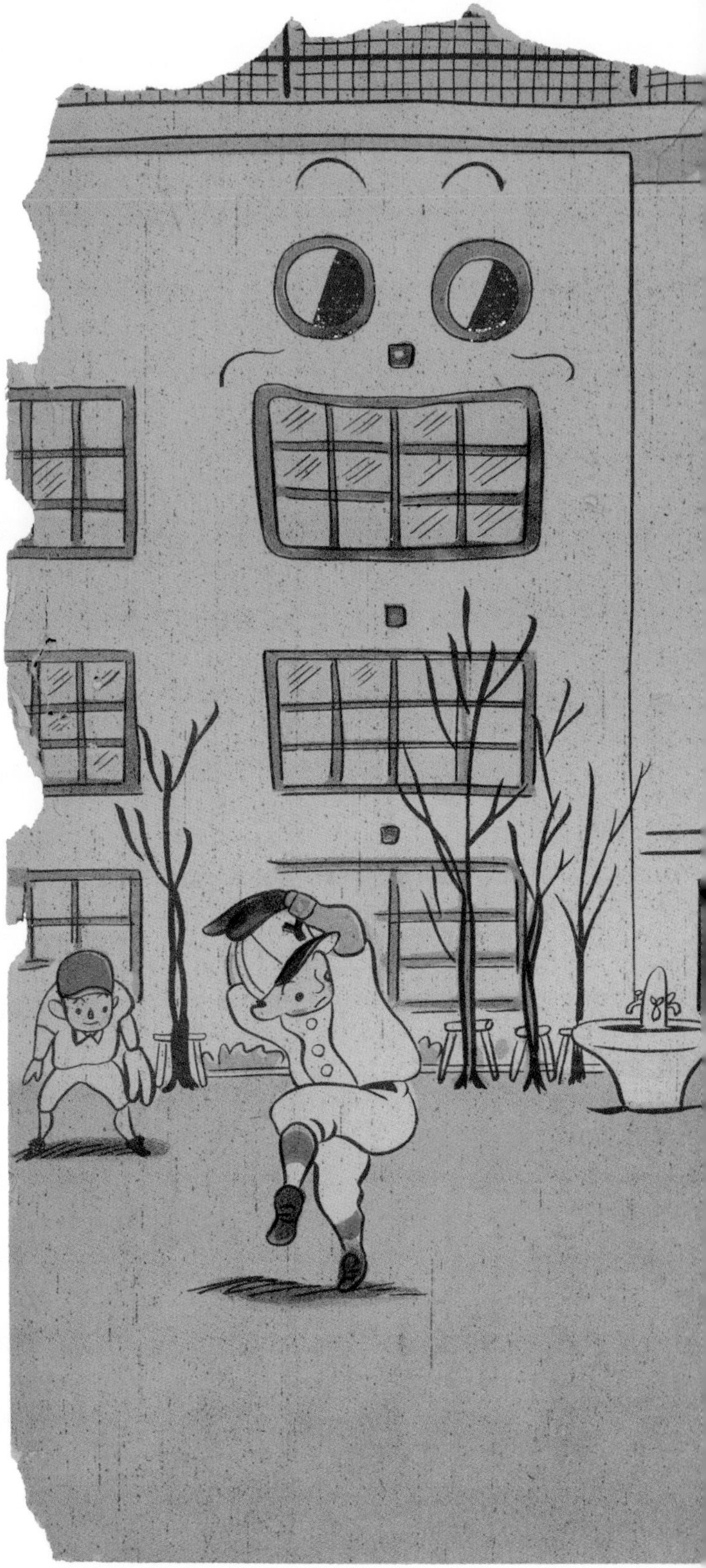

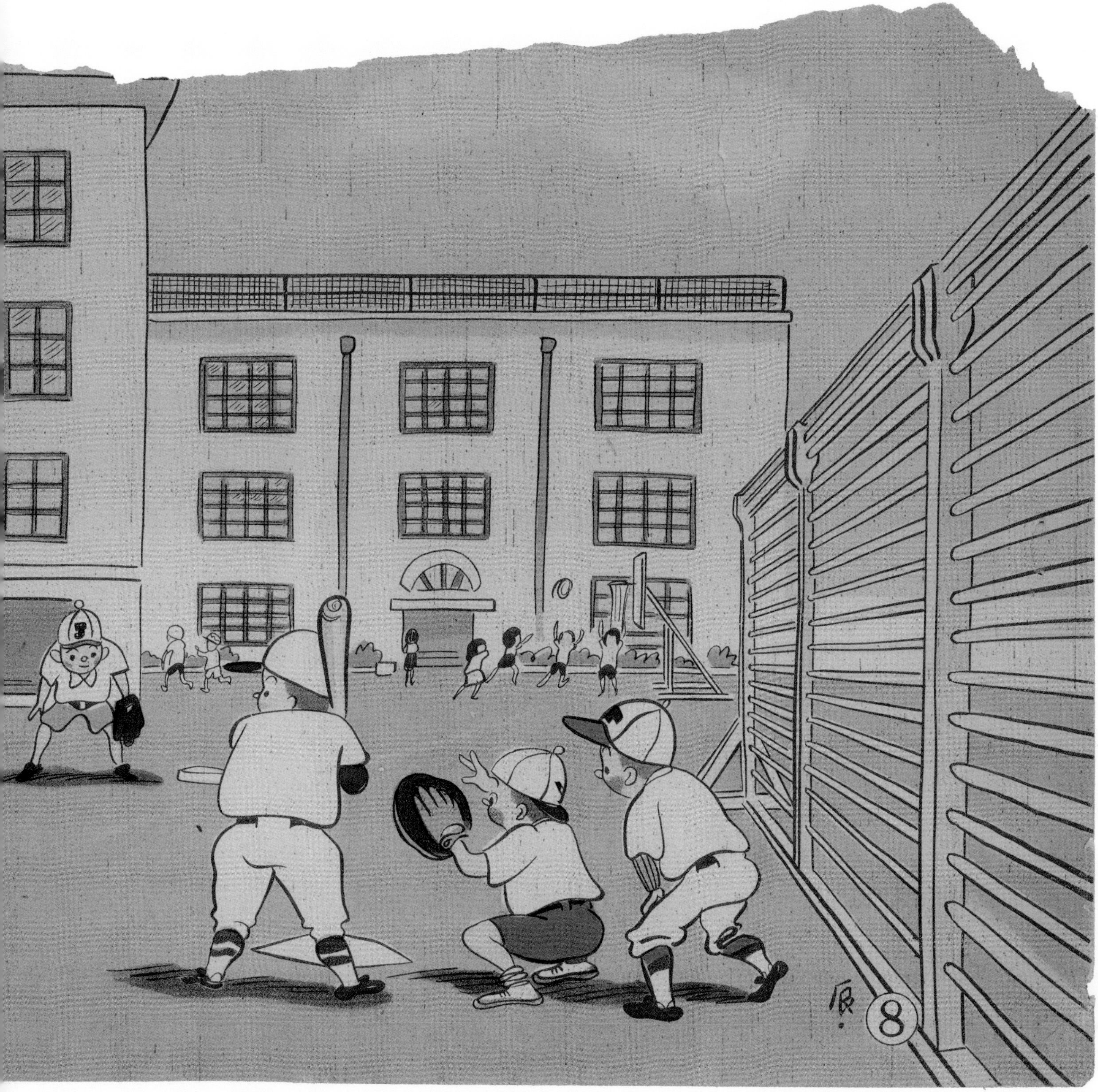
8

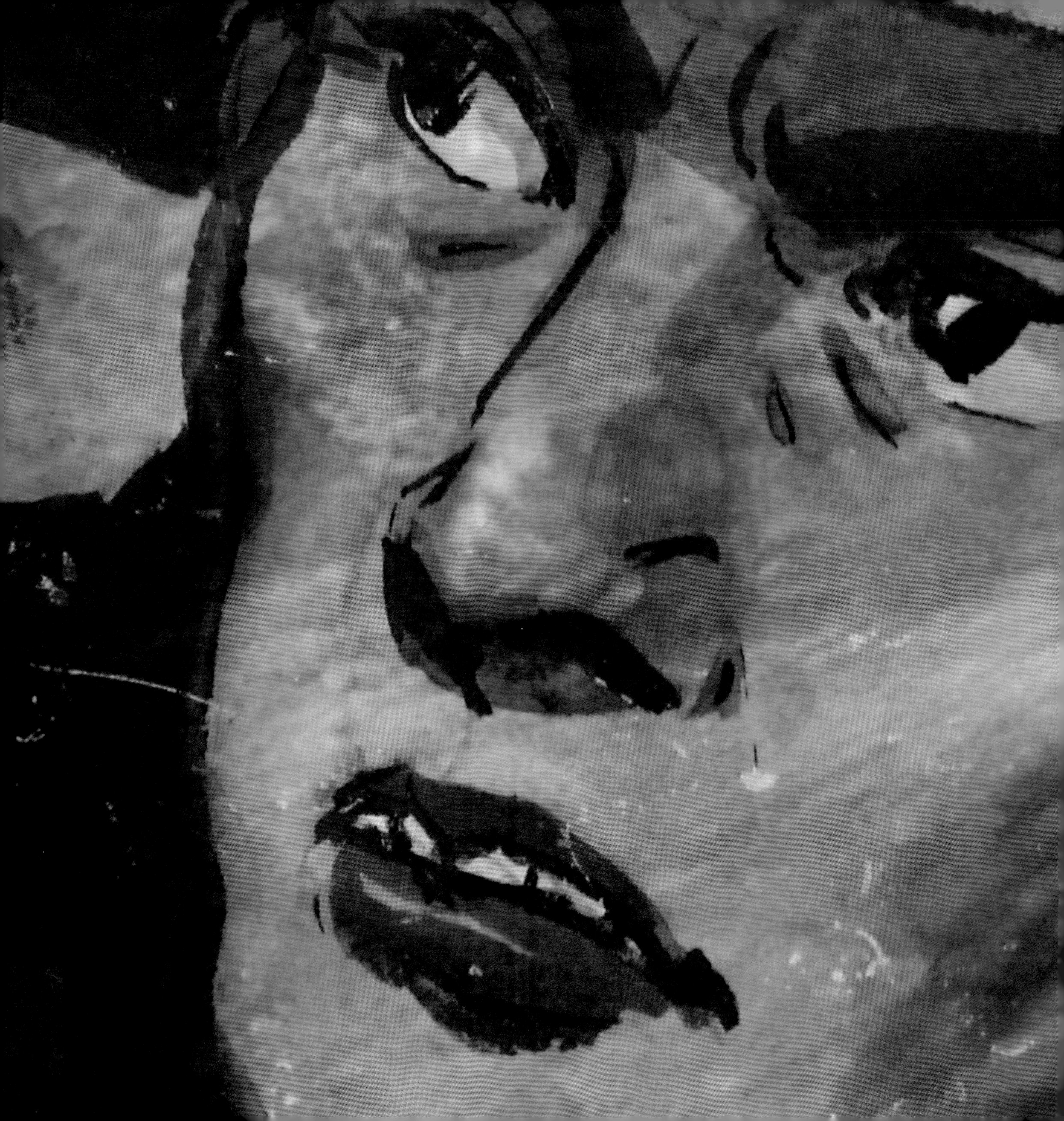

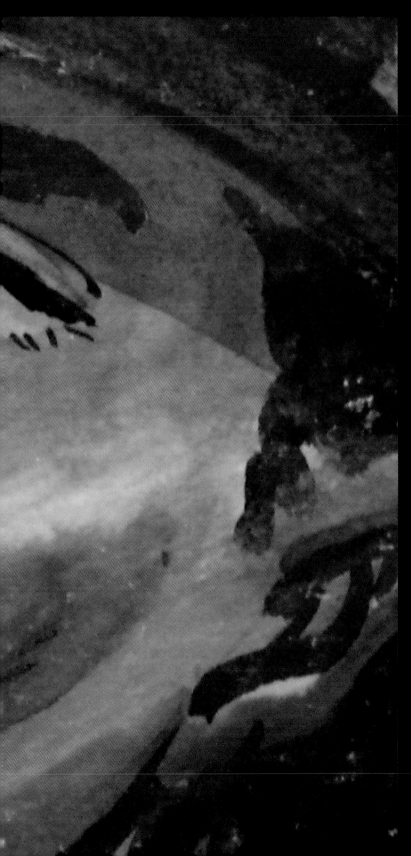

TV KILLED THE KAMISHIBAI MAN

◀ **Hard-Boiled**: *Kamishibai* artists paid tremendous attention to detail: outlines of the facial features of the character Detective Kenji are rendered with subtly varying ink brush lines and filigree work like the shadow under the lower lip, the teeth within the mouth, and the reflection in the eye. Reds and yellows model the volume of the face with highlights on the nose and cheekbone. Even the shadow under the brim of the hat is portrayed.

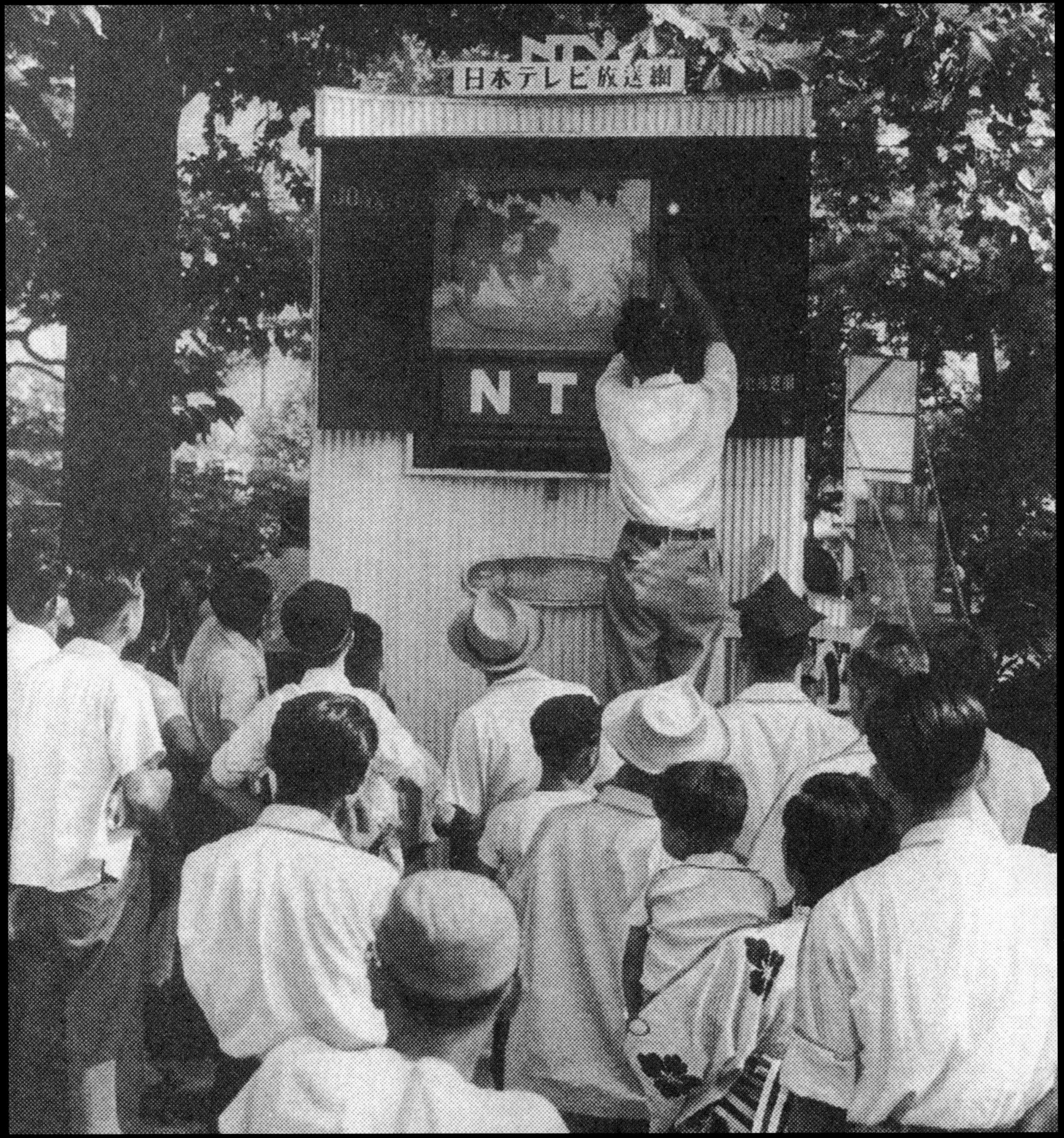
日本テレビ放送網
NT

*T*elevision directly replaced the role *kamishibai* played in Japanese society. A year after the American occupation ended in 1952, **NHK** (Japan's public broadcaster) began broadcasting to a total of 866 sets in the country. Many of these sets were mounted in open-air public spaces in parks and near train stations, so that television was a group experience, much like *kamishibai*.

The first mass phenomenon on television was *Mitsubishi Faitoman Owa* (*Fighterman Hour*) in 1952, a rigged wrestling show featuring a scrappy Japanese wrestler named Rikidozan who underwent untold indignities at the hands of a lumbering American opponent until he emerged triumphant in the last round. Largely unemployed crowds, who had little to cheer about, wept openly at the rare display of Japanese victory. By 1953 there were only three dozen *kamishibai* creators left in the once-active center of Osaka. The penetration of television continued to grow to seventeen thousand sets in 1954, and more than 4.5 million sets by the time Astro Boy made his debut in 1963. *Kamishibai* storytellers tried desperately to keep up with the new medium, adding lights, loudspeakers, and gramophone records to their presentations.

Electric *Kamishibai*: When television was first introduced to Japan in 1952, many of the sets were viewed in public places, like *kamishibai*. Viewers associated the novelty with the small screen of the *kamishibai* stage, and TV was first called *denki kamishibai*—electric paper theater.

"Then kids started watching cartoons," said a veteran storyteller who recalled performing *kamishibai* for eighty children at a time. "And in the meantime, the birthrate fell, and parents got obsessed with education and started sending their children to cram schools," putting an end to the child's world of idle afternoons.

About 5 percent of *kamishibai* creators turned to manga as increasing numbers of *kamishibai* men folded up their miniature stages. By the mid-1950s, there were only half a dozen *kamishibai* printing companies left and twenty production companies. The sanitized genres included a series of biographies of classical composers, and moral tales of Japanese heroes. *Kamishibai* also appeared in schools as a tool for language studies, becoming established as a children's medium and teaching method in the early 1960s. Cartoon characters like AnPan Man, a round-faced caped crusader made of bread who flies through the air, continued to appear in *kamishibai* on language, nature, exploration, current events, health, and historical themes from the Stone Age to the atom bomb.

"*Kamishibai* was in a declining state," in the late 1950s, says Yoko Taniguchi, the daughter of Golden Bat's creator Takeo Nagamatsu. "There were still street *kamishibai* men performing with pictures a bit larger than the older ones, but my father had moved on from this and mainly worked for manga magazines. Many people who had previously done *kamishibai* were doing manga work at our house. This was the time that TV had begun to spread and people could see that *kamishibai*'s time was ending."

Despite *kamishibai*'s decline, there were still a few colorful holdouts. Like *Blondie* and *Beetle Bailey*, who endured long after the dramatic strips *Apartment 3-G* and *Kerry Drake* fell victim to TV soaps and cop shows, programs featuring funny personalities were among the most enduring in Japan. The longest-running *kamishibai* character was Chon-Chan, a rotund, mischievous little boy whose idea of a good time was fooling a grown-up into eating a bar of soap. Chon-Chan's sandlot stories ran for twenty-five years, from 1950 to 1975, for a record 5,200 episodes. Crime and horror continued to be popular genres in the 1950s, just as they were in the United States. One serial combined the two, as the fedora-wearing detective Kenji battled a finned monster who looked suspiciously like the Creature from the Black Lagoon. There was even an Eastern Western in 1962, *Ron Renja* (pronounced with a long

"*O*" sound), with backgrounds that looked like a sketchy impression of John Ford's Monument Valley. One of the last true street-corner *kamishibai* was a delightful rendition of the Adam West *Batman* TV series of 1966–68, done in opaque primary colors with authentic period costumes (blue cowl with outlined eyebrows, black and yellow bat symbol, purple tights) and a sporty bubble-domed Batmobile with red racing trim.

Mass Medium: Huge crowds gathered in outdoor places to watch one of the early hits, a wrestling show where the Japanese hero defeated his American opponent. Television soon replaced *kamishibai*.

"Television became popular when the current emperor got married in April 1959," Yoko Taniguchi says. Sales for fourteen-inch, black-and-white television sets doubled in anticipation of the event. "Street-corner *kamishibai* gradually decreased," Tangiguchi continues. "*Kamishibai* men stopped coming, and children turned to TV. At the same time many manga magazines emerged.

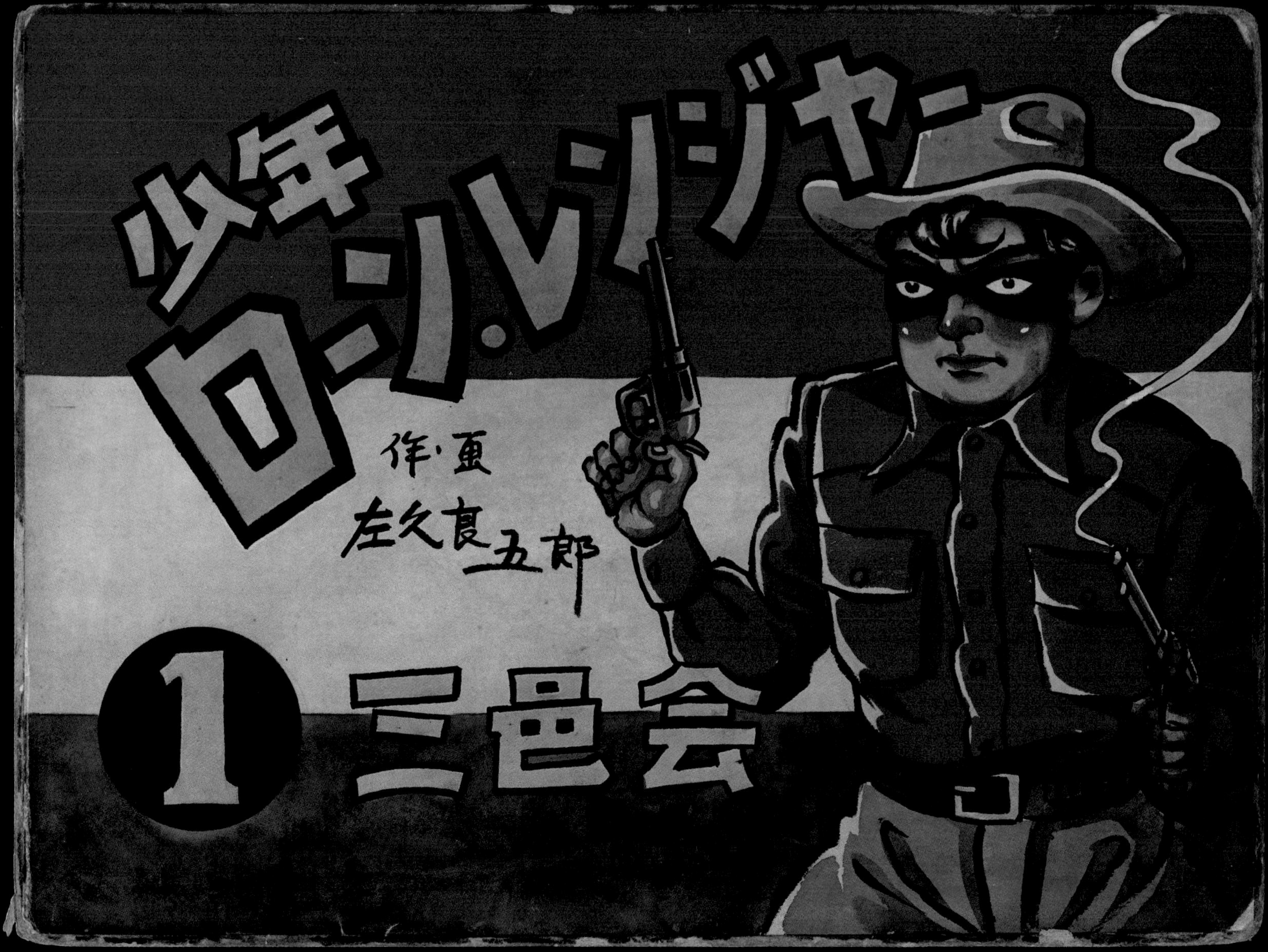
少年ローン・レンジャー
作・画
左久良五郎
1
三邑会

Hi-Yo Silver!: Desperate to compete with the wealth of TV Westerns imported from America in the early 1960s, longtime *kamishibai* artist and writer Sakura Goro, who created *Ninja Woman* in the 1930s, came up with the two-gun masked cowboy Ron Renja (pronounced with a long O sound) in 1962.

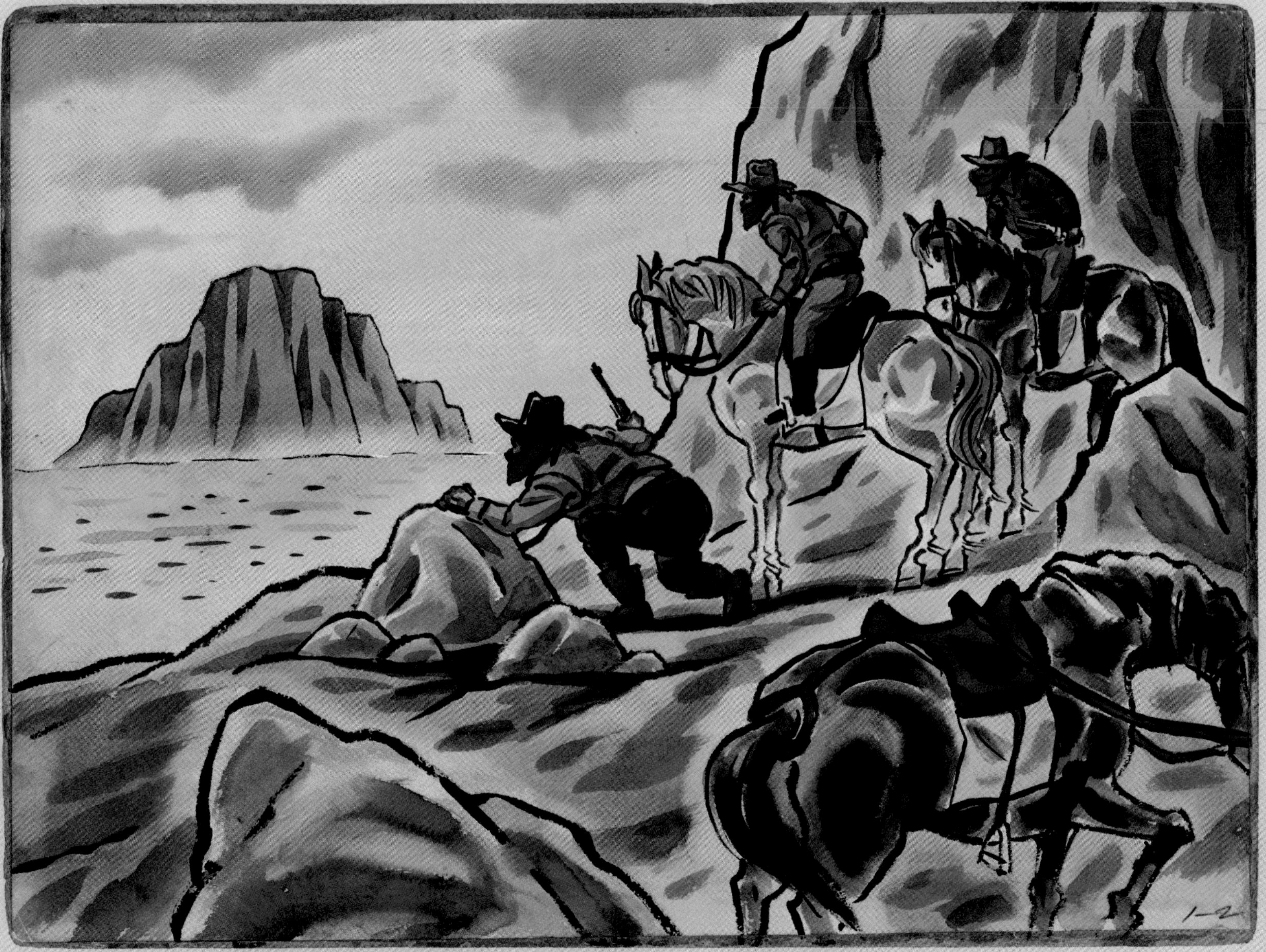

The Wild, Wild East: Bad guys in black hats wait to ambush Ron Renja in a pastiche of Monument Valley Westerns and Eastern treatment of the horses and rocks.

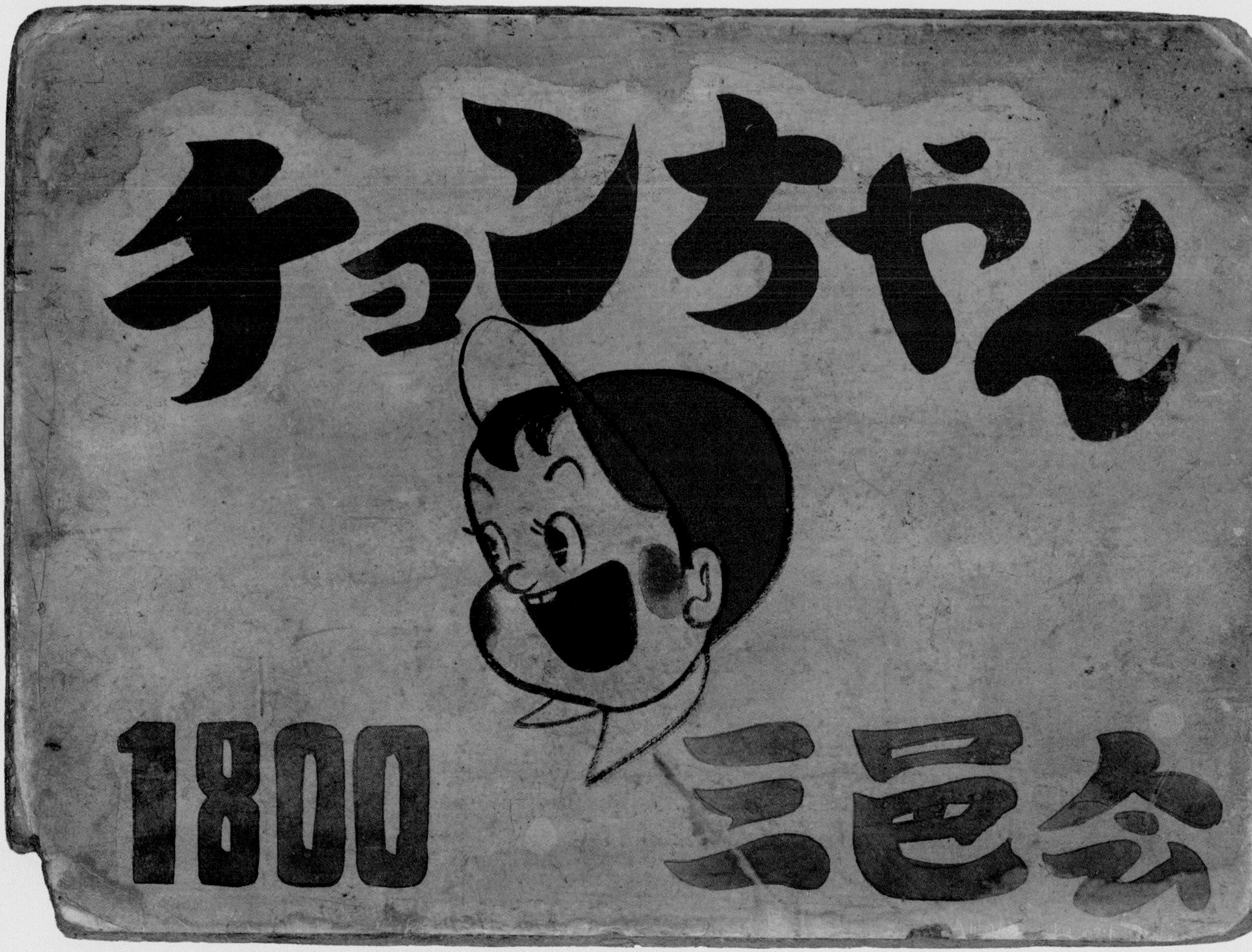
チョンちやん
1800

Chon-Chan, sandlot stories about a mischievous young boy whose idea of a good time was conning an adult neighbor into eating a bar of soap, was the longest-running *kamishibai*, with more than 5,200 episodes from 1950 until 1975. Since the late eighteenth century, the Japanese public has been fans of *gesaku* or (playful stories), published in as many sequels as there was demand for.

Kamishibai men would occasionally come, but it was hard to get the kids to gather like before. I think this made my father sad. Previously you could find children gathered on street corners everyday to hear *kamishibai*, and they looked forward to this."

The death knell for *kamishibai* sounded on New Year's Day 1963, when Osamu Tezuka's Astro Boy made his television debut—the zero hour of Japanese anime. The anime process has its roots in *kamishibai*: Astro Boy's animators, Tezuka and his colleague Sakamoto Yusaku, could not afford the full, fluid animation characteristic of deluxe Disney productions, and instead relied upon what is called limited animation, where fewer drawings are used. In *Astro Boy* (known as *Atomo* in Japan), Tezuka used many still frames of a character's face to fill out the time, much the way a *kamishibaiya* would pause on a particular drawing for dramatic effect. Sakamoto said this method of animation would be received as "electric *kamishibai*."

"TV is a reality factory," one *kamishibai* writer said about the new medium, "whereas *kamishibai* is a factory of dreams."

PRAYER FOR PEACE

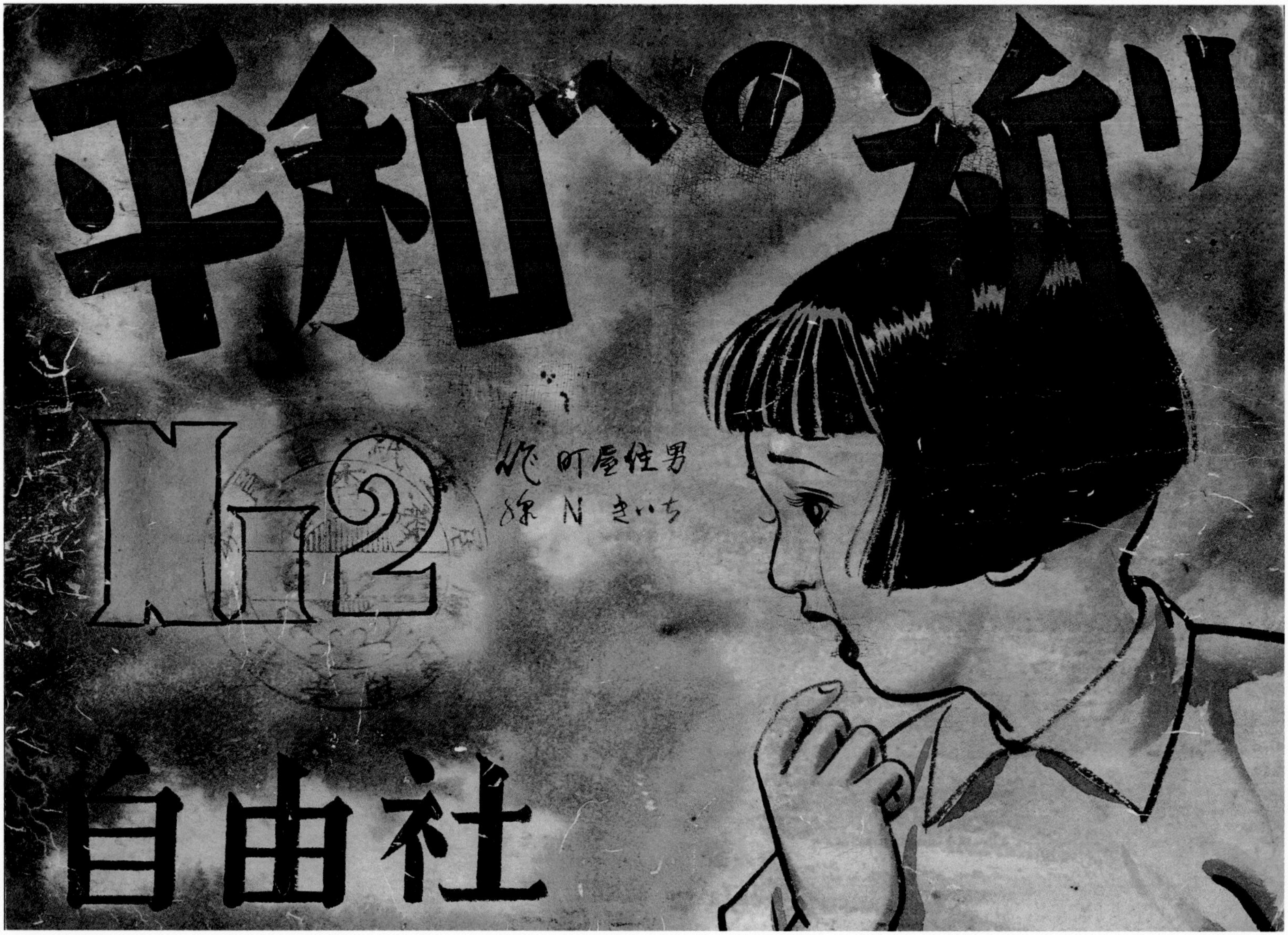
平和への祈り
自由社

Prayer for Peace: References to the atomic bombing were forbidden by SCAP censors but reemerged after the occupation as a means of coping with the tragedy.

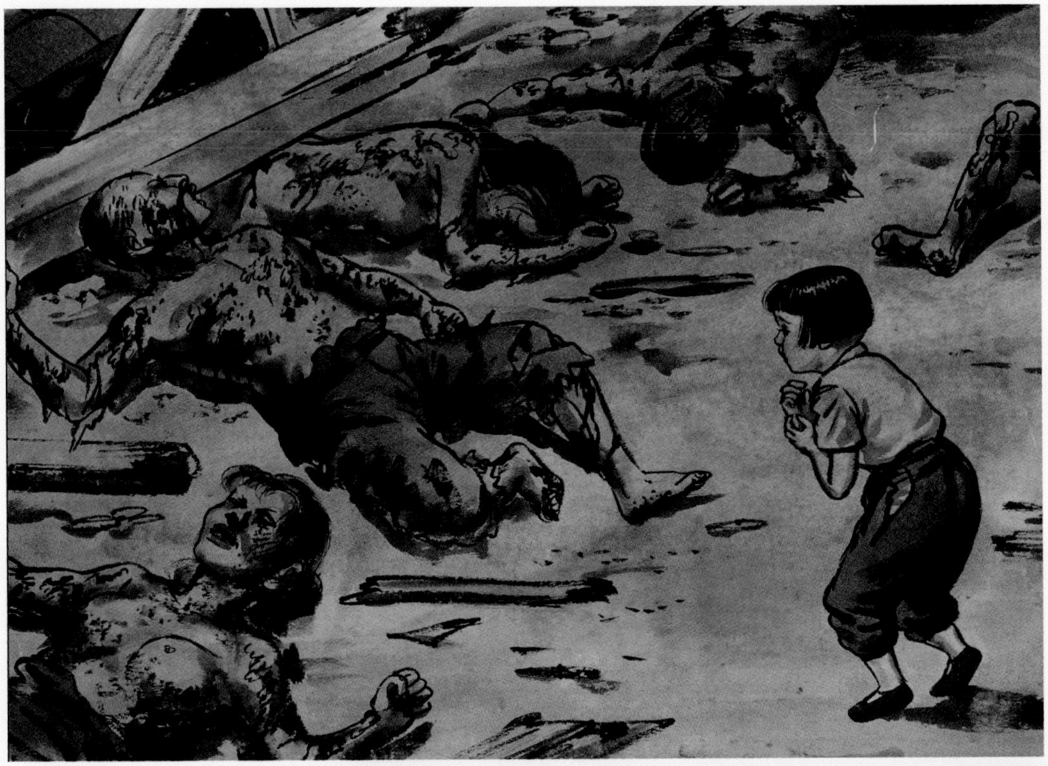

LEFT A young girl looking for her mother in the minutes after the blast is the sole survivor in a landscape of gruesomely charred bodies. Miraculously untouched by the blast, the girl is a vivid spot of color in an ashen scene of carnage.

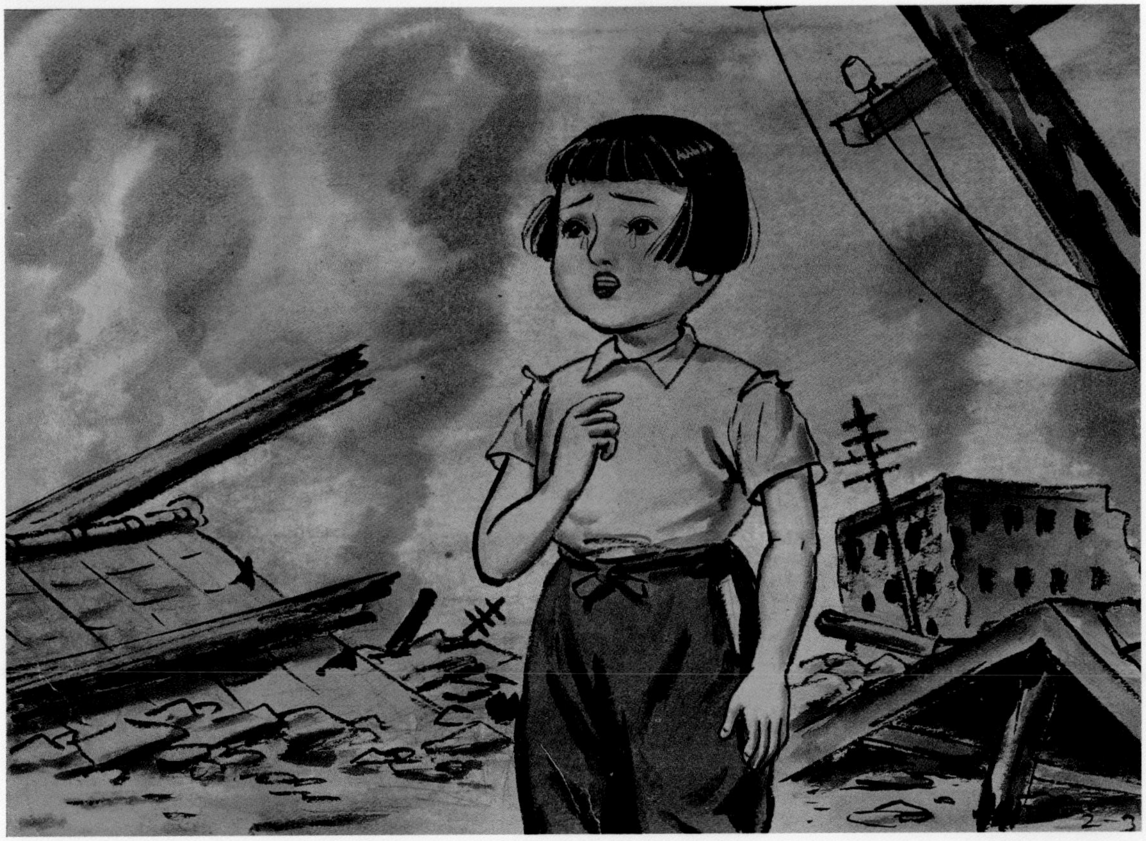

RIGHT Against a shattered cityscape of leaning utility poles and smoking ruins, the girl cries out for her mother. Her centrality in the frame shows her isolation as the last living person, and her worried expression would speak directly to children in the audience.

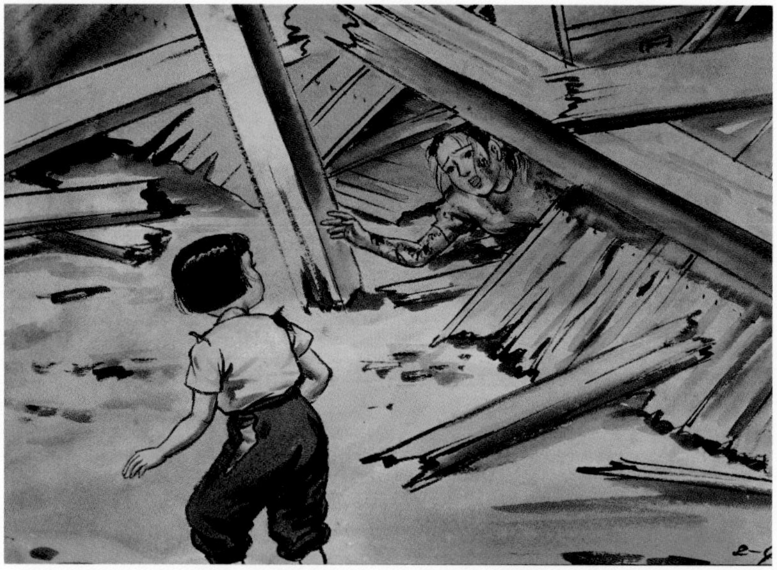

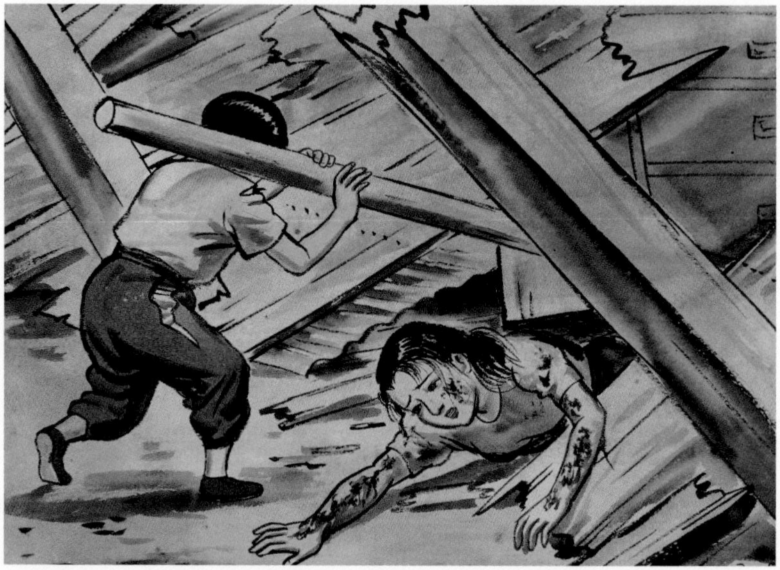

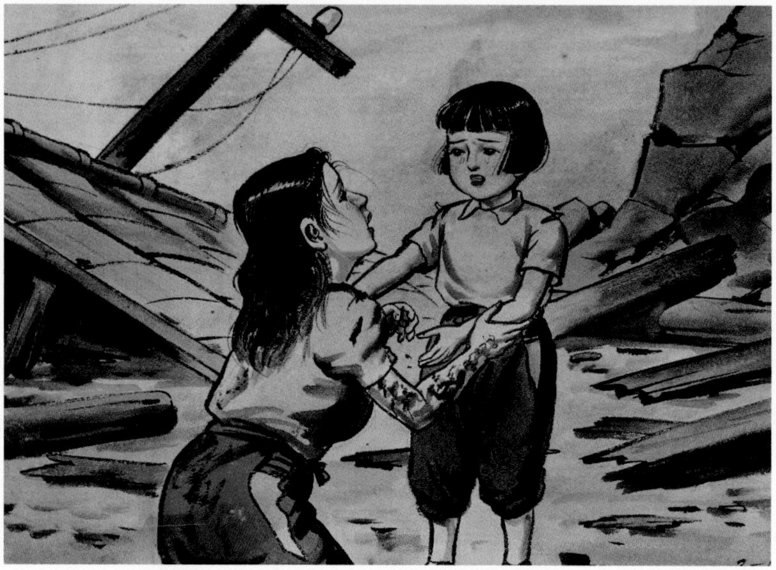

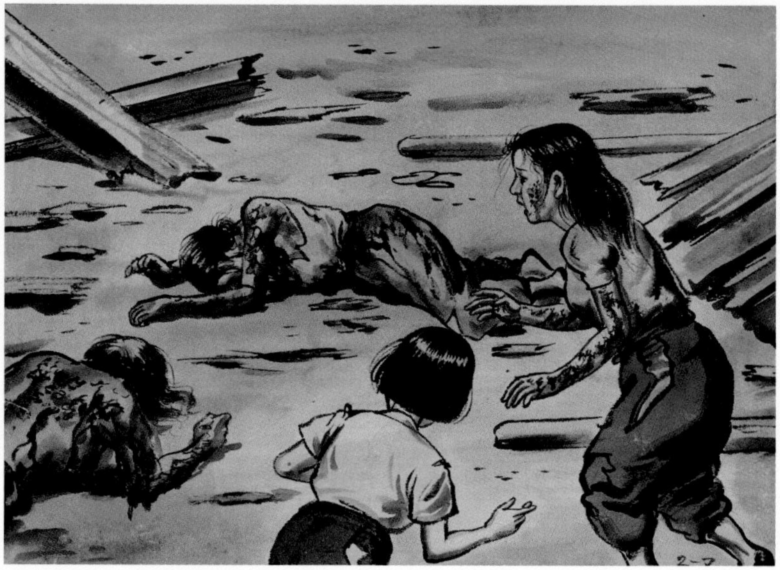

TOP LEFT The girl hears her mother's voice emanating from a jumble of fallen beams that emphasizes her entrapment.

BOTTOM LEFT Kneeling, the mother expresses her gratitude that the girl is still alive and thanks her for rescuing her. Their relative positions show that girl is taking on the role of an adult.

TOP RIGHT Using a beam as a lever, the girl frees her mother, whose skin is covered in radiation burns. *Genbaku no ko* (children of the bomb), are shown literally shouldering the burden of adult responsibilities in the postwar society. "The day before the bomb was dropped on Hiroshima," John Hersey wrote in *The New Yorker*, "the city, in fear of incendiary raids, had put hundreds of schoolgirls to work helping to tear down houses and clear fire lanes. They were out in the open when the bomb exploded. Few survived."

BOTTOM RIGHT Mother and daughter search through the charred wreckage for surviving relatives and neighbors. The mother comes across the body of a friend sprawled on the ground. The holocaust is unsparingly portrayed: the figure in the foreground bears wounds that burn through to the bone.

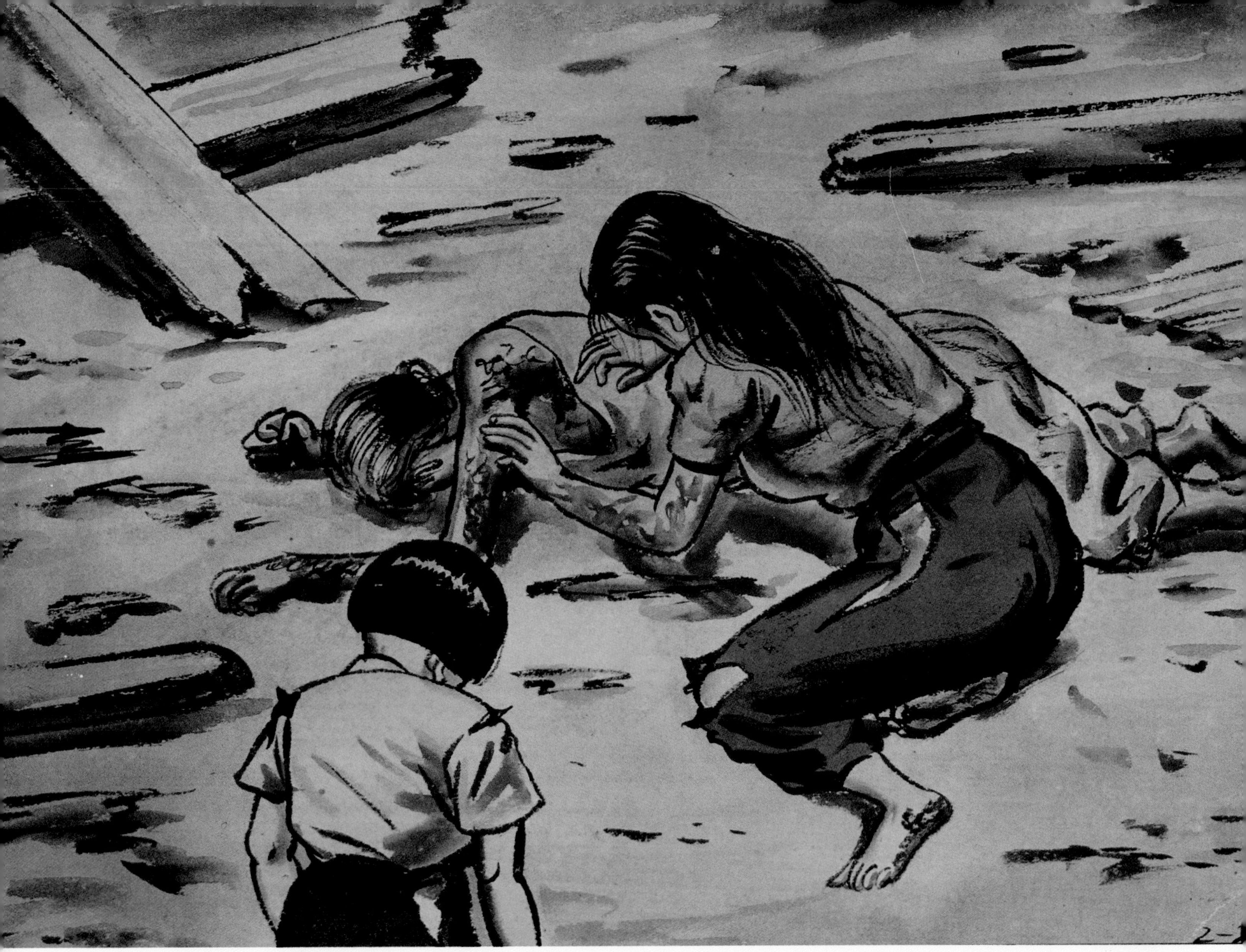

The neighbor is dead, and the mother and daughter drop their heads in sorrow. The angle of the girl's pageboy haircut is especially expressive.

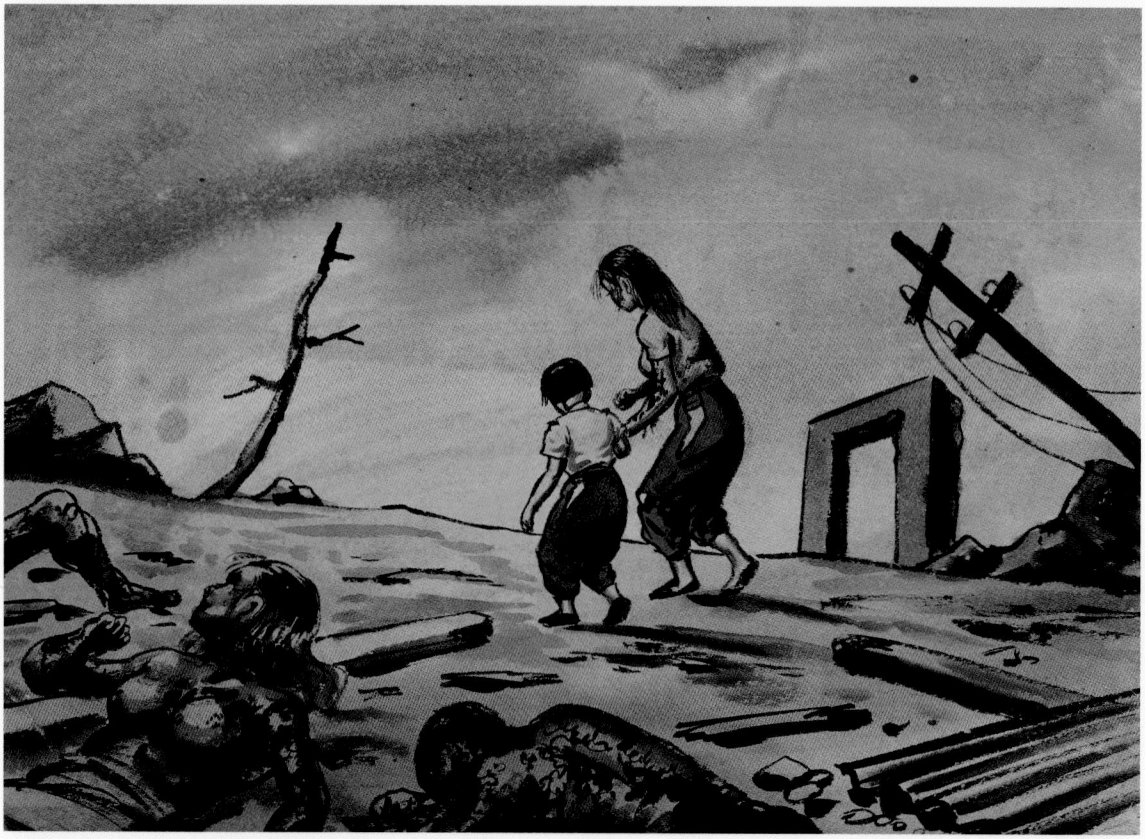

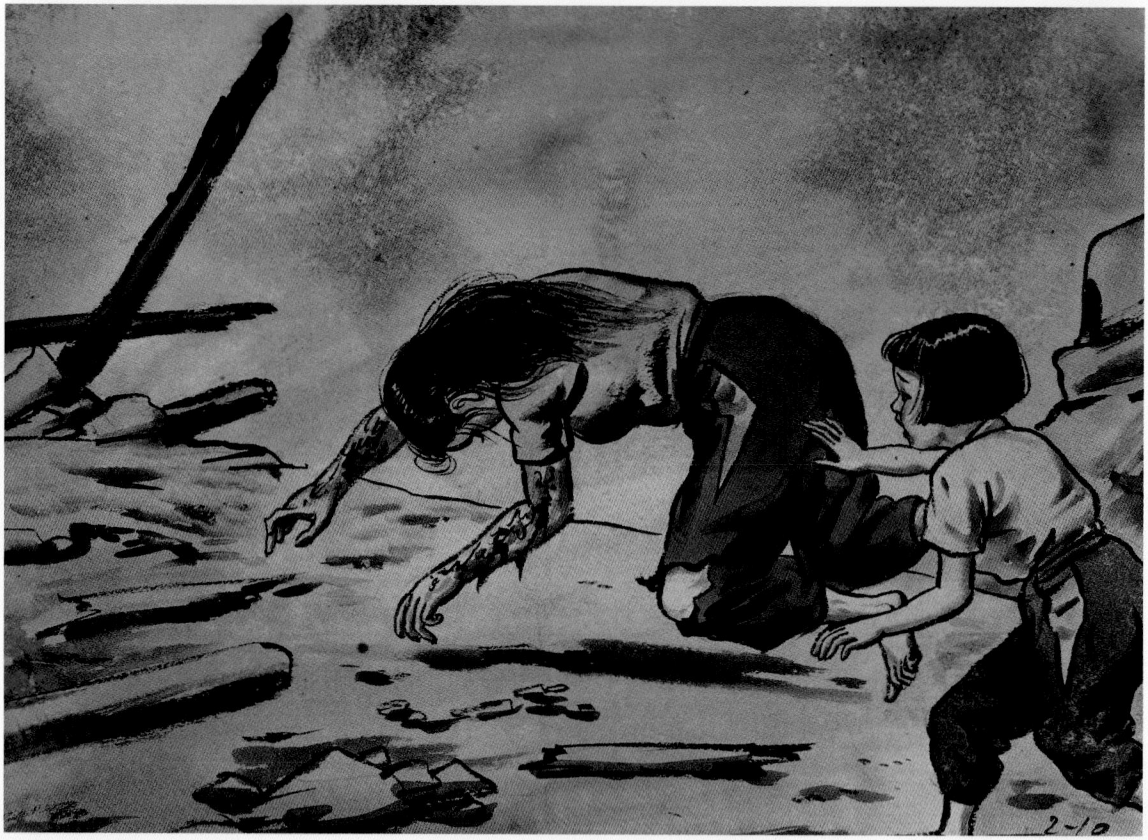
2-10

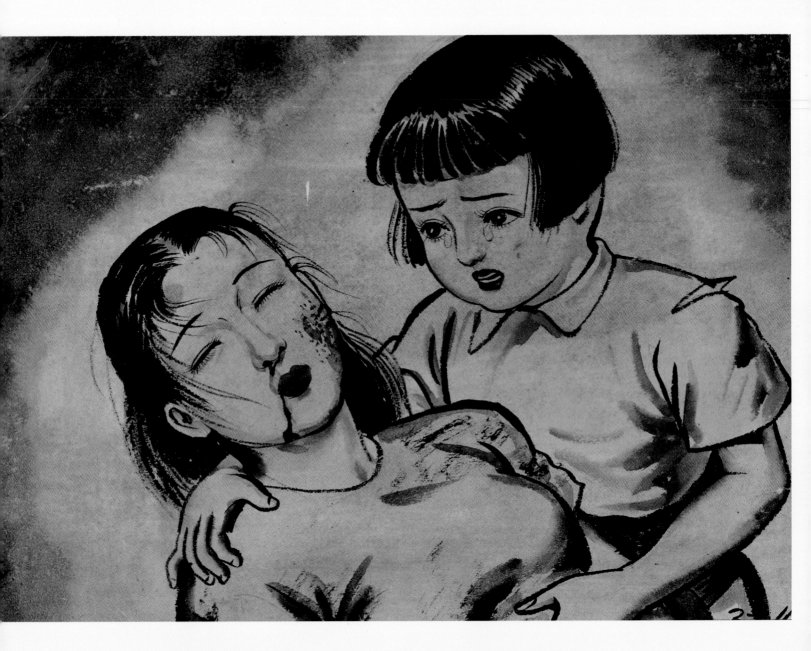

OPPOSITE, TOP Ash-covered corpses loom in the foreground as the pair wanders through the ruined landscape of a leafless tree in August, a tottering electrical pole, and an askew door frame.

OPPOSITE, BOTTOM The girl reaches out as the mother stumbles. The narrative is framed in medium shots, emphasizing the human scale.

ABOVE The mother dies in her daughter's arms with a few last words, as blood trickles from the corner of her mouth. The story ends with this devastating image.

PRINCE GAMMA VS. THE GIANT ALIEN

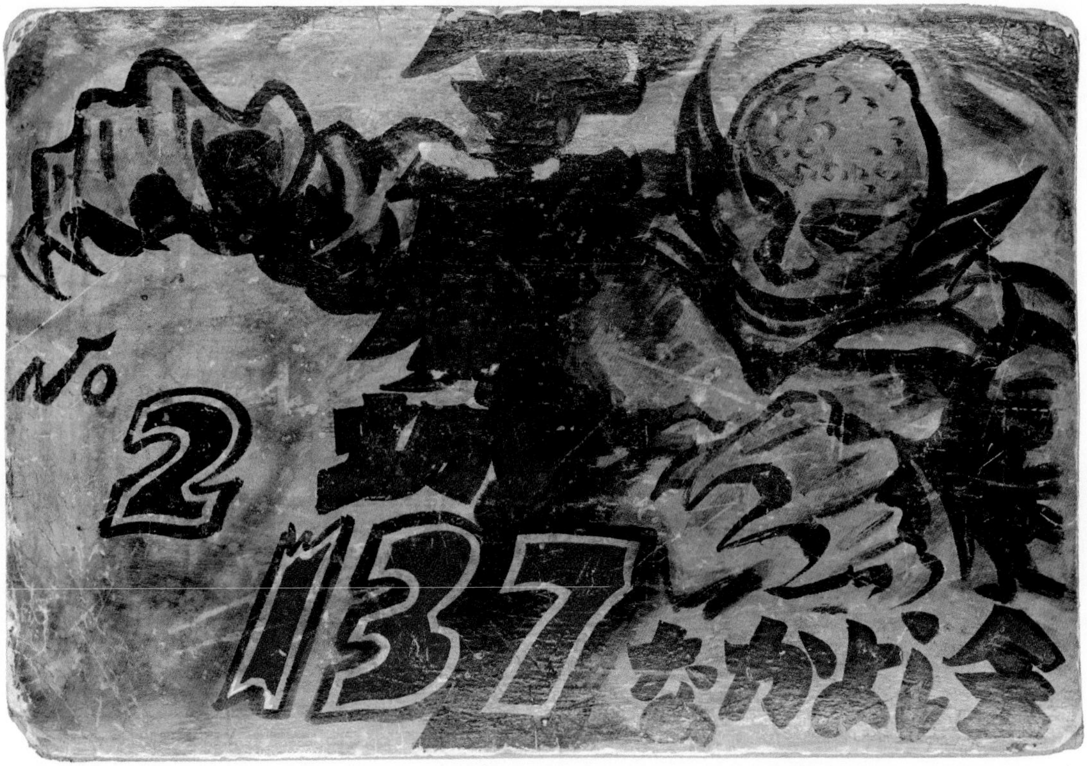
No 2

ABOVE Creature Feature: The title card for this episode of *Demon Castle of Outer Space* features an extraterrestrial who looks suspiciously like the Creature from the Black Lagoon.

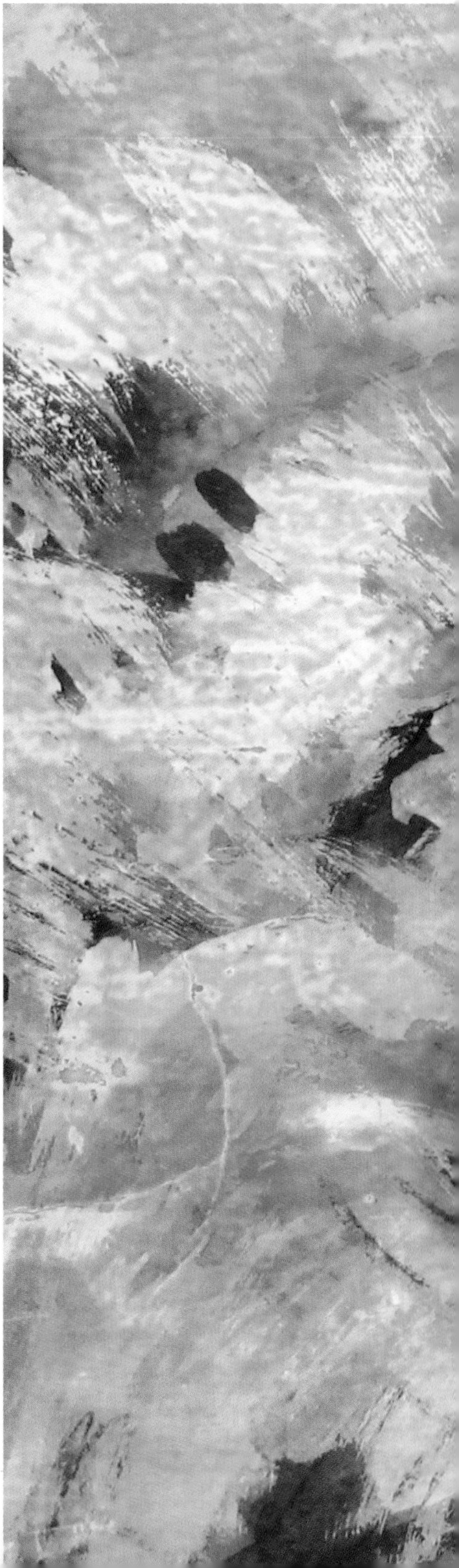

RIGHT Fintastic: The grinning alien pops his head above water in a rainbow of color.

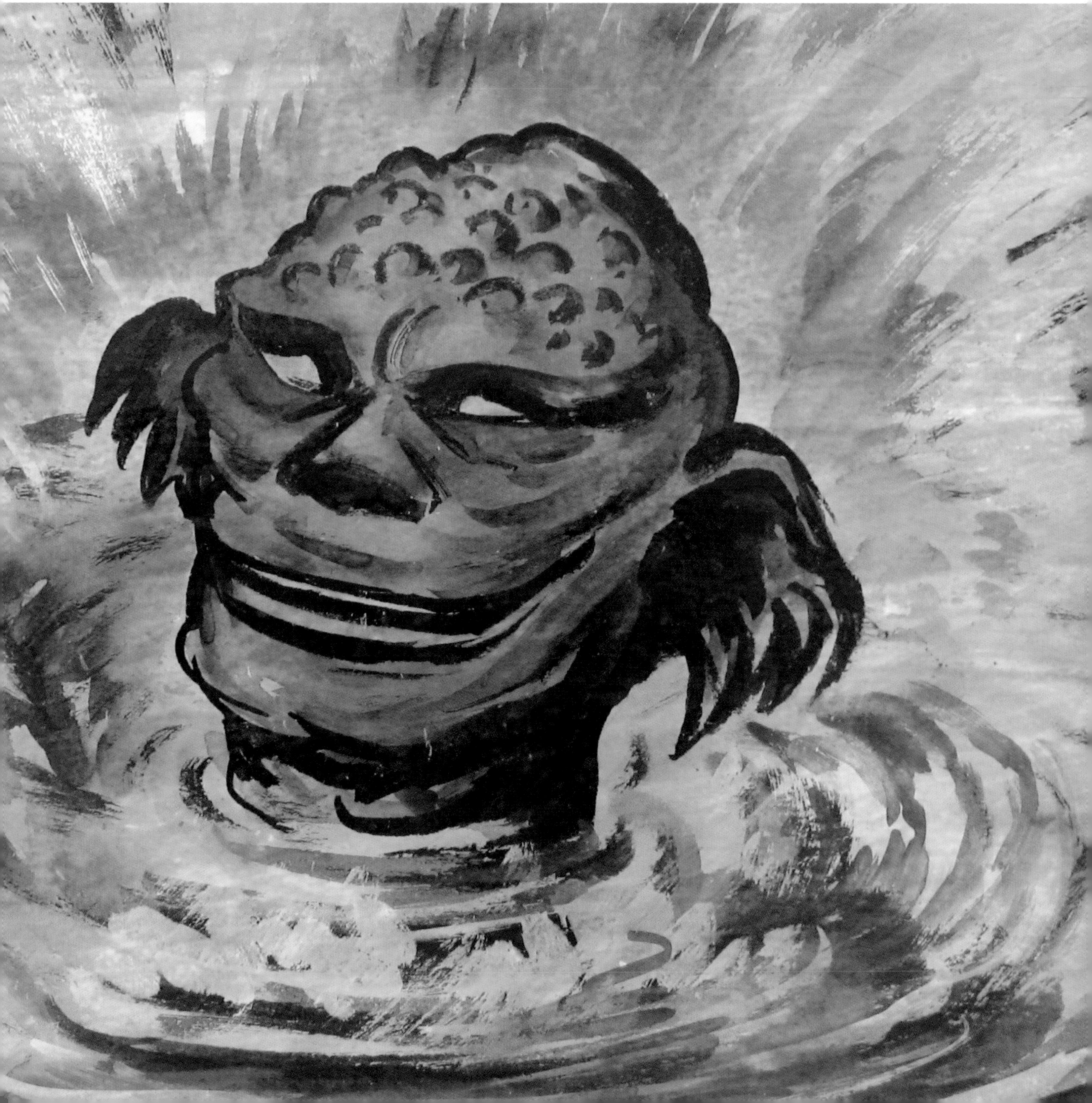

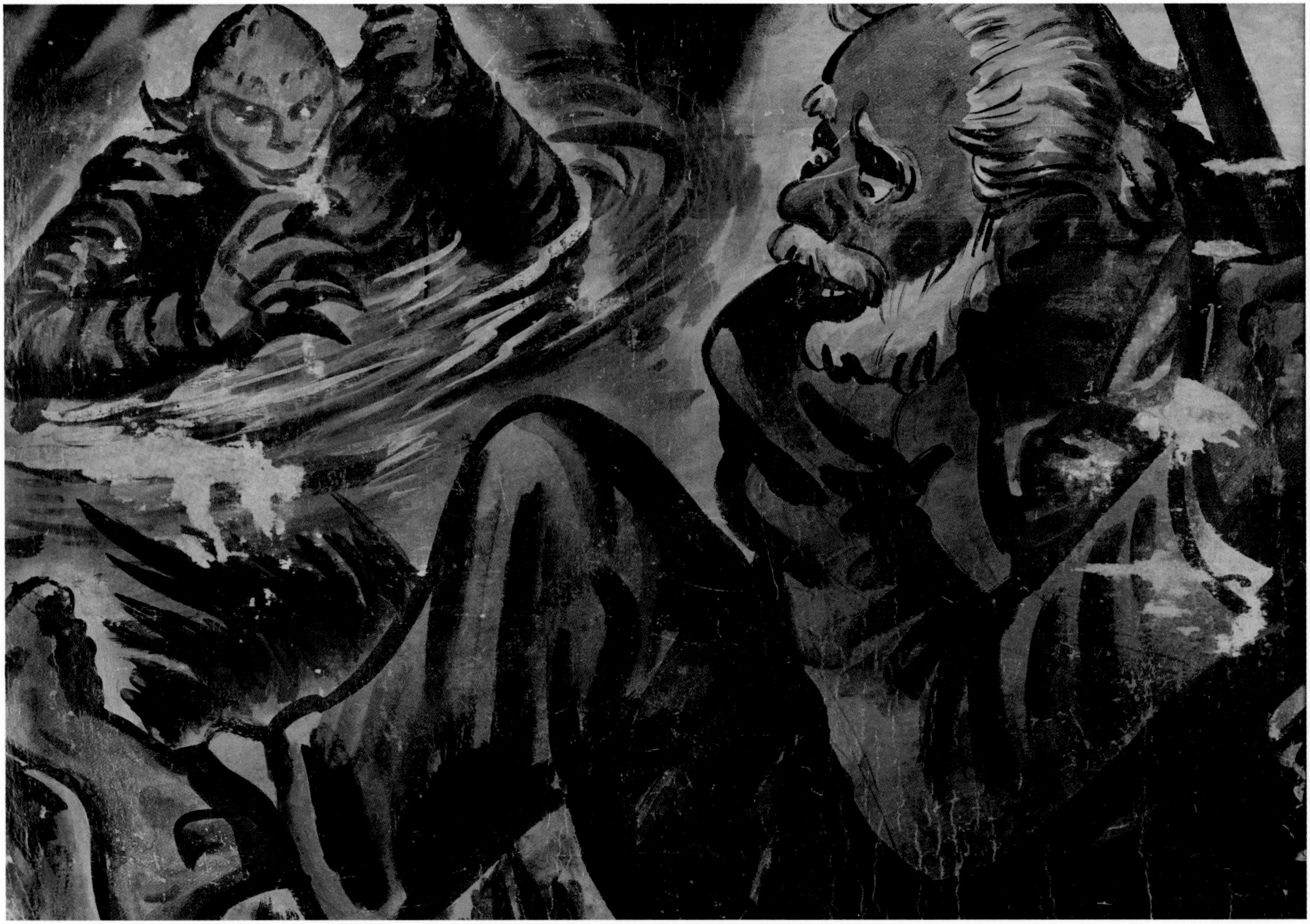

ABOVE Fish Tale: The monster surprises a barefoot fisherman, who could have been a stock character in an ancient folktale.

OPPOSITE, TOP Claws and Effect: A syndactyl claw reaches for the unsuspecting hard-boiled hero Kenji.

OPPOSITE, BOTTOM Screen Grab: The creature snatches Kenji to the horror of the little girl. Children are most commonly witnesses in *kamishibai* stories and see more than adults.

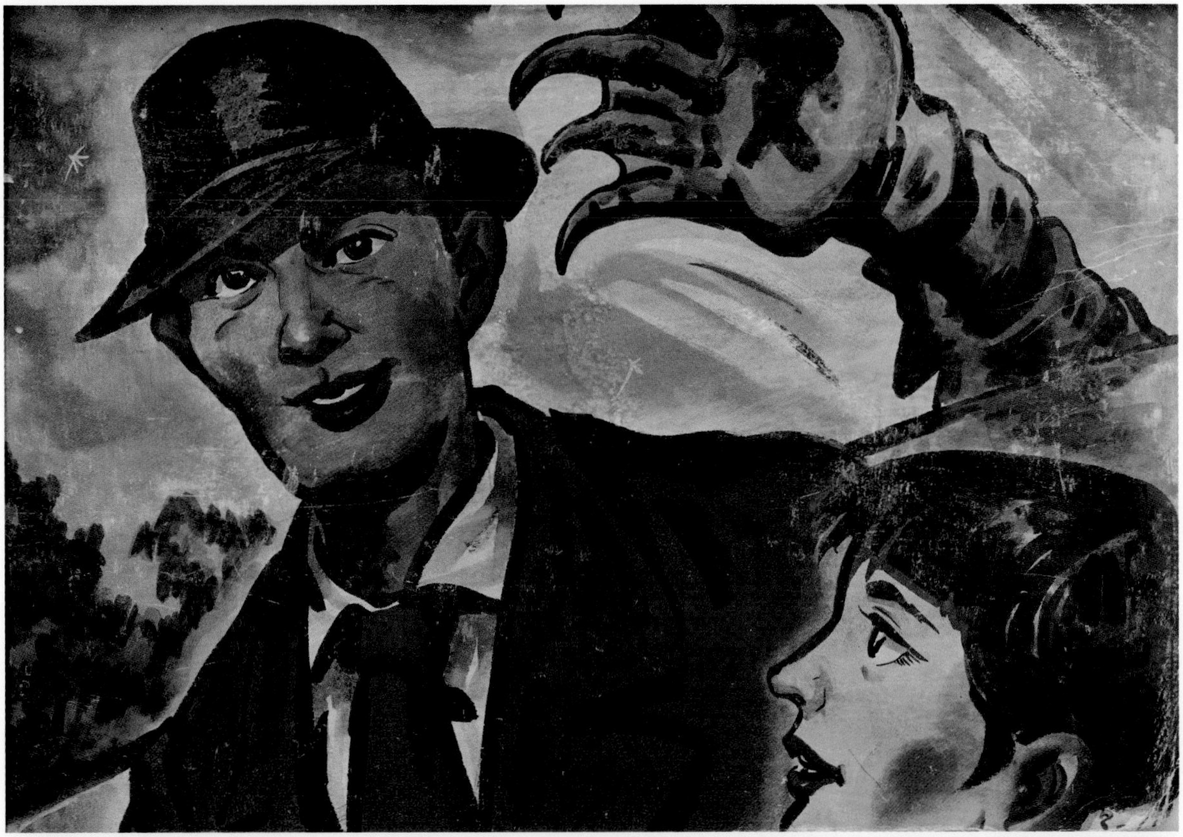

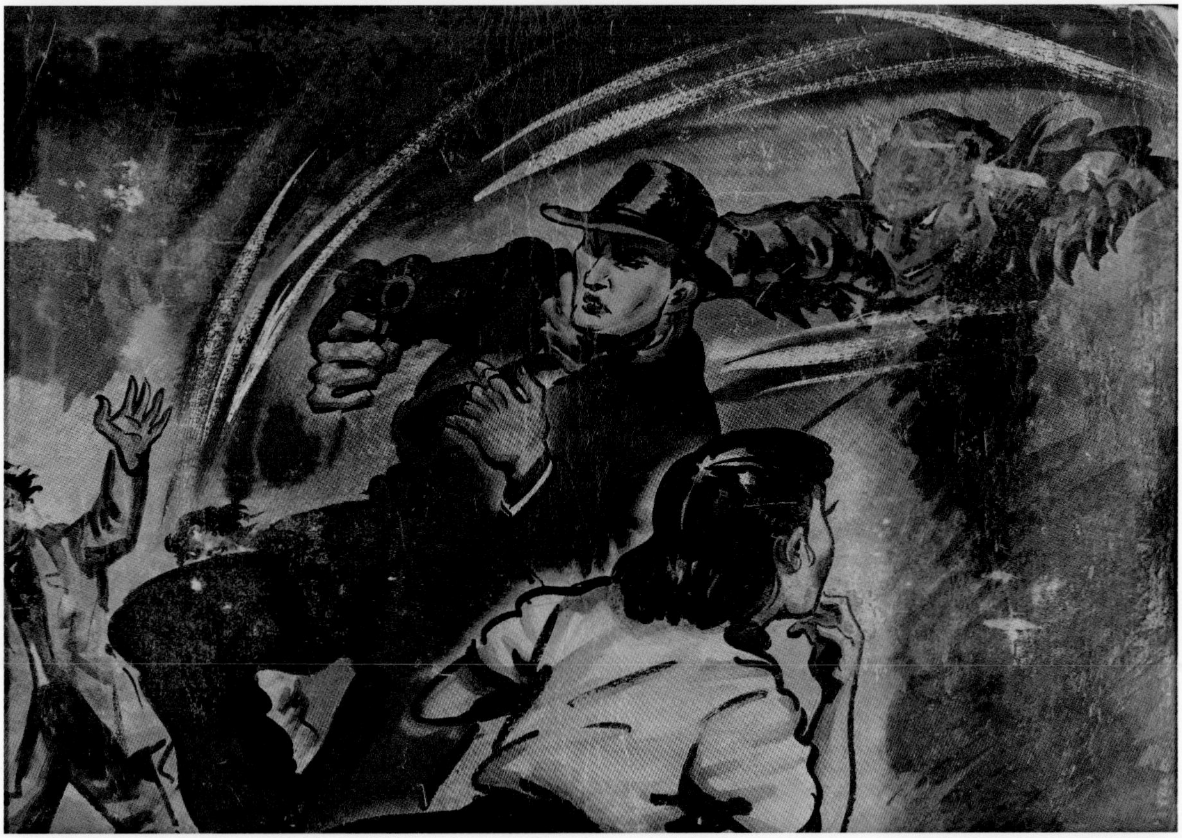

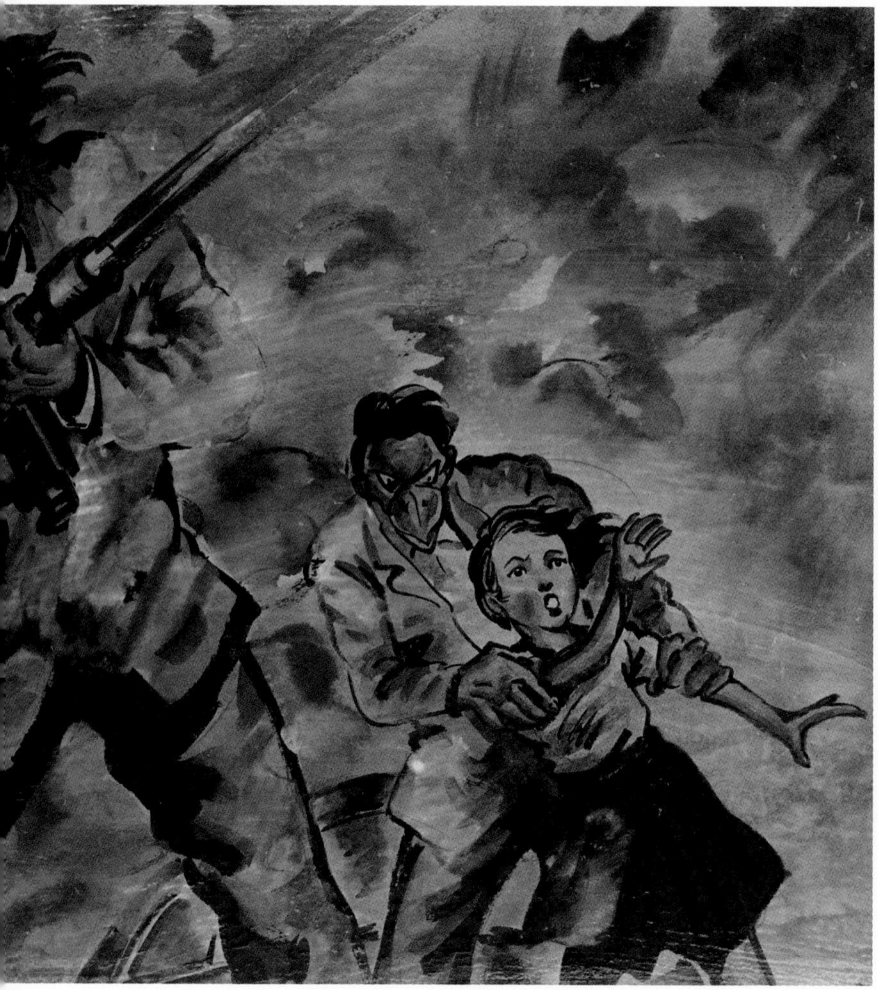

ABOVE Duck, Little Girl: Duck-billed bank robbers take a girl hostage in this crime *kamishibai.*

RIGHT Wipeout: With his fedora, pistol, and motorbike, hard-boiled Kenji is a delirious mix of detective and science-fiction hero as he investigates the crash of a flying saucer in a lake. Here he loses traction on his motorcycle in a swirl of tempera brush strokes.

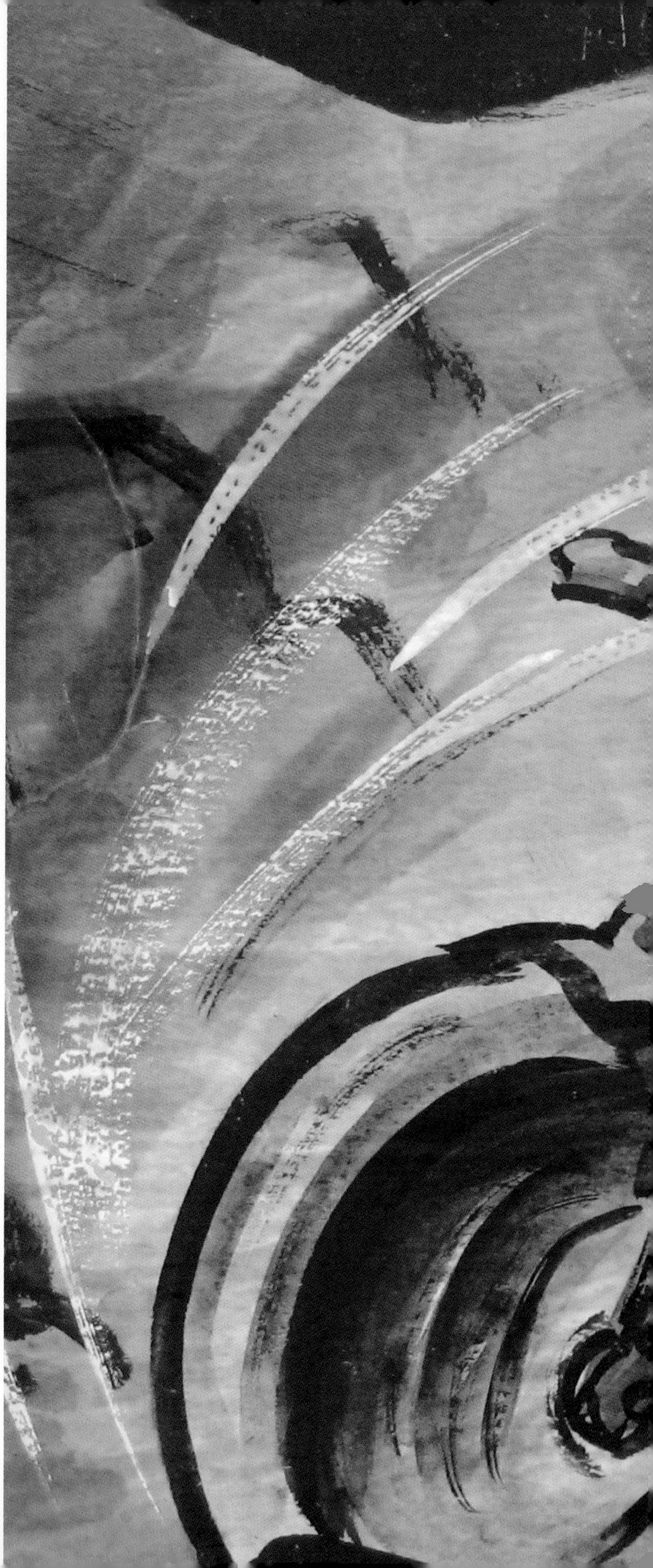

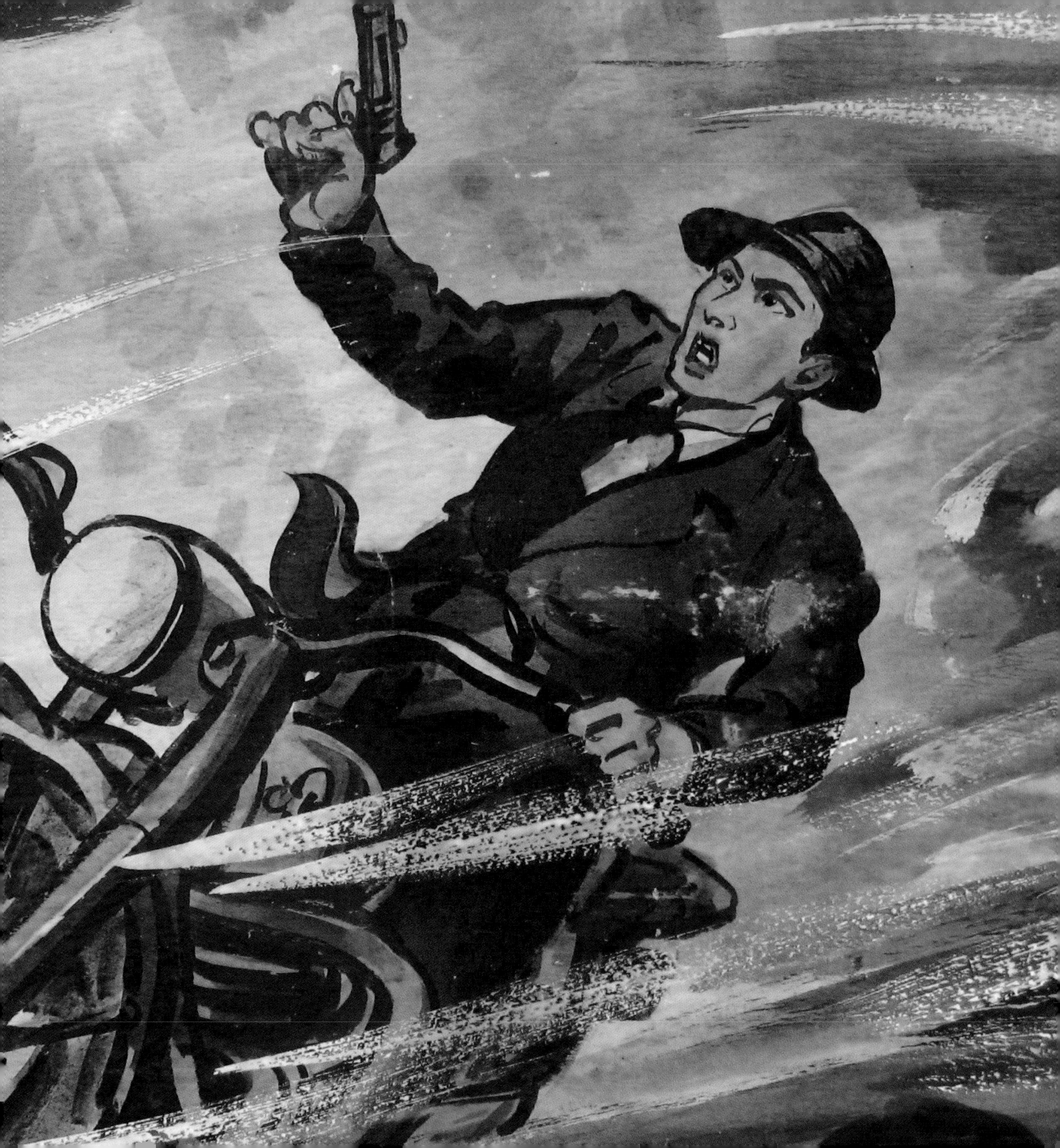

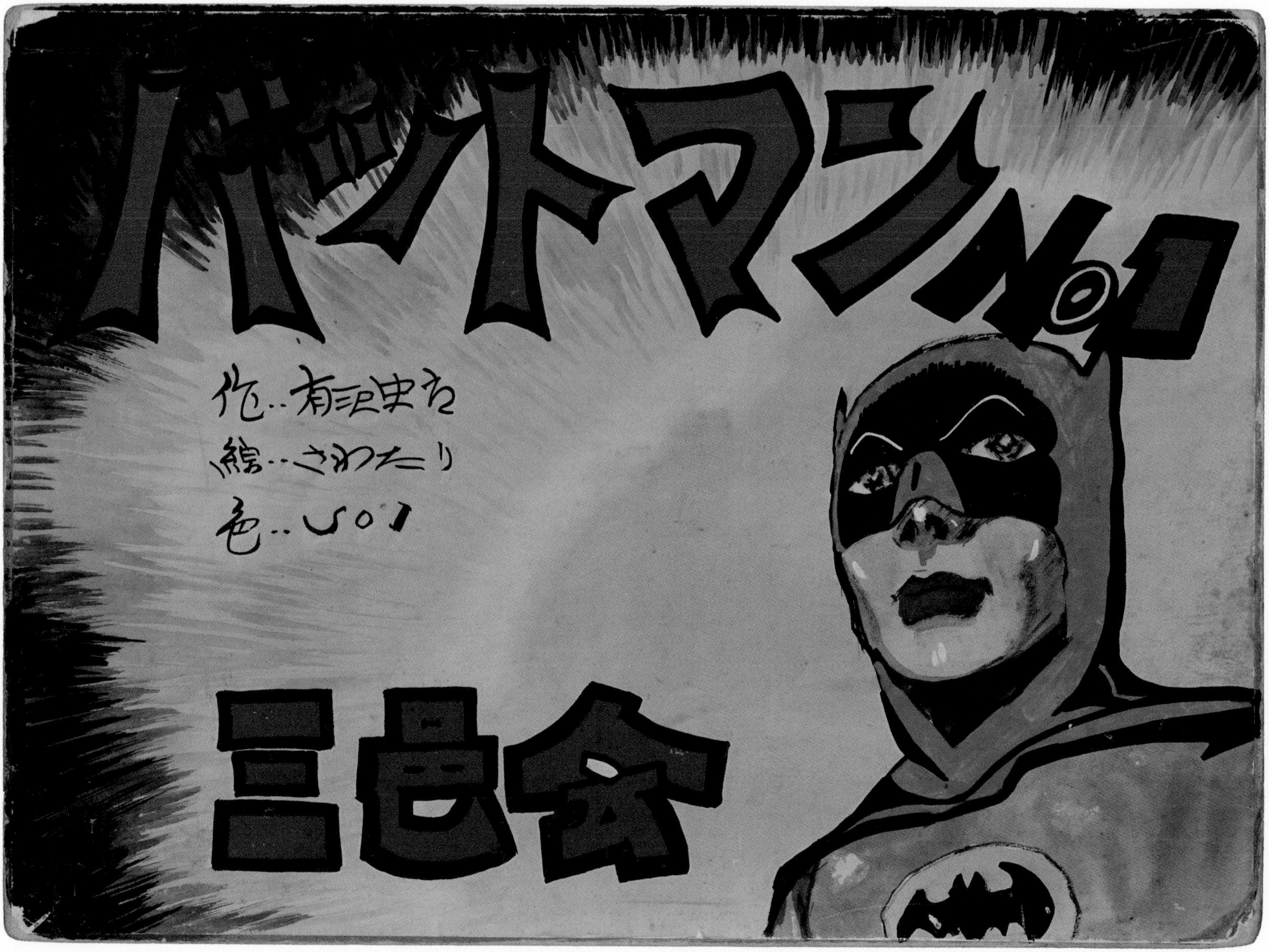
バットマン No.1
絵..さわたり

Batmanga: Creators made sporadic attempts to keep pace with imported American TV shows as late as the mid-1960s. This brightly colored *kamishibai* was inspired by the hit *Batman* series of 1966–68 starring Adam West and Burt Ward, but a distinctly Japanese Batman looks back at us.

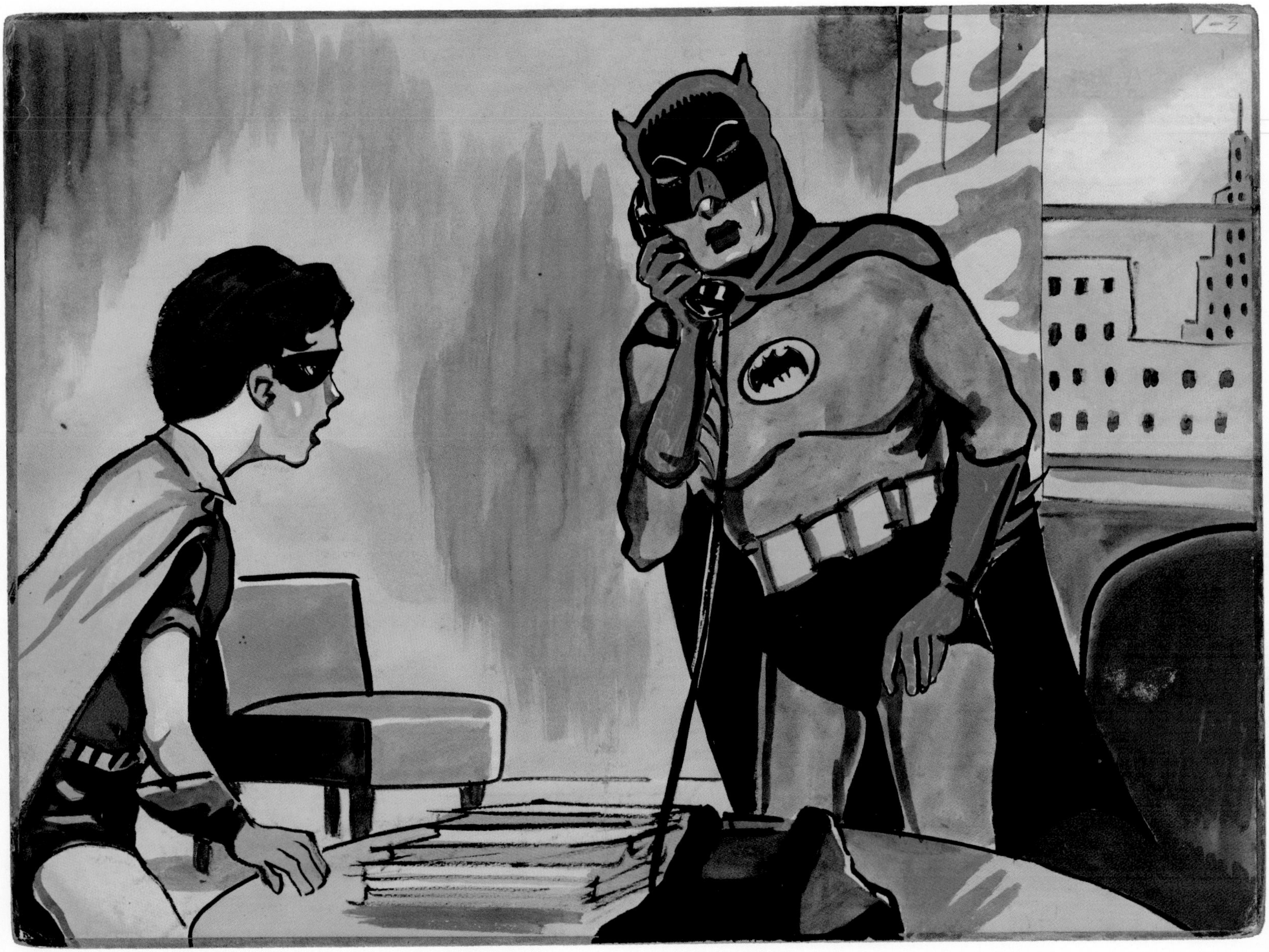
1-3

Holy Simulacre, Batman!: The Caped Crusader answers a call from Police Commissioner Gordon as a Burt Ward–era Robin looks on. Batman usually answers the call in his alter ego as Bruce Wayne, but the pace is sped along for the *kamishibai*. Wayne Manor is located in the outskirts of Gotham City, rather than downtown, as the skyscraper through the window makes it appear.

From Golden Bat to Silver-Age Batman: The Dynamic Duo jumps out of a bubble-domed Batmobile, remarkably faithful to the 1966 TV version, with a red bat emblem on the door, red racing trim, and long, low fins. The Batmobile in the television series was a Ford concept car called the Futura, stylized by Kustom Kar designer George Barris. The scenery is as spotless as a generic New York street backlot.

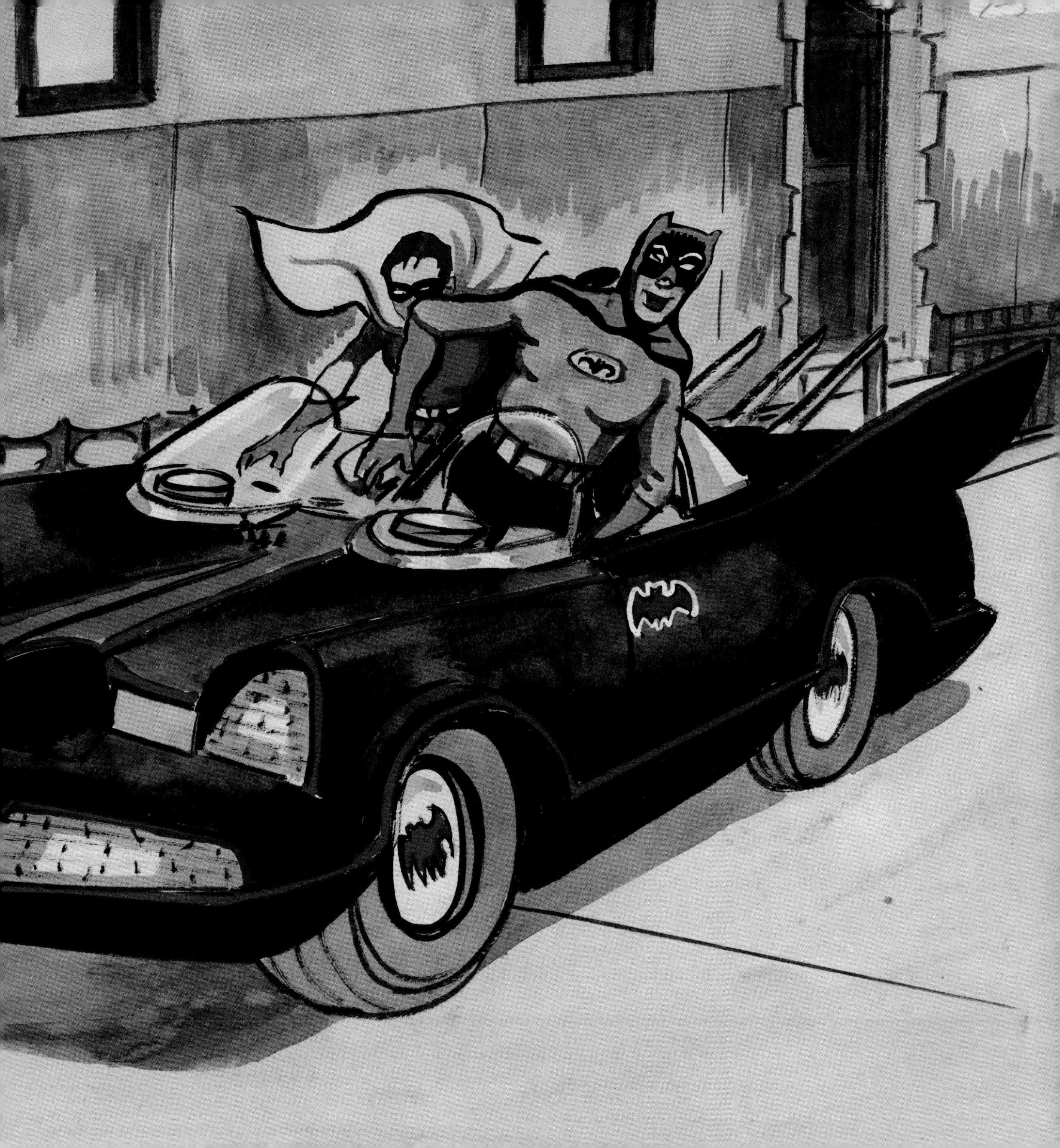

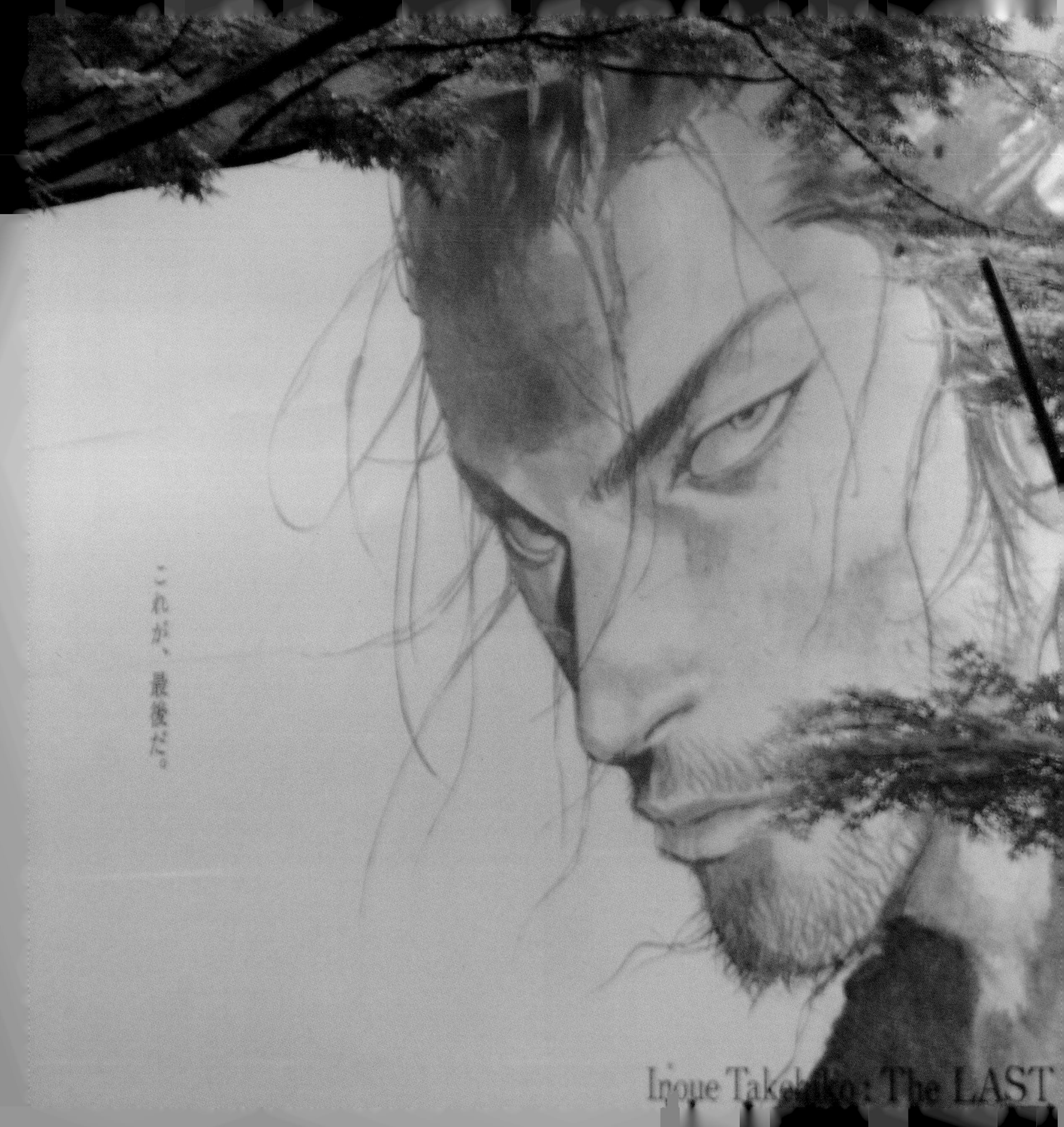
これが、最後だ。
Inoue Takehiko : The LAST

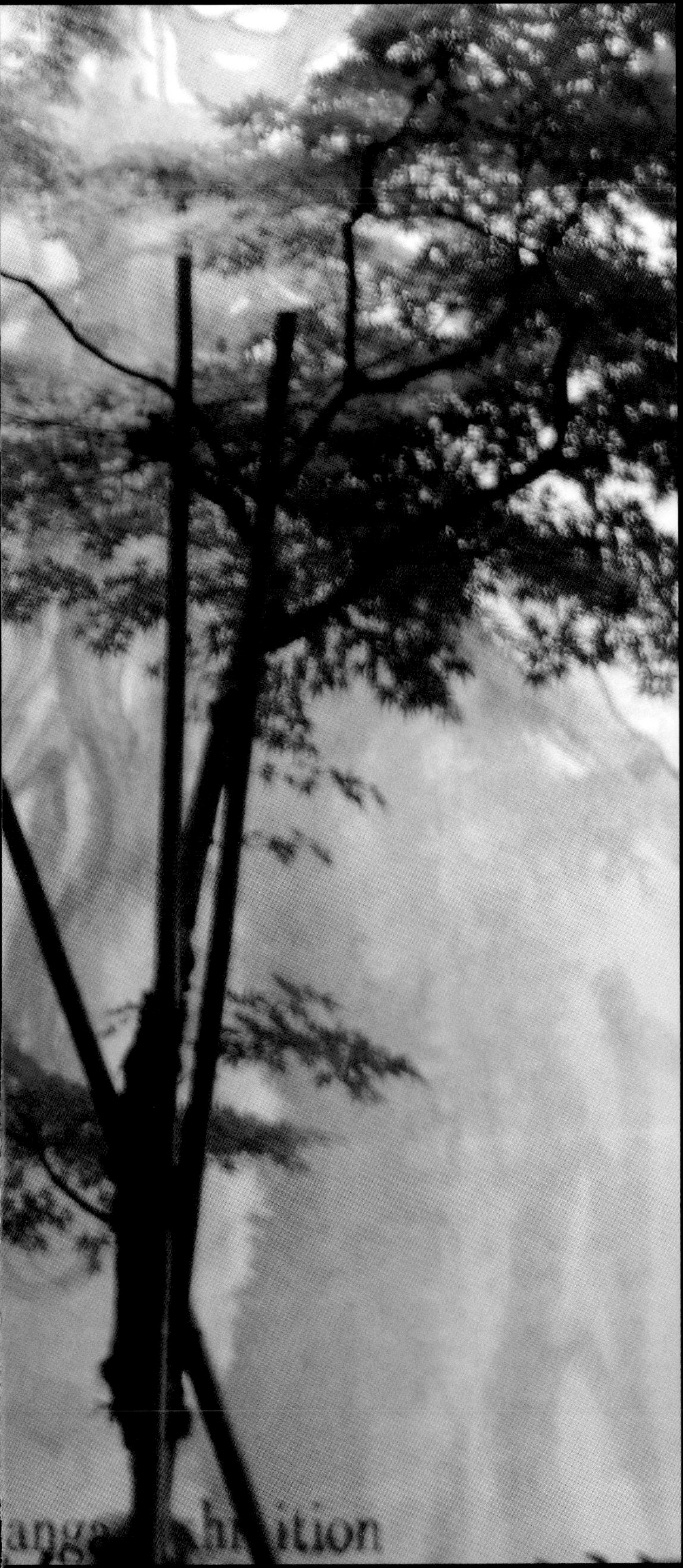

ACROSS THE MANGAVERSE

4 **Samurai Mural:** Takehiko Inoue, a rock star among mangaka with his series *Slam Dunk* and *Vagabond*, has made the leap from comics to fine art, as seen in this mural of Musashi at the Ueno Museum of Art.

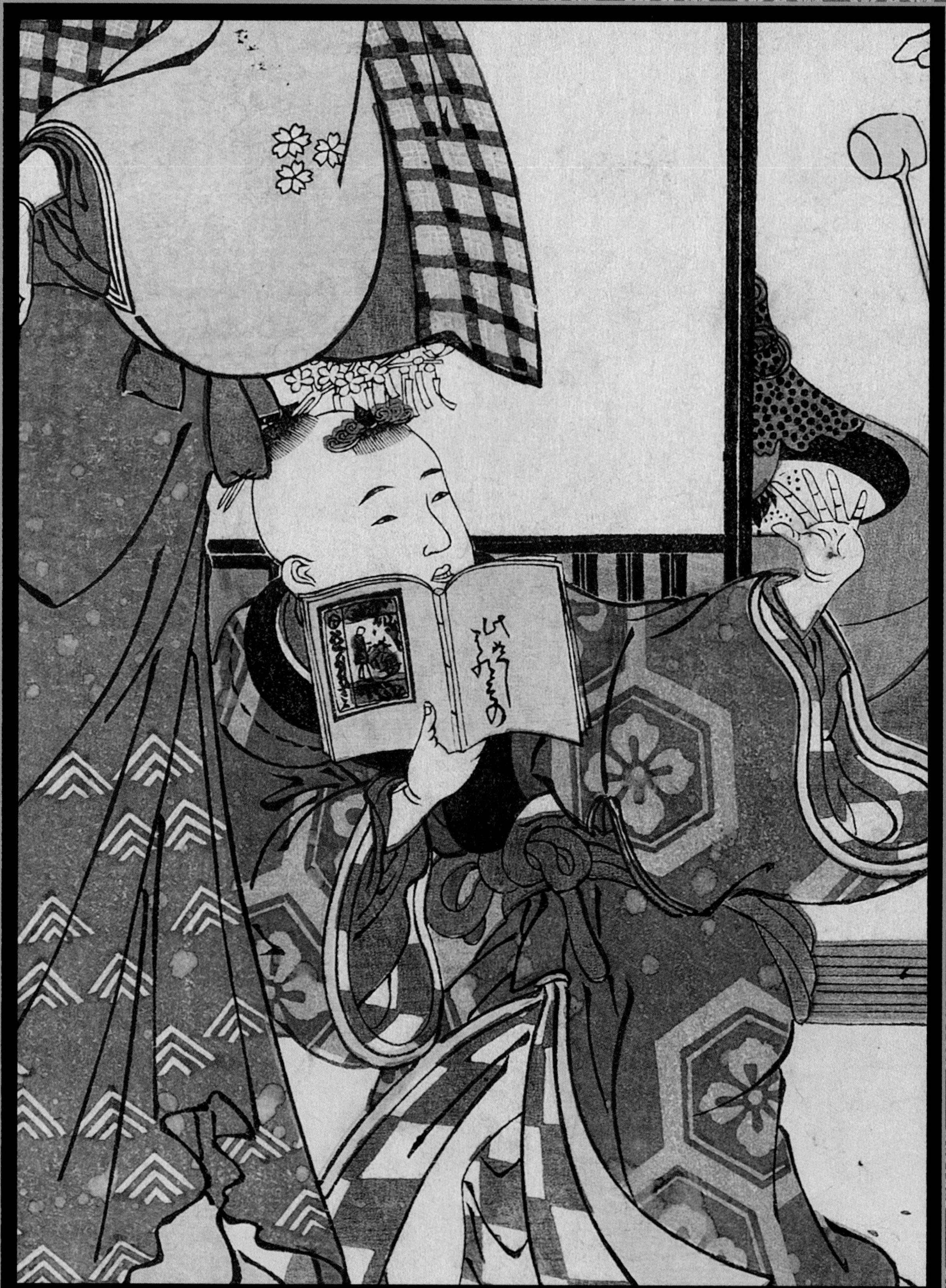

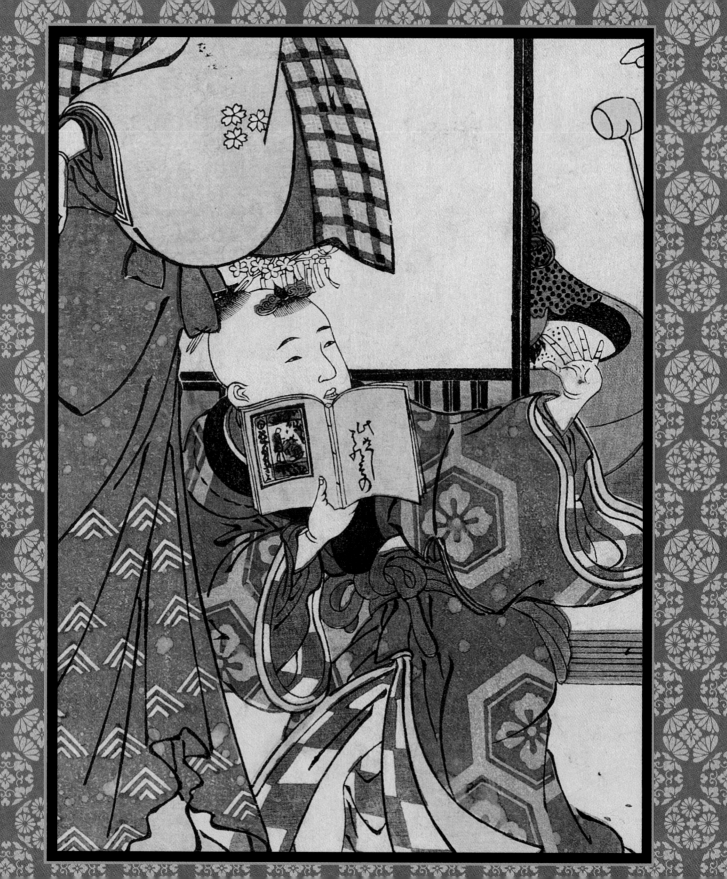

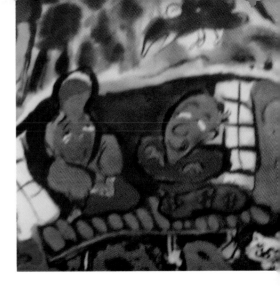

> We are now in an age when we breathe manga as air.
> —OSAMU TEZUKA

> Manga is a very strange form. You either like it
> or you hate it. I haven't made up my mind.
> —STAN LEE

The first thing a newcomer to kamishibai, manga, and anime asks is, What's with the wide eyes?

Osamu Tezuka: the godfather of manga grew up in a well-to-do family in Tokyo and shared with his father a passion for screening Walt Disney and Max Fleischer shorts on a home projector. Astro Boy, with his button nose and delicately lashed, jeepers-creepers-size eyes, is a direct descendent of Betty Boop with a touch of early Mickey Mouse in his bare torso and two horns of hair—always visible from any angle, instead of mouse ears. Boop's oversized orbs resemble nothing so much as the expressive eyes of the original sweetheart of the silent screen, Mary Pickford, who was the subject of the first cinematic close-up. Needless to say, Pickford was huge in Japan. Another influence on cutesy characters with eyelashes as big as Venus flytraps was the ubiquitous Depression fad of kewpie dolls. Even today Japanese toy stores feature kewpie-doll trinkets of major manga characters.

A cultural variant that may be lost on Western readers who tend to associate big eyes with the kitschy Keane portraits of doe-eyed waifs in the 1960s, is that the Japanese divide social relations into "dry" or formal interaction, and "wet" or more intimate connections. The term wet is literal; tears are seen as the ultimate expression of sincerity and depth of emotion. The limpid eyes of manga and anime characters are ideal

Detail from *A Pageant of the Latest Beauties, Their Calligraphy Mirrored*, by Kitao Masanobu (page 52). A young handmaiden reads a kibyoshi (yellow-covered) comic book.

for communicating wet emotions with tears glistening at the welling point, the glint of hard resolution, or the sparkle of delight. In contrast, villains are frequently depicted with emotionless, pinprick pupils. When the good guys get down to business and transform into super heroes, their eyes are often shielded with visors or slits to project power.

Another explanation for the near-universal appeal of cartoon characters like Mickey Mouse and Japan's Doraemon, a magical blue cat from the future, is neoteny—the human instinct to be drawn sympathetically toward infant traits, specifically large, round heads, small bodies, and disproportionately large eyes. Indeed, a newborn who has not quite mastered the art of focusing and appears to be all humectant eyes very much resembles a manga character.

The circular and rounded shapes that make up many popular characters from Charlie Brown to Astro Boy also appeal as a Jungian symbol of wholeness. One of Japan's most popular exports, Hello Kitty, has big eyes, no discernible mouth, and virtually no backstory. Unlike Mickey Mouse or Bugs Bunny, who have a full repertoire of stories, next to nothing is known about Hello Kitty, except that she was born in London, has a little sister, is fond of eating yummy cookies, and is responsible for 1 billion dollars in revenues worldwide.

The level of audience projection required by a tabula rasa like Hello Kitty accounts in part for manga's success. Manga gives the reader just enough visual information to fill in the picture. Recent anime and manga strive for a look of *mukokuseki*, a quality of statelessness, so that the characters are racially ambiguous. The characters in Ghibli Studios anime like *Princess Mononoke* and *Howl's Moving Castle* are vaguely Caucasian looking, yet exhibit distinctly Japanese mannerisms. The stateless stakes are heightened by manga characters' wild coifs in platinum and purple, like the blond, blue-eyed ninja Naruto, and the sexually ambiguous features of the elven-eared warrior InuYasha.

Even more startling to the casual reader are the Jessica Rabbit-esque proportions of fighting female characters, who make Barbie dolls look like

Raggedy Ann. The degree of eroticism ranges from naughty "good girl" art known to readers as "fan service," to X-rated anime called *hentai* (perverted), like the tits-and-tentacles spectacle of *Demon City Shinjuku*. Dressing up like as erotic manga characters has caught on in *cosplay*—or costume-wearing events, at comics conventions—where the customers are as well inked as the comics. *Cosplay* steps out on the streets of the Shibuya section of Tokyo, where young women dress up in the *Rori-kon*, Lolita style, and wear full *maido*—French maid outfits. The combination of sex appeal and juvenescence may serve to make women less threatening.

Epicene characters in *yaoi* manga (chaste love stories between pretty boys) directed toward female readers may fulfill similar wishes. In Japan, *yaoi* tales of doomed love in defiance of societal conventions have a particular appeal. Manga is growing exponentially in the United States and bringing a new audience to comics: young females. An increasing number of young women are invading the previously male enclaves of comic book specialty shops. The sea change is also evident in burgeoning manga sections throughout chain bookstores, where you can see young women sitting cross-legged with stacks of manga in their laps. Manga love stories may be tapping into the taste for romance novels that dominates the women's market. Lonely hearts devour *yaoi* manga by the dozen, like oysters on the half shell. Midori Komatsubara, a skilled artist in the field,

Curb Appeal: A current-day *kamishibai* man announces his presence in Tokyo's Ueno Park by clapping together traditional *hiyogoshi* sticks. He promises a tale of marvels set in ancient, ghost-ridden Kyoto.

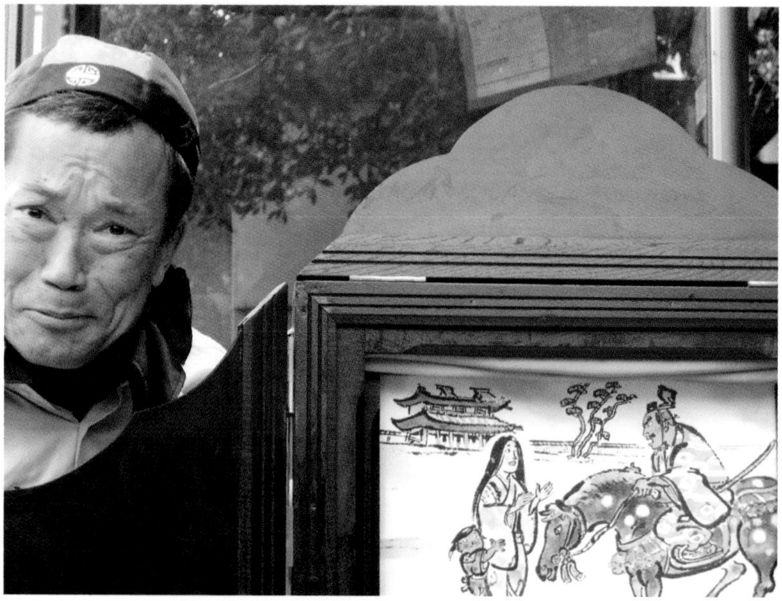

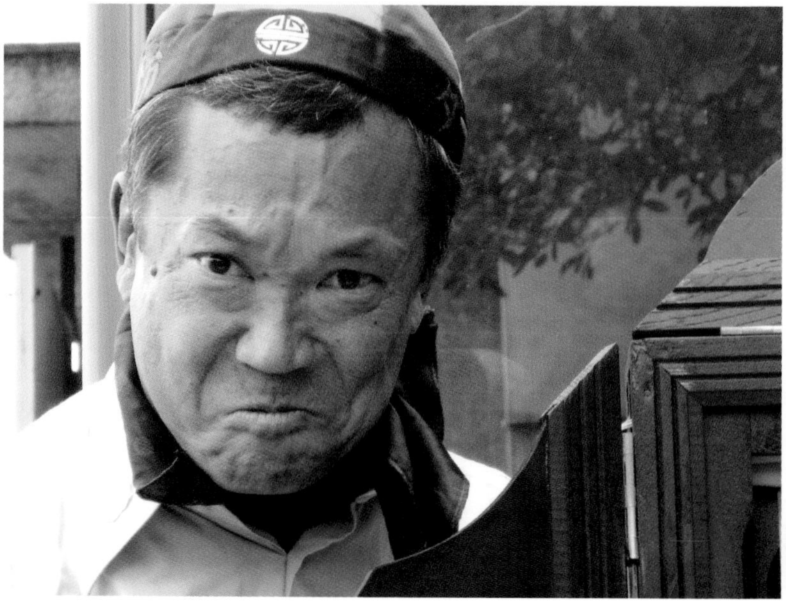

has reinterpreted *yaoi* imagery in fine-art photography by digitally imposing women's heads on male bodies.

Sex is less of a factor in *kamishibai* because much of it was produced in the more chaste decade of the 1930s, and because it was largely a children's medium before the war. However, *kamishibai* are rightly seen as the forerunner of *gekiga*, which branched out into more adult subjects of adventure and eroticism. Shirato's ***Kamui-dan*** is filled with enough dismembering and skull splitting to make Quentin Tarantino blanch. Manga and film highlight the freeze-frame moment after the sword strike—when both duelists stand until the vanquished falls like timber. The champion chambara ***Shogun Assassin***, first in a series of films based on ***Lone Wolf and Cub***, is drenched in the arterial blood spray that inspired ***Kill Bill***.

The barriers between manga, graphic novels, anime, and film are highly permeable. ***Lone Wolf*** inspired Max Allan Collins's graphic novel ***Road to Perdition***, which later became a feature film, about the Kansas City mob days. Tatsuo Yoshida's ***Speed Racer*** has led many lives, first in the kinesthetic draftsmanship of Tatsuo Yoshida's manga ***Mach GoGoGo*** in the 1960s; then in a turbocharged 1967 anime series in which the characters speak nearly as fast as they race because of hasty dubbing; and finally in a 2008 candy-colored CGI-driven, live-action film by the Wachowski

LEFT The *kamishibaiya* uses facial expressions and vocal inflections to enact his story about a village preyed upon by a terrible ogre.

ABOVE With a gruff demeanor, the samurai agrees to fight the ogre.

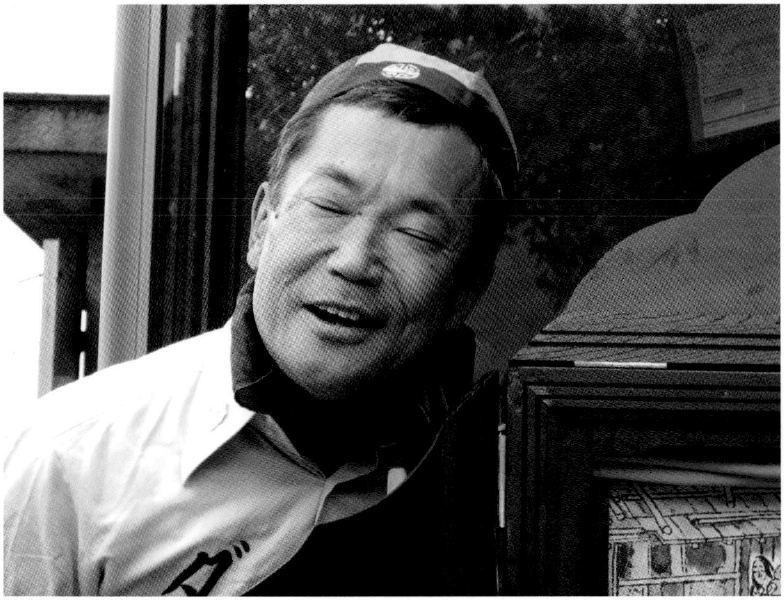 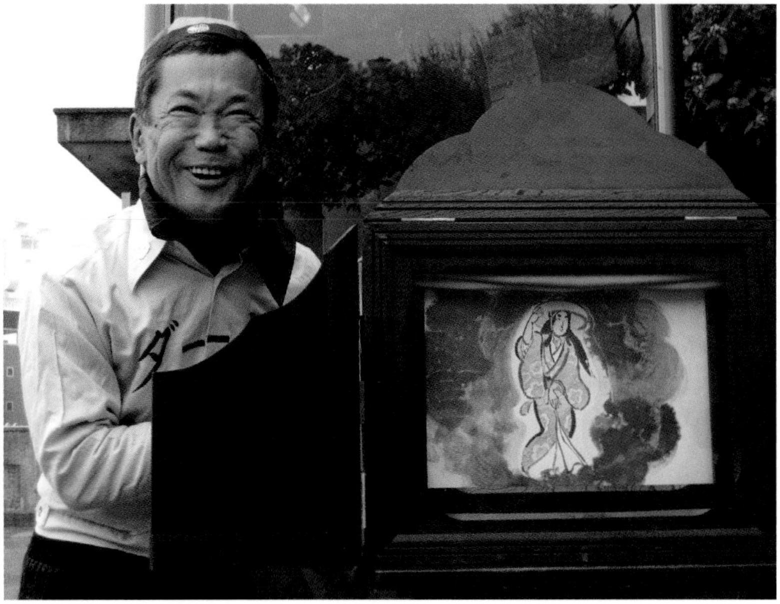

brothers—who in turn owe some of their *Matrix* moves to the anime *Ghost in the Shell* based on Masamune's cybernetic manga. *Speed Racer* was inspired by two popular 1964 films, *Viva Las Vegas*, with Elvis Presley as a race-car driver, and *Goldfinger*, with James Bond's gadget-laden Aston Martin. With his soft pompadour, stray forelock and red neckerchief, Speed looks like a pie-eyed Presley. The anime's opening credits, when Speed hurtles from the powerful Mach-5 (a tricked-out Corvette), may be the first example of frozen action combined with continual camera movement that has become a staple of Hong Kong action movies and Wachowski films like *The Matrix*.

Clearly, we are in a cultural spin cycle. Some critics have suggested that nations now lead by "soft power"—the act of winning the hearts and minds of people through cultural means. And in this contest American military might is losing in a judo maneuver to the Japanese culture of *kawaii*—meaning cute.

More than ever, it is easy for artists to move between manga, cinema, and fine art, and across cultures. Recently the art photographer Mika Ninagawa turned the popular manga series *Sakuran*, about a young prostitute in the Edo era, into a live-action film.

Though he was too young to be influenced by kamishibai, Satoshi Kon started in the 1980s as a *manga-ka* and went on to create the anime series

LEFT In a soft voice and with exquisite grammar, the noble-woman thanks the samurai.

ABOVE The ogre appears from a bank of clouds disguised as an enticing woman before revealing his true self.

Paranoia Agent and the acclaimed anime *Millennium Actress*—a kaleido-scopic recap of Japanese film history, including the years in frozen Manchuria. Marvel Comics' Iron Man and Spider-Man have been retrofitted to have a more Japanese sensibility by Madhouse Studios, a renowned Tokyo-based animation company. As a man protected by a metal suit, Iron Man appeals to fans of animes featuring mechanized characters like *Mobile Fighter G Gundam* and *Appleseed*.

Takehiko Inoue, the rock star of *manga-ka*, bridged into fine art with his 2008 one-man show at the Ueno Royal Art Museum. On exhibit were drawings from *Vagabond*, his manga series about the life of Musashi, interspersed with large-scale paintings presented in the context of narrative sequential art, though the story is told by moving through the gallery, rather than turning pages. The exhibition literally drew the observer into the manga world, with a heavy *bokken* lying on the floor, which seemed to have dropped from the swordsman's hand, and a bed of sand spread in front of a final beach scene for gallery-goers to walk through. Golden Bat's creator Takeo Nagamatsu used to take his young daughter Yoko to look at art in the Ueno Museum; now the museum features manga as fine art.

Kamishibai is an unusual interstitial medium between comics and theater, in that the pacing of the story is entirely under the control of the live narrator. The medium is truest to its derivation of paper theater in that it is a performed act, meant to be appreciated over a controlled period of time. Manga writers who grew up with *kamishibai* had essentially a theatrical or cinematic sense of action and timing, drawing out each image as much as possible, relying on the suspense and expectation between images.

One critical distinction between manga and American comics is the speed at which they are meant to be consumed. American comics tend to be text dense, like the Shakespearean sonority of Stan Lee's scripts, or the claustrophobic captions of the old E.C. comics. Unlike manga, American comics are fully illustrated in each panel so that the reader may linger over subtle articulation, in-depth compositions and realistically rendered emotions. American comic book artists like Wally Wood had a kind of horror vacui

Detail from *Prince of Gamma* (page 32).

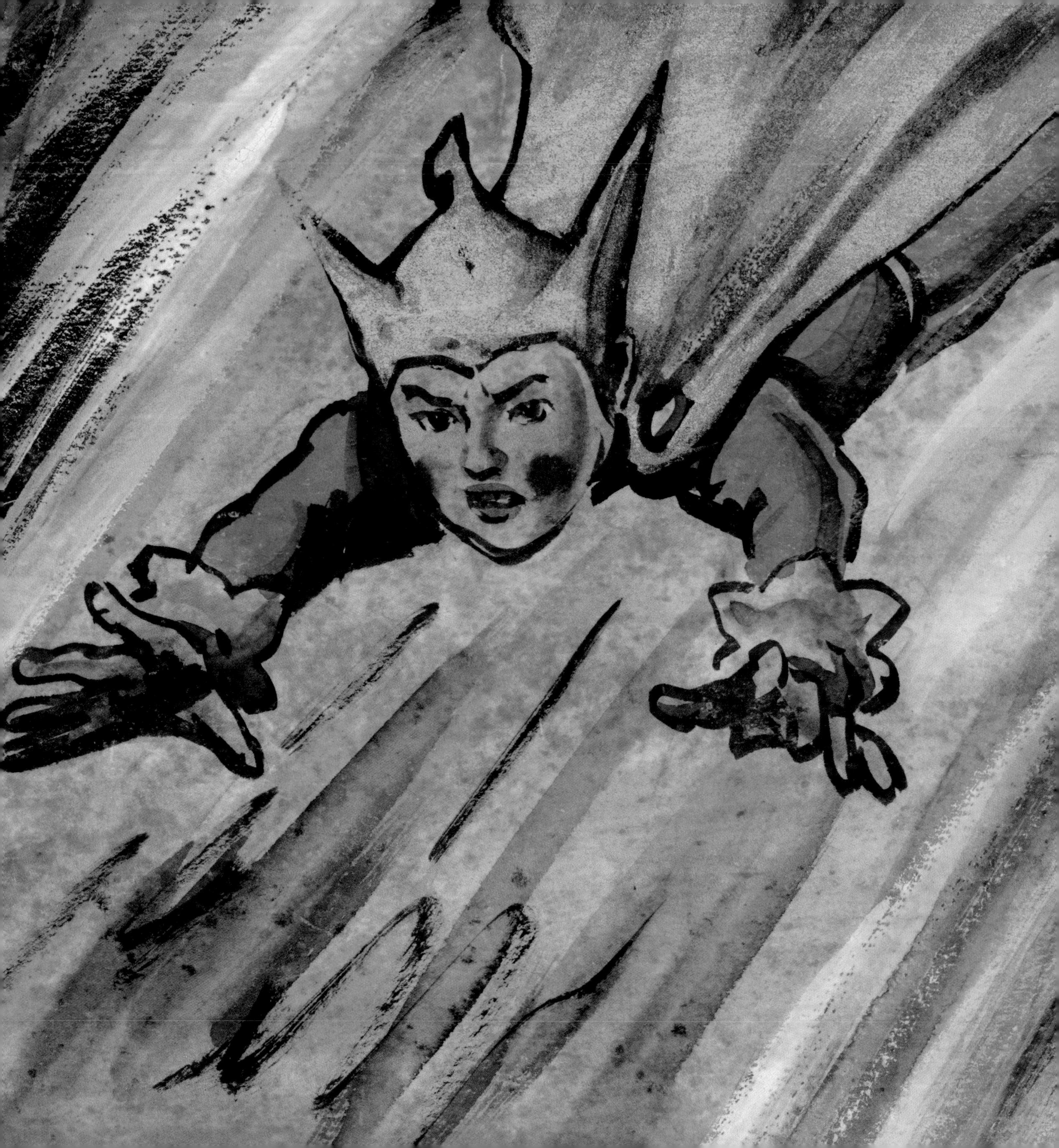

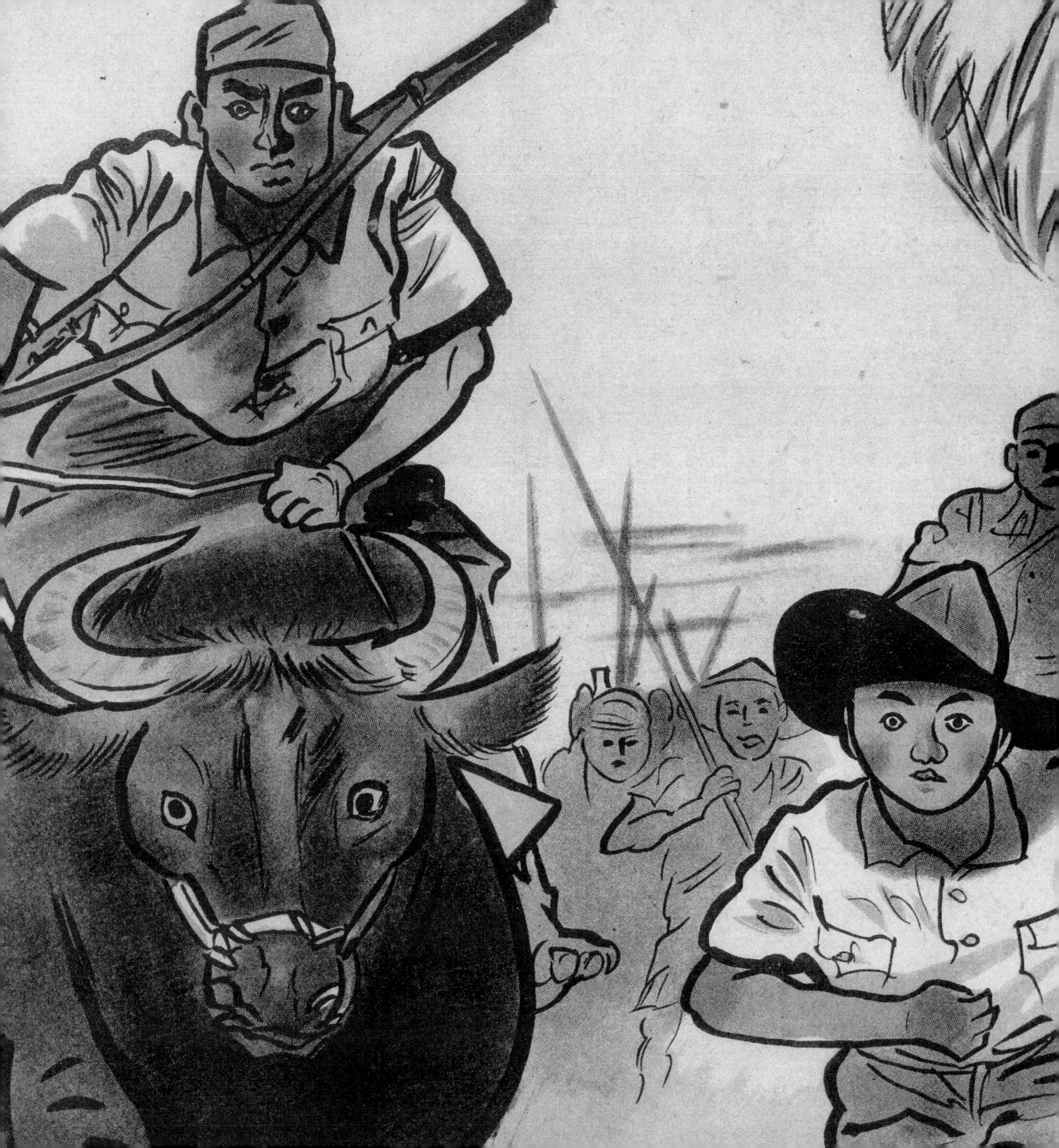

and left no square inch of their panels unfilled with lavish detail. Jack Kirby pioneered the Marvel Comics house style with fantastically foreshortened figures and elastic imbalances in foreground and background composition, giving the sense that the characters are leaping off the page. The sense of time in the way the images are experienced, rushing through some, pausing over others on the full-size page, is at the reader's discretion. American scripters and artists can build up suspense and relief so that a turn of the page is like turning a line in poetry.

In contrast, manga, generally consumed in a flip-book format, are designed to be slurped up like a bowl of ramen. A Japanese reader zips through a page of manga in an average of three seconds. The images are deliberately flat and simple, with all the action in the foreground so that the reader can concentrate on the most salient story elements. A wide range of nonverbal symbolic shorthand is used: simplified, big foot facial expressions when the characters are enraged or happy, and superdeformation of the figures into Bat-Mite-size *chibi* (little) characters for humorous effect. Speed lines take the place of foreshortening to indicate action. Other conventions include a sweat drop for emotional exertion, a mark that looks like a plus sign to represent a throbbing temple vein for anger, and a mute ellipsis when characters are mulling over their feelings. Flying sweat has long been a symbol in American funnies, but the pregnant pause of the ellipsis is catching on.

The sense of timing in manga is completely different from that of American comics: Relatively brief events like sword fights or sports action scenes are e-x-p-a-n-d-e-d over many panels and pages so that more attention is paid to the buildup of emotions each step of the way. This method of presenting a story is called decompression, meaning that quick sequences are unpacked for all the little moments they contain, rather than told in a more rapid, compressed form. Unlike rumbles in Marvel Comics, where characters exchange quips between fisticuffs, extended fight sequences in manga are more often silent. Manga has in turn influenced the look of American comic books in long-running Ameri-manga like *Ninja High School* and *Usagi Yojimbo*, about a *ronin* rabbit. Frank Miller was heavily influenced by *Lone Wolf and Cub*, as

Detail from page 189.

A *kamishibaiya* relates a comic tale to a group of schoolchildren in a Yokohama park. His performance includes funny masks and talking in silly voices. The children call him *kamishibai oji*—Uncle *Kamishibai*.

seen in the wordless breakdowns of action sequences in his *Daredevil*, particularly those featuring Elektra, and in the stark, black and white storytelling of *Sin City*. **WARNING**: Switching too rapidly between American comics and manga, arranged back to front and right to left, can leave you cross-eyed, reading a page boustrophedonically.

Manga and anime have grown in depth and scope over the years, taking on corrosive subjects like abortion, incest, and sexual delusion in Yoshihiro Tatsumi's *Push-Cart Man* and other stories. Anime like *Grave of the Fireflies* (1988), a ground-eye view of two orphans in the firebombing raids during World War II, extend the emotional resonance of the medium.

Manga have so long been a part of the cultural ecosystem in Japan that it is a mature market experiencing decline rather than growing each year. Although manga still account for one fifth of publications of all kinds in Japan, and best-sellers like *Bleach* have sold more than 46 million copies,

The *kamishibaiya* slides the colorful boards in and out of his miniature wooden stage called a *butai*. This *kamishibai* man arrived by car rather than bicycle, and his performance was sponsored by the local school rather than the sale of sweets.

sales of the major weekly manga omnibus magazines like *Weekly Shonen Magazine* and *Weekly Shonen Jump*, a vital sign of the industry's health, have dropped off by half over the last decade, and book sales have plateaued in the same period. Nonetheless, popular manga series like *Galaxy 999* about an interstellar train trip, continue to feed the 3-billion-dollars-a-year *Pachinko* industry and a burgeoning toy and figurine market.

Part of manga's appeal is the sheer diversity of publications, what might be called narrowcasting to a highly specific audience. Like *kamishibai*, there are manga for every taste and pastime: tennis (*Prince of Tennis*), garage bands, cooking, the gritty neo-noir realism of Garon Tsuchiya and Nobuaki Minegishi's *Old Boy*, games of *Pachinko* and Go (*Hikaru no Go*, a spritely series featuring a middle-school player with eyes the size of Go stones). Got a thing for homicidal saucer-eyed schoolgirls? *Gunslinger Girl* is just for you. There are even manga about *doujinshi*, comics by amateurs who

Classroom *Kamishibai*: *Kamishibai* lives on as an educational tool. A librarian at the International Children's Library in Osaka performs a *kamishibai* with press-on felt characters for young children.

adapt popular characters like Sailor Moon. Created for sale at conventions attended by more than two hundred thousand people, *doujinshi* provide a near-real-time feedback on popular trends and are followed avidly by established *manga-ka* to see the future of the industry.

Factors in the increasing popularity of manga in the United States include the rise of video games, which are always in search of new characters and story lines, and the proliferation of cable channels that demand more product. There is also the Japanese cool factor in everything from sushi to sudoku. Nostalgia of an older generation for black and white cartoons from the dawn of consciousness, like *Astro Boy*; *Tobor the 8th Man*; and *Gigantor*, who looks like an overgrown water heater tank, also play a part.

Judging by young Tokyoites on the endless train rides between home, school, and work, manga is giving way to cell phone games, texting, and even "mobile manga" or manga created for cell phones, like the popular *J-Pop Idol*. One subway ad even addressed the trend: A macho manga hero in a rumpled trench coat exhorts a slouching hipster with a cell phone to be a man and read! Texting and gaming may kill off manga magazines, as Victor Hugo wrote of the printed Bible replacing the centricity of cathedral buildings, *ceci tuera cela* (this will kill that), but it is guaranteed that there will be a *chibi* figurine from *GeGeGe no Kitaro*, hearkening all the way back to *kamishibai*, dangling from their latest cell phones.

Manga transforms everything it touches, like Jiro Kuwata's lost Bat-Manga from the mid-60s, unearthed in 2008 by Chip Kidd, which has the charming purity of line of a simple woodblock stamp combined with flat poster-style coloring. A distinctly Japanese Batman looks back at us forty years later. Del Rey Manga and Marvel in the United States have started a new line of *shonen* Ameri-manga with Wolverine, and *Spider-Man J*, about a cross-eyed *chibi* Spider-Manga.

Despite competition from other media, *kamishibai* has flourished in the form of educational stories for children (*kyoiko kamishibai*). Publishers like Doshinsha print new children's stories, as well as classics like *Sleepy Potato and Angry Carrot*, that date back to the peace and prosperity of late 1950s Japan. Educational *kamishibai* has a more rounded style, simpler shapes, and the softer palette that is expected of children's stories. *Kyoiko kamishibai* editions are gaining popularity around the world, and are currently printed in Vietnamese, Dutch, and Basque. One new *kamishibai* story relates the trauma of the Vietnam War as seen from the Vietnamese side, so the stories are by no means strictly kids' stuff.

This rich tradition of storytelling is still a part of Japan. Once in a while, you can still hear the exciting clack of *hiyoshigi* sticks as a *kamishibai* man drums up business in a Tokyo park. We never tire of hearing a good story—no matter our age.

BIBLIOGRAPHY

Allison, Anne. *Permitted & Prohibited Desires: Mothers, Comics, and Censorship in Japan.* Boulder, CO: Westview Press, 1996.

Allison, Anne. *Millennial Monsters: Japanese Toys and the Global Imagination.* Berkeley and Los Angeles, CA: University of California Press, 2006.

Cathorne, Nigel. *Reaping the Whirlwind: The German and Japanese Experience of World War II.* Cincinnati, OH: David & Charles, 2007.

Craig, Timothy J., ed. *Japan Pop! Inside the World of Japanese Popular Culture.* Armonk, NY: M.E. Sharpe, 2000.

Dower, John W. *War Without Mercy: Race & Power in the Pacific War.* New York: Pantheon Books, 1986.

Dower, John W. *Embracing Defeat: Japan in the Wake of World War II.* New York: W. W. Norton & Company, 1999.

Drazen, Patrick. *Anime Explosion!: The What? Why? & Wow! of Japanese Animation.* Berkeley, CA: Stone Bridge Press, 2003.

Ferguson, Niall. *The War of the World: Twentieth-Century Conflict and the Descent of the West.* New York: The Penguin Press: 2006.

Gravett, Paul. *Manga: Sixty Years of Japanese Comics.* New York: Harper Design International, 2004.

Grayling, A.C. *Among the Dead Cities: The History and Moral Legacy of the WWII Bombing of Civilians in Germany and Japan.* New York: Walker & Company, 2006.

Harries, Meirion and Susan. *Soldiers of the Sun: The Rise and Fall of the Japanese Imperial Army.* New York: Random House, 1991.

Jones, James. *WWII.* New York: Ballantine, 1975.

Kelts, Roland. *Japanamerica: How Japanese Pop Culture Has Invaded the U.S.* New York: Palgrave Macmillan, 2007.

Kern, Adam L. *Manga from the Floating World: Comicbook Culture and the Kibyoshi of Edo Japan.* Cambridge, MA: Harvard University Press, 2006.

Koerner, Brendan I. *Now the Hell Will Start: One Soldier's Flight from the Greatest Manhunt of World War II*. New York: The Penguin Press, 2008.

Koyama-Richard, Brigitte. *One Thousand Years of Manga*. Paris: Flammarion, 2007.

Kushner, Barak. *The Thought War: Japanese Imperial Propaganda*. Honolulu: University of Hawaii Press, 2006.

Napier, Susan J. *From Impressionism to Anime: Japan as Fantasy and Fan Cult in the Mind of the West*. New York: Palgrave Macmillan, 2007.

Schodt, Frederik L. *Dreamland Japan: Writings on Modern Manga*. Berkeley, CA: Stone Bridge Press, 1996.

Thompson, Jason. *The Complete Guide to Manga*. New York: Del Rey Books, 2007.

Versaci, Rocco. *This Book Contains Graphic Language: Comics as Literature*. London: The Continuum International Publishing Group, 2007.

Whiting, Robert. *Tokyo Underworld: The Fast Times and Hard Life of an American Gangster in Japan*. New York: Vintage, 2000.

ACKNOWLEDGMENTS

To get anywhere in Japan, you first need to have someone draw you a map. My thanks to Kumiko Yoshino for her gracious hospitality and for drawing my first maps of how to get to the *kamishibai* collections at Tama Library and the Osaka International Children's Library. Also thanks to Hiro Sato, the best guide anyone could have to Japan, for introducing me to expert translator Stacy Smith—without whose help translating the map titles this book would not be possible. Thanks to Yoko Taniguchi for filling in the blank areas of the map about the history of Golden Bat. I am grateful to Charles Kochman, Sofia Gutiérrez, and Laura Lindgren for helping me navigate the way from simple map to finished copy.

CREDITS

Thanks to the following organizations for allowing us to photograph and scan kamishibai images from their collections:
Jungle Boy: Distributed by the Fuji Society, 13; *Gee, How I'd Like to Be A G-Man*: Distributed by the Brotherly Love Society, 23; *Demon Castle of Outer Space*, Produced by the Good Friends Society, 37; *The Story of Nazo*: Distributed by Tales of Japan, 97; *The Burmese Boy and the Tanks*: Produced by the Great Japan Company, 188; *We are Fighting a War*: Produced by the Japanese Educational Kamishibai Society, 192; *Incendiary Bombs*: Produced by the Great Japan Air Defense Society, 194.

All characters, their distinctive likenesses, and related elements are ™ and © 2009. All rights reserved. Reprinted with permission:

Bibliotheque nationale de France: 59, 60; Chiba City Museum of Art: 58; Dark Horse Productions: Kazuo Koike photograph, 122; Kawanabe Kyosai: *Kyosai Hyakki Gadan (Kyosai's Illustrations of the Hundred Demons)* illustrated book, 1889, Copyright Kawanabe Kyosai Memorial Museum, 116 (top); Batman copyright DC Comics: 259, 278, 279, 280; Konzanji: 54; Courtesy Shigeru Mizuki: 114, 115, 118, 119, 120, 121; Copyright Mizuki Productions: 116 (bottom); Museum of Fine Arts Boston: 56, 284; Eric P. Nash: v, 177, 186 (right), 256, 277, 287, 288, 289, 294, 295, 296; National Archives: 228, 233, 238, 239, 246, 247, 250, 251, 252, 253, 254, 255; Omachi-Town: 16 (right); Osaka International Children's Library Collection, Osaka: i, 15, 22 (left and right), 23, 106, 108, 164, 166, 167, 170, 171, 173, 174, 175, 178, 180, 181, 182, 184, 185, 186 (left), 188, 189, 190, 191, 194, 195, 196, 197, 198, 199, 200, 201, 202, 203, 204, 205, 206, 207, 208, 209, 210, 211, 212, 213, 214, 215, 216, 217, 218, 219, 220, 221, 223, 224, 225, 226, 227, 231, 236, 237, 259, 262, 263, 264, 266, 267, 268, 269, 270, 272, 274, 278, 280, 282, 292; Asahi Shimbunsha: 25 (left); Mainichi Shimbun: 261; Tama Library Collection, Tokyo: iii, 12, 19, 24, 27, 28, 29, 30, 31, 32, 33, 34, 35, 36, 37, 38, 39, 40, 41, 42, 43, 44, 45, 46, 47, 48, 49, 50, 51, 52, 53, 62, 63, 64, 65, 66, 67, 68, 69, 70, 71, 72, 73, 74, 75, 76, 77, 78, 79, 80, 81, 82, 83, 85, 86, 88, 89, 90, 91, 92, 93, 94, 95, 96, 99, 113, 148, 150, 151, 152, 153, 154, 156, 158, 159, 160, 161, 162, 163, 168, 176, 240, 241, 242, 243, 244, 245, 272, 273, 274, 275, 276, 291; Courtesy Yoko Taniguchi: 20, 21, 97, 98, 103, 105, 110, 124, 125, 126, 127, 128, 129, 130, 131, 132, 133, 134, 135, 136, 137, 138, 139, 140, 141, 142, 143, 144, 145, 146, 147; U.S. Army Signal Corps: 234, 235

INDEX

Page numbers in *italics* refer to illustrations.

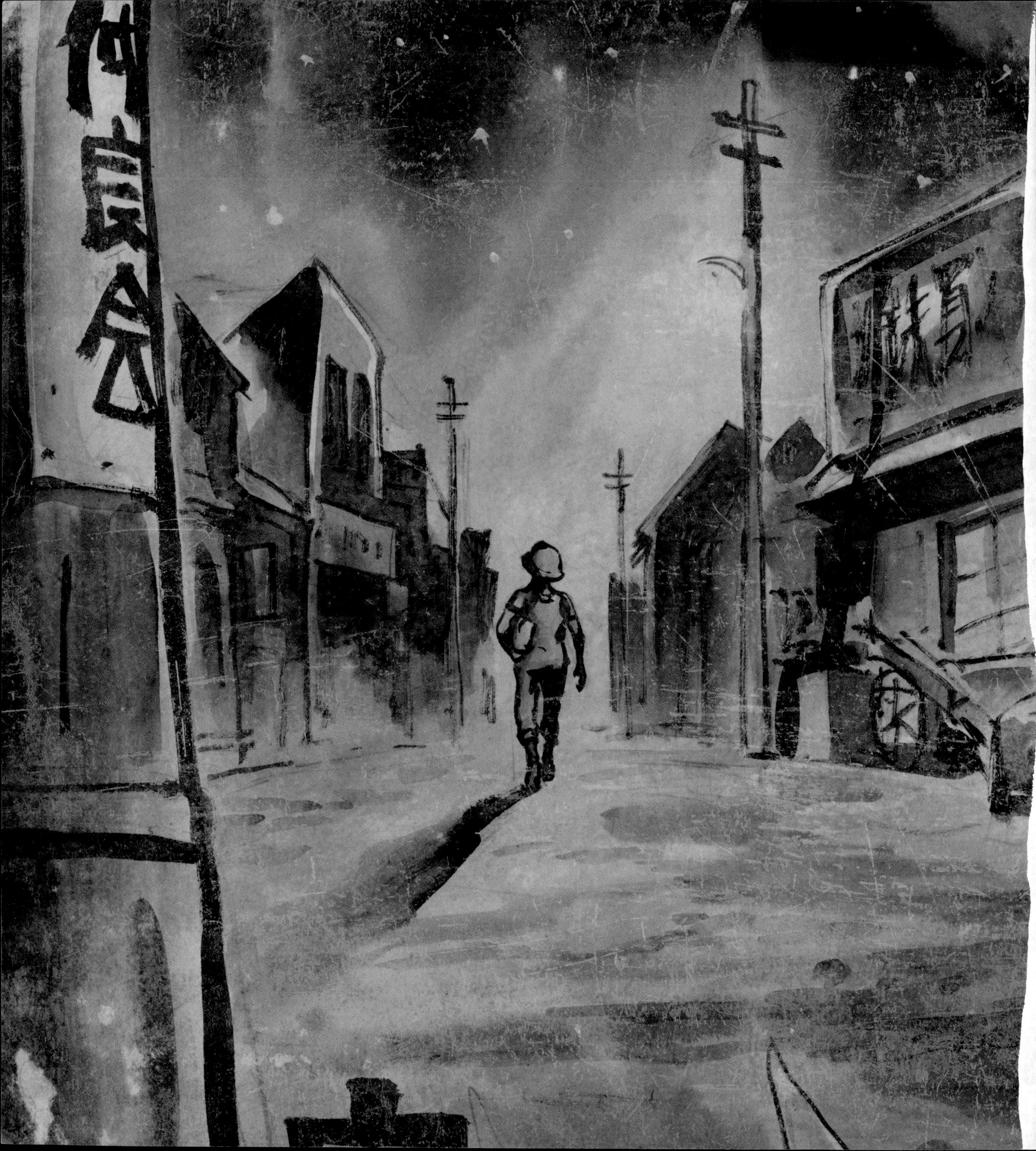